Paths of Inequality in Brazil

Marta Arretche
Editor

Paths of Inequality in Brazil

A Half-Century of Changes

Springer

Editor
Marta Arretche
Department of Political Science
University of São Paulo
São Paulo, Brazil

Translated from the Portuguese language edition: "Trajetórias das desigualdades: como o Brasil mudou nos últimos cinquenta anos" by Marta Arretche (Ed.). Copyright (c) Editora Unesp, 2015. All rights reserved. Translated by Paulo Scarpa with the support of the grant 2013/07616-7 from the São Paulo Research Foundation (Fundação de Amparo à Pesquisa do Estado de São Paulo - FAPESP). The opinions, hypotheses and conclusions expressed in this material are the author's responsibility and don't necessarily reflect FAPESP's vision. Translation revised by Kim Olson.

ISBN 978-3-030-08635-0 ISBN 978-3-319-78184-6 (eBook)
https://doi.org/10.1007/978-3-319-78184-6

Printed on acid-free paper

This Springer imprint is published by the registered company Springer International Publishing AG part of Springer Nature.
The registered company address is: Gewerbestrasse 11, 6330 Cham, Switzerland

Preface

From the 1970s on, democracies in the developed world have witnessed a substantial increase in income inequality. Although the level of inequality and the speed of such upward progress differ among countries (Piketty and Saez 2014), the path has been the same whether observed by means of the share the top richest obtain from total income (Piketty 2014) or by the relative income gains enjoyed by different economic strata (Milanovic 2016). Not surprisingly, inequality has turned out to be one of the most salient topics in public affairs around the world today.

Under democracy, Brazil headed in the opposite direction. Income inequality systematically declined after reaching a peak in 1989, at the end of the Sarney administration, when the average income of the richest 10% (as measured by surveys) was 71 times higher than the average income of the poorest 10%. Since then, this ratio has presented a systematic decrease. In 2014, when this number reached its lowest level, the average income of the richest 10% was 32 times that of the poorest 10%.[1] Despite this trend, there is no doubt that the income gap remains very high. Latin America has the highest inequality rates in the world (Ravallion 2014), and Brazil ranks among one of the most unequal countries in Latin America.[2]

Both pathways – of developed countries and of Brazil – subverted well-established theories and raised important questions for democratic theory. In the history of political ideas, liberals and conservatives feared universal suffrage in view of the risk that struggles for income redistribution would gain political momentum and that the possible outcomes would be disastrous on property and the social order. The trajectory of post-World War II democracies seemed to confirm the claim that in the long run, universal suffrage would lead to a reduction in social and economic inequalities. Given that in the overwhelming majority of democracies the

[1] Calculations based on data from the National Household Sample Surveys. As this introduction was written, IBGE data was available up to the year 2015.

[2] The inequality-adjusted income index calculated by the 2012 United Nations Program for Development indicates that in Latin America, only Colombia, Paraguay, Venezuela, and Ecuador have worse income distribution than Brazil. Source: https://data.undp.org/dataset/Inequality-adjusted-income-index/kgcz-8b4v

median voter's income is below the average income, collective social choices under universal suffrage would lead to an increase in the State's redistributive role (Meltzer and Richard 1981).

Contrary to these expectations, evidence displayed by mature democracies in the early twenty-first century has revealed that middle-class society, which emerged in the post-World War II period, may not endure. Has the golden age (Hobsbawn 1994) been just a pause along the path of wealth concentration rather than an expression of structural changes in capitalist societies? If democracy can give way to either inequality reduction or long-run increasing impoverishment, it appears that it is not a sufficient condition for redistribution to occur. If so, what is it that drives politics to affect an individual's well-being?

Such facts seem no less challenging for economic theory. Even if Simon Kuznets had been far more cautious than his observers, his preliminary speculations (1955, p. 7) gave rise to a research agenda that sought evidence and reasons for an inverted-U in the long-term trajectory of income inequality: the increase in inequality would only occur during the early stages of industrialization; more advanced developmental stages would be accompanied by a reduction in inequality (Kuznets 1955, p. 18).

The fact is that the factors leading to inequality reduction are still the subject of on-going debate among social scientists. That is why Brazil's story of success deserved to be scrutinized, even if the path we observed from the early 1990s to the mid-2010s does not continue into the future. Inequality and poverty has long been a constraint on the country's economic and human development, a pattern shared by many other countries in Latin America. As a result, different dimensions of exclusion in Brazil have also long been at the center of the political debate and academic agenda.

Indeed, many analysts were quite skeptical about the prospects of redistribution in Brazil under democracy. Some shared the assumption further elaborated by Boix (2003), according to whom it is not rational for elites to accept democratization in highly unequal societies due to the risk of future expropriation. Others were disappointed by the constancy of inequality and poverty that took place in Brazil during the transition to democracy (Barros et al. 2000; Carvalho 2001; Reis and Cheibub 1993). Finally, still others acknowledged that institutions inherited from a previous context where exclusion was the rule would impede the adoption of inclusion policies (Carvalho 2001; Lamounier 1992; Stepan 1999).

As this book shows, inequality in Brazil affected much more than simply income inequality. Market forces along with social policies, whose origins date back to the early 1930s and whose main pillars remained in place up to the late 1980s, set in motion a mechanism of fusion of advantages through which roughly the same categories of individuals acquired better positions in the job market along with entitlement to social rights such as worker protection and social security, access to health care, and home ownership. The result was the emergence of a monumental divide between insiders and outsiders. In turn, starting in the early 1990s, economic inequality reduction, along with factors exogenous to policies themselves, was a by-product of the inclusion of outsiders, a mechanism through which access to different social benefits were incrementally, albeit at different speeds, de-linked from income and social background. Such a process entitled those in the middle and bottom strata of income distribution to social rights.

This book hopes to contribute to the overall understanding of the trajectory of inequalities. In a gathering at the Center for Metropolitan Studies (CEM), the authors of this volume were exhilarated by the availability of six editions of the Demographic Censuses compiled by the Brazilian Institute of Geography and Statistics (IBGE), for the 1960–2010 period. The opportunity encouraged us to undergo a collective effort to analyze the changes over a period of Brazilian history comprising very distinct economic and political contexts: rural-urban transition, industrialization, rapid economic growth and economic slowdown, inflation and monetary stability, authoritarianism, and democracy. Even though these transitions have been extensively covered by the specialized literature, a systematic assessment of the trajectory of inequality during this period has yet to be carried out.

Brazil in 1960 was a rural country where inequalities regarding income and the provision of infrastructure services were limited in scope throughout the vast national territory. This was, however, a relative equality in poverty insofar as low income and lack of essential public services were more or less evenly distributed throughout the country. The labor market was predominantly male. In 1970, in an overwhelmingly Catholic country, women bore an average of six children, but the better educated had a fertility rate of two children per woman. At each end of the income and education scale, the predominant arrangement was the traditional family, in which females were confined to domestic work.

Over three quarters of the Brazilian population was functionally illiterate, i.e., they had 0–3 years of study. Only 20% of youth between the ages of 12 and 15 had completed 4 years of schooling. Universities were restricted to the admission of white men from upper strata environments. Inequality between whites and nonwhites began as early as the access to elementary education.

The short supply of skilled professionals ensured male providers with major advantages in the labor market and in the social protection system, since entitlement to pensions and health care was linked to formal inclusion in the job market. In a context of limited size of the urban industrial sector and high levels of chronic unemployment, social policies themselves were a source of inequality.

In 2010, Brazil was extremely urbanized: 85% of the country's population lived in cities. Educational levels had changed radically. Functional illiteracy had dropped to below 20% of the economically active population, mostly concentrated among the elderly. Among youth, completion of elementary education was virtually universal – almost 70% of youth completed eight years of schooling. Therefore, the completion of primary education was increasingly less dependent on family origin. At the other end of the educational system, the population over age 18 that reached high school went from 6.2 million in 1980 to 39.7 million in 2010; the population reaching university studies went from 3.4 million in 1980 to 21.5 million in 2010. Both numbers increased more than sixfold. During the same period, Brazil's infant mortality rate fell from 69 to 16 per 1000 live births and life expectancy increased from 62 to 73 years.

However, protagonists of the feminist as well as civil rights movements of the 1960s, women and non-whites, did not enjoy the same success in their respective emancipatory agendas. From 1970 on, women massively began to attend universities to the point of becoming the majority of university students in 2010, and to substantially reducing the differences between typical male and female occupations. The female fertility rate fell at a fast pace since poorer women began to adopt the reproductive behavior of highly schooled women. Having children became a choice!

Alongside these changes in women's behavior emerged a multitude of family arrangements – the traditional family ceased to be the predominant grouping. Likewise, a marked decline in Catholicism, far from signaling the end of this religion, in fact established religious pluralism.

Although the black and brown population has progressively enrolled in universities in recent decades, the fact remains that in 2010, whites still made up 75% of the university population. Moreover, when non-whites entered the higher education system, they tended to enroll in programs leading to less prestigious occupations. Consequently, the reduction of inequality for non-whites within the educational system continued to be restricted to where access had become universal, that is, at elementary schools.

However, the mass entry of women in school and work did not translate into equal wages. Women and blacks still earned less than white men in 2010, even when they possessed the same level of education.

In 2010, illiteracy was no longer an exclusion criterion for voting: costs of voter registration, turnout and obtaining information about competitors had been considerably reduced. Furthermore, there were countless opportunities for extra-parliamentary participation, whether through councils or a variety of associations.

Some conclusions can be drawn from this brief summary. Firstly, the term "inequality" remains overly abstract. The social world presents multiple inequalities: between rich and poor, men and women, between categories of race, which in turn are expressed through income, access to services, and political participation. In fact, the centrality of the income factor in comparative studies on inequality is most often the result of data availability, not the fact that income is the only relevant factor. Inequality is much more complex and goes well beyond its sheer monetary dimension. Therefore, knowledge of inequality demands that we analyze its multiple dimensions. Moreover, far worse than income inequality is the fusion of disadvantages upon the same individuals, that is, the mechanism through which someone's capacity to have a decent life is impeded by several layers of deprivation.

Secondly, the Brazil of 2010 still suffered from many unacceptable inequalities. Its course, however, was far from steady. The brief summary outlined above reveals that major offsets took place in the distances between social categories. Moreover, as one can observe in this volume, these shifts are unquestionably tied to democracy. The 1964 authoritarian regime expanded access to education, urban infrastructure services, and entitlement to social security and health care. But, contrary to the aphorism attributed to John F. Kennedy, this wave of supply expansion did not raise every boat to the same level. The increase in inequality, marked by inequalities between individuals and regions in terms of household infrastructure as well as status distinctions in social security rights, accompanied both the economic growth and the expansion of the military regime's social policies. In contrast, the accelerated decline in poverty levels, income inequality within the labor market, and inequalities in access to services among individuals and regions would only emerge under the democratic regime. The 1990s introduce a shift in the history of inequality in Brazil.

Democracy, however, is not a sufficient condition to affect long-established patterns of income distribution and access to public goods. The evidence presented in this volume confirms the findings of a traditional line of research in the social sciences, emphasizing the need for continuous policies for substantial changes in the economic and social order to occur (Glaeser et al. 2004; Esping-Andersen 1985a, b, 1990). The long-term trajectory of inequalities in Brazil reveals there is no determinism – economic or political – in this process. Policies matter! Moreover: displacements in inequality patterns demand that policies be implemented over a long period of time.

The existence of continuous policies is precisely what allows one to explain the puzzle expressed by Kingstone and Power (2008, pp. 2–5), for whom in contemporary Brazilian democracy, "progress in some areas is offset by stagnation in others. (…) Some dimensions of democratic governance have improved rapidly and dramatically, while some have improved very little or not at all." Dimensions of deprivation and inequality which displayed a dramatic decline – such as income, access to education, health, and electricity, as well as barriers to political participation – were those subject to continuous policies from the 1990s on. A number of chapters use a different lens to examine the improvements in these dimensions and point toward a steady path through which policies of inclusion incrementally reached those who were once considered outsiders. In fact, those areas have had greater centrality in the national political agenda.

Conversely, the reduction of inequality levels was considerably slower in those areas – such as access to water and sewage networks – marked by a lack of continuity between presidential terms or even due to decisional paralysis.

The emphasis on continuous policies does not imply that they exhaust the necessary conditions to reduce inequalities, however. A number of factors exogenous to policies also combined in a way that contributed to this downward progress. Besides market forces, such as the commodity boom that favored the increasing demand for jobs, this book also reveals that an individual's behavior can also affect redistributive patterns. In the Brazilian case, a silent revolution in women's behavior on different fronts – massive entry into the educational world and the labor market, changing choices concerning family arrangements, and even in religious choices – played a major role in reducing inequalities. Income inequality declined because a great number of women no longer received zero earnings in spite of the scale of the gender income gap. Changes in reproductive behavior on the part of poor women reduced the abundant supply of low-skilled workers in the job market. In contrast, prejudice and self-exclusion also limited the effect of opportunities brought about by policies regarding individual choice.

This is not a book on policies. Instead, it is an effort to examine inequality through several of its facets and more precisely, to describe its trajectory over the course of 50 years. Collectively, this volume shows that these different dimensions cannot be directly inferred from one another. Each dimension has its own particular path and pace. For example, while the income gap between the rich and the poor started declining from the early 1990s on, the gender earnings gap only began to display some reduction in 2001. The income gap among races in turn did not diminish at the same pace. Therefore, it seems evident that these different trajectories are affected by different factors, which justifies that we examine them separately.

The independent pace of the various dimensions as well as the role of public policies in dissociating income from inequality is even clearer when we look at what happened with regard to citizens' voting. The 1985 removal of the literacy barrier for the right to vote was an important step toward universal suffrage. Still, a number of policy decisions concerning detailed rules for exercising this right – such as holding elections on Sundays, free access to electoral campaigns through the media, and the electronic voting system – were just as decisive in reducing electoral participation costs for the poor. As a result, there was a significant reduction in the weight income and education exercised on electoral participation.

By the same token, the path toward access to public services in Brazil reveals an incremental dissociation from income. However, this de-linking effect is only eradicated under universalization. The negative association between household income, on the one hand, and unequal access to education, health care, and electricity, on the other, is only reduced if and when such policies become universal. The path toward universalization, however, reveals that the poorest are the last to be included. Once universalization is reached, inequality is displaced to a new frontier, where social origin and income continues to have a significant impact.

Book Contents

This book is organized into five parts, each corresponding to a dimension considered to be central by the literature.

The first part deals with political participation. It reveals that major changes occurred in this sphere, whether observed from the perspective of electoral participation or in the form of extra-parliamentary participation. The chapter "Political Participation in Brazil," by Fernando Limongi, José Antonio Cheibub, and Argelina Cheibub Figueiredo, analyzes the dimensions and mechanisms behind the incorporation of voters: Brazil went from 7.4 million voters in 1945 to 135.5 million in 2010. These numbers are not a mere consequence of demographic growth. Instead, their main explanatory factor was the elimination of the educational barrier in 1985 in view of the high illiteracy rates that still prevailed in Brazil at that time. The authors argue, however, that evidence shows that legislation excluding illiterates was bypassed during the military regime (1964–1985). Therefore, considering the impossibility of knowing for sure the extent to which the legal exclusion of illiterates was indeed complied with until 1988, the real impact of the fall of the educational barrier as well as its effect on political decisions is debatable.

However, the elimination of legal barriers to electoral participation is not enough for effective inclusion of the underprivileged. As shown by the authors, those included in the voting world must overcome obstacles – regarding registration, displacement to polls, and information retrieval – in order to cast their vote in the ballot box. Electoral codes have been the subject of intense political dispute precisely because they are not neutral. Income and education unevenly enable voters to afford such costs. The chapter shows that decisions concerning electoral rules removed many of these obstacles, which greatly reduced electoral participation costs for the poorest and least educated, with obvious consequences on the act of voting.

The contemporary democratic regime was also witness to dramatic growth in the number of civil society associations. This is clearly demonstrated in the chapter "Councils, Associations and Inequality," by Adrian Gurza Lavalle and Leonardo Sangali Barone. Between 1988 and 2009, local-level policy councils expanded throughout the country, converting into reality the provisions envisaged in the 1988 Federal Constitution. The course of this expansion reveals the interactions between civil society and Brazilian State institutions since expansion is affected by the federal government's induction policies. The presence of councils in all municipalities is limited to policy areas in which the federal government harnessed its spending power to condition federal transfers for their establishment though. In the absence of such federal induction mechanisms, territorial penetration of councils is affected by cross-municipality inequality: there is a clear association between citizens' education and income, as measured by the Human Development Index (HDI), and the presence of local-level councils.

Between 1999 and 2009, the number of civil society associations increased at a faster rate than did population in all municipalities, regardless of socioeconomic conditions. However, the authors show that a greater presence of associations in more advantaged municipalities is essentially an effect of the indicator used to measure the phenomenon, that is, under the condition that registry offices and condominium associations, which tend to flourish in urban agglomerations, are recognized as civil society associations. By adopting an indicator better suited to measuring the type of associations described by the literature on political participation –associations for the protection of rights – the authors reveal that in the 2000s, such proliferation was most remarkable in municipalities that had the lowest HDI indexes.

The book's second part deals with the relationship between education and income, a classic theme in the literature on inequality. It shows that this association is twofold, that is, social origin has an effect on an individual's access to school as well as on her educational performance. Besides, there is a prize associated with education that distinguishes individuals with different educational levels in the labor market. Education is among the factors that most strongly determine better opportunities in the labor market, just as there is a close relationship between education and political participation. For this reason, any comprehensive study on inequality should carefully examine the behavior of access to education and its impact on income as well as the trajectory of the connection between family origin and access to education.

In the chapter "Educational Stratification Among Youth in Brazil: 1960–2010," Carlos Costa Ribeiro, Ricardo Ceneviva, and Murillo Marschner Alves de Brito examine the impact socioeconomic background has on educational progression and access to education among youth. The authors show that substantial changes have occurred over the course of the past 50 years regarding the magnitude by which social inequalities affect educational opportunities. Universal access to primary education – almost 70% of youth who enrolled in the school system completed eight years of schooling in 2010 in contrast to 10%, which was the rate in 1960. The subsequent massive entry of young people into high school education resulted in a saturation effect-induced displacement of the educational level in which socioeconomic origin operates as a constraint on school progression.

With regard to concluding primary school, the factors – rural origin, parents' educational level, family income, gender, and skin color – which in the 1960s and 1970s acted as constraints on educational progression were virtually eliminated. However, these effects have not entirely disappeared. They were instead displaced to the upper levels of the educational trajectory. Albeit an increasing number of youths have enrolled in high school and university, graduation rates at this level are far below admissions rates. Moreover, inequalities of opportunity – the link between failure to complete these educational levels and family background –proved to be resilient for high school or even increased in terms of holding a university diploma.

In the chapter "Education and Inequality in Brazil," Naercio Menezes Filho and Charles Kirschbaum analyze the connections between the relative supply of a skilled and schooled workforce and income inequality in the labor market, even as the authors acknowledge that this trajectory is also affected by other factors. Based on the evidence that the labor market is the main element behind the reduction in income inequality, the authors attempt to unravel what happened to change the previous pattern of steady inequality increase. Their core argument is that both trajectories – the rise and fall of income inequality – are directly linked to educational gains, which in turn can be explained by the supply and demand for skilled labor.

According to the authors, Brazil's educational lag – extremely low educational levels – and the consequent shortage of skilled workers is responsible for the high wage disparities in the labor market. They demonstrate how an increased supply of education increased the supply of more skilled workers, and thus reduced the prize obtained by those holding more education. Hence, wage compression in the labor market has its origins in the expanded supply of education among the economically active population.

In the chapter "Horizontal Stratification in Brazil's Higher Education (1960–2010)," Carlos Antonio Costa Ribeiro and Rogerio Schlegel provide an additional analytical step. If, as shown by Naercio Menezes Filho and Charles Kirschbaum, the correlation between education and income differentials in the labor market holds true, it is also true that individuals with the same educational level obtain different earnings in the job market. This horizontal stratification can be seen in university careers, that is, through professional titles obtained by individuals. The authors therefore examine how gender and race affect university enrollment. Horizontal stratification means that individuals at the same educational level are differentiating by means of occupations of quite diverse prestige.

Carlos Antonio Costa Ribeiro and Rogerio Schlegel reveal that between 1960 and 2010, increasing numbers of poor, women, blacks, and browns were admitted to universities. Women, however, were more successful than other population segments. Not only was the rate of female enrollment in higher education much higher than the rate for blacks and browns, to the point that the former surpassed men in terms of percentage as of 1991, but women also enrolled in programs leading to careers once typically considered to be male and more prestigious, such as medicine, dentistry, and architecture. If, on the one hand, there was reasonable equalization of university careers between men and women, inequality between races remained fairly stable. Blacks are not only less likely to enroll in universities, but when they do so, it is usually in programs that lead to less prestigious occupations. However, women, blacks, and browns receive lower income, even when holding the same diploma as white men.

In the chapter "Racial Inequalities in Brazil: A Persistent Challenge," Marcia Lima and Ian Prates draw our attention to the inequality of different skin colors in the school system and labor market. Their results tread in the same direction as previous chapters: the authors show that in the age bracket between 7 and 14 years, which corresponds to primary education, universal access had already eradicated racial inequalities in 2000. However, inequality in the access to high school by non-whites would only present a downward trend from 2000 on, after showing reasonable stability between 1980 and 2000. In higher education, on the other hand, despite the expansion of enrollment rates, in 2010 there was still a substantial gap between whites and non-whites, where blacks and browns presented very similar trajectories. In addition, in 2010 there was still an overlay of disadvantages by color and income, since poor blacks encountered greater difficulty in achieving higher levels of education than poor whites.

Thus, according to the authors, declining racial inequality does not mean that it was eliminated. Instead, there has been a displacement of the point at which race inequality manifests itself in the educational system. Brazilian universities are no longer predominantly white, but non-whites still have a lower share of university spots. One's family background still affects the odds for enrollment in higher education. Moreover, when non-whites enter the university, they tend to concentrate in programs that lead to less prestigious careers.

The third part of the book examines the path taken by public policies whose outcomes critically affect an individual's well-being.

In the chapter "The Geography of Access to Basic Services in Brazil," Marta Arretche examines the trajectory of access to infrastructure services and its association with poverty from 1970 to 2010 by using Brazilian municipalities as units of observation. The chapter shows that living conditions have improved considerably from 1970 to 2010. There was a decrease in the unequal access to basic services such as electricity, water and sewage, garbage collection, and schools among Brazilian municipalities. However, access to services has expanded in close connection with the expansion of per capita income as well as the concentration of the poor in Brazilian municipalities, although the causal mechanism behind such dramatic changes is not clear.

The path of improvement had notable regional expression however. In other words, the territorial expansion of services revealed a very similar pattern across policies. The expansion of supply began in affluent municipalities where universalization of services significantly preceded expansion in poorer jurisdictions. Coverage expansion in the South and Southeast regions is the first expansion cycle for all policies. Policies of the military regime and the re-democratization period were of greater benefit to the South and Southeast. Supply expansion for cities in the Central-West region constitutes the second expansion cycle for all policies, albeit in different periods for each region. Finally, the North and Northeastern regions are the last expansion zone. Whether for water or for energy – whose universal access was in place in the Southeast since 1980 – access only became universal in the Northeast beginning in 2010. In fact, rural populations and the poor who lived in less advantaged areas, especially in the Drought Polygon, would only gain access to water and electricity in the twenty-first century.

In the chapter "Housing and Urban Conditions in Brazil," Eduardo Marques argues that housing inequalities cannot be captured by indices of housing ownership. The high rates of housing in private residential property in the country since 1950 are explained by a recording problem: one that concerns ownership of buildings rather than ownership and legalization of the land on which a building is erected. Housing inequality therefore must be examined according to household occupancy density – which shows a downward trajectory – the existence of a bathroom – which is strongly associated with income – and access to essential services, such as water, sewage, garbage collection, and electricity.

The author shows that between 1960 and 2010, there was a significant improvement in urban conditions, with the exception of sewage collection coverage, which still remained very low in 2010. This reduction in access inequalities, however, varied considerably between policies. Electricity and garbage collection have become almost universal in urban areas, whereas water coverage has stagnated in the 90% range since the 1990s. The chapter reveals that two factors intersect in producing inequalities for infrastructure access in urban households. The first is household income: coverage for poorer households is systematically inferior to that for richer households, a factor that only disappears under the condition of universal access. The second is city size: larger cities tend to have higher coverage rates. The overlay of these two factors can be the source of a third expression in urban infrastructure access inequality: inequality between regions. Poverty and smaller towns are a feature concentrated in the North and Northeastern regions, therein producing situations of greater urban precariousness.

In the chapter "Health and Inequalities in Brazil," Vera Schattan Pereira Coelho and Marcelo F. Dias analyze the trajectory of health inequalities in Brazil. They show that health indicators improved considerably after re-democratization: between 1980 and 2010, the infant mortality rate fell from 69.1 to 16 per 1000 live births and life expectancy increased from 62.6 years in 1980 to 73.4 years in 2010.

Moreover, these indicators were accompanied by a reduction in inequalities among regions, states, and municipalities.

The authors found a solid and statistically significant association between these health indicators, on the one hand, and the average income of municipalities and level of schooling of women on the other. Furthermore, higher income inequality rates were associated with higher infant mortality rates and lower life expectancy. The strength of this association was, however, modest and declined throughout the period.

The fourth part of the book addresses the links between demographics and inequality. Recent decades have witnessed intense demographic changes in the form of major population displacements, profound changes in conditions for women, a decline in fertility rates along with significant changes in religious behavior. These changes were both the expression and cause of the path of inequality examined in this book.

In the chapter "Brazil's Internal Migration in 50 Years: (Dis)continuities and Ruptures," José Marcos Pinto da Cunha, in addition to describing the intensity of population displacements, shows how their scope and direction were closely associated with the dynamics of the Brazilian economy and the spatial distribution of employment opportunities. Industrialization – and, therefore, the rural-urban transition – was the main driving force for the country's massive population displacements that peaked in the 1970s.

This transition, however, is not enough to account for the volume or the direction of internal migration in each decade. In the 1970s, the accelerated growth of the Southeastern region (Sao Paulo in particular) greatly appealed to massive contingents of population living in expelling regions, given the scarce employment opportunities and poor housing conditions therein present. The same nature of motivations explains why the economic downturn – in the 1980s, but especially during the 1990s – intensified return migration. Employment opportunities had become limited in the Southeast. In the 2000s, this return migration decreased in intensity due to the recovery of economic activity in wealthier regions.

The rural-urban transition was not the only driving factor for migration in Brazil, however. In the 1970s, massive groups also moved to the North and Midwest as a result of agricultural modernization in the South and poverty in the Northeast. This rural-rural migration expanded the agricultural frontiers and made migration pressure toward the Southeast less dramatic.

The strength of both factors – jobs in the Southeast and the expansion of agricultural frontiers in the North and the Midwest – was less intense in the 1990s, resulting in a reduction in the volume of migration flows. From then on, the de-concentration of economic activity has changed the intensity of migration flows. More importantly, it has upset the hegemonies of the Southeast region and of the agricultural frontier areas as privileged migration destinations.

The chapter "Fifty Years of Gender Relations and Generation in Brazil: Changes and Continuities," by Maria Coleta Oliveira, Joice Melo Vieira, and Glaucia dos Santos Marcondes, describes the silent revolution in private life that occurred in Brazil over 50 years, a revolution where women were the main protagonists. The authors unravel the extent of demographic changes in Brazil between 1970 and 2010. Not only did life expectancy increase but inequalities among those living longer decreased. In parallel, there has been a decline in progeny, i.e., there was a significant decrease in the number of children per woman of childbearing age. This drop in the fertility rate was an expression of the widespread adoption of a behavior typical to more schooled women in the past. This behavioral change displaced the association between income and education across different types of inequality affecting women. The act of having children became a choice as did factors such as the widespread presence of women in the labor market and the proliferation of females in education.

No less intense were the changes in family arrangements. There is an increasing heterogeneity in family configurations. The number of formal marriages dropped significantly just as marital separations increased although this does not mean that the nuclear family model is less important. In contrast, consensual unions have grown exponentially, revealing the coexistence of multiple and changing forms of cohabitation and parenting. The authors show that, regardless of the persistence of inequalities, the scope of women's freedom and choice greatly increased over the course of a half-century.

In the chapter "Religious Transition in Brazil," Ronaldo Almeida and Rogério Barbosa describe the path of conversion from a heavily Roman Catholic country in rural 1960s Brazil to a country marked by religious pluralism in a highly urbanized environment. For the authors, the religious history of the half-century has been the history of progressive loss of hegemony on the part of the Catholic Church, which has not only lost members outright but has also maintained a large number of non-practicing members.

This route, however, far from signifies the end of religion, especially if we consider that the nonreligious population only modestly increased throughout this period. The gradual decline in the importance of Catholicism led to the proliferation of many diverse religious affiliations. The authors indicate that religious pluralism has established itself in Brazil as a result of intense societal transformations as well as the proselytizing strategies employed by the religions themselves. Such a plurality in religious affiliations, however, is not without its own stratification. Catholic hegemony remained restricted to rural areas. In urban areas, evangelicals increased at a rapid pace, especially in large metropolises, given their greater presence – particularly on the part of Pentecostals – at the base of the social pyramid. Spiritists, in turn, are mostly concentrated among the most educated and higher income populations.

Last but not least, changes in the composition of the labor market comprise the central theme in the trajectory of inequality and constitute the main subject in Part Five.

In the chapter "Economic Development and Inequalities in Brazil: 1960–2010," Alvaro Comin begins with an unsettling observation: income inequality in Brazil is perpetually high in spite of its downward trend from the 1990s on. Based on evidence that the main factor that explains income inequality lies in the labor market, the author attempts to reveal this phenomenon by analyzing changes in the occupational structure. In his approach, preexisting agrarian structures and the industrialization model along with educational and social rights policies assume a central role.

The author shows that the macro process of rural-urban transition, which accompanies industrialization, a combination of superimposed factors concerning the stratification of occupations, explains the persistence of an unequal and polarized labor market. The agrarian structure was only marginally altered by the modernization process. Rural populations were excluded from access to education as well as from social rights and worker protection. As a result, they had very limited opportunities for integrating themselves into the urban economy. Oversupply and low qualifications translated into low wages and below subsistence conditions in the urban economy. The path this significant segment of the population found through which to integrate themselves into the economically active population – especially women, the less schooled, and non-whites – was the service sector in low-skilled manual occupations.

For the author, the great challenge in reducing income inequality consists of reducing the wage disparity among these segments in comparison to the privileged portion, which succeeded in obtaining higher levels of education and, by extension, occupying nonmanual professions.

In the chapter "Commodification of Labor in Brazil's Labor Market (1960–2010)," Nadya Araujo Guimarães, Leonardo Sangali Barone, and Murillo Marschner Alves de Brito unravel the paths by which commodification of labor established itself in Brazil. According to the authors, in order to analyze this process one must first understand the processes by which the labor market, which in 1960 had not yet spread the typically capitalist wage labor dynamics to the entire workforce, became, in 2010, a place where most of the population of working age sought the conditions for their survival. For the authors, answering this question required an understanding of the trajectory of potential labor supply, i.e., the configuration of the economically active population.

The authors show that the most significant change in the consolidation of commodification of labor in Brazil in the last 50 years is linked to the integration of women into the labor market. Even though women reached the same levels of participation as men in 2010, the growth of opportunities for women has been remarkable. This, in turn, is associated with variations in the expected return as a result of labor market participation.

This book was only possible thanks to the generous contributions by a number of people. Rogério Jerônimo Barbosa has been an anchor in the production of all chapters. He has led a brilliant team of young researchers of the Center for Metropolitan Studies (CEM), composed by Diogo Ferrari, Ian Prates, Leonardo Sangali Barone, Murillo Marschner Alves de Brito, and Patrick Silva, who were in charge of the statistical support for data production. In addition, he actively collaborated in resolving several key methodological issues that emerged during the project. Finally, he coordinated the dataset of all editions of the Brazilian Census (1960, 1970, 1980, 1991, 2000, and 2010) as well as all editions of the *National Household Sample Survey* (from 1974 to 2015), which are available on the CEM website for open access. The resolution of several challenges in handling data also benefited from the always-competent collaboration of Edgard Fusaro. The CEM transfer team, José Donizete Cazzolato and Daniel Waldvogel Thomé da Silva, was very helpful in producing the maps.

The Portuguese edition largely benefited from two seminars held at CEBRAP in September 2012 and March 2013. The generous contribution of André Portela, Claudio Amitrano, Daniel Hidalgo, Eduardo Rios Neto, Elza Berquó, Marcelo Ayres Camurça Lima, Maria Herminia Tavares de Almeida, Nelson do Valle, and Ricardo Mariano were tremendously helpful. Initial versions of the chapters largely benefited from their input. The competent support of Mariza Nunes and Paula Zucaratto provided us the conditions to undertake these seminars.

The English edition was updated after a seminar held at the Brazilian Institute of the Woodrow Wilson Center in February 2016. We are particularly grateful to the generosity of Paulo Sotero in hosting and organizing this seminar. Moreover, comments and suggestions by Maria Herminia Tavares de Almeida, Daniel Gingerich, Matthew Taylor, David Lam, Carlos Eduardo Lins da Silva, Paulo Sotero, Peter Ward, Kenneth Roberts, and Sergei Soares pointed toward key aspects we should address. Comments from the Woodrow Wilson Center Press anonymous reviewers were very important in reframing the original version of the book. The editing support of Kim Olson has surely made our ideas understood by the English audience.

Last but not least, this project would not have been accomplished without the support of the São Paulo Research Foundation (FAPESP) through its Research, Innovation and Dissemination Centers (RIDCs), which have funded this and many other projects at the Center for Metropolitan Studies. Funding provided by the National Council for Scientific and Technological Development (CNPq) to the National Institutes of Science and Technology was also very helpful.

We are thankful to all of these sources of support over the many years of research, as we have attempted to comprehend the paths through which this very shameful phenomenon known as inequality can be overcome.

São Paulo, Brazil Marta Arretche

References

Barros, R. P. , Henriques, R., & Mendonça, R. (2000). Desigualdade e Pobreza no Brasil: retrato de uma estabilidade inaceitável. *Revista Brasileira de Ciências Sociais, 15*(42), 123–142.

Boix, Carles (2013). *Democracy and redistribution*. Cambridge: Cambridge University Press.

Carvalho, J. M. (2001). *Cidadania no Brasil*. São Paulo: Civilização Brasileira.

Esping-Andersen, G. (1985a). *Politics against markets. The social democratic road to power*. Princeton: Princeton University.

Esping-Andersen, G. (1985b). Power and distributional regimes. *Politics & Society, 14*(2), 223–256.

Esping-Andersen, G. (1990). *The three worlds of welfare capitalism*. Princeton: Princeton University.
Glaeser, E. L., La Porta, R., Lopez-De-Silanes, F., & Shleifer, A. (2004). Do institutions cause growth? *Journal of Economic Growth, 9*, 271–303.
Hobsbawn, E. (1994). *Era dos Extremos. O Breve século xx (1914–1991)*. São Paulo: Companhia das Letras.
Kingstone, P. R., & Power, T. (2008). *Democratic Brazil revisited*. Pittsburgh: University of Pittsburgh Press.
Kuznets, S. (1955). Economic growth and income inequality. *The American Economic Review, 45*(1), 1–28.
Lamounier, B. (1992). Estrutura institucional e governabilidade na década de 90. In J. P. dos Reis Velloso (org.). *O Brasil e as reformas políticas*. Rio de Janeiro: José Olympio.
Meltzer, A. H., & Richard, S. F. (1981). A rational theory of the size of government. *Journal of Political Economy, 89*, 914–927.
Milanovic, B. (2016). *Global inequality: A new approach for the age of globalization*. Cambridge/ London: The Belknap Press of Harvard University Press.
Piketty, T. (2014). *Capital in the twenty-first century* (Kindle ed.). Cambridge, MA: Harvard University Press.
Piketty, T., & Saez, E. (2014). Inequality in the long run. *Science, 344*(6186), 838–842.
Ravallion, M. (2014). Income inequality in the developing world. *Science, 344*(6186), 851–855.
Reis, E., & Cheibub, Z. B. (1993). Pobreza, Desigualdade e Consolidação Democrática. *Dados, 36*(2), 233–260.
Stepan, A. (1999). Para uma nova análise comparativa do federalismo e da democracia: Federações que restringem ou ampliam o poder do *demos*. *Dados, 42*(2), 197–252.

Contents

Part I
Political Participation

Political Participation in Brazil

Fernando Limongi, José Antonio Cheibub, and Argelina Figueiredo

Abstract This chapter analyzes the expansion of political participation in Brazil between 1945 and 2010. During this time, the country lived under three different political regimes: two democratic (1945–1964, 1985–2010) and one authoritarian (1964–1985). The analysis focuses on electoral participation, showing how social inequality impacted voters' ability to register, turn out, and ultimately cast a valid ballot. The chapter shows how extensive voting restrictions in 1945 were along these three dimensions and how they declined over time. It also calls attention to the impact of changes in the electoral legislation on different social groups' ability to exercise their voting rights.

Keywords Suffrage expansion · Electoral participation · Electoral integrity · Political incorporation · Political inequality

On October 3, 2010, just over 111 million Brazilians went to the polls. The vast majority of the adult population had no trouble registering and voting. Election results were released within a matter of hours and were not contested by parties or individual candidates. The electoral process in its multiple and complex stages, from voter registration to swearing-in the elected, was subject to no political or legal disputes.

We thank Marta Arretche, Maria Hermínia Tavares de Almeida, Daniel Hidalgo and the participants in the II Census Project Workshop (held in the Center for Metropolitan Studies, CEBRAP, March, 2013) for helpful comments. We gratefully acknowledge the research assistance of Diogo Ferrari. José Antonio Cheibub acknowledges support from the Lemann Institute of Brazilian Studies, University of Illinois at Urbana-Champaign.

F. Limongi (✉)
Universidade de São Paulo, São Paulo, Brazil

J. A. Cheibub
Texas A&M University, College Station, TX, USA
e-mail: cheibub@tamu.edu

A. Figueiredo
Instituto de Estudos Sociais e Políticos, Universidade Estadual do Rio de Janeiro, Rio de Janeiro, Brazil
e-mail: argelina@iesp.uerj.br

M. Arretche (ed.), *Paths of Inequality in Brazil*,
https://doi.org/10.1007/978-3-319-78184-6_1

Brazil is currently a democracy with one of the largest electorates on the planet (135.5 million registered voters), ranking only behind India, the United States, and Indonesia,[1] and is renowned for its efficiency in organizing the electoral process. Elections take place without violence or disputes regarding the legitimacy of their results. Due to the electronic voting system adopted in 1998, results are known within hours of polls' closing.

The growth of the Brazilian electorate between 1945 and 2010 is striking and could be viewed as extraordinary.[2] In 1945 the total electorate was 7.4 million people, 18.2 times smaller than it is today. Within this period, the population quadrupled. The ratio between registered voters and total population went from 16% to 70%. The increase in the number of voters as a proportion of voting age population (adults over the age of 18) is no less remarkable, having gone from 42.6% in 1950 to almost 100% in 2010. Even if we account for the legal restrictions that prohibit illiterate adults from voting, the percentage of registered voters compared with the literate adult population reached 87% in 1950.

Thus, expansion of the electorate was not simply a result of demographic growth, changes in the age composition of the population, or even educational expansion and the enfranchisement of illiterate adults. Rather, the period since 1945 is marked by an intense process of political incorporation. Transformations were not only of a quantitative nature: institutional and social contexts also underwent radical changes. With this in mind, the goal of this chapter is to document this process and underscore the connections between political disputes, changes in electoral legislation, and social changes. Throughout the text, we distinguish three political periods: the first democratic experience (1945–1964), the authoritarian period (1964–1985), and the current period (1985–2010).

Components of Electoral Participation[3]

In order to participate in politics, even if only through the act of voting itself, a citizen has to incur some costs. The act of registering to vote, showing up at the voting booth, and making a specific choice are activities that demand time and resources. Costs may be higher or lower depending on the legal specifications and context in which these three activities take place. Even if legally eligible to vote, a citizen may

[1] The number of registered voters in the last election covered by IDEA data in these countries was 716.9 million, 190.4 million, and 171.2 million, respectively. Available at: http://www.idea.int/resources/databases.cfm#vt. Last accessed: 02/27/2013. Regime classification is based on Cheibub et al. (2010).

[2] There have been no changes in the electoral calendar for legislative elections since 1945, when the first democratic elections were held in Brazil, despite periods of military rule. All census data used in this chapter begin in 1950.

[3] For convenience, we use the terms *electoral* participation and *political* participation interchangeably, although the latter encompasses forms of action that go beyond electoral participation.

be unable to register because she cannot gather together all the documents required to do so, for instance, or because she simply cannot physically get to the registration offices. Voters may be registered by people who expect to control their behavior at the polls, just as they can be prevented from registering by people who do not expect to get their votes. The most direct and forceful exclusion occurs when the law denies voting rights to specific groups as in the case of Brazil's illiterate population before 1985.

In order to vote, citizens have to physically go to the polls, an effort that could entail missing a day of work. For those living in rural areas, travel costs are high and are unlikely to be absorbed by the voter. In cases such as this, consideration should be given to the actions of organized political groups who seek to reduce or increase these costs perhaps by transporting those whose vote they expect to get or by intimidating those expected to vote for opponents.

Finally, in order to cast a valid vote, citizens have to know how to do so, that is, they have to process information about the available alternatives and be able to express their preferences adequately. The very type of ballot used in an election directly affects these costs and can lead to the exclusion of voters with low levels of education.

Therefore, participation costs may involve overcoming a variety of obstacles related to registering, getting to the voting site, and actually casting a ballot. It is important not only to analyze these costs directly but also to determine how their unequal distribution affects the way citizens participate in politics. Voters rarely bear participation costs voluntarily; if they do it is because they have been convinced that they have to. In many cases, parties and candidates register voters and take them to the polls, instructing them – when not outright coercing them – to vote in a certain way.

Voting has been mandatory in Brazil since the 1930s. This is a critical factor that has to be considered throughout this analysis. The adoption of mandatory voting was part of an electoral reform package designed to eliminate fraud and corruption. These problems were perceived to have marred the country's elections, which at that point in history had already been held for a century. Mandatory voting was the least debated aspect of the reform package, which also included such things as establishment of a judiciary body dedicated to electoral issues (the Superior Electoral Court, TSE), measures to guarantee the secrecy of the vote, and the "invention" of the open list system of proportional representation (Pires 2009). These measures were aimed at undermining the electoral foundation of state-level oligarchies (Melo Franco 2005).

Mandatory voting is implicitly justified by the assumption that electoral participation would not be universal if it remained voluntary. Voluntary participation would mean that the poorest members of the electorate would be kept away from the polls since they would vote only when and if transported to the voting stations by their "superiors" (the bosses). When everyone is forced to vote, those who control a chunk of votes become less advantaged. Thus, when compulsory voting was adopted, some advocates believed that its effects would only be felt when and if registration costs were entirely assumed by the state (Pinto Serva 1931, p. 250).

When viewed in light of institutional changes that have occurred since 1945, the data indicate a marked increase in electoral participation. This increase was the result of a general decrease in the costs of registration, attendance, and expression of a political preference. But the increased participation did not go unchallenged nor was it the product of an idealism that saw electoral integrity as a condition for the country's political progress. In Brazil, gradual expansion of political participation as well as fluctuations in it over the years is the result of clashes of partisan forces, which projected the effects the measures they advocated would have on their supporters and positioned themselves accordingly.

The Right of Suffrage and Voter Registration

The right of suffrage defines the potential electorate, i.e., the share of the population able to register and legally participate in the political process. Contemporary democracies are characterized by the adoption of universal suffrage, which in practical terms means conferring the right to vote on adults and, in general, on those over the age of 18. Restrictions pertaining to gender, income, education, and race, common during the nineteenth century, were gradually eliminated.[4]

In Brazil, gender-based restrictions were abolished in the 1930s. The reforms responsible for extending the vote to women also established mandatory voting, reduced the minimum voting age, introduced the secret ballot, and established the TSE as the sole competent body responsible for organizing elections. The same reforms, however, restricted voting on the basis of education. The 1946 Constitution retained basic elements of the model established after the Revolution of 1930, preserving mandatory voting and excluding illiterate persons from the electoral process. However, the constitutional text allowed for statutory exceptions to mandatory voting; in this way, the 1950 Electoral Code made the vote of housewives optional.[5] The exclusion of illiterate persons was upheld until 1985, when a constitutional amendment granted them the right to vote. The legal enfranchisement of illiterates was confirmed in the 1988 Constitution although in a decision that is quite indicative of the way this segment of the population is viewed by Brazilian politicians: their vote is not mandatory, like that of everyone else. Similarly, individuals over the age of 70 and between the ages of 16 and 18 are also allowed to vote, but not required to do so.

In light of these changes, it is natural for composition of the potential electorate to vary over time. For the period prior to 1985, the potential electorate excluded illiterates, although this legal restriction should be considered in light of the practices associated with formal qualification, that is, determination that voters have met legally established requirements. There is always a certain amount of fluidity when one goes from theoretical to practical legal exclusion. That is why the actual

[4] See Przeworski (2010, Chapter 3).

[5] Article 4 Code stipulates that only women in paid professions were required to vote.

electorate does not necessarily correspond to the potential electorate. The procedures designed to provide proof of an individual voter's literacy never required more than a simple signature on the registration form. Prior to 1950, this requirement was not even necessary since a third party could register voters. Proof of literacy, such as a diploma or a certificate of school attendance, has never been required. Proof of age and residence, on the other hand, were thoroughly defined by law. Thus, assessment of the degree to which the electorate approaches the universe of potential voters – literate citizens over the age of 18 – is not as clear as the legal exclusion suggests.[6] These considerations affect how the data presented below should be read.

Data on voter registration is presented by using a reference population defined in three different ways: total population, adults over the age of 18, and literate adults over the age of 18 (Graph 1). Between 1950 and 2010, the proportion of registered voters increased regardless of the reference population. However, this increase is minimal in the first democratic period (1950–1964), during which we actually observe a reduction in the number of registered voters as a proportion of the total population and total literate adult population. This reduction was caused by the differential growth rates of each of these populations. Thus, while the registered electorate grew by 35.7% between 1950 and 1960, during the same period, the gen-

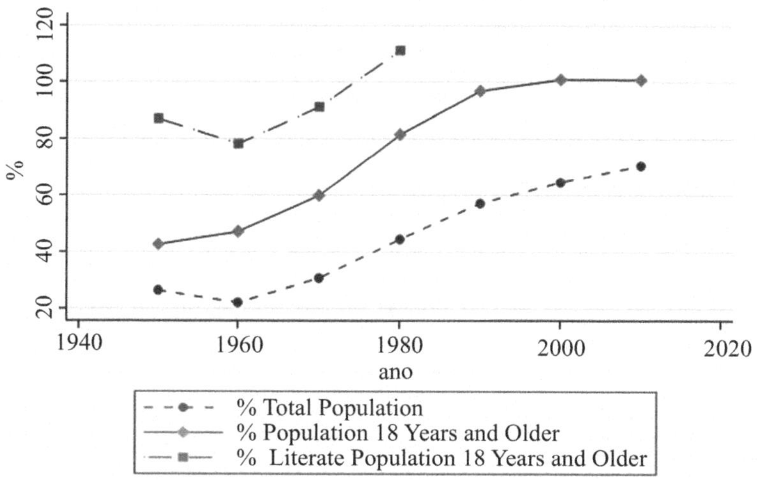

Graph 1 Vote registration rates, 1950–2010. (Source: Superior Electoral Court (TSE); Brazilian Institute of Geography and Statistics (IBGE))

[6] Note that fluidity involved in translating legal requirements into practice is common in any electoral system, even those based on ascriptive criteria (Horowitz 1985). In systems based on non-ascriptive criteria, however, this fluidity is even greater since it is subject to objective changes in their distribution among the population.

eral population increased by 61.9%, and the eligible population increased by 50.9%. Since total adult population did not grow as fast as the electorate, a steady increase was noted in the number of registered voters in this population. One can therefore infer that both the literate and the young populations (younger than age 18) grew rapidly between 1950 and 1960. As we will see below, relative growth of the electorate was the result of the 1956–1957 voter relisting.

The legal exclusion of illiterates eliminated a significant portion of the adult population from political life. Data in Graph 1 suggest that if voting rights were granted to illiterates, approximately 13 million more people would be able to vote. However, this exclusion was commonly circumvented. Analysis of demographic data by state confirms violation of the constitutional precept, since the number of registered voters exceeds that of potential voters in several states (Table 1). This result could possibly be due to the fact that the numerator and denominator used to calculate the registration rate come from different sources (the Brazilian Institute of

Table 1 Percentage of registered voters listed by state – 1950–1980

	% pop 18 years of age or older				% pop 18 years of age or older and literate			
State	1950	1960	1970	1982	1950	1960	1970	1982
AC	21.8	16.0	42.6	75.6	58.0	56.4	90.8	139.9
AL	27.2	19.9	36.0	66.0	112.3	130.3	95.7	149.3
AM	29.8	20.2	61.6	71.5	65.0	76.1	99.4	103.2
AP	35.5	15.5	42.7	74.6	80.1	62.8	66.9	101.7
BA	35.5	25.3	53.7	81.2	106.9	122.4	111.6	147.0
CE	52.2	30.3	57.1	84.4	157.3	147.0	131.2	160.9
DF		7.2				13.1		
ES	43.3	29.9	64.2	78.2	91.3	101.2	98.6	105.7
GO/TO	36.9	28.7	62.4	92.2	106.1	111.5	105.1	133.5
MA	32.8	26.5	32.6	66.8	126.4	150.1	84.2	142.8
MG	50.5	38.0	65.3	84.2	113.8	137.9	102.3	114.7
MT/MS	51.5	26.7	48.1	87.4	99.3	90.9	73.9	121.8
PA	48.3	30.9	57.9	79.3	96.6	102.8	87.4	112.0
PB	40.5	29.3	52.5	83.3	135.5	158.9	120.4	171.2
PE	25.9	25.9	50.5	73.3	78.5	121.5	103.4	130.2
PI	44.2	29.8	57.6	86.6	160.5	151.5	148.0	181.4
PR	35.2	26.2	62.3	107.4	67.0	82.6	92.6	138.0
RJ	53.1	36.2	64.1	80.9	73.7	77.4	77.9	93.7
RN	49.7	35.0	55.8	87.1	154.1	187.8	126.7	163.4
RO	24.5	16.3	29.0	70.9	37.9	43.5	46.1	106.6
RR	38.2	29.1	42.3	83.9	80.3	96.9	66.7	115.8
RS	45.6	40.0	65.7	83.8	69.4	102.1	82.0	97.6
SC	49.3	42.5	75.0	95.9	80.9	122.8	94.5	111.6
SE	45.8	34.1	59.2	75.1	139.1	167.6	131.1	146.6
SP	40.0	34.3	64.1	77.2	63.0	85.4	80.5	90.7
Brazil	**42.6**	**32.2**	**59.8**	**81.5**	**87.0**	**101.9**	**91.1**	**111.1**

Source: Superior Electoral Court (TSE); Brazilian Institute of Geography and Statistics (IBGE)
Note: The series refers to the period before the incorporation of illiterate adults, which occurred in 1986

Geography and Statistics (IBGE) and TSE) and that these sources use different definitions of illiteracy. More realistically, we think that registration rates above 100% result from the fact that the definition of illiteracy for purposes of voter registration was left deliberately vague; the boundaries of political citizenship were far from being objectively defined. As might be expected, this definition has been at the center of the partisan-political debate since 1945 when the first democratic elections were held.

Castro Gomes (2005) has shown that as World War II drew to a close, Brazil's federal government seized the political initiative by proposing that presidential elections be held after having been "provisionally" suspended by the 1937 Constitution. The government's original transition strategy rested on two pillars: control of voter registration and prompt and noncompetitive elections. The plan devised by Minister of Labor Marcondes Filho was to use government-controlled labor unions to register voters en masse for compulsory voting and even considered the creation of rural labor unions. The government's goal was to neutralize the electoral strength wielded by state "oligarchies."

The government lost control of the transition process it had set in motion, at least partially, when opposition forces launched their candidate, Brigadier Eduardo Gomes (Castro Gomes 2005). By February 1945, it was already clear to everyone involved that the December elections would be competitive. At that point, forces inside the government started organizing the Social Democratic Party (PSD) to face the opposition candidate, but not without first turning to the "oligarchies," which Marcondes Filho had sought to weaken.

The narrow deadline for composing voter rolls – around 6 months[7] – allowed the government to preserve a key part of its original plan: ex officio registration, i.e., the collective and nonvoluntary registration of employees of private firms and public agencies, including trade unions. Thus, the electorate formed in 1945 was a result of the combination of ex officio registration, which was predominantly urban, and "voluntary" registration, which mainly took place in rural areas. The latter should not be interpreted as resulting from autonomous individual decision, however. Third parties could request registration, and the physical presence of the potential voter was not even required at all points of the process. As a result, voter registration in large sections of the country occurred under the strict control of local political machines connected to both the PSD and the National Democratic Union (UDN), although government control favored the former.

Carvalho (1958, p. 27) illustrates the intense government involvement taking place during the process of registration in the state of Minas Gerais. State funds were often misused in an attempt to favor incumbents and hinder the opposition.[8] Table 2 presents evidence of the importance of ex officio voter registration on the total number of voters registered per state, distinguishing state capitals, invariably

---

[7]The last national election had taken place in 1935, and presidential elections scheduled for January 1938 were suspended with the 1937 coup that established the *Estado Novo* regime.

[8]Carvalho (1958, p. 27) states that: "The questionnaires declare with no discrepancy that the incumbent party's expenses were paid by the mayors' office, if not by the State; but they did not obtain proof to support a peremptory statement." Subsequently the author states: "The first sign that the administrative apparatus favors the incumbent party came with the appointment of low level officials to be in charge of voter registration and qualification" (Carvalho 1958, p. 52).

Table 2 % of ex-officio registered voters by state and city status

Capital cities			Other cities			Total		
Ex-officio	Application	Total	Ex-officio	Application	Total	Ex-officio	Application	Total
11.0	13.4	24.4	11.6	64.0	75.6	22.7	77.3	100.0
22.5	31.6	54.1	4.5	41.4	45.9	27.0	73.0	100.0
7.4	11.7	19.1	9.9	71.0	80.9	17.3	82.7	100.0
4.8	9.2	14.1	3.4	82.5	85.9	8.3	91.7	100.0
54.1	45.9	100.0	0.0	0.0	0.0	54.1	45.9	100.0
6.8	9.8	16.6	8.3	75.1	83.4	15.1	84.9	100.0
2.3	7.0	9.3	5.1	85.6	90.7	7.4	92.6	100.0
7.9	7.8	15.8	3.9	80.4	84.2	11.8	88.2	100.0
2.9	4.5	7.4	11.7	80.9	92.6	14.6	85.4	100.0
4.0	16.4	20.4	11.7	67.9	79.6	15.7	84.3	100.0
13.8	27.0	40.7	3.7	55.6	59.3	17.4	82.6	100.0
4.4	6.5	10.8	5.3	83.9	89.2	9.6	90.4	100.0
13.9	13.2	27.1	7.2	65.7	72.9	21.1	78.9	100.0
10.7	11.5	22.2	10.9	66.9	77.8	21.7	78.3	100.0
6.3	6.2	12.5	25.4	62.1	87.5	31.7	68.3	100.0
2.9	10.3	13.2	5.9	81.0	86.8	8.7	91.3	100.0
7.4	8.0	15.4	13.6	71.0	84.6	21.0	79.0	100.0
2.2	4.5	6.7	17.2	76.1	93.3	19.3	80.7	100.0
9.2	10.2	19.4	6.1	74.5	80.6	15.3	84.7	100.0
18.3	20.4	38.7	14.7	46.5	61.3	33.0	67.0	100.0
12.7	14.3	27.0	11.1	62.0	73.0	23.8	76.2	100.0

Source: Superior Electoral Court (TSE)
Note: Information for the state of Piauí is not included, due to nonavailability

the state's largest city, from other municipalities. The government's control over the composition of the electorate is significant in the capitals, especially in large urban centers such as Rio de Janeiro and São Paulo. In Rio (then Brazil's capital), for example, 54% of voters were registered ex officio. After the 1945 election, the opposition claimed that the magnitude of the vote obtained by Getúlio Vargas in the capital was evidence of the strong relationship between official control of electoral registration and support for the government. The former president was elected as federal deputy by the Brazilian Labor Party (PTB) with more than 100,000 votes. Because of the electoral rules, Vargas' win swept into office eight other deputies from the PTB, five of whom obtained fewer than 1000 votes.

Ex officio registration is seen as one of the many ways the government manipulated electoral law for the purpose of ensuring its own victory (Campello de Souza, 1976, Chap. V). However, government control of voters registered ex officio is not as readily apparent as commonly assumed.[9] As Campello de Souza has argued (1976, p. 121), ex officio registration is certainly the means through which

[9]According to Kinzo (1979, p. 81), ex officio registration "acted as a control mechanism over the urban electorate, tying it to the government since voters often felt obligated to vote with those responsible for their registration."

"'Getulism' expands the electorate while at the same time keeps it under its control."[10] However, academic analyses seem to give more weight to ex officio registration as a mechanism of control than does contemporary opposition itself. For the opposition, the main issue with ex officio registration was not that the government would control the way they voted but that it illegally included illiterates and foreigners on the electoral rolls. Since its defeat in the 1945 elections, the UDN strongly advocated for a new process of electoral registration aimed at "purging the rolls of its criminal aspects: illiterates and foreigners" (Franco 1946, p. 29).

Thus, the dimensions of the institutional debate concerning the right to vote are clear: while Getulist forces sought to simultaneously expand and control the electorate, the UDN sought to restrict it by defending stricter enforcement of the legal exclusion of illiterates. The importance of ex officio registration in this debate therefore needs to be reexamined because it occurred most often where a minority of the electorate resided at the time. In the 1940s, most voters lived in rural areas and small towns. This is indicative of the success of local political machines in mobilizing the support of rural workers, most of whom were illiterate.

Electoral legislation, debated generically in drafting the 1946 Constitution, took center stage during the Dutra administration, especially over the course of debating the Electoral Code set forth in the constitutional provisions. At that time, there was no heated confrontation between the two major parties, since the debate took place under the aegis of the coalition formed by the PSD and the UDN to support the Dutra government (Leal 1993, p. 239). Many of the UDN demands were met, including adoption of the D'Hondt method for allocating remaining seats in elections for national and state-level legislatures, and prohibition of the elimination of "multiple candidacies," under which one individual could run for different offices in more than one electoral district. Topics such as voter transportation and introduction of the official (Australian) ballot were discussed, but proposals associated with them were easily defeated. Ex officio registration was eliminated for new voters, but nothing was said about voters who had already been registered. Note that the electorate grew from 7.4 to 11.2 million voters between 1945 and 1950 and to 15.2 million in 1955. Thus, despite elimination of ex officio registration, the number of registered voters doubled over the course of a decade.

Following the 1954 suicide of Vargas, the UDN chose electoral reform as one of its main issues. Strengthened by its proximity to President Café Filho, the party supported the establishment of a joint congressional committee (consisting of members of the Chamber of Deputies and the Senate) charged with "purifying" the electoral process. Two concrete measures were proposed in one bill: adoption of the official ballot and creation of a new electoral roll. The first measure will be discussed in the section that follows. As for the electoral roll, its goal was to impose stricter standards for certifying literacy and thus prevent the registration of illiterate and semiliterate individuals.[11]

---

[10] Campello de Souza (1976, p. 121) goes as far as to say that the manipulation of electoral rules gave the 1945 elections "if not an air of downright official fraud, then at least one of considerable bias in favor of the government."

[11] See Bloem (1955) for more details concerning these proposals.

Establishment of a new electoral roll had the expected results. The total number of registered voters dropped in nearly all states (Table 3). As a result, the new roll had 1,462,786 fewer voters, even though the country's population had increased by almost six million people between when the new registration process began (1955) and ended (1958). The states of Maranhão, Pernambuco, and Amazonas lost about a third of their voters, while many other states experienced a decrease of over 20% in the size of their electorate. Only a small number of states saw an increase in the number of registered voters, Ceará standing out with a somewhat questionable expansion of 29% in the size of its electorate.

Electoral reform approved in 1955 included a number of measures designed to ensure strict enforcement of registration requirements. It also determined that all existing registration cards would become invalid as of December 1955. As previously noted, the new law categorically adopted voluntary (as opposed to ex officio) registration, which required that voters complete registration forms in person, in front of the electoral official, thus making it harder to register illiterate and semiliterate persons. Additionally, the new voter registration card would require a photograph of the voter that had to be provided by the voter himself. Thus, registration costs increased, not only for those who were illiterate or semiliterate but also for low-income voters living in rural areas who were particularly hard hit. The overall reduction in the number of voters was thus the result of both the purging of fraudulent voters and more effective exclusion of less privileged citizens. The UDN's goal in electoral reform was to limit the size of the electorate. In contrast, possibly due to pressure from the PSD, punishment for those failing to vote became more severe.

Whether due to stricter requirements or some other reason, the fact is that the process of electoral registration dragged on for some time. Under pressure from local political forces usually identified with the PSD, which had won the 1955 presidential elections, the National Congress extended the validity of the old voter registration cards, which were then used for the 1957 mayoral elections. Consequently, the new electoral roll only became ready in 1958.[12]

Viewed together, the first democratic experience in Brazil unfolded within a framework of limited political participation. There was an initial mobilization effort that originated in the political forces identified with followers of Vargas. The response to the political polarization that characterized the first half of the 1950s was clear: it increased control over the addition of new voters thus limiting the electorate. With completion of the new registration, the electorate again began to grow but at a significantly slower pace than the one observed during the first decade of the democratic regime. Evidence suggests that the expansion of the electorate at that point in time was the product of demographic and education factors: respectively, the growth of voting age population and improvements in Brazil's system of basic education. The political polarization of the 1960s did not affect the rate with which new voters were included in the political system.

[12] The same law that extended the validity of old voter registration cards also determined that the official (Australian) ballot would be used in all majoritarian elections beginning in 1958.

Table 3 Electorate by state, absolute number and growth, 1946–2010

Estado	1946	1950	1954	1955	1958	1960	1962	1966	1970	1974	1978	1982	1986	1989	1990	1994	1996	1998	2000	2002	2004	2006	2008	2010
Acre		**12284**	50.0	−6.2	−13.6	0.0	30.8	39.7	46.9	47.9	53.3	27.0	22.7	29.0	8.2	33.1	9.4	10.8	4.3	11.1	4.8	6.5	7.3	6.3
Alagoas	**82068**	78.1	33.4	−2.6	−29.0	14.6	24.3	17.0	22.2	36.9	38.3	41.0	32.6	24.4	7.7	−11.3	9.7	9.0	10.0	5.1	10.6	5.1	6.3	2.9
Amazonas	**31948**	135.9	61.3	−1.5	−25.9	3.6	49.4	17.1	65.0	4.2	41.0	39.1	21.8	27.5	5.1	25.0	11.3	11.1	3.0	8.2	8.9	7.3	7.1	6.4
Amapá		**6737**	48.2	−7.5	−16.4	2.0	73.5	19.6	31.1	38.3	49.2	58.5	20.7	39.7	15.1	45.0	−11.8	22.7	17.2	16.0	13.3	9.8	6.7	9.3
Bahia	**440621**	96.8	25.7	0.3	−15.9	2.5	27.9	15.6	40.1	24.1	33.0	32.1	13.8	21.6	2.1	16.8	8.6	3.9	3.8	4.1	4.5	1.7	0.5	4.3
Ceará	**369550**	84.9	0.0	−25.5	29.0	1.8	27.6	8.6	33.6	10.9	40.5	29.5	14.1	17.6	4.2	14.7	8.3	−0.8	7.5	3.9	6.9	4.4	5.0	4.4
Brasília						**23564**							**733112**	16.9	4.2	18.9	1.5	17.7	1.6	17.8	−0.5	9.6	0.5	10.4
Espírito Santo	**122281**	47.7	45.0	−4.9	−6.5	0.9	30.6	23.1	31.0	16.7	26.1	33.4	19.3	21.4	1.1	20.2	11.2	0.8	6.1	5.5	4.2	4.5	4.5	3.4
Guanabara	**549353**	52.4	15.3	2.8	−1.5	12.4	9.0	24.9	18.8	24.4														
Goiás	**103079**	111.3	67.0	0.0	−10.1	24.7	25.1	27.3	37.1	27.5	39.0	29.8	5.4	1.9	2.0	16.8	5.2	6.9	7.0	6.7	7.3	3.4	3.7	4.8
Maranhão	**109101**	140.4	53.9	5.6	−34.7	38.2	29.4	−41.2	61.0	43.5	60.7	33.4	19.3	24.2	5.2	15.9	6.4	7.4	6.1	7.0	10.4	4.7	6.1	4.0
Minas Gerais	**1231251**	57.3	22.2	3.9	−17.2	5.7	19.3	19.6	22.9	18.8	20.6	26.9	16.3	18.4	0.6	11.2	6.5	5.1	3.8	3.4	4.7	3.0	2.9	3.2
Mato Grosso do Sul											**517923**	44.8	9.3	22.2	2.3	13.3	2.2	5.9	5.9	6.0	5.7	4.6	3.7	5.2
Mato Grosso	**59121**	123.3	38.4	6.2	−8.8	15.2	28.9	21.1	16.5	56.3	−35.9	56.1	42.4	24.4	6.0	17.4	11.9	6.0	8.4	5.2	6.1	5.7	2.7	5.2
Para	**159395**	74.2	24.5	8.0	−27.3	19.6	29.9	13.6	24.7	26.2	38.0	46.5	14.8	25.1	5.6	20.5	8.9	6.2	3.6	6.9	11.5	4.5	8.6 5.6	
Paraíba	**175634**	97.1	27.0	1.9	−35.0	21.4	14.7	36.4	14.0	32.3	21.9	25.4	14.8	20.0	3.1	15.5	6.0	0.3	−2.6	7.2	6.3	4.3	3.2	3.2
Pernambuco	**321736**	40.7	85.0	4.3	−29.6	10.0	25.9	17.4	31.7	21.6	26.2	25.8	23.9	19.5	3.2	15.0	8.6	5.5	2.6	2.7	4.7	3.2	4.0	3.2
Piauí	**132455**	66.1	32.9	4.1	−23.7	5.1	29.0	9.8	32.6	30.3	27.3	27.5	12.0	22.7	5.7	15.7	9.6	−0.4	−4.4	8.6	7.5	4.4	5.4	3.5
Paraná	**229672**	62.3	63.6	10.3	1.8	29.3	24.3	34.1	40.5	29.8	66.8	−7.0	3.4	16.9	1.3	12.4	5.8	5.0	1.9	2.4	3.7	3.1	2.5	4.1
Rio de Janeiro	**383100**	64.9	44.2	−7.5	−6.2	4.6	34.8	18.7	20.9	25.1	156.8	20.7	15.1	14.8	1.0	10.3	6.0	3.1	−0.4	2.9	3.0	3.6	3.4	2.9

Table 3 (continued)

Estado	1946	1950	1954	1955	1958	1960	1962	1966	1970	1974	1978	1982	1986	1989	1990	1994	1996	1998	2000	2002	2004	2006	2008	2010
Rio Grande do Norte	**131560**	84.9	33.3	−9.1	−22.2	21.2	15.8	23.7	11.0	27.8	27.6	32.5	11.8	21.5	2.5	12.0	9.4	6.0	4.3	6.3	5.6	3.8	3.4	3.4
Rondônia				**6995**		19.2	53.0	25.8	−2.0	107.8	187.2	148.5	91.7	24.7	5.5	17.6	12.0	7.9	−0.4	6.0	7.8	3.9	4.0	4.9
Roraima				**5675**		0.4		18.4	15.5	58.2	123.1	35.6	40.5	39.4	18.1	39.0	17.2	21.4	9.0	12.1	2.9	8.8	6.1	9.7
Rio Grande do Sul	**753232**	31.1	22.8	8.8	−3.4	10.6	10.8	23.5	24.6	20.4	22.4	22.2	15.2	14.3	0.8	9.6	4.7	3.8	3.9	3.4	2.6	2.7	2.3	2.4
Santa Catarina	**248086**	48.2	29.0	4.1	6.1	10.9	9.8	23.4	33.3	26.9	24.1	29.1	8.4	17.8	1.5	14.0	6.2	4.9	3.1	5.3	4.7	4.3	4.5	4.2
Sergipe	**97089**	51.6	48.7	−8.2	−27.7	3.3	28.3	13.3	15.7	7.0	30.6	33.3	34.3	22.8	3.5	17.3	9.2	5.1	0.5	5.7	8.3	4.5	5.4	4.1
São Paulo	**1688598**	20.9	35.0	1.0	2.6	19.5	12.0	28.2	33.6	22.5	27.7	28.3	21.8	15.6	1.2	10.9	6.4	5.5	4.0	5.7	5.5	3.6	3.9	4.0
Tocantins														**464060**	7.5	29.9	2.8	−6.3	16.0	8.4	7.4	4.7	5.0	2.4
Brasil	**7418930**	54.3	31.8	1.0	−9.7	12.9	19.2	20.9	29.4	23.6	31.2	25.3	17.8	18.3	2.1	13.0	6.9	4.7	3.5	4.9	5.3	3.7	3.7	3.9

Source: TSE, Dados Estatisticos. Numbers in bold represent the number of voters; other numbers represent the rate of growth of electorate

Moderate expansion of the electorate persisted during the early years of the military regime but picked up in the mid-1970s. By 1980, only three states seemed to have any literate adults who had not yet been formally incorporated into the political process.[13] In fact, the data indicate that the number of registered voters surpassed the number of voters permitted to register in almost every state.

Between 1974 and 1986, the electorate practically doubled in size (from 35.8 million to 69.3 million), paradoxically indicating that the rate of expansion of the electorate accelerated during the military period. Demographic and educational factors obviously continued to play a role in this expansion, and increased urbanization may have contributed to reducing the costs of registration. But purely political factors should not be entirely disregarded, especially the effect of regular elections and mobilizing campaigns promoted by the Brazilian Democratic Movement (MDB). The rate of electoral registration increased once elections became more important with the beginning of the process of political liberalization in 1974.

The return to democracy in 1985 was accompanied by the extension of voting rights to illiterates. The measure was overdue in more than one sense. First, at the time only a few countries in the world still prevented illiterates from participating in elections.[14] Moreover, electoral exclusion of illiterates had already ceased to be seriously enforced throughout Brazil, and if enforced at all, it affected a declining proportion of the population. Still, its effect should not be minimized. Once the right to vote was made universal, the TSE implemented new voter registration, requiring, in the process, that individuals state their level of formal education. Of the nearly 70 million voters then registered, 9.72% declared themselves illiterate and a stunning 30% declared that they had only very basic reading and writing skills; 28% declared having some but not complete primary education. The extension of voting rights to illiterates, thus, was no trivial matter, even if we can never be sure of the number of people who actually registered for the first time as a result of its implementation.

The current period does not really require systematic treatment with regard to electoral registration. As shown in Graph 1, voter registration has been almost universal since the return to democracy in 1985. Registration barriers today are minimal, the costs involved are low, and the composition of the electorate is not a topic of contention among the forces engaged in elections. However, the legal inclusion of illiterates does not guarantee their actual political participation. As we will discuss below, the type of ballot adopted in elections for the Chambers of Deputy, both at the national and state levels, acts as a barrier to the expression of political preferences on the part of voters with less schooling.

---

[13] Electoral data for 1980 is actually an average of data from 1978 and 1982.

[14] In India, a country with high rates of illiteracy, universal suffrage has been constitutionally guaranteed since 1950.

Voter Turnout

Voter turnout rates in Brazil are relatively high. As shown in Graph 2, the majority of registered voters comply with mandatory voting.[15] Two factors explain the bulk of the less than complete turnout: lags in the upkeep of voter rolls and the nonexistence of absentee ballots. As time goes on, electoral rolls accumulate voters who cannot turn out to vote, either because they died or because they moved out from the district where they registered. Since voters are not always weeded out, their presence inflates the rates of abstention. This is why turnout rates were the highest in elections that immediately followed the 1958 and 1986 national registration efforts. According to data from the Institute for Democracy and Electoral Assistance (IDEA), turnout rates in Brazil are similar to those observed in other democracies where voting is mandatory.

Transportation costs are a major barrier to voter turnout in rural areas. At the beginning of the period under analysis, the majority of the population lived in rural areas and was employed in the primary sector. Relatively high costs were therefore involved for a significant proportion of citizens to vote. A large number of them relied on receiving free transportation and would vote only if actually taken to the polling places. Taking voters to vote implied more than simply providing transportation to the voting precinct. Although the vote was secret, ballots were

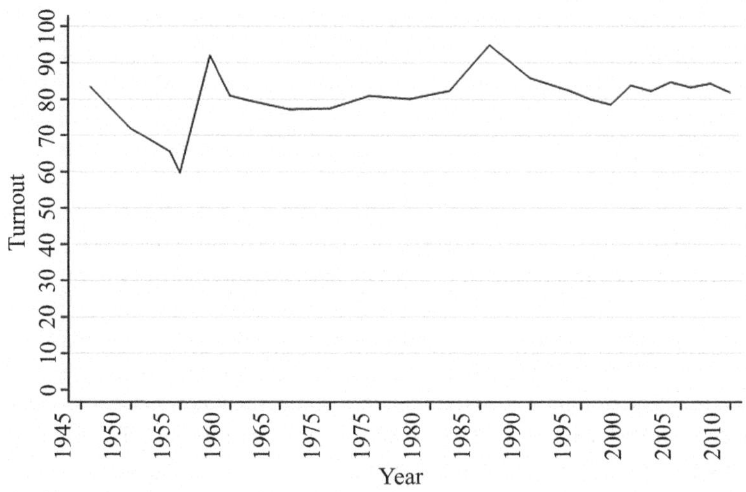

Graph 2 Voter turnout (Votes cast/Registered voters), 1946–2010. (Source: Superior Electoral Court (TSE)

[15] Between 1945 and 1964, the electoral calendar varied across states since it was the states that decided when their governors and mayors were to be elected. Voter turnout rates presented in Fig. 2 are computed only for the years when elections took place on the same date throughout the entire country.

printed and distributed by the parties. Thus, taking the voter to the polling station also meant making sure that the voter was given the "right" type of ballot, and watching to see that this ballot was deposited in the ballot box. For this reason, voters needed to be "protected" in order to prevent rival parties from gaining access to them. This was done by sequestering the voters in shelters, away from other candidates. This practice was widely and publicly acknowledged, and both the UDN and the PSD engaged in it. Proposals to limit the degree of coercion that voters were subject to were debated in connection with the 1950 Electoral Code, but as previously noted, this was an overriding concern of neither the UDN nor the PSD.

In 1954, after the suicide of Vargas, the UDN proposed a number of electoral reforms, which in addition to establishing a new electoral roll and adopting the official (Australian) ballot included the creation of new rules for organizing the transportation of voters on election day.[16] For the party, the latter was to be immediately implemented as it would effectively "sanitize" the electoral process and remove the base upon which Getulism had constructed its electoral hegemony.

The proposed reform was only partially approved to include a new voter roll, new rules for voter transportation on election day, and tougher penalties for voters who failed to appear. Adoption of the official ballot, however, was vehemently rejected by a coalition of parties led by the PSD. Party leaders argued that because of its complexity, the official ballot would prevent less educated citizens from casting a valid vote. They argued that adoption of the official ballot would be akin to instituting voting restrictions based on income.

The UDN, in turn, pushed for approval of the official ballot, supporting a modified proposal in 1955 that limited the official ballot to presidential elections, but adopted it immediately, so that it would be used in the race already underway at the time. Negotiations over the issue were tense. The PSD claimed that the goal of the UDN in pushing for immediate adoption of the official ballot was to rig the election. The measure was only approved when assurances were given that ballots would be designed and distributed in a way that would not favor the UDN candidate. Instead, candidates would be listed in the order in which they registered their candidacies and parties would be allowed to print and distribute their own ballots if the official ones were not distributed in a timely fashion.[17]

As part of negotiations to delay the new voter registration, the official ballot was adopted for all majoritarian elections. In proportional elections, it was used in 1962, the last to take place before the military coup in 1964, and only in capital cities. Only in the state of São Paulo was the official ballot used in all municipalities.[18] That is, the instrument was adopted where it was least necessary: in urban areas and in the most industrialized state of the federation. In smaller towns, where the majority of

[16] Melo Franco (1965, p. 454) discusses the options considered by UDN at that moment in time.

[17] For further details, see Costa (1964, p. 268).

[18] The law also stipulated that in the 1966 election only cities with more than 500,000 inhabitants would use the official ballot; all other cities would continue to use the old system, under which parties provided voters with the ballots.

the rural population resided, voters remained subject to traditional control mechanisms, which included the distribution of ballots printed by the political parties.

The official ballot was used for the first time across the entire country in the legislative elections of 1966, which took place under the military regime. There was, of course, a new political context wherein the military regime, among many other limitations, imposed a two-party system by means of highly restrictive electoral and party legislation. The simplification of the party system and reduced number of candidates that it implied facilitated adoption of the official ballot.

Notwithstanding the existence of a military regime, voter turnout did not change significantly. Turnout fell in 1966 when compared to the 1962 elections, but the change was small, particularly when viewed in the context of the drastic intervention of the military rulers in the electoral and party systems. Elections had little political meaning, yet voters for the most part continued to turn out to vote in proportions similar to those observed under the democracy.

The process of political liberalization that began with the 1974 election had little impact on voter turnout. If turnout fell by 2% in the first two elections under the dictatorship, it recovered when political liberalization started. Therefore, if we consider growth in terms of both turnout and number of registered voters, we can say that the process of liberalization was accompanied by increasing voter mobilization.

Regardless of whether mobilization actually occurred, the fact is that general voter registration implemented in 1985 accounts for high voter turnout in the 1986 election. Turnout rates later declined, mostly due to the lag in the upkeep of the electoral roll. Fluctuations observed after 1994 can be explained by localized administrative measures taken by the TSE to clean the voter registration records. For example, individuals who had failed to vote in three consecutive elections were removed from the rolls, while municipalities with an "excessive" voter/population ratio were required to reregister their entire electorate.

Lastly, it should be noted that turnout has been consistently high in more recent elections across all Brazilian states (Graph 3). This indicates that the conditions enabling electoral participation have become more or less uniform across the country. Voting costs are no longer higher for particular population sectors.

Valid Votes

Exercising the right to vote is directly associated with a voter's competence. Even when there are legal limitations with regard to age, competence remains the guiding principle. Minors do not vote since they do not have enough discernment to form their political will autonomously. The same applies to those considered insane: they do not vote because they are legally incapable of doing so (Przeworski 2010, p. 74).

The competence assumed under the law may be denied, deliberately or not, in practice. The type of ballot used in an election can have major political consequences because it affects the costs that different voters must pay to effectively express their preference. In this sense, depending on its design, the official ballot

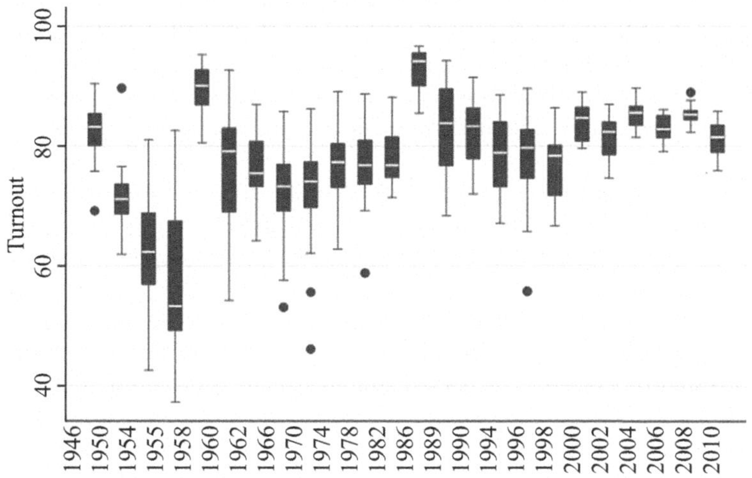

Graph 3 Average and dispersion of voter turnout in states, 1946–2010. (Source: Superior Electoral Court (TSE))

may constitute an obstacle to the electoral expression of less educated voters. Thus, it is possible that the right guaranteed by law is denied in practice. As we described above, the PSD and the UDN, the two major parties of the 1945–1964 period, were acutely aware of this possibility and understood how different alternatives would affect their partisan strength.

Recent studies (Gingerich 2012; Hidalgo 2010; Fujiwara 2010) have shown that changes in the way that votes are cast – e.g., introduction of the official ballot in the 1955 presidential elections or introduction of electronic voting machines in 1988 – directly affected the rate of valid votes. Adoption of the official ballot had an obvious impact on the rate of invalid votes, which went from 9% in 1958 to 17.7% in 1962. Gingerich (2012) provides strong evidence that this increase was actually a result of introducing the official ballot and that it had significant and broad political consequences. According to him, the official ballot weakened conservative parties by removing a mass of rural, poorer and less educated voters from under their control. At the same time, it effectively disenfranchised these voters, whose ballots were more likely to be invalid. Thus, the relative empowerment of the left occurred because a large segment of its constituency was disenfranchised. If introducing the official ballot is viewed as progressive reform that limits voter control and violence, its practical effects reinforce a typical elitism within the Brazilian political system since it invalidates the vote of those with lower levels of education.

Advocates of the official ballot were well aware that it would represent an obstacle to participation on the part of less educated voters, but there were disagreements as to who would actually benefit from the new method. Melo Franco, a leader of the opposition to Vargas that sought to sanitize the political system from what the opposition viewed as immoral practices, made no bones about listing the quartering of voters as one of his campaign expenses in his memoirs of the 1954 campaign.[19] Both the UDN and the PSD knew the measure would require an adjustment to their electoral strategies, especially among the rural electorate. Voters would now need to be told how to vote. Many were not while others could not be, given their low level of education.

Thus, education comes to represent a de facto limitation on the exercise of voting rights. Since 1985, the limits for effective participation of less educated voters became clear when suffrage became formally universal. Although illiterate persons had the right to vote, the first elections in which they could legally participate in order to have their preferences registered required them to write the names of their candidates. It is no wonder there was an increased number of invalid votes in both majoritarian and proportional elections, although many more in the latter than in the former.

The numbers are alarming. Nearly one out of every five votes cast in the 1994 presidential elections was invalid. In the 1990 and 1994 elections for the Chamber of Deputies, more than four out of every ten voters wasted their votes. The number of blank and null votes dropped to 20% of votes cast in the 1998 election for the Chamber of Deputies, a rate that was similar to the one observed in the presidential election. The rate of invalid votes declined even further in 2002 for both proportional and majoritarian elections and since then has remained static at around 10%.

Graph 4 provides basic information regarding the evolution of invalid votes since 1946. As depicted, the introduction of electronic voting in 1998 served as a turning point. Hidalgo (2010) and Fujiwara (2010) unequivocally demonstrate that the decline in the number of invalid votes in proportional elections was a result of the introduction of electronic voting. The same level of certainty does not exist, however, when it comes to determining which social sector was effectively excluded from participation with the old ballot or, more generally speaking, the broader consequence of the increased participation under the political system. Nor did these studies deal with majoritarian elections.

The authors do agree on key points, however. For both, the high rates of invalid votes were a result of the type of ballot and the difficulties they entailed for less educated voters. While it is not possible to rigorously prove this point, identification of the causal mechanism and empirical evidence does corroborate the hypothesis. Both authors believe that effective incorporation of less educated voters through the introduction of electronic voting had important political consequences. In an analysis of elections for state-level assemblies, Fujiwara (2010) claims that health policies were more in tune with the needs of low-income voters. Hidalgo (2010), in turn, concludes from his analysis of elections for the national Chamber of Deputies that the effect of electronic voting was to strengthen ideological parties and weaken parties based on traditional political machines. For this reason, he argues, introduction of electronic voting should be seen as equivalent to Europe's elimination of

[19] The actual passage reads: "registration, assistance to voters and their families, the prudent courage to face the authorities linked to the opposition, not to mention the expenses with transportation, food, clothing and sheltering of voters in the *quarters*" (Melo Franco 1965, p. 292).

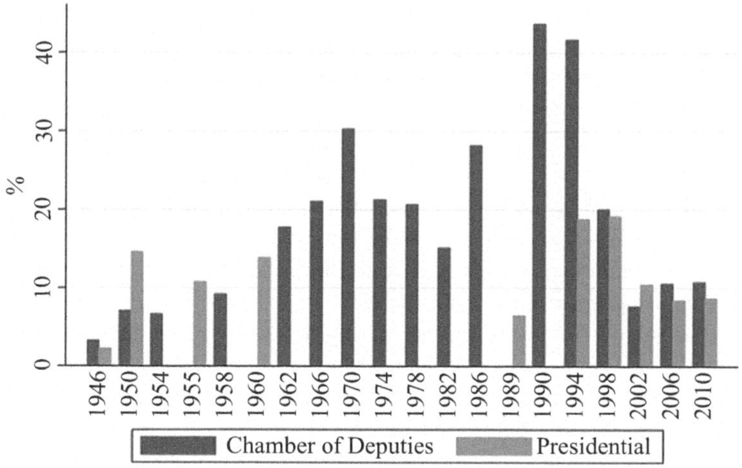

Graph 4 Invalid vote as a percentage of total vote, 1945–2010. (Source: Superior Electoral Court (TSE)

restrictions based on income. Both effectively incorporated less privileged members of the population into the electoral process, leading to changes in the nature of political parties and the direction of public policies. The difference, he argues, is that Brazil was able to accomplish this in 8 years while it took Europe nearly a century to do so.

Intriguing as they are, these conclusions should be taken with a grain of salt. Since analyses by Hidalgo and Fujiwara focus exclusively on legislative elections (in a presidential system), they may well exaggerate the actual impact of the reform. The number of invalid votes has often been lower in presidential elections. In 1994, for instance, it was over 40% in the election for the Chamber of Deputies but less than 20% in the presidential election of that same year. Thus, the effective exclusion of those who failed to cast a valid vote in the legislative election was not absolute, even without electronic voting. Given the fact that presidents are vital in defining public policies in Brazil, there is no reason to believe that politicians were not taking into consideration the preferences of the poorest voters.

Therefore, it is not the official ballot itself that explains the relatively high rates of invalid votes, but rather what casting a valid ballot requires from voters. Note that the number of invalid votes has increased over time, even after adoption of the electronic vote. The 1994 elections represent a turning point because it was the first time that presidential and legislative elections were held together and the number of simultaneous races increased to five (president, senators, governors, federal and state-level representatives). The need to mechanically allow for so many choices led to the creation of two ballots: one for the majoritarian races (president, senators, and governors) and one for proportional races (federal and state deputies). In the majoritarian ballot, voting required selecting one candidate from among a list of multiple alternatives. The proportional ballot, in turn, was blank, listing neither candidates nor parties. Voters were required to write in the name and/or number associated with their choice. It is not surprising, therefore, that voters have had greater difficulty in expressing their preference in proportional elections.

In any case, it is undeniable that the adoption of electronic voting has led to a significant expansion of political participation, altering the social composition of those who actually vote. There has been a significant decline in the number of invalid votes even in presidential elections. It is worth noting that since 2006, the rate of invalid votes has been more or less the same for majoritarian and proportional elections. This suggests that it is the type of ballot rather than the intrinsic importance of a given election that has led to the differences observed between the two. The open list proportional representation system adopted in legislative elections may have many shortcomings, but raising the costs of the decision for voters is not among them. The sharp decline in the number of invalid votes since introducing electronic voting demonstrates that voters are capable of choosing among the many candidates who participate in the race.

The contrast in the nature of the political debate involving ballot reforms of 1955, 1962, and 1998 is striking. At that time, the PSD and the UDN, the two major parties, were the main protagonists, and their positions were determined by strategic anticipation of the reform's impact on their own electorate. As far as we know, the later reform did not involve any significant partisan disagreement. Existing evidence indicates that the reform was entirely initiated by the TSE, motivated less by the need to reduce the number of invalid votes and more by the need to simplify the counting of votes, making it more secure and accurate.

Conclusion

It is no simple task to organize an election in which the majority of voters are able to attend, vote, and have their preferences counted. It is even harder to make it such that, in the end, interested parties do not claim that they were improperly harmed or their opponents favored. From this perspective, Brazil can be considered a success story. Elections take place with an overwhelming turnout and are recognized as free and fair.

During the period analyzed here, barriers to political participation were significantly reduced. The most significant legal restriction was removed in 1985, when illiterate persons were finally allowed to vote. From 1946 to 1964, efforts were mostly in the opposite direction, that is, in the direction of effectively excluding, as parties sought to impose stricter de facto standards to weed out less educated (i.e., poorer) voters.[20]

Nonetheless, it is significant that the rebirth of democracy in 1985 was accompanied by expansion of voting rights. True, the restriction was not actually as impor-

[20] Interestingly, one of the first reform packages sent to Congress by President Castello Branco shortly after the 1964 military coup included the extension of voting rights to illiterates. He made no explicit effort to have this measure approved and Congress, ultimately, rejected it.

tant then as it had been in 1945 since the percentage of voting age illiterates had sharply declined and legal exclusion was no longer rigorously implemented. Still, the generally low educational level of the population, combined with ballots that were not user-friendly, prevented a significant proportion of voters from effectively expressing their preferences. The right to participate acquired in 1985 was denied in practice by the ballot requirements. The fear expressed by members of the PSD in the 1950s would, thus, come true: the official ballot would represent a surreptitious way to impose income-based political exclusion. Regardless of whether ballot-related exclusion reached the magnitude of this kind of exclusion, the fact is that the barrier was removed with the introduction of electronic voting in the late 1990s. It is interesting to underscore the contrast between the intense politicization surrounding the introduction of the official ballot in the 1950s and the technical nature of the manner in which electronic voting was introduced.

Today, the costs faced by voters in registering to vote, going to the polls, and expressing their preference are low. The barriers preventing widespread electoral participation have been increasingly removed since the first democratic election in 1945. The social and institutional context in which electoral participation takes place today has been completely transformed. In the 2010 presidential elections, 99.2% of the 134 million members of the potential electorate were registered, 82.6% of these turned out to vote, and 75.4% cast a valid ballot. By comparison, in the 1950 presidential election, 42.6% of the 26.9 million adults were registered to vote, 30.7% of these attended, and only 29.1% cast a valid ballot. The contrast between the two periods reflects the intense transformation in the way electoral participation takes place. Between the "quartering" of voters and electronic voting, a profound and positive change has taken place.

References

Bloem, R. (1955). *A crise da democracia e a reforma eleitoral*. São Paulo: Livraria Martins Fontes.

Campello de Souza, M. d. C. (1976). *Estado e partidos políticos no Brasil (1930 a 1964)*. São Paulo: Alfa-Ômega.

Carvalho, O. (1958). *Ensaios de sociologia eleitoral*. Belo Horizonte: Edições da Revista Brasileira de Estudos Políticos.

Castro Gomes, A. (2005). *A invenção do trabalhismo* (3ª ed.). Rio de Janeiro: FGV Editora.

Cheibub, J. A., Gandhi, J., & Vreeland, J. R. (2010). Democracy and dictatorship revisited. *Public Choice, 143*, 67–101.

Costa, E. (1964). *A Legislação Eleitoral Brasileira: (histórico, comentários e sugestões.)*. Rio de Janeiro: Departamento de Imprensa Nacional.

Franco, V. d. M. (1946). *A campanha da UDN (1944–1945)*. Rio de Janeiro: Livraria Editora Zelo Valverde S.A.

Fujiwara, T. (2010). *Voting technology, political responsiveness, and infant health: Evidence from Brazil*. Vancouver: University of British Columbia.

Gingerich, D. W. (2012). Can institutions cure clientelism? Assessing the impact of the Australian ballot in Brazil. In *70th Annual Midwest Political Science Association Conference*, Chicago, IL, April 11–15.

Hidalgo, D. (2010). *Digital democracy: The consequences of electronic voting technology in Brazil*. Berkeley: University of California.

Horowitz, D. (1985). *Ethnic groups in conflict*. Berkeley: University of California Press.
Kinzo, M. D. G. (1979). *Representação Política no Brasil*. São Paulo: Símbolo.
Leal, V. N. (1993). *Coronelismo, enxada e voto* (3rd ed.). São Paulo: Editora Alfa-Omega.
Melo Franco, A. A. (1965). *A Escalada (memórias)*. Rio de Janeiro: Livraria José Olympio Editora.
Melo Franco, A. A. (2005). *Evolução da crise brasileira* (2nd ed.). Rio de Janeiro: Topbooks.
Pinto Serva, M. (1931). *A reforma eleitoral*. São Paulo: Livraria Zenith.
Pires, J. M. (2009). *A invenção da lista aberta: o processo de implantação da representação proporcional no Brasil*. Biblioteca digital da Câmara dos Deputados.
Przeworski, A. (2010). *Democracy and the limits of self-government*. New York: Cambridge University Press.

Councils, Associations, and Inequality

Adrian Gurza Lavalle and Leonardo Sangali Barone

Abstract There is broad consensus in the literature concerning the singularity of the Brazilian experience in the post-transition period. The increasing number of institutional channels where non-electoral participation and extra-parliamentary representation takes place – the so-called Brazilian model – would find no parallel in other latitudes. Likewise, the evolution of civil organizations would have become a major phenomenon. Against the backdrop of such expansion, this chapter systematically describes the evolution of councils in Brazilian cities from 1988 to 2009 and associations over one decade (1999–2009) to shed light on the implications this evolution has had on territorially measured socioeconomic inequality. Two questions are put forth: have councils and associations expanded and favored the most prosperous municipalities, thus becoming an additional item on the list of factors reproducing inequality, or have them, at least in principle, allowed their possible effects of inclusion to act as a counterbalance, however modest? What factors are associated with the presence of councils and associations in the socioeconomic "geography" of Brazilian municipalities? The answers vary, sometimes surprisingly, among types of councils and sets of civil organizations.

Keywords Participation · Democratic innovation · Councils · Civil society · Brazil · Inequality

We are grateful for the suggestions from Monika Dowbor, Lizandra Serafin, and Rosangela Paz for interpretation of the findings presented here. The first author is also grateful to the Institute for European Studies and the Centre for the Study of Democratic Institutions, both at the University of British Columbia, for institutional support during the writing of this chapter as well as to the São Paulo Research Foundation (FAPESP) for providing a research grant abroad (Grant No. 2012/18439-6).

A. G. Lavalle (✉)
Political Science Department, University of São Paulo, São Paulo, Brazil

Center for Metropolitan Studies (CEM), São Paulo, Brazil

L. S. Barone
Political Science Department, University of São Paulo, São Paulo, Brazil

M. Arretche (ed.), *Paths of Inequality in Brazil*,
https://doi.org/10.1007/978-3-319-78184-6_2

Over the course of about two decades, since the pioneering experiences of participatory budgeting gained notability after implementation in Porto Alegre (Rio Grande do Sul State), the scenario for innovation in institutional participation has become varied and taken on proportions that would have seemed unlikely during the early 1980s. Not only did participatory bodies assume new formats and more institutionalized features and gain wider dissemination and territorial scope, but organizations of civil society established their presence within such bodies, thus subjecting their very status and direct or indirect access to public resources to new regulations and making their role in implementing various functions in policy management, training, advocacy, and knowledge production a natural element of Brazilian democracy and its public sector.

There is broad consensus in national and international literature concerning the singularity of the Brazilian experience in the post-transition period, although in different theoretical accounts and with varying emphasis on the value and limitations of participatory institutions and the role of civil society. The increasing number of institutional channels where non-electoral participation and extra-parliamentary representation takes place – the so-called Brazilian model – would find no parallel in other latitudes. Equally uncommon in the Brazilian experience would be the vitality and influence civil society holds over discussions of policy. The narrative commonly associated with this consensus is well known: the emergence of a civil society committed to democratization gave way to a trajectory of institutionalization thanks to civil society's capacity to mobilize during the Constituent Assembly. The demands of civil society extolled in the Constitution – particularly the democratization of the State through participation – in turn, would have gained momentum due to the progressive expansion of the Workers' Party (PT), whose election to the presidency defined the favorable environment in which the architecture of participatory institutions and the expansion of civil society's role acquired their current features.

National conferences increased exponentially and participation became mandatory when formulating master plans, multi-annual plans, and annual finance acts for municipal budgets. Public hearings became required for approving investments and executing projects in several areas. Committees and other forms of consultation acquired widespread dissemination in federal programs. The most notable case concerns policy management councils. In 1991, only Brazil's southern region had an average of more than one council per municipality. Nine years later, all Brazilian regions had more than 1.5 councils per municipality, and in 2010 that number rose to 3.9 in the Northeast, 4 in North, and over 5 in the Central-West (5.2), Southeast (5.7), and South (5.7). At the beginning of the same period, only the states of Espírito Santo (1.16), Rio de Janeiro (1.35), and Rio Grande do Sul (1.45) had more than one council per municipality, but nine years later, all states found themselves in this situation and, in 2010, only the states of Alagoas and Roraima registered fewer than three councils per municipality.[1]

---

[1] Excluding the Federal District, which lacks municipalities and is home to all national councils. Thus, in 1991, it had 4 councils, and 15 councils in 2010.

Likewise, the evolution of civil organizations has become a major phenomenon, judging by the more systematic data available with greater territorial scope. Between 1996 and 2002, the number of entities classified as Private Foundations and Non-Profit Associations (FASFIL) by the Brazilian Institute of Geography and Statistics (IBGE) increased from 107,000 to 276,000, reflecting 109% higher growth than all other private and public institutions registered in the Central Register of Enterprises (CEMPRE), increasing its share from 3% to 5% (IBGE, 2002, p. 43–45). In 2005, FASFIL experienced 9% more expansion than all other CEMPRE entities, increasing its share in the registration to 5.6% (IBGE, 2005, p. 46). Our findings show that the number of associations per capita has grown at least a third in Brazil's various regions over the years 2000 to 2010. In the North, which has the lowest number of associations per 1000 inhabitants (18.53) in 2000, the increase was 75%, reaching 32.75 associations per 1000 inhabitants in 2010. In funding terms, the outlook also indicates growth. The annual transfer of federal funds to nonprofit entities (NPE) increased from R$2106 million in 1999 to R$4106 million in 2010, and the increase in transfers from states and municipalities to such entities was proportionally higher (Lopez and Bueno 2012).

Against the backdrop of such expansion, this chapter has a twofold objective: to systematically describe or establish facts concerning the evolution of councils in Brazilian cities over the years 1988 to 2009 and to do the same for associations over one decade (1999–2009) all in an effort to shed light on the implications this evolution has had on territorially measured socioeconomic inequality. Two questions are put forth: have councils and associations expanded and favored the most prosperous municipalities, thus becoming an additional item on the list of factors reproducing inequality, or have they, at least in principle, allowed their possible effects of inclusion to act as a counterbalance, however modest? What factors are associated with the presence of councils and associations in the socioeconomic "geography" of Brazilian municipalities? The answers vary, sometimes surprisingly, among types of councils and sets of civil organizations.

Our analysis illustrates the evolutionary patterns of councils and associations in municipalities across different positions in synthetic indicators of inequality, especially the municipal Human Development Index (HDI). Data from councils and associations have been aggregated in temporal series by quintiles of municipalities, according to different inequality variables, which imposed several methodological requirements. In the following section, we briefly discuss the main sources of data and their contributions to this chapter.

The analysis then goes on to show the evolution of councils since the 1980s, focusing on the general trend of expansion that can be better understood when broken down into three patterns: i) convergence toward universalization, ii) average and highly unequal expansion, and iii) low uneven expansion. We subsequently analyze the evolution of four sets of civil society organizations, starting with all FASFILs and successively defining subsets to apply more restrictive or demanding concepts of civil society. We then address the relationship between socioeconomic and demographic variables stemming from the censuses and the presence of councils and rights advocacy organizations in Brazilian municipalities. Lastly, we examine the implications of our findings for territorial inequality.

Sources and Choices

It is notoriously difficult to study associations and councils using systematic evidence and temporal series. With regard to associations, most studies on the composition of civil society in Brazil have worked with lists, and to a much lesser extent, with notary office records and nonrandom samples. In all cases, the data is spatially and temporally limited. In this chapter, we used the Annual Social Information Report (RAIS), prepared by the Ministry of Labor and Employment (MTE), to identify civil society associations because it has been the longest avaliable series and is one of the sources used to update CEMPRE. The sets of associations classified as civil organizations were made compatible with the categories developed by the IBGE for the FASFIL research.[2] Data from the RAIS allows us to observe different sets of nonprofit entities from their economic activities and compare them with each other.

The study of councils, on the other hand, has largely benefited from the introduction of questions from the Survey of Basic Municipal Information series (MUNIC) – IBGE. A substantial part of the progress in the literature evaluating the effects of participatory institutions is due to the information on councils or the municipal administrative capacity raised by this research. MUNIC allowed us to identify the founding dates for 17 different councils and examine their expansion over time in Brazilian municipalities.[3] Lastly, the censuses allowed for a detailed characterization of the sociodemographic profile of municipalities in 1991, 2000, and 2010 in order to use variables to systematically explore the relationships found in the annual series between the position of municipalities according to their HDI and the evolution of councils and associations. We also incorporated variables from other sources in order to introduce the electoral-political dimension to the analysis.

---

[2] The term FASFIL denotes both research and researched entities. FASFIL is a reclassification of the information contained in CEMPRE, which combines information from the RAIS, the Ministry of Labor and Employment's general registry of employment and unemployment (CAGED), and other IBGE sectoral surveys. CEMPRE microdata are not public, which enhanced the convenience of using RAIS microdata regarding establishment of organizations provided by the Ministry of Labor and Employment and organized by CEBRAP and the CEPESP-FGV.

[3] Changes in the MUNIC questionnaire in its various editions prevent construction of a temporal series on municipal councils. However, in 2009, municipalities were asked about the year of creation of 17 councils. Based on this information, an annual series was rebuilt. However, the series could only consider the year of creation and not the actual existence of councils in each year. Furthermore, the absence of questions regarding some councils in 2009, notably the municipal councils for social assistance, also imposes limitations on this analysis.

Evolution of Councils

Policy management councils succeeded participatory budgeting as the second generation of increasingly institutionalized channels of participation. The council format became the preferred option for regulating the constitutional mandate, which established participation as a feature of policy sectors defined as strategic. However, the establishment of councils was not only gradually implemented in sectors such as health, welfare, and education or areas that cover a cross section such as the rights of children and adolescents but also eventually gained presence in a wide range of other sectors and fields. Thus, the designation of councils refers to those situated within policy systems, provided with funds and organized into three levels according to the federal structure, as well as those with less structured connections to their respective policy areas, with uneven access to resources, and uneven presence across the federal structure, or even those created by discretion by some municipalities or states to support the political priorities of local executive powers.[4]

The general trend in the expansion of councils is represented in Graph 1a. Using as starting point the year 1988 when promulgation of the Constitution mandated participation in policy areas and sectors considered strategic, and when councils were practically nonexistent in all municipalities, we witness a clear expansion of councils in each municipal HDI quintile, calculated in the 2000 Census.[5] However, when considering the period under analysis, we note a systematic increase in the gap among municipalities with different socioeconomic characteristics in establishing councils. In 2009, a municipality with a high HDI (fifth quintile) was expected to have twice the number of councils as a municipality with a low HDI (first quintile). There is indeed a close correlation between municipal HDI and expansion of councils, indicating a proportionally smaller gap between intermediate quintiles.

Although the variety of existing councils in municipalities is greater than the 17 councils surveyed by MUNIC/IBGE, the latter raised information about those

---

[4] There are also guardianship councils, administrative councils for local facilities, and program councils, but they go beyond the scope of this chapter.

[5] In MUNIC/IBGE we found some councils created prior to 1988, but this year was defined as the basis since there is little empirical or analytical relevance in differentiating previous years. In addition, we decided to use the HDI calculations based on the 2000 census, the midpoint of our series. At the time of writing this chapter, the 2010 HDI had not yet been released by the UNDP. We chose to use only the 2000 HDI to rank municipalities between quintiles. There are four reasons for this choice, which seemed to us the most prudent. The first is that if we varied the HDI according to each year, in 1991 we would have quintiles eventually composed of municipalities different from the quintiles established with the 2000 HDI (which due to the lack of data would also be the 2010 quintiles). The second reason is the absence of 1991 data on associations, which, according to the limitations of RAIS, could only be used from 1999 onward. It would only be possible to vary the HDI when analyzing the evolution of councils. The third reason is that, empirically speaking, it makes little difference to use either 1991 or 2000 as the initial year of the data series on councils. As we note below, the number of councils in the early 1990s is low and HDI groups are not easily distinguishable. Lastly, we can vary the socioeconomic conditions of the municipalities by examining the variables in the 1990, 2000, and 2010 censuses. The results, presented in the penultimate section, confirms the patterns found using 2000 HDI.

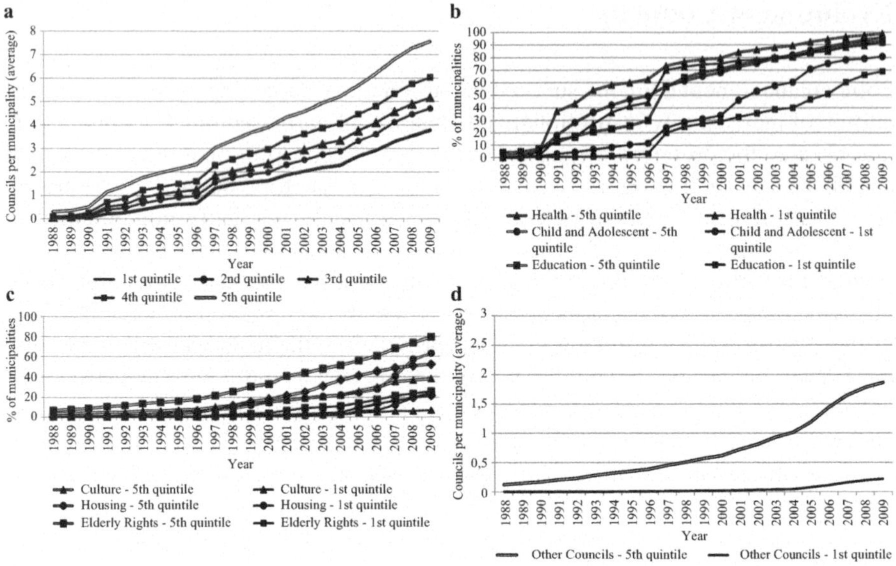

Graph 1 Evolution of municipal councils, according to municipality's HDI quintiles Brazil – 1988–2009. (**a**) Councils by municipality's HDI quintile. (**b**) Councils by municipality's HDI quintile: Health, Education, and Child and Adolescent Rights. (**c**) Councils by municipality's HDI quintile: Culture, Housing, Elderly Rights, and Environmental. (**d**) Councils by municipality's HDI quintile: other policy areas (Source: IBGE. Demographic Census and MUNIC; UNDP. HDI (special tabulations by CEM)

known to be more relevant or those expected to expand further.[6] Thus, the growth trend presented in Graph 1a expresses the general evolution of councils in Brazil. Nevertheless, we should underscore the presence of a factor favoring the expansion of councils in all HDI quintiles which becomes clearer in the graphs that follows. As explained below, this refers to the effect of federal induction.

The general evolution of councils is the aggregated result of three different patterns. First, we find a small set with a convergent trend toward universalization: Health, Education, and Child and Adolescent Rights (Graph 1b). These are traditional councils that are provided with sector funds corresponding to areas deemed strategic under the Constitution, in which participation has been mandated. Because of their similarities, it seems plausible to assume that, if information were made available, social assistance municipal councils would fall into this group. In order to facilitate the visualization of this and subsequent trends, only the first and fifth quintiles were represented, assuming that the trajectories of intermediate quintiles follow the same pattern and preserve the expected order among the strata of

[6] With the exception of the social assistance municipal council. See footnote 4.

municipalities. For example, the double line with a triangle mark in Graph 1b corresponds to the percentage of municipalities that have Health councils within the highest HDI quintile group, while the solid line corresponds to the lowest quintile group. Between those two lines we find the remaining omitted quintiles. Thus, the exclusion of the second, third, and fourth quintiles from Graphs 1b, c, and d does not affect interpretation of the results.

The universalization of councils followed two different paths. Health councils expanded simultaneously across municipalities with high and low HDI, although growth in the former was higher in the first half of the 1990s. There are factors with a remarkable induction capacity operating in 1990 and 1996 in such a way that, in the second case, municipalities with the worst conditions for human development practically reached those of the fifth quintile. Since then, evolution has been constant regardless of municipal characteristics. Among municipalities with the highest HDI, 99% had Health councils in 2009 versus those with the lowest HDI where 92.2% had Health councils.

The sharp induction registered in these two years has federal origins and derives from regulation of the Unified Health System (SUS), specifically with regard to decentralization and participation. Law No. 8080 of September 19, 1990, established community participation as a SUS principle and assigned councils the power to oversee the sector's funding resources. In turn, Law No. 8142 of December 28 of the same year regulated participation by defining councils as a collegiate body of the health system and, above all, conditioning federal transfers to the existence of local councils – the second of six conditions (Duarte 2000). Several directives were introduced by the Federal Ministry of Health in the 1990s in the form of Basic Operational Standards (NOB) aiming at inducing municipalities toward joining the SUS. A NOB introduced in 1996 strengthened the role of councils in the local management of SUS provision of services (Scatena and Tanaka 2001, p. 73). Municipalities in turn complied to federal-driven rules so as to have access to federal transfers (Arretche and Marques 2003, p. 467).

The councils on Education and Child and Adolescent Rights expanded at a slower pace, most notably in municipalities with a higher HDI. A reduction of the gap between municipalities with the highest and lowest HDI occurred in the 2000s, although such councils attained levels of presence equivalent to Health in only the top quintile. There is a general trend toward universalization, albeit slower than what can be seen in the Health councils. There, acceleration induction factors operated only in 1996 and had a more attenuated effect on the Child and Adolescent Rights councils, whose biggest boost came in 1990, with the enactment of the Child and Adolescent Statute (Law No. 8069). The boost in Education councils also seemed to be driven by induction mechanisms similar to those seen in Health councils, thus are federal in origin, although the temporal connection is less clear. This refers to the regulation of constitutional provisions on education and, specifically, the establishment of educational systems in municipalities (Sarmento, 2005). The National Education Council was established by enactment of Law No. 9131 November 24, 1995. One year later, Law No. 9394 defined democratic management as a guiding principle of the educational system and considered councils part of the educational structure.

The second pattern observed in the general evolution of councils corresponds to a set of councils with average and highly unequal expansion (Graph 1c). Culture, Housing, Elderly Rights, and Environmental councils expanded mainly from the late 1990s onward, but did so unevenly and without reaching levels even close to universal. In 2009, almost two-fifths of municipalities in the highest HDI quintile had Culture councils, more than half had Elderly Rights councils, two-thirds had Housing councils, and nearly 80% had Environmental councils. However, the presence of these four councils in municipalities in the lowest quintile is currently modest and rarely exceeds 20% of municipalities, and was nearly nonexistent for most of the 1990s. Despite recent expansion in low HDI municipalities, trajectories are increasingly divergent. With the exception of Housing councils in 2006, we witness no sharp federal induction. The jump in Housing councils coincides with the first year of the National Social Housing System, enacted in 2005 through Law No. 11.124, defining municipal councils as an integral part of the system (Maricato 2006). The absence of strong induction mechanisms conditioning the transfer of federal resources to the creation and operation of such councils is one explanation for its limited expansion.

The third pattern corresponds to low and unequal expansion and includes most of the councils. In this case, municipalities in the lower quintile recorded a minimum presence of Human Rights councils as well as councils for Sports, Youth, Rights of Disabled Persons, LGBT, Women's Rights, Promotion of Racial Equality, Urban Policy, and Safety and Transportation. In 2009, in the quintile of municipalities with the highest HDI, the average presence of these nine councils is only 1.7, indicating their reduced incidence and great distance from universalization (Graph 1d). In the remaining quintiles, this value is less than 1 and only 0.2 in the lowest quintile.

The overall expansion of councils is an uncontroversial fact in the specialized literature, and the data confirms this trend. However, the diversity of councils and the role they perform in the regular operation of their corresponding policy area show distinct patterns. Universalized councils have been subjected to strong federal inductions to the point of neutralizing the effects associated with HDI differences. Councils with average and highly uneven expansion are less articulated in their respective policy areas largely because of the less structured nature of the policies themselves – compared to de facto organized policies within systems – and weak or absent induction from the federal government. Lastly, councils with a low and highly unequal expansion progressed only in municipalities with a higher HDI. The less structured nature of policies associated to this set of councils was accompanied by the transversal or cross-sectional nature of the issues many of them deal with, which, one can assume, hinders coordination, distribution of costs, and definition of the benefits sought through potential implementation of centralized induction mechanisms.

Evolution of Associations

Theoretical reasons and their underlying normative assumptions give life to more or less demanding concepts of the characteristics that define an association, instituting looser or more restrictive compositions on the universe of actors under consideration. Thus, associations, in a pluralist approach, include every effort toward consociation, making it impossible to clearly distinguish between associations that are purely economic or simply market associations and those whose primary purpose is not profit, or between those that are primarily political associations and those whose purpose is not to govern. In turn, contemporary theories of civil society focus only on civil organizations, excluding any market or State actors – and the political system and its actors are conceived as part of the State. However, neither of these theories reach any consensus regarding the constellation of organizations to whom the adjective "civil" is fitting, although we may clearly see that the more normative the understanding, the more restrictive becomes the universe of selected actors and the most virtuous is the behavior expected from them.

It is not suitable for the purposes of this chapter to adopt a specific definition of civil society, since many of the shortcomings in this field of research lie in the variability between the concept and its empirical referents. Instead, the analytical strategy adopted was to define and examine four sets of associations, starting from the broadest category and narrowing it down to the subsets of the most restrictive civil organizations subsets – all of which are contained in the upper contingent.[7]

The first broad set encompasses *all nonprofit entities* (NPE) as classified by their legal status in the RAIS and according to criteria used by the IBGE.[8] All national organizations that cannot be classified as companies or public administration – "market" or "State" – are included in this category.

The second set – *debugged nonprofit entities* – excludes condominium associations and notary offices, entities that would hardly be understood as civil society.[9] The third set comes closer to the *standard contemporary definition of civil society*: voluntary, noncorporate associations that are not integrated into the market, the State, or the political system. We therefore do not include political parties, workers, professional and employers associations, professional unions, or churches, which together make up somewhere between 16.5% and 19.5% of the NPE during the 1999–2009 period. This is a very heterogeneous group of organizations, involving hundreds of economic categories classified under the legal nature of private domestic and foreign associations and foundations.[10]

Lastly, the fourth set is designated as a *demanding definition of civil society* and limited to the subcategories of rights advocacy associations and other associative

---

[7] The formation of these sets is limited by the national classification of the entities' economic activity (CNAE) found in the RAIS (Ministry of Labor and Employment), by changes in classification over time, and by the vagueness or inaccuracy of some categories.

[8] Only from 1999 onward does it become possible to separate establishments registered in the RAIS based on their legal status and reliably obtain the universe of nonprofit organizations. Thus, this is a limit in data availability one faces when analyzing associations.

[9] Condominiums and notary offices represent approximately one-fifth to one-quarter of the 1999 NPE onward, and their presence correlates with factors such as city size and level of urbanization.

[10] Most of the economic categories included within this definition contain few organizations, with the exception of the entities in the fourth set.

activities.[11] Unlike the other groups, which are defined by the NPE as a whole or by excluding subsets of organizations whose economic nature are known, this contingent is established in a very restrictive manner, selecting only organizations classified in these two subcategories. They correspond to 35% to 40% of the total NPE and to 65% to 70% of the third set, which varies according to year.

Since only those entities with a CNPJ[12] are listed in the RAIS, there is some bias in the composition of the universe that tends to favor organizations with some level of institutionalization. However, there are no nationwide data sources that can analyze the myriad of informal associations potentially comprising a category such as civil society. Nevertheless, incentives for registering associations in Brazil are extensive.

Graph 2a describes the general evolution of all NPE between 1999 and 2009, preserving the municipal HDI as an ordering variable for the quintiles and controlling the number of nonprofits by the total population of the municipality. Two findings stand out when considering this universe. First, the initial decade of the 2000s registered an increase in NPE across all quintiles, despite a small drop at the end of the decade. Second, the presence of these entities covaries positively with the HDI, especially in the differences favorable to the fifth quintile, which featured an extra association per 1000 inhabitants over the analyzed period. The gap between municipalities with lower HDI and municipalities in intermediate positions is smaller, but remained stable during the period observed, while among municipalities of the second, third, and fourth quintiles, this gap decreased. At this level of aggregation, associations and their potential effects operate largely in municipalities with a higher HDI.

However, as shown in Graph 2b, the NPE universe, especially among municipalities with the highest HDI, behaves very differently if we disregard condominium associations and notary offices – two types of associations that are very sensitive to urban agglomeration, one mandatory by law (condominium associations) and the other the product of legal concessions that sets NPEs with an idiosyncratic status (notary offices). Indeed, if we exclude such associations from the universe, not only do we witness a decrease in the difference in the number of entities per 1000 inhabitants in the top quintile, but the trajectory also becomes convergent. That is, the gap between quintiles becomes smaller or disappears over the decade, and the second and third quintiles reverse their position compared to the fourth quintile.

Surprisingly, the trajectory of civil organizations becomes partly reversed if we also exclude labor unions, professional and employers' associations, political

[11] From 1999 to 2005, we only have what CNAE lists as "other associative activities." From 2006 onward, with changes in the legal classification of organizations, a new category was established, "rights advocacy organization," which is of special interest to this analysis. The reduced number of organizations classified as "other associated activities," from 2005 to 2006, when the change occurs, corresponds almost entirely to the new category of "rights advocacy organizations." Thus, we deemed it safe to treat the sum of these categories from 2006 onward as equivalent to the preexisting category, even if this procedure leads to marginal inaccuracy. Throughout the text this set is referred to as "rights advocacy organizations."

[12] CNPJ is the Brazilian taxpayer ID and stands for "National Registry of Legal Entities."

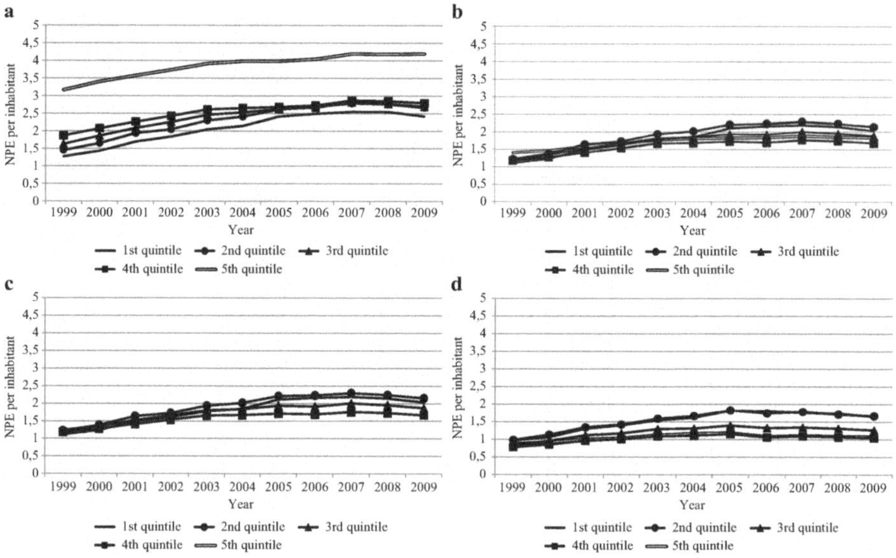

Graph 2 Nonprofit entities (NPE) per 1000 inhabitants according to HDI quintiles Brazil – 1999–2009. (**a**) All nonprofit entities. (**b**) NPE (excluding condominium associations and notary offices). (**c**) NPE (excluding condominium associations and notary offices, labor unions, professional and employers' associations, political parties, and churches). (**d**) Rights advocacy associations. (Source: IBGE. Censuses and MUNIC; UNDP. HDI; RAIS (special tabulations by CEM)

parties, and churches (Graph 2c). The initial gap in the number of associations per 1000 inhabitants between the different municipal HDI quintiles is relatively small, only marginally higher than the final gap between municipalities in the previous graph – after a convergent trajectory. In this case, the path becomes divergent and not only do we witness a greater final gap between quintiles, but also the quintile with municipalities with the lowest HDI shows higher numbers of associations per capita. Thus, over the decade, organizations that correspond to a standard contemporary definition of civil society further increased and gained a comparatively greater presence in municipalities with a lower HDI.

The divergence and reversal of trend described above becomes clearer in the last set of civil organizations – closer to a prescriptively more demanding definition of civil society. These are rights advocacy organizations and other associative activities, whose trajectory in Graph 2d begins in 1999 with a relatively similar starting point for all municipal HDI quintiles, but evolves into three clearly distinct routes. On one side, 40% of municipalities with the highest HDI show a moderate increase in the number of rights advocacy organizations, registering nearly one organization per 1000 inhabitants. Then, municipalities in the third quintile, since 2000, present a higher level of associations per inhabitants compared to those with a higher HDI. Lastly, municipalities in the two quintiles with the lowest HDI present higher growth in their NPE per capita. After a few years, these municipalities

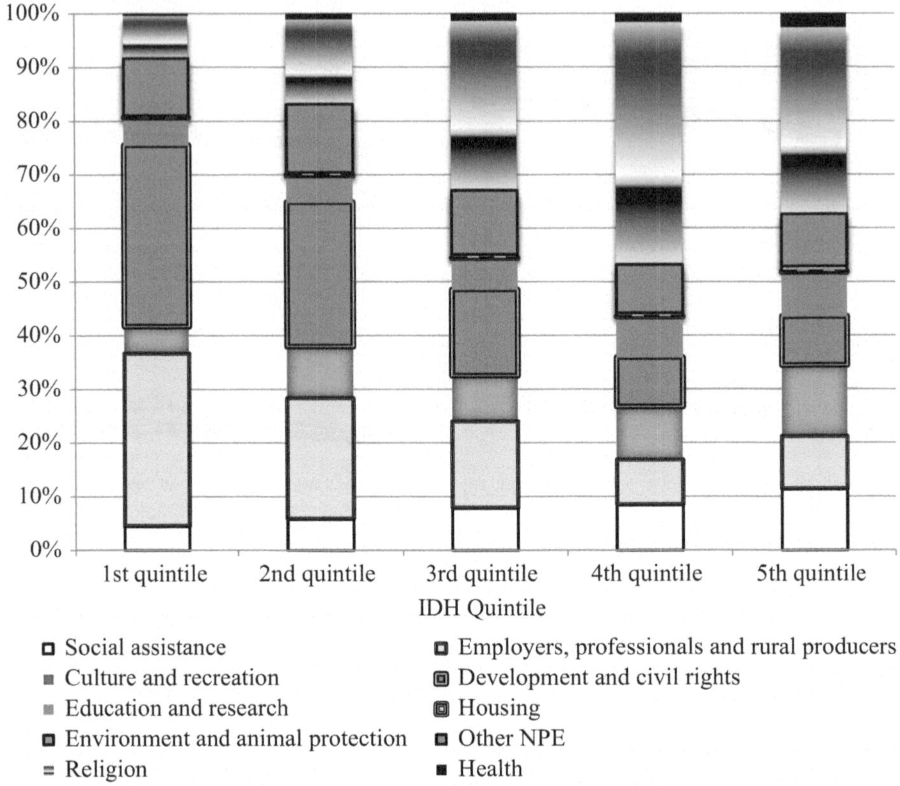

Graph 3 Distribution of nonprofit entities (NPE) per HDI quintile, according to the FASFIL classification Brazil – 2010. (Source: IBGE. Censuses and MUNIC; UNDP, HDI; FASFIL (special tabulations by CEM)

register 80% more organizations than those belonging to the fourth and fifth quintiles. We should also note that the trajectories of the first two and the last two quintiles are tangential.

As previously stated, the sets of civil organizations analyzed were selected based upon information available in the RAIS, which allowed us to observe the temporal evolution of the number of organizations with definitions close to the categories used by IBGE for FASFIL studies. The classification categories created by IBGE, however, are more accurate due to access to detailed information not available in the RAIS. Only for 2010 did we observe the distribution of different categories of organizations by municipal HDI groups in FASFIL, allowing us to compare the results from both sources in order to verify the accuracy of the previously presented results.

The share of rights advocacy organizations is markedly higher in municipalities with a lower HDI, representing a third of the nonprofit entities. As for the quintile of municipalities with the highest HDI, these NPE account for only 9% in 2010. On the other hand, the share of health organizations, churches, and social assistance organizations increases according to the municipal HDI (Graph 3).

Unfortunately, we are unable to isolate professional and employers' organizations from rural producers' associations in the FASFIL data. As we can see in the graph, the set formed by these three types of entities represents a larger share in the universe of organizations the smaller the municipal HDI, an indication that, in these municipalities, rural organizations carry significant weight. Indeed, when one looks at the municipalities with the lowest HDI, two-thirds of organizations are either in this category or in the rights advocacy category. In the municipalities in the fourth and fifth largest HDI quintiles, these institutions do not amount to a fifth of the total.

The number of per capita associations in Brazil increased over the decade observed. This increase indicates different patterns according to the set of civil organizations analyzed. The relationship between the propagation of associations and greater wealth, cultural infrastructure, and services in the cities seems intuitively correct. However, this connection only appears significant in the total universe of NPE, where building construction and urban agglomeration outweigh the presence of notary offices and condominium associations. If we exclude them, the gap between the number of associations in municipalities with low and high HDI fell remarkably in a convergent trend among the quintiles. Even when we continue to include entities with alleged "urban dependency" and "demographic dependency," such as trade unions or employers' associations, professional associations, political parties, and churches, we notice reduced discrepancies in the number of organizations per capita at the end of the period. In addition, the more the universe of NPE approaches the demanding definition of civil society, the more prominence they gain in municipalities with the lowest HDI. The results appear consistent when the analysis is replicated using classification categories developed by IBGE for FASFIL studies.

Factors in the Evolution of Councils and Associations

Thanks to use of the HDI, it was possible to characterize the relationship between the expansion trajectories of councils and associations and the socioeconomic conditions of Brazil's municipalities. However, since the index aggregates three components with equal weights, namely, economic, educational, and health components, the specific factors operating in this relationship continue to be assumed. Moreover, any changes in the effects of such components over time remain hidden. Furthermore, the HDI correlates with various sociodemographic and economic variables, which could likely find indirect expression in the index, in addition to factors other than sociodemographic or economic that are omitted by the index. In this regard, we are particularly interested in the political-electoral dimension.

In order to systematically explore the connections found in the annual series between the position of municipalities according to their HDI and the trajectories of councils and associations, we examined the behavior of the dependent variables, aggregated here in municipal quintiles in keeping with different variables from the 1991, 2000, and 2010 censuses and a few other sources that will be discussed later. This procedure offers the advantage of taking into account variations in the social and economic conditions of the municipalities, whereas when using HDI, the characteristics of municipalities were set out in the year 2000.

Table 1 summarizes the major results of this test and shows, for each variable, the averages of councils per municipality and associations per 1000 inhabitants for the first and fifth quintiles. We also present the correlation coefficient for each variable, but expose only the averages for each category in the case of discrete variables. In all cases, we included all councils and the set of rights advocacy associations. This is the same data used in producing Graphs 1a and 2d, respectively.

Generally speaking, the main socioeconomic variables – per capita municipal income, educational level of the population, and percentage of urban population – display a consistent association with the average number of councils and per capita rights advocacy associations, positive for the former and negative for the latter. Since councils only began to be established in the late 1980s, we also note that the correlation between the variables used and the municipal average of councils generally grows over time, an indication that the process of dissemination of such participatory institutions follows very clear socioeconomic patterns. As shown in Graph 1a, there is a correlation between these factors if we observe the entire set of councils in the municipalities.

Starting with per capita municipal income, an intuitively clear variable as to its expected effects, we observe that at the beginning of the last three decades, councils were significantly more numerous in municipalities whose population had higher income in relation to those of the first quintile with the lowest income. In 1991, the municipalities with wealthier inhabitants had on average 1.13 councils compared to only 0.3 with higher concentration of poor inhabitants. The gap between municipalities whose population income is higher than those sheltering people with the lowest per capita earnings increased over time, and in 2010, the municipalities in the fifth per capita income quintile had 3.4 councils more on average than those of the first quintile. The correlation between income and average number of councils grows every year, reaching 0.52 in 2010, a strong indication that the presence of councils is associated with population income.

In turn, the incidence of rights advocacy associations holds an inverse relationship to population income. In 2000, the average number of associations per 1000 inhabitants was higher in municipalities with lower income (1.11 compared to 0.87 in the last quintile) and the gap between the two groups of municipalities increased from 0.24 to 0.52 over the course of a decade.

The proportion of people with complete secondary education provides a good approximation for assessing the effects of education and shows a very similar pattern to that of population income. Thus, the number of councils is greater in municipalities whose residents have completed higher levels of education, and inequality

Table 1 Councils and associations, according to social, economic, and political characteristics of municipalities Brazil – 1991–2010

Characteristics of the municipalities	Measurement	Councils per municipality			Rights advocacy associations per 1000 inhabitants	
		1991	2000	2010	2000	2010
Municipal income[a]	Average first quartile	0.30	1.43	3.40	1.11	1.62
	Average fifth quartile	1.13	3.50	6.89	0.87	1.10
	Correlation	0.35	0.48	0.52	0.12	0.18
% of inhabitants with complete secondary education	Average first quartile	0.30	1.51	3.44	1.08	1.53
	Average fifth quartile	1.21	3.51	6.94	0.81	0.97
	Correlation	0.39	0.48	0.54	0.02	−0.01
% of rural population	Average first quartile	0.54	3.31	6.87	0.73	0.89
	Average fifth quartile	0.59	2.09	4.15	1.72	2.46
	Correlation	−0.02	−0.26	−0.36	0.30	0.35
% of white population	Average first quartile	0.32	1.59	3.87	0.83	1.28
	Average fifth quartile	1.06	3.14	5.98	1.51	1.84
	Correlation	0.28	0.35	0.30	0.31	0.34
% of male population	Average first quartile	0.87	2.94	6.38	0.81	0.98
	Average fifth quartile	0.45	1.92	4.20	1.03	1.46
	Correlation	−0.17	−0.23	−0.26	0.00	0.02
% of population in the EAP[b]	Average first quartile	1.10	3.24	6.93	0.78	0.98
	Average fifth quartile	0.46	2.09	4.35	2.23	3.24
	Correlation	−0.16	−0.14	−0.20	0.29	0.38
PT once between 1997 and 2008[c]	Average PT	0.74	2.86	6.16	1.47	2.02
	Average other parties	0.51	2.24	4.80	1.36	2.03

Source: IBGE; TSE; MUNIC; RAIS. (Special tabulations by CEM).

[a]R$ in 2012 values.

[b]EAP = Economically active population.

[c]"PT" are those municipalities in which the PT won mayoral elections in any of the three years, 1996, 2000, or 2004. In other words, municipalities governed by PT at least once between 1997 and 2008.

between quintiles increases over time. The correlation between the municipal education indicator and the number of councils is even greater than that observed between the latter and income. Rights advocacy associations, in contrast, established a greater presence in municipalities that had the lowest percentage of people with complete secondary education in the year 2000. The correlation between these variables, however, is practically null. When examining the other quintiles (omitted from the table), it can be observed that, in fact, only the fifth quintile presents an average below the total for all municipalities. If education is measured under a less demanding method, using the percentage of people with complete primary education, the results show the same pattern.

A third variable indicates a similar pattern to income and education: the proportion of rural population. More urbanized municipalities (first quintile) have, on average, more councils and fewer associations than those where the rural population is higher (fifth quintile). Interestingly enough, in 1991, the correlation between the average number of councils and the proportion of rural population was null, and in 2010, it dropped −0.36, suggesting that the dissemination of councils follows an urban path.

The dimensions represented by the first three variables in Table 1 do not differ, therefore, from what we would expect by merely looking at the HDI of the municipalities. However, there are demographic variables whose relationship with the presence of councils or the number of associations in Brazilian municipalities do not conform with the pattern described by the HDI: proportion of groups by color/race, gender, and economically active population (EAP), showing that the pattern revealed is not maintained through other dimensions of inequality not covered by the HDI.

Finally, the expansion of councils and associations may have been spurred by a diverse set of effects associated with political-electoral competition. The main political-electoral factor of interest refers to the possible favorable relationship between the Workers' Party (PT) administrations and the expansion of councils and associations. Municipalities governed by the PT at least once between 1997 and 2008 display a systematically higher average number of councils.[13] Particularly between 2000 and 2010, the PT strongly distinguishes itself from other parties: while in 2000 the difference was only 0.62, in 2010 it rose to 1.36. In that decade, the Municipal Health, Education, and Child and Adolescent Rights councils headed toward universalization, and Housing, Environment, Culture, and Elderly Rights councils became more frequent. Municipalities governed by the PT at least once between 1996 and 2004[14] had an average of 6.16 councils in 2010 against 4.80 in other municipalities.[15]

[13] Sources for the electoral data: Superior Electoral Court (TSE). The TSE does not provide data for the 1992 municipal elections. We expected few municipalities governed by the PT in this mandate however.

[14] Since data on councils and associations are from the late 2009, we decided not to include the 2008 elections. Mayors elected in 2008 took office in 2009 and its inclusion would increase the number of municipalities governed by the PT, albeit without enough time for the expected effects to manifest themselves in the variables of interest.

[15] Our interest here is merely to observe the association between variables – PT administration and

As for the number of associations in municipalities governed by the PT between 1997 and 2008, there are no significant differences compared to municipalities that were not governed by this party. Apparently, there is no evidence that the PT has any greater chance of victory where more associations per capita exist or, conversely, that a municipal government of this party will result in more organizations per capita.

The pattern described in this section registers a positive and growing correlation between the socioeconomic variables considered and the evolution of councils in general, but this relationship is reversed and decreases when it comes to rights advocacy associations. We now know that this behavior has remained stable over the period analyzed. Other social inequality factors, such as race, gender, and inclusion in the EAP, differ from the pattern found. Thus, we can reasonably assert that these social stratification factors would not covary with the HDI in relation to the presence of councils and associations. Only one political variable was incorporated, with interesting results: PT governments show a favorable relationship with the expansion of councils in Brazil's municipalities, but, counterintuitively, hold no apparent correlation with the expansion of associations.

Councils, Associations, and Inequality

Despite their diversity and the variety of their potential effects, councils operate as extra-parliamentary channels of representation and are expected to give rise to at least two scenarios: rationalization of policies and inclusion of groups affected by such policies. Both effects presumably imply a favorable relationship with the reduction of inequality. The literature assessing the effectiveness of participatory institutions constitutes cutting-edge efforts to deal with the effects of rationalization and, although still a relatively new body of research, it has indicated correlations between the presence of these institutions and better public policy performance indicators (Pires 2011; Pires and Vaz 2010). On the other hand, the effects of inclusion have been the subject of the literature for longer, and the summary of characteristics emphasizes two complementary aspects: participatory elitism, which is the socioeconomic gap between the average council member and the average citizen, and pluralization of representation, which is the difference in the makeup of councils and parliamentary bodies with regard to the increased presence of women, and the lower income and schooling of the former (Almeida et al. 2012). Either because policies better respond to the needs of the social groups affected by them or because there is an outlet for minimally present voices in traditional channels of representation, the expected effects of councils assume a favorable relationship with inequality reduction, and not the other way around. It is worth mentioning that the assumption of a favorable relationship between councils and inequality reduction is found at the level of institutional values and regulatory bases that guide the

number of councils or associations per inhabitant. The available instruments do not allow us to assess causality.

literature, although research reveals the presence of adverse factors or of findings contrary to such an assumption.[16]

Inequality, however, functions on a different scale, and its reduction at the municipal level may cause it to rise in comparisons among municipalities or regions. Between 1988 and 2009, councils have expanded in Brazil's municipalities, and what was once a constitutional provision has become an institutional reality of considerable reach. Within this general trend, the penetration of councils has occurred unevenly, following a trend that associates – systematically and steadily over two decades – improved human development conditions (HDI) and socioeconomic variables in the greater presence of councils. One group of councils escapes this trend and follows a trend toward universalization – Health, Education, and Child and Adolescent Rights – thanks to the incidence of strong federal induction mechanisms. The other councils, fourteen out of a total of seventeen examined, established in fields with less structured policies or transversal issues, registered lower, selective, or exclusionary expansion in the Brazilian municipal geography. In such cases, the possible effects of rationalization and inclusion of councils enhance the list of factors that reproduce territorial inequality. Thus, where decentralized participatory institutions such as councils are not subject to federal induction, the divergence favoring municipalities with a higher income and better educated population risks turning out to be the norm. The PT administrations hold a positive relationship with the expansion of councils.

At the same time, associations can be understood as drivers of both equality and inequality, since they use different approaches on different scales. Greater benefits for affiliates of specific associations are often achieved by disputing and appropriating scarce resources, which other associations are then deprived of. For different theoretical reasons, however, associations often appear in the literature as sources of mechanisms that mitigate political, economic, and social inequalities. Even when one presumes that associations are quintessential vehicles for promoting collective private interests, as distinctively occurs in pluralism, it is subsequently assumed that the best antidote against the domination of organized private interests is associative pluralism (Dahl 1991). Although the correlation between socioeconomic status and the propensity to participate in associations is well established in the literature, the same literature also presents associations as sources for acquiring resources and skills to compensate for social inequalities on an individual basis (Verba et al. 2005). At the opposite end of the spectrum, normative theories define associations for their authenticity and genuine interest in issues relevant to society as a whole, or as a vehicle par excellence of genuine self-determination (Cohen and Arato 1992; Hirst 1994). These are simply diametrically opposed positions within a range of possible positions. In Latin America, largely due to a negative consensus engendered by dictatorships as well as the prevalence of more demanding conceptions of civil society, associations were considered to be closer to the second regulatory extreme

[16] See, for example, the tone of complaint in the first generation of studies on councils in Tatagiba (2002), or even in more recent studies (Tatagiba 2005), some with fierce criticisms (Neto 2012).

rather than the first – realist, liberal, and focused on interests. Brazil is no exception in this regard and, in fact, rarely do studies focus on associations, descriptions of their various forms, organizational logic, or the impact of their composition (Lüchmann 2013; Gurza Lavalle and Bueno 2011; Gurza Lavalle et al. 2012).

The level of aggregation in this analysis and the implications of the relationship between associations and territorial inequality depends on at least two factors: the availability of the former to citizens and the types of entities locally available. In the decade studied (1999–2009), the vast universe of associations included under the category NPE expanded beyond the population growth across all municipalities, regardless of their status in the human development conditions. This expansion was higher in cities with better conditions due to the relationship between urban agglomeration, notary offices, and condominium associations. If we disregard both types of entities, however, differences in the presence of associations between municipalities with the worst and best HDI not only drop dramatically but also decrease over the decade. Moreover, an inversion occurs when we adopt demanding definitions of civil society to select the universe to be analyzed. The set of entities that excludes trade unions, professional employers' associations, political parties, and churches as well as the most restrictive set of claiming rights associations predominates in municipalities with lower HDI. The inverse also holds true when we consider socioeconomic variables. Thus, territorial inequality, in terms of the availability of associations in municipalities, is counterintuitively moderated even when we consider a large contingent of entities. Moreover, the distribution of rights advocacy associations follows a pattern opposite to that of territorial inequality.

The path of expansion of councils and civil society associations presents a stable pattern: divergent between both and inverted when we consider its relationship with synthetic indicators of economic inequality. The territorial equalization trends found are of two types: institutional and societal, both consonant with Brazil's politics and policies over the last two decades. On the one hand, municipal councils which followed a path toward universalization did so in the presence of strong federal induction; on the other hand, distribution of associations across "municipal geography" closer to the standard understandings of civil society followed a pattern opposite to that of territorial socioeconomic stratification, though for reasons that still require further clarification, and which apparently hold no connection to the "electoral cartography" of PT victories in local governments.

Will that pattern remain stable in the foreseeable future? Although no social science is at its best looking forward, it seems reasonable to wonder if the dramatic end of the federal PT administrations and the rise of a right-wing coalition would affect the expansion trends of councils and associations. As for the former, uneven and weak expanded councils, which are less articulated in their respective policy area, seem more vulnerable to drastic shifts in Congress and in federal offices. Universalized councils, however, are now highly integrated into the regular functioning of sectoral policies and seem to be in a safer position. Because the mechanisms that operate behind the expansion of rights advocacy associations are not clear, educated guessing is harder. Nonetheless, if public money is playing an important role among those unknown mechanisms, it would be wise to expect a sharp decline in the number of associations.

References

Almeida, C., Lüchmann, L., & Ribeiro, E. (2012). Associativismo e representação política feminina no Brasil. *Revista Brasileira de Ciência Política*, (8), 237–263.

Arretche, M., & Marques, E. (2003). Municipalização da saúde no Brasil: diferenças regionais, poder do voto e estratégias de governo. *Ciência e Saúde Coletiva, 7*(3).

Cohen, J., & Arato, A. (1992). *Civil society and political theory*. Cambridge: MIT Press.

Dahl, R. A. (1991). *Los dilemas del pluralismo democrático. Autonomía versus control*. México: Alianza Editorial/Conaculta.

Duarte, C. M. R. D. (2000). Equidade na legislação: um princípio do sistema de saúde brasileiro? *Ciência e Saúde Coletiva, 5*(2), 443–463.

Gurza Lavalle, A., & Bueno, N. (2011). Waves of change within civil society in Latin America: Mexico City and Sao Paulo. *Politics & Society, 39*(3), 415–450.

Gurza Lavalle, A., Houtzager, P., & Castello, G. 2012 La construcción política de las sociedades civiles. In *El horizonte de la política – Brasil y la agenda contemporánea de investigación en el debate internacional.* 1a ed. México: CIESAS, pp. 207–268, 2011. 1ª ed. São Paulo: CEM/ Unesp, 2012, pp. 185–259.

Hirst, P. (1994). *Associative democracy. New forms of economic and social governance*. Amherst: University of Massachusetts Press.

IBGE. 2002. Central Register of Enterprises (Cempre). Rio de Janeiro.

IBGE. 2005. Central Register of Enterprises (Cempre). Rio de Janeiro.

Lopez, F., & Bueno, N. (2012). *Transferências federais a entidades privadas sem fins lucrativos (1999–2010)*. Brasília: IPEA. (Textos para discussão, no. 1778).

Lüchmann, L. (2013). Impactos democráticos do associativismo: questões teóricas e metodológicas. In *Encontro Internacional Participação, Democracia e Políticas Públicas*. Araraquara: Unesp. April 2013.

Maricato, E. (2006). O Ministério das Cidades e a política nacional de desenvolvimento urbano. Cidades brasileiras: a matriz patrimonialista. *Políticas Sociais, 12*, 211–220.

Neto, A. F. P. (2012). *Conselho de favores – Controle social na saúde: a voz dos seus atores*. Rio de Janeiro: Garamond.

Pires, R. R. (Org.). (2011). *Efetividade das instituições participativas no Brasil: Estratégias de Avaliação* (Vol. 7). Brasília: IPEA.

Pires, R. R., & Vaz, A. C. N. (2010). Participação faz diferença? Uma avaliação das características e efeitos da institucionalização da participação nos municípios brasileiros. In *In A dinâmica da participação local no Brasil*. São Paulo: Cortez.

Sarmento, D. C. (2005). Criação dos sistemas municipais de ensino. *Education and Society, 26*(93), Campinas, 1363–1390.

Scatena, J. H. G., & Tanaka, O. Y. (2001). Os instrumentos normalizadores no processo de descentralização da saúde. *Saúde Soc., 10*(2).

Tatagiba, L. (2005). Conselhos gestores de políticas públicas e democracia participativa: aprofundando o debate. *Revista de Sociologia e Política*, (25), 209–213.

Tatagiba, L. (2002). Os conselhos gestores e a democratização das políticas públicas no Brasil. In *Sociedade civil e espaços públicos no Brasil*. São Paulo: Paz e Terra.

Verba, S., Schlozman, K. L., & Brady, E. H. (2005). *Voice and equality – Civic voluntarism in American politics*. London: Cambridge University Press.

Part II
Education and Income

Educational Stratification Among Youth in Brazil: 1960–2010

Carlos Antonio Costa Ribeiro, Ricardo Ceneviva, and Murillo Marschner Alves de Brito

Abstract The chapter investigates patterns of inequalities of educational opportunities (IEO) among young men and women who lived with their parents in Brazil from 1960 to 2010. We used educational transition models (ETM) applied to census data (1960, 1970, 1980, 1991, 2000, and 2010) in order to analyze socioeconomic inequalities of access and completion of primary, secondary, and tertiary education. We documented how socioeconomic origins shape educational opportunities of young people in Brazil during five decades of intense educational expansion and social change. Our analysis reveals a mixed pattern of changes: inequality of educational opportunities (in terms of parental income and region of birth) decreased at basic educational levels, persisted at secondary level, and increased in terms of access to higher education.

Keywords Educational stratification · Inequality of educational opportunities · Educational system in Brazil

Inequality of educational opportunity (IEO) is measured by the effect parents' socioeconomic and cultural characteristics have on the educational accomplishment of their children. We know that the education attained by an individual is the primary source of social mobility in modern societies; thus, a decreasing IEO is essential for increasing social mobility. Several studies on this topic in Brazil have

This chapter benefited from comments and suggestions from participants of the first seminar project "Census: how much has Brazil changed in the past 50 years" held by the Center for Metropolitan Studies (CEM) in September 2012. We sincerely thank Marta Arretche for her invitation and support for the accomplishment of this work.

C. A. C. Ribeiro (✉) · R. Ceneviva
Instituto de Estudos Sociais e Políticos, Universidade Estadual do Rio de Janeiro, Rio de Janeiro, Brazil
e-mail: carloscr@iesp.uerj.br; ceneviva@iesp.uerj.br

M. M. A. de Brito
Department of Education, Pontifical Catholic University of Rio de Janeiro, Rio de Janeiro, Brazil
e-mail: murillo-marschner@puc-rio.br

M. Arretche (ed.), *Paths of Inequality in Brazil*,
https://doi.org/10.1007/978-3-319-78184-6_3

revealed that this type of inequality has remained practically unchanged over the years. Although there has been expansion in all educational levels, individuals from families with more socioeconomic resources continue to have advantages when progressing through the system. This conclusion is based chiefly on data pertaining to birth cohorts observed in sample surveys, which introduce retrospective information about families of origin (mainly occupation and educational level of the parents while their children were growing up). To understand this effect on the likelihood of an individual's educational progression, one must have access to information concerning the family's socioeconomic conditions, which, in the case of the census, is available to children in the family (sons and daughters). Thus, the objective of this chapter is to use the microdata from Brazilian censuses for the period of 1960–2010 to assess the evolution of the effects that socioeconomic background has had on the educational progression of Brazilians age 12–25, in order to understand what has changed in Brazil over the past 50 years regarding educational stratification among youth.

Educational Progression Models

A commonly used method to measure IEO in sociological literature on social stratification consists of analyzing educational progression as a string of decisions (Mare 1980, 1981). During the 1980s and 1990s, several studies on the subject resulted in a compilation edited by Shavit and Blossfeld (1993) in which the determinants of educational stratification in 13 countries are comparatively examined through highly standardized tests. The main question was to what extent the association between socioeconomic origin and educational attainment changed over time. The national cases investigated included Western capitalist societies (the United States, the former West Germany, England and Wales, Italy, Switzerland, the Netherlands, and Sweden), non-Western capitalist societies (Japan and Taiwan), and countries having a socialist legacy (Poland, Hungary, and the former Czechoslovakia). Four major educational transitions were analyzed: completion of primary education, entry into secondary education after having completed primary education, completion of secondary education, and entry into postsecondary (university) education after having completed secondary education. The main conclusion reached in this comparative study was that there was no change in inequality over time, regardless of the educational expansion, a claim further supported by Mare (1980) when researching the US case. Indeed, these studies suggest that there was a pattern of persistent inequality, assuming that class differences in completing transitions tend to be constant across older and younger birth cohorts in the twentieth century. Even though school participation rates have increased for all classes at practically every level, the advantages associated with privileged socioeconomic backgrounds remained unchanged. Only the Netherlands and Sweden seemed to escape this general pattern: in these countries, the association between schooling and social origin witnessed a downward trend throughout the twentieth century.

Given that this evidence seemed fairly consistent across the various countries, researchers began to develop models to explain the empirical patterns observed, especially the patterns of persistent inequality. Since then, research efforts in investigating class determinants in educational stratification have produced a fair amount of empirical evidence that attempts to explain persistent inequality. Among the most prominent explanatory hypotheses we find is the maximally maintained inequality (MMI) hypothesis (Raftery and Hout 1993), which states that changes in the correlation between social origin and educational fate tend to occur only in circumstances where transition rates for certain educational levels reach saturation levels that prevent its increase among classes of a privileged socioeconomic background due to a "ceiling effect." If, on the one hand, this process reduces class inequalities across educational levels where one observes saturation of access for the upper classes, on the other hand, it displaces inequality toward higher educational levels. Thus, where saturation exists, there is no inequality for any class of origin. In this regard, a uniform decrease in educational costs tends to maintain inequalities at a constant level, since its impact is uniform among all classes. Research on the Brazilian case (Valle Silva and Souza 1986; Hasenbalg and Valle-Silva 2002; Fernandes 2004; Torche 2010; Ribeiro 2011; Montalvão 2011) greatly contributed to the understanding of the major patterns of IEO evolution. The fact that disparities are especially prominent among individuals with urban and rural origins and that race inequality, especially at higher educational levels, places the black and brown populations at a disadvantage became firmly established. Furthermore, class-based inequality is pervasive and persists over time. In the past three decades, expansion of Brazil's educational system primarily targeted lower stages of progression, thus decreasing class inequality in educational access and shifting it, to a large extent, to higher educational levels. It is now possible to demonstrate the correlation between social origin and educational attainment at higher educational levels. From this perspective, the pattern of persistent inequalities remains applicable for studying the evolution of educational stratification in Brazil, and MMI continues to be a thought-provoking research hypothesis for analyzing the effects that expansion of the system has had on the lowest levels of educational opportunities.

Because these studies use information that cover an extended period of time, we plan to investigate the extent to which the conclusions reached, based on birth cohort analysis and retrospective data on class origin (questions regarding parents' occupation and educational level), can be observed when analyzing educational progression of youth over a long period.

We initially present descriptive statistics regarding the evolution of youth educational level and odds of youth progression within the Brazilian educational system during the period analyzed, regardless of social origin. Then we demonstrate the educational progression model applied to the microdata from Brazilian censuses between 1960 and 2010 and the main results of analysis on the probabilities of youth educational progression in view of socioeconomic background.

Educational Transitions in Brazil: Operational Definitions and Data Description

During the period analyzed, the Brazilian educational system underwent major reforms through enactment of the Directives and Foundations Laws (LDB 1961, 1971, and 1996), which had an impact on the regulatory structure of the scope of education and, consequently, on how educational levels are measured in censuses. Even though significant changes have occurred, it is possible to devise a set of suitable educational transitions that can be applied to all censuses to represent the levels of education in Brazil since the 1960s. In its most detailed version, the structure contains seven transitions (Chart 1).

Level	Transition	Description	T1	T2	T3	T4	T5	T6
Unschooled	**Outside the educational system**	Illiterate/Never attended school	-	-	-	-	-	-
Primary/Basic Ed.	**T1 - Entered the educational system**	Entered educational system and completed the 1st, 2nd and 3rd grades (does not include pre-school, day-care, literacy class and adult literacy course)	V	-	-	-	-	-
	T2 -Completed four years of schooling	Entered the Educ. Syst. (T1) and completed the first 4 years of Prim. Ed. (T2)	V	V	-	-	-	-
	T3 - Completed primary education	Entered Educ. Syst. (T1), completed four years of Prim. Ed (T2), and completed Prim. Ed. (up to 8th grade) (T3)	V	V	V	-	-	-
Secondary Ed.	**T4 - Completed PEd. and entered SEd.**	Entered Educ. Syst. (T1), completed four years of Prim. Ed (T2), completed Prim. Ed. (up to 8th grade) (T3), and entered Sec. Ed. (T4)	V	V	V	V	-	-
	T5 - Completed SEd.	Entered Educ. Syst. (T1), completed four years of Prim. Ed (T2), completed Prim. Ed. (up to 8th grade) (T3), entered Sec. Ed. (T4), and completed Sec. Ed. (T5).	V	V	V	V	V	-
Higher Ed.	**T6 - Completed SEd. and entered university**	Entered Educ. Syst. (T1), completed four years of Prim. Ed (T2), completed Prim. Ed. (up to 8th grade) (T3), entered Sec. Ed. (T4), completed Sec. Ed. (T5), and entered university (T6)	V	V	V	V	V	V
	T7 - Completed Higher Ed.	Entered Educ. Syst. (T1), completed four years of Prim. Ed (T2), completed Prim. Ed. (up to 8th grade) (T3), entered Sec. Ed. (T4), completed Sec. Ed. (T5), entered university (T6), and completed university (T7)	V	V	V	V	V	V

Chart 1 Educational transition model: Brazil

An illiterate individual or one who has never been enrolled in the educational system made none of the defined transitions; therefore, his or her educational level assumes a value of 0 for any of the transitions. In turn, someone who completed higher education has passed through all the transitions measured by the model (i.e., for this person $T_1 = 1$, $T_2 = 1,..., T_7 = 1$). Other educational levels occupy intermediate positions.

The position of individuals within the educational trajectory basically depends on their age. Just as certain educational levels are not accessible to individuals in some age brackets, we can roughly guess an individual's age by his or her position in the educational trajectory. The association between age and educational progression is particularly true in the early stages of youth educational trajectory, in which age-grade distortion tends to be smaller. It becomes less evident as individuals become older and move forward (or not) in school. We therefore attempted to structure analysis of the evolution of educational transitions starting from the comparison between significant population categories from the standpoint of evolution of individuals' educational trajectories. For presentation purposes, this meant selecting some age brackets within the population spectrum that carry certain expectations regarding position in the educational trajectory that can be used as reference to evaluate the empirical results observed.

The age brackets selected are the following:

1. **Population, age 12–15**: this population is expected to complete T_1 (entry into the educational system) and T_2 (4 years of schooling completed). Since higher educational levels are not accessible to all individuals in this age group, the analysis is limited to these two transitions.
2. **Population, age 16–18**: all individuals within this age bracket were considered to have reached a position in their life cycle that enabled them to have completed T_1, T_2, and T_3 (8 years of schooling completed); thus, the analysis is restricted to these three transitions.
3. **Population, age 19–20**: in this age bracket, we analyzed the odds of completing T_1, T_2, and T_3, as well as T_4 (entry into secondary education), T_5 (completed secondary education), and T_6 (entry into university).
4. **Population, age 21–25**: for this age range, we evaluated the odds of someone completing the entire transition spectrum, which includes, in addition to those previously described, T_7 (completed higher education).

Youth Education

Youth Educational Level (Age 12–25)

Analysis of the evolution of indicators compares the population age 12–25 in the 1960 census, the population age 12–25 in the 1970 census, and so on, demonstrating that it is not the same population or even the same cohort. Since the objective is to

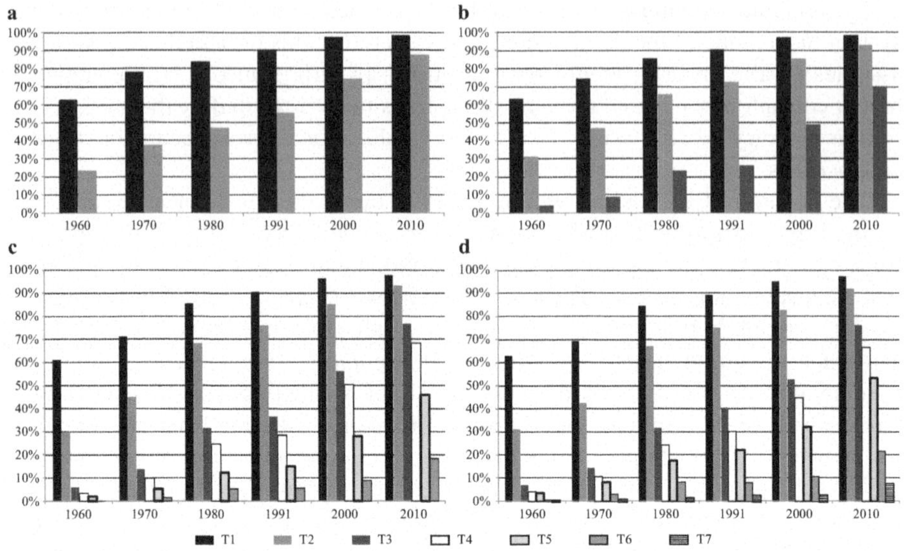

Graph 1 Youth educational level, according to the age groups of interest Brazil (1960–2010). (**a**) Population age 12–15. (**b**) Population age 16–18. (**c**) Population age 19–20. (**d**) Population age 21–25. (Source: IBGE Demographic Censuses 1960, 1970, 1980, 1991, 2000, 2010 (special tabulations by CEM)

verify the effects of parental resources on their children's odds of progressing through the educational system (IEO), we only worked with individuals who still resided with their families of origin. This is another factor that limits the analysis to the age brackets previously described. While the vast majority of children still reside with their parents, the same cannot be said for adolescents, especially from the age of 19 onward. Consequently, the results are more reliable for early educational transitions since they are based on children and young people who still reside with their parents.

Graph 1 shows improvements in the youth educational level for all age ranges analyzed between 1960 and 2010. The proportion of the population entering the educational system becomes virtually universal between 2000 and 2010 for all age ranges. This did not occur at the beginning of our series. Among the youth population, age 12–15, almost 90% entering the school system completed 4 years of study in 2010. This proportion was just over 20% in 1960. This same movement occurs between 1960 and 2010 regarding these educational levels in all age groups, thus demonstrating the process of universalization of access to the educational system, which is ultimately consolidated within the 2000–2010 period.

We also note significant improvements in the portion of the population that attains 8 years of schooling for groups above age 16. Among the population age 16–18 in 1960, less than 10% of individuals completed their primary education, while nearly 70% did so in 2010. Graphs referring to populations age 19–20 and age 21–25 provide evidence that gains in education also extended to entry into and completion of secondary and higher education, although by varying degrees across these levels. The results for these populations indicate that a growing number of individuals who complete primary education tend to continue on to secondary education.

On the other hand, completion of secondary education continues to be a relevant barrier to young people age 19–25. Entry into and completion of higher education has also shown gains over the years, although access to university education continues to be limited, even in 2010.

The results show significant changes in youth educational levels, with a constant upward trend between 1960 and 2010. Moreover, universalization of access for the first two educational levels and very significant advances in completion of secondary education were noted. Even if the educational trajectory of many young people still ends at these levels, there has been an increase in the number of young people attaining access to higher education between 1960 and 2010.

Youth Educational Progression (Age 12–25)

Little has been said regarding the likelihood of actually accomplishing the transitions, i.e., the proportion of individuals who complete transition T_n to go on to actually complete T_{n+1}. We could refer to the population that completes T_n as the one with the probability of completing T_{n+1}, and accessibility to different educational levels can be measured by the system's ability to transform the population at a probability of T_{n+1} into one that actually completes it. The relation between the total number of individuals capable of completing T_{n+1} and those who actually complete it may be measured by conditional transition rates. These are important indicators of the educational system's capacity to absorb populations across several levels. Thus, the population completing T_{n+1} is always decreasing in relation to those who actually complete T_n, since the latter constitutes a subset of the former (only individuals who complete T_1 are capable of completing, e.g., T_2, and so on).

In the transitional structure used here, there are six educational transition movements, ranging from T_0 to T_1 (entry into the educational system) and from T_6 to T_7 (completed higher education once having entered university). In Graph 2, we can see the conditional transition rates for the age brackets to which a transitional movement pertains.

Analysis of conditional transition rates illustrates the differences in the evolution of parameters for youth educational progression in Brazil across basic levels (up to T_3), middle levels (T_4 and T_5), and advanced levels (T_6 and T_7). Transition rates between T_0 and T_1 are virtually universal in 2010 for all age brackets (Graph 2a), and their increase indicates that the educational system had a progressive capacity to absorb individuals since 1960, with the same occurring in movements from T_1 to T_2 (Graph 2b) and from T_2 to T_3 (Graph 2c). In the first case, this is almost universal, like the transition from T_0 to T_1, indicating continuity in the educational progression up to 4 years of schooling in 2010 for practically all individuals entering the system.

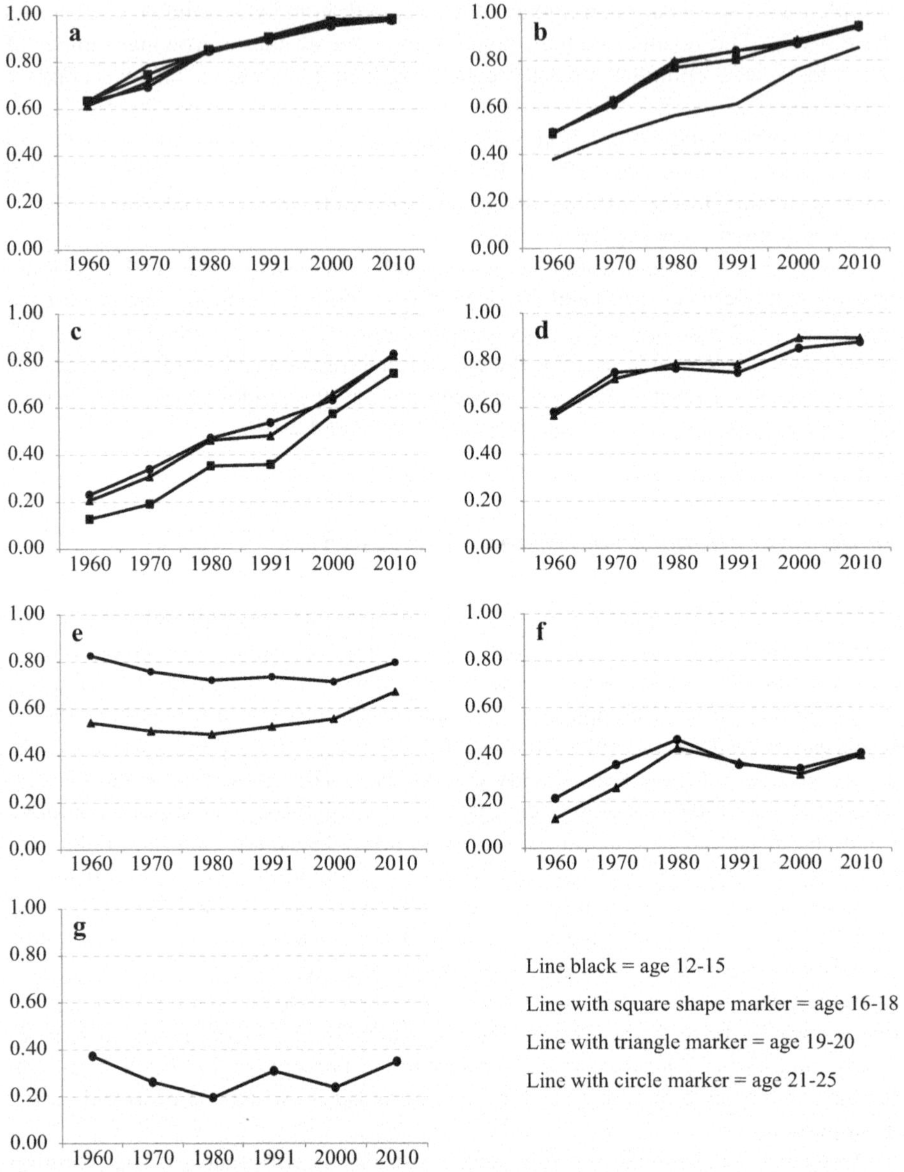

Graph 2 Conditional transitional rates, by age brackets and transitional movements Brazil (1960–2010). (**a**) T_0 to T_1. (**b**) T_1 to T_2. (**c**) T_2 to T_3. (**d**) T_3 to T_4. (**e**) T_4 to T_5. (**f**) T_5 to T_6. (**g**) T_6 to T_7. (Source: IBGE Demographic Census (special tabulations by CEM)

Completion of primary education, once an individual has finished 4 years of schooling (transition from T_2 to T_3), also became, over the course of this period, a very common educational target under which we find more than 70% of the population within the age brackets analyzed. Up to 1970, only the first 4 years of primary education were compulsory, but in 1971 the Brazilian government expanded the minimum level of schooling to 8 years of primary education. An increase in completion of this transition (T_2 to T_3) really occurred after 1970. However, even in 2010 only around 20% of people who had finished 4 years of schooling managed to complete primary education (8 years).

As for the intermediate and advanced levels of youth educational progression, trends are somewhat different. The conditional transition from T_3 to T_4 (Graph 2d), which indicates entry into secondary education after completion of primary education, shows a growth rate similar to those found at basic levels, thus indicating a considerable accessibility gain with very high growth rates throughout the period. However, it is in the transition from T_4 to T_5 (completed secondary education, on Graph 2e) that trends shown by the conditional transition rates are more clearly distinguished than those observed for basic levels. The behavior of these rates indicates that the system's ability to transform the population eligible for T_5 into one that actually completes the transition remained constant between 1960 and 2000, recovering slightly in 2010. Thus, the proportion that completes this movement remained unchanged – which can be explained by the increasing number of individuals eligible for this transition coupled with the educational system's inability to increase the number of vacancies at this educational level at the same rate of growth as the eligible population.

At higher educational levels, we find the lowest conditional transition rates among Brazilian youth. The transition for entry into university, after completion of secondary education (from T_5 to T_6, on Graph 2f), was very low in 1960: within the population age 19–20, only 12.9% of those who completed secondary education went on to university. As for the population age 21–25, this proportion was 21.5% in 1960, rising in 1970 and reaching its peak in 1980, when it was approximately 40%. From 1991 on, there is a drop in the rate of conditional transition to T_6, with a slight recovery through 2010. In this case we also observe that the evolution of the educational system in terms of absolute numbers was unable to increase the conditional transition rate, that is, the proportion of students entering university. Among all the transitional movements, the conditional rate for completing higher education demonstrated the most erratic behavior. It is also the transitional movement that has the lowest conditional rates, indicating that Brazilian youth (up to age 25) who reach university frequently fail to complete this educational level (or complete T_7). The only age bracket that allows assessment of the transition rates from T_6 to T_7 (age 21–25) shows results that indicate a decrease in the odds of completing university (once having entered). Between 1960 and 1980, only 19.6% of entrants completed higher education, with the rate recovering from 1991 through 2010 when it reaches 35% of young people in the age bracket of 21–25 years (Graph 2g).

The evolution of transition rates among young Brazilians shows that the capacity of the educational system increased substantially between 1960 and 2010 at the basic educational levels. If in 1960 it was highly unlikely for young people to complete 8 years of study, by 2010 the odds of educational progression for T_1, T_2, and T_3 are practically universal. Regarding intermediate levels, there are important gains for conditional access to entry into secondary education (T_4), but it is not yet possible to identify movements with the same magnitude in the transition toward T_5 (completed secondary school), for which the Brazilian educational system continues to present transitional parameters in 2010 similar to those observed in 1980. When looking at higher levels, access restriction decreased within the period of 1960–2010. Throughout almost this entire period (except for 1960), the odds of young people completing university – once admitted – are smaller than the odds of entry into university after having completed secondary education.

Statistical Analysis and Results

Among the restricted set of variables available in census data, we decided to use those with the fewest compatibility problems:

- *Gender*: in light of the evolution of average educational levels for women in Brazil (a phenomenon also observed in other countries), to a point where it has surpassed the level of men, we believe women have a higher likelihood of completing transitions.
- *Color*: color/race is a dimension that is very present (and relevant) in studies on educational inequality in Brazil, ranging from dichotomous specifications that separate whites and nonwhites (Hasenbalg and Valle-Silva 2002) to those that distinguish brown, black, and white (Fernandes 2004; Ribeiro 2011; Montalvão 2011). The results of these studies demonstrate the relevance of the operationalization of race by using a three-category variable due to significant differences found in the educational opportunities for blacks and browns. We use this variable to classify three categories: black, brown, and white.
- *Residence status*: differences in the educational supply of rural and urban areas justify the inclusion of a control variable for region of residence. Results of Brazilian studies demonstrate a significant effect that decreases the likelihood that students who live in rural areas will complete transitions (Hasenbalg and Valle-Silva 2002; Montalvão 2011). Rural or urban origin (and not necessarily current residence) is also used as a social origin indicator in international studies (Mare 1981; Hout et al. 1993; Lucas 2001) and in studies dealing with the Brazilian case (Fernandes 2004; Ribeiro 2011), generally presenting an effect of decreasing the odd of completing transitions.
- *Family composition*: we chose to incorporate two indicators concerning family composition when estimating the odds of someone reaching a particular educational transition – (1) the absence of a spouse, an indicator of single-parent families, and (2) a variable indicating whether the individual is the firstborn child.
- *Family income*: per capita household income is commonly used as an indicator of the family's economic status. National and international studies that have introduced this variable have demonstrated its positive effects on the odds of transition (Lucas 2001; Hasenbalg and Valle-Silva 2002, Milesi 2010; Montalvão 2011; Roksa and Velez 2010). The income variable employed in this study under-

went a monotonic transformation using a logarithmic transformation to reduce excessive data dispersion.
- *Mother's educational level*: the total number of years of education attained by the parent is a commonly used variable to indicate an individual's social origin. Most studies use the total number of years of schooling attained by both the father and the mother (Mare 1981; Hout et al. 1993; Lucas 2001; Hout 2006; Fernandes 2004; Torche 2010; Ribeiro 2011). Valle-Silva and Hasenbalg (2000) use only the mother's educational level and, in other cases, employ variables that summarize schooling by the average of both parents (Ayalon and Shavit 2004) or by using the highest level of education attained between the two (Kesler 2003; Milesi 2010; Roksa and Velez 2010; Karlson 2011). This study uses the mother's educational level, operationalized via dichotomous variables for complete or incomplete educational levels. Regardless of how this variable is used, studies indicate that the higher the educational level, the greater the odds of completing transitions at the basic educational level.

Statistical Models

The basic model, adjusted to capture correlations between observable attributes of youth, their family, social and economic environment, and the likelihood of completing educational transitions, is described by Eq. (1) below.

$$T_{ij} = \alpha_0 + \beta_1 S_{ij} + \beta_2 C_{ij} + \beta_3 R_{ij} + \beta_4 F_{ij} + \beta_5 Lg\left(R\right)_{ij} + \beta_6 \mathrm{E}_{ij} + \varepsilon_{ij} \quad (1)$$

where, in Eq. (1):

- T_{ij} is an ordinal categorical variable (with eight levels), which identifies whether individual i from age bracket j completed a particular educational transition.
- α_0 is a constant that indicates the cutoff point between the different levels in ordinal models.
- S_{ij} is a dummy variable that identifies whether individual i from age bracket j is female.
- C_{ij} is a vector of dummy variables that identifies whether individual i from age bracket j is black, brown, or white.
- R_{ij} is a dummy variable that identifies if the residence of individual i from age bracket j is located in the rural area.
- F_{ij} is a vector of dummy variables that identifies whether individual i from age bracket j lives in a single-parent family and if he or she is a firstborn child.
- $Lg(R)_{ij}$ is a scalar variable indicating the natural log of per capita household income of the residence of individual i from age bracket j.
- E_{ij} is a vector of dummy variables identifying the educational level of the mother of individual i from age bracket j and if she concluded primary, secondary, and higher education.

- ε_{ij} is the random error term.

The variable of interest in this chapter, T_{ij} – educational level of an individual – was built as a series of educational transitions that an individual *i* from age bracket *t* could complete throughout his or her academic life. Therefore, transitions have a dichotomous outcome: an individual completes a given educational transition, for example, primary school, within the appropriate age bracket,[1] or an individual does not complete it until the age of 18. Thus, educational transitions have been operationalized as an ordered categorical variable – with levels from zero to seven – indicating the highest transition completed by an individual within a certain age bracket. In other words, educational transitions assume discrete values, which correspond to sortable categories *k*. While it is possible to organize categories *k* in the shape of educational transitions, the actual distance between each category is ignored, and, most importantly, we cannot presume that the distance between categories remains constant.

In this chapter, we opted to use a proportional odds model (POM), mainly because of two characteristics present within the educational transition data in Brazilian censuses: (1) this type of model is more suitable for analyzing ordinal variables derived from a continuous variable, which, in turn, was grouped in the same manner as the educational transitions analyzed in this chapter[2]; (2) the POM rests on the assumption that proportional odds between categories are empirically valid. Recent uses of this type of model when analyzing educational transitions may be found in Hauser and Andrew (2006) and Torche (2010).

Results

Tables 1, 2, 3 and 4 show the results of estimates obtained by the proportional odds model (POM) fit to census data from 1960 to 2010.[3] The results report the odds ratios of educational progression of young people, age 12–25, for the covariates that refer to personal characteristics, family environment, and social origin.

[1] In this chapter, we considered broader age brackets than those employed by the Ministry of Education (MEC) for measuring the age-grade distortion rate. For example, according to MEC criteria, the ideal age for completing primary education (transition T3, according to the classification hereby adopted) is age 15. In the present analysis, we consider that the individual can complete T3 up to the age of 18. We make use of broader age brackets because it is not our intention to measure the age-grade distortion rate but rather to examine the factors associated with the social and economic status of families that can affect youth educational performance and progression.

[2] This methodological choice is theoretically justified in section "Educational Transitions in Brazil: Operational Definitions and Data Description" of this chapter.

[3] All models had controls for state, since we consider that Brazilian states played a relevant role in providing basic education. More importantly, the coverage of state-level public supply shows significant variations across the different states as well as throughout the period analyzed (1960–2010). Consequently, standard errors were clustered by states. Cutoff points for the categories have been omitted so as to preserve greater simplicity in presenting the results.

Table 1 Estimated odds ratios for completing T_2 Brazil (1960–2010)

	1960	1970	1980	1991	2000	2010
Women	1.203***	1.264***	1.510***	1.667***	1.687***	1.739***
	(0.0408)	(0.0524)	(0.0544)	(0.0549)	(0.0524)	(0.0723)
Blacks	0.341***	NA	0.543***	0.532***	0.638***	0.772***
	(0.0254)	NA	(0.0165)	(0.0150)	(0.0219)	(0.0182)
Browns	0.548***	NA	0.687***	0.713***	0.816***	0.912***
	(0.0306)	NA	(0.0166)	(0.0153)	(0.0101)	(0.0206)
Rural	0.202***	0.298***	0.394***	0.524***	0.607***	0.875**
	(0.0256)	(0.0380)	(0.0503)	(0.0565)	(0.0382)	(0.0356)
Monoparental	0.740***	0.808***	0.884***	0.949*	1.0100	0.9950
	(0.0267)	(0.0186)	(0.0200)	(0.0252)	(0.0217)	(0.0264)
Firstborn	1.215***	1.111***	1.151***	1.245***	1.238***	1.216***
	(0.0304)	(0.0224)	(0.0406)	(0.0381)	(0.0198)	(0.0203)
Income (Log)	0.614***	0.552***	0.545***	0.434***	0.437***	0.283***
	(0.0334)	(0.032)	(0.043)	(0.024)	(0.0133)	(0.0154)
Mother Prim. ed.	4.399***	2.919***	2.091***	1.731***	1.723***	1.563***
	(0.6910)	(0.1870)	(0.1040)	(0.0556)	(0.1110)	(0.0662)
Mother Second. ed.	0.9830	1.1700	1.376***	1.571***	1.401***	1.533***
	(0.1860)	(0.1050)	(0.0732)	(0.0927)	(0.0721)	(0.0555)
Mother Higher ed.	0.8460	0.7060	0.9670	1.2270	0.819***	1.332***
	(0.4410)	(0.1510)	(0.0739)	(0.1290)	(0.0432)	(0.1010)
N	67.482	403.119	423.313	205.853	206.605	162.826
Control p/ FU (state)	Yes	Yes	Yes	Yes	Yes	Yes

Standard errors in parentheses
Source: Census data (IBGE); IBGE Demographic Census (special tabulations by CEM)
$*p < 0.05$, $**p < 0.01$, $***p < 0.001$

These results can be read both synchronously, by analyzing the effects of each covariate (while all others are kept fixed) over the odds of success in completing certain transitions, and diachronically, by analyzing the dynamics of specific covariates throughout the 50 years of the 1960–2010 censuses.

Over 50 years, Brazil has experienced significant changes in its social and economic structure. Once predominantly agricultural, the economy has now become mostly industrial, and the population went from essentially rural to urban. Women gained ground in the labor market and, most importantly, a major expansion took place in public basic educational systems.

Table 1 shows the odds ratios estimated for a successful transition from T_1 to T_2. The odds ratio compares the odds of success – that is, the odds that an individual i from age bracket j will complete 4 years of education and fall in a category greater than or equal to T_2 – from one group over another group. An odds ratio of 1 indicates that the odds of completing transition T_2 is just as likely to occur in both groups compared. A ratio greater than 1 indicates a higher probability of transition in the first group. Therefore, an odds ratio of 1.20 for women in 1960 means that the odds of success in completing transition T_2 is 1.20 times higher for women than for men,

Table 2 Estimated odds ratios for completing T_3 Brazil (1960–2010)

	1960	1970	1980	1991	2000	2010
Women	1.219***	1.341***	1.568***	1.586***	1.440***	1.381***
	(0.0652)	(0.0744)	(0.0898)	(0.1020)	(0.0767)	(0.0468)
Blacks	0.323***	NA	0.577***	0.605***	0.757***	0.863**
	(0.0225)	NA	(0.0224)	(0.0261)	(0.0307)	(0.0473)
Browns	0.522***	NA	0.755***	0.768***	0.873***	0.9740
	(0.0255)	NA	(0.0189)	(0.0161)	(0.0133)	(0.0283)
Rural	0.186***	0.242***	0.372***	0.483***	0.720***	1.0520
	(0.0205)	(0.0252)	(0.0390)	(0.0438)	(0.0560)	(0.0481)
Monoparental	0.629***	0.724***	0.866***	1.0050	1.0120	0.9920
	(0.0230)	(0.0189)	(0.0203)	(0.0265)	(0.0176)	(0.0193)
Firstborn	1.145***	1.062**	1.0350	1.183***	1.102***	0.909***
	(0.0249)	(0.0194)	(0.0232)	(0.0216)	(0.0186)	(0.0155)
Income (Log)	0.587***	0.525***	0.433***	0.351***	0.268***	0.135***
	(0.0462)	(0.0349)	(0.0402)	(0.0255)	(0.0134)	(0.0164)
Mother Prim. Ed.	6.220***	2.937***	1.368***	3.095***	2.444***	3.286***
	(1.2930)	(0.2020)	(0.1090)	(0.2170)	(0.1020)	(0.1900)
Mother Second. Ed.	1.0230	1.261***	0.8950	0.493***	0.553***	0.377***
	(0.3280)	(0.0523)	(0.0711)	(0.0361)	(0.0506)	(0.0227)
Mother Higher Ed.	0.151***	1.2100	0.717***	0.757***	0.460***	0.8220
	(0.0799)	(0.1350)	(0.0672)	(0.0590)	(0.0623)	(0.0876)
N	39.993	230.974	216.761	111.518	95.523	50.169
Control p/ FU (state)	Yes	Yes	Yes	Yes	Yes	Yes

Standard errors in parentheses
Source: Own calculations based on Census data (IBGE); IBGE Demographic Census (special tabulations by CEM)
$*p < 0.05, **p < 0.01, ***p < 0.001$

that is, approximately 20% higher for women. An odds ratio of less than 1, on the other hand, indicates that the probability is lower in the first group. For example, an odds ratio of 0.53 for black youths in 1991 means that the odds of success in completing T_2 among young blacks is 0.53 times the chance of young whites – the reference category – in completing the same transition in 1991. In other words, the odds of success among young blacks is approximately 47% lower than among young whites.

Graph 1 shows that in 1960 nearly 25% of young people age 12–15 had completed 4 years of education. That means that for every 100 young people who entered the school system, only 25 completed four school years before the age of 16. The estimated odds ratio of 1.20 for women, therefore, means that in a sample of 200 young people, consisting of 100 men and 100 women, we would expect an average of 25 men to have completed T_2 before reaching age 16, while 30 women would have the same success in completing 4 years of study by age 15. Similarly, in 1991, only 55% of young people up to age 15 completed T_2. That means that out of every 100 young people who entered the school system, only 55 completed 4 years

Table 3 Estimated odds ratios for completing T_5 Brazil (1960–2010)

	1960	1970	1980	1991	2000	2010
Women	1.428***	1.586***	1.788***	1.489***	1.672***	1.687***
	(0.054)	(0.070)	(0.079)	(0.065)	(0.061)	(0.059)
Blacks	0.321***	NA	0.501***	0.585***	0.690***	0.758***
	(0.024)	NA	(0.025)	(0.015)	(0.028)	(0.028)
Browns	0.533***	NA	0.676***	0.761***	0.822***	0.847***
	(0.038)	NA	(0.022)	(0.020)	(0.013)	(0.015)
Rural	0.195***	0.234***	0.311***	0.414***	0.537***	0.805***
	(0.022)	(0.027)	(0.033)	(0.034)	(0.037)	(0.040)
Monoparental	0.642***	0.708***	0.812***	1.099***	1.046	1.008
	(0.021)	(0.020)	(0.023)	(0.030)	(0.028)	(0.016)
Firstborn	1.030	1.068	1.067	1.672***	1.791***	1.643***
	(0.040)	(0.036)	(0.046)	(0.065)	(0.064)	(0.033)
Income (Log)	0.671***	1.177***	0.736***	0.545***	0.584***	0.369***
	(0.056)	(0.0359)	(0.0659)	(0.0369)	(0.0232)	(0.022)
Mother Prim. Ed.	7.342***	3.245***	2.030***	2.453***	1.845***	1.441***
	(1.616)	(0.117)	(0.123)	(0.111)	(0.160)	(0.093)
Mother Second. Ed.	1.442	1.507***	1.284***	2.296***	2.318***	3.634***
	(0.322)	(0.100)	(0.058)	(0.168)	(0.131)	(0.187)
Mother Higher Ed.	0.461*	0.910	0.869**	0.595***	0.657***	0.527***
	(0.156)	(0.121)	(0.045)	(0.038)	(0.064)	(0.052)
N	18,813	114,851	125,914	79,654	98,396	74,629
Control p/ FU (state)	Yes	Yes	Yes	Yes	Yes	Yes

Standard errors in parentheses

Source: Own calculations based on Census data (IBGE); IBGE Demographic Census (special tabulations by CEM)

$*p < 0.05, **p < 0.01, ***p < 0.001$

of study before age 16. An odds ratio of approximately 0.53 for blacks, therefore, means that in a sample of 200 young people, made up of 100 blacks and 100 whites, we would expect, on average, that only 30 blacks would achieve success, whereas approximately 55 whites would complete T_2.

In Table 1 we can see that the gender variable played a relevant role in the odds of completing this transition as early as the 1960s. The estimated effect indicates that the odds of women completing 4 years of school prior to age 15 was approximately 20% higher than men, a trend accentuated between 1960 and 2010. Women's advantage over men in such early decades as the 1960s is a noteworthy finding, since in most countries around the world, men tended to have an advantage until at least the 1970s.

Comparisons between racial groups demonstrate that inequality in educational opportunities among browns, blacks, and whites (the reference category) in completing T_2 is stable throughout the entire period analyzed and may be considered one of the striking characteristics of the Brazilian educational stratification structure, even if such inequality has decreased significantly since the beginning of this

Table 4 Estimated odds ratios for completing T_7 Brazil (1960–2010)

	1960	1970	1980	1991	2000	2010
Women	1.266***	1.566***	1.871***	1.457***	1.749***	1.776***
	(0.0485)	(0.0721)	(0.0717)	(0.0745)	(0.0552)	(0.0502)
Blacks	0.328***	NA	0.527***	0.647***	0.700***	0.714***
	(0.0264)	NA	(0.0136)	(0.0178)	(0.0211)	(0.0136)
Browns	0.493***	NA	0.662***	0.756***	0.777***	0.768***
	(0.0287)	NA	(0.0196)	(0.0198)	(0.0180)	(0.0145)
Rural	0.205***	0.254***	0.321***	0.458***	0.525***	0.726***
	(0.0225)	(0.0268)	(0.0341)	(0.0345)	(0.0287)	(0.0236)
Monoparental	0.617***	0.713***	0.800***	1.177***	1.082***	1.047*
	(0.0240)	(0.0159)	(0.0135)	(0.0381)	(0.0231)	(0.0195)
Firstborn	0.9940	1.062*	1.104**	3.093***	2.979***	2.822***
	(0.0433)	(0.0258)	(0.0383)	(0.1740)	(0.1770)	(0.0762)
Income (Log)	0.763***	0.879***	1.023***	0.668***	0.747***	0.631***
	(0.0608)	(0.0544)	(0.0804)	(0.0289)	(0.0367)	(0.0356)
Mother Prim. Ed.	6.663***	3.105***	2.419***	3.214***	2.502***	1.911***
	(0.8590)	(0.1500)	(0.1440)	(0.1370)	(0.1040)	(0.1100)
Mother Second. Ed.	1.666***	1.371***	1.330***	3.066***	3.100***	3.491***
	(0.2050)	(0.0495)	(0.0359)	(0.0834)	(0.1200)	(0.1020)
Mother Higher Ed.	0.6310	0.9520	1.0320	2.870***	2.512***	3.240***
	(0.1950)	(0.0532)	(0.1010)	(0.1590)	(0.1220)	(0.1130)
N	26.013	152.283	192.828	200.252	237.026	229.691
Control p/ FU (state)	Yes	Yes	Yes	Yes	Yes	Yes

Standard errors in parentheses
Source: Own calculations based on Census data (IBGE); IBGE Demographic Census (special tabulations by CEM)
$*p < 0.05, **p < 0.01, ***p < 0.001$

historical series. The same could be said for inequality pertaining to residence in rural areas, even though we can observe a more drastic decrease for this inequality throughout the 50 years analyzed here.

Among family characteristics, we observe that inequality in the odds of completing T_2 as a result of belonging to a single-parent family declined between 1960 and 1991 and from 2000 onward. This effect is no longer significant, thus indicating the inexistence of inequalities in the odds of completing this transition among individuals from single-parent families, or families with a relative and spouse. On the other hand, the effect of being the eldest child in the family remains relatively constant throughout the historical series, and the firstborn have significantly higher odds of completing T_2. The effect of per capita household income clearly decreases during the period, suggesting that completing T_2 was increasingly less a condition of family income due to the expansion of access to primary education (completion of the first 4 and 8 years of school, which currently make up the basic education system in Brazil).

The mother's educational level shows the expected effect, suggesting that children born to mothers who completed primary education (8 years) are more likely to complete T_2. For other levels of maternal education, the effects are ambiguous and sometimes even contradictory, which is probably due to the variation in maternal levels of schooling throughout the period.

Table 2 presents the odds ratios of completing T_3, which indicates the completion of primary education (8 years).

Just as in the case of T_2, women display a greater likelihood of completing T_3, although one can observe a decreasing trend in inequality among men and women since 1991. Racial inequalities in completing T_3 also persist but decrease between 1960 and 2010 and disappear among browns and whites in 2010. Significant inequalities still persist in 2010 among blacks and whites. Disadvantages associated with rural residence for the completion of primary education, very prominent in 1960, declined during the period and since the last census are no longer statistically significant.

The effect of family characteristics indicates a decrease in the negative effect of belonging to a single-parent family – a trait that ultimately has no influence on the odds of completing primary education as of 1991 – and a change in such an effect among the eldest child and other siblings: even if inequalities associated with this trait are small, the odds that the eldest child will complete T_3 are higher in every year except 2010, when they actually become lower. Inequality as a condition of income, on the other hand, undergoes a monotonic decline and demonstrates that, just as in the case of T_2, the completion of primary education is increasingly dissociated from household income levels. The effect of maternal levels of schooling indicates higher odds for individuals whose mothers completed at least primary education, with the effects being less clear for other categories of mother's educational level.

Table 3 presents the odds ratios for completing T_5, indicating completion of secondary education. As in all other transitions, women maintained their advantage in the odds of completing secondary education throughout the entire period, even though it is not possible to identify a clear upward or downward trend in inequality compared with men. Even if racial inequalities have been decreasing since 1960, they are still significant when we analyze completion of secondary education, and both browns and blacks are less likely than their white counterparts to complete this level. The negative effect of living in a rural residence suffers a considerable decrease, accompanying the general observations regarding the completion of T_1 and T_2.

The odds of completing secondary education for individuals from single-parent families are significantly lower until 1980. In 1991, the odds are slightly higher, but since 2000 the differences are not significant. The effect of being the eldest child presents the opposite dynamic; it becomes significant as of 1991, when there are greater odds of completion for the firstborn, which indicates prioritization of the firstborn in the family's educational investment for progression to this level. Household income has an increased effect between 1960 and 1970, from which point it declines, undergoing a period of stability between 1991 and 2000, and reaching its lowest historical levels in 2010. Regarding the effect of the mother's educational level, individuals whose mothers have completed primary and secondary education are more likely to complete secondary education. Inequalities based on maternal levels of schooling are especially prominent among individuals whose mothers completed secondary education, and the results indicate that the general trend points to an increase in these inequalities.

Table 4 shows the odds ratios of completing T_7, i.e., holding a university degree. The odds of completing this transition are also significantly higher for women. Gender inequalities also tended to widen throughout the period, except for 1980. Racial inequalities are also significant for this level and at higher levels than those observed for other transitions, although there has been a decrease in inequality between the beginning and the end of the period. Evolution of rural residence coefficients also indicates a decrease in inequality pertaining to the odds of completing higher education among rural and urban residents.

Individuals from single-parent families had significantly lower odds of completing higher education. Since 1980, these odds increased, although the difference is still not very prominent. On the other hand, the effect of being the eldest or only child, which was not significant at the beginning of the period, becomes highly relevant for the odds of completing higher education as of 1991.

Finally the effect of household income displays a different behavior for this transition when compared to other transitions analyzed here. Besides being significantly higher, thus indicating a stronger correlation between income and odds of completion, inequalities tended to increase in 1960 and 1980 – when they reach their peak – and decline thereafter but still at levels above those seen in other transitions. Finally, the effect of the mother's educational level on the odds of completing higher education is the most stable among all transitions analyzed, indicating that the higher the mother's educational level, the higher the odds of holding a university degree, especially for offspring of mothers who have completed secondary and higher education.

In general, the main findings of the analysis indicate that women have always presented positive and statistically significant coefficients, indicating that, when compared to men (omitted category), they presented higher odds of completing educational transitions.

Over the 50 years we observed, in all age brackets and educational levels considered, the race/color variable demonstrates that the odds of access and ascent by young blacks and browns within the educational system are considerably lower when compared to the progression of whites (category omitted). Moreover, young blacks have even lower odds than browns when attaining access to and progressing through Brazil's educational system. We can see that over time, there is a decrease in the magnitude of the effect that race has on the estimated odds of success in completing educational transitions, meaning that there has been a slight improvement in access to and progression through on the part of blacks and browns over these 50 years.

The residence status variable indicates that individuals living in rural areas have much lower access and educational progression odds than urban youth. Odds ratios lower than 1, statistically significant for all the transitions analyzed, show that inequality by census residence status operates across all educational levels and all age brackets. The behavior of this variable indicates that there is a significant increase in the odds of success, suggesting that educational opportunities for young people in rural areas have improved throughout the period, although their odds of progressing are persistently lower. Variables related to family status of young people show that in 1960, the odds of access and educational advancement for children of single-parent families were smaller when compared to children of families with two parents, a trend that continues into the 1980s but decreases from 1991 onward. This variable has a significant negative effect when not controlled by socioeconomic background covariates (i.e., income and mother's educational level); however, it loses explanatory strength once inserted in the models. This fact may indicate that the effect of this variable is subject to covariates pertaining to income and the mother's educational level.[4]

The second variable pertaining to family situation, indicating whether a young person is a firstborn or only child, displays different effects for educational access and progression, especially when analyzing the data from 1960 and 1970. Being the first or only child increases the odds of completing the first three educational transitions, but from then on the effect is no longer detected. It could be speculated that in the 1960s and 1970s, the opportunity cost of a job for the first or only child was very high and it would not have been worthwhile to delay entry into the labor market at the expense of progressing in educational levels, especially in a context where the presence of young people in the labor market was more prevalent. However, as the country became progressively modernized, being the first or only child began to have a positive effect on the chances of access and educational progression. From the 1990s on, this status greatly increases the likelihood of access and especially of progression within the educational system, a trend that has intensified in the decades of 2000 and 2010.

Estimates for covariates pertaining to socioeconomic background, income, and mother's educational level displayed the expected signs and effects, especially concerning completion of secondary and higher education. From a synchronic point of view, we note a decrease in its effect on the odds of youth educational development, especially from the 1990s on, particularly for primary levels – up to 8 years of school. We should stress that for (the natural logarithm of) per capita family income, we have reported the coefficients and not the odds ratios. In relation to the basic transitions, the level of household income since 1960 has been associated with the odds of entry into and completion of 4 years of study among young Brazilians. However, this effect has been decreasing for the two basic transitions since 1980, which indicates gains in accessibility at these levels for people who come from poorer families. For completion of 8 years of study, the effect of income is generally smaller than in transitions that pertain to entrance and completion of 4 years of study, and it tends to decline monotonically between 1960 and 2010, indicating greater equality of access among the income strata with regard to completion of

[4]This effect becomes clear in the linear and binomial regression models when different specifications are tested. These were omitted in the present analysis.

basic education. The odds of completing secondary education are increasingly associated with family income between 1960 and 1980, decreasing from 1980 onward. The evolution of the effect of family income on secondary education completion is quite similar to that on primary education and even greater on the educational progression points on which young people obtain credentials. The acquisition of a university degree, on the other hand, which is strongly related to income levels at the beginning of the historical series, displays a downward trend starting in 1991.

The second variable of social origin, the mother's educational level, was operationalized in three dichotomous categories, indicating the mother's highest level of education attained. Yet the category for uneducated was omitted and serves as basis for comparing the results of the other categories. When examining the effect of the mother's educational level on the odds of youth educational progression, we notice that completion of *at least* basic education is significantly associated with progression across all educational levels, for all analyzed age ranges and all years. As for higher educational level coefficients, the effects are less clear and sometimes even contradictory. It can be argued, especially for 1960, 1970, and 1980, that this is attributable to the very low percentage of mothers with higher education in the samples analyzed.

In the transitional movement of secondary school completion, evidence of correlation between mother's educational level and educational progression of her children is also quite robust. As of 1970, the positive effect of the mother having completed secondary education over the odds of her offspring also completing secondary education is significant, with an upward trend between 2000 and 2010, especially among older age groups. For upper level transitions, for which only one age bracket observed is eligible, we note that especially as of the 2000 census, youth whose mothers held college degrees are significantly more likely to complete higher education.

Final Considerations

In this chapter, we presented the initial results of an analysis concerning the correlation between socioeconomic characteristics of families and the odds of youth educational progression over 50 years. From an operational standpoint, the exercise has shown to be successful and demonstrates that it is possible to conduct a comparative analysis both from a synchronic and a diachronic perspective based on census data.

The main descriptive results confirm the process of expanded access to basic educational levels in Brazil over the past 50 years. Barriers to entry into the educational system, and especially to completion of primary education, which were so prominent in 1960, 1970, and 1980, are gradually being replaced by obstacles that stand in the way of educational progression toward secondary education completion and university entrance, especially since the 1990s. Brazil's recent history of educational opportunities shows signs of very substantial gains in basic level education access and less obvious gains in access to other levels.

Over the 50 years examined, a youth's social origin has significantly shaped his or her odds of educational progression although differently and depending on the educational level considered or period analyzed. With gains in accessibility, the effects of social origin tended to decrease at basic levels, indicating a decrease in inequality of educational opportunities at these stages. This is the case in the first three transitions in Brazil's educational progression structure, where gains in accessibility derived from educational expansion tended to decrease the effects of social origin. Upon entry into secondary education, the decrease in unequal educational opportunities subject to social origin is not as clear, and inequality levels tended to stabilize throughout the period analyzed.

The effects of the mother's educational level, per capita family income, and social characteristics of the family environment demonstrate that in these 50 years, the social origin of young Brazilians had a strong impact on their educational trajectory, whether it was in educational access or educational progression. While in the past, barriers to educational progression were imposed on youth at the early stages of their educational trajectory, throughout this half-century they have been displaced to more advanced stages of progression. Currently, educational system access up to completion of the first 8 school years is much less conditioned by the social background of young people than in the past. The same cannot be said for the highest educational levels, for which the effect of social origin on the odds of progression among young people has had a historical tendency to be stable or even to display signs of worsening inequality, as is the case with higher education.

Consequently, the analysis presented here suggests a mixed pattern and not one of persistent inequalities. It could be said that from 1960 to 2010, there has been a decrease in inequality of educational opportunity at basic educational levels, persistent inequality across middle levels, and an increase in inequality at the upper level.

References

Ayalon, H., & Shavit, Y. (2004). Educational reforms and inequalities in Israel. The MMI hypothesis revisited. *Sociology of Education, 77*, 103–120.

Fernandes, D. C. (2004). Estratificação educacional, origem sócio-econômica e raça no Brasil: as barreiras da cor. In IPEA. *Prêmio IPEA 40 Anos*. Monografias premiadas. Brasília.

Hasenbalg, C., & Valle-Silva, N. (2002). Recursos familiares e transições educacionais. *Cadernos de Saúde Pública, 18*, 67–76.

Hauser, R. M., & Andrew, M. (2006). Another look at the stratification of educational transitions: the logistic response model with partial proportionality constraints. Sociological Methodology, 36, 1–26.

Hout, M. (2006). Maximally maintained inequality and essentially maintained inequality cross-national comparisons. *Sociological Theory and Methods, 21*(2), 237–252.

Hout, M., Raftery, A. E., & Bell, E. (1993). Making the grade. Educational stratification in the United States, 1925-1989. In Y. Shavit & H. P. Blossfeld (Eds.), *Persistent inequality. Changing educational attainment in thirteen countries*. Boulder: Westview Press.

Karlson, K. B. (2011). Multiple paths in educational transitions. A multinomial transition model with unobserved heterogeneity. *Research in Social Stratification and Mobility, 29*, 323–341.

Kesler, C. (2003). Educational stratification and social change: Evidence from German unification. *European Sociological Review, 19*(5), 467–482.
Lucas, S. (2001). Effectively maintained inequality: Education transitions, track mobility, and social background effects. *American Journal of Sociology, 106*(6), 1642–1690.
Mare, R. (1981). Change and stability in educational stratification. *American Sociological Review, 46*(1), 72–87.
Mare, R. (1980). Social background and school continuation decisions. *Journal of the American Statistical Association, 75*, 295–305.
Milesi, C. (2010). Do all roads lead to Rome? Effect of educational trajectories on educational transitions. *Research in Social Stratification and Mobility, 28*, 23–44.
Montalvão, A. (2011). Estratificação educacional no Brasil no século XXI. *Dados, 54*(2), 389–430.
Raftery, A., & Hout, M. (1993). Maximally maintained inequality: Expansion, reform, and opportunity in Irish education, 1921-75. *Sociology of Education, 66*(1), 41–62.
Ribeiro, C. A. C. (2011). Desigualdade de oportunidades e resultados educacionais no Brasil. *Dados, 54*(1), 41–87.
Roksa, J., & Velez, M. (2010). When studying schooling is not enough: Incorporating employment in models of educational transitions. *Research in Social Stratification and Mobility, 28*, 5–21.
Shavit, Y., & Blossfeld, H. P. (1993). *Persistent inequality. Changing educational attainment in thirteen countries*. Boulder: Westview Press.
Torche, F. (2010). Economic crisis and inequality of educational opportunity in Latin America. *Sociology of Education, 83*(2), 85–110.
Valle Silva, N., & Hasenbalg, C. (2000). Tendências da desigualdade educacional no Brasil. Dados, 43(3), 423–425.
Valle Silva, N., & Souza, A. M. (1986). Um modelo para a análise da estratificação educacional no Brasil. *Cadernos de pesquisa,* Fundação Carlos Chagas, no. 58.

Education and Inequality in Brazil

Naercio Menezes Filho and Charles Kirschbaum

Abstract Brazil is widely known for its high levels of social inequality and poor rates of education. In the late twentieth century, it was still among the nations with the highest income inequality and lowest average educational levels among the poor in the world. This chapter shows that the standard model of supply and demand for skills appears useful when analyzing the evolution of wage differentials by education and income inequality in Brazil over the last 50 years. The results show that the increase in relative supply of education, especially high school graduates, was responsible for the reduction of wage differentials associated with education throughout the period, which has contributed to the decline in inequality.

Keywords Education · Inequality · Wage differentials · Brazil

Brazil is widely known for its high levels of social inequality and poor rates of education. In the late twentieth century, it was still among nations with the highest income inequality and lowest average educational levels among the poor in the world. For example, while those born in the United States had 14 years of education on average in 1980, in Brazil this cohort had received only 9 years of education, the same level as that received by people in the United States born in 1900. In terms of income inequality, the wealthiest 10% in Brazil at the end of the last century had an average income 70 times higher than that of the poorest 10%, well above the levels prevailing in countries with similar per capita income.

It is important to emphasize that social inequality is also the result of factors not directly related to education. They include wage differentials by gender or race, across occupations or fields of activity (Barros et al. 1995), differentials in wages

N. Menezes Filho (✉)
Insper, Sao Paulo, Brasil

University of São Paulo, São Paulo, Brazil
e-mail: naercioamf@insper.edu.br

C. Kirschbaum
Insper, Sao Paulo, Brasil
e-mail: charlesk1@insper.edu.br

M. Arretche (ed.), *Paths of Inequality in Brazil*,
https://doi.org/10.1007/978-3-319-78184-6_4

and full retirement benefits provided to public employees (Hoffman 2009), or a specific macroeconomic context that affects certain groups more severely than others, such as hyperinflationary periods in which the poorest cannot preserve the value of their real income (Ferreira et al. 2006).

During much of the twentieth century, the focus of public policies was on economic development, (Kerstenetzky 2008). Starting in the 1980s, the primary goal of economic policy was to stabilize the economy, given that hyperinflation had hampered any economic planning. With the Real Plan and the stabilization of inflation, attention then turned toward fighting poverty and income inequality (Neri 2006). In recent decades, a consensus has emerged around the idea that inequality was "unacceptable," either because of its economic consequences or concerns about social justice (Barros et al. 2000; Kerstenetzky 2000). In this regard, different sectors of society have identified education as a priority in the fight against inequality (Reis 2000).

Thus, more recently, the reduction of income inequality has become a focus of government concern. The *Bolsa Familia* program, for example, reorganized and expanded several preexisting income transfer policies as a way to link income transfers with compliance with health and education goals (Soares et al. 2010). Aligned with the latest generation of income transfer programs, the goal of the *Bolsa Família* program is to relieve poverty while generating opportunities for social mobility through increased schooling for the most disadvantaged strata of society (Silveira Neto 2010).

However, recent studies show that despite their relevance, income transfer programs are not the most important factor explaining the recent reductions of income inequality in Brazil. These reductions mainly originated in the labor market (Hoffman 2005). Consequently, if the main dynamics that led to the decrease in inequality are to be found in the labor market, it is important to take a closer look at the evolution of the supply and demand for skilled labor in Brazil's economy in recent periods, since wage differentials by skill are key determinants of income inequality generated the labor market (Menezes-Filho 2001).

The association between inequality and education has been the subject of intense debate in Brazil since the late 1970s, when the first empirical studies were conducted using data from the 1960 and 1970 censuses (Hoffman and Duarte 1972; Langoni 1973). This chapter does not intend to debate this issue at length (for that purpose, see Menezes-Filho 2001) but instead aims to present the viewpoint of one of its proponents (Langoni 1973), who largely predicted the conclusions presented here. Following the ideas of Kuznets (1955) and provoking an intense debate among those in Brazil's academic community,[1] Langoni (1973, p. 97) states:

> The classic changes accompanying economic development lead to an increase in the aggregate concentration rates (of income), without the possibility of assigning to them any sense of deterioration of well-being. This is a typical case of a workforce flow leaving regions and sectors where real income is relatively low; of youth and women entering the labor market, and especially of educational improvement or ascent by the existing and future workforce. (p. 97)

[1] See Tolipan and Tinelli (1978).

More recently, there seems to have been a convergence among the different social sciences in Brazil towards a common set of propositions with respect to social inequality. One of the main arguments states that income inequality is affected by education. Therefore, educational policies are directly responsible for the reduction of inequality in Brazil (Reis and Barros 1990). This theoretical formulation was accompanied by findings on the education gap yet to be covered in Brazil, as well as by estimations of the effects of education on wages, after controlling for the individual characteristics and socioeconomic context (Barros and Lam 1993; Ribeiro 2010).

The goal of this chapter is to examine how the evolution of the supply of workers with varying educational levels affected the behavior of wage differentials and, consequently, income inequality in the Brazilian labor market during the last 40 years. More specifically, we argue that an increase in educational levels, especially at the secondary school, led to a drop in educational returns and, therefore, to a drop in income inequality.

Theoretical Framework: Education and Income Distribution

The relationship between education and income distribution has long been a topic of analysis by researchers in different fields. One of the first scholars to analyze the relationship between economic growth and income distribution was Kuznets (1955), who found an inverted U-shaped relation between these two factors. According to him, the development process initially causes an increase in income inequality, since industrialization requires workers achieving higher educational levels, whose offer is usually limited in poorer countries. This leads to a situation where the demand for such workers exceeds the supply, at first leading to a wage increase among more educated workers (compared to less educated), which in turn leads to further inequality. But, at a second stage, the expectation is that inequality will be reduced when most workers are incorporated into the more advanced production process.

At the same time, with economic development the educational level of workers tends to increase, since the widening of wage differentials leads to more investments in education. Moreover, the very demand for more educated workers leads to institutional changes and policies that promote an increase in educational levels. With the increase in the supply of skilled workers, wage differentials tend to fall.

The current theoretical framework used to analyze the relationship between education and income distribution employs a similar argument: wage differentials in the labor market are the result of a "race" between education and technology (Goldin and Katz 2008). Based on a terminology coined by Tinbergen (1975), the idea is that while education increases the supply of skilled labor, technology increases the demand for these skills if it is geared toward more qualified work. This occurs, for example, when skilled workers are the only ones able to handle technological advances introduced at a certain point in time. This phenomenon seems to have occurred at the end of the last century in several countries due to the widespread use of computers (e.g., Goldin and Katz 2008).

Thus, if the relative supply of an educational stratum increases at a greater rate than growth in the relative demand for this stratum, wage differentials should decrease and vice versa. For example, Goldin and Katz (2008) show how the rapid educational progress in the United States during most of the twentieth century caused a reduction in wage differentials associated with education and, consequently, a decrease in inequality. However, starting in the 1980s, the slowdown in the rate of education growth in the country, especially among minorities, coupled with firms' intensive use of computers, which increased the demand for skilled workers, led to an increase in wage differentials and to higher levels of income inequality.[2]

The evolution of the demand for skills can be inferred from the evolution of the educational composition and of the wage differentials associated with each educational level. For example, if the wage differential of workers with higher educational levels increases during a certain period (in relation to the less educated) while the supply of this group also increases (also in relation to the less educated), we can infer that there has been an increased demand for workers from this group. The magnitude of the impact of relative supply on wage differentials between two educational groups depends on the elasticity of substitution between these types of workers, that is, the extent to which firms can substitute one type of worker for another in the production process without affecting the amount produced (see proof in the Appendix).

We emphasize that we are interested only in *relative* measures of income; therefore, what matters is the *relative* scarcity (availability) and relative demand, that is, the comparison between supply and demand of two (or more) worker groups with different educational levels. For example, if the supply of workers with secondary education and workers with higher education increases in the same proportion, then there is no change in the relative supply and, therefore, if the relative demand also remains constant, the wage differential between workers in these two groups should not change.

[2]The technical appendix presents a formal model to analyze this relationship, but it would be beyond the scope of this chapter to describe it or use it in a formal analysis of the behavior of the labor market in 50 years (see Goldin and Katz 2008). The analysis becomes more complicated once we work with more than two educational groups because it then requires an examination of the interrelationship of supply and demand of these groups (see Fernandes and Menezes-Filho 2012).

Results

Graph 1 shows the evolution of income inequality from all sources in Brazil from 1970 to 2010. We can observe that inequality – expressed by the ratio between the income of a person situated in the 90th percentile of income distribution and the income of a person situated in the 10th percentile – was 11 times higher in 1970, increased to over 12 times higher in 1980, and peaked at 14 times higher in 2000. However, this ratio fell sharply between 2000 and 2010, reaching a level lower than that seen in the early 1970s. The same trend, albeit to a lesser extent, can be seen in the curve expressing the ratio between the income of the median person and a person who belongs to the 10th percentile. After a period of continuous growth between 1970 and 2000, this ratio went from 3 to 2.6 times between 2000 and 2010. A similar pattern occurred when we observe the ratio between the 90th and 50th percentiles, which declined from 4.8 to 3.8 over the 2000 decade.

The evolution of the same measurements of inequality, but now using labor income alone instead of income from all sources (which includes rent, interest, pensions and transfers),[3] is displayed in Graph 2. We can observe that labor income inequality presents an evolution similar to that depicted for all sources, displaying an increase in the first period followed by a decrease in more recent periods. The reduction in labor income inequality began earlier, however, between 1991 and 2000. Thus, the factors that influence the decrease in inequality in the labor market seem to have been triggered earlier than what we observed for income inequality from all sources. One possible explanation for this fact may lie in the inflationary process that dominated Brazil in the 1990s and that has stabilized since 1994 with the introduction of the Real Plan. Reduced inflation resulted in a real income gains for low-income workers (Ferreira et al. 2006).

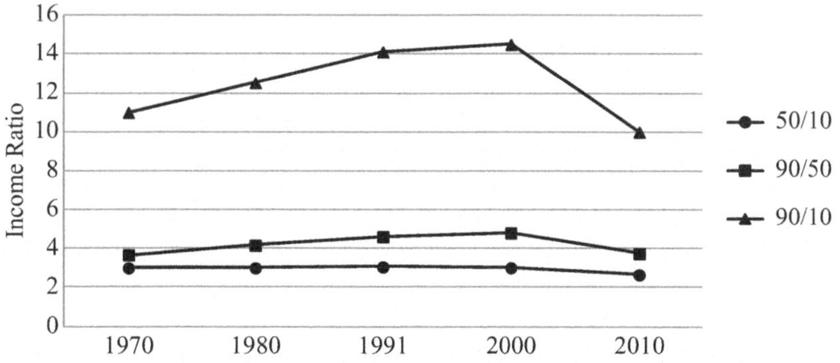

Graph 1 Evolution of income inequality from all sources – ratio between percentiles (Brazil, 1970–2010) (Source: IBGE. Demographic censuses 1970–2010 (special tabulations by CEM))

[3] Unfortunately, there is no information on labor income in the 1970 Demographic Census.

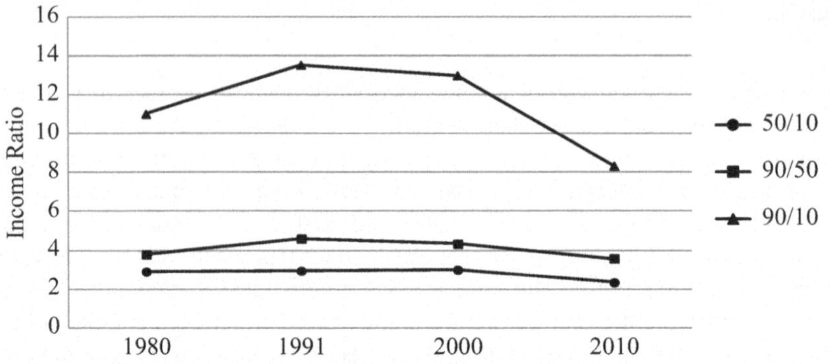

Graph 2 Evolution of labor income inequality – ratio between percentiles (Brazil, 1980–2010). (Source: IBGE. Demographic censuses 1970–2010 (special tabulations by CEM))

Next, we analyze the behavior of labor supply by education, which, according to the canonical model presented earlier, must have played an important role in reducing inequality. In Graph 3, we clearly see that within the economically active population (EAP), there was a relative decrease in the number of people with 0–3 years of education, which went from 75% in 1960 to approximately 26% in 2010.[4] This decline was significant, in spite of the extremely high starting point as compared to other countries. It is worth noting that this decrease has slowed down slightly since 2000, as it becomes more difficult to reduce illiteracy when rates are already very low.[5]

In contrast, the share of the population with 4–7 years of education increased rapidly between 1960 and 1980, stabilized from 1980 to 1990, and has declined since then. This decline occurred because the majority of youth who used to interrupt their studies at this stage moved on to complete fundamental and secondary school from 1990 onwards. In turn, the share of the population with 8–10 years of education (complete fundamental and incomplete secondary education) increased until the year 2000, stabilizing from then on, when the majority of the Brazilian youth began to stay in school until the end of secondary school. This movement is reflected in the behavior of the share of the population with complete secondary education and incomplete university education (11–14 years), which displayed a slight increase between 1960 and 1970, then increased faster between 1970 and 1990, before "taking off" from 2000 onward, becoming the majority in the population. Lastly, the portion with complete university education (15 or more years of schooling) slowly increased between 1960 and 2000, accelerating only in the first decade of the new century.

[4] In this case, zero refers to those who have not successfully completed any year of school.

[5] We emphasize that changes in participation rates in the workforce throughout the period may affect changes in education if they occur differentially between groups, such as an increase in the participation rate of women, for example. Graph 11 of the appendix reproduces the same curves using the working age population (WAP), which show very similar behavior.

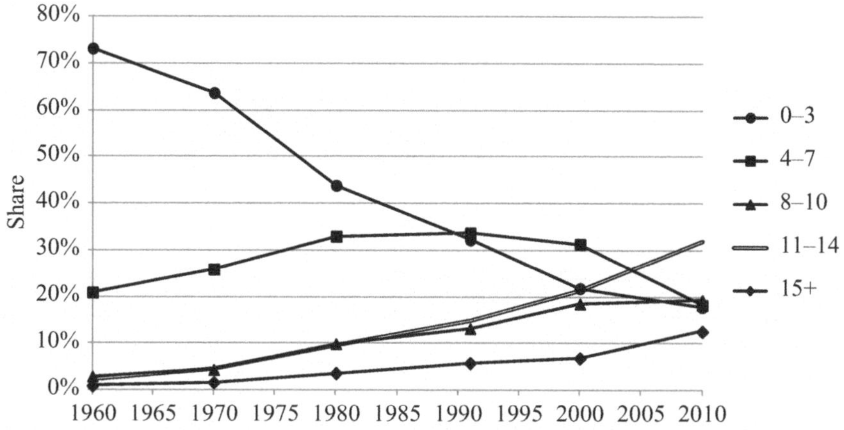

Graph 3 Distribution of the population by years of education (Brazil, 1960–2010). (Source: IBGE. Demographic censuses 1970–2010 (special tabulations by CEM))

These educational changes are important for explaining how Brazilian society has evolved over these 40 years, because education affects fertility, criminality, civic engagement, concern for the environment, etc., beyond having an impact on the labor market. Several factors explain the educational increase observed, such as: accelerated demographic transition due to reduced fertility rates between 1960 and 1991; decentralization of public education management and resources under the 1988 Constitution; the establishment of the Fund for the Maintenance and Development of Basic Education and Teacher Valorization (FUNDEF), responsible for transferring funds from wealthy districts with few students to poor municipalities with many students; conditional income transfer programs (*Bolsa Escola* and *Bolsa Familia*) that require students to stay in school in order to receive federal transfers for their families; and the no-grade repetition programs that were introduced throughout the 1990s. Lastly, the increase in the share of the population with college education is due, in large part, to the easing of rules for opening new private colleges, which occurred since the 1990s and primarily served the lower middle classes longing for access to a diploma.

In parallel with the changes in educational composition, this chapter tries to understand the behavior of relative income between the different education groups. This investigation involves two steps. First, it explores the evolution of education groups in relative terms, that is, how one group increased in relation to the group directly below it, indicating an increase in relative supply. Next, it describes the evolution of the relative income between two adjacent groups for the purpose of investigating how wage differentials evolved and impacted income inequality.

Graph 4 shows that the supply of workers in the 4–7 schooling group (incomplete primary school) compared to the lower group (0–3 schooling) increased from 28% to 140% between 1960 and 2000, decreasing thereafter until it reached the same number of people as in the lower group in 2010 (ratio equal to 1). As previously

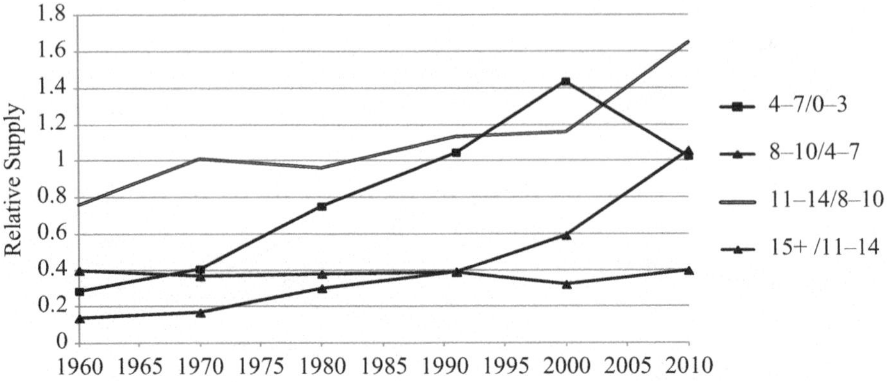

Graph 4 Relative supply of education (Brazil, 1960–2010). (Source: IBGE. Demographic censuses 1960–2010 (special tabulations by CEM))

noted, this decline reflects the fact that new generations no longer discontinue studies at this stage and advance toward secondary school. Thus, there was substantial growth of the 8–10 schooling group (complete fundamental school and incomplete secondary education) over the 4–7 group, especially after 2000. It is worth noting that both groups had the same size in 2010.

Similarly, it turns out that the relation between the 11–14 schooling group (complete secondary school and incomplete university studies) and the 8–10 group increased throughout the entire period, with spells of greater or lesser acceleration, reflecting Brazil's institutional and economic developments as previously noted. At the end of the period, the group with secondary education is 70% higher than the one who completed fundamental school. Lastly, it is interesting to note that the ratio between the number of people holding a university degree and those having concluded secondary education remained relatively stable over the years, with small short-term fluctuations in this trend. This shows that the two strata expanded in a very similar manner throughout the period.

Taken together, these trends show a population shift from lower educational levels toward higher ones. It is possible that this migration is the result of efforts by policymakers to alleviate the educational bottleneck that prevented the supply of skilled labor (Steiner 2006) after decades of neglect toward education in Brazil. Furthermore, families themselves decided to increase their children's schooling given the high returns obtained on investment in education. However, such evidence may also be taken critically since this shift encounters a ceiling around the 11–14 years of education. The relation between the 15 or more schooling group and the 11–14 group remained fairly stable throughout the period (around 40%), which means that the groups increased at the same rate over these years, and therefore, the bottleneck effect remains virtually unchanged for access to college.

In Graph 5, we can observe the behavior of relative labor income between the education groups so as to examine the extent to which it reflects the behavior of the relative supply of workers with different schooling levels.[6] We find that income

[6]Graph 13 of the appendix presents the same calculations using income data from all sources.

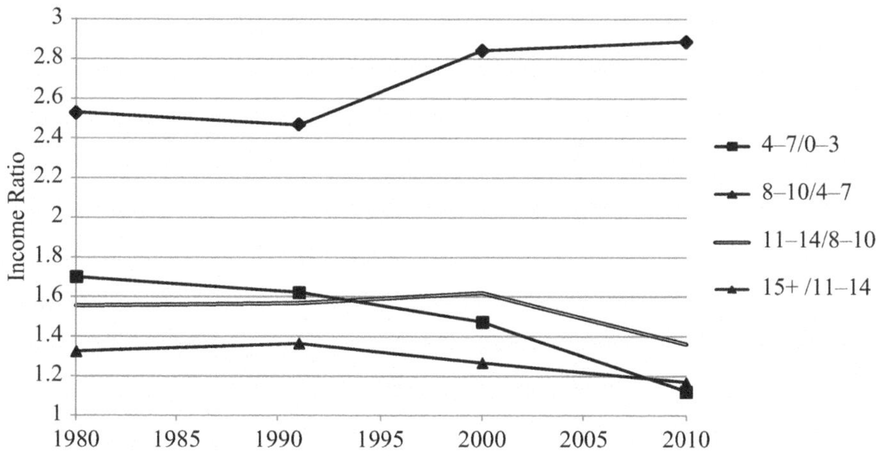

Graph 5 Ratio between average labor incomes by years of education (Brazil, 1970–2010). (Source: IBGE. Demographic censuses 1970–2010 (special tabulations by CEM))

of the 4–7 schooling group (compared to the 0–3 schooling one) has been declining, as has the relative income between the 8–10 schooling group and the 4–7 one. The gap in favor of the 8–10 group was 33% in 1980, decreasing to 17% in 2010, despite having slightly increased between 1980 and 1991. The gap between the 4–7 group and the lowest schooling group, which had previously been at 70%, decreased to only 12%. It seems clear that this decrease stems from an increase in the relative supply of this group over time, as shown in Graph 4. The magnitude of the response by the wage gap to changes in supply depends on the elasticity of substitution between the groups (see the Technical Appendix). One exception is found in the final period (between 2000 and 2010), when reductions in the relative supply of the 4–7 schooling group were not accompanied by an increase in relative wages. This may reflect a demand shock favoring the unskilled in recent years or could be due to the large real minimum wage increases that took place in the last 15 years.

It is interesting to note that the income gap between the group that concluded secondary school (11–14 schooling years) and the one who concluded fundamental education increased between the years 1980 and 2000 and then decreased significantly from 2000 to 2010, reaching approximately 37%, just when the relative supply of this group showed an accelerated increase. It is also interesting to note that while in 1980 a higher premium was associated with incomplete fundamental, meaning that in the past this first level of formal education brought more returns when compared with the second and the third levels, by 2010 the largest wage gap (excluding higher education) is to be found in complete secondary education. The rearrangement of these curves reflects the educational advancements in the period as well as the new demands from Brazilian society, creating greater incentives for staying in school.

Finally, the ratio between incomes of the 15 or more schooling group and the 11–14 schooling group fell at modest rates between 1980 and 1990, accelerated between 1990 and 2000, and continued to increase more recently. Compared with

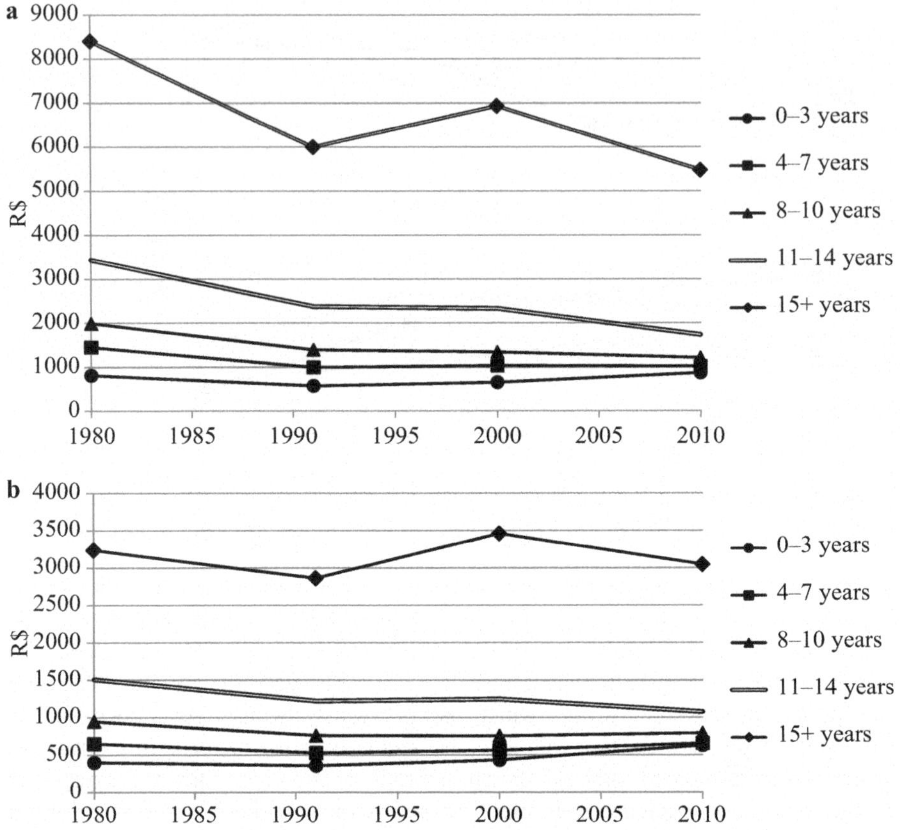

Graph 6 Average labor income by gender and years of education – Brazil – 1980–2010. (**a**) Men. (**b**) Women. (Source: IBGE. Demographic censuses 1970–2010. (Special tabulations by CEM))

the stability of supply between these strata in the past decades, the increase of this gap means that the relative demand for this group is increasing, possibly due to the use of technologies that favor skilled labor.

Next, we investigated the evolution of educational wage gaps by individual attributes, in order to explore whether there are important and persistent differences between the groups. In Graph 6, which presents the evolution of income for each educational group disaggregated by gender, we observe that men earn higher incomes than women for all educational groups, but especially those with university education. However, women's income increased more than men's in all strata. The differences in the level of income by gender can be understood in different ways.[7] First, it could be explained by the occupations sought by women compared to men. Second, labor market discrimination is always a possibility. Also, depending on the type of education received, returns to education could be different by gender.[8]

[7] See Leme and Wajnman (2001), for example.

[8] See Costa Ribeiro and Schlegel, in this volume.

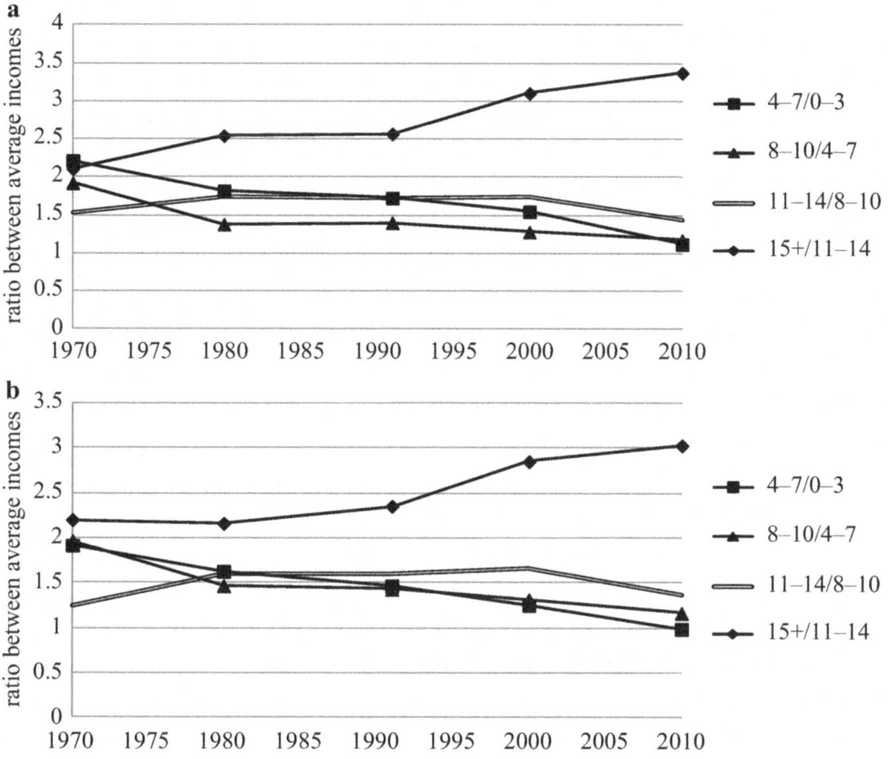

Graph 7 Ratio between the average labor incomes by gender and years of education (Brazil, 1980–2010). (**a**) Men. (**b**) Women. (Source: IBGE. Demographic censuses 1970–2010 (special tabulations by CEM))

At the same time, however, we know that active involvement of women in the workforce, i.e., their willingness to work outside home, has changed significantly throughout the period. As Araujo Guimarães, Barone, and Brito show (in this volume, chapter "Commodification of Labor in Brazil's Labor Market (1960–2010)"), women's active involvement more than doubled from 1980 to 2010 at the same time that the average fertility rate suffered a drastic drop. Therefore, if the supply of female labor has increased sharply, the decrease in the gender wage differentials over this period (especially of those in the 15 or more years of education group) could signal that women are increasingly competing with men for better-paying jobs. To put it in another way, the glass ceiling may have gradually shifted in recent decades.

It is noteworthy to observe that the evolution of wage differentials through education has been similar for both men and women in the past 30 years (Graph 7), in spite of major changes in their respective participation rates. Thus, it seems that the effect of evolution in the educational supply is prevalent over the effects of composition and other factors in determining wage differentials.

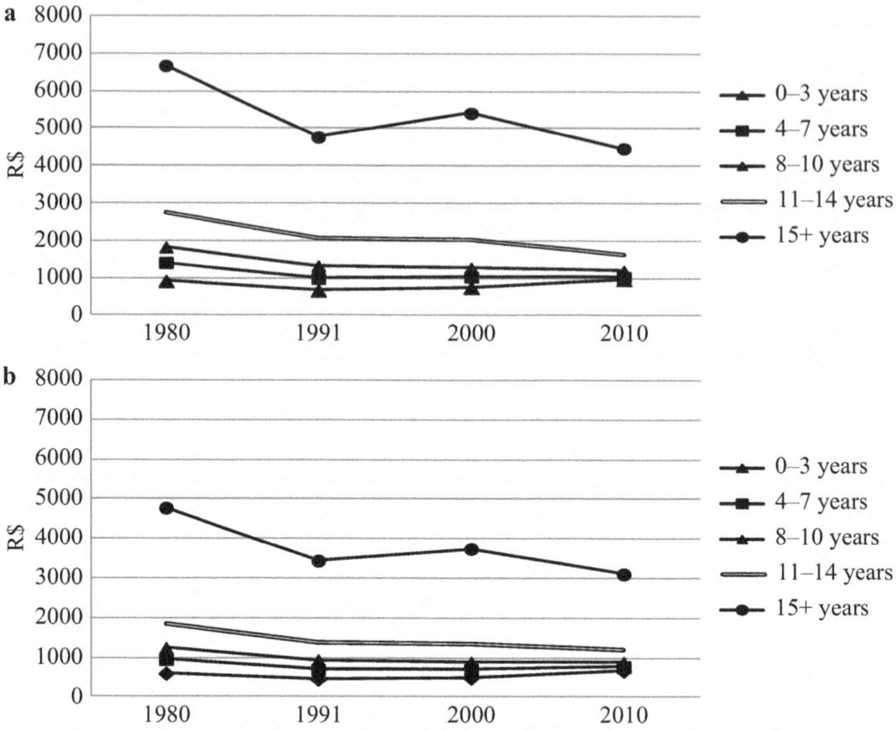

Graph 8 Average labor income by race and years of education (Brazil, 1980–2010). (**a**) Whites/Asians. (**b**) Blacks/Browns. (Source: IBGE. Demographic censuses 1970–2010 (special tabulations by CEM))

Analogously, Graph 8 shows the evolution of income by education group according to race (see also Soares et al. 2007).[9] We note that whites and asians earn higher income than blacks and browns, and this difference becomes more pronounced when we look at the higher educational strata, which may reflect discrimination in the labor market as well as the poor quality of education received by blacks and browns, who largely have attended public schools. We know that there is a significant gap in quality between public and private schools and that whites are overrepresented in the latter. Lastly, the educational level of the parents tends to be higher among whites than among blacks and browns.[10]

When analyzing the income ratio between the educational strata by race (Graph 9), two facts call our attention. First, while we see a constant growth in the ratio between the 15 or more schooling stratum over the 11–14 one for whites and Asians, this is not the case for blacks and browns, as this ratio decreased between 2000 and 2010,

[9]The 1970 Demographic Census contains no information on race.

[10]See Albernaz et al. (2002).

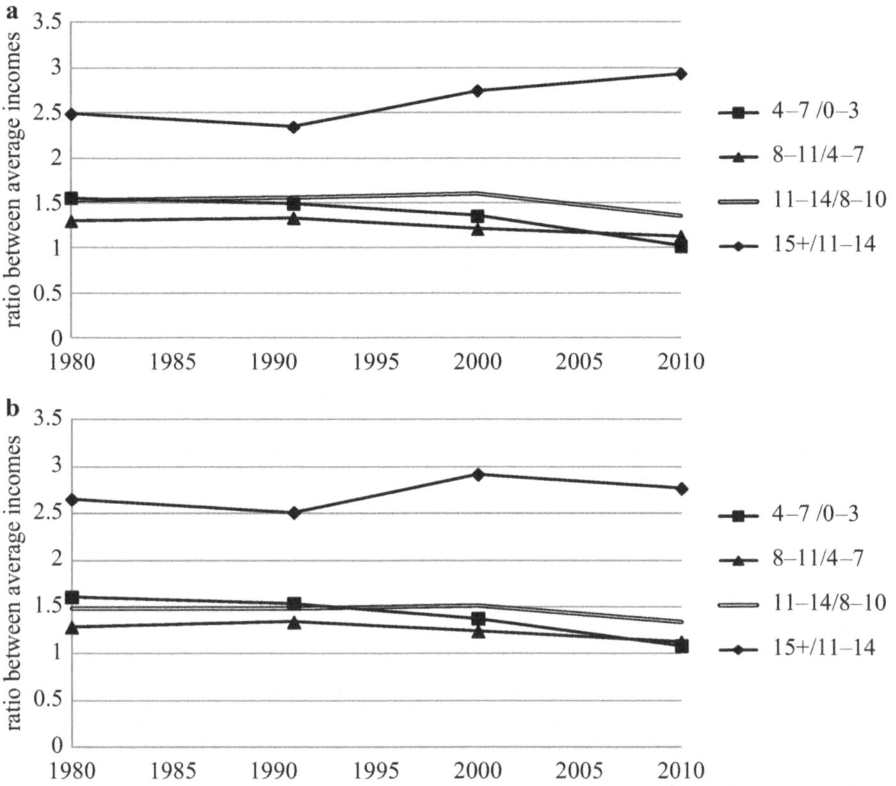

Graph 9 Ratio between the average incomes from all jobs by race and years of education (Brazil, 1980–2010). (**a**) Whites/Asians. (**b**) Blacks/Browns. (Source: IBGE. Demographic censuses 1970–2010 (special tabulations by CEM))

suggesting that fluctuations in the supply and demand for skilled individuals are different across these racial groups. The second fact to catch our eye refers to the relative wages earned by the 4–7 schooling stratum over the 0–3 years one, which was higher than the 11–14 schooling premium until the mid-1990s for blacks and browns, while in the case of whites and asians, this decline had already occurred starting in the 1980s. The trends depicted here corroborate studies on racial inequality in Brazil. Even though we find a relative decline in inequality between races, we may wonder to what extent residual inequality (caused, for instance, by the existence of few parents holding university diploma) might be reversed in the future (see the chapter "Racial Inequalities in Brazil: A Persistent Challenge" in this book by Marcia Lima and Ian Prates).

Graph 10 shows the ratio between relative wage differentials and relative supply disaggregated by educational strata. The purpose here is to summarize the results described thus far and attempt to infer the behavior of relative demand from

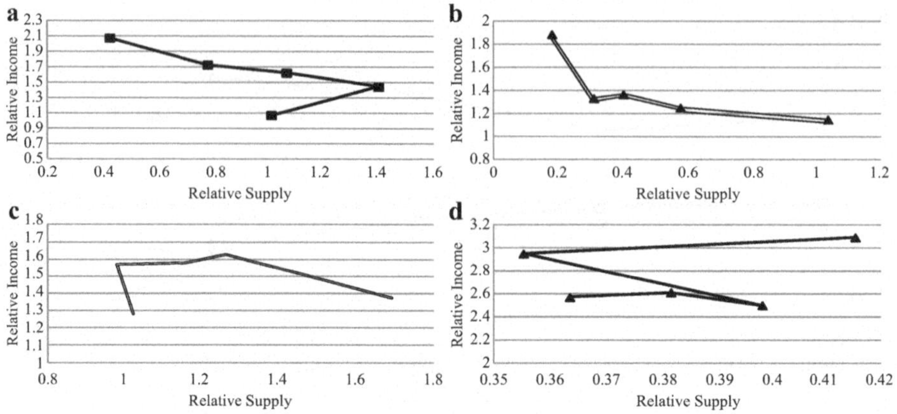

Graph 10 Relationship between relative income from all sources and relative supply by years of education (Brazil, 1970–2010). (**a**) 4–7/0–3 years. (**b**) 8–10/4–7 years. (**c**) 11–14/8–10 years. (**d**) 15+/11–14 years. (Source: IBGE. Demographic censuses 1970–2010)

the behavior of relative supply and relative income for each group.[11] Whenever a line connecting two points has a negative slope, it means that relative income and supply between the two groups went in the opposite directions during the decade analyzed.[12] This means that there were likely no shocks in demand that could favor either group within the period and that supply shifts alone could explain the wage movements. When relative supply and relative income move in the same direction (positive slope), relative demand necessarily plays a significant role, unless the elasticity of substitution between groups is less than one (see the Appendix).

An example of this can be seen by examining the movements of supply and demand for the groups with lower educational levels (4–7/0–3), which shows that until 2000 there was always a negative relationship between them (as indicated by the line). However, between 2000 and 2010, relative supply decreased substantially, as did relative income, which may be a reflection of an increase in the relative demand for less skilled workers. It is possible that such behavior occurred because of growth in the service sector (which intensively employs unskilled labor), or the behavior is reflecting the increase in the real value of the minimum wage, which grew 74% in real terms over the 2000 decade.

The negative relationship between supply and income is also evident for the group with complete fundamental school (8–10) compared with the group with 4–7 years of schooling. Despite small deviations in the general trend (such as the one that occurred between 1980 and 1991), it seems clear that there is a fairly strong

[11] It is worth noting that we are using income from all sources, not just labor income, in order to increase the period of analysis. The results are very similar when we use labor income only.

[12] If we are moving to the right along the line with a negative slope, the relative wage falls and relative supply increases. But, if we are moving to the left (going straight up the line), the relative wage increases while relative supply drops.

relation between the increase in relative supply and the decrease in relative income among these groups during the entire period.

The negative relationship is not as clear, however, with regard to the group with complete secondary education (11–14) and the group with complete fundamental education (8–10). Between 1970 and 1980, there was a decrease in supply accompanied by strong income growth, which seems to indicate that the decrease in supply was accompanied by an increase in relative demand for this group at the height of the Brazilian economic miracle. Nevertheless, between 1980 and 2000, income differentials expanded together with relative supply. This means that there must have been an increase in the relative demand for people with complete secondary education. More recently, however, with the rise in the rate of innovation and economic growth based on knowledge, the demand shifts may have moved to a higher skill level. Thus, the income differential in favor of high school education more clearly reflects the evolution of relative supply and therefore has dramatically fallen between 2000 and 2010.

The behavior of income and supply differentials between the most educated group (15 or more years) and those with complete secondary education appears symmetrical in relation to what was previously stated. It seems that between 1980 and 2000, there was a fairly clear negative relationship between supply and relative wages, even though the scale of the graph can be somewhat misleading (the movements of supply are in fact much smaller than in the previous groups). However, between 2000 and 2010, relative supply increased significantly along with relative income. Therefore, it seems that there was an increase in the relative demand for workers with higher education between 2000 and 2010.

Conclusions

The evidence presented in this chapter shows that the standard model of supply and demand for skills appears useful when analyzing the evolution of wage differentials by education and income inequality in Brazil over 50 years. The results show that the increase in relative supply of education, especially in the intermediate groups (4–7, 8–10, and 11–14 years of education), seems to have been responsible for the reduction of wage differentials associated with education throughout the period.

In order to make the connection between the behavior of wage differentials by education and income inequality, however, we need to go beyond the scope of this chapter. Income inequality depends not only on wage differentials but also on the educational inequality of the population (see Menezes-Filho et al. 2007), in addition to all other economic and social factors. For example, between 1970 and 1990, even though wage differentials derived from fundamental education were already on a downward trend (Graph 5), wage differentials due to secondary education were growing and educational inequality (access to school) was increasing. Thus, it was only from 2000 onward when inflation stabilized and educational inequality (in terms of access) and high school wage differentials began to decline that income inequality dropped significantly.

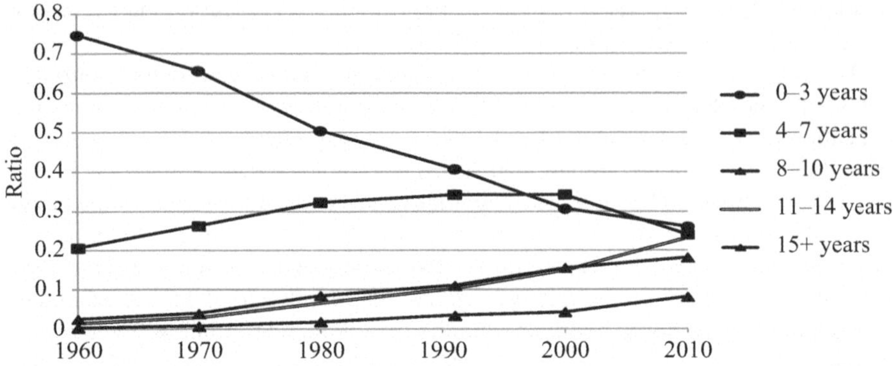

Graph 11 Distribution of WAP by years of education (Brazil, 1960–2010). (Source: IBGE. Demographic censuses 1960–2010)

It is also important to emphasize that this chapter did not produce direct evidence concerning the behavior of demand for skill. Thus, it is quite plausible that other economic and social factors have also contributed to the behavior of wage differentials among the various educational groups over time, influencing income inequality.

Finally, there is a need for further research in order to interpret the movements of educational supply during particular periods in recent Brazilian history, especially for those periods in which wage differentials between groups moved in the same direction as relative supply. Between 2000 and 2010, for example, relative supply as well as wage differentials associated with the 4–7 schooling years of education group declined. This might be due to increased demand for less skilled groups in the economy. As previously stated, this growth could be the result of an increase in consumption of services, a sector that intensively employs this group, or to statutory minimum wage increases.

Between 1980 and 2000, there seems to have been an increase in the demand for workers with complete high school education. Lastly, in the most recent period, there appears to have been wider demand for university education in Brazil, possibly associated with a new type of economic growth that is increasingly based on innovation and ideas. Thus, there seems to be evidence indicating polarization in Brazil, with expansion in the demand for the most and least educated groups and excess supply of the intermediate groups (Autor and Korn 2012).

From now on, we need to associate the shifts in educational supply and demand with political, institutional, and economic changes throughout specific periods of the Brazilian economy in order to shed more light on the important transformations Brazilian society has undergone in recent decades.

Technical Appendix

We assume that aggregate output can be represented by a Cobb-Douglas production function with constant scale returns and two production factors: physical capital and labor. This aggregate can be represented by a constant elasticity substitution (CES) production function with skilled and unskilled workers:

$$Y = K^{1-\theta}\left(\left[A_1(t)L_1\right]^{\frac{\sigma-1}{\sigma}} + \left[A_2(t)L_2\right]^{\frac{\sigma-1}{\sigma}}\right)^{\frac{\theta\sigma}{\sigma-1}} \tag{1}$$

where Y is aggregate output, K is aggregate capital, L_l is the supply of unskilled labor, L_2 is the supply of skilled labor, Ai are the factors of productivity, σ is the elasticity of substitution between the two types of labor, and θ is the elasticity of aggregate labor output.

Starting from (1), the marginal productivities of skilled and unskilled labor are

$$\frac{\partial Y}{\partial L_1} = K^{1-\theta}\frac{\theta\sigma}{\sigma-1}\left(\left[A_1(t)L_1\right]^{\frac{\sigma-1}{\sigma}} + \left[A_2(t)L_2\right]^{\frac{\sigma-1}{\sigma}}\right)^{\frac{\theta\sigma-\sigma+1}{\sigma-1}}\frac{\sigma-1}{\sigma}\left[A_1(t)L_1\right]^{\frac{-1}{\sigma}}A_1(t)$$

$$\frac{\partial Y}{\partial L_2} = K^{1-\theta}\frac{\theta\sigma}{\sigma-1}\left(\left[A_1(t)L_1\right]^{\frac{\sigma-1}{\sigma}} + \left[A_2(t)L_2\right]^{\frac{\sigma-1}{\sigma}}\right)^{\frac{\theta\sigma-\sigma+1}{\sigma-1}}\frac{\sigma-1}{\sigma}\left[A_2(t)L_2\right]^{\frac{-1}{\sigma}}A_2(t)$$

If wage rates are equal to marginal productivities, relative wages will be given by

$$\frac{W_2}{W_1} = \left[\frac{A_2(t)}{A_1(t)}\right]^{\frac{\sigma-1}{\sigma}}\left[\frac{L_2}{L_1}\right]^{\frac{-1}{\sigma}}$$

In logs

$$\ln\left(\frac{W_2}{W_1}\right) = \frac{\sigma-1}{\sigma}\ln\left[\frac{A_2(t)}{A_1(t)}\right] - \frac{1}{\sigma}\ln\left[\frac{L_2}{L_1}\right]$$

That is,

$$\ln\left(\frac{W_2}{W_1}\right) = \frac{1}{\sigma}\left[D(t) - \ln\left(\frac{L_2}{L_1}\right)\right] \tag{2}$$

The demand for qualification will be given by

$$D(t) = (\sigma-1)\left(\frac{A_2(t)}{A_1(t)}\right)$$

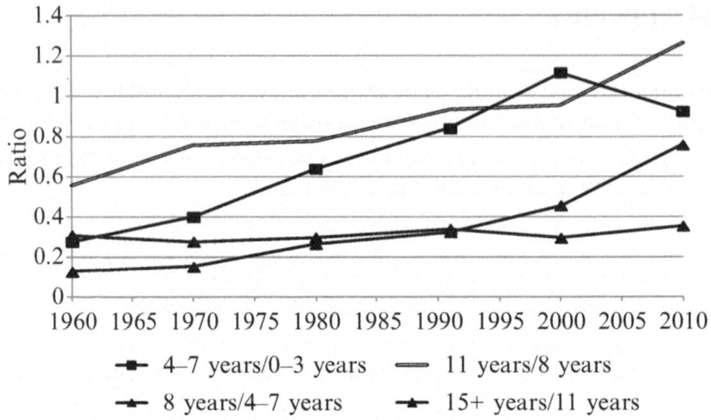

Graph 12 Relative supply of education within WAP (Brazil, 1960–2010). (Source: IBGE. Demographic censuses 1960–2010)

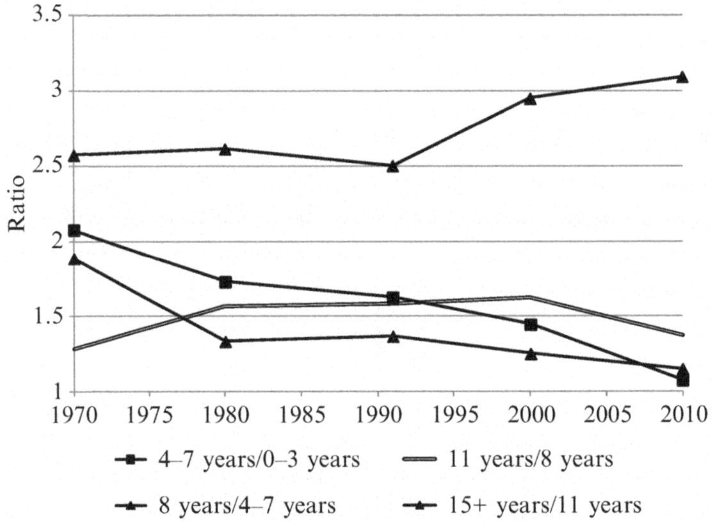

Graph 13 Ratio of average incomes from all sources by years of education (Brazil, 1970–2010). (Source: IBGE. Demographic censuses 1960–2010)

Equation (2) indicates that the log of relative wages between skilled and unskilled workers depends on the elasticity of substitution, the demand for skills, and the log of relative supply. Thus, if relative supply and relative wage move in the same direction and the elasticity of substitution is greater than 1, the relative demand must also follow this direction (Graph 12).

References

Albernaz, A., Ferreira, F., & Franco, C. (2002). Qualidade e Eqüidade no Ensino Fundamental Brasileiro. *Pesquisa e planejamento econômico, 32*(3).

Autor, D., & Korn, D. (2012). *The Growth of Low Skill Service Jobs and the Polarization of the U.S. Labor Market* (IZA Discussion Paper, 7068).

Barros, R. P., & Lam, D. (1993). Desigualdade de renda, desigualdade em educação e escolaridade das crianças no Brasil. *Pesquisa e Planejamento Econômico, 23*(2).

Barros, R. P., Franco, S., & Mendonça, R. (1995). *Os determinantes da desigualdade no Brasil.* Brasília: IPEA (Texto para Discussão no. 377).

Barros, R. P., Henriques, R., & Mendonça, R. (2000). Desigualdade e pobreza no Brasil: retrato de uma estabilidade inaceitável. *Revista Brasileira de Ciências Sociais, 15*(42).

Fernandes, R. E., & Menezes-Filho, N. (2012). Educação, Salários e a Alocação de Trabalhadores entre Tarefas: Teoria e Evidências para o Brasil. *Pesquisa e Planejamento Econômico, 42*(3).

Ferreira, F. H. G., Leite, P. H., Litchfield, J. A., & Ulyssea, G. (2006). Ascensão e queda de desigualdade no Brasil. *Economica, 8*(1).

Goldin, C., & Katz, L. (2008). *The race between education and technology*. Harvard: Harvard University Press.

Hoffman, R. (2005). As transferências não são a causa principal da redução da desigualdade. *Economica, 7*(2), 335–341.

Hoffman, R. (2009). Desigualdade da distribuição da renda no Brasil: a contribuição de aposentadorias e pensões e de outras parcelas do rendimento domiciliar per capita. *Economia e Sociedade, 18*(1 (35)), 213–231.

Hoffman, R., & Duarte, J. C. (1972). A distribuição de renda no Brasil. *Revista de Administração de Empresas, 12*, 46–66.

Kerstenetzky, C. L. (2000). Desigualdade e pobreza: lições de Sen. *Revista Brasileira de Ciências Sociais, 15*(42), 113–122.

Kerstenetzky, C. L. (2008). Redistribuição e desenvolvimento? A economia política do programa bolsa família. *Revista Dados, 51*(1).

Kuznets, S. (1955). Economic growth and income inequality. *American Economic Review, 45*, 1–28.

Langoni, C. G. (1973). *Distribuição da renda e desenvolvimento econômico do Brasil.* Editora Expressão e Cultura.

Leme, M. C., &Wajnman, S. (2001). Diferenciais de rendimentos por gênero**.** In M. B. Lisboa & N. A. Menezes-Filho (Orgs.). *Microeconomia e sociedade no Brasil.* Rio de Janeiro: Contraponto.

Menezes-Filho, N. 2001. Educação e Desigualdade**.** In M. B. Lisboa& N. A. Menezes-Filho (Orgs.). *Microeconomia e sociedade no Brasil.* Rio de Janeiro: Contraponto.

Menezes-Filho, N., Fernandes, R., & Picchetti, P. (2007). Educação e a queda da desigualdade no Brasil**.** In R. P. de Barros, M. N. Foguel& G. Ulyssea(Orgs.). *Desigualdade de Renda no Brasil: uma análise da queda recente* (vol. 2, pp. 285–304). Brasília: IPEA.

Neri, M. (2006). Desigualdade, estabilidade e bem-estar social. *Ensaios Econômicos*, Fundação Getulio Vargas, no. 637.

Reis, E. P. (2000). Percepções da elite sobre pobreza e desigualdade. *Revista Brasileira de Ciências Sociais, 15*(42), 143–152.

Reis, J. G. A., & Barros, R. P. (1990). Desigualdade salarial e distribuição de educação: a evolução das diferenças regionais no Brasil. *Pesquisa e Planejamento Econômico, 20*(3), 415–478.

Ribeiro, C. A. C. (2010). Desigualdade de oportunidades e resultados educacionais no Brasil. *Dados – Revista de Ciências Sociais*, (1), 41.

Silveira Neto, R. (2010). Impacto do programa Bolsa Família sobre a frequência à escola: estimativas a partir de informações da Pesquisa Nacional por Amostra de Domicílio (PNAD). In J. A. de Castro & L. Modesto, (Orgs.) *Bolsa Família 2003–2010: avanços e desafios* (pp. 25–52). Brasília: IPEA.

Soares, S., Fontoura, N.,& Pinheiro, L. (2007). Tendências Recentes na escolaridade e no rendimento de negros e de brancos. In R. P. de Barros, M. Foguel, & G. Ulyssea (Orgs). *Desigualdade de renda no Brasil: uma análise da queda recente* (vol. 2, pp. 285–304). Brasília: IPEA.

Soares, S., De Souza, P. H. G. F., Osório, R. G., & Silveira, F. G. (2010). Os impactos do benefício do programa Bolsa Família sobre a desigualdade e a pobreza. In J. A. de Castro & I. Modesto (Orgs.). *Bolsa Família 2003–2010: avanços e desafios* (pp. 25–52). Brasília: IPEA.

Steiner, J. E. (2006). Conhecimento: gargalos para um Brasil no futuro. *Estudos Avançados, 20*(56), 75–90.

Tinbergen, J. (1975). *Income distribution: Analysis and policies*. Amsterdam: North Holland.

Toilpan, R., & Tinelli, A. (1978). *A controvérsia sobre distribuição de renda e desenvolvimento*. Rio de Janeiro: Zahar Editores.

Horizontal Stratification in Brazil's Higher Education (1960–2010)

Carlos Antonio Costa Ribeiro and Rogerio Schlegel

Abstract Using census' data from 1960 to 2010, the study focuses on the horizontal stratification in Brazil's higher education – i.e., inequalities among sex and race groups which completed the superior level of schooling. Three major trends, not in the same direction, were detected. First, university access has been democratized, with an increase in the relative share of women, blacks, browns, and indigenous people. In the general population, 9.4% of the women and 7.2% of the men had a college degree in 2010. Whites were 95% of the college graduates in 1960; in 2010, they represent three out of four graduates – although whites are less than half the Brazilian population. Second, this inclusion does not imply equal access to all university careers; it took place more intensely in fields less valued by the labor market. Brazil has a stratification pattern similar to that of the United States: education, humanities, and health – with Medicine as an outlier – are fields with a larger concentration of women, while careers related to business, engineering, and technology attract more men. In terms of race, there is a higher concentration of brown and black people in careers in applied social sciences and humanities and especially in the field of Religion. Finally, inferential analysis revealed persistent wage inequalities. Women with university degrees still earn less than her male counterparts in the same career, despite the decrease in the wage gap. More dramatically, disadvantages related to race fluctuated but did not undergo significant changes throughout these decades.

Keywords Higher education · Horizontal stratification in education · Gender inequalities in education · Race inequalities in education · Affirmative action

---

C. A. Costa Ribeiro (✉)
Instituto de Estudos Sociais e Políticos, Universidade Estadual do Rio de Janeiro, Rio de Janeiro, Brazil
e-mail: carloscr@iesp.uerj.br

R. Schlegel
Federal University of São Paulo, São Paulo, Brazil
e-mail: rschlegel@unifesp.br

M. Arretche (ed.), *Paths of Inequality in Brazil*,
https://doi.org/10.1007/978-3-319-78184-6_5

The trajectory of higher education in Brazil over 50 years reveals two clear trends that travel in opposite directions. On the one hand, university access has been democratized and has led to an increase in the relative share of women, blacks, browns, and indigenous included among its population. On the other hand, while this inclusion does not represent equal access to all university careers, it occurred more intensely in fields less valued by the labor market.

This has had an unequal effect on wages: women with university degrees still earn less, but there has been a decrease in the wage gap between women and men. Disadvantages related to race fluctuated but did not undergo significant changes. When they do manage to complete higher education, blacks, browns, and indigenous still earn less than whites and Asians with the same educational level.

Census data reveal that Brazil shows a pattern similar to the United States when it comes to career stratification. The fields of Education, the Humanities, and Health – with Medicine being the outlier – have larger concentrations of women, while careers related to Business, Engineering, and Technology attract more men and have higher average incomes. In terms of race, there is a higher concentration of browns and blacks in careers in Applied Social Sciences and the Humanities, especially in the field of Religion.

Census data also provide a unique opportunity for understanding changes and continuities in Brazil's higher education in the long term. Since 1960, the census sample questionnaires have identified career choices by those who completed higher education. This is a powerful tool, especially for evaluating what is known as horizontal stratification – the hierarchy that exists within a single educational level – a term that runs counter to the idea of vertical stratification, which refers to the unequal chances of individuals progressing in the educational system. This chapter is devoted to the study of horizontal stratification in higher education.

In general, studies that address the Brazilian case compare higher education and other educational levels without considering relevant differences within university education itself. Differentials are considered vertically by comparing higher, secondary, and primary education or by considering years of schooling as an educational variable. If we just consider differentials among educational levels, this could lead us to attribute wage differentials to the labor market when instead they may better be explained by the educational system, as we discuss below.

Horizontal stratification is not only relevant but also contains multiple dimensions. In Brazil, one crucial marker refers to the type of institution of higher education – whether it is private or public and, in case of the latter, whether it is maintained by the federal government or by other government bodies. Among private universities there are differences in reputation or in the quality of the education offered. International research on this topic explores other factors, such as the course's intensity (whether part time or full time) and the existence of research and postgraduate programs at the institution.

By using census data, we can observe horizontal stratification in terms of university careers and understand how gender and race are associated with different careers and salaries.

The next section will discuss the mechanisms behind stratification and the theories to explain them. We then describe the census data involved in the analysis. Subsequently, we present analyses concerning participation in particular careers and their associated incomes. Lastly, we close the chapter with a brief conclusion.

Understanding Horizontal Stratification

Education is the single most important factor for determining opportunities within the labor market, and it plays a decisive role in social stratification. Access to education does not occur uniformly across different social segments. Individuals with a privileged origin are more likely to study for longer periods of time, in better quality institutions and in the company of equally privileged people, to mention just a few factors that can influence success in the working world.

Traditionally, when looking at inequality across educational distributions, the focus falls on vertical stratification. For example, it answers the questions about how individuals with different personal characteristics face and overcome (or fail to overcome) different transitions within the educational system or how characteristics associated with personal origin impact the number of years of education one is able to complete.

The focus on horizontal stratification in higher education in Brazil gains importance because of advances in vertical equalization, largely due to expansion in the system of higher education. The hypothesis of effectively maintained inequality predicts that horizontal inequality tends to increase whenever vertical inequality decreases (LUCAS 2001, p. 1652), since the socioeconomically privileged would be tempted to secure leverage for themselves and their children in this setting. If quantitative differences are common, then these people would pursue quantitative advantages; when these cease to exist, they would then aim for qualitative advantages. In educational terms, this mechanism would mean that when access to a certain educational level is not universalized, the privileged would use their advantaged position to secure its completion. However, when a certain educational level comes closer to being universalized, the strategy then becomes one of ensuring access to qualitative differences.[1]

Studies by Karen (1991, 2001) suggest that factors related to origin became less important in determining access to elite universities in the United States in the 1970s, but the trend has been neutralized in subsequent decades with regard to blacks and poorer students. In a comparative analysis involving 12 countries, Charles and Bradley (2002) found that vertical and horizontal inequalities have their own dynamic and may be positively or negatively associated. Thus, democratization of access to higher education is not always accompanied by greater differentiation between careers. The Brazilian case allows us to incorporate evidence into the discussion of this hypothesis.

[1]These are the predominant paths; as stated by Lucas himself (2001, p. 1652), there is nothing that would prevent qualitative differences from being pursued even when universalization is not present.

Differences in University Careers

The analysis seeks to understand how gender and race impact the placement of individuals within the labor market according to their choice of university career.

There has traditionally been a concentration of women in the fields of Education, the Humanities, Arts, and Health, while men have been largely concentrated in Engineering, Math, Business, and Science (Physics, Chemistry, and Biology). These patterns have been verified in previous studies about Brazil and are similar to those observed in the United States. Recently in the United States, women have achieved significant advances in the fields of Business, Math, and Science. They are already overrepresented in Biology and the Social Sciences (with the exception of Economics), but in Physics, Engineering, and Computer Science, they still lag behind in terms of participation in university degree programs (Gerber and Cheung 2008).

Why do women choose certain fields in universities more intensely and with relative stability over time? Research into this matter is far from being able to provide clear explanations. Some hypotheses point to differing values that socialization sows in future professionals. Young men prioritize economic success and prestige when defining their ideal job, while young women mostly value the social and altruistic opportunities offered by the profession (Fiorentine 1987; Marini et al. 1996; Jonsson 1999; Van de Werfhorst and Kraykamp 2001; Daymont and Andrisani 1984).

An alleged difference in skills between genders is another suggested explanation. This argument states that the labor market tends to pay better wages for mathematical skills compared with other skills. Studies have shown that in many countries men perform better than women on tests involving mathematical thinking at different stages of the educational trajectory. However, there are major variations between nations as to the magnitude of these differences: not only do they not repeat themselves in all countries, but they have also declined in recent decades (Baker and Jones 1993; Xie and Shauman 2003).[2]

There has been a trend toward a gradual reduction of disparities between men and women in terms of choice of university careers in different types of society (Bradley 2000; Charles and Bradley 2002; Ayalon 2003). The number of women studying science or engineering grew by a third between 1972 and 1992 on a global scale (Ramirez and Wotipka 2001). Around the world, the wage gap between men and

[2]The gender difference in mathematical skills is lower in countries where there are more equal opportunities for men and women. By conducting a review of the research in this field, Gerber and Cheung (2008, p. 312) concluded that there is no clarity as to which decisive mechanisms are responsible for these differences to emerge so early in the life of college students. So, more research is needed on this front.

women decreased between the decades of 1960 and 1980 (Gunderson 1989, p. 47). In the United Kingdom, remuneration of women increased from 61% of the amount received by men in 1960 to 75% in 1980, while their share in the labor force increased from 29.5% to 55.4%. In Sweden, average income for women increased from 72% of the men's income to 90%. However, this is not a predictable process, as shown in the example of the United States. In 1980, American women earned 66% of the average income earned by American men – the same percentage as two decades before.

Race is a characteristic much less explored in studies of stratification caused by university careers. This is not only the case in Brazil, but also internationally (Gerber and Cheung 2008, p. 308). This kind of research is usually concentrated in the United States – and this is why it is an ideal country for comparisons in this chapter.

In Brazil, differences in participation in higher education and concentration in a variety of fields of study according to race tend to be interpreted in line with studies on domination – following in the footsteps of Bourdieu (1999) and Bourdieu and Passeron (1992). According to this argument, blacks, like women, are stigmatized and display a negative symbolic coefficient applied to everything they do.

Less privileged race groups present several similarities with women in their choices of university career. The main hypothesis used to explain this occurrence relies on status and lower market value for female professions. Given the difficulties in achieving access to higher education, less privileged social groups opt for less prestigious and less male-dominated careers. In the past, the selection represented by the college entrance exams (in Brazil these exams were called *vestibular*) kept out those who defied this logic. Nowadays it is possible to consider that the proliferation of private institutions of higher education that focus on offering low-cost courses is among the mechanisms able to explain this horizontal stratification.

The stratification observed in university degree programs naturally has an impact on wages. Generally speaking, careers in Engineering offer the highest returns, while those related to Education provide the lowest wages. Degree programs in Business and Economics tend to offer above-average incomes, while those in the Humanities offer below-average pay.

A question that still must be answered is which mechanism could explain these wage differences. One hypothesis involves the fact that these career paths attract more men (or women, in the case of underpaid fields). According to the human capital theory, skills associated with various careers would represent different types of capital, and the returns for a given career would depend on the type of capital associated with it. Paglin and Rufolo (1990) argue that human capital related to mathematical competence is scarcer than that associated with verbal skills and therefore better paid. Grogger and Eide (1995) found indications that more specialized careers (e.g., associated with Engineering and Business) offer greater rewards in the labor market than less specialized careers (such as in the field of Education). Van Werfhorst (2002) suggested four different dimensions for individual abilities: cultural, economic, communicative, and technical, where each career would require different combinations of these abilities and those closer to Economics, for example, would provide higher economic returns.

Inequality in Higher Education Over 50 Years

Brazil has experienced visible progress in the participation of women, blacks, browns, and indigenous people at different levels of the educational system. In the early 2000s, blacks and browns left the educational system having an average of 1.5 fewer years of participation than whites, earned only 53% of the amount whites earned, and were twice as likely to live in poverty. Most of the income disadvantage is attributed to educational differences (Hasenbalg 1979; Soares 2000; Campante et al. 2004; Reis and Crespo 2005).

Although the increase in the participation of brown, black, and indigenous is a very relevant phenomenon, there is no doubt that the greatest change observed over the 50 years we focused on is the marked increase in women's participation in higher education. This is directly linked to expansion of education at the earlier levels but also due to women's growing participation in the labor market and the dramatic change in their role in contemporary Brazilian society. Even though the increase in female participation is an indisputable fact, there is still a great deal of horizontal stratification as we shall see.

When looking at census data from 1960 to 2000, Beltrão and Teixeira (2004) found that the concentration of blacks and browns in university degree programs follows the hierarchy observed in female participation. In women's careers, the largest relative presence of blacks and browns appeared in Nursing, Geography, and History. Among courses perceived as male dominated, which could be considered exceptions due to the large proportion of blacks and browns, careers in the Military and Theology stand out. The authors note that these are fields that do not fit in a *stricto sensu* capitalist production chain.

Another key component to understanding the Brazilian case is seeing how higher education has expanded. Some specific degree programs – such as Nursing, Business, Tourism, Pharmacy, Marketing, and Therapy and Rehabilitation – have greatly expanded among graduates. In general, they are fields in which the relatively low cost of training new professionals boosts the establishment of new degree programs, particularly among private institutions. In these areas, average wages have suffered a steep drop. Other careers reported an increase in wages, following the decrease in participation among graduates – such as Medicine, Architecture, Engineering, Economics, and the Social Sciences (Menezes-Filho 2012).

Public policies geared toward inclusion may have played a special role in the 2000 decade. Since 2005, the University for Everyone Program (ProUni) has granted scholarships at private institutions of higher education in exchange for tax exemption status. Anyone may apply as long as he or she has completed secondary education at a public school or has received a full scholarship at private school and has family income below the amount corresponding to three statutory minimum wages. There are specific quotas for indigenous, blacks, and browns, but in practice, there is a surplus of scholarships and quotas need not necessarily be applied. In its first year of operation, the initiative offered 112,300 scholarships. There was steady growth until 2009, when it reached 247,600, followed by some fluctuation in 2010 (Brasil 2009, 2013).

The mid-2000s also witnessed the expansion of affirmative action policies in higher education. In 2010, 51,494 students enrolled in vacancies reserved for specific groups. Nearly two-thirds of these vacancies benefited public school students, and 27% were reserved for specific ethnic groups. The bonus system became widespread. While quotas reserve a fixed percentage of vacancies for certain population segments, bonuses add extra points to the entrance examination score obtained by students within a certain group so that the proportion of beneficiaries varies each year according to merit (Brasil 2011).

Most of these policies of inclusion steadily improved until the mid-2010s. ProUni's scholarships increased by 20% between 2010 and 2014. From 2016 on, every federal public university is required by law to reserve 50% of their vacancies for graduates of public high schools – the federal higher education system accounted for 15% of the 7.8 million students at this level (2014). At the same time, economic crises in the middle of the decade threatened the pace of expansion in private universities, previously boosted by scholarships sponsored by the federal government. This means that part of the impact of these policies is likely reflected in 2010 census data, but the other part will be better assessed in the next version.

Data and Careers

The analyses focus on census variables regarding education, gender, race, and income. Data represent a unique source of information for analyzing higher education stratification but carry some restrictions.

The censuses analyzed deal with four main categories of race: whites, blacks, Asians, and browns. From 1960 to 1980, the censuses identified indigenous as brown. It was only in 1991 that indigenous populations came to be identified under a specific category. The 1970 census did not have a variable for race. In all Brazilian censuses, data regarding race are only obtained in the sample and is not included in the basic questionnaire applied to the entire population. In this chapter, we distinguish between blacks and browns rather than merging both groups under the category black, as has been the practice in many studies on race relations in Brazil. As we shall see below, the distinction proved to be analytically justified.

Since the 1960s, the portion of women university graduates has increased, seeing a sharp upturn in the 1970s, overtaking men in the 1991 census, and currently doing so by a wide margin (Graph 1). Data on the general population provides further confirmation of this trend: in 1960, only 0.14% of women had college degrees, a figure that rose to 9.4% in 2010 compared with 7.2% of men.

In terms of race, there are two well-defined groups: whites and Asians on one side with a higher proportion of graduates and blacks, browns, and indigenous on the other. Despite the downward trend, differences remain significant. In the 2010 census, 12.8% of whites and 14.4% of Asians completed higher education, compared with 4% of blacks and browns and 2.7% of indigenous.

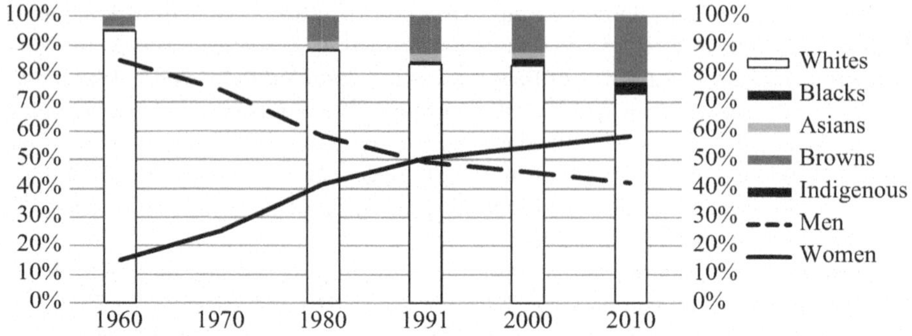

Graph 1 Distribution of the population with diplomas in higher education, by race and gender Brazil – 1960–2010 (%). (Source: IBGE. Demographic Censuses 1960–2010. (Special tabulations by CEM)

The share of whites among graduates has declined, but the group continues to be overrepresented. In 1960, the group accounted for 95% of those with a college degree; currently three out of four graduates are white (Graph 1), even though the share of whites in the total population does not exceed 47.5%. Browns make up the segment that has made the most progress, rising from 3.6% to 20.8% of college graduates, but within the total population, browns represent only 43.4%. Less than 1% of graduates were black up until 1991; they currently make up close to 4% of those with a college degree and represent 7.5% of the population.

As for educational level, all the censuses provide information on post-secondary education, but there are limitations. In censuses from 1980 to 2000, information pertaining to a complete degree program in higher education was only available for those who were not currently studying – and the census left out those who were pursuing a master's degree, doctorate, or a second undergraduate degree. In those censuses as well as in the 2010 one, the question asked about the highest level of degree program completed; for those pursuing a master's or doctorate, the career chosen could only be assigned by approximation from the graduate field declared, which proved to be acceptable due to the great convergence found whenever there is information on graduate and postgraduate levels.

Accompanying the increasing complexity of Brazil's higher education, the number of careers has expanded throughout the period: in 1960, there were 29 careers and 1 category for "other;" in 1970, there are 20 careers and one "other" category; in 1980, 40 careers; in 1991, there were 42 careers and 1 category for "other higher education courses;" in 2000, there were 45 programs plus the categories "other graduate programs" and "other master's/doctoral programs;" and in 2010, there were 89 programs in addition to the category "does not know/unspecified."

Given this increasing diversification, we chose to work with two subgroups of typical careers – those that have demonstrated a higher degree of continuity throughout the period studied and have a higher percentage of graduates: 1 group includes 16 careers for the entire period (1960–2010) for analyses involving gender and another group that includes 25 careers for 1980 to 2010, for analyses related to race

1	Medicine	
2	Architecture	
3	Dentistry	
4	Law	
5	Engineering	
6	Economics	
7	Military	16 careers for analysis
8	Pharmacy or Biochemistry	from 1960 to 2010
9	Veterinary Medicine	
10	Agronomy	
11	Geography or History	
12	Mathematics, Physics, Chemistry or Statistics	
13	Religion and Ecclesiastical	25 careers for analysis
14	Fine Arts	from 1980 to 2010
15	Languages	
16	Biology or Natural History	
17	Physical Education	
18	Nursing	
19	Management	
20	Pedagogy	
21	Psychology	
22	Philosophy	
23	Social Sciences	
24	Accountancy or Actuarial Science	
25	Social Service	

Chart 1 University careers analyzed. (Source: IBGE. Demographic Censuses, 1960–2010)

(Chart 1). The proportion of college graduates in the 16-career group varied from 94.5% in 1960 to 38.2% in 2010 and in the 25-career group, from 94.5% to 83%.

In virtually every career, the proportion of women graduates has increased during these 50 years (Graph 2), even in fields that are still predominantly male, such as Engineering and Religion. Languages and Literature are mostly female fields, with men constituting less than one-fifth of participants in the program according to the last three censuses. Three careers should be featured for having once been considered male but now have female majority: Pharmacy/Biochemistry, Architecture, and Dentistry.

Only a few fields clearly fall outside the general pattern of feminization. In biology, for example, women's participation has fluctuated – in 2010 it was lower than in the previous census. Arts and History/Geography showed a peak in the female participation ratio in 1991, but it has declined ever since. In all of these programs, however, women continue to graduate at rates higher than men.

In Graph 3, the 25 careers used in the analysis involving race are arranged according to their proportion of whites – from lowest to highest – verified in the most recent census. At one end we find Religion, with 54.8% of whites, 37.2% of browns, 1.6% of Asians, and 6.5% of blacks. At the other end, we have Architecture, with 85.5% of whites, 10% browns, 3.4% Asians, and 1.3% blacks. For greater

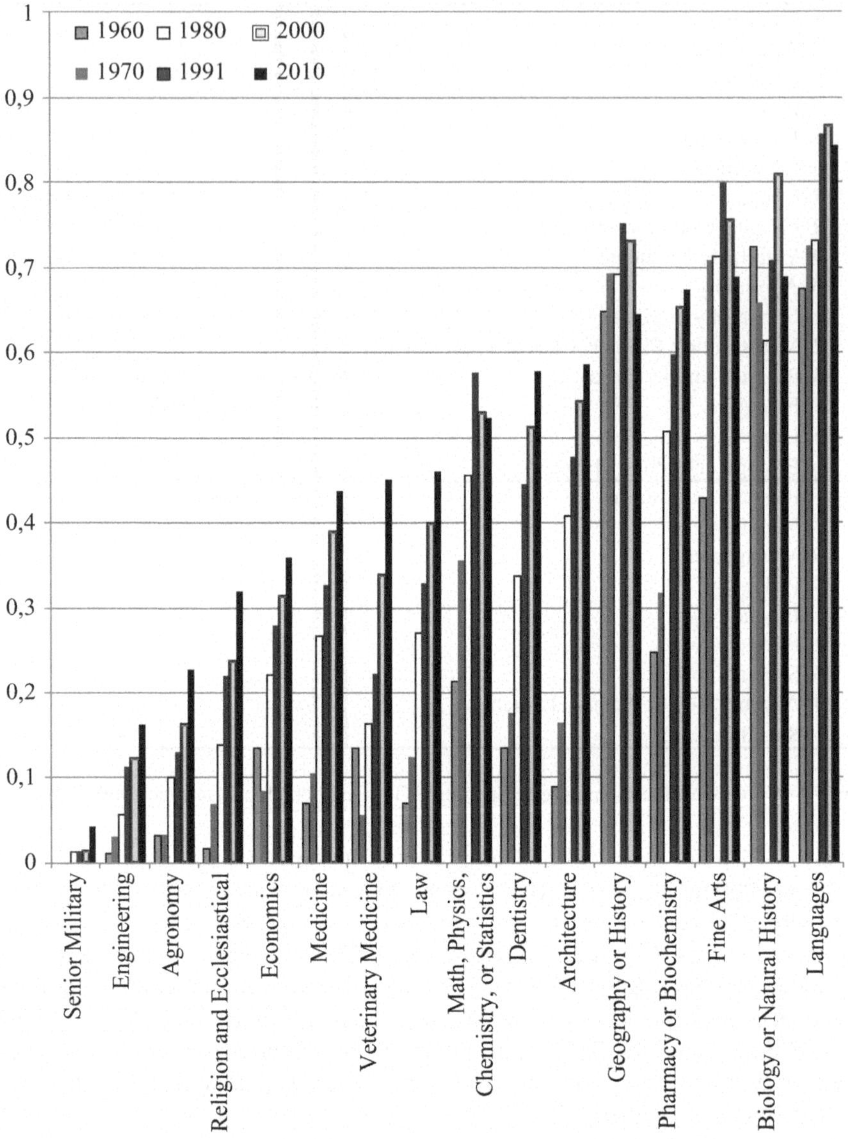

Graph 2 Participation of women among graduates in 16 higher education courses Brazil – 1960–2010. (Source: IBGE. Demographic Censuses 1960–2010. (Special tabulations by CEM)

accuracy in making comparisons with the 1980 census and because of its limited size, we chose to include indigenous and browns as a single group beginning with the 1991 census.

The predominant pattern is one of increasing diversification, with whites ceding ground to other races from 1980 to 2010. Medicine is the only field that differs from other careers in that it has maintained the same proportion of whites from 2000 on.

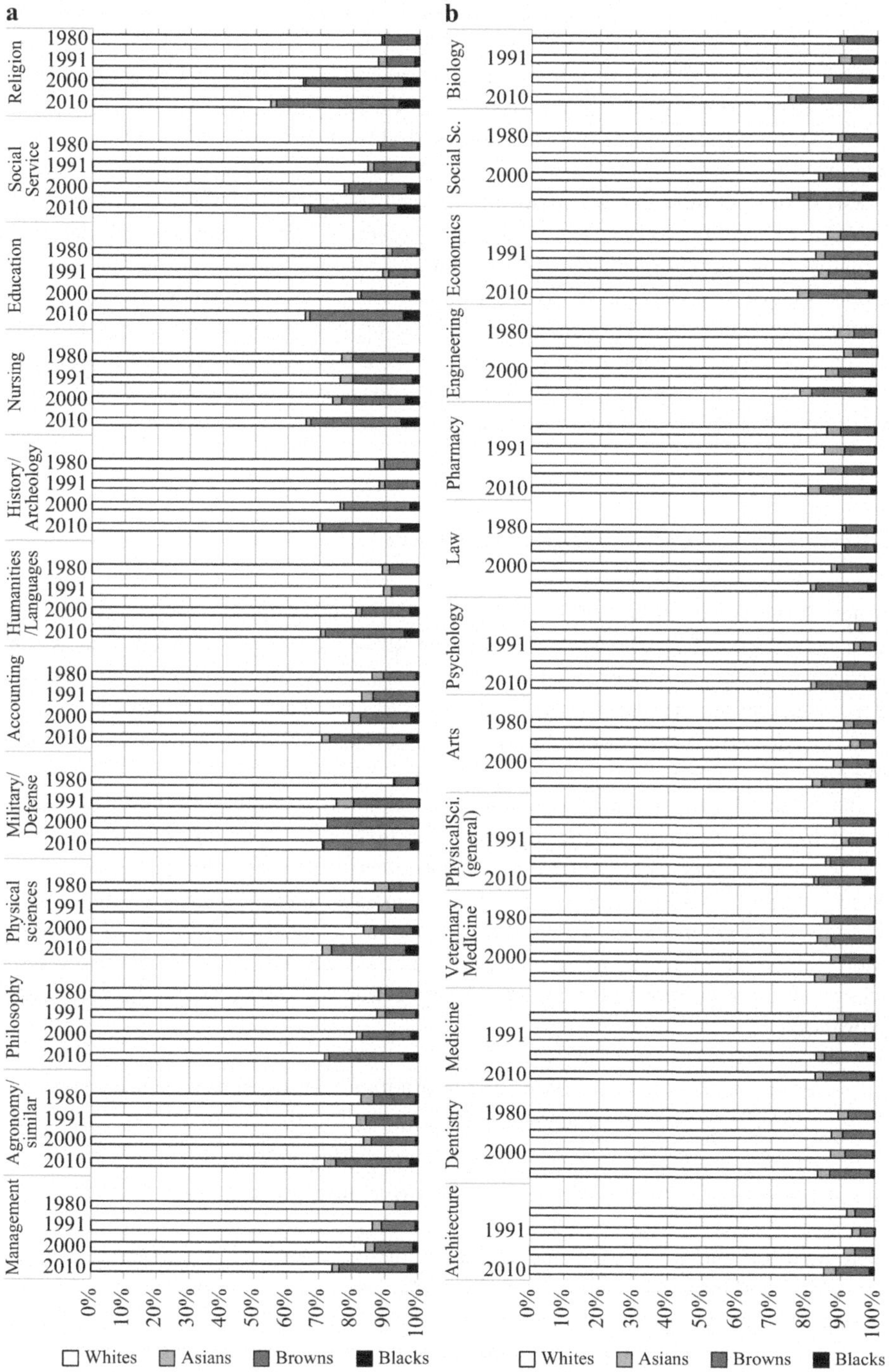

Graph 3 Distribution of graduates among 25 higher education courses according to race Brazil – 1980–2010 (Source: IBGE. Demographic Censuses, 1960–2010. (Special tabulations by CEM))

Notice that the inclusion of once-excluded segments was often concentrated in fields that experienced a large increase in the number of college graduates within the period. Education (Teaching), for example, was the field with greatest proportional growth from 1980 to 2010: going from 7.2% of total graduates to 19.5% of them. In this field, the proportion of browns increased almost threefold, while blacks saw a sevenfold increase.

Only three other careers saw an increase in their share of the total number of graduates: Nursing, Accounting, and Management (the latter saw almost 6% growth). It is significant that in Management, there was a twofold increase in the proportion of browns and a fivefold increase in the proportion of blacks; in Accounting, there was a twofold increase in the proportion of browns and a fourfold increase in the proportion of blacks. All other careers experienced stability or saw reductions in their share of total graduates, especially in traditional fields like Medicine (9.6–2.6%) and Law (from 14.9% to 10%).

University Careers, Gender and Race

Graph 2 shows the sharp rise in female participation in various university careers between 1960 and 2010. Graph 3, however, shows a less pronounced increase in participation on the part of blacks and browns in university careers from 1980 to 2010. To complement the stratification analysis, we used log-linear models to estimate the strength of the association between gender and university career and race and university career.

The strength of association is obtained by odds ratios in these models. For example, if the odds of men completing Medicine instead of Languages and Literature are 20 times higher than women, and decrease to 5 times higher in a subsequent period, it can be said that there was a reduction of gender inequality in obtaining a diploma in Medicine when compared to Languages and Literature. Working with odds ratios (OR) enables us to set a reference career and retrieve results, which account for the proportion of graduates by gender, as reflected in the following expression:

$$OR_{MW/ML} = \frac{\dfrac{\text{Men college graduates in Medicine}}{\text{Men college graduates in Languages}}}{\dfrac{\text{Women college graduates in Medicine}}{\text{Women college graduates in Languages}}}$$

In addition, the models provide a measure of statistical association between gender or race and university career regardless of the size of the career. The stronger the association, the greater the inequality of gender or race and vice versa. Two models were estimated: the first (constant association) tests the hypothesis that the association between gender or race and careers has remained constant over the years; the second (log-multiplicative or uniform change) tests the hypothesis that there was a change in the strength of the association between gender or race and careers in the period, in addition to providing a parameter for measuring the change in this strength of association.

More specifically, these models have been adjusted to the two tables obtained listing the 16 and 25 careers. The adjustment of both models to each table was evaluated using the statistic L^2, which is distributed as X^2, and the Bayesian information criteria (BIC), a statistical measure that takes into account the sample size (the more negative the BIC value, the better adjusted is the model to the data). By using these measures, we selected the model that best fits each of the two tables in order to interpret trends in gender and race inequalities among careers – a formal way to measure horizontal stratification by gender and race across university careers between 1960 and 2010.

Gender and Careers

To analyze the change in the strength of the association between gender and careers from 1960 to 2010, the two models were adjusted to the first table. In this case, the model that tests the hypothesis of change throughout the year gives a better fit ($L^2 = 89.9$; g.l. = 71; BIC = −609) than the constant association model ($L^2 = 167.1$; g.l. = 74; BIC = −561). In other words, there was a significant decrease in gender inequality in completion of 16 university careers between 1960 and 2010.

This change is mainly due to the expansion of women's access to university in Brazil during the period under review. Here we are able to see the advantages of this research strategy: the proportion of women with a college diploma increased over the course of the 50 years analyzed, but the models reveal that a reduction of inequalities between genders only took place between 1960 and 1980 and 2000–2010, remaining constant between 1980 and 2000. This reduction in the association between gender and career is summarized by the unidiff parameter (Graph 4), a factor that multiplies all odds ratios in each year analyzed. The parameter is set at 1 for the first year (1960) and varies upward or downward according to the data analyzed. In this case, the unidiff parameter decreased from 1 to 0.7 between 1960 and 1980 and from 0.7 to less than 0.6 between 1980 and 2010. Given that this parameter is in a logarithmic scale, the reduction was quite substantial.

In order to verify the size of this reduction in inequality, it is appropriate to assess the change in odds ratios between 1960 and 2010. Table 1 compares the odds for men and women enrolled in Medicine (the reference career) compared to other programs in each year analyzed. The change in the odds ratios follows the pattern indicated by the unidiff coefficient. For example, in 1960, men were 26 times more likely than women to get a diploma in Medicine rather than a diploma in Pharmacy. In 2010, this value decreased to only 6.3 times more.

Reductions in the same direction, although at different levels and always in comparison to Medicine, can be seen in Military, Law, Veterinary Medicine, Biology, Engineering, Agricultural Science, Geography or History, and Mathematics/

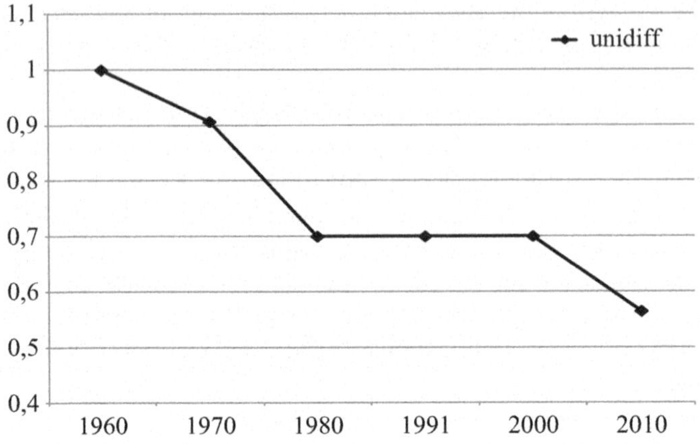

Graph 4 Change in the strength of the association between genders in 16 careers Brazil – 1960–2010. (Source: IBGE. Demographic censuses 1960–2010. (Special tabulations by CEM))

Table 1 Odds ratio of men having studied Medicine in relation to other careers, compared with women Brazil – 1960–2010

Careers	1960	1970	1980	1991	2000	2010
Medicine (base category)						
Pharmacy or Biochemistry	26.2	19.3	9.8	9.8	9.8	6.3
Military	14.9	11.6	6.6	6.6	6.6	4.6
Law	13.1	10.3	6.1	6.1	6.1	4.3
Veterinary Medicine	12.3	9.7	5.8	5.8	5.8	4.1
Biology or Natural History	4.2	3.7	2.7	2.7	2.7	2.2
Engineering	3.1	2.8	2.2	2.2	2.2	1.9
Agronomy	2.3	2.1	1.8	1.8	1.8	1.6
Geography or History	1.9	1.8	1.6	1.6	1.6	1.4
Math, Physics, Chem. or Stat.	1.1	1.1	1.1	1.1	1.1	1.1
Architecture	0.8	0.8	0.9	0.9	0.9	0.9
Fine Arts	0.8	0.8	0.8	0.8	0.8	0.9
Economics	0.4	0.5	0.5	0.5	0.5	0.6
Dentistry	0.2	0.2	0.3	0.3	0.3	0.4
Religion and Ecclesiastical	0.1	0.2	0.2	0.2	0.2	0.3
Languages	0	0	0	0	0	0.1

Source: IBGE. Demographic Censuses, 1960–2010. (Special tabulations by CEM)

Physics/Chemistry/Statistics. Even though these careers continue to offer easier access to men, they have gradually become more open to women.

Other careers continued to be defined as mostly female, although there has also been equalization as they became more open to men. For example, in 1960, women were 112.7 (1/0.009) times more likely than men to get a degree in Languages instead of Medicine. This number decreased to 14.4 (1/0.069) times more likely in 2010. Decreases in the relative advantage of women and increased participation of men also occurred in the following careers compared to Medicine: Architecture, Arts, Economics, Dentistry, and Religion.

The findings presented here reveal that there was a considerable process of equalization between men and women in the completion of several university degree programs between 1960 and 2010. There are still degree programs that are distinctly female (Languages, Biology, Arts, Geography, and History), others that have ceased to be male and have become female (Architecture, Dentistry and Mathematics/Physics/Statistics/Chemistry), and others that despite the large increase in female participation between 1960 and 2010 are still predominantly male (Law, Veterinary Medicine, Medicine, Economics, Religion, Agronomy, Engineering, and Military).

Race and Careers

In Graph 3 we see an increase in the percentage of blacks and browns in most university degree programs between 1980 and 2010. But to what extent can this increase be understood as a reduction of racial inequality in the completion of university degree programs? To answer this question, we again made use of log-linear models, testing the hypotheses of continuity and change in the association between race and careers.

In this case, it was the constant association model that hypothesizes continuity in the association between race and careers over the years that fit the data better ($L^2 = 1018$; g.l. = 216; BIC = −1471) than the model hypothesizing changes over the years ($L^2 = 1001$; g.l. = 213; BIC = −1453). This means that the odds ratios are not statistically different in 1980, 1991, 2000, and 2010. In other words, racial inequality in completion of several university degree programs has not changed since 1980.

In general, Asians are more likely to complete university degree programs than whites, who in turn are more likely to do so than browns, while blacks are the least likely. This result, however, should be treated with a degree of caution since in some careers, the advantages of whites, browns, and Asians in comparison to blacks are similar, while in others these differences are extremely disparate. In any event, in all comparisons, blacks have the lowest odds of being in any university degree program. It should be noted that in this chapter, we make a distinction between blacks and browns, which allows us to conclude that blacks accrue most of the disadvantages while browns sometimes face similar odds as those of whites and Asians.

According to the data, the career that offers the greatest likelihood of completion for Asians and whites is Dentistry, and it has therefore been chosen as our basis for comparison. The reference category is that of blacks (see Graph 5).

Asians are 15 times more likely than blacks to have completed Dentistry than Social Service, while whites are 6 times more likely to have done so, and browns are 3 times more likely to have done so. In Engineering, the level of inequality is differ-

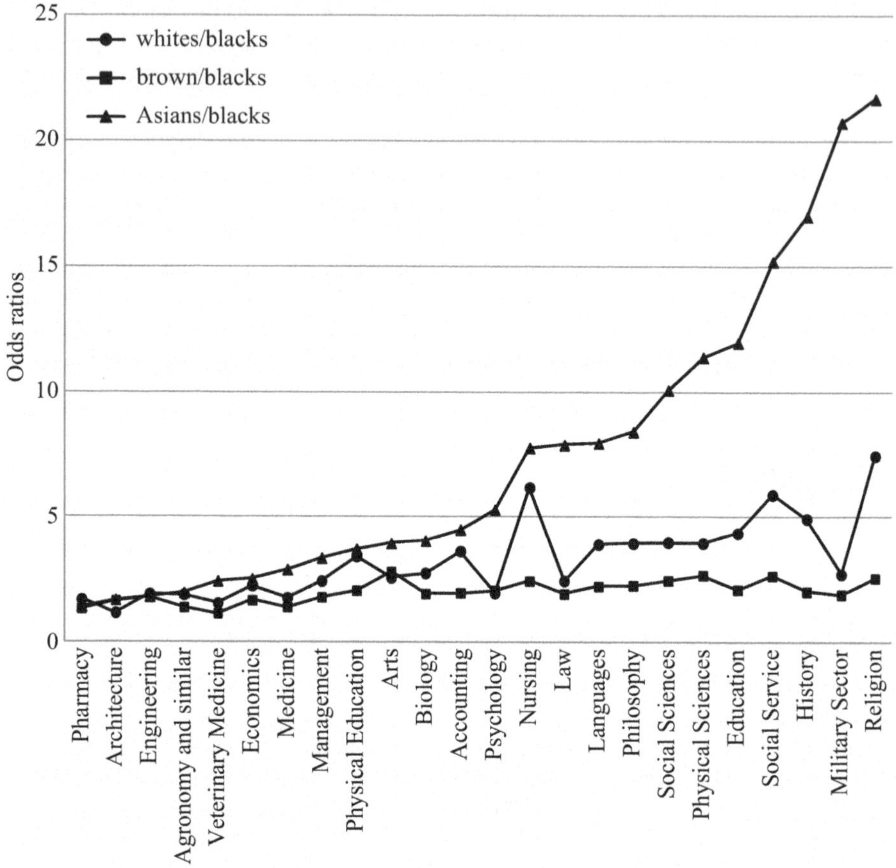

Graph 5 Odds ratios of Asians, whites, and browns, in comparison to blacks, having studied Dentistry compared to other careers Brazil – 1960/2010. (Source: IBGE. Demographic Censuses, 1960–2010. (Special tabulations by CEM))

ent since the advantages of whites, Asians, and browns in completing Engineering instead of Dentistry in comparison with blacks are the same: twice as likely.

Graph 5 also indicates that the inclusion of blacks in higher education occurs in less prestigious careers. The racial difference using Dentistry as the base course – a career with a majority of white graduates – is higher when the comparison is made with less prestigious programs such as Social Service, History, Education, Religion, Military, Physical Sciences, Social Sciences, Philosophy, and Languages. On the other hand, the differences are smaller when drawing comparisons between Dentistry and the most prestigious careers, such as Architecture, Engineering, and Medicine. Thus, the racial inequality indicator is larger when comparing high-prestige careers (such as Dentistry) with careers that are less valued (such as Social Service). That is to say, whites and Asians have more advantages in high-prestige careers.

Income and University Career

Career prestige is ultimately defined by the income gains and subsequent labor market placement it provides. These gains may be fairly modified over the years according to the supply and demand mechanisms for professionals in the labor market. Graph 6 shows the average income for careers analyzed in each of the years for which there are observations. The first nine careers displayed at the top of the chart (Teaching, Philosophy, Social Service, Nursing, Accounting, Psychology, Physical Education, Management, and Social Sciences) were only observed for the

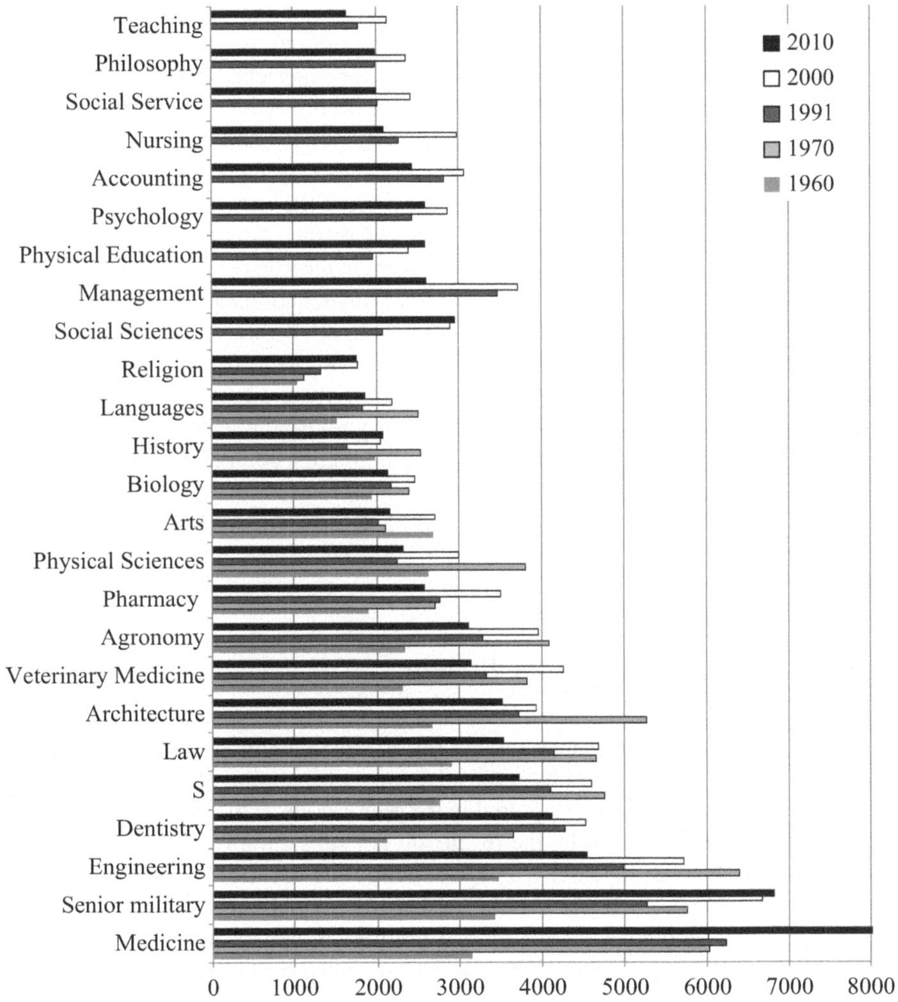

Graph 6 Average predicted income per career Brazil – 1960–2010 (in 2012 R$). (Source: IBGE. Demographic Censuses, 1960–2010. (Special tabulations by CEM))

years 1991, 2000, and 2010. The other 16 careers in the graph below were observed in the years 1960, 1970, 1991, 2000, and 2010. In addition, Graph 6 ranks the careers by average income, from lowest to highest, in 2010. Thus, the graph provides two sets of information: first, career hierarchy by income and second, the increase and decrease in average income over the years. Some careers, such as Medicine and Social Sciences, saw their average income steadily increase over the decades, while others, such as Engineering and Accounting, witnessed fluctuations over the years.

The following analyses are quite straightforward. We initially estimated several linear regressions by using the logarithm of income as the dependent variable and careers, gender, race, and age as independent variables. However, we found that there was not much difference between the results obtained by regressions and those obtained by a simple comparison of the average income for gender and race groups. In other words, the effect of age (used as a proxy for experience in the labor market) tends to be less relevant. Therefore, in order to verify return on income, we compare average income for university career (divided by gender and race) from 1960 to 2010. We actually calculated the average labor earnings logarithm per career for each census between 1960 and 2010, but we present the data on a normal income scale. We initially analyzed the data for men and women between 1960 and 2010. Following the same logic, we calculated the average income per career (1991, 2000, and 2010) for each racial group (Asian, white, brown, and black).

For every year, incomes were deflated relative to 2010 values. This exercise does not present many problems for the 1970, 1991, 2000, and 2010 census but is less reliable for the 1960 census since income data is only available in ranges for that year. Therefore, income estimates behave in a very unusual manner for 1960 and do not follow the same pattern as other years. Even though a comparison with the 1960 results is not strictly valid, we present the results here so as to verify horizontal stratification in 1960, i.e., while it is not possible to compare 1960 with other years, it is possible to observe income differentials between careers at that point in time.

Gender, Careers, and Labor Income

The initial strategy of using linear regressions to calculate the predicted income for graduates in each career would have the advantage of including the impact of experience (modeled as age and age squared in the regressions of the income logarithm). While this caution is justifiable, the results do not substantially differ from simple calculations of average income, which is a simplified form of analysis because it considers all graduates at a single point in their life, equalizing careers with recent expansion – and younger graduates – and traditional careers, which tend to offer higher wages at the beginning of the period analyzed and have a stock of older graduates. By taking these precautions, we reached an income-based career order not too far from a simple comparison of averages. Therefore, we decided to only present the differences in average income per career.

Table 2 Differences in the predicted income of women compared to men according to careers Brazil – 1960–2010 (in %)

Careers	1960	1970	1991	2000	2010
Higher Military		0.24	0.35	0.45	0.41
Economics	0.62	0.45	0.54	0.54	0.61
Management			0.53	0.57	0.63
Physical Education			0.69	0.71	0.63
Religion	0.49	1.22	0.72	0.72	0.64
Medicine	0.61	0.53	0.58	0.54	0.64
Accounting			0.58	0.60	0.66
Agronomy	0.8	0.69	0.63	0.64	0.66
Veterinary Medicine	0.56	0.59	0.66	0.63	0.67
Biology	0.48	0.57	0.56	0.72	0.67
Social Sciences			0.53	0.64	0.69
Engineering	0.54	0.51	0.58	0.59	0.69
Physical Sciences	0.73	0.56	0.58	0.62	0.70
Law	0.74	0.47	0.61	0.66	0.71
Dentistry	0.67	0.54	0.67	0.69	0.74
Architecture		0.54	0.61	0.69	0.75
Teaching			0.61	0.71	0.76
History	0.68	0.53	0.68	0.75	0.79
Languages	0.55	0.56	0.64	0.78	0.80
Pharmacy	0.64	0.56	0.59	0.68	0.80
Psychology			0.67	0.76	0.80
Philosophy			0.79	0.94	0.84
Arts	0.81	0.49	0.65	0.75	0.86
Nursing			0.82	0.94	0.89
Social Service			0.66	0.82	0.95

Source: IBGE. Demographic Censuses, 1960–2010. (Special tabulations by CEM)

Table 2 indicates that women have systematically earned less than men in all careers across all censuses. There is one exception: Religion in the 1970 census, where women earned 22% more than men. In 2010, the greater distance was found in senior military careers (predicted female earnings equivalent to 41% of males), followed by Economics (61%). Following the trend in feminization of careers, we also observed reduction of wage differentials over time. Women with a diploma in Medicine, for example, had earnings that were 53% of men in 1970 (remember that 1960 numbers have to be interpreted with caution since they are measured using a different scale), a number that increased to 64% in the most recent census. The data indicate that income differences tend to be smaller in careers perceived as female and that this approximation was also more prominent in these careers. In Languages, the career having the highest number of females among all those analyzed since 1960, women's income departed from 55% of male earnings to reach 80% in 2010. In Social Service, the career having the second highest number of females, women earned an income equivalent to 95% of the income earned by men in 2010 – the smallest difference found. Approximation occurred even in careers perceived as male. Women with a diploma in Engineering in 2010 had predicted income at 69% of male income, a ratio that were 51% in 1970.

In order to verify the association between average career income and the percentage of women within these careers, we used a linear regression model where average income by career (in logarithmic form) is a function of the percentage of women and the census year. These analyses clearly indicate a considerable increase in average income per career over time (which is also evident in Graph 6), as well as the fact that careers with higher average incomes tend to have a lower percentage of women. In other words, women tend to pursue careers where the average income is lower. Their entry into these careers tended to increase over the decades.

Race, Careers, and Labor Income

In the analysis concerning wage differentials due to race, we analyzed 25 careers for 1991, 2000, and 2010. Once again, the average income per career without a divider by racial group can be seen in Graph 6 above. Graph 7 below shows the average income for each racial group per career between 1991 and 2010.

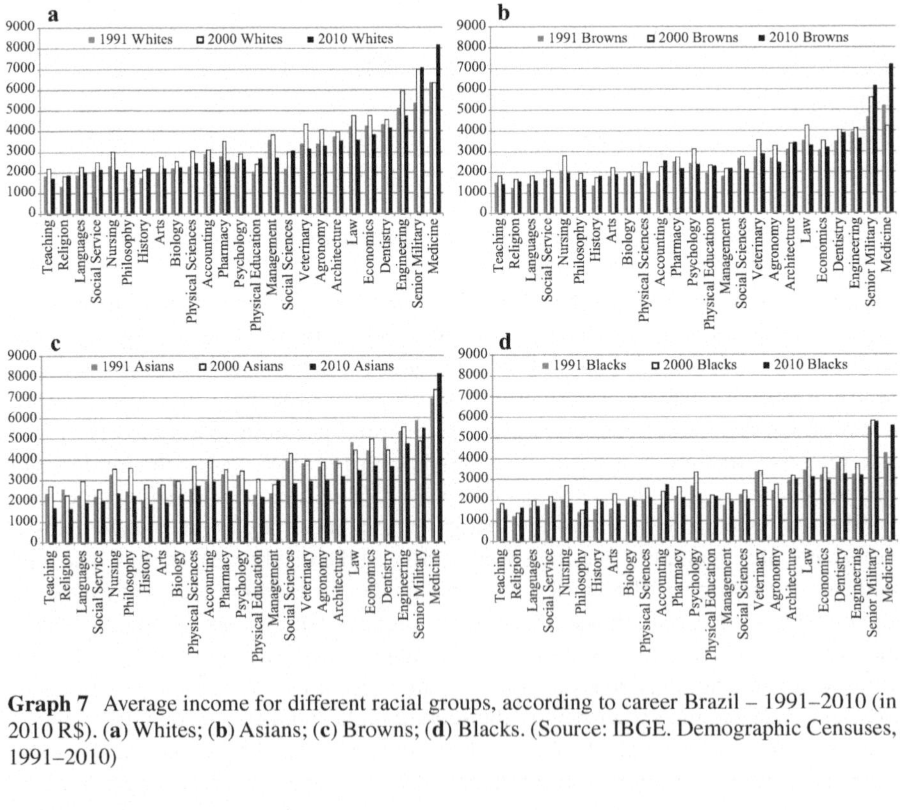

Graph 7 Average income for different racial groups, according to career Brazil – 1991–2010 (in 2010 R$). (**a**) Whites; (**b**) Asians; (**c**) Browns; (**d**) Blacks. (Source: IBGE. Demographic Censuses, 1991–2010)

There is relative coincidence in the ranking of careers with regard to wages (Graph 7 is organized on the basis of average income for 2010) and participation of nonwhites (shown in Graph 3). Three of the five careers with lowest income according to this criterion are among the five that have the highest concentration of nonwhites: Religion, Education, and History/Geography. At the opposite end, we find careers that have the highest concentration of whites: Architecture, Dentistry, and Medicine. These coincidences depict an unusual situation for military career: with one of the highest rates of blacks and browns graduating (almost 30%), the field offers one of the best predicted incomes, and as Beltran and Teixeira (2004) point out, the career holds the promise of social mobility for these racial groups.

The comparison of average incomes across racial groups shows the most striking results. Not only is there a smaller concentration of browns and blacks in prestigious fields such as Medicine, Engineering, and Dentistry, but also those who manage to complete these degree programs still tend to earn less than whites and Asians within the same career.

Graph 7 clearly shows the existence of racial inequality on income returns. Whites and Asians systematically tend to earn higher wages, on average, than browns and blacks who hold the same university program diploma. Moreover, by using a linear regression (not displayed), we can see that the average income of careers has increased between 1991 and 2010 and that the percentage of Asians and whites is larger in careers that provide higher income. Browns are in an intermediate position between whites and blacks, that is, they tend to be in careers with lower average incomes than careers with a higher share of whites and in careers with a higher average income than those with a higher share of blacks. In other words, the expansion in participation of blacks and browns in universities occurs most of all in careers with lower average incomes. Racial inequality according to career income is systematic. Table 3 below shows average income by race between 1991 and 2010.

By comparing the differences between whites on the one hand and Asians, browns, and blacks on the other, we find a clear trend of lower income for the latter two groups. It is equally clear that Asians often tend to earn more than whites. For Engineering in the 1991 census, for example, browns received income equivalent to 77% of that earned by whites, while blacks received income equivalent to 63%. Whites and Asians had almost identical average incomes. In the same census, incidentally, only the Military career diverged from the general pattern where income earned by blacks surpassed that earned by whites.

In the 2000 census, we find a slight downward trend in racial inequality to the extent that income disparity between racial groups diminished in comparison to the 1991 census. In 2010, racial income inequality continues to decrease. However, throughout the entire period, the average income per career remains higher for Asians, closely followed by whites. Further away we find browns and blacks, the latter which continue to have the lowest average income of all racial groups. In addition, there is a strong correlation between average income and percentage of whites, Asians, browns, and blacks for each career. The more whites and Asians within a career, the higher the average income tends to be; conversely, the higher the percentage of blacks and browns, the lower the average income. Racial inequality decreases slowly precisely because browns and blacks tend to be in careers with lower incomes, and even within these careers, they tend to earn less than whites and Asians.

Table 3 Average income of Asians, browns, and blacks compared to whites according to career Brazil – 1991–2010

	1991			2000			2010		
Career	Asians/whites	Browns/whites	Blacks/Asians	Asians/whites	Browns/whites	Blacks/whites	Asians/whites	Browns/whites	Blacks/whites
Agronomy	1.07	0.79	0.72	0.94	0.80	0.67	0.91	0.74	0.61
Engineering	1.04	0.77	0.63	0.93	0.69	0.63	1.00	0.76	0.67
Medicine	1.09	0.82	0.67	1.16	0.67	0.58	1.00	0.88	0.68
Physical Education	1.20	0.90	0.88	1.16	0.89	0.95	1.11	0.81	0.72
Management	1.10	0.74	0.63	1.11	0.71	0.64	1.03	0.77	0.74
Economics	1.03	0.71	0.74	1.05	0.74	0.74	0.96	0.83	0.76
Dentistry	1.15	0.81	0.87	0.97	0.88	0.87	0.88	0.94	0.78
Military	1.10	0.86	1.02	0.70	0.80	0.83	0.78	0.87	0.81
Veterinary Medicine	1.11	0.80	0.98	0.90	0.81	0.78	0.92	0.91	0.82
Psychology	0.93	0.78	0.79	1.03	0.80	0.75	0.82	0.86	0.82
Arts	1.30	0.87	0.78	1.01	0.80	0.83	0.86	0.85	0.82
Accounting	1.13	0.86	0.76	1.13	0.86	0.83	0.98	0.86	0.84
Architecture	1.05	0.82	0.78	0.95	0.85	0.79	0.89	0.97	0.85
Languages	1.22	0.77	0.87	1.31	0.81	0.89	0.96	0.79	0.85
Physical Sciences	1.13	0.84	0.86	1.19	0.80	0.84	1.11	0.79	0.86
Nursing	1.42	0.89	0.85	1.17	0.92	0.90	1.09	0.90	0.86
Law	1.14	0.84	0.81	0.93	0.89	0.84	0.97	0.92	0.86
Biology	1.34	0.79	0.89	1.16	0.77	0.83	1.03	0.79	0.87
Religion	1.91	0.94	0.91	1.24	0.90	0.74	0.87	0.83	0.87
Social Service	1.06	0.81	0.86	1.02	0.83	0.86	0.94	0.80	0.88
History	1.17	0.77	0.90	1.32	0.83	0.94	0.84	0.82	0.88
Pharmacy	1.16	0.86	0.96	0.97	0.88	0.94	0.98	0.91	0.88
Social Sciences	1.36	0.72	0.82	1.31	0.74	0.79	0.96	0.82	0.89
Teaching	1.28	0.82	0.88	1.24	0.83	0.83	0.95	0.82	0.89
Philosophy	1.19	0.79	0.69	1.44	0.78	0.60	1.04	0.76	0.91

Source: IBGE. Demographic Censuses, 1960–2010

Conclusions

Analysis of horizontal stratification in higher education reveals that 50 years of changes have been enough to modify the amount of elitism within this educational level but not enough to overcome inequalities in completing and obtaining diplomas across different careers. Gains were larger for women, both in access to different careers as well as in income. There is still a notable gap between genders, but important steps have been taken.

From a racial standpoint, advances were more limited. Generally speaking, career diversification has increased in terms of proportionality, but the statistical models more suited to the temporal data show stability in inequality. Much more serious is the determination that browns and blacks systematically have lower incomes than whites, even if they follow the same university career path.

In this sense, the evidence clearly shows significant horizontal stratification in Brazil's higher education. This type of stratification can be seen in both completion of degree programs as well as returns in the labor market. Even though gender inequalities have decreased and racial inequalities have remained unchanged, lower prestige degree programs continue to be the ones to include more women, blacks, and browns. Moreover, earnings are unequal in terms of gender and race. Women, blacks, and browns earn lower average incomes than men and whites who have completed the same academic programs. Careers that have more women are also the ones with more browns and blacks and tend to provide lower average incomes than careers with more men, Asians, and whites.

Although these inequalities have decreased over the years, they persist. As shown in this chapter, a relevant portion of the inequality between segments with different observable characteristics can be accredited to the educational system, even though asymmetries are visited among higher education graduates – a group that has already completed several transitions within the educational system. By failing to take this into account, policies pursuing further equality may miss their target and fall short of being effective.

References

Ayalon, H. (2003). Women and men go to university: Gender differences in choice of field in higher education. *Sex Roles, 48*, 277–290.

Baker, D. P., & Jones, D. P. (1993). Creating gender equality: Cross-national gender stratification and mathematical performance. *Sociology of Education, 66*(2), 91–103.

Beltrão, K. I., & Teixeira, M. de P. (2004). O vermelho e o negro: gênero na universidade brasileira – uma análise da seletividade das carreiras a partir dos Demographic Censuses de 1960 a 2000. Rio de Janeiro: IPEA (Texto para discussão, no. 1052).

Bourdieu, P. (1999). *Escritos de educação* (2ª ed). Petrópolis: Vozes.

Bourdieu, P., & Passeron, J. C. 1992. *A reprodução: elementos para uma teoria do sistema de ensino* (3ª ed.). Rio de Janeiro: Francisco Alves.

Bradley, K. (2000). The incorporation of women into higher education: Paradoxical outcomes? *Sociology of Education, 73*(1), 1–18.

Brasil. (2011). *Censo da Educação Superior (CES) de 2010*. Resumo técnico.

Brasil. *Bolsas ofertadas por ano*. Disponível em: http://prouniportal.mec.gov.br/images/arquivos/pdf/Representacoes_graficas/bolsas_ofertadas_ano.pdf. Accessed 12 Apr 2013.

Brasil. Instituto Nacional de Estudos e Pesquisas Educacionais Anísio Teixeira (INEP). (2009, September). Avaliando o desempenho no ENADE de bolsistas do ProUni. *Na Medida, 1*(3).

Campante, F. R., Crespo, A. R. V., & Leite, P. G. (2004, June). Desigualdade salarial entre raças no mercado de trabalho urbano brasileiro: aspectos regionais. *Revista Brasileira de Economia*, Rio de Janeiro, *58*(2). Available at: http://www.scielo.br/scielo.php?script=sci_arttext&pid=S0034-71402004000200003&lng=en&nrm=iso. Accessed 27 Mar 2014. https://doi.org/10.1590/S0034-71402004000200003.

Charles, M., & Bradley, K. (2002). Equal but separate? A cross-national study of sex segregation in higher education. *American Sociological Review, 67*(4), 573–599.

Daymont, T. N., & Andrisani, P. J. (1984). Job preferences, college major, and the gender gap in earnings. *Journal of Human Resources, 19*, 408–428.

Fiorentine, R. (1987). Men, women, and the premed persistence gap: A normative alternatives approach. *American Journal of Sociology, 92*, 1118–1139.

Gerber, T. P., & Cheung, S. Y. C. (2008). Horizontal stratification in postsecondary education: Forms, explanations, and implications. *Annual Review of Sociology, 34*, 299–318.

Grogger, J., & Eide, E. (1995). Changes in college skills and the rise in the college wage premium. *Journal of Human Resources, 30*, 280–310.

Gunderson, M. (1989). Male-female wage differentials and policy responses. *Journal of Economic Literature, 27*, 46–72.

Hasenbalg, C. (1979). *Discriminação e desigualdades raciais no Brasil*. Rio de Janeiro: Graal.

Jonsson, J. (1999). Explaining sex differences in educational choice: An empirical assessment of a rational choice model. *European Sociological Review, 15*, 391–404.

Karen, D. (1991). The politics of class, race and gender access to higher education in the United States, 1960–1986. *American Journal of Education, 99*, 208–237.

Karen, D. (2001). Changes in access to higher education in the United States: 1980–1992. *Sociology of Education, 75*(3), 191–210.

Lucas, S. (2001). Effectively maintained inequality: Education transitions, track mobility, and social background effects. *American Journal of Sociology, 106*, 1642–1690.

Marini, M. M., Fan, P., Finley, E., & Beutel, A. M. (1996). Gender and job values. *Sociology of Education, 69*(1), 49–65.

Menezes-Filho, N. (2012, December). *Apagão de mão de obra qualificada? As profissões e o mercado de trabalho brasileiro entre 2000 e 2010* (Policy Paper no. 4). São Paulo: Insper.

Paglin, M., & Rufolo, A. (1990). Heterogeneous human capital, occupational choice, and male-female earnings differences. *Journal of Labor Economics, 8*, 123–144.

Ramirez, F., & Wotipka, C. M. (2001). Slowly but surely? The global expansion of women's participation in Science and Engineering Fields of study, 1972–92. *Sociology of Education, 74*, 231–251.

Reis, M. R., & Crespo, A. R. V. (2005). *Race discrimination in Brazil: An analysis of the age, period and cohort effects* (Texto para Discussão IPEA, no. 1.114). Rio de Janeiro: IPEA.

Soares, S. S. D. (2000). *O perfil da discriminação no mercado de trabalho: homens negros, mulheres brancas e mulheres negras* (Texto para Discussão IPEA, no. 769). Brasília: IPEA.

Van de Werfhorst, H. G., & Kraykamp, G. (2001). Four field-related educational resources and their impact on labor, consumption and sociopolitical orientation. *Sociology of Education, 74*(4), 296–317.

Van der Werfhorst, H. G. (2002). Fields of study, acquired skills, and the wage benefit from a matching job. *Acta Sociol., 45*(4), 287–303.

Xie, Y., & Shauman, K. A. (2003). *Women in Science: Career processes and outcomes*. Cambridge, MA: Harvard University Press.

Racial Inequalities in Brazil: A Persistent Challenge

Marcia Lima and Ian Prates

Abstract This chapter analyzes racial inequalities in Brazil along 50 years exploring the superposition of race and class. How has the topic of race relations and inequalities been addressed in Brazil? Has the inequality situation changed from 1960 on? If so, how have those changes been interpreted? Despite the numerous social changes Brazil has undergone in 50 years, the vast majority of blacks were hold at the bottom of the social pyramid. First, the chapter briefly reviews how the literature on race relations and inequalities has addressed the issue of black social status in Brazil. Second, the chapter examines racial disparities over time, taking into account the fundamental factors and effects relating to the reproduction of racial inequality in Brazil, such as educational opportunities and holding a university degree.

Keywords Racial inequalities · Higher education · Brazilian race relations · Labor market · Schooling

How has the topic of race relations and inequalities been addressed in Brazil? Has the inequality situation changed in recent decades? If so, how have those changes been interpreted? In an attempt to answer these questions, this chapter describes the scenario of racial inequalities in Brazil in recent decades. The aspects it considers are drawn from the literature on the mechanisms of social reproduction that, despite the numerous social changes Brazil has undergone in 50 years, hold the vast majority of blacks at the bottom of the social pyramid.

The chapter first approaches the discussion by briefly reviewing how the literature on race relations and inequalities has addressed the issue of black social status

M. Lima (✉) · I. Prates
Department of Sociology, University of Sao Paulo, Center for Metropolitan Studies, São Paulo, Brazil
e-mail: mrlima@usp.br

M. Arretche (ed.), *Paths of Inequality in Brazil*,
https://doi.org/10.1007/978-3-319-78184-6_6

in Brazil, particularly with regard to changes that have taken place since 2000. It then examines racial inequalities over time, taking into account the key factors and their effects that relate to their reproduction, such as educational opportunities and holding a university degree.

Social Construction of the Race Versus Class Dilemma: Origins and Effects of Discrimination

Studies to identify the effects of race in a class society are essential for understanding the race issue in Brazil since the abolition of slavery. An exhaustive review of the literature on race relations and inequalities is beyond the scope of this chapter. However, we decided to choose at least three of the major interpretative approaches in studies of black social status and race relations in Brazil: (i) blacks occupy the worst social status because they have emerged from slavery, a time that, although had no racial prejudice, did have class prejudice; (ii) racial prejudice is a vestige of slavery, incompatible with development of a class society; and (iii) racial discrimination is a mechanism that leads to inequality by disqualifying blacks from competition, thus preserving privileges, as well as material and symbolic gains, for whites.

These perspectives began to take shape in the 1930s with Donald Pierson's 1935–1937 study, which resulted in the book *Brancos e pretos na Bahia* (Blacks and whites in Bahia) (Guimarães 2002). In that study, he concluded that Brazil represented a multiracial class society and that, although the upper classes were very light-skinned, prevailing prejudice was grounded not in race but in class.

In the 1950s, the issue of race and class was revisited from another perspective, this time in connection with what was known as the UNESCO project (1953–1956).[1] Although its original purpose was to investigate race relations in Brazil, particularly the absence of conflict, the results pointed in a different direction: its authors agreed that race affected the likelihood of social mobility and class structure as a result of both racial prejudice and the individual status of Afro-Brazilians following abolition. Nonetheless, there was no consensus as to the persistence of prejudice and its long-term effects as class society developed.

The study *Relações raciais entre negros e brancos em São Paulo*: *ensaio sociológico sobre as origens, as manifestações e os efeitos do preconceito de cor no município de São Paulo* (Race relations between blacks and whites in São Paulo: sociological essay on the origin, manifestations and effects of racial prejudice in the city of SP) by Florestan Fernandes and Roger Bastide, published in 1955, proved to be the landmark. Fernandes undertook a historical and sociological study in the city

[1] The UNESCO project was a series of UNESCO-funded studies on race relations in Brazil. The proposal rested on the belief, following studies in Brazil during the 1930s and 1940s that the tendency there was to unparalleled racial harmony. Studies were conducted in the cities of Recife, Salvador, Rio de Janeiro, and São Paulo.

of São Paulo, while Roger Bastide took a sociographic approach to describe the diversity of attitudes in race relations.

In the chapter *Cor e estrutura social em mudança* (The changing color and social structure), Florestan Fernandes considered the effects of racial prejudice on class society, calling this process one of accommodation between blacks and whites. He concluded that stratification, as reflected in the composition of the labor force, did not respond primarily to criteria of workers' race. He also asserted that the social conditions in which slave labor was exploited economically favored the formation of social symbols and behavior patterns that polarized the issue of race (Fernandes and Bastide 1955, p. 67). That is to say, prejudice existed, but it was not enough to explain the unequal status of blacks in the social structure.

Roger Bastide's research addressed the manifestations and effects of racial prejudice in everyday life and individual experience. Using various analytical techniques, he pointed to the societal factors that led to external manifestations of prejudice: the industrialization and urbanization of the city of São Paulo, the flow of immigrants, and the emergence of stratified social classes. These manifestations, however, coexisted with differential social conditions, a factor that masked conflict. Bastide argued that only in horizontal relations – that is, within the same social class – is it possible to distinguish racial prejudice from class prejudice.

In the 1970s, a new framework emerged in these studies, which continued to question the lower social positions of blacks in class society and the effects of racial prejudice in shaping that society. In this new line of research, the expression "racial prejudice" gave way to the term "discrimination," and the term "racial inequalities" became increasingly recurrent. A 1979 study by Hasenbalg established a dialog with studies of models of slavery from the standpoint of the relationship between slave and slave-owner and the process of transition to freedom, with a view toward developing an analysis of social relations after emancipation. That dialog paved the way to establishing his critique of both the theoretical approach that explained contemporary race relations as the after effect of slavery in the past and the perspective that argued that racism was incompatible with industrialization. To Hasenbalg, on the contrary, industrialization did not eliminate race as a criterion on which social relations were structured.

That study framed a new line of investigation, which became established in the 1980s and 1990s and was firmly grounded in statistical data and the increasingly refined use of quantitative analyses. Its results indicated extreme racial inequalities in a number of different fields.

During that period, demographic studies pointed to marked racial inequalities, especially with regard to the likelihood of surviving the first year of life and life expectancy at birth. Berquó (1988) examined data on mortality, marriage, and fertility rates to highlight the high levels of infant mortality in the poorer – mostly black- and brown-skinned – portions of the population. She reports that, in 1980, levels of infant mortality in these groups were the same as those among whites in 1960.

Studies of education and work have also highlighted strong inequalities among black and white children in completing fundamental education, even when class characteristics – such as social origin and per capita family income – are similar (Barcelos 1990; Hasenbalg and Silva 1988, 1990). Even wider disparities were found in access to, attendance at, and completion of secondary and higher education.

These educational inequalities are thought to affect access by different racial groups to employment and the occupation structure. Studies of blacks' share in the labor market, in examining the conditions surrounding their entry, have shown that differences in access to education decisively reflect access to employment (higher rates of unemployment) and the occupational structure, resulting in disproportionate confinement of blacks to less-skilled, lower-paying manual occupations (Bairros et al. 1992; Castro and Guimarães 1993; Hasenbalg 1979; Oliveira 1985; Silva and Lima 1992).

In addressing the relationship between family origin and racial inequality, Silva (1988) asks whether social heritage alone is enough to explain social differences between blacks and whites in Brazil, given that whites come from families that are better positioned in the social hierarchy, making it easier for them to reproduce their status. He divides his study into two stages: the first examines intergenerational social mobility and the second examines earnings to observe how monetary returns differ among people holding similar positions in the occupational hierarchy.

By examining intergenerational mobility for 1996, he concludes that whatever occupational group of origin is used as reference, blacks were concentrated in the lower occupational strata. Accordingly, considering the social mobility of racial groups distributed by occupation, blacks were exposed to a lesser likelihood of upward social mobility. The difficulties increased with stratum of origin, and those born into the higher strata were exposed to greater risks of downward mobility.

In looking at income, Silva suggests that earnings differentials by race are largely unrelated to the fact that whites were positioned primarily in the upper occupational strata, given that he compared differences in earnings among whites, blacks, and browns in the same occupational strata.

It can thus be seen that, throughout the 1980s and 1990s, a major analytical effort was made to identify the influence of the race attribute in the unequal position of blacks in school and in the labor market. The more recent agenda of studies has pursued that same question while advancing in empirical and methodological terms. It has also encountered significant changes in social structure in Brazil, as will be seen in the next section.

Racial Inequalities: Recent Changes

From mid-1990s on, especially since Brazil achieved economic stability, a series of changes have added to a process that has reduced social inequalities. The changes have been structural (economic stability and growth and their effects on the labor market) and demographic (declining fertility and alterations in the pattern of the working-age population). Changes have also resulted from the introduction of extremely important social policies to reduce the number of people in situations of poverty and to narrow inequalities in educational opportunity. Affirmative action policies in higher education have been especially important with regard to racial inequalities.

Two complementary analytical perspectives have considered changes in racial inequalities: (i) the reduction in inequalities is seen as resulting from advances in education and a narrowing of income inequalities, and (ii) diminishing differences among racial groups have contributed to reducing overall inequalities.

Paixão (2009) examined changes in the levels of poverty and extreme poverty in Brazil by comparing figures from the 1995 to 2006 National Household Sample Surveys (PNAD) and examining information on the race of government program beneficiaries (by household reference person). With regard to extreme poverty, he pointed out that participation by the white population in the extremely poor group had declined by 30.4%, while among blacks and browns, the percentage was slightly higher, at 33.4%. Despite this scenario, he showed that in 2006, 18.8% of blacks and browns and 8.0% of whites were still below the extreme poverty line. In 1995, 27.9% of whites and 43.6% of blacks and browns were below the poverty line, while in 2006, these percentages were 21.6% and 43.1%, respectively. He concludes that:

> Despite the percentage reduction in inequalities by color or race, when analyzed in terms of the respective paces at which the relative proportions of people below the poverty line declined, the asymmetries can be seen to have grown. Thus, in 1995, the proportion of poor blacks and browns was 93.9% greater than of poor whites. In 2006, meanwhile, the proportion of blacks and browns below the poverty line was 99.5% greater than the same proportion among whites. (PAIXÃO 2009, p. 9)

With regard to income transfer programs, Paixão reported that in 2004, in 67.6% of the households benefiting from some program of this nature, the household reference person was black or brown. What can be seen then is that a policy benefiting the poorest of the poor will almost certainly reflect in racial inequality. However, because the level of inequality was extremely high when these changes began, even though significant advances have been made, the black population still displays strong disadvantages. According to projections by the Institute for Applied Economic Research (IPEA), at the rate at which racial inequality in income diminished between 2001 and 2007, it would take 30 years before these groups had the same mean income (IPEA 2008).

Another useful perspective from which to understand the changes is given by considering to what extent racial inequality contributes to the trajectory of overall inequality. Ferreira et al. (2006) examined income inequality in Brazil from 1981 to 2004. They defined changes in groups' relative incomes as income effect changes and changes in the composition of the groups' characteristics (such as levels of education), as allocation-effect changes. By breaking down income levels and income variations across the entire period, they arrived at results showing that income effects and allocation effects were trending in the same direction as the reduction in inequalities. They argue that racial inequalities are diminishing (income effect), and at the same time, the groups' compositions are improving (allocation effect), which may be related to educational advances among non-whites.

Lastly, studies deploying various analytical models to examine processes of educational transition and social mobility are unanimous in finding that educational difficulties coincide with racial barriers. However, the race effect is more evident in odds of social mobility, the likelihood of losing social status, as well as in point toward larger racial inequality among those who are better educated and in higher-status occupational positions. Ribeiro (2006), who examined the effects of race and class of origin on the likelihood of making educational transitions, demonstrated unequal opportunities for making transitions from school to work, where the effects of class of origin were stronger than the effects of race. However, while the effect of class of origin diminished progressively over the various transitions, the effect of race increased in transitions at the higher levels, especially with regard to completing the first year of university and completing a university education. He reports that:

> The analyses indicated that there is inequality, by race and class of origin, in the likelihood of making transitions, although the latter type of inequality is greater than the former. In addition, while class inequality diminishes over the course of the transitions, racial inequality increases at transition five (completing the first year of university). Up to the fourth transition (completing middle school), the effects of class of origin are at least six times greater than the effects of race. In other words, up to the fourth transition, class inequality is greater than racial inequality. At the fifth and sixth transition (completing the first year of university and completing university), racial inequality becomes more similar to class inequality, given that the weight of class of origin is only 2.5 times greater than that of race. (Ribeiro 2006, pp. 863–864)

Race and Access to Education in Brazil

As mentioned in the previous section, the core objective and purpose of the sociology of race relations and racial inequalities, as it has been constituted, has been to establish the boundaries between race and class. The main challenge has been to contribute to an understanding of the relationship between discrimination and inequalities. While on the one hand, pioneering studies on the subject pointed to race and class as overlapping one another, more recent research claims that the persistence of racial inequalities does not come about solely as an effect of class. Discrimination becomes evident to the extent that the more salient aspects of class status are controlled and the racial inequalities endure.

Hasenbalg and Silva (2005) developed a model for analyzing socioeconomic accomplishment, so as to characterize a cumulative process of disadvantages with differential effect on blacks and browns. Their idea was to consider all the important factors in the trajectory toward individual socioeconomic fulfillment, with a view toward identifying the influence of race in that process.

The analysis began with the individual's family origin (observing the family's social status and the resources available to its members), continuing on through educational accomplishment, entry into and position in the labor market, and ending by analyzing the effects of these stages on the composition of income.

It is beyond the scope of this chapter to cover the cycle in full, but certain analytical options have been used here in light of the authors' intent, especially the stage dealing with internalization of resources. Access to formal education is considered to be an inequality-producing mechanism that affects racial inequality. Three aspects were chosen for the analysis presented here: first, the scenario of changes regarding access to school in Brazil; second, access to higher education and its effects in terms of income and the labor market; and, third, differences in the educational accomplishments of children of parents with higher education.

Some preliminary remarks are in order. The first has to do with racial classification. For nearly 30 years, studies of racial inequalities found that blacks (*pretos*) and browns (*pardos*) displayed similar socioeconomic profiles, leading a number of statistics analysts to aggregate these two categories (black and brown) and classify them as non-whites or negroes (Silva 1986). It is important to emphasize that this classification is not synonymous with race identity in Brazil and that current policy-related categories involve classification by both race (blacks and browns considered to be negroes or non-whites) and identity (indigenous people and quilombo descendants).[2] In the first analyses, the black and brown groups will be presented separately to highlight the similarity between them, and from then on, the text will refer to them as blacks, understood here as a descriptive category, aggregating the black and brown groups. The study period covers the 1980, 1990, 2000, and 2010 censuses.

The information to be treated falls into three distinct datasets. The first refers to Brazil's overall population, highlighting educational characteristics, particularly educational accomplishment among those of age 15–17 and age 18–24. A second dataset considers only those individuals who completed higher education. The third reports on education accomplishment among children whose parents completed higher education.

The educational landscape in Brazil should be understood both in terms of improvements to the education system and considering trends in Brazil's demographics and the effects of socioeconomic changes. The demographic feature that has most left an imprint on this process is population age structure, measured not only by age but also by cohort, which helps understand the phenomena associated with the period in which each individual gained access to (or should have gained access to) education (Collares 2009).

---

[2] Note here the peculiar status of indigenous groups in statistics. Underrepresentation of the indigenous population is associated with a number of factors. As a segment separate from other groups, they were first recorded in 1872 and 1890 as *caboclos* (mestizos) and, in subsequent censuses, in residual categories or together with "yellows" [Asians]. From the 1940 census onward, indigenous people and *caboclos* became "brown," an indistinct category that could also refer to *mulattos*, *morenos*, etc. It was not until the 1991 census that the category of "indigenous" was introduced. We decided to exclude the group from analysis in this study.

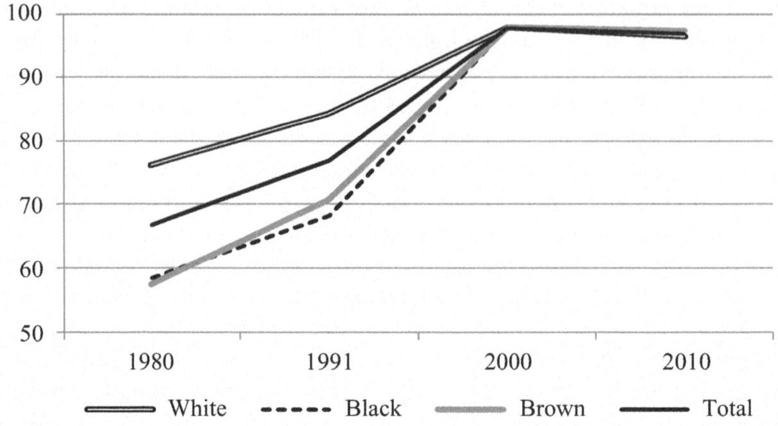

Graph 1 Net enrolment rates in primary school (age 7–14), by race Brazil, 1980–2010 (%). (Source: IBGE. Demographic censuses 1980–2010 (tabulation by CEM))

The graphs below show changes in net enrolment rates by level of education and race.[3] In the case of primary education, Graph 1 shows a trend toward universalization in all racial groups, indicating that by the 1980s, performance by the black and brown groups was already very similar and considerably inferior to the white groups. These figures show that school attendance is practically universal (98%) only in primary school, corresponding to the age range of 7–14. Studies nonetheless indicate that the challenges facing education in Brazil begin with progression at this level. In a study of access to school in Brazil, by income and race, Andrade and Dachs (2007) found that access to the early years of primary school is practically universal among age 7–10, regardless of class and race, but in the age 11–14, the situation strays from the universal, and there is stronger variation by income and race (Andrade and Dachs 2007, p. 405).

With regard to the participation by students age 15–17 in high school (Graph 2), the changes have not altered the situation, which remains highly unequal. From 1980 to 1990, enrolment rates changed little, but then expansion in the 1990s gave whites a significant advantage over blacks and browns (23.8%, 6.4%, and 8.7%, respectively). In 2000, all groups benefited from the expansion of coverage in the 1990s, but the gap between racial groups continued to be wide, with blacks and browns displaying similar trends. It was only in 2010 that racial inequalities declined more significantly: among those ages 15–17, 68.1% of whites attended high school, while the percentages of blacks and browns were 49.3% and 53.7%, respectively.

[3] Net enrolment rate refers to students' participation in the level of education considered appropriate to their age group, i.e., age 7–14 at primary school, age 15–17 at high school, and age 18–24 enrolled in higher education. The rate is calculated by dividing the total number studying at the appropriate level of education in each age group by the total number of individuals in that age group.

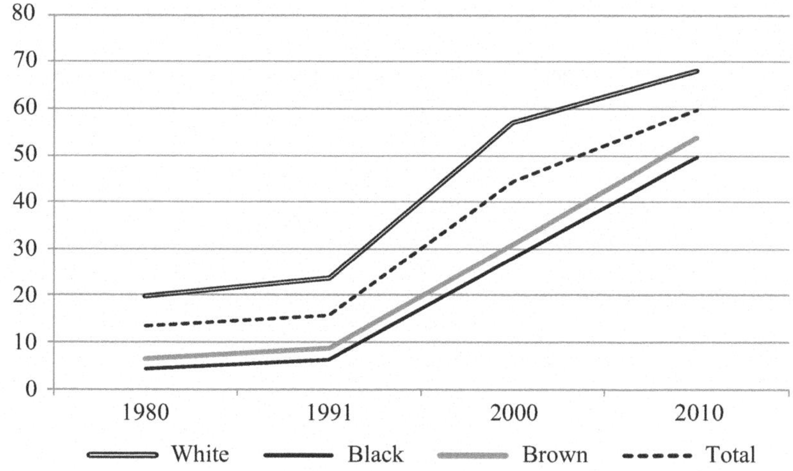

Graph 2 Net enrolment rates in high school (age 15–17), by color/race Brazil, 1980–2010 (%). (Source: IBGE. Demographic censuses 1980–2010 (tabulation by CEM))

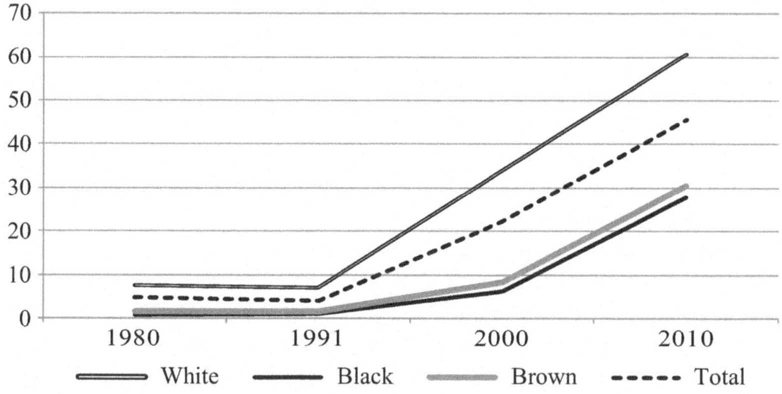

Graph 3 Net enrolment rates in higher education (age 18–24), by race Brazil, 1980–2010 (%). (Source: IBGE. Demographic censuses 1980–2010 (tabulation by CEM))

The participation of black and brown students in high school has certainly increased. That change is extremely important to the discussions of access to higher education that have taken shape from 2000 on. Growth in access to high school has driven demand for access to higher education, which grew only slightly over the course of the 1990s.

Among students age 18–24, as can be seen in Graph 3, net enrolment rates are lower and racial inequalities even more considerable. Once again, participation by all groups can be seen to grow strongly, starting from their clearly differentiated shares by race in the 1980s, at which point the rates among blacks and browns were practically null. Even though enrolment rates have increased by 2010, however,

Table 1 Net enrolment rates in higher education (age 18–24), by income quintile and race Brazil, 1990–2010 (%)

Level	Income	Race/color	1991 (%)	2000 (%)	2010 (%)
Higher – age 18–24	1st quintile	White	1.2	3.7	25.5
		Black	0.1	0.4	8.1
		Brown	0.2	0.8	8.4
		Total	0.5	1.7	13.5
	2nd quintile	White	1.3	5.7	30.3
		Black	0.3	1.3	14.4
		Brown	0.5	2.0	17.0
		Total	0.8	3.4	21.6
	3rd quintile	White	2.6	12.8	49.3
		Black	0.7	3.5	25.9
		Brown	1.2	5.5	34.4
		Total	1.9	9.1	41.2
	4th quintile	White	6.5	30.4	68.7
		Black	2.1	12.0	49.2
		Brown	3.1	15.4	54.8
		Total	5.2	24.8	63.0
	5th quintil	White	19.3	66.0	86.0
		Black	4.9	33.0	73.5
		Brown	6.1	41.5	76.5
		Total	15.2	61.3	83.5

Source: IBGE. Demographic censuses, 1990–2010 (tabulation by CEM)

there was still a wide gap between the racial groups, with blacks and browns displaying very similar trends.[4]

When race groups' participation in higher education is examined by income quintile (Table 1), considerable changes can be seen to have occurred.[5] First, note the low participation by all race groups in the poorest (first income quintile) up to 2000. Not until 2010 can participation by this quintile be seen to grow, most significantly among whites. To summarize, in 2010, among the poorest 20%, the enrolment rate among white students age 18–24 was 25.5% and among blacks and browns, 8.1% and 8.4%, respectively. That is quite significant inequality for such a recent period.

Meanwhile, the population figures for the upper income quintile (fifth quintile) reveal that from 1991 on, racial inequalities in this group have declined significantly. In 1980, 18.5% of white students age 18–24 in the wealthiest quintile attended higher education. Among blacks and browns, the rates were 4.0% and

[4]The chapter by Carlos Costa Ribeiro and Rogerio Schlegel points to significant differences between blacks and browns in terms of the university degree programs chosen. There seems to be a trend for the gap between blacks and browns to widen (the advantage being with the latter) in the upper strata, whether educational, via university degree, or in the labor market.

[5]In calculations by income quintile, the values express the percentages of people within each quintile who reached higher education. Each quintile represents 20% of the population, the first comprising the poorest 20% and the fifth, the wealthiest 20%.

7.3%, respectively. In 2010, the rates were 86% among whites, 73.5% among blacks, and 76.5% among browns, the slight difference persisting between the latter two groups (blacks and browns).

In sum, when racial inequalities are compared by quintile (among the wealthiest and the poorest), poor Afro-Brazilians can be seen to encounter greater difficulties in attaining higher levels of education than poor whites.

Reproduction of Inequalities: The Race Attribute Among University Graduates

In order to examine the reproduction of racial inequalities and bearing in mind that formal schooling and access to the various levels of education constitute one of the key mechanisms in such process, this section will focus primarily on university graduates. To analyze type of occupation and income of university graduates, all individuals who had completed any undergraduate program in each of the study years were considered.

This study is divided into two parts. It first highlights the differences in the labor market for those with higher education, focusing on their socioeconomic destination and controlling for academic field (degree) and occupation, with a view toward highlighting inequalities in access to stratification mechanisms (schooling). The second part then considers differences in educational accomplishment among children of parents who are university graduates, that is, children and young people with quite similar socioeconomic origins.

Table 2 shows changes in the population with higher education in Brazil and its racial makeup, in absolute and relative terms. Despite the undeniable increase in participation by blacks, the composition is still clearly unequal. In 1980, Afro-Brazilians accounted for 9.3% of university graduates and, in 2010, 24.7%; that is, whites were still in a substantial majority. Meanwhile, what is striking about percentage growth within the groups is that the group of black university graduates increased with the same considerable intensity – nearly three times (growth of 290%) – in both the 1980s and the 2000s. Although there is a certain similarity in percentage growth among blacks, the difference that emerges is that, among whites, the increase in the 2000s (102%) is significantly smaller than in the 1980s (133%), suggesting a different dynamic in the decrease in inequalities. Note also the peculiarity of the 1990s: in proportional terms, the composition does not change over the decade, and growth rates are much lower.

Graph 4, below, which also considers only university graduates, offers two types of information: the bars show the proportion of blacks within occupational strata over time and the lines show the proportion of blacks among total university graduates by year. The previous table showed that participation by Afro-Brazilians in this educational stratum grew from 9.3% in 1980 to 24.7% in 2010. By combining these two datasets, Graph 4 makes it possible to indicate whether the variations within the occupational strata are more or less marked than the variation in the proportion of

Table 2 Distribution of population with complete higher education and growth rates, by race Brazil, 1980–2010

	1980		1991		2000		2010		Growth rates (%)		
Race	N	%	N	%	N	%	N	%	1980–1991	1991–2000	2000–2010
Blacks	140,449	9.30	547,572	14.60	853,539	14.50	3,326,957	24.70	290.0	56.0	290.0
Whites	1,372,813	90.70	3,198,828	85.40	5,014,281	85.50	10,136,734	75.30	133.0	57.0	102.0

Source: IBGE. Demographic censuses 1980–2010 (tabulation by CEM)

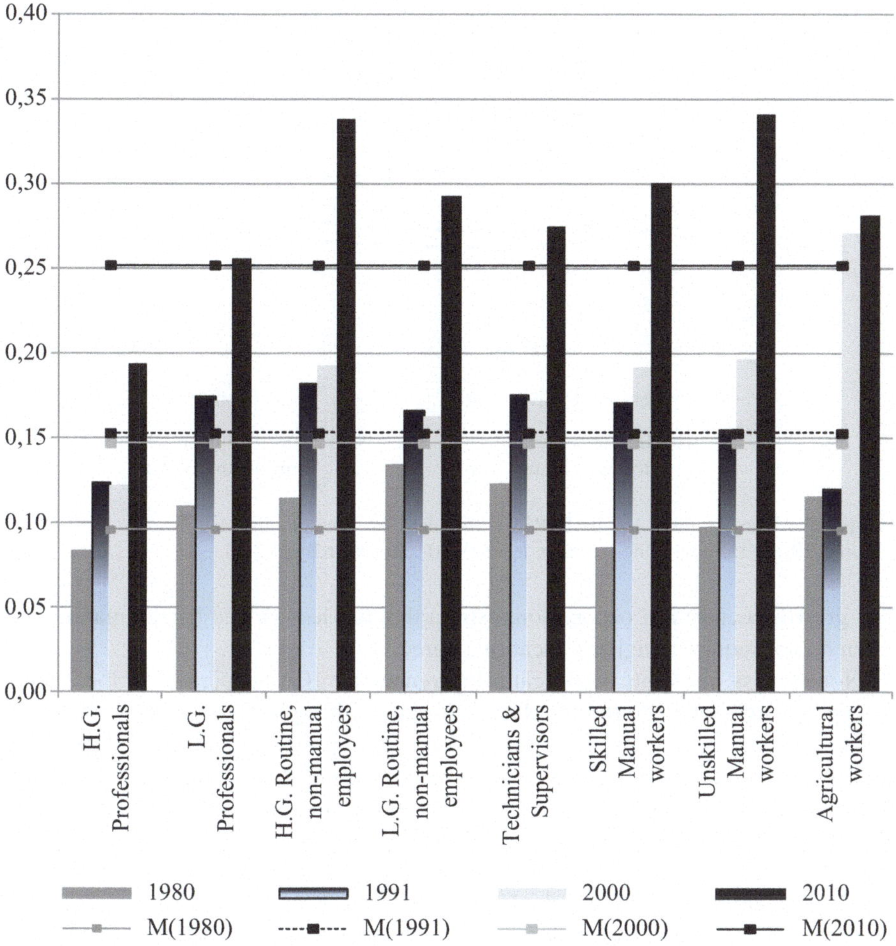

Graph 4 Percentage of black university graduates, by occupational group Brazil, 1980–2010 (Source: IBGE. Demographic censuses 1980–2010 (tabulation by CEM))

blacks in total university graduates. This avoids possible interpretative bias, which could result from the process of racial reclassification that has taken place, particularly from the mid-2000 on.

Looking at the differences between the beginning and the end of the period, it is in the higher-grade routine non-manual, skilled manual, and unskilled manual occupational classes that participation by blacks (in percentage terms) grew more than their overall participation among university graduates. The proportion of blacks in each of these occupational strata, in 1980, was 11.5%, 8.5%, and 9.8%, respectively, and in 2010, it was 33.8%, 30%, and 34.2%, respectively. This shows that the changes that occurred over these 30 years produced varying degrees of permeability to entry by blacks into the university graduate occupational field. Their participation

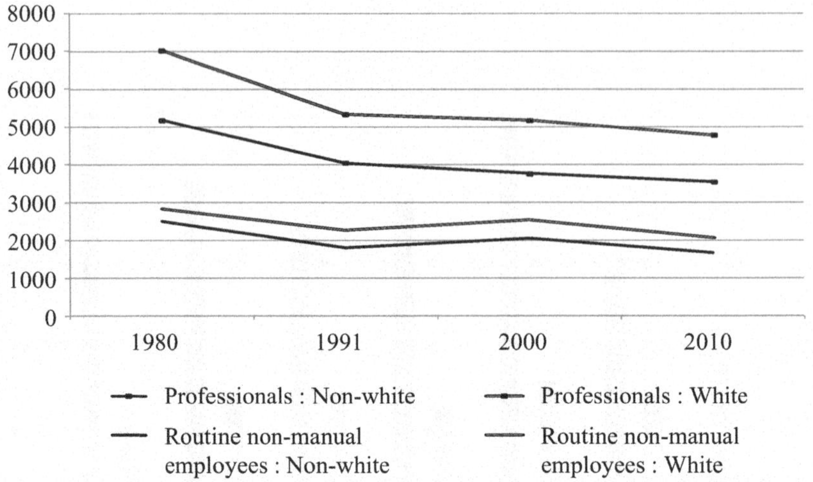

Graph 5 Mean earnings (in BRL R$) from main occupation, by race Brazil, 1980–2010. (Source: IBGE. Demographic censuses 1980–2010 (tabulation by CEM))

and growth occurred in occupational strata that are less valued by the market and often do not require a higher education degree.

Nonetheless, there are significant differences by 10-year period. In the 1980s, despite strong growth in the number of blacks with higher education, only in the skilled manual workers group (8.6%) did the increase exceed the overall mean by more than 1%, indicating a relatively stable situation. Meanwhile, to some extent, the 1990s reflect the labor market characteristics at the time. Although the percentage of blacks among total graduates remained practically constant, there was considerable growth in occupation in the unskilled and agricultural manual workers categories, which are precisely the lowest occupations in the social hierarchy.

Lastly, the 2000s mark an increase in the percentage of blacks in all occupational strata, but (as mentioned earlier) that result has to be offset against overall growth in the black population. If that dimension is discounted, it can be said that it was among the higher- and lower-grade routine non-manual workers and unskilled workers that growth in occupation actually occurred. Accordingly, although the occupational structure proved more receptive to a less disproportionate entry by black graduates, inequality in access to the upper levels of the hierarchy persisted.

The next step offers a more detailed analysis of the dynamics of inequality among the groups of professions, more precisely those where blacks are more under-represented. Graph 5 shows differences in earnings within the professional and routine manual occupational groups, considering only university graduates. Although there is a clear downward trend in earnings in all strata, blacks in these two groups earn less than whites. That difference can be seen to be greater in the upper group (professionals), reinforcing the idea that racial inequality tends to increase; the higher up one is in the social hierarchy.

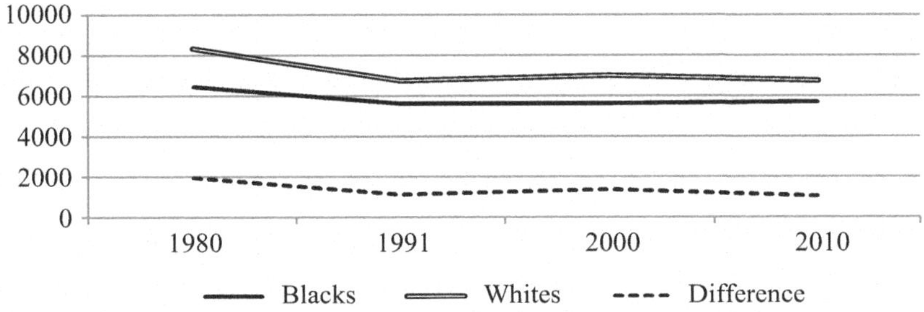

Graph 6 Mean earnings (in BRL R$) in the main occupation of graduate in "imperial professions," by race Brazil, 1980–2010. (Source: IBGE. Demographic censuses 1980–2010 (tabulation by CEM))

One possible objection to this interpretation may be that earnings inequality within the major occupational groups is due to the fact that whites tend to hold more highly-valued degrees than blacks. These differences can be controlled for, as in Graph 6, which shows earnings within occupational groups, while controlling for degree type.

This analysis will be even more specific in order to facilitate the comparison of earning differences within groups. For that purpose, certain professions have been selected. First, mean and median earnings within the occupational group were considered, by university graduate program, and the upper and lower limits of the distribution were identified, aggregating into two groups:

- Group 1: "Imperial professions": Medicine, Engineering, and Law (three highest mean salaries in 1980)[6]
- Group 2: "Low-prestige professions": Languages, History, and Education (three lowest salaries in 1980)

Graphs 6 and 7 corroborate the interpretation that there are differences in earnings between blacks and whites among individuals who hold the same degree and are in the same occupational category. Among professionals with less valued degrees, the difference in earnings is practically constant over time (around R$500.00). For those with degrees in the "imperial professions," there is a decline in the 1980s, slight growth in the 1990s, and a discreet drop in the 2000s.

Taking into account that there were still earning gaps between whites and blacks, although quite small, among those in the low-prestige professions, the point turns out to be what is the participation by Afro-Brazilians in these groups. Table 3 displays information about that.

[6] Medicine, Engineering, and Law were established as university programs at the imperial period (1822–1889). At that time, holding a degree meant a higher status than having a profession. Nonetheless, holding a diploma worked as a strong instrument of exclusion (COELHO 1999).

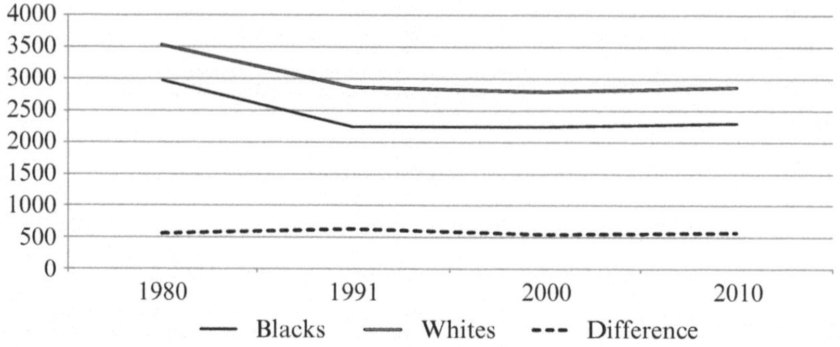

Graph 7 Mean earnings (in BRL R$) in the main occupation of graduate in "low-prestige professions," by race Brazil, 1980–2010. (Source: IBGE. Demographic censuses, 1980–2010 (tabulation by CEM))

Table 3 Distribution of population with higher education, by selected courses and race Brazil, 1980–2010

Selected courses and race	1980	1991	2000	2010
Medicine, Law, Engineering				
Total	100	100	100	100
Blacks	8.7	12.9	11.8	17.9
Whites	91.3	87.1	88.2	82.1
Languages, History, Education				
Total	100	100	100	100
Blacks	11.2	19.9	21.5	35.7
Whites	88.8	80.1	78.5	64.3

Source: IBGE. Demographic censuses 1980–2010 (tabulation by CEM)

Table 3 shows that change was underway; but once again, note that the prestige of a degree is an important component in the composition of racial inequalities. Blacks are managing to expand their participation in higher education but, among those who complete higher education, significant differences can be seen in terms not only of occupation but also of university degree program. Their participation has expanded faster in less prestigious degree programs, and they still get differentiated earnings.

Educational Accomplishment of Children of University Graduates

From the foregoing, it can be said that racial barriers turned out to be lower, given the expansion of educational opportunities at the fundamental level from the 1980s onward and, at the middle and higher levels, from 2000s on. However, a closer look

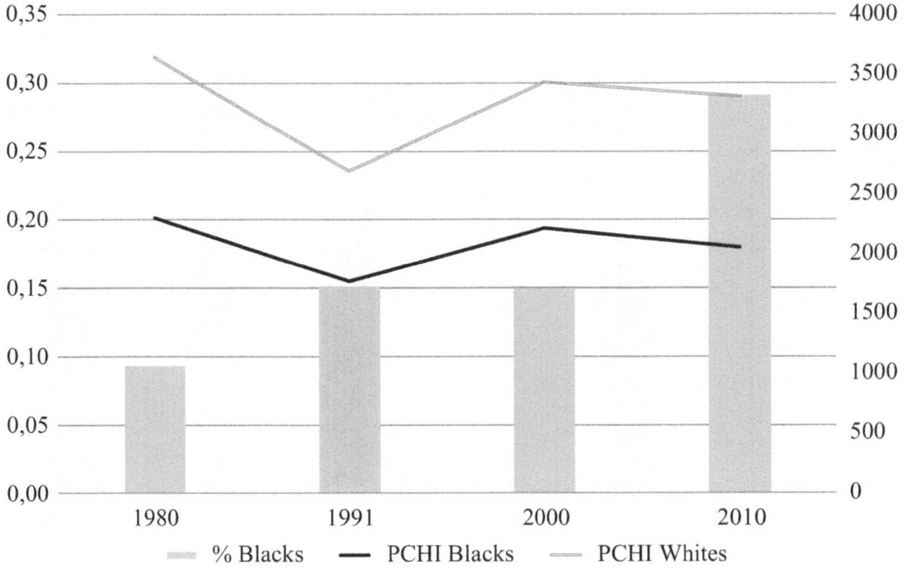

Graph 8 Percentage of blacks in families with graduate parents and family per capita household income by race Brazil, 1980–2010. (Source: IBGE. Demographic censuses 1980–2010 (Special Tabulation by CEM))

at higher education graduates reveals the persistence of significant racial inequalities. Considering the prominence given to the issue of social origin in this book and in the literature on the subject, we examined the educational accomplishment of those who are children of university graduates.

Households were selected where at least one reference person or spouse had completed higher education. In this case, the race of the household reference person was then considered. In light of that information, the educational accomplishments of the children were analyzed. We selected households in which there was at least one child older than age 14 (analyses were not conducted to examine the transitions "entrance to primary education" and "completion of 4 years of school"). Graph 8 shows the proportion of blacks in this group (whose parents hold university degrees) and per capita household income of whites and blacks. In 1980, only 9.3% of children among university graduates were black; in 1990, that percentage had risen to 15.1% and held steady in 2000 (14.9%). In 2010, the percentage had jumped to 29.1%. In terms of income, children in the white group are seen to be at a significant advantage. In 2010, per capita household income among whites was R$3,313.14 and, among blacks, R$2058.10.

These figures show that among children of university graduates, whites have an overwhelming presence, with strong advantages in terms of income. That scenario reveals the likelihood of educational accomplishment on the part of the children. The idea of this longitudinal analysis is to capture how the educational accomplishments of children of graduates were differentiated by race.

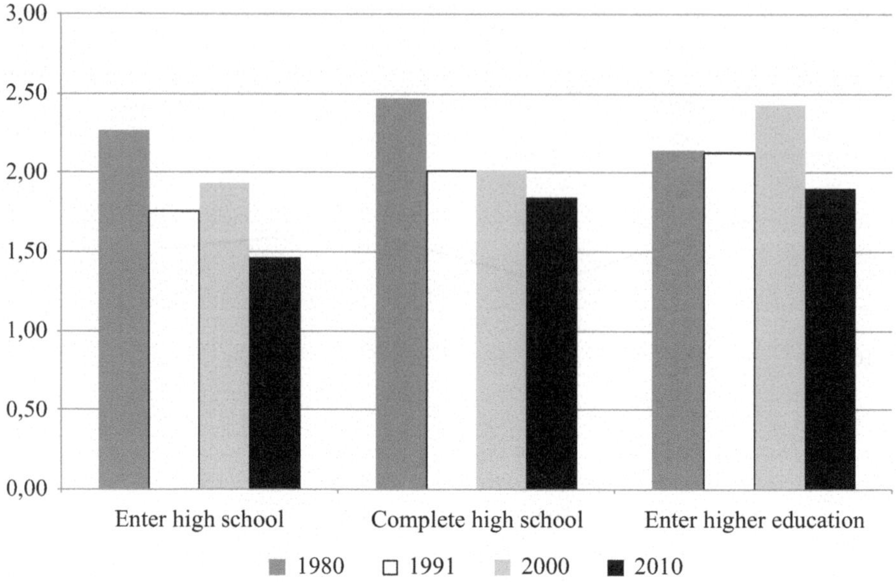

Graph 9 Odds ratios of whites making the education transitions Brazil, 1980–2010. (Source: IBGE. Demographic censuses, 1980–2010 (tabulation by CEM); Note: Considering only those who made the previous transition)

Graph 9 shows the odds ratios[7] of children of university graduates completing the three education transitions (entering high school, completing high school, and entering higher education). This graph answers the following question: considering only individuals who completed one stage of schooling, what are the odds of their entering the subsequent stage?

Overall, racial inequalities diminished over time at the three transition points, although with some specific features. Advantage by whites at entrance to high school declined (from 2.25 times to 1.5) and then increased slightly between 1990 and 2000. The position of whites at completion of high school declined abruptly between 1980 and 1990 and then steadied between 1990 and 2000, before falling slightly between 2000 and 2010. The advantage of white children at entry to higher

[7]The odds ratio analysis considered "success rate" within each group and the ratios among the groups. That is:

$$\text{Odds ratio} = \left(\text{Pw}/1-\text{Pw}\right)/\left(\text{Pn}/1-\text{Pn}\right) = \text{Pw}\times\left(1-\text{Pn}\right)/\text{Pn}\times\left(1-\text{Pw}\right),$$

where Pw is the proportion of whites who reached the level of schooling and Pn is the proportion of Afro-Brazilians who reached the same level of schooling. Lower values mean smaller inequalities.

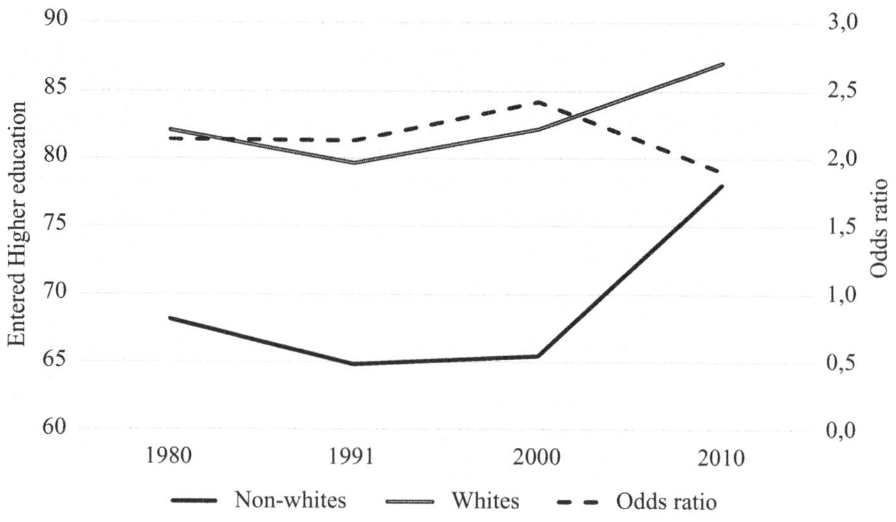

Graph 10 Proportion and odds ratio of entrance to higher education among children of university graduates by race (1) (over age 18) Brazil, 1980–2010. (Source: IBGE. Demographic censuses 1980–2010 (tabulation by CEM); Note: (1) Completed high school and entered higher education)

education was unchanged between 1980 and 1990, increased between 1990 and 2000, and diminished between 2000 and 2010.

This analysis is concerned about highlighting the odds of children's managing to follow their parents into higher education. The graph below shows specific data on that transition. Slightly greater inequality can be seen among those who completed high school and entered higher education. Among whites, 87.1% entered university and among blacks, 78.1% (Graph 10).

By analyzing the odds ratio curve, we can see that from 1980 to 1990, the advantage on the part of whites did not change; from 1990 to 2000, it increased, and from 2000 to 2010 it diminished, again underscoring the specific features of the latter period with regard to the changing trend in the racial landscape of Brazil.

Conclusion

This chapter has attempted to show that race is an important attribute in understanding overall social inequalities. This research agenda has always faced the need to address the core issue of race and class. That difficulty is not exclusive to Brazilian society but does gain very specific features there. This becomes clear when reviewing classic studies on the subject in Brazil, where distinctions are made between analysis of inequalities and analysis of race relations.

With regard to racial inequalities, the data are clear and show how the cumulative process of socioeconomic disadvantage not only maintained the black population at the base of the social pyramid but also displayed a strong capacity for reproduction, causing several generations of this group to encounter increased difficulty in social mobility (Lima 2001; Hasenbalg et al. 1999). Based on the census data, this chapter has examined educational accomplishment, occupational placement, and earnings by blacks and whites who belong to the same income quintile or hold a higher education diploma or still have parents who are university graduates in an effort to investigate the race effect within similar conditions.

The most significant findings indicate that, although racial inequalities have diminished from the high levels seen in the 1980s, impressive rates are still to be found in 2010. Also, family income affects the reduction in inequalities, resulting in fewer imbalances within income quintiles.

In the case of education accomplishment, it is important to highlight how trends in racial disparities are linked to configuration of the school system over the time. At the primary level, for example, the expansion of the public provision after 1990 has led to universalization of access. On the other hand, even though a significant increase in entrance to high school has also occurred, the levels of inequality by race in 2010 are still higher. This demonstrates that public policy has been more successful in mining inequalities at the base of the system than at the intermediate levels.

A different pattern regarding entrance to higher education has also been found. At the beginning of the period, less than 5% of the population had the opportunity to access the university (and white people made up nearly 100% of this group). With the beginning of expansion of the university system in 1990, the levels of inequality increased, demonstrating that whites benefited most from this process. After the 2000s, however, the scenario changed, and a downward trend in racial inequalities at this level has appeared. However, even considering these improvements, racial and social disparities persist.

In sum, educational accomplishment on the part of blacks has improved during this period. However, these improvements should be considered from three aspects. First, there has been improvement of the school system as a whole. That is, all racial groups improved. Second, at some educational levels, especially high school and higher education, blacks had an insignificant net attendance participation rate (less than 1% in the 1980s). Thus, any gain exerts a substantial impact. Third, although affirmative action policies are recent in Brazil, their impact has already been perceived regarding the flow of young blacks into higher education after 2000. A good example of the effects of these policies is the number of students who attend higher education because of the university program for all, ProUni.[8] Between 2005 and 2015, the program distributed one million scholarships, half of them targeting black and brown students.

---

[8] ProUni (Programa Universidade para Todos/University for All) was established in 2004. The program seeks to provide full or partial scholarships to low-income students to pursue undergraduate programs at private colleges and universities. The candidate for a ProUni scholarship must have graduated from a public primary school and high school and must have per capita family income of no more than the equivalent of three minimum wages. ProUni has adopted the quota system for candidates self-identified as black, brown, or indigenous at the time of applying for the scholarship. The percentage of scholarships reserved for those groups is determined by the proportion of these groups in the population of the candidate's state.

Considering the current economic crisis and government budget cuts, it is possible that these recent gains will be hampered by the low priority given to social programs in Brazil at times of crisis.

With regard to return on investment in higher education, belonging to the university graduate group is an important – but not decisive – factor in reducing racial inequality. Among the university degree programs selected, there are differences in placement in occupational strata, while wage distortions continue even among individuals with similar qualifications and placement.

Lastly, having university graduates as parents has a decisive impact on the educational progress of children. In this item, racial inequality is expressed in the small percentages of blacks whose parents hold university degrees and in the greater inequality that these young people encounter in making the transition from high school to entrance to university. Even so, those differences have diminished over time.

References

Andrade, C., & Dachs, J. (2007, May/August). Acesso à educação por faixas etárias segundo a renda e a cor. *Cadernos de Pesquisa, 37*(131).

Bairros, L., et al. (1992). *Negros e brancos num mercado de trabalho em mudança* (pp. 32–54). Rio de Janeiro: ANPOCS.

Barcelos, L. (1990). Raça e oportunidades educacionais no Brasil. *Estudos Afro-Asiáticos*, Rio de Janeiro, *18*, 73–91.

Berquó, E. (1988). Demografia da desigualdade: algumas considerações sobre os negros no Brasil. *Anais da Abep*. Olinda, *3*, 89–110.

Castro N., Guimarães, A. S. (1993). Desigualdades raciais no mercado e nos locais de trabalho. Estudos Afro- Asiáticos, Rio de Janeiro, 24, 23–60.

Coelho, E. (1999). *As profissões imperiais: medicina, engenharia e advocacia no Rio de Janeiro (1822–1930)*. Rio de Janeiro: Record.

Collares, A. C. (2009). *The Expansion of Higher Education in Brazil between 1982 and 2006: Disentangling age, period and cohort effects*. Paper presented at the 33rd Meeting of the Associação Nacional de Pós Graduação e Pesquisa em Ciências Sociais, Caxambu.

Fernandes, F., & Bastide, R. (1955). *Relações raciais entre negros e brancos em São Paulo: ensaio sociológico sobre as origens, as manifestações e os efeitos do preconceito de cor no município de São Paulo*. São Paulo: Anhembi.

Ferreira, F., et al. (2006). Ascensão e queda da desigualdade de renda no Brasil. *Econômica*, Rio de Janeiro: Universidade Federal Fluminense (UFF), *8*.

Guimarães, A. S. A. (2002). *Classes, raças e democracia*. São Paulo: Editora 34.

Hasenbalg, C. (1979). *Discriminação e desigualdades raciais no Brasil*. Rio de Janeiro: Graal.

Hasenbalg, C., & Silva, N. (1988). *Estrutura social, mobilidade e raça*. São Paulo/Rio de Janeiro: Vértice/IUPERJ.

Hasenbalg, C. & Silva, N. V. (1990). Raça e oportunidades educacionais no Brasil. Estudos Afro-Asiáticos, 18, 73–91.

Hasenbalg, C. et al. (1999). Cor e estratificação social. Rio de Janeiro, Contra Capa Livraria.

Hasenbalg, C., & Silva, N. (2000). Tendências da desigualdade educacional no Brasil. *Dados – Revista de Ciências Sociais, 43*(3), 423–445.

Hasenbalg, C., & Silva, N. (orgs.). (2005). *Origens e destinos: desigualdades sociais ao longo da vida*. Rio de Janeiro: Topbooks.

IPEA. (2008). Educação, Juventude, Raça/cor. *Comunicados da Presidência*. Brasília.

Lima, M. (2001). Serviço de preto, serviço de branco: representações sobre cor e trabalho no Brasil. Tese (Doutorado) - IFCS/UFRJ.

Oliveira, L. et al. (1985). O lugar do negro na força de trabalho. Rio de Janeiro: IBGE, 1985.

Paixão, M. (2009, June). Níveis de intensidade da pobreza e indigência sobre os grupos de cor ou raça no Brasil e estimação dos efeitos das políticas governamentais de transferências de rendimentos sobre as desigualdades. In Congresso da Associação de Estudos Latino-Americanos. Rio de Janeiro.

Ribeiro, C. A. C. (2006). Classe, raça e mobilidade social no Brasil. *Dados* [online], *49*(4), 833–873. ISSN 0011–5258.

Silva, N. do V. (1986). Updating the cost of not being white in Brazil. In P. M. Fontaine (Ed.), *Race, class and power in Brazil* (Vol. 1, 1st ed., pp. 42–55). Los Angeles: UCLA/CAAS.

Silva, N. do V.. (1988), "Cor e Processo de Realização Socioeconômica", in C. Hasenbalg e N. V. Silva (eds.), Estrutura Social, Mobilidade e Raça. Rio de Janeiro, Vértice.

Silva, D. F., & Lima, M. (1992). Raça, gênero e mercado de trabalho. *Estudos Afro-Asiáticos, 23*, 97–111, Rio de Janeiro.

Part III
Public Policies

The Geography of Access to Basic Services in Brazil

Marta Arretche

Abstract This chapter analyzes the long-term path of access to public services in Brazil from 1970 to 2010. It shows that the supply of services completely changed over this period, from widespread lack of basic services in 1970 to high levels of coverage in 2010. However, the path of such expansion had a distinctly regional pattern, to the extent that it cannot be fully explained by an individual's income. Instead, the path of coverage expansion is characterized by a strong association between access to services, on the one hand, and the wealth of jurisdictions along with the profile of its population income on the other hand. Progress in the production of wealth tends to be accompanied by reduction in the percentage of poor and by expansion in the supply of basic services. Improvements in coverage rates also followed a fairly clear spatial pattern: the Southeast region, Brazil's wealthiest, and particularly the state of São Paulo, was better served in the 1970s and moved toward universalization as early as the 1980s. The expansion of coverage toward universalization occurred subsequently in the South and Central-West regions, which happen to be in an intermediary position with regard to wealth and concentrated poverty. Yet the North and Northeast regions, Brazil's poorest, only achieved high coverage levels when the service in question had already achieved universal levels in the three previously mentioned regions. This chapter relies on data collected in Brazilian censuses from 1970 to 2010.

Keywords Territorial inequality · Access to services · Water · Sanitation · Electricity

---

The author thanks Patrick Silva, Rogerio Barbosa, and Edgard Fusaro for their valuable collaboration in preparing the statistical data, as well as Jose Donizete Cazzolato in the production of the maps. This final version has benefited from comments by Argelina Figueiredo, Edgard Fusaro, Eduardo Marques, Kenneth Roberts, Patrick Silva, and Peter Ward as well as the participants of the "II Workshop of the Census Project," held in March 2013 at CEBRAP, and the Seminar "Trajectories of Inequality in Brazil," held at the Brazil Institute of the Woodrow Wilson Center, in Washington, DC in February 2016.

M. Arretche (✉)
Department of Political Science, University of São Paulo, São Paulo, Brazil
e-mail: arretche@usp.br

M. Arretche (ed.), *Paths of Inequality in Brazil*,
https://doi.org/10.1007/978-3-319-78184-6_7

Territorial inequality in the provision of public goods is an understudied topic in social science. Literature on inequality has focused on income, while literature on public service provision favors inequality of access among individuals. What is more, literature on territorial inequality tends to concentrate on either fiscal transfers or economic growth.

There are good reasons to scrutinize the long-term path of both access to public services and their territorial distribution though. First of all, the concept of well-being entrenched throughout the twentieth century as a result of the incorporation of social rights into the notion of citizenship (Marshall 1967) does not refer to income alone. Instead, it is associated with citizens' rights to civilized life according to the current societal standards to which all citizens are entitled. As a result, a decent life should also include access to a number of collective goods, which citizens have right to enjoy regardless of personal income (Esping-Andersen 1985, 1990; Marshall 1967; Rawls 1971; Sen 1999).

Although the literature concerning the welfare state presents evidence that income inequality does not necessarily translate into inequality in living conditions, provided the latter are designed as a way to reduce inequality, it seldom examined within-country distribution of public services. Instead, this literature assumes a variant of methodological nationalism, according to which a given phenomenon is assumed to display even distribution across the territory.

This chapter attempts to fill the gap by analyzing the long-term path of access to public services in Brazil in the past 40 years. First and foremost, we begin by noting that the supply of services completely changed over this period. In the 1970s, the lack of basic services – water, sewage, and electricity – along with low educational levels were widespread in nearly the entire country. In 2010, on the other hand, at least 90% of the population in 91% of Brazil's municipalities had access to electricity.[1] In 1,868 municipalities – out of 5,564 – at least 80% of citizens were supplied with water. In 2,190 municipalities – 40% of the total – at least 80% of the population had garbage collection services. Between 1980 and 2010, the infant mortality rate in Brazil fell from 69 to 16 per 1,000 live births, and life expectancy rose from 62 to 73 years.[2] The population age 18 and older who attained secondary education went from 6.2 to 39.7 million, and those attaining higher education went from 3.4 to 21.5 million. Both populations enjoyed a sixfold increase during the period.

Secondly, and even more importantly, the path of expansion in the provision of services has shown a distinctly regional pattern to the extent that it cannot be fully explained by an individual's income. Instead, the path of coverage expansion is characterized by a strong association between access to services, on the one hand, and the wealth of jurisdictions along with the profile of its population income on the

[1] The differences in coverage rates reported in the chapter "Housing and Urban Conditions in Brazil" by Eduardo Marques (in this volume) refer to the inclusion of the rural population in my analysis.

[2] See the chapter "Health and Inequality in Brazil" by Vera Schattan Coelho and Marcelo Dias in this volume.

other hand. While it is impossible to determine the direction of this causality, the fact remains that improvements within these different dimensions of well-being tended to occur together. Progress in the production of wealth tends to be accompanied by a reduction in the percentage of poor and by expansion in the supply of basic services.

Improvements in coverage rates also followed a fairly clear spatial pattern: the Southeast region, Brazil's wealthiest, and particularly the state of São Paulo, was better served in the 1970s and moved toward universalization as early as the 1980s. The expansion of coverage toward universalization occurred subsequently in the South and Central-West regions, which happen to be in an intermediary position with regard to wealth and concentrated poverty. Yet the North and Northeast regions, Brazil's poorest, only achieved high coverage levels when the service in question had already achieved universal levels in the three previously mentioned regions.

As a result, the geography of public service supply in Brazil shows that nationwide, medium to high coverage rates of access can be associated with an unequal spatial distribution, meaning that some regions display very low provision rates, while others enjoy nearly universal access. Therefore, the question to be answered is not whether territorial inequality did in fact decrease, but rather, what direction did the decrease take? In other words, what is the association between such coverage expansion and the wealth of the jurisdiction or the population benefited?

This chapter relies on data collected in Brazilian censuses from 1970 to 2010. It is therefore possible to explore the extent to which key contexts in Brazilian history contributed to the incremental expansion of citizens' access to public services. These contexts are the military regime, whose legacy can be observed in 1980; redemocratization and the first civilian government under President José Sarney, the outcome of which can be observed in 1991; and, finally, the recent democratic period. For the latter, we are able to analyze the contributions of two administrations: Fernando Henrique Cardoso (1995–2002) and Luiz Inácio Lula da Silva (2003–2012). The years 2000 and 2010, respectively, will be taken as legacies from each of these administrations.

Studies on the relationship between income and access to services typically use households as the unit of observation. This chapter demonstrates that this association, while essential, is not enough to explain the factors that affect inequalities in access to services. Unlike private goods, consumption of collective goods is not determined solely by an individual's purchase decisions. Instead, the consumption of services with respect to electricity, water, sewage and garbage collection, healthcare, and education requires that said services be made available within a reachable distance of households. Therefore, where an individual lives matters in obtaining access to these services, i.e., the spatial distribution of supply has an independent effect over individuals' payment capacity. Although the territorial distribution of service supply has consequences for an individual's access, providers make their supply decisions based on the characteristics of jurisdictions. The wealth of the jurisdiction and the income of their population were revealed to be key factors in the geography of public services supply, and consequently, in individuals' access to such services. Therefore, this study will consider municipalities as the analytical unit since they are the most plausible units of observation for disaggregated statistical treatment in the census data.[3]

The Trajectory of Territorial Inequality

In the 1970s, access to public services in Brazil was not only very limited; it was a privilege enjoyed almost exclusively in the South and Southeast regions. A large portion of the population living above the twentieth parallel simply did not have access to water, sewage collection, and electricity. Even middle- and high-income individuals had no access to such services. High poverty rates were widespread throughout the country. As a result, the country displayed low levels of inequality since this relative equality meant that the overwhelming majority of municipalities were inhabited by vast swathes of the poor. Wealth, in turn, was concentrated in a small number of municipalities in the South and Southeast regions.

Between 1970 and 2010, patterns of wealth inequality among Brazilian municipalities remained unchanged, while territorial inequality regarding poor concentration increased. In turn, territorial inequality regarding access to key services, except for the supply of physicians, dropped. This trajectory can be seen in Graph 1, which shows the Gini coefficients for the coverage rates in selected policies, as well as poor concentration[4] and municipal per capita GDP.

The graph shows that inequality in per capita GDP suffered only a slight drop from 1970 to 2010, from 0.494 to 0.403. In 1970, a few municipalities in the South and Southeast had the highest per capita GDP levels, while the poorest municipalities were concentrated in the Northeast. In 1980, there was an increase in the

---

[3]The smallest analytical unit available in the 2000 and 2010 censuses is the weighting area. However, it is not available in other censuses. To aggregate the information from the last five censuses, two procedures were adopted. First, the number of municipalities systematically increased throughout the period. They totaled 3,991 in 1970, reaching 5,564 in 2010. Converting the universe of municipalities in each census – maintaining the 1970 value or taking a fraction of the municipal population derived from dissecting each census – entails unavoidable methodological difficulties. Thus, the universe for each census was maintained, which implies that results for each period are not directly comparable to others. The year 1960 was not included in the analysis since the available data does not allow for a disaggregation of the municipalities.

[4]The variable was calculated from the demographic censuses. Fogel and Corseuil deflators (2002) were applied for the 2010 values. Per capita household income was calculated (excluding nonfamily residents, pensioners, domestic workers, or relatives of domestic workers), and a cutoff point was made between individuals with per capita household income above and below R$255.00 (half the legal minimum wage value for 2010). Individuals with income below this value were considered "poor" and received one in the indicator variable for poor. Individuals with income above this value were called "nonpoor" and received a score of zero. To calculate the proportion of poor per municipality, the values of this indicator variable per municipality were added together, resulting in the number of poor individuals. The value obtained was then divided by the total population of the municipality.

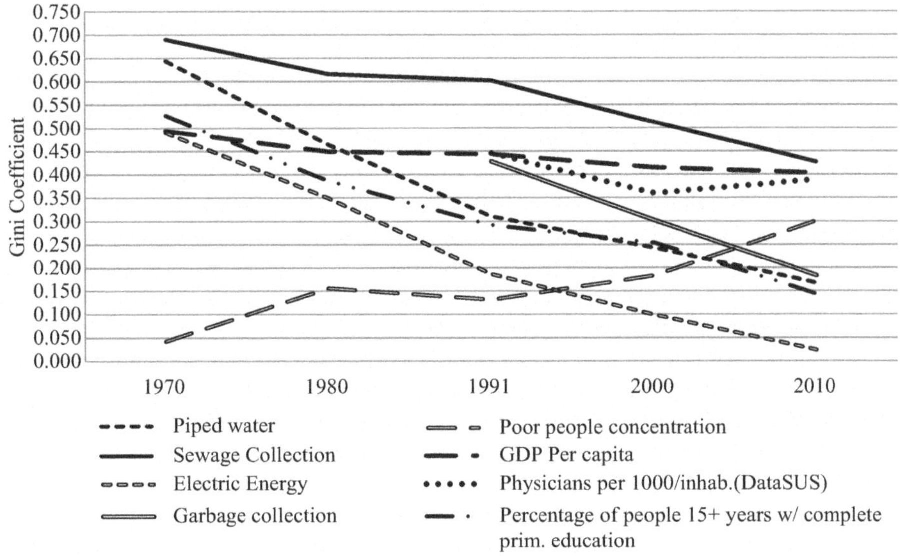

Graph 1 Gini coefficient, per capita GDP, and access to public services Brazilian municipalities – 1970–2010. (Source: IBGE. Demographic Censuses 1970–2010; PNAD (special tabulations by CEM))

number of municipalities in the South and the Southeast with higher rates of wealth, as well as some expansion of wealth in the Central-West region. The Northeast, however, continued at levels quite similar to 1970, i.e., with the lowest per capita GDP values nationwide.

It is startling to see the resilience of the per capita GDP geography. As Map 1 shows, a clear divide that emerges early in 1980, between the affluent South, Southeast, and Central-West regions, on the one hand, and the Northeast and North regions in which islands of wealth are surrounded by poorer municipalities, on the other, is still evident in 2010. Indeed, the Northeast region shows a stable pattern: it is the poorest region over the entire period. Therefore, despite general economic growth, inequality remains unchanged when it comes to the wealth of Brazilian jurisdictions.

These data confirm what regional economic studies say about the trajectory of regional inequality in Brazil. Regions have become more unequal among themselves and more internally homogeneous. Economic growth favors the Southeast region (Azzoni 1997). There are "convergence clubs": the federal district and the state of São Paulo lead the group with the highest income (concentrated in the Southeast), while Northeastern states form the "low-income club" (Magalhães et al. 2005). Among municipalities there are also "convergence clubs" that are regional in nature, i.e., low-income municipalities are located in the North and Northeast regions, while their high-income counterparts are concentrated in the Southeast, South, and Central-West regions (Araujo et al. 2010; Chein et al. 2007; Coelho and Figueiredo 2007; Laurini et al. 2003; Ribeiro and Almeida 2012).

Despite the stability of the geography of wealth, the inequality of poor concentration, as measured by the share of individuals living at an income below half the minimum wage in 2010 values (see footnote 5), increased among Brazilian municipalities from 1970 to 2010. The result seems paradoxical if one considers the steady decline in income inequality among individuals in the past decades (Neri and Souza 2012; Soares 2010). The data therefore suggest that long-term changes in poverty and income inequality are not distributed in the same way throughout Brazil. Although average levels of poverty in the country diminished from the early 1990s on, the spatial concentration of poverty increased. A greater number of municipalities display lower rates of poor concentration, but quite a few still shelter extreme poverty. In other words, poverty has turned out to be territorially concentrated.

This trajectory is visible in Map 2. One can observe that low inequality in poor concentration in 1970 expresses its widespread presence throughout the entire territory. The lowest Gini we see on Graph 1 means that the vast majority of municipalities hosted large strata of poor. As for the 1980s, increasing inequality in the geography of poverty distinguishes the South, Southeast, and Central-West regions, which display lower levels of concentrated poverty, from the North and Northeast regions, which have the highest levels of poor concentration. In 1991, poverty rates were high in all regions – including the South and Southeast – as a result of the low economic growth rates experienced during the so-called lost decade of the 1980s. However, the geography of inequality remains, given that the North and Northeast regions (and the northern part of the Southeast region) display the highest levels of poor concentration. Although poverty rates fell in the North region in 2000, the territorial divide between the North-Northeast region, on the one hand, and the South-Southeast region, on the other hand, remains constant. The fact is that although poverty rates have come down in the North and Northeast regions in 2010, they have dropped even further in the South and Southeast regions.

Given the definition of poverty adopted here (individuals living with an income of half the statutory minimum wage),[5] the behavior of this indicator is not affected by the *Bolsa Familia* program, the conditional cash-benefit program adopted by President Lula, whose entitlement rules require household earnings to be below one quarter of the minimum wage. It does, however, capture the impact of all income benefits pegged to the statutory minimum wage, such as pensions and unemployment compensation, as well as earnings by low-skilled workers have on poverty rates in Brazilian municipalities.

Thus, if per capita income is kept constant, the variation on poverty rates among Brazilian municipalities can be explained by differences in income distribution, that is, concentrated poverty is not a function of low income but rather of how income in each jurisdiction is distributed (Barros et al. 2000). Brazilian regions do not only display different levels of wealth. They also display different patterns of income distribution.

The decrease in income inequality we observed from the 1990s on was not evenly distributed throughout Brazil. Instead, it was more intense in the Southeast region, possibly due to higher productivity gains on the part of the poor in this

[5] The statutory minimum wage of reference is 2010.

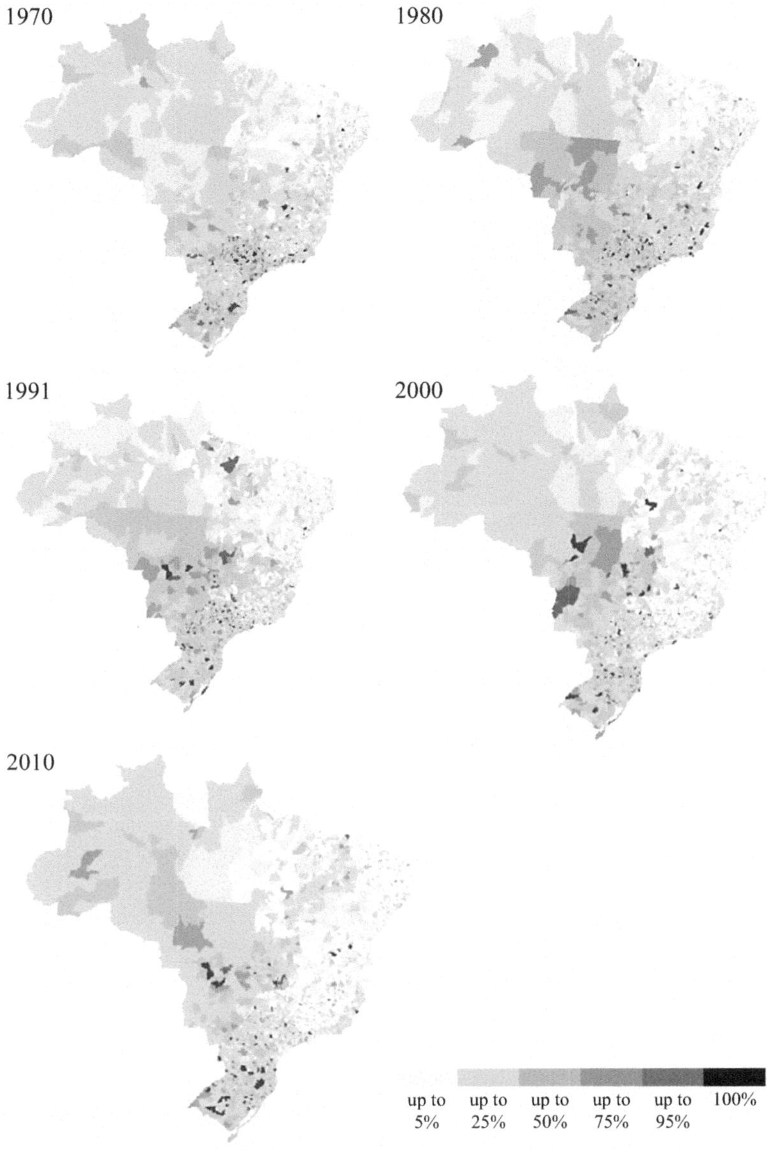

Map 1 Per capita GDP (standardized) (For municipal GDP, we used the 2000 value of the Brazilian *real* (R$) available on the IPEAData website (www.ipeadata.gov.br) and in IBGE research on municipal GDP. The values were deflated by these institutions (IPEA and IBGE) based on the implicit GDP deflator. This measure was left at 2000 fixed prices. The population data came from the demographic censuses. After calculating per capita GDP, standardization of values was performed for a range of 0 to 100, using the formula below:

$$\text{Standardized GDP per capita} = \frac{\text{GDPper capita}_i - \text{GDPper capita}_{\min}}{\text{GDPper capita}_{\max} - \text{GDPper capita}_{\min}} * 100.$$

In order to control variations in the standardization, GDP values greater than the 99th percentile were removed from the calculation and reinserted with the value of 1 upon standardization) Brazil – 1970–2010 (Source: IBGE. Demographic Censuses 1970–2010; PNAD. (Special tabulations by CEM))

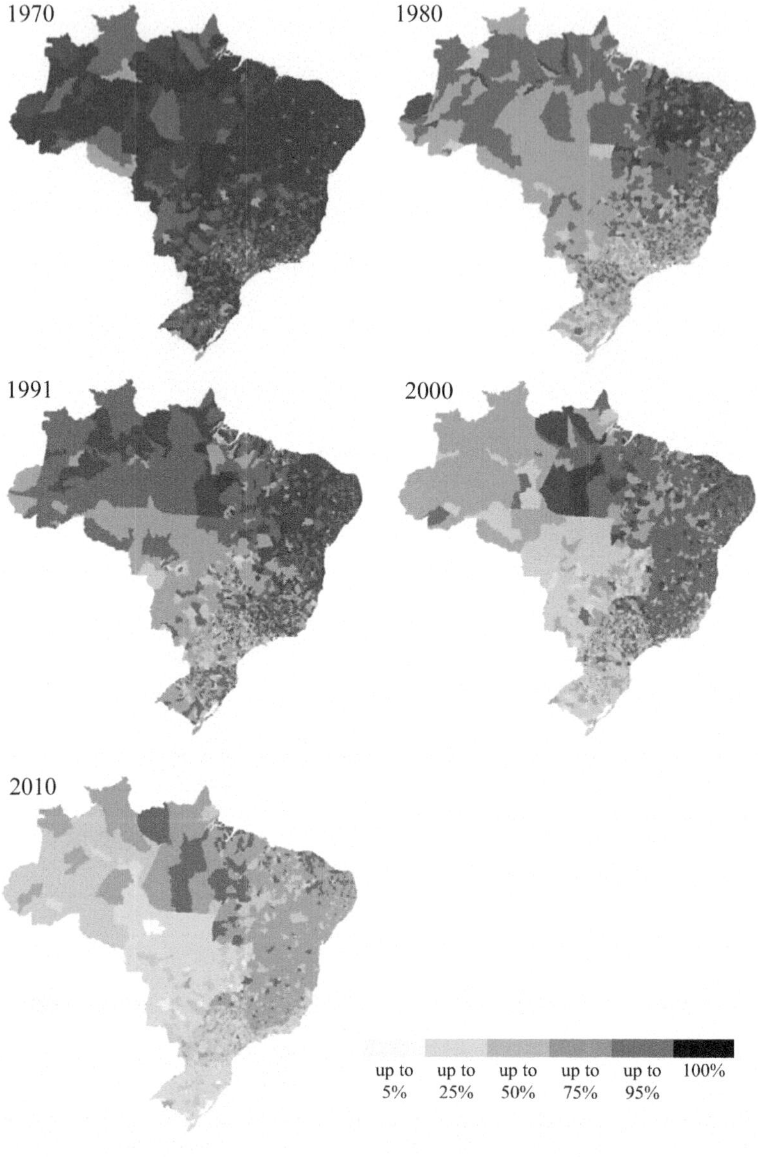

Map 2 Percentage of poor people Brazil – 1970–2010. (Source: IBGE. Demographic Censuses 1970–2010; PNAD. (Special tabulations by CEM))

region (Manso et al. 2010a, b; Pinto and Oliveira 2010). As a result, income inequality is higher in the Northeast and the states of Rio de Janeiro, Espírito Santo, and Minas Gerais and lower in Sao Paulo and the Southern region (Hoffmann 2010). We therefore saw an increase in the Gini coefficient for poor concentration among

Brazilian municipalities from the 1990s on (Graph 1) because income inequality within regions began to take different paths.

From 1970 to 2010, there was a significant reduction in poverty since the share of the poor systematically dropped across all regions. However, low regional inequality due to widespread poverty in 1970 was replaced by a huge divide between the Northeast-North, on the one hand, and the Southeast-South, on the other, because such reduction went faster in the latter.

Finally, Graph 1 also shows that the geography of access to public services presents quite a different trajectory from the one observed with regard to wealth and poverty. First, inequality in coverage rates drops systematically from the 1970s on for all services, although the pace of such similar downward trend is not the same among policies. On the one hand, inequality in the supply of electricity, piped water, basic education, and garbage collection present an incremental decline resulting in the fact that in 2010, the Gini coefficients for these policies were the lowest in Brazilian history, below 0.200. On the other hand, the downward trend in the supply of doctors and sewage collection was consistent but less steep. As a result, cross-municipality Gini coefficients with regard to these two policies in 2010 were even higher than those found for poor concentration and similar to the values found for municipal per capita GDP.

In sum, despite a similar downward trend in cross-municipality inequality of service supply, there may be policy-specific reasons hindering the provision of doctors and sewage collection. This point will be the subject of further discussion later in the chapter.

Does Geography Matter?

Evidence presented thus far suggests that access to public services was incrementally delinked from the income of jurisdictions in 40 years, since the Gini coefficient for per capita GDP remained fairly steady, and the Gini coefficient for poor concentration increased, while the coefficients for the various policies dropped. Even if such downward trend occurs at a different rate among policies, the overall trend is still toward a reduction of cross-municipality disparities in access to services. This conclusion is *false* however. It does not stem from the evidence presented, and the reason for this is simple: the data presented refers to inequality in coverage rates for each of the observed dimensions and for each census year, not to any potential association between the two.

In order to observe the relationship between these dimensions, factor analysis was applied to all variables for the period 1970–2010. The variables "garbage collection" and "physicians per 1,000 inhabitants" were excluded because this data is only available for the 1990s on. To make the variables comparable, they were converted to express the fact that higher values correspond to more privileged positions.[6] The variable "poor concentration" was therefore operationalized to "the percentage of individuals living at more than half the minimum wage."[7] As a result, when calculating the synthetic indicators, all variables change in the same direction.

The methodological procedures were operationalized as follows: factor analysis was conducted for the 1970 census data. We then replicated the weighting structure obtained from this modeling for the remaining census data in order to observe how the synthetic indicator behaved in each census year. In this modeling, we extracted a single factor, whose total explained variance was 80.4%.[8] This result therefore indicates an association between the expansion of coverage in some basic public goods, GDP per capita, and income inequality in Brazilian municipalities over the past 40 years.

Association does not mean causality, however. It is not possible to claim if improvements in income account for the expansion of access to services or if the contrary holds true. The fact is that improvements (or lack thereof) tended to occur in all dimensions simultaneously. Affluent municipalities and regions have also seen a reduction in poverty rates and in the coverage of those services. In other words, wealth, poverty reduction, and access to services had similar territorial paths in Brazil over these 40 years.

From the results obtained by the factor analysis, we generated a synthetic indicator, which is a reparametrization of "factor scores" for each of the census years.[9] The resulting index varies on a scale of 0 to 100, where the value zero (0) represents the worst situation, and one hundred (100) represents the best.[10] Graph 2 shows the box plot of the trajectory of this synthetic indicator obtained for Brazilian munici-

---

[6] I thank Edgard Fusaro for this methodological solution, especially for its implications in the analysis that follows.

[7] For the economic wealth dimension, we performed a mathematical transformation so that the variable that was part of the modeling was the "natural logarithm of municipal GDP per capita."

[8] The coefficients of the factor scores, in their original form, are as follows: (i) percentage of individuals living in households with sanitary sewage: 0.193; (ii) percentage of individuals living in households with water supply (general network): 0.185; (iii) percentage of individuals living in households with electricity: 0.194; (iv) percentage of individuals age 15 or older that have completed primary school: 0.187; (v) percentage of individuals living at more than half the minimum wage in 2010 values, with 2010 wages: 0.190; and (vi) natural logarithm of municipal GDP per capita (BRL R$1.00 in the year 2000): 0.165.

[9] Mathematically, the synthetic indicator was obtained as:

$$Y = \frac{EF_{original} - EF_{orignal,mínimo}}{EF_{orignal,máximo} - EF_{orignal,mínimo}} * 100$$

where Y is the synthetic indicator on the scale 0–100, and EF corresponds to the original "factor score."

[10] It is worth noting that although it is possible to sort municipalities according to synthetic indicators, these indicators can only be quantified comparatively, not in absolute terms of "large" or "small" values.

palities by major geographic region. Thus, the data presented can be read as expressing inequality across all dimensions taken together, i.e., GDP per capita, presence of nonpoor population, and access to infrastructure services (electricity, water, sewage collection, and population age 15 or older with complete basic education, meaning 8 years of schooling).

Graph 2 shows that, as already observed, 1970 can be described as displaying relative territorial equality in deprivation. Median values are low for all regions, where they range from 10% to 25% of households in the municipality displaying the presence of the synthetic indicator, and their respective box sizes are small, meaning that variation within regions was not large. Despite all that, the South and Southeast regions presented higher median values, meaning that municipalities situated in these regions had the best income and living conditions as compared to the others in 1970.

In fact, in 1970, the supply of public services in Brazil was simply terrible. Municipalities in which more than half the population had access to electric power were rare and concentrated mostly in São Paulo and in the Southern states. Even in the most affluent regions that enjoyed greater supply of services, the rule of thumb was that less than half of the population obtained access to electricity. In the North and Northeast, there was almost a complete lack of access to electricity, except for a few cities along the coast (Map 3).

Scarcity was even more pronounced with regard to water supply and sewage collection. Supply was heavily concentrated in the Southeast and some cities in the South, but even there it did not exceed more than half the population. In the North, Northeast, and Central-West regions, however, there was an almost absolute lack of access to water supply and sewage collection (Maps 4 and 5).

Data clearly show that the policies of the military regime mostly benefited the South and Southeast regions, even though within-region inequality remains. Box plots for 1980 (Graph 2) show that median values for the two regions increased faster than for the remaining ones, compared to 1970 box plots. The size of the boxes for these regions was also larger in 1980 compared to 1970. That means that some municipalities within these two regions have greatly improved their income and living conditions, while others within them, along with municipalities in the North, Northeast, and Central-West regions, have not experienced similar rates of improvement.

By 1980, water and electricity supply had greatly expanded, when compared to 1970. But in both policies, supply expansion was concentrated in the South and Southeast regions, despite an extension to almost the entire national territory (Maps 3 and 4). The result is a clear territorial divide. Cities in the South and Southeast move toward universalization, while in the North, Northeast, and Central-West, only rarely do we find municipalities where the coverage rate exceeds over half the population. Lastly, the provision of sewage collection showed coverage expansion only in the South and Southeast regions, keeping the remaining regions almost entirely without such services (Map 5).

The great achievements of the military regime, namely, the National Sanitation Plan (PLANASA) for water and sewage services as well as the creation of Eletrosul

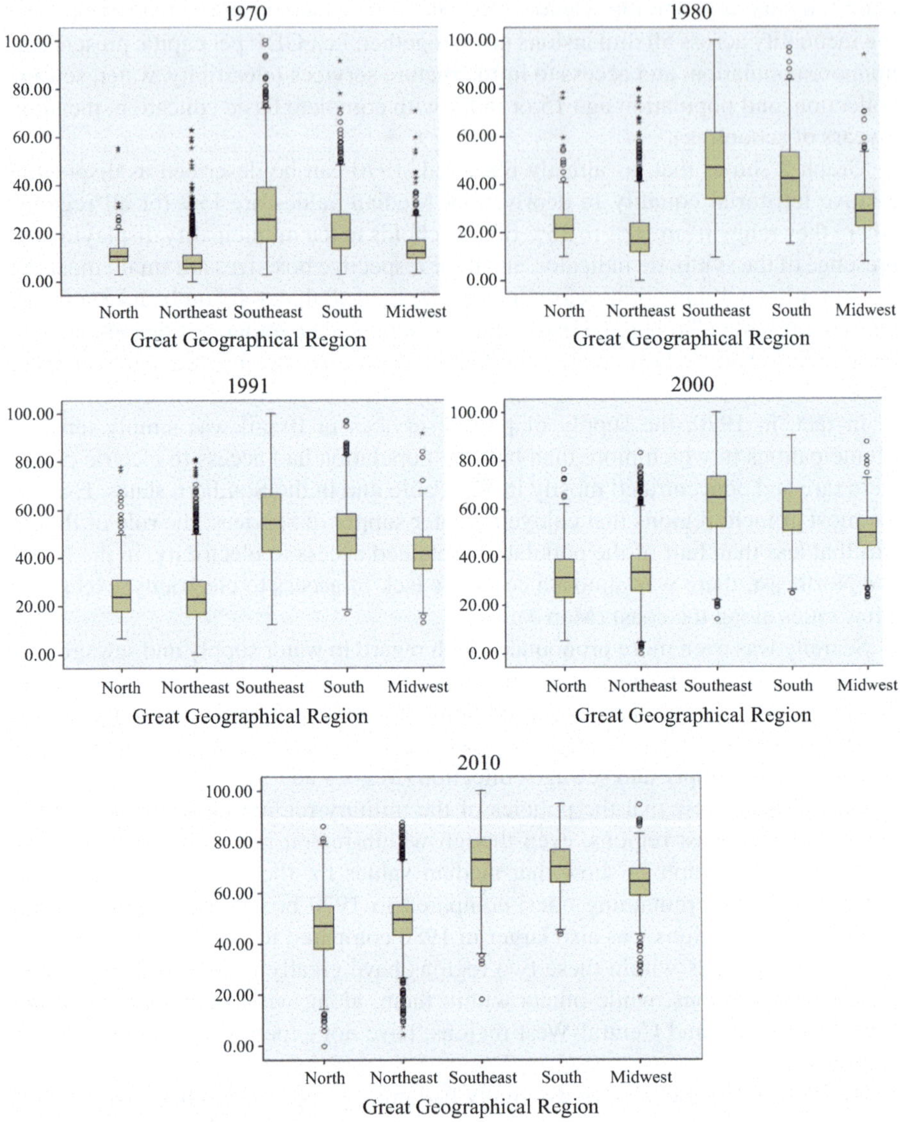

Graph 2 Box plot of well-being (synthetic indicator). All municipalities by major geographic regions – 1970–2010. (Source: IBGE. Demographic Censuses 1970–2010. (Special tabulations by CEM))

(1968), Eletronorte (1973), and the binational Itaipu Dam for electricity services, in fact allowed for the expansion of coverage. This varies between policies, however, since policies to supply electricity and water moved much faster than the provision of sewage collection. Furthermore, this expansion accentuates regional disparities, given that the South and Southeast regions move toward universalization, while the Central-West, North, and Northeast regions present very low coverage rates.

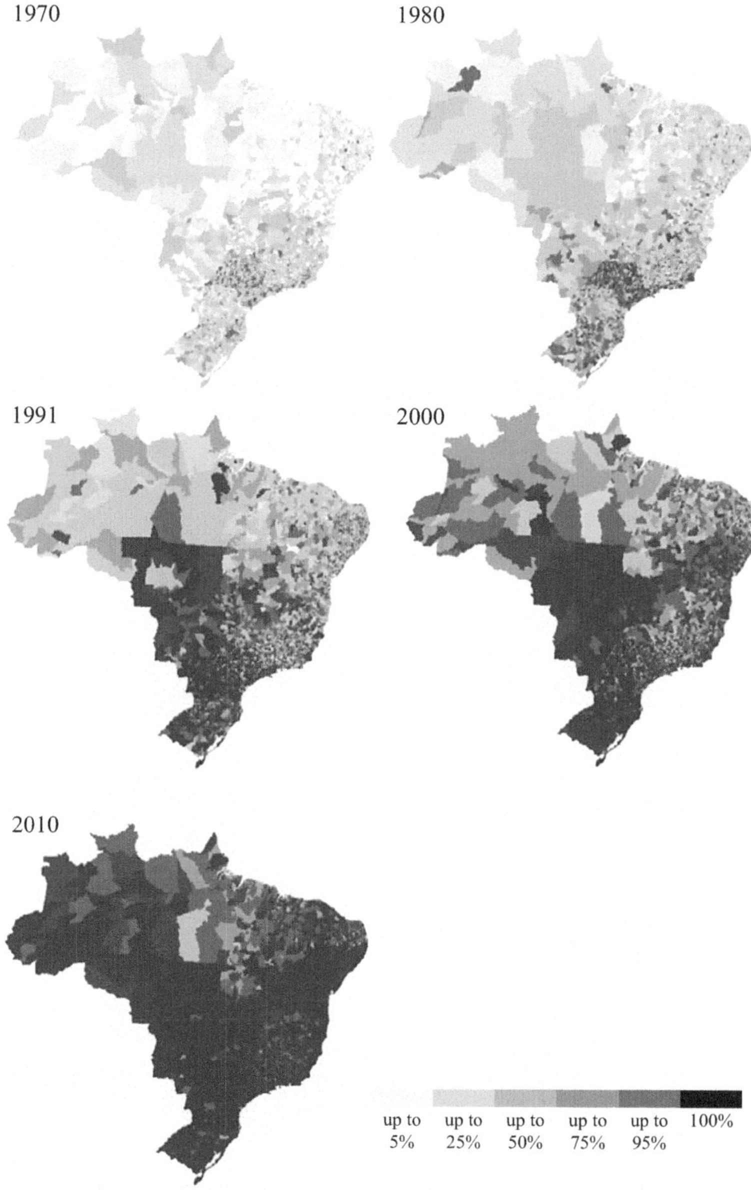

Map 3 Coverage rates of electricity by municipality Brazil – 1970–2010. (Source: IBGE. Demographic Censuses 1970–2010; PNAD. (Special tabulations by CEM))

In 1991, we can see some improvement in the spatial distribution of the synthetic indicator. However, there is a notable distinction in the geography of this progress. The median overall indicator was eminently higher in the South and Southeast regions, while the North and Northeast regions were left behind. Indeed, in the latter, both the median position and the size of the box remained quite similar to the 1980s.

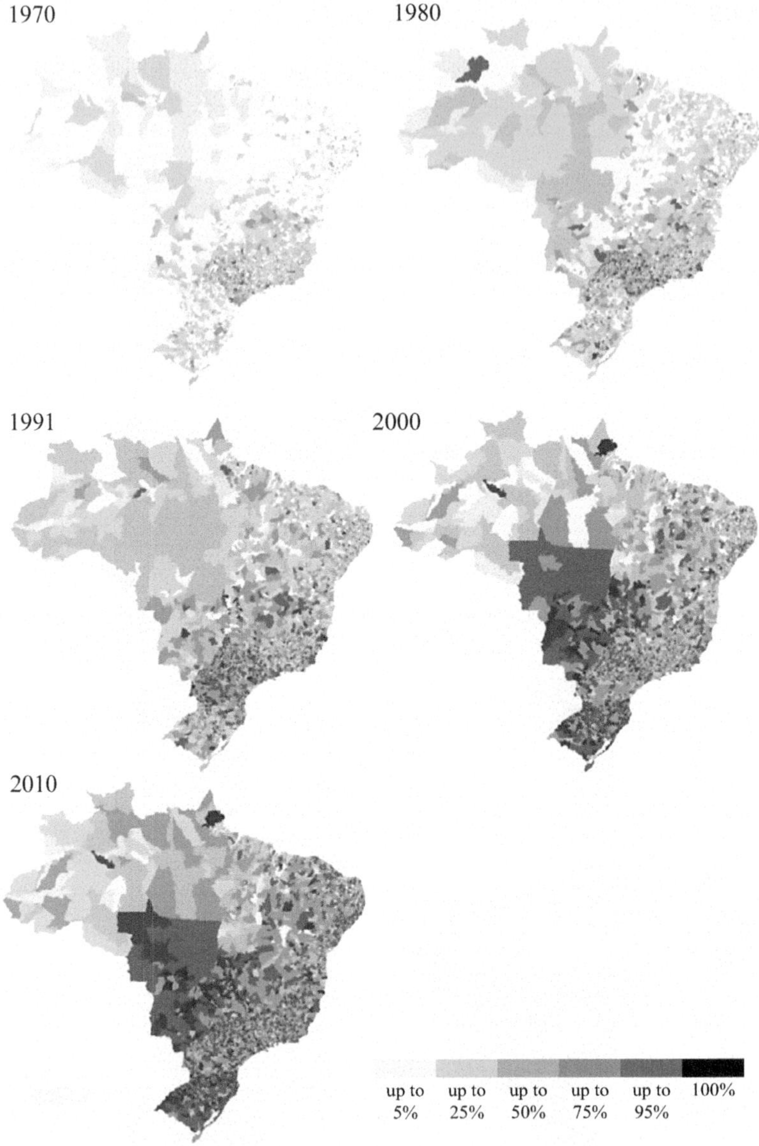

Map 4 Coverage rates of water supply by municipality Brazil – 1970–2010. (Source: IBGE. Demographic Censuses 1970–2010; PNAD. (Special tabulations by CEM))

In 1991, the different policy trajectories become even clearer. Access to electricity was practically universal in the South, Southeast, and Central-West regions. Still less than half of the population had coverage in large areas of the Northeast and Northern regions (Map 3) however. This expansion can be attributed to the completion of two large-scale projects initiated under the military regime: (i) the aforemen-

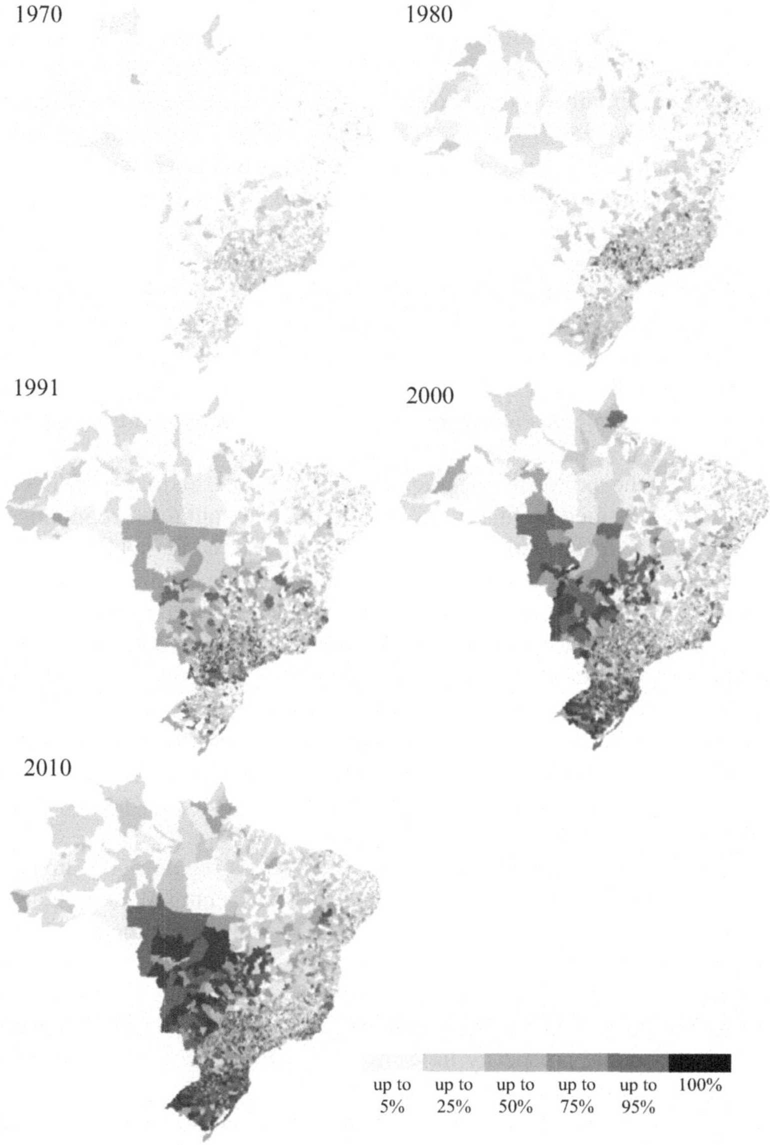

Map 5 Coverage rates of sewage collection Brazil – 1970–2010. (Source: IBGE. Demographic Censuses 1970–2010; PNAD. (Special tabulations by CEM))

tioned Itaipu, the largest hydroelectric dam in the world at the time, which had supplied the Southeast since 1986, and (ii) the first section of the North-Northeast transmission system, which allowed for energy generated in the Amazon basin to be distributed across the Northeast region.

Water and sewage policies, in turn, have followed quite different trajectories, albeit implemented and funded as part of the same PLANASA inaugurated by the military regime, established in 1969 and implemented in 1971. Sewage collection coverage remained confined to almost the same areas in which it was already available in 1980 (Map 5), while water supply reached nearly universal levels in the Southeast – most of the municipalities had coverage rates for over 75% of households – and was greatly expanded in the North and Northeast regions, although coverage rates in these regions were generally below 50% of the households (Map 4).

The year 1991 also displays data on garbage collection and on the number of physicians per 1,000 inhabitants (Maps 6 and 7). While this information is not used in calculating the synthetic indicator, it can be noted that distribution at the time was very similar to the water and electricity coverage levels: higher in cities of the South and Southeast regions along with very low rates in the North and Northeast regions.

In the 1980s, the political transition toward the first civilian president, José Sarney, was accompanied by high rates of inflation and continued economic crisis. It was considered a "lost decade" in economic terms. Vilmar Faria (1992), however, denied that this had been a lost decade when it came to the supply of basic services and argued that significant expansion in coverage had indeed taken place during this period. He argued that the return of free elections had produced incentives for governments to expand provision. The main evidence, however, took the form of increases in the coverage percentages of household services on a national scale. Nevertheless, spatial disaggregation of data reveals that the 1980s was undeniably a lost decade for residents in the North and Northeast regions. The virtual universalization of coverage was concentrated in the Southeast and somewhat less sharply in the South.

Data suggest that throughout the 1990s, such cross-region and within-region inequality remained, although municipalities in the Central-West regions more clearly joined the affluent ones. In 2000, median values of the synthetic indicator for the South, Southeast, and Central-West regions were far superior to the traditionally underdeveloped regions. This means that during the Fernando Henrique Cardoso administration, the former regions, and especially cities in the Central-West, experienced reasonable prosperity in terms of wealth, poverty, and reduction and increased coverage rates for basic services.

In 2000, access to electricity was practically universal in the South, Southeast, and Central-West regions. However, in much of the Northeast and North, it did not reach half the population, although the region witnessed coverage expansion when compared to 1990 (Map 3). Territorial inequality of coverage expansion also occurred in relation to garbage collection: it expanded significantly when compared to 1991, but universal coverage remained concentrated in cities in the South, Southeast, and Central-West. This expansion did little to alter low coverage rates in the North and Northeast (Map 6).

In the 1990s, the expansion of water supply toward universal coverage occurred only in the South and Southeast regions. The North and the Northeast regions altered

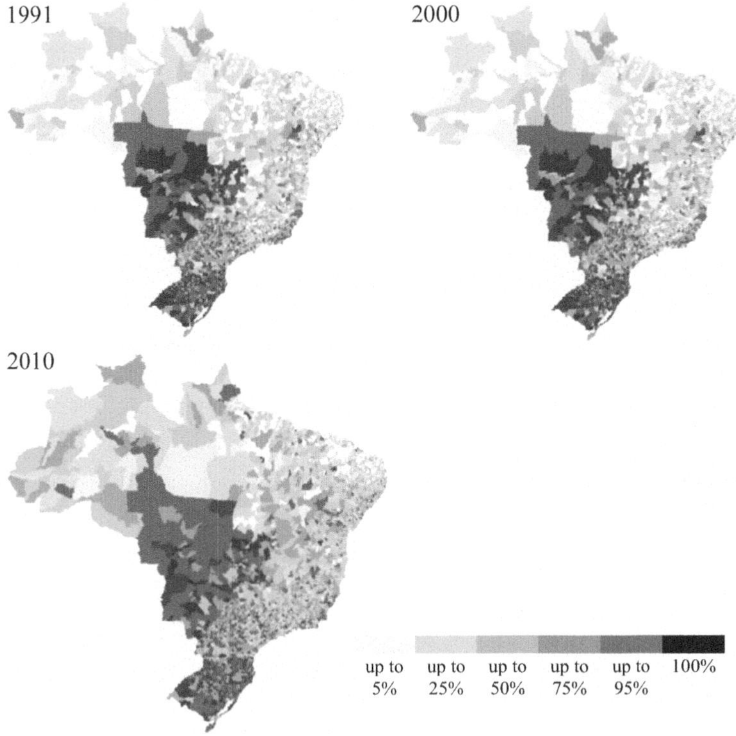

Map 6 Population with garbage collection services, Brazil – 1991–2010. (Source: IBGE. Demographic Censuses 1970–2010; PNAD. (Special tabulations by CEM))

their position when compared to 1991 but at a much slower pace. Some expansion in sewage coverage was also registered, but this primarily affected the South and Central-West regions (Map 4).

The year 2000 can be interpreted as the legacy of Fernando Henrique Cardoso's presidency for the territorial distribution of infrastructure services. There is no doubt that there was an expansion in services pertaining to water supply, sewage collection, electricity, and garbage collection, but this expansion mostly benefited the Central-West and the South, since the Southeast was already well served in 1980. While the North and Northeast regions saw some expansion in coverage, it is most striking with regard to access to electricity. The difference in coverage compared to 1991 is much less noticeable in other services.

Lastly, municipalities in the North and Northeast regions experienced an increase in their rates of well-being – in terms of income and services – during the Lula administration. In 2010, these regions showed a significant increase in the synthetic indicator for median values, even if internal inequality within these areas remained similar to that observed in 2000 (expressed by an increase in the size of the box).

In 2010, access to electricity was truly universal in Brazil, regardless of per capita income of a given jurisdiction (Map 3) as a result of the National Program for

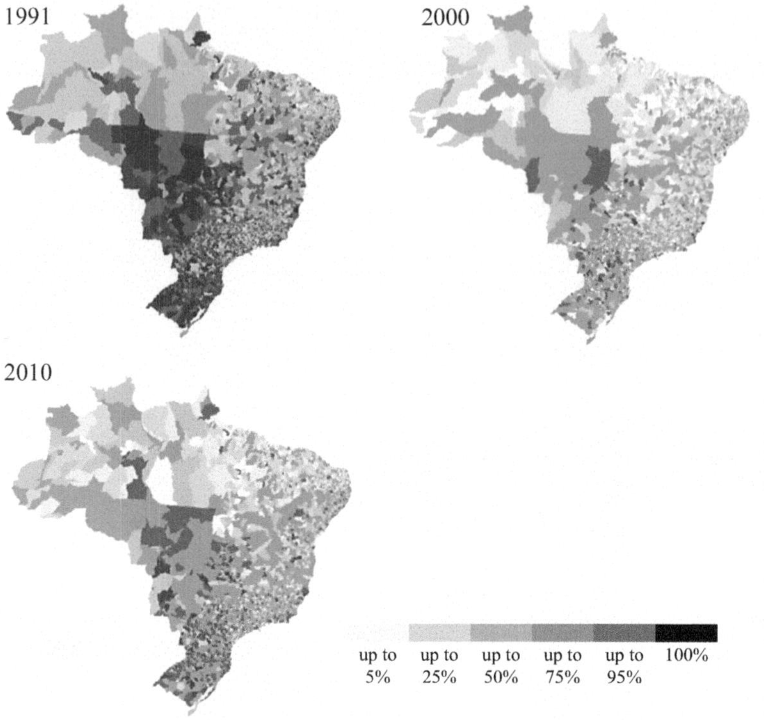

Map 7 Number of physicians per 1000 inhabitants, Brazil – 1991–2010 (DATASUS). (Source: IBGE. Demographic Censuses 1970–2010; PNAD. (Special tabulations by CEM))

Universalization and Use of Electricity (*Programa Nacional de Universalização e Uso de Energia Elétrica*), launched in 2003. Garbage collection was practically universal in cities of the Southeast and Central-West regions, with a small expansion in coverage in the South. Even though coverage has been expanding in the North and Northeast regions, there is still a significant variation in coverage rates (Map 6). In relation to water supply, coverage in municipalities in the North and Northeast regions increased, and rates close to 75% in several locations were maintained in the nearly universal provision of the South, Southeast, and Central-West regions. Municipalities in these regions, where coverage was quite variable in 2000, have seen rates reach levels higher than 75% (Map 4).

Sewage collection services, however, remained virtually unchanged except for a marginal increase in coverage rates in municipalities already receiving services. Universalization in the Southeast and the virtual lack of sewage collection services in the North and the Northeast continue to be a trademark in this policy (Map 5).

The year 2010 can be considered the legacy of the Lula administration in the struggle against territorial inequality in access to essential services. In territorial terms, the Northeast is the region that most benefited from the expansion of coverage rates: it expanded its services for water supply and garbage collection and registered universal access to the electricity network.

In a nutshell, during these 40 years, prosperity – understood as income and access to services – has considerably expanded, but its geography is clearly unequal. During the military regime and the turbulent 1980s, which coincided with the process of democratization, municipalities in regions of the South and Southeast experienced improvement rates higher than those in other regions. During the Cardoso administration in the 1990s, municipalities in Brazil's Central-West displayed a more significant increase in income and access to services. Finally, during the Lula administration in the 2000s, municipalities in the North and the Northeast regions experienced the most significant increases in their income conditions and coverage rates for essential services.

In short, from 1970 to 2010, cross-municipality inequality in the production of wealth in Brazil remained almost unchanged despite general economic growth. Poverty, in turn, defined as the percentage of households earning less than minimum wage, turned out to be increasingly concentrated in poorer municipalities. Finally, although cross-municipality inequality in the provision of infrastructure services declined, such downward trend is clearly biased in favor of more affluent regions, that is, service supply inequality reduction among municipalities mainly occurred within regions with higher wealth growth and lower levels of poor concentration. Furthermore, infrastructure improvements were clearly driven by expansion in electric power and water supply, meaning that some area-specific factors seem to hinder the expansion of physicians and sewage collection. The result is a clear divide between affluent regions – the South, the Southeast, and Central-West – and poor regions of the North and Northeast.

Policies Also Matter

As stated above, the Brazilian trajectory clearly shows an association between the wealth of jurisdictions, poverty rates, and the geography of basic services. As expected, there is a systematic negative correlation between poverty and coverage rates for basic services, as shown in Table 1. In other words, high levels of poor concentration are associated with low levels of coverage in services.

Even though such association rates drop systematically for most of the policies analyzed, it is still high. In 2010, the negative association between both indicators is the lowest in Brazil's history. Without a doubt, this is explained, as previously shown, by the gradual expansion of coverage in poorer municipalities. However, in any case, poor concentration seems to be an important factor hindering supply coverage.

Can these trends be explained solely by the attributes of municipalities? Can the geography of inequalities described in this chapter be explained only on the basis of local factors, be they economic – such as wealth and poverty, as seen up to now – or political – such as political competition, administrative capacity, or the ideological orientation of mayors?

A good amount of research has shown that neither political competition nor administrative capacities, let alone party affiliation of mayors, fully explain the

Table 1 Correlation between access to essential services and the percentage of poor people Municipalities – 1970–2010

Basic services	1970	1980	1991	2000	2010
Access to general sewage collection (1)	−0.739	−0.618	−0.598	−0.583	−0.548
Access to electric power (1)	−0.745	−0.811	−0.795	−0.758	−0.599
Access to general water (1)	−0.615	−0.643	−0.636	−0.461	−0.439
Percentage of the population 15+ years with basic education (1)	−0.772	−0.773	−0.797	−0.866	−0.712
Garbage collection (1)	–	–	−0.693	−0.699	−0.7
Physicians per 1000 inhabitants (DATASUS)	–	–	−0.404	−0.425	−0.5

Source: IBGE. Demographic Censuses 1970–2010; DATASUS (Special tabulations by CEM)
(1) Variables measured in percentage were transformed into Logit: Ln (p / [1-p])

supply of services at the local level although they may play some role in the final outcome (Arretche 2016a; Arretche et al. 2012; Loyola 2014; Marques and Arretche 2004; Satyro 2013). So, if for instance affluent municipalities display higher rates of service supply, it does not necessarily follow that this association is explained by their ability to deliver services due to better administrative capacity or fierce political competition.

First of all, note that the policies examined display different paces under a common downward trend in inequality. The negative association between poverty concentration and the territorial distribution of physicians per 1,000 inhabitants as well as garbage collection has remained stable, since we are able to measure it from 1991 on. The negative correlation between poverty and level of schooling of the population age 15 or older has increased systematically between 1970 and 2000. In fact, it reaches its highest point in 2000 and actually only falls during the decade of 2000. Only in 2010 does it present lower values than in 1970. Access to electricity in 1980 also presents values above those of 1970, indicating that the beginning of the coverage expansion process could increase rather than decrease the negative association between poor concentration and access to services.

If read through the lens of political periods, the negative association between poverty, on the one hand, and the supply of physicians and garbage collection, on the other, remains stable despite democracy and under the administrations of both Cardoso and Lula. The Lula administration alone was responsible for the sharp reduction of the negative association regarding schooling and access to electricity, while Cardoso's contribution to such drop refers only to the supply of water. In short, there is no straightforward way to associate turning points along the path of the negative association between poor concentration and scarcity of services to a specific point in time. Besides geography, policies themselves also matter!

In fact, everything being equal, the attributes of municipalities cannot fully explain why policies display such different paths. Indeed, focusing the explanation on the attributes of the municipality requires ignoring how the institutional framework of these policies affects the role municipalities have in the provision of services.

First of all, funding schemes and policy entitlement go hand in hand. As we saw, the significant expansion of major services took place in Brazil beginning with the very low baseline of 1970. The expansion of coverage at that time cannot be understood without taking into account the policies designed by the military regime and its commitment to economic growth through a developmental state. In such a state model, the role of the federal government in funding urban infrastructure policies served as a key dimension. In the face of the blossoming urbanization that resulted from massive flows of workers from less developed regions migrating to wealthier ones in order to at least gain entry to the labor market (see chapter on "Brazil's Internal Migration Over the Past 50 Years: (Dis)continuities and Ruptures" by José Marcos Cunha), the urban infrastructure policies advanced by an authoritarian and centralized political regime sought to install state-level companies as providers of services, and so, municipalities had a very subordinate role.

By that time, water, sewage collection, and electric power supply were seen as requirements for economic growth. For water and sewage collection, federally managed funds were launched to fund investments through state-level companies. The main source of revenue for federal funds earmarked for water supply and sewage collection came from formal employee unemployment insurance. The construction of hydroelectric power plants, in turn, was funded mainly by means of foreign investment and public debt, once again at the behest of the federal government. State-level company funding was obtained through loans with federal-led funds, which had to be repaid in order to enable payment of either the public debt or unemployment insurance for entitled workers. Then, user's fees became the state-level strategy that needed to be adopted to provide for the payment of loans, although many of them were constantly undergoing political negotiation. Above all, expenditure on urban infrastructure policies had to be profitable.

Hence, the attributes of municipalities cannot fully explain the trajectory observed in this chapter because services were provided by state-level companies. These companies in turn benefited affluent municipalities because the strategy they employed was the most efficient way to get profitable returns on investments, given the design of urban infrastructure policies under the military regime.

The democratization period that extended from the mid-1980s on was followed by an economic downturn accompanied by high rates of unemployment. This led to the collapse of the Brazilian State's capacity for further spending on urban infrastructure policies due to declining revenue collection, increasing demand for unemployed insurance payments, and mounting difficulties in servicing the foreign debt. The adverse macroeconomic context reinforced the strategy of state-level companies to favor both affluent municipalities and affluent areas within cities.

Under the democratic regime, the dimensions of these policies, as framed by the military regime, did not undergo paradigmatic changes to the extent that the main funding sources and the role of state-level companies in service provision remained untouched. Nonetheless, the two parties that led the competition for the presidency had different program guidelines regarding infrastructure policies. The Brazilian Social Democratic Party (PSDB), the party of Cardoso, favored a regulatory role for the State, meaning that provision of services should largely be put in the hands of private corporations. Cardoso's policies envisioned privatization of state-level companies, an orientation that was meant to both address the federal government's limited capacity to invest and avoid politicization of urban infrastructure expenditure. A number of state-level companies were indeed privatized, in both the electric and sanitation sector. In contrast, the Workers' Party (PT), the party of Lula, held that the provision of urban infrastructure should be in the hands of the public sector and that subsidies should be guaranteed to poorer beneficiaries as a way to delink access to services from income. As a result, universal access was made possible by subsidy policies adopted by the Lula government, under the National Program for Universal Access and Use of Electric Power.

In short, urban infrastructure policy design, particularly funding schemes and the absence of subsidies, implied that the capacity to pay service fees has usually been a condition for the selection of new areas to be served, despite mounting pressure for expansion of coverage. The path of incremental expansion and its territorial divide was not the result of paradigm shifts in policy templates deployed by the military regime under democracy (if we exclude privatization implemented by Fernando Henrique Cardoso). It was the result of endogenous changes implemented via layering processes by which new layers of legislation were added to the existing models (Mahoney and Thelen 2010), particularly subsidy policies to the poorest (Dias 2012; see chapter "Housing and Urban Conditions in Brazil" by Eduardo Marques).

Policy-specific production costs can also explain why these infrastructure policies display such different speeds with regard to expansion in services. Once large investments in electric power plants are made, distribution costs turn out to be much lower (see also the chapter "Housing and Urban Conditions in Brazil" by Eduardo Marques). The provision of sewage collection, however, requires substantial installation costs anytime a new area needs to be served, a technical factor that, along with deadlock arising out of disputes regarding which level of government has actually the authority to grant services (Arretche 2014), explains why this policy lags behind, despite the fact that water and sewage disposal policies are under the same institutional framework, launched during the military regime.

As for the healthcare policies, the constitutional earmarking of municipal income in the form of federal transfers for health and induction mechanisms for integrating the Unified Health System (SUS) have an important effect on the territorial distribution of physicians (Arretche 2016a, b), although cross-municipality inequality in supply is largely affected by proximity to medical schools (Marques and Arretche 2014).

Two separate factors may be at work with regard to those policies in which this negative association remains high (around −0.7), namely, basic education and garbage collection. For garbage collection, this is most likely explained by the fact that since its origin, this service has been organized under the exclusive responsibility of municipal governments. The impossibility of cross-subsidies and the absence of federal regulation – whether by encouraging universal access or associating resources to services – may be the origin of the high negative correlation between poverty rates and coverage rates for this service.

The high negative correlation between educational level and poverty rates is more readily explained. There is solid evidence that indicates the association between education and income in that these two phenomena represent two sides of the same coin. Municipalities where populations present lower levels of schooling – even if these are a result of the migration of better educated individuals to areas with higher levels of activity – also present higher rates of concentrated poverty.

Conclusions

In the 1970s, Brazil was more than simply a poor country. The majority of municipalities were inhabited by high concentrations of poor people, and lack of basic services was widespread. From 1970 to 2010, there have been noticeable improvements in the living standards of Brazilian cities. There was an increase in per capita income, a decrease in poor concentration, and significant improvements in the coverage of physical infrastructure services, the provision of physicians, and educational levels. In the meantime, wealth inequality among Brazilian municipalities remained rigorously stable, territorial inequality in poor concentration increased, and there was a decrease in inequality with regard to access to basic services pertaining to electricity, water and sewage, garbage collection, and educational levels.

Prosperity – understood here as a synonym for well-being and involving income and access to services – arose within a scenario of close association between expansion of per capita income and reduction in the percentage of poor people although it is impossible to determine the causality direction. The fact remains that improvements in the wealth of jurisdictions were generally accompanied by reductions in poverty concentration and expansion in coverage rates for services. When a municipality experienced improvements in one dimension, it would very likely lead to progress in other dimensions of well-being.

In this way, individuals with similar income levels may display unequal access to public services, depending on the supply in the jurisdiction in which they reside. This supply is closely associated with the wealth and poverty rate of the municipalities.

Moreover, the trajectory of improvements shows marked regional expression. Territorial expansion of services began in the wealthiest municipalities where universal service supply preceded – by a significant margin – coverage expansion in the remaining regions. Improvements in coverage in the South and Southeast regions constituted the first cycle of expansion for all policies, even if at different rates for each policy area. It could be said that the policies of the military regime – and even those during the redemocratization period – were of greater benefit to the South and Southeast regions.

The 1980s was not in fact a lost decade in the social field as Vilmar Faria (1992) stated. However, advances in the coverage of social services in this period mainly benefited the poor within the wealthiest municipalities, where access to water and electricity were practically universal by the early 1990s.

Improved coverage for the South and Central-West regions constitutes the second cycle of expansion for all policies, albeit in different periods for each policy area.

Finally, the North and Northeast regions constitute the last area for service expansion. For both water and electricity – universal in the Southeast since 1980 – access would only become universal in 2010. In fact, the rural population and the poor in the neediest municipalities, especially in the Drought Polygon (equivalent to over half of the Northeast region), would only obtain access to water and electricity in the twenty-first century. However, garbage collection and sewage remain unfulfilled promises for these populations.

References

Araujo, H., et al. 2010. Desigualdade da renda no território brasileiro. *Comunicados do IPEA*, no. 60.

Arretche, M. (2016a). Federalism, social policy, and reductions in territorial inequality in contemporary Brazil. In B. R. Schneider (Ed.), *New order and progress. Development and democracy in Brazil* (pp. 162–186). Oxford: Oxford University Press.

Arretche, M. (2016b). The Brazilian place equality regime. In J. Sellers, M. Arretche, D. Kubler, & E. Razin (Eds.), *Inequality and governance in the Metropolis: Place equality regimes and fiscal choices in eleven countries*. London: Palgrave Macmillan.

Arretche, M., Cordeiro, B. de S., Fusaro, E., Dias, E. C., & Bittar, M. (2012). *Capacidades Administrativas dos Municípios Brasileiros para a Política Habitacional.* Brasília/São Paulo: Ministério das Cidades/Centro de Estudos da Metrópole.

Azzoni, C. R. (1997, September/December). Concentração de renda regional e dispersão das rendas *per capita* estaduais: análise a partir de séries históricas estaduais de PIB, 1939–1995. *Estudos Econômicos, 27*(3), 341–393.

Barros, R. P. de, Henriques, R, & Mendonça, R. (2000). Desigualdade e Pobreza no Brasil: retrato de uma estabilidade inaceitável. *Revista Brasileira de Ciências Sociais, 15*(42), 123–142.

Chein, F., Lemos, M. B., & Assunção, J. J. (2007, July/September). Desenvolvimento desigual: evidências para o Brasil. *Revista Brasileira de Economia, 61*(3), 301–330.

Coelho, R. L. P., & Figueiredo, L. de. (2007, July/September). Uma Análise da Hipótese da Convergência para os Municípios Brasileiros." *Revista Brasileira de Economia, 61*(3), 331–352.

Dias, E. C. (2012). *Do Plano Real ao Programa Minha Casa, Minha Vida: negócios, votos e as reformas da habitação.* Master Dissertation, University of São Paulo.

Esping-Andersen, G. (1985). Power and distributional regimes. *Politics & Society, 14*(2), 223–256.

Esping-Andersen, G. (1990). *The three worlds of welfare capitalism.* Princeton: Princeton University Press.

Faria, V. (1992). A conjuntura social brasileira. *Novos Estudos CEBRAP,* no. 33.

Foguel, M. N., & Leite Corseuil, C. H. (2002, July). *An alternative income deflator for some Brazilian Household Surveys.* Discussion Paper No. 897. Available at SSRN: https://ssrn.com/abstract=374561; https://doi.org/10.2139/ssrn.374561.

Hoffmann, R. (2010, December). Desigualdade da renda e das despesas *per capita* no Brasil, em 2002–2003 e 2008–2009, e avaliação do grau de progressividade ou regressividade de parcelas da renda familiar. *Economia e Sociedade, 19*(3) (40), 647–661.

Laurini, M., Andrade, E., & Pereira, P. L. V. (2003). *Clubes de Convergência de Renda para os Municípios Brasileiros: Uma Análise Não-Paramétrica.* Insper Working Paper, WPE: 048, Mimeografado.

Loyola, P. C. P. (2014). *Partidos e políticas nos governos subnacionais brasileiros* (Master's dissertation). University of São Paulo.
Magalhães, A., Hewing, G. J. D., & Azzoni, C. R. (2005). Spatial dependence and regional convergence in Brazil. *Investigaciones Regionales, 6*, 5–20.
Mahoney, J. & Thelen (ed.) (2010). *Explaining Institutional Change: Ambiguity, Agency, and Power.* Cambridge, Cambridge University Press, pp. 236.
Manso, C. A., Barreto, F. A., & França, J. M. S. de. (2010a, April/June). Retornos da Educação e o Desequilíbrio Regional no Brasil. *Revista Brasileira de Economia, 64*(2), 115–133.
Manso, C. A., Barreto, F. A., & França, J. M. S. de. (2010b, April/June). Bem-Estar Social, Mercado de Trabalho e o Desequilíbrio Regional. *Estudos Econômicos, 40*(2), 401–443.
Marques, E. & Arretche, M. (2004). Condicionantes Locais da Descentralização das Políticas de Saúde. In *Cadernos CRH,* (39), 55–81.
Marshall, T. H. Cidadania e classe social. (1967). *Cidadania, classe social e status*. Rio de Janeiro: Zahar.
Neri, M. C., & Souza, P. H. C. F. de. (2012). A Década Inclusiva (2001–2011): Desigualdade, Pobreza e Políticas de Renda. *Comunicados do IPEA*, no. 155.
Pinto, M. S., & Oliveira, J. C. de. (2010, May/August). Crescimento Pró-Pobre: Análise dos Estados Brasileiros entre 1995 e 2007. *Revista de Economia Contemporânea, 14*(2), 327–358.
Rawls, J. (1971). *A Theory of Justice*. Cambridge, MA: Belknap Press of Harvard University Press.
Ribeiro, E. C. B. de A., & Almeida, E. S. de. (2012). Convergência Local de Renda no Brasil. *Economia Aplicada, 16*(3), 399–420.
Satyro, N. (2013). Política estadual e desigualdade: por que alguns estados redistribuem mais do que outros? *Dados*. Rio de Janeiro. Impresso, *56*, 497–530.
Sen, A. (1999). *Desenvolvimento como liberdade*. São Paulo: Companhia das Letras.
Soares, S. S. D. (2010, July/September). O ritmo na queda da desigualdade no Brasil é aceitável? *Revista de Economia Política, 30*(3) (119), 364–380.

Housing and Urban Conditions in Brazil

Eduardo C. L. Marques

Abstract The chapter discusses the trajectory of urban conditions in Brazilian cities from 1960 to 2010, based on data from the IBGE demographic censuses. The study focused especially on information about households and access to urban infrastructure, such as the coverage of water supply services, sewage networks, garbage collection, and electric power supply. On average, urban conditions have improved substantially over time, and there is no question of the reduction of inequalities in access to better urban conditions in a general sense. However, the analysis indicates the persistence of two kinds of problems. Firstly, the data shows obvious difficulties in the provision of certain services, especially sewage networks, still marked by very low coverage. Additionally, there are still high and persistent regional and social inequalities in access to services, when we combine in the analysis the most important metropolitan regions with the social groups that compose them. The Brazilian urban trajectory, therefore, is marked in the period by significant improvements, but with still substantial persisting inequalities.

Keywords Urban conditions · Urban infrastructure · Metropolitan regions · Inequalities · Access to policies

This chapter focuses on the trajectory of urban conditions in Brazilian cities from 1960 to 2010, based on information from the Brazilian Institute of Geography and Statistics (IBGE) censuses, particularly those relating to households and access to urban infrastructure, such as coverage of water supply services, sewage systems, garbage collection, and electricity supply. Even though census data present limitations when analyzing urban conditions, especially with regard to urban services,

E. C. L. Marques (✉)
Department of Political Science, Center for Metropolitan Studies (CEM), University of São Paulo (USP), São Paulo, Brazil

M. Arretche (ed.), *Paths of Inequality in Brazil*,
https://doi.org/10.1007/978-3-319-78184-6_8

it is the only information collected comprehensively, using a unified methodology. There is no systematic information on precarious housing in particular, but the chapter does discuss the research findings for these 50 years. On average, urban conditions have improved substantially over time, and there has been an unquestionable reduction in inequalities of access to improved urban conditions in a broader sense. However, analysis indicates that there are still problems attributable to two factors: the difficulties in providing certain services, especially sewage collection, given the prevalence of very low coverage rates, and the persistence of important regional and social inequalities (among groups) in obtaining access to services. The goal of this chapter is to analyze this improved coverage scenario in the presence of persisting inequalities.

This analysis is organized into three sections. In the first section, the historical trajectory of Brazil's urban conditions is discussed. In the second section, the temporal trajectory of indicators is analyzed, showing average improvement in access, but also revealing the persistence of localized problems in certain policies as well as continuing inequalities among regions, states, city size, metropolitan areas, and social groups. The third section takes a more detailed look at regional and social inequalities by combining comparisons of the most important metropolitan regions with observations of the social groups that comprise them.

The Legacy of Urban Conditions in Brazil

Most studies on this topic consist of monographs that analyze specific cities at precise points in time. Few works have attempted to track the more general dynamics of Brazilian cities over long periods. Even though it would be impossible to cover such a broad field of research in a single chapter, a brief historical overview of academic literature that pertains to Brazilian cities is definitely worthwhile.

The first group of works focused on the prevailing conditions in Brazilian cities during the late nineteenth century and early twentieth century, when major urban reforms were carried out in an effort to erase colonial traces from cities, to embellish them (the specific wording at the time), and to provide them with infrastructure (Abreu 1987; Leme 1999). The predominant form of housing, at least for the working class, was the tenement (Vaz 2002), although a few working-class villages were constructed in outlying areas (Bonduki 1998). The supply of urban infrastructure began in the second half of the nineteenth century, particularly in Rio de Janeiro, but also in other cities mainly through concessions to foreign private companies (Marques 1995; Carone and Der 1989). Transport followed the same typical trajectory, starting with concessions to domestic private companies and then to foreign companies. Service coverage was low and highly selective in spatial and social terms, and in addition, it was entirely in the hands of local governments and thus was highly concentrated in major affluent cities.

Initial federal actions targeting cities took place in the late 1930s with the creation of housing departments by the Retirement and Pensions Institutes (IAPs). The Low-Income Housing Foundation (FCP) was established in 1945 (Azevedo and Andrade 1981; Bonduki 1998). In both cases, the volume of public housing produced was minimal in quantitative terms and highly concentrated in the cities of Rio de Janeiro, Belo Horizonte, and São Paulo. Remaining cities produced even less and more selective local-led policies and interventions. The Brazilian urban population went from 12.9 million in 1940 to 31.3 million in 1960 (Baeninger 2011), with practically no national urban policy.

In 1960, when the first massive federal policies emerged, Brazilian cities had already accrued high levels of precarious housing and lacked state policies capable of produce actions to provide suitable urban conditions. The military governments established a complex centralized institutional apparatus to promote urban policies, such as creating the National Housing Bank (BNH) in 1964, setting up the Housing Finance System (SFH) and the Sanitation Financial System (SFS) in 1967, and formulating the National Sanitation Plan (PLANASA) in 1971 (Maricato 1987; Rezende and Heller 2002). From then on, prompted by the federal government, state and municipal enterprises were established to implement nationally administered policies on housing, water supply, sewage, and electricity. Garbage collection remained entirely under the responsibility of local jurisdictions as did urban planning, although the latter was subject to the policies of the Federal Service for Housing and Urbanism (SERFHAU), which had little impact (Maricato 1987). Public wheeled transportation, widely prevalent in post-World War II Brazilian cities (Brasileiro and Henry 1999), remained entirely local with no federal regulation, while rail transportation became regulated and partially funded by the federal government.

Policies introduced by the military regime led to a significant increase in coverage, changing the benchmark for public intervention in Brazilian cities, but their framework was shaped by excessive centralization of decision-making, high levels of corruption, and clientelism. All this ended up substantially reducing the potential redistributive effects of such policies (Draibe 1989; Maricato 1987; Rezende and Heller 2002). As for the public served, policies were highly selective, even mistargeting, as in the case of housing policies where considerable subsidies benefited the middle classes at the expense of the poorest (Maricato 1987). It is worth noting that only 33.1% of units built by the BNH system between 1964 and 1986 targeted low-income populations (Royer 2009). Moreover, what was produced in terms of low-income housing focused almost exclusively on a single product – new units in housing projects located on the periphery, for sale through long-term housing loans, excluding a sizeable portion of the population (whose demand was not for purchase through loans) and reinforcing the already substantial residential segregation patterns in metropolitan areas.

As a result, the policies failed to address preexisting precarious housing conditions not to mention the growing demand since Brazil's urban population had increased from 31 million inhabitants in 1960 to 80 million in 1980 (Baeninger 2011). The data analyzed here partially capture this dynamic, indicating an increase in coverage as of 1960, but this occurred at a pace slower than what was needed and in a highly selective path, amassing inequalities of access across social groups. Both international comparative studies (Gilbert and Gugler 1992; Gilbert 1996) and Brazilian urban studies alike accumulated a wide array of evidence regarding the segregation consequences of such policies on the country's metropolitan areas

(Kowarick 1979, 2011; Bonduki and Rolnik 1982), housing (Valladares 1980; Cardoso 2007), *favelas* (Taschner and Baltrusis 2007), the structure and form of urban settlements (Abreu 1987), and the impact of such patterns on poverty and inequalities (Marques and Torres 2005).

From the early 1980s, the BNH policy models quickly fell into turmoil, leading to that agency's extinction in 1986. Even though the period that followed demonstrated acute volatility with regard to government involvement in the sector (Arretche 1995), it was accompanied by important innovations and activism in policies at the local level, especially when it came to housing (Cardoso 2007). Despite existing policies that attempted to address demand as a result of the increase in urban population, which went from 80 to 161 million between 1980 and 2010, precarious urban conditions continued to worsen.

It was only in the early 2000s that the federal government returned to this sector. This began with the City Statute in 2001, followed by the establishment of the Ministry of Cities, which was successful at conducting several national city conferences and organizing numerous important institutions, such as councils, funds, and the national plans for housing, sanitation, and solid waste (Maricato 2006; Heller 2010). It also introduced important regulatory changes, allowing for a strong uptick in housing investments, including those from the private sector (Dias 2012). On the other hand, local administrative capacity, still very low, had been growing steadily, due in part to federal induction policies (Arretche et al. 2007, 2012). Development of a national urban policy appears key to reducing the level of precarious housing and providing better urban conditions, but this is far from being well-established and rife with challenges to be faced in the coming years (Heller 2009; Maricato 2011; Roberts 2005).

Brazilian Urban Conditions Between 1960 and 2010

First and foremost, some methodological caveats are necessary concerning the limitations of the census data employed in this study, meaning that there are trade-offs involved in their use. With regard to disadvantages, as widely discussed in the research on Brazilian cities, census data have some limits (Taschner and Baltrusis 2007; Heller 2009). First, available information is of limited range and does not cover key dimensions, such as the legal conditions of land and real estate, construction densities and other building details, conditions of urban mobility, urban standards of settlements, or the quality of the environment. Moreover, the available information does not allow us to make a distinction among the details and features of service coverage (and their environmental or urban impact) – such as sanitary drainage and combined sewer networks, any existing sewage treatment, or specifications regarding solid waste disposal. In fact, no systematic information is available to describe these dimensions for Brazil as a whole.

It is impossible to determine the quality of the policies and services provided, the frequency in water supply, or the regularity of garbage collection, differences that could lead to significant inequalities of service in terms of sanitation and comfort.

This chapter puts forward arguments related to service quality whenever possible, but in general this issue is not addressed.

It is likely that such limitations have stronger than anticipated effects when analyzing recent periods. In the 1960s and 1970s, the lack of services was the main dimension differentiating locations and social groups. More recently, however, as they come into existence, differences in quality are the most important sources of inequality. It makes sense to consider that patterns of social and territorial inequalities specified throughout this chapter are even stronger when it comes to service quality, but it is impossible to empirically test this claim in a systematic manner.

Lastly, a large number of these inequalities occurs at a very disaggregated level and can only be analyzed by means of detailed intra-urban investigations. This will not be done here for several reasons. First, it would impossible to carry out such an analysis for all urban spaces or even for a large group of metropolitan areas in Brazil.[1] Second, geo-referenced databases are only available for Brazilian cities after 1991. As for census sample information, the situation is even worse since area weighting is only spatially identifiable from 2000 on. Therefore, intra-urban and intertemporal comparisons are possible for only 2000 and 2010, which greatly reduces the scope of the temporal comparative exercise in this chapter, although it would improve social and spatial detail.[2] Nevertheless, a methodological device was used to explore existing social inequalities by disaggregating information by income groups and separately analyzing the poorest 40%, the intermediate 50%, and the wealthiest 10% in each metropolitan area, region, and country. Even in the case of cities, these groups cannot be distinguished in detail using existing information, making it impossible to analyze intertemporal behavior in residential segregation for the country as a whole.

Census information does, however, present national and temporal coverage, since it is the only standard data for the entire country besides being collected consistently over time.

Given these initial caveats, we begin the analysis by observing the changes in urban conditions over time, beginning with data on buildings. Occupancy in Brazilian cities over the past decades predominantly occurred through owner-occupancy, even if ownership conditions often involved various types of irregularities or urban illegalities. In the early twentieth century, Brazilian urban residents lived in rented real estate, both in the form of houses for the middle class and tenement rooms for the working class (Bonduki 1998; Vaz 2002). From the 1940s on, however, there was a significant upward trend in the proportion of owner-occupancies and a gradual decline in renter-occupancies (Graph 1). Until 1940, owner-occupied housing was less common than renter-occupied or other types of occupancy (assigned, licensed, and others). Between 1950 and 1960, owner-occupied housing became more prevalent, making up more than 75% of property available in 2000.

---

[1] A detailed analysis of the nine most traditional metropolitan areas defined by Law 14/73 is provided: Belém, Fortaleza, Recife, Salvador, Belo Horizonte, Rio de Janeiro, São Paulo, Curitiba, and Porto Alegre.

[2] This type of comparative exercise was done for the cities of São Paulo and Rio de Janeiro (Marques et al. 2012; Marques 2015).

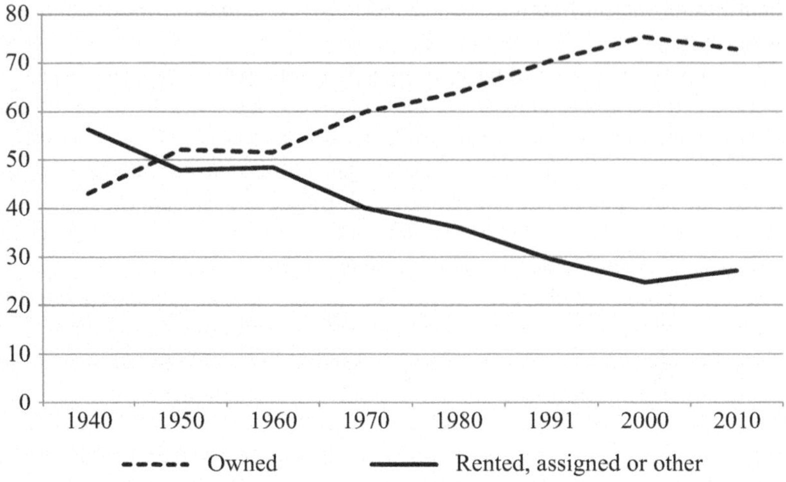

Graph 1 Household occupancy Brazil: 1940–2010 (%). (Source: IBGE Demographic census (special tabulations by CEM))

During the 2000s, there was a slight reduction (73%), but available information does not allow us to analyze what was entailed in the reduction or the reasons for it.

From 1980 on, houses also became more prevalent than apartments in Brazilian cities, although the latter form of residence is slowly increasing. Proportions have shown little variation: private housing was 91.9% in 1981, going to 90.3% in 1992, and 90.7% in 2009. Apartment dwelling increased slowly but steadily: from 7.1% in 1981 to 8.7% in 1992, reaching 9.2% in 2009 (PNAD, IBGE).

This general trend can be seen in all regions of Brazil, including its major metropolitan regions. At the state level, the proportion of renter-occupancies among the urban population in 2010 is constantly between 20% and 30%, except in the states of Maranhão and Piauí, where rates were about 19%, Goiás (33%), and Brasilia (40%). At the end of the period, one can observe a convergence of renter-occupancies at about 20% in all metropolitan areas analyzed. Furthermore, the increase in owner-occupancies remains practically the same when isolating for high- and low-income households.

This dynamic includes at least two simultaneous and specific movements by different social groups. On the one hand, it is a result of the establishment of local real estate construction markets between the 1930s and the 1970s (Ribeiro 1997), which are also involved in the gradual increase in the proportion of available apartments. Even in the case of public housing construction, the option for financed sale is at the root of Brazil's popular housing policies (Bonduki 1998). On the other hand, the increase of owner-occupancies actually conceals a problem with this information, since residents of *favelas* and settlements declare themselves owners (except when they pay rent) regardless of the status of the building, land, or allotment. Thus, the development of low-income housing in *favelas* and squatter settlements throughout Brazil, dating back to the time of rapid urbanization in the 1950s, also explains the increase in owner-occupancies.

Another process that contributes to the relative reduction of rentals involves the apparent decline in single-room households or tenement rooms, a highly precarious and unhealthy housing solution. According to the information found in the PNAD, in 1982, 2.1% of Brazilian households were of this type, falling to 1.0% in 1992, 0.3% in 2001, and 0.1% in 2009. Monographic studies suggest higher numbers for metropolitan areas, leading us to believe that such information is underestimated (Schor and Borin 1997; Bianchini and Schicchi 2009). Nevertheless, regardless of the extent of the phenomenon, the data suggest a downward trend in this precarious housing solution.

Information about precarious housing classified in census tracts as substandard, which is only available from 1991 on, reports that the proportion of households considered substandard went from 4.5% in 1991 to 3.7% in 2000 and 5.6% in 2010 for Brazil as a whole (IBGE 2010). However, it is very difficult to analyze this information over time because the data is quite sensitive to the classification strategy – and the operational definition of substandard – adopted by IBGE in each census.[3] A study conducted in 2007 by the Center for Metropolitan Studies (CEM) for the Ministry of Cities showed that 13% of households in Brazil had similar social, urban, and housing characteristics to those 6.7% classified by the IBGE as being substandard. It means that the phenomenon of precarious housing is much more prevalent than the information on substandard sectors would lead us to believe. According to the IBGE, in 2010 the metropolitan regions with the highest proportion of households in substandard sectors were Belém (53.9%), Salvador (26.1%), Recife (23.2%), and Rio de Janeiro (14.4%). This ranking had already been identified by CEM in a study using the 2000 data, indicating Belém (51.3%), Fortaleza (25.4%), Salvador (24%), and Rio de Janeiro (21%) as cities with the largest presence of substandard sectors (Marques et al. 2007). The greatest difference between the CEM 2000 study and the 2010 IBGE data refers to Fortaleza, where IBGE claimed that there were only 11.9% of households in substandard sectors in 2010. In addition to the nine metropolitan areas that are the focus of this chapter, São Luiz do Maranhão appeared in the CEM study as being characterized by an increased presence of substandard sectors in 2000 (27.9%), data that is confirmed by the 24.5% credited to the city in the 2010 IBGE Census. Although caution regarding the use of this information on substandard sectors is needed, the elevated presence of precarious housing in Brazilian cities is clear, being Belém, most cities in the Northeast cities, and Rio de Janeiro those in the worst situation.[4]

[3]The substandard classification has an administrative and objective nature: extra pay for census workers assigned to sectors with precarious conditions, since their job is considered more difficult. Therefore, although there is a definition of substandard sector (and entire sectors rather than as households are defined as such) in each census, sectors are classified as substandard before the fieldwork by considering locally available data and financial availability for the fieldwork. For further details on the issue, see Marques et al. (2007) and Costa and Nascimento (2005).

[4]The only study that uses the same methodology over time but does not rely strictly on the substandard classification concerns the metropolitan regions of the state of São Paulo, reproducing the CEM methodology for 2000 and 2010. The results suggest proportional reduction of precarious housing in São Paulo and an increase in the other three metropolitan areas (Marques et al. 2014).

Another piece of information regarding the general conditions of households is the average density of urban households, which tended to increase until 1970, but monotonically declined thereafter. Even when disaggregating this information and looking only at the poorest 40%, densities peaked in 1970 with nearly 3.2 people per household, then dropped steadily until reaching 2.2 in 2010. The same trend can be seen in the nine major metropolitan regions in Brazil, although densities are always higher on average in the poorest ones, especially Belém, which had an average density of 2.2 in 2010, similar to that of the poorest 40% of the country. In 2010, the average household density in substandard sectors was still 3.5 (IBGE 2010).

Lastly, an important indicator of housing quality refers to sanitary installations, the absence of which constitutes one of the most intense forms of precarious housing. Information pertaining to the presence of bathrooms is only found in the 1991 census onward, but even for such recent data, levels of precarious housing were very high. Households without bathrooms numbered more than 20% among the poorest 40% of Brazil in 1991, while this condition was present in only 5% among the intermediate 50% in 1991 and virtually nonexistent among the wealthiest 10%. The situation progressively improved from the 1990s on, so as that in 2010, only 5% of the poorest 40% of households had no bathrooms. However, this proportion reached about 20% of the poorest (40%) in the North.

If we disaggregate this data for the states, we find that more than 10% of the urban population in Amazonas, Pará, and Amapá in 2010 did not have bathrooms in their homes, and over 20% of the urban population in the states of Acre and Maranhão lived in extreme conditions of precarious housing. Among the metropolitan areas analyzed, the worst conditions were found in Belém, where almost 12% of the poorest 40% lived in households without bathrooms. As a sign of the inequalities found in Brazilian metropolitan areas, only 35% of households in Belém not classified among the poorest 40% in 2010 had two or more bathrooms. Among the remaining metropolitan areas, this proportion was very low in 2010, but still reached nearly 5% of the poorest 40% of Salvador, Recife, and Fortaleza. Therefore, despite substantial improvements in the averages, housing inequalities remain significant both regionally and across social groups. The distance between these regions and groups presents a downward trend.

A similar result is obtained when comparing cities of different sizes. Although the greatest presence of households without bathrooms occurs in cities with fewer than 500,000 inhabitants, mainly on cities with fewer than 100,000 inhabitants, the distances between types of cities have declined over time. In 1991, approximately 22% of households in municipalities with a population of fewer than 20,000 and 17% of households in cities that had between 20,000 and 100,000 inhabitants had no bathrooms, while in cities with over 500,000 inhabitants, this proportion did not reach 10%. In 2010, we find that smaller municipalities presented rates close to 5%, while in larger municipalities, this rate was around 1%. It should be emphasized here that rates fell little between 1991 and 2000, and greater improvements occurred in the 2000s, possibly more as a result of improvements in the labor market and income rather than as a specific outcome of urban and housing policies.

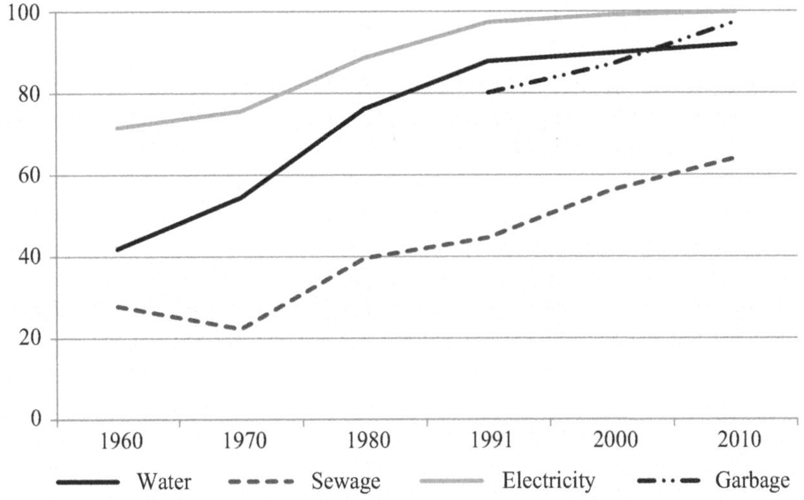

Graph 2 Evolution of urban infrastructure, according to service coverage Brazil: 1960–2010 (% of urban households). (Source: IBGE Demographic census (special tabulations by CEM))

Consequently, the presence of urban precarious housing coexists with the improvement of specific indicators. This becomes even clearer when housing conditions are complemented by urban infrastructure, as we will see below. While it may seem contradictory, it is in fact quite understandable. Although access to land and regular housing have historically been a major problem in Brazilian cities, housing and infrastructure conditions have tended to improve on average, even in the *favelas* and poor regions. This holds particularly true for the post-democratization period, when average conditions are likely to improve for most precarious housing situations – particularly *favelas* and squatter settlements. These improvements were related to a combination of factors: pressures from social movements, especially during the 1980s, and changes in state agencies involved in promoting services in a political environment increasingly regulated by regular and competitive elections (Farias 1992; Silva 1992; Marques and Bichir 2003).

Graph 2 shows the evolution in the coverage of water, sewage system, electricity, and garbage collection,[5] considering that data for the latter is only available as of 1991.

The overall trend indicates increased coverage, but sanitary sewage services show a slower expansion rate by comparison. The expansion of water supply was significant in the 1970s and 1980s – certainly as a result of a nationwide restructuring of the sector starting with the Sanitation Financial System in 1967 and the PLANASA in 1971 – but decreased in the 1990s when it registered a stagnant rate of around 92%. Sewage system coverage is still expanding at a reasonable rate, but at a very

[5] Water supply, households connected to a water supply system; sewage, households covered by a sewage system, even if combined (unitary); garbage collection, households with regular direct garbage collection; electricity, households connected to a distribution grid, with or without individual meter.

low threshold, reaching only 64% of urban households in 2010. It greatly increased in the 1970s and 1990s, but remained stagnant during the 1980s, at the height of the BNH national funding crisis, as well as the 2000s. Energy services and garbage collection tended toward universalization in 2010. The expansion of the latter was very significant, especially among the poorest – in 1991 at the beginning of the series for this indicator, only 40% of households among the poorest 40% of Brazil had access to this service, while in 2010, 95% of households within this group were served.

The scenario regarding sewage system coverage would be even more dramatic had we considered only properly treated separate sanitary sewage systems, an even more uncommon situation, but one not distinguishable using census data. Heller (2012) worked with census and PNAD data, estimating service coverage to precarious housing for the year of 2008 at 33% for water supply, 44% for sewage system, and 27% for garbage collection. According to estimates from the Ministry of Cities (SNIS 2011), in 2010 only 54% of sewage collected in urban areas was properly treated. The situation surrounding garbage collection is also not as favorable as it appears in the graph because it does not identify suitable final disposal. Even though all domestic waste is being collected, a significant portion might continue to be disposed in a manner detrimental to health and the environment. The same source reports that in 2010, 78% of the urban population was located in cities that claimed to have some type of selective garbage collection (SNIS 2012), highly concentrated in larger cities (garbage collection only served 39% of municipalities). On the other hand, in 22% of the cities, the garbage collected was disposed of in landfills. Therefore, after the near universalization of garbage collection, the barriers to progress with regard to recycling and proper disposal remain very distant goals (SNIS 2012).

When we regionally disaggregate the information by social group, city size, and metropolitan area, clear patterns of inequality appear, except for access to electricity, which has virtually become universal for urban households. The first axis of inequality involves Brazil's major regions. While on average, coverage for the Southeast, South, Midwest, and Northeast regions converges toward universalization, except for sanitary sewage coverage; the North presents rates quite distant from this threshold, including rates for water supply coverage, which remain at around 65%. The second axis of inequality refers to social groups. Even with water supply coverage close to universal levels, the difference between coverage for the wealthiest 10% and poorest 40% is 7% points, increasing substantially for sewage, since while the wealthiest 10% have service in 83% of households, the poorest 40% only have it in 53% of households. As for garbage collection, although service is almost universal for the wealthiest 10% and the intermediate 50% of the population, nearly 10% of households among the poorest 40% of the North and Northeast regions are not served.

In terms of the states, water supply coverage remained below 60% for the urban population in 2010 in only four states, all in the North – Rondônia, Acre, Pará, and Amapá – whereas in the remaining states, there was clear convergence of rates close to 95%. Sanitary sewage coverage for the urban population, on the other hand, was very low in 2010 for all states in the North – 32% in Amazonas and Acre – and below 20% in others. The rates were also very low for the remaining states, only reaching above 60% in the four states of the Southeast as well as in Paraná, Rio Grande do Sul, and Bahia and in the Federal District. As for the provision of electricity, there was a trend toward universal coverage for the urban population by 2000 in all of Brazil's states, with the same occurring with garbage collection, although in two states in the Northeast, services have remained lower – at only 80% in Maranhão and 88% in Piauí in 2010.

Generally speaking, states in the Southeast and Midwest showed significant improvement in water supply coverage in the 1960s and in sewage coverage in the 1970s and 1980s, while although the South saw improvements in water supply coverage in the 1960s, it was only in the 1980s that the same progress was seen in sanitary sewage networks. In the states of Brazil's Northeast, water supply coverage improved significantly in the 1960s and again in the years 1990 and 2000, and the region experienced limited improvement in sewage coverage during the 1990s.

Another interesting way to analyze the information is to observe city size, presented in Table 1 for the period between 1970 and 2010. The exercise presents a certain degree of artificiality, however, because cities are classified under a particular size, which could change over time and thus place them into a different category. Despite that, the analysis provides us with a notion of how urban conditions were gradually transformed in the Brazilian urban network. Overall, the table indicates that small cities have lower coverage rates when compared to very large cities,

Table 1 Service coverage averages by city size Brazil: 1970–2010 (%)

		City size (in inhabitants)				
Service coverage	Years	Up to 20,000	20,000–100,000	100,000–500,000	500,000–1 million	Over 1 million
Water supply	1970	24.74	43.74	64.66	58.21	60.54
	1980	60.99	67.85	78.39	73.62	85.75
	1991	78.38	81.67	88.97	88.78	95.04
	2000	86.81	86.17	89.68	89.98	95.17
	2010	90.03	88.42	91.31	91.68	95.01
Sanitary sewage	1970	6.83	17.11	34.77	29.73	7.77
	1980	19.97	26.22	39.49	34.43	57.11
	1991	22.44	29.80	47.00	49.02	61.64
	2000	37.73	47.57	60.01	58.57	75.85
	2010	41.33	49.34	61.48	66.46	80.90
Electricity	1970	46.05	61.01	81.85	84.67	91.95
	1980	71.60	79.89	91.24	95.37	96.93
	1991	92.63	94.84	98.30	99.06	99.51
	2000	97.69	98.45	99.51	99.80	99.84
	2010	99.36	99.53	99.72	99.86	99.92
Garbage collection	1991	60.82	69.58	83.05	85.66	91.32
	2000	75.87	82.40	90.88	90.07	92.40
	2010	93.91	95.73	97.18	98.18	98.87

Source: IBGE Demographic census (special tabulations by CEM)

especially in recent years. The relative position of average-sized cities changes over time, starting better in general, but eventually being overtaken by very large cities.

Nonetheless, different services display their own dynamics. Water supply coverage has always been higher for large cities, with substantial progress occurring in cities of all sizes during the 1970s and 1980s, and much slower growth thereafter. At the end of the period, services are still low in the smaller cities, but gaps have been greatly reduced. Electricity coverage follows a very similar path, albeit starting at a higher point and achieving nearly universal access to services in 2010 for cities of all sizes. If we look at the different dynamics for sewage coverage, we notice that at the beginning of the period, the highest coverage rates are in cities whose population numbers between 100,000 and 1 million inhabitants. In the 1970s and 1980s, larger cities showed giant leaps in coverage, ending the period with rates that were high but still far from universal. Although the problem of sewage networks is widespread, it tends to be even more severe in small- and medium-sized cities. If it were possible to discriminate between separate and combined sewage networks, we would certainly see a much more precarious situation for smaller cities. With regard to garbage collection services, higher rates have always been present in large cities, but in the years 1990 and 2000, the numbers in smaller cities rose substantially, almost matching the others.

In 2010, for all regions analyzed, even among the poorest, electricity and garbage collection services also appear to be practically universal. This suggests that the aforementioned garbage collection problem refers to poor populations in non-metropolitan urban areas within the North and Northeast regions.

For the remaining services, Belém and Recife and, to a lesser degree, Rio de Janeiro, show the worst conditions. In Recife, water supply coverage does not exceed 85% even among the wealthiest 10%, and in Belém, it stands at less than 70% for all social groups. If we disaggregate the three groups for each metropolitan area, the poorest 40% of Rio de Janeiro are also negatively significant, thus expressing the worst coverage supply to slum areas and the Baixada Fluminense. In Rio de Janeiro, great inequalities persist across social groups, and while the wealthiest 10% have universal access, the poorest 40% are served in only 83% of households in 2010. As for sewage coverage, the situation presents very low rates for all regions. Although service is far from being universal in all regions, situations are worse in Belém, Recife, and Fortaleza. In these regions, the wealthiest 10% register coverage rates between only 55% and 72%, and the poorest 40% have rates of only 24% in Belém and 42% in Fortaleza. In Curitiba as well, coverage rates are only 70% among the poorest 40%.

A good strategy to measure inequalities between groups is to subtract the coverage rates of the poorest 40% from the coverage of the wealthiest 10%. Table 2, which shows this data, omits differences less than 10%, showing only the first and last years for each indicator. The general trend shows a reduction of inequalities over time. In addition, certain services, such as electricity and garbage collection, no longer display significant inequalities with regard to access. Sanitary sewage is the service with most unequal access and still displays major gaps. In the recent period, inequalities have remained significant in terms of sewage network, water supply, and lack of bathrooms. Belém, Fortaleza, and Recife are the most unequal metro-

Table 2 Differences between coverage of the wealthiest 10% and the poorest 40% by metropolitan region: 1970–2010 (%)

Service coverage	São Paulo	Rio de Janeiro	Porto Alegre	Curitiba	Belo Horizonte	Fortaleza	Recife	Salvador	Belém
Water – 1970	56	44	52	68	61	49	69	58	49
Water – 2010		15							
Sewage – 1970		71	63	58	71	14	53	23	32
Sewage – 2010	15	17	22	22	14	31	40	15	33
Electricity – 1970	11	18	27	31	71	59	36	35	29
Electricity – 2010									
Garbage – 1991		32	9	11	37	31	37	34	29
Garbage – 2010									
Bathrooms – 1991			20	18	11	22	22	22	28
Bathrooms – 2010									11

Source: IBGE Demographic census

politan regions, but Rio de Janeiro still presents major inequalities in access to water supply. If it were possible to rely on indicators that allow analysis of the quality of services provided, these inequalities would certainly be even greater.

All these services are produced by different public agencies at various levels of government, which greatly explains the differences. Since the 1960s, electric power distribution, which is the responsibility of state companies, has expanded steadily to groups and regions not yet covered by this service, most notably the poorest populations and those in the North and Northeast regions. In the case of street sweeping, a responsibility reserved for municipal governments, a significant effort was apparently made to expand coverage among the poorest, especially in cities in the North and Northeast, where service was very precarious until 1991 and where the largest expansion in coverage took place. The most complex situation pertains to sanitary sewage, which, since the late 1960s, was under the responsibility of state-owned companies financed by the federal government and administered through the BNH until 1986 and, more recently, funded by a federal arrangement under the Ministry of Cities. In this case, considerable differences remain across metropolitan regions, indicating diverse state policies. Even though sanitary sewage rates the worst in all regions of Brazil, service is provided even less frequently in Belém and in the northeastern metropolitan areas of Recife and Fortaleza, suggesting in the case of these capitals, ineffective policies on the part of their respective state companies.

In summary, one can say that there is a strong trend toward universalization – practically complete for electricity and nearly achieved for garbage collection coverage. As for water supply, coverage is widespread and very high, but the sector has had trouble in achieving universalization over the past decade. With regard to sanitary sewage, coverage rates are still low and major challenges remain. However, regardless of the differences between policies, significant inequalities persist between regions – with conditions being worse in the North – as well as within social groups, especially among the poorest populations of the North and Northeast. Metropolitan areas with the greatest differences in terms of coverage between the wealthy and the poor are Belém, Recife, and Fortaleza, where there is twice as much sewage coverage and 10% more water supply coverage for the wealthy compared to the poor. Generally speaking, the further away from universal service coverage, the greater the inequality of access between the wealthy and the poor.

Cities Within Cities

Another way to analyze existing urban conditions in Brazil's major metropolitan areas is to compare different coverage profiles, which allows not only an assessment of patterns of inequality and different levels of service across cities and groups but also an observation of the trajectories of urban settlements and their social groups in terms of urban infrastructure. To this end, I conducted a cluster analysis of the regions, according to the coverage profile in each year for which census data was available. However, as previously noted, different social groups have very different conditions of access within each region; so, three different social groups were separately considered for each of them – the poorest 40%, the intermediate 50%, and the wealthiest 10%. In this way, the analysis compared the profile of coverage in 27 "regions," which actually consist of the nine metropolitan areas previously mentioned divided further according to household income and coverage for water supply, sewage, electricity, garbage collection as well as the lack of bathrooms in the home.

We began by performing a factor analysis of the 21 variables, obtaining four factors with eigenvalues greater than 1, which explained 89% of the variance. These factors were then subjected to a cluster analysis, which resulted in four groups. Each of them is comprised of "regions" with different profiles regarding coverage among services and over time, combining the effects of regional and social inequalities. Detailed below are the composition and characteristics of each group.

Group 1

Included in this group are the poorest of Belém, Fortaleza, and Recife – the poorest 40% in these metropolitan areas and the intermediate 50% in Belém.

Here we find a concentration of the worst infrastructure conditions among all metropolitan regions analyzed. Water supply increases slowly and remains low in 2010 (75.7%). Sanitary sewage begins extremely low (3.6%) and remains so to the end of the period (31.6%). Additionally, we find an average of 6.4% of households without bathrooms in 2010 (in 1991, this figure stood at 22.1%). The supply of electricity and garbage collection began with intermediate values (around 63.9% and 70.6%, respectively), but achieved universal levels by 2010.

This is the only group that continues to be characterized by highly precarious access to infrastructure. The worst infrastructure conditions, however, are those provided to the poorest groups in the poorest, most remote cities of the North and Northeast. Here, we find social and income inequalities combined with regional inequalities. Particularly notable is the intermediate social group in Belém because it displays access rates similar to the poorest among all cities.

Group 2

Included here are poor groups from various metropolitan areas (the poorest 40% of Salvador, Belo Horizonte, Rio de Janeiro, and Porto Alegre) and those of average income (the intermediate 50% of Fortaleza, Recife, and Salvador), as well as those with highest income in Belém (the wealthiest 10%).

Water supply begins at low levels (46.9%), but increases substantially to 88.9% in 2010. Sanitary sewage starts extremely low (13.3%), but greatly increases in relative terms, coming close to Brazil's average (67.8%). Electricity and garbage collection also begin at relative low levels (71% and 78%, respectively), but achieve universal levels. The percentage of households without bathrooms is very high at the beginning of the period – 10.8% in 1991 – and although it decreases, it remains at 1.5% of households in 2010.

This group displays highly precarious conditions at the beginning of the historical series, which persist throughout the military regime, although it experienced major improvements since re-democratization. Represented here are mainly areas of poverty where coverage was once low, but where services have improved significantly. Noteworthy is the presence of Belém's elite and average income groups of metropolitan areas in the Northeast region that display coverage rates similar to the poorest groups within these same cities or in metropolitan areas of the Southeast region. The blending of regional and metropolitan inequalities with social and income inequalities is also evident.

Group 3

Included here are the poor in cities in the South and Southeast (the poorest 40% of São Paulo and Curitiba), intermediate groups in southern metropolitan areas (Curitiba and Porto Alegre), and the wealthiest 10% in Fortaleza and Recife. Noteworthy is the presence of wealthy social groups in Fortaleza and Recife whose urban conditions are similar to those of the poorest in São Paulo and Curitiba as well as to intermediate groups in southern metropolitan areas, once again indicating combinations of inequality patterns.

Trajectories that refer to sewage and water supply are higher than in the previous group, starting with coverage slightly inferior to Brazil's average in 1970 (55.6% and 24.8%, respectively, compared with 59.8% and 26.6% for all regions), but surpass them at the end of the period (92.5% and 76.1% versus 90.6% and 72.3% in an overall average). Electricity starts high (90.2%) and becomes universal as does garbage collection, which begins with a 95.3% coverage rate. There were about 6% of households without bathrooms early on the period, but they practically disappeared by 2010.

As in the previous group, this group also displays an expansion in infrastructure after the post-democratization period. However, if policies succeeded in increasing coverage for this group and the previous one, they still do not materialize in the first group where regional and social inequalities appear combined. Generally speaking, it can be said that the increase in coverage affected the middle and lower-middle strata of society, but did not affect the poorest strata in the poorest cities.

Group 4

This group includes the intermediate strata (intermediate 50%) in the cities of Belo Horizonte, Rio de Janeiro, and São Paulo and the wealthiest 10% of Salvador, Belo Horizonte, Rio de Janeiro, São Paulo, Curitiba, and Porto Alegre.

This is the group that presents the best urban and housing conditions. Water supply achieved universal levels as early as 1991 and even sewage coverage starts at 49.9% in 1970, reaching 91.9% of households in 2010. Electricity achieves universal levels in 1980 and as does garbage collection in 1991. The presence of households without bathrooms is negligible, even early in the series.

Thus, we can see that social and regional/metropolitan inequalities are cumulative. Even in the case of the elites, the wealthiest groups in the poorest metropolitan areas do not display the same trajectory or the same conditions as those observed in the wealthiest metropolitan areas. Intermediate and poor groups also display specific trajectories, depending on the coverage displayed in the 1970s and on the subsequent progress pace. Finally, the poor in more peripheral metropolitan areas continue to have very low coverage rates, even when we consider Brazil's overall progress in coverage.

From the standpoint of service provision, despite the existence of centralized national systems for generating policies regarding water, sewage, and electricity since the military dictatorship, regional differences have not yet been eliminated. On the other hand, policies have followed a clear social hierarchy: services provided to poor social groups progressed slower and remained more precarious. As certain services tended to become universal, even the poorest groups were able to obtain access to them. The overlapping of these inequalities is still visible in 2010 in the less universalized services.

Conclusion

Throughout the period analyzed, urban conditions have improved substantially with regard to levels of coverage. Census data does not allow for a systematic analysis of service quality, but existing information attests to the presence of high inequalities pertaining to service quality. Brazilian metropolitan areas still exhibit high rates of precarious housing, but the presence of tenements, excessive density, and lack of bathrooms has declined substantially over 50 years. Significant inequalities still persist, however.

We begin by referring to inequalities among services. While electricity and garbage collection have become practically universal, coverage of sanitary sewage remained low. Water supply coverage is high, but tends to stagnate, especially in smaller towns and poorer states in Brazil's North and Northeast.

In addition, significant inequalities persist across Brazil's regions, especially in the North, most notably in the states of Rondônia, Pará, Amapá, and Acre, and in the Northeast, particularly in Maranhão and Piauí. The cities with the most precarious conditions are also located in these regions – Belém, Fortaleza, and Recife. When observing cities by size, the worst conditions can be found in smaller cities. Furthermore, the provision of services continues to follow a clear hierarchical logic in terms of social groups, with the poorest being served at the lowest proportions and served last when services are scarce. Existing studies also suggest that services to these groups are of inferior quality.

Finally, it can be said that these regional, metropolitan, and social inequalities combine and accumulate, with a resulting impact on the services provided not only to the poorest but also to the elite, who tend to have worse access in more remote towns than in the cities of Brazil's South and Southeast. However, it is the poor in peripheral metropolitan areas who face the most precarious urban conditions.

References

Abreu, M. (1987). *Evolução urbana do Rio de Janeiro*. Rio de Janeiro: Iplan Rio/Zahar.

Arretche, M. (1995). Políticas de desenvolvimento urbano na crise: descentralização ou crise no modelo do BNH? In E. Reis, M. Almeida, & P. Fry (Eds.), *Pluralismo, espaço social e pesquisa*. São Paulo: Hucitec/Anpocs.

Arretche, M., Vasquez, D. E., & Fusaro, E. (2007). *Capacidades administrativas, Déficit e efetividade na política habitacional*. Brasília: Ministério das Cidades/Centro de Estudos da Metrópole. Available at: http://centrodametropole.org.br/v1/mc/assets/pdfs/capacidades_web.pdf. Accessed 29 July 2013.

Arretche, M., Cordeiro, B., Fusaro, E., Dias, E., & Bittar, M. (2012). *Capacidades Administrativas dos Municípios Brasileiros para a Política Habitacional*. Brasília: Ministério das Cidades/ Centro de Estudos da Metrópole.

Azevedo, S., & Andrade, L. (1981). *Habitação e poder: da fundação da casa popular ao Banco Nacional da Habitação*. Rio de Janeiro: Zahar.

Baeninger, R. (2011). Crescimento da população da região metropolitana de São Paulo: desconstruindo mitos do século XX. In L. Kowarick & E. Marques (Eds.), *São Paulo: novos percursos e atores*. São Paulo: Ed. 34.

Bianchini, L., & Schicchi, M. (2009). *Cortiços no centro de São Paulo*. Cuadernos de vivenda y urbanismo, v. 2, n. 3, p. 12–37.

Bonduki, N. (1998). *As origens da habitação social no Brasil*. São Paulo: Estação Liberdade.

Bonduki, N., & Rolnik, R. (1982). Periferia da Grande São Paulo: reprodução do espaço como expediente de reprodução da força de trabalho. In Maricato, E. (Org.). *A produção capitalista da casa (e da cidade) do Brasil industrial*. São Paulo: Alfa-ômega.

Brasileiro, A., & Henry, E. (Org.). (1999). *Viação ilimitada: ônibus das cidades brasileiras*. São Paulo: Cultura Editores Associados.

Cardoso, A. (Org.). (2007). *Habitação social nas metrópoles brasileiras*. Rio de Janeiro: IPPUR/ Habitare.

Carone, E., & Dér, R. (1989). Light versus Guinle. In *Memória da Eletropaulo*. Ano II, no.3.

Costa, V., & Nascimento, J. (2005). O conceito de favelas e assemelhados sob o olhar do IBGE, das Prefeituras do Brasil e da ONU. Trabalho apresentado no X Encontro de Geógrafos da América Latina, São Paulo, USP.

Dias, E. (2012). *Do Plano Real ao Programa Minha Casa, Minha Vida: negócios, votos e as reformas da habitação*. MSc dissertation, DCP/University of São Paulo.

Draibe, S. (1989). O *Welfare State* no Brasil: características e perspectivas. *Ciências Sociais Hoje*, Rio de Janeiro: Anpocs/Ed. Rio Fundo.

Farias, V. (1992). A conjuntura social brasileira: dilemas e perspectivas. *Novos Estudos CEBRAP*, São Paulo, no. 33.

Gilbert, A. (1996). *The megacity in Latin America*. Tokyo: UN Press.

Gilbert, A., & Gugler, J. (1992). *Cities, poverty and development: Urbanization in the third world*. Oxford: Oxford University Press.

Heller, L. (2009). Estudo 20: Saneamento ambiental e recursos hídricos. BNDES/Cedeplar. *Relatórios Perspectivas dos Investimentos Sociais no Brasil* – PIS. Disponível em: www.cedeplar.ufmg.br/pesquisas/pis/Estudo%2020.pdf. Accessed 29 July 2013.

Heller, L. (2010). *Estudo 20: Saneamento ambiental e recursos hídricos*. BNDES/Cedeplar.

Heller, L. (2012). Saneamento para todos com equidade: desafios contemporâneos para o Brasil. Accessed: mimeo. Available at: http://www.assemae.org.br/arquivoArtigos/saneamentoparatodos.pdf. Accessed 29 July 2013.

IBGE. (2010). *Censo demográfico 2010*. Aglomerados subnormais, primeiros resultados. Rio de Janeiro: IBGE.

Kowarick, L. (1979). *A espoliação urbana*. Rio de Janeiro: Paz e Terra.

Kowarick, L. (2011). *Viver em risco* (p. 34). São Paulo: Ed.

Leme, M. (Org.). (1999). *Urbanismo no Brasil 1895/1965*. São Paulo: Nobel.

Maricato, E. (1987). *Política habitacional no regime militar*. Petrópolis: Vozes.
Maricato, E. (2006, February). O Ministério das Cidades e a política nacional de desenvolvimento urbano. IPEA. *Políticas Sociais – Acompanhamento e Análise*, Brasília, IPEA, no. 12.
Maricato, E. (2011). *Os impasses da política urbana no Brasil*. Rio de Janeiro: Vozes.
Marques, E. (1995). Da higiene à construção da cidade: a constituição do setor saneamento no Rio de Janeiro. *Revista História, Ciência, Saúde-Manguinhos, 2*(2).
Marques, E., & Bichir, R. (2003). Public policies, political cleavages and urban space: State infrastructure policies in São Paulo, Brazil – 1975–2000. *International Journal of Urban and Regional Research, 27*(4), 811–827.
Marques, E., & Os espaços da metrópole. (2015). *A metrópole de São Paulo no século XXI: espaços, heterogeneidades e desigualdades*. São Paulo: Editora Unesp/CEM.
Marques, E., & Torres, H. (Org.). (2005). *São Paulo: segregação, pobreza urbana e desigualdade social*. São Paulo: Senac.
Marques, E., Gomes, S., Gonçalves, R., Toledo, D., Moya, E., Cazolato, D., & Ferreira, P. (2007). *Assentamentos precários no Brasil urbano*. Brasília: Ministério das Cidades/CEM, 390 p.
Marques, E., Bichir, R., & Scalon, C. (2012). Residential segregation and social structure in São Paulo: Continuity and change since the 1990s. In T. Maloutas & K. Fujita (Eds.), *Residential segregation around the world: Why context matters*. London: Ashgate Publishing.
Marques, E., Bittar, M., Cazolato, D., Fusaro, E., & Waldvogel, D. (2014). *Diagnóstico dos assentamentos precários nos municípios da Macrometrópole Paulista*. São Paulo: CEM/Emplasa. Available at: www.fflch.usp.br/centrodametropole/upload/aaa/655-Relatorio_I_Assentamentos_Fundap_Final_logo.pdf
Rezende, S., & Heller, L. (2002). *O saneamento no Brasil. Políticas e interfaces*. Belo Horizonte: UFMG/Ingenium.
Ribeiro, L. (1997). *Dos cortiços aos condomínios fechados*. Rio de Janeiro: Civilização Brasileira.
Roberts, B. (2005). Globalization and Latin American cities. *International Journal of Urban and Regional Research, vol., 29*(1), 110–123.
Royer, L. (2009). *Financeirização da política habitacional: limites e perspectivas*. Doctoral Dissertation – FAU/USP, São Paulo.
Schor, S., & Borin, M. (1997, January/March). Cortiços adaptados e concebidos na cidade de São Paulo. *São Paulo em Perspectiva*, São Paulo, Fundação Seade, *11*(1), 152–159.
Silva, L. (Org.). (1992). O que mostram os indicadores sociais sobre a pobreza na década perdida. Brasília: IPEA. Relatório de pesquisa IPEA.
SNIS. (2011). *Diagnóstico dos serviços de água e esgotos, 2010*. Brasília: Ministério das Cidades. Available at: www.snis.gov.br/PaginaCarrega.php?EWRErterterTERTer=95. Accessed 29 July 2013.
SNIS. (2012). *Diagnóstico do manejo de resíduos sólidos, 2010*. Brasília: Ministério das Cidades. Available at: www.snis.gov.br/PaginaCarrega.php?EWRErterterTERTer=93. Accessed 29 July 2013.
Taschner, S., & Baltrusis, N. (2007). Um olhar sobre a habitação em São Paulo. In Cardoso, A. (Org.). *Habitação Social nas Metrópoles Brasileiras*. Rio de Janeiro: IPPUR/HABITARE.
Valladares, L. (Org.). (1980). *Habitação em questão*. Rio de Janeiro: Zahar.
Vaz, L. (2002). *Modernidade e moradia. Habitação coletiva no Rio de Janeiro, séculos XIX e XX*. Rio de Janeiro: 7 Letras/FAPERJ.

Health and Inequalities

Vera Schattan P. Coelho and Marcelo Dias

Abstract This study describes the behavior of health inequalities in Brazil between 1980 and 2010 and revisit theoretical and methodological difficulties on researching this topic. The behavior of infant mortality and life expectancy in Brazil's municipalities was investigated, attempting to identify the relationship between these indicators, on the one hand, and income, income inequality, supply of public health services and basic sanitation, and education, on the other. Over the course of that period, considerable improvements were recorded in both infant mortality rates and life expectancy at birth as well as in reducing the inequalities in these indicators among Brazil's regions, states, and municipalities. A robust and statistically significant association was found between health indicators and mean income in the municipalities. That association was also positive for women's level of education. Contrary to expectations, no association was found between expansion of public health care service supply and improvement in health indicators. An exercise to deepen the analysis, considering health inequalities between socioeconomic and racial groups, was made by calculating mortality rates directly, which yielded unsubstantial results. Improvement in Brazil's vital statistics recording systems will make it possible – beyond the reach of this study – to examine the contribution made by the Brazilian public health system, the SUS, to improving health conditions and reducing health inequalities.

Keywords Health inequalities · Brazilian public health system · SUS · Infant mortality · Life expectancy

We are grateful to Patrick Silva, who organized the material presented in this chapter, for his thorough, painstaking work, and to Rogério Barbosa, for his invaluable contribution to processing and analyzing the data. We thank Elza Berquó, Jane Greve, Marta Arretche, Argelina Figueiredo, José Marcos P. da Cunha, Estela M. G. P. Da Cunha, Carlos Eugenio de C. Ferreira, and Cristina Guimarães for their careful reading of preliminary versions and their valuable suggestions. The chapter presents results of FAPESP projects 2013/07616-7 and 2011/20641-5.

V. S. P. Coelho (✉)
Federal University of ABC, Santo André, Brazil

Centre for Metropolitan Studies, São Paulo, Brazil

CEBRAP, São Paulo, Brazil

M. Dias
CEBRAP, São Paulo, Brazil

M. Arretche (ed.), *Paths of Inequality in Brazil*,
https://doi.org/10.1007/978-3-319-78184-6_9

The book *Prevenir e Curar* (Singer et al. 1988) grew out of research by the Brazilian Center for Analysis and Planning (CEBRAP) to investigate relations among mortality and morbidity, socioeconomic status, and access to health-care services. Twenty-five years later, we revisited that discussion to examine the trajectory of inequalities in health.[1]

Between 1980 and 2010, the infant mortality rate in Brazil fell from 69.1 to 16 per 1000 live births. Life expectancy also showed substantial gains, increasing from 62.6 years in 1980 to 73.4 years in 2010. Meanwhile, however, the evidence is that considerable health inequalities have persisted. In the 1990s, the likelihood of a black child dying before completing 1 year of life was 1.8 times higher than for a white child, while maternal mortality among black mothers was 3.6 times higher than for white mothers (Cunha 2008). Menegolla (2008) reported that infant mortality among indigenous children was double the rate for white children, while tuberculosis rates among indigenous people were three times higher than rates in the overall population.

Evidence of this kind is at the root of discussions over which factors explain health indicators and inequalities (Castro and Simões 2009; Costa et al 2001; Duarte 2007; Pellegrini et al 2011). This chapter revisits the theoretical and methodological difficulties of that discussion and attempts to move forward in describing the trajectory of health inequalities in Brazil, as well as in discussing the factors that affect it.

The chapter is divided into five parts, in addition to this introduction. Section "Literature Review" reviews the literature on the determinants of health inequalities. Section "Infant Mortality and Life Expectancy: 1980–2010" describes the trajectories of infant mortality and life expectancy by Brazil's major regions, states, and municipalities from 1980 to 2010.[2] Section "Health Conditions in the Municipalities and Their Determinants" investigates the behavior of infant mortality and life expectancy in Brazil's municipalities overall in the period 1980–2010, attempting to identify the relationship between these indicators, on the one hand, and income, supply of public health services and basic sanitation, and education, on the other. Section "Challenges in Analyzing Health Inequalities" outlines the methodological difficulties involved in further analysis of health inequalities over the period. Lastly, section "Conclusions" discusses the study results and points to challenges to be met by those interested in this subject.

Literature Review

Until the mid-1970s, the dominant hypothesis in social medicine was that raising people's income and lifting them out of poverty would assure them decent health conditions. From 1985 on, some studies began to admit that socioeconomic conditions had broader impact, that is, their effects appeared not only in adverse

[1] Health inequalities are the differences, in descriptive terms, in levels of health among population groups identified on the basis of socioeconomic, gender, race, color, and ethnic characteristics.

[2] As municipal-level mortality data are available only from 1979 onward, our study period starts in 1980.

conditions associated with poverty but also in more favorable socioeconomic conditions. For instance, mortality tends to decrease steadily with improving socioeconomic conditions as measured by indicators like education, occupation, or income, which are generally used as interchangeable markers (Marmot 2002).[3]

A similar discussion is ongoing over how racial, ethnic, and gender differences relate to health conditions. This has become emblematic in the United States, where mortality rates, for practically all the main causes of death, are higher among African-Americans. Since the mid-1990s, in parallel with studies examining health conditions by individual attributes (income, education, occupation, race/color, age, gender), increasing importance has been given to research highlighting how individual health is affected by inequalities internal to countries, states, or towns (Wilkinson 1996, 2000). In studies of the United States, Kaplan et al. (1996) and Kennedy et al. (1996) demonstrated that populations living in areas with greater income inequality live fewer years, regardless of income in those areas. Characteristics of area of residence are thought to be better predictors of rates of individuals' morbidity and mortality than their socioeconomic characteristics (Adler and Ostrove 1999).[4] In this way, the social determinants of health have gained prominence in discussions of the mechanisms that associate economic, psychological, cultural, behavioral, and biological determinants with individuals' health conditions (WHO 2005; Pellegrini Filho and Vettore 2011).

At the same time, the relations between the health-care system, health-care spending, and health conditions have also gained importance (Nolte and McKee 2004; Moreno-Serra and Smith 2012). Crémieux et al. (1999), who compared Canadian provinces, found a clear association between lower health-care spending and higher infant mortality rates and shorter life expectancy. Gupta et al. (2003) examined the relation between public health-care spending and health conditions in 70 developing or transitional economies, concluding that health conditions of the poor are significantly worse than those of the nonpoor; that the former benefit most from public health spending; and that this effect is reinforced by schooling and economic growth. Moore et al. (2003) examined the influence of primary health care on infant mortality indicators in 22 Latin American countries between 1990 and 1998. They highlighted the importance of investing in primary care, women's education, and access to drinking water. Even though these studies have produced advances, there has been no lack of criticism of their methodological rigor (Martin et al. 2008).

Offsetting this, Hitris and Posnett (1992), Filmer and Pritchett (1999), and Young (2001) have concluded that increased health-care service supply is not associated with better conditions of health.

---

[3] There are no definitive conclusions, however, on the direction of the causal association: do socioeconomic conditions impact health or vice versa?

[4] Kondo et al. (2009) concluded that each 0.05 increment in the Gini coefficient is associated with a 7.8% higher mortality hazard, even though there is no consensus as to the geographical areas where this relationship holds. They suggest that, if the relationship between inequality and mortality is in fact causal, 1.5 million deaths (9.6% of adult mortality) could be prevented in 30 OECD countries by reducing the Gini coefficient to below the 0.3 threshold.

In Brazil, there is heated discussion over the factors that explain the decline in infant mortality since the 1990s, as well as over health-care inequalities.[5] Sousa et al. (2010) found that, from 1991 to 2000, neonatal and early childhood mortality rates fell more in wealthier municipalities, accompanied by increasing relative inequality, measured as the ratio between rates in the poorest 20% of municipalities to those in the wealthiest 20%. Along the same lines, Castro and Simões (2009), who examined infant mortality between 1980 and 2005, concluded that the best outcomes were concentrated in the wealthiest regions of Brazil; the relative inequality between the wealthiest and poorest regions remained unchanged, and, accordingly, infant deaths continued disproportionately concentrated in the poorest regions. Garcia and Santana (2011), after investigating infant and child mortality trends between 1993 and 1998, pointed in a different direction. They concluded that inequalities in infant and child mortality had diminished at the individual level, when examined by mothers' education and per capita household income.

With regard to metropolitan regions, the conclusions also vary. Costa et al. (2001) found that although infant mortality had decreased in Salvador between 1990 and 1997, the health-care inequalities between wealthy and poor areas had persisted. Goldani et al. (2001) investigated infant mortality in Porto Alegre from 1995 to 1999 on the basis of a geographic measure of mothers' education. They observed that mortality had declined more markedly in the poorest regions and that inequalities in the neonatal and postneonatal components of mortality had narrowed. Holcman et al. (2004), who studied infant mortality in the São Paulo metropolitan region from 1980 to 2000, concluded that the drop in infant mortality rates in nearly all municipalities of the metropolitan region was accompanied by a leveling of their values.

Costa et al. (2001) argued that the decrease in infant mortality during the 1980s was due primarily to declining fertility. Holcman et al. (2004) attributed this decrease to expansion of the drinking water system. In more recent years, Macinko et al. (2006, 2012) and Rocha and Soares (2009) have pointed to health-care policy – and particularly the Family Health Program – as one of the key determinants of decreased infant mortality rates.

Mortality in the adult population has received much less attention, with few nationwide studies relating it to inequality. Singer et al. (1988) concluded that the population's health status depended chiefly on education and income levels and was much less affected by health-care services (beds and appointments). Duarte et al. (2002) observed important gains in life expectancy at birth, especially among men, in the period 1991 to 1999, as well as greater homogeneity in this indicator in more recent years. Chiavegatto et al. (2012), in examining the impact of inequalities on mortality in the municipality of São Paulo, showed that areas with greater income inequality displayed worse health-care indicators; once controlled for socioeconomic and demographic variables, mortality from all causes was greater in the more unequal districts.

[5] Duarte (2007) identified more than 60 original studies of infant mortality published between 1998 and 2006. These studies examined the relations between infant mortality rates and the following factors: (i) total fertility and birth rate, (ii) unemployment, (iii) illiteracy, (iv) per capita GDP, (iv) Gini coefficient, (v) connection to public drinking water supply and sewage system, (vi) health facilities, and (vii) vaccination coverage.

To summarize, there is no consensus in the literature as to the process of change in health inequalities or as to the relative importance of the factors that affect them. Accordingly, the question posed by Singer et al. (1988) remains.

This chapter picks up that challenge, returning to the debate over the relative effects of income, income inequality, supply of public health services and sanitation, and education on population health status. To that end, it examines a body of demographic and health data provided by the Brazilian Institute of Geography and Statistics (IBGE), the Institute of Applied Economic Research (IPEA), the United Nations Development Program (UNDP), and the Ministry of Health (DATASUS), for Brazil's regions, states, and municipalities for the years from 1980 to 2010. These units of analysis – rather than individuals – were chosen because of the limited availability of mortality data in population censuses and the difficulties involved in calculating mortality rates directly.

The next section describes the variation in infant mortality rates and life expectancy. It then examines the relation between the independent variables – income, income inequality, education, sanitation, and health-care system – and their behavior in Brazil's municipalities. It thus represents a significant gain over current analyses, most of which considers the major regions and states.

Infant Mortality and Life Expectancy: 1980–2010

This section traces the trajectory of infant mortality and life expectancy at birth in Brazil's major regions, states, and municipalities over the past 30 years.

Between 1980 and 2010, infant mortality in Brazil fell from 69.1 to 16 per 1000 live births. That 77% reduction ranks Brazil among the emerging countries that have most reduced rates during this period – ahead of Mexico (−74%, from 54.8 to 14.1), China (−71%, from 47.9 to 13.7), India (−52%, from 101.9 to 48.6), and South Africa (−47%, from 67.2 to 35.5).

Brazil has also made substantial gains in terms of life expectancy, which rose from 62.6 years in 1980 to 73.4 years in 2010, a 10.8-year increase in 30 years. Those gains were greater than among other Latin American countries (where the mean gain was 9.6 years, from 64.5 to 74.1) or in the set of low- and medium-income countries (mean gain of 7.4 years, from 60.3 to 67.7) (World Bank 2012).

Although showing considerable improvements in key health indicators, these data say nothing of the inequalities within Brazil. The behavior of the indicators in the various regions, states, and municipalities also reflects important progress.

Graph 1, which shows how infant mortality rates behaved in Brazil's five major regions, indicates that inequalities among regions have declined considerably. Between 1980 and 2010, in comparing the region where infant mortality rates have historically been the worst (Northeast) with the region exhibiting the best rates (South), it can be noted that the ratio between the mean rates of the former and latter fell from 2.4 to 1.6, respectively, equivalent to a reduction of 33%.

Similar, although less marked, behavior can be seen in Graph 2, which shows data on life expectancy at birth in Brazil's five major regions. Once again, life

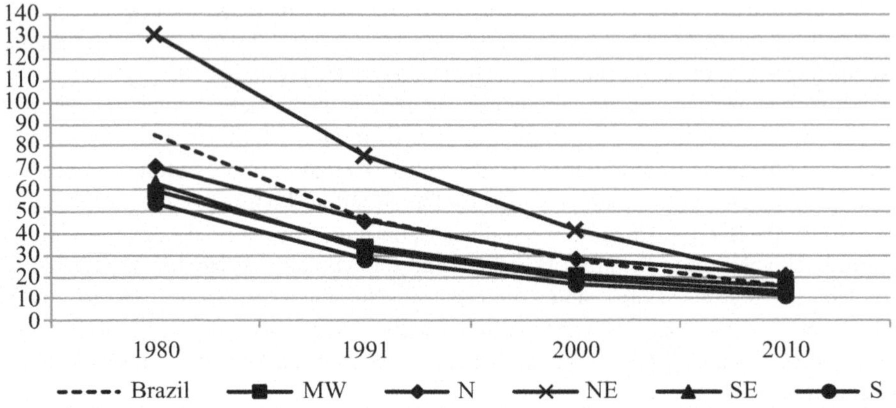

Graph 1 Infant mortality rate (per 1000 live births): Major regions of Brazil, 1980 to 2010. (Sources: Infant mortality (IPEAData); MS/SVS, Mortality Information System (SIM) and live birth information system (SINASC); life expectancy (IBGE/United Nations Population Fund – UNFPA/Brazil))

expectancy differences between the South and Northeast regions of Brazil decreased (from 7.7 years in 1980 to 4.7 in 2010).

The fact that these indicators are converging can also be seen in Table 1, showing the national mean, standard deviation, and coefficient of variation by Brazilian state. Between 1980 and 2010, the standard deviation among states' infant mortality rates fell by 84% (from 24.6 to 3.8 years). Meanwhile, in terms of life expectancy, the drop was 33% (from 3.3 to 2.2 years). This narrowing in inequalities can also be seen in the coefficient of variation, which in the same period fell by 33% for infant mortality and 40% for life expectancy at birth.

Accordingly, the improvement in infant mortality and life expectancy between 1980 and 2010 was accompanied by greater homogeneity in the indicators among Brazil's 5 regions and 27 states.

These indicators also improved solidly among the municipalities (ranked according to per capita income in Tables 2 and 3),[6] together with a small reduction in inequalities. In terms of infant mortality, between 1980 and 2000, municipalities with higher per capita income advanced more than municipalities with lower income, but that situation was inverted in the 2000s. As a result, by 2010 the gap between the mortality rates of the poorest and wealthiest municipalities had narrowed. Nonetheless, in 2010, the infant mortality rate of the municipalities with lowest per capita income was 27.8 deaths per 1000 live births, more than double the 13 deaths per 1000 live births recorded in the municipalities with highest mean income.

[6] In each period, municipalities were ranked by mean per capita household income and divided into quartiles. This chapter describes only the first (the poorest municipalities) and last quartiles (the wealthiest municipalities). The makeup of these quartiles changes over time, not just because new municipalities have been created but also because municipalities may change position in the ranking from 1 year to the next.

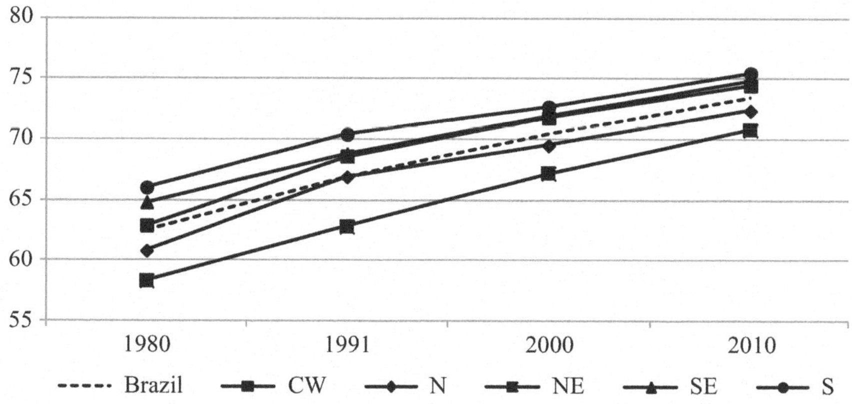

Graph 2 Life expectancy at birth (years): Major regions of Brazil, 1980 to 2010. (Sources: Infant mortality (IPEAData; MS/SVS, Mortality Information System (SIM) and live birth information system (SINASC); life expectancy (IBGE/United Nations Population Fund – UNFPA/Brazil))

With regard to life expectancy at birth (Table 3), since 1991, municipalities with lower per capita income have advanced more quickly than higher-income municipalities, reducing the inequality between the quartiles in 2010. In municipalities with lower per capita income, life expectancy at birth was 70 years, compared to 75.7 years among the higher per capita income municipalities (a difference of 8.1%, and thus smaller than the 10.8% recorded in 1980).

The maps below show how these indicators evolved in Brazil's municipalities between 1980 and 2010.

The maps above show that in 1980, the South region was notable for having the lowest rates of infant mortality. By 1991, the Southeast and Central-West regions displayed indicators closer to those of the South. In 2000, the municipalities of the North region had improved considerably. That year, 87.8% of the region's municipalities reported infant mortality rates lower than 60 per 1000 live births, in stark contrast with 1980, when rates in 84.3% of the municipalities were above that level. In 2010, the municipalities of the Northeast region attained the level that the municipalities of the Central-West had achieved in 2000. Only five of Brazil's municipalities, all in the Northeast, showed infant mortality rates in excess of 45 per 1000 live births. In 2010, despite the enormous advances achieved over the period, inequality still persisted between the municipalities of the North, Northeast, and part of the Central-West, on the one hand, and those of the South and Southeast, on the other.

The maps above show how life expectancy behaved at the municipal level. The dynamics are similar to that of infant mortality. In 1980, the South and Southeast regions displayed the best indicators. In 1991, values in the Central-West region were closer to those of the South and Southeast. In 2000, the North region showed remarkable improvement: 62.2% of its municipalities reported life expectancy of 66 years or more; in 1980, none of the municipalities were in that position. In 2010,

Table 1 Infant mortality rate and life expectancy at birth, Brazilian states, 1980 and 2010

	Infant mortality rate (per 1000 live births)			Life expectancy at birth (years)		
	1980	2010	Diff (%)	1980	2010	Diff (%)
Mean (Brazil)	69.1	16	−77	62.6	73.4	+17
Standard deviation (states)	24.6	3.8	−84	3.3	2.2	−33
Coefficient of variation	36%	24%	−33	5%	3%	−40

Sources: Infant mortality (IBGE/DPE/COPIS); MS/SVS, Mortality Information System (SIM) and Live Birth Information System (SINASC); Life expectancy (IBGE/United Nations Population Fund, UNFPA/Brazil)

Table 2 Infant mortality rate (per 1000 live births): Municipalities, Brazil, 1980–2010

	Infant mortality rate							
	Rate (per 1000 live births)				Diff (%)			
	1980	1991	2000	2010	1980–1991	1991–2000	2000–2010	1980–2010
Municipalities of the 1st income quartile (poorest)	133.8	76.4	55.4	27.8	−42.9	−27.5	−49.8	−79.2
Municipalities of the 4th income quartile (wealthiest)	55.6	27.9	17.4	13.0	−49.8	−37.6	−25.3	−76.7

Sources: IPEAData; United Nations Development Program (UNDP)

Table 3 Life expectancy at birth: Municipalities, Brazil, 1980–2010

	Life expectancy at birth (years)							
	Years				Diff (%)			
	1980	1991	2000	2010	1980–1991	1991–2000	2000–2010	1980–2010
Municipalities of the 1st income quartile (poorest)	53.7	58.4	62.5	70.0	8.8	7.0	12.0	30.3
Municipalities of the 4th income quartile (wealthiest)	59.5	68.2	72.2	75.7	14.6	5.9	4.8	27.2

Sources: IPEAData; United Nations Development Program (UNDP)

inequality among the municipalities of the South, Southeast, and Central-West regions was very small: all, except for 13 municipalities in the Southeast, displayed life expectancy of more than 70 years. Life expectancy in more than half the municipalities of the South was greater than 75 years; in the Southeast, life expectancy in 44% of municipalities was greater than 75 years; and in the Central-West, life expectancy in 26% of municipalities was greater than 75 years. Notwithstanding these undisputed advances, in 2010, life expectancy in Central and Southern Brazil still differed greatly from expectancy in the North and particularly the Northeast. In the latter region, 40.6% of municipalities reported life expectancy of less than 70 years

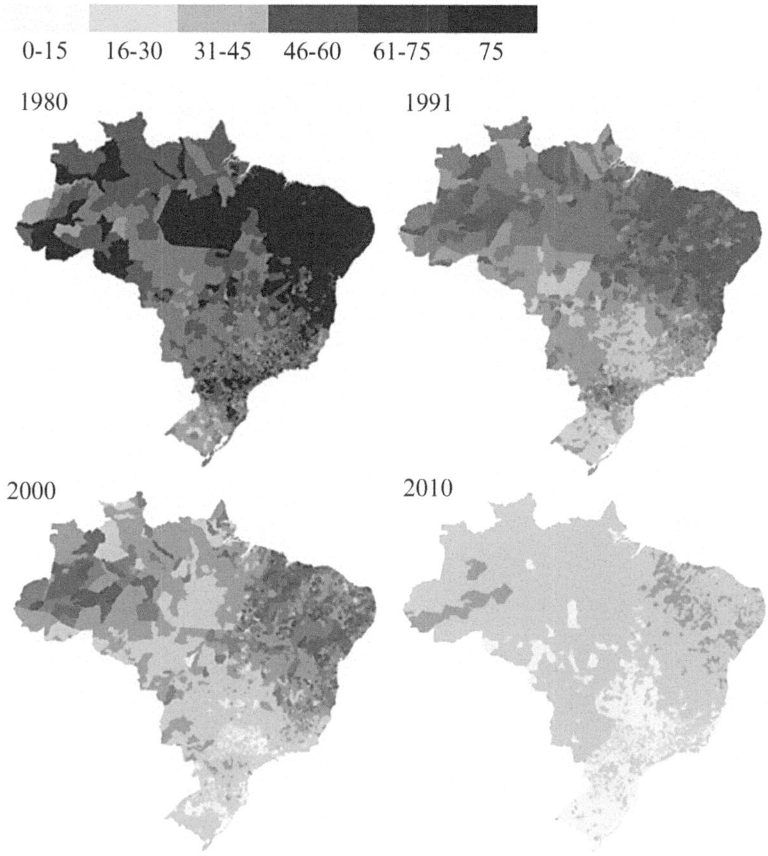

Map 1 Infant mortality: Municipalities, Brazil, 1980 to 2010. (Sources: Institute of Applied Economic Research (IPEA); United Nations Development Program (UNDP))

(i.e., 90% of the municipalities nationwide with this level of life expectancy). In terms of life expectancy too then, the ongoing challenge is to close the gap between rates in the North and Northeast with those of the other regions of Brazil.

The next section examines factors that may influence the behavior of health indicators. The unit of observation is municipal rates of infant mortality and life expectancy at birth.

Health Conditions in the Municipalities and Their Determinants

Before proceeding with the analysis, an overview of the behavior of key features at the municipal level between 1980 and 2010 is necessary, as is a brief history of the public health-care system in Brazil.

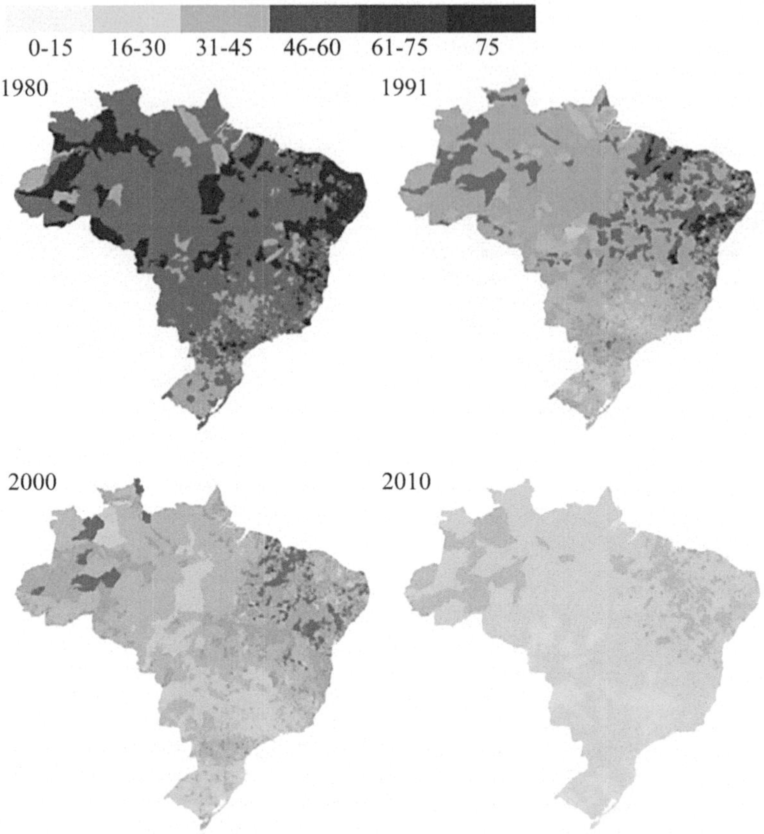

Map 2 Life expectancy at birth: Municipalities, Brazil, 1980 to 2010 (Sources: Institute of Applied Economic Research (IPEA); United Nations Development Program (UNDP))

Map 3 shows the trajectory of mean income in Brazil's municipalities between 1980 and 2010 (corrected to 2012 values): over the period, it grew by 56%. In relative terms, individual income grew more among municipalities in the (poorest) first quartile than in the (wealthiest) fourth quartile. While municipalities of the first quartile saw incomes rise by a mean 92%, in the last quartile, mean income grew by 46%. That dynamic, however, was not uniform over the period. Between 1980 and 1991, income grew more quickly in the wealthiest municipalities. Since then, the trend has reversed, particularly since the 2000s: in 2010, income in the poorest municipalities was 22% that of the wealthiest, compared to 16.7% in 1980.

Map 4 shows how income inequality, as measured by the Theil index, evolved in Brazil's municipalities between 1980 and 2010.[7] In 1980, income inequality was

[7]The Theil index, which measures inequality in income distribution among individuals, is calcu-

more pronounced in the South, Southeast, and Central-West regions. In 1991, inequality worsened in the North and Northeast, while in 2000 it advanced more in the North and Central-West. Between 2000 and 2010, there was a 10.5% reduction in income inequality among municipalities, and the Theil index fell from 0.76 to 0.68. That progress appears more clearly in the South, Southeast, and Central-West regions and is slightly less clear-cut in the North and Northeast regions, where a significant portion of the most extremely unequal municipalities is concentrated.

In parallel with improved income, health-care service supply was considerably expanded in Brazil. The Brazilian health-care system, established in 1930, grew substantially during the 1970s. However, it was not until promulgation of the 1988 Constitution (often referred to as the Citizen Constitution) that health care came to be considered a universal right for all citizens, to be provided by the state, which formally established the Unified Health System (SUS), involving the three levels of government (federal, state, and municipal), governed by the principles of service universality, equity, and comprehensiveness. The SUS offers all Brazilians, free of charge, access to doctor's appointments, tests, hospitalization, and a wide range of medicines, in addition to vaccination campaigns and prevention and health-care surveillance actions. At present, about 70% of Brazil's population depends exclusively on the SUS. The rest has some form of private health insurance (Agência Nacional de Saúde Suplementar (National Agency for Supplemental Health) (ANS) 2013).

Although the SUS still has important challenges to meet, a great deal of progress has been made. Between 1995 and 2010, the number of medical appointments per inhabitant per year increased from 2.21 to 2.71, prenatal care coverage increased from 49% to 61% (the proportion of live births with seven or more appointments), and practically universal vaccine coverage was attained for major diseases and epidemics (DATASUS 2011). The fact that the system is universal and free of charge has also contributed to the success of national programs, such as the program to fight HIV/AIDS (levels of incidence and mortality in Brazil are considered low), and the Family Health Program, which served 34 million families in 2010.

Health-care funding has also improved: between 1995 and 2010, health-care spending rose from 6.7% to 8.9% of GDP, with the public sector portion of that total rising from 43% to 47%. That increase drove expansion in the supply of public health-care facilities. From 1991 to 2010, the number of public outpatient health-care facilities rose from 1.52 to 2.49 per 10,000 inhabitants. That development can be seen in Map 5.

Sanitation has also improved greatly: between 1980 and 2010, the percentage of the population covered by the public sewage system, rainwater drainage system, and septic tanks rose from 19.2% to 41.7%. Meanwhile, coverage by the public drinking water system expanded from 29.2% to 67.8%. That is, despite considerable improvements, coverage is still low in both cases. In the field of education, illiteracy has fallen from 36.8% to 15.8% of the population in the period. Taking schooling among women age 15 or older as the basis, the percentage of those who completed

---

lated on the basis of per capita household income. The calculation does not include those with null per capita household income. The index is null when there is no income inequality among individuals and increases as the inequality among them increases.

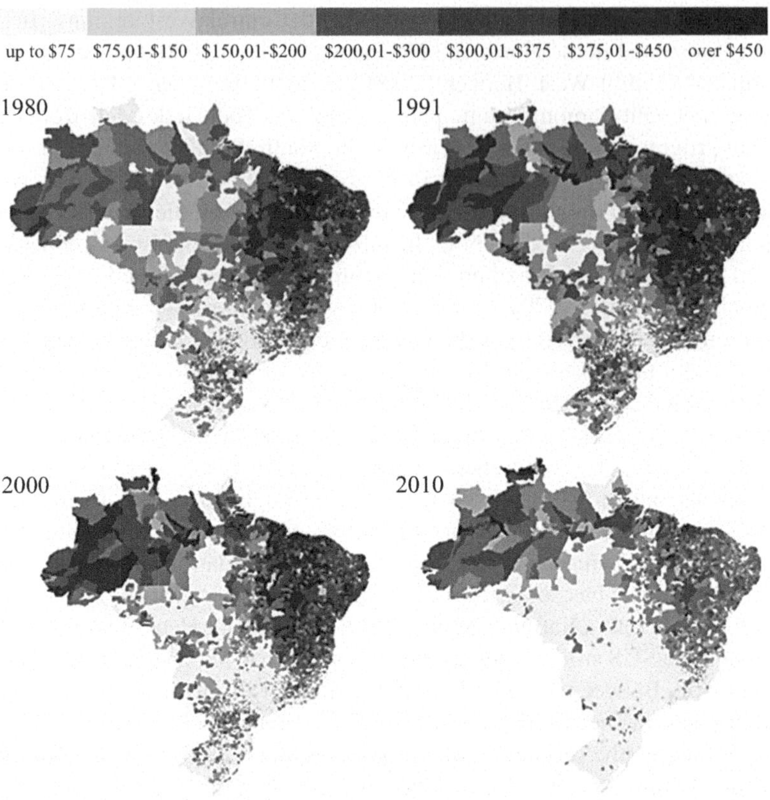

Map 3 Mean income: Municipalities, Brazil, 1980–2010(2012 BRL R$). (Source: IBGE. Demographic censuses, 1980–2010)

basic education (the first 9 years) has more than tripled, increasing from 16.1% to 55.5% in the period.[8]

The dependent variables used in analyzing relations between these factors and health conditions were infant mortality rate and life expectancy at birth, as provided, respectively, by the DATASUS and IBGE and corrected by the IPEA and UNDP. The explanatory variables used were (a) economic and sociodemographic characteristics (population size, mean income, inequality in per capita household income, education), (b) infrastructure and sanitation (coverage by the public drinking water and sewage systems), and (c) information on the SUS (number of medical

[8] For more in-depth analysis, see the accompanying chapters by Marta Arretche, Naercio Menezes Filho, and Charles Kirschbaum and Carlos Antonio Costa Ribeiro and Rogerio Schlegel.

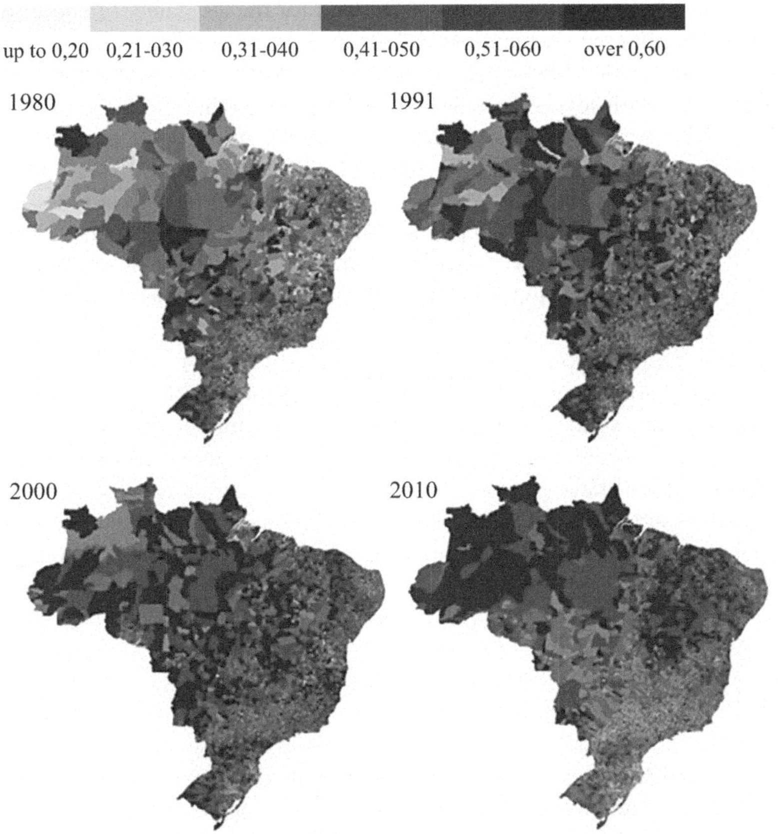

Map 4 Theil index: Municipalities, Brazil, 1980–2010. (Source: IBGE. Demographic censuses, 1980–2010)

employees in the SUS and number of active outpatient facilities, and Family Health Program coverage rate).[9]

For each census year (1980, 1991, 2000, and 2010), two types of multiple linear regression model were constructed. Because information on health-care services is not available for all years, the models constructed were minimally comparable for all years (using variables from only the first two blocks, sanitation and socioeconomic characteristics) and complete for only the years for which all data were available. Missing data for some health variables were replaced by their mean values.[10]

[9] For items (a) and (b), census data were used; for item (c), the data used were provided, respectively, by the Medical Assistance Research, IBGE, and the Ministry of Health.

[10] Infant mortality and life expectancy do not fit a normal distribution among municipalities –they

In both models, fixed effects were also added for the 27 states.[11] In addition, all variables were centered on the mean values of each of the census years. The first model was designed to show whether the values of the explanatory characteristics were associated with levels of mortality and life expectancy. The second model took the difference between the values observed for the dependent and independent variables between two census years (1991–1980, 2000–1991, and 2010–2000); that is, the intention was to observe whether there was any association between the variation in each independent variable and the selected health indicators. Models of differences like these implicitly include effects by municipality.[12]

Although the second model is theoretically more appropriate for analyzing associations that relate to variations in the study variables over time, preference was given to the first model. This was because difference-in-differences models contemplate variation over a very wide period (10 years), with no values available for the intervening years. During that interval, any number of unobserved phenomena may have occurred, in addition to which the number of units of analysis (municipalities) will have grown. Thus, there may be errors associated both with all the changes not captured by the data and with variation in the universe itself. Nevertheless, the two models pointed in the same direction, making for greater confidence in the results of the first model. These results are discussed below.

Infant Mortality

Models 1 and 1A indicate a systematic and statistically significant association between higher mean income in the municipalities and lower infant mortality rates. This association grew in strength in 1991 and 2000 and weakened in 2010. Additional tests (not displayed) suggest that positive variations in the mean income of municipalities show statistically significant associations with negative variations in infant mortality rates in only two of the four periods examined (1980–1991 and 2000–2010).

These results point to two different dynamics. Models 1 and 1A reflect increased inequality between infant mortality rates in the municipalities with highest and lowest mean incomes, which occurred in both 1991 and 2000. Meanwhile, additional tests (not displayed) show both the growth in mean income and the decline in infant mortality that occurred, particularly among municipalities in the North region, from 1980 to 1991, and the coincidence between income gains and falling infant mortal-

are right-skewed – and the convention is to observe heteroscedasticity in distribution of the regression residuals. Least squares regression analysis presents non-skewed values for the point estimates, even given asymmetry and heteroscedasticity; accordingly, preference was given to use of the log of the dependent variables (in line with models widely used in the literature on the subject). In order to obtain non-skewed estimates of the coefficient distribution statistics, robust errors were calculated (Huber-White).

[11] The control exerted by the fixed effects is similar to what is obtained when including indicator variables for each state, except for the fact that the implicit fixed effects are not taken into account in calculating the coefficient of determination (R^2).

[12] Here too, these effects did not enter into the calculation of R^2.

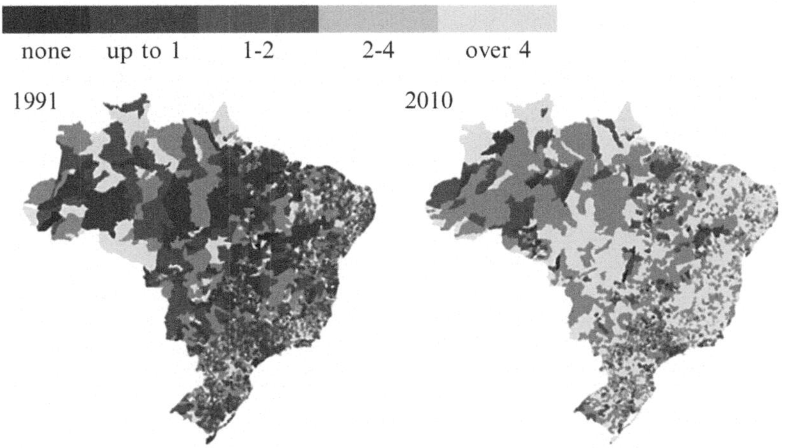

Map 5 Public outpatient health facilities per 10,000 inhabitants: Municipalities, Brazil, 1991 and 2010. (Sources: Medical Assistance Research; IBGE. Demographic censuses, 1980–2010)

ity rates that occurred in the municipalities of the North, and particularly Northeast, regions of Brazil between 2000 and 2010.

Models 1 and 1A also point to a systematic and statistically significant association between higher proportion of women who completed fundamental education and lower infant mortality rates. However, the strength of that association diminished over the period. From 1991 onward, a systematic and significant association can also be seen between higher income inequality and infant mortality rates.

These models also yield information on the association between infant mortality and sanitation services. It was expected that the greater the supply of such public service, the lower the infant mortality rates. That relationship was not confirmed to exist with either drinking water supply or sewage.

In terms of municipal population size, populous municipalities displayed higher infant mortality rates in 1980, but that situation has changed over the past 30 years, until reversing in 2010.

Model 1A also yields information on the relation between public health-care supply and the behavior of infant mortality. The number of public outpatient health-care facilities per 10,000 inhabitants is the only health indicator that appears in robust and statistically significant association with lower infant mortality rates and then only in 2000. The association between the presence of the Family Health Program and lower infant mortality rates is in the direction expected, but its intensity is weak.

The models thus point to a strong association between growth in municipalities' mean income and lower infant mortality rates in Brazil. They also display an association that is statistically significant, but lose strength over the period, between infant mortality rates, intra-municipal income inequality, and the percentage of

Models 1 and 1A: Infant mortality, Brazilian municipalities, 1980–2010

	Model 1	Model 1A (Model 1 + Health Variables)					
	1980	1991	2000	2010	1991	2000	2010
Public drinking water system	−0.018	0.017	0.010	0.012*	0.017	0.009	0.012*
	(0.019)	(0.017)	(0.015)	(0.006)	(0.017)	(0.014)	(0.006)
Sewage, drainage, and septic tank	−0.009	0.003	0.003	−0.003	0.004	0.003	−0.003
	(0.032)	(0.017)	(0.011)	(0.003)	(0.017)	(0.011)	(0.003)
Log population	3.487***	1.482***	1.167***	−0.147*	1.429***	1.061***	−0.184**
	(0.733)	(0.264)	(0.251)	(0.080)	(0.278)	(0.282)	(0.088)
Theil index	−0.052	0.057*	0.144***	0.010*	0.057*	0.145***	0.010*
	(0.049)	(0.028)	(0.019)	(0.005)	(0.028)	(0.018)	(0.006)
% over-14 women with complete fundamental education	−0.590***	−0.385***	−0.188***	−0.089***	−0.376***	−0.187***	−0.089***
	(0.203)	(0.086)	(0.041)	(0.027)	(0.083)	(0.042)	(0.027)
Log mean income	−1.529	−11.467***	−14.024***	−4.640***	−11.406***	−14.182***	−4.666***
	(3.815)	(1.060)	(1.025)	(0.566)	(1.083)	(1.025)	(0.562)
Doctors/1000 population					−0.482	0.183	0.021
					(0.437)	(0.115)	(0.025)
% population covered by Family Health Program						−0.001	−0.002
						(0.003)	(0.002)
Public outpatient health facilities/10,000 inhabitants						−1.029**	−0.177
						(0.475)	(0.151)
Constant	85.306***	48.742***	34.083***	19.247***	48.742***	34.083***	19.247***
	(0.000)	(0.000)	(0.000)	(0.000)	(0.000)	(0.000)	(0.000)
N	3991	4491	5507	5565	4491	5507	5565
r2	0.034	0.166	0.292	0.243	0.166	0.293	0.243
rmse	18.718	11.123	8.408	3.254	11.122	8.407	3.254

Standard errors in parentheses
*$p < 0.10$; **$p < 0.05$; ***$p < 0.01$.

women age 15 or older who completed fundamental education. Lastly, these models do not capture significant associations between expansion in the supply of public health services and lower infant mortality rates.

Life Expectancy at Birth

Models 2 and 2A point to a systematic and statistically significant association between higher mean income in the municipality and greater life expectancy at birth. That association grew stronger between 1991 and 2000, but weakened in 2010. Additional tests (not displayed) suggest that positive variations in mean income of municipalities had statistically significant associations with the gains in life expectancy recorded between 1980 and 2010.

In order to understand these differences, we have to remember that models 2 and 2A show that, although from 1991 onward, municipalities with lower mean income reported greater gains in life expectancy at birth than municipalities with greater mean income, it was not until 2000 that the former municipalities began to show substantial income gains.

Models 2 and 2A also point to a systematic and statistically significant association between higher percentages of women over age 15 who completed fundamental education and greater life expectancy at birth. The strength of that association diminished over the period, however. Additional tests (not displayed) show that gains in educational accomplishment varied in the same direction as gains in life expectancy and that the strength of the association was statistically significant in two periods: 1980–1991 and 2000–2010.

From 1991 onward, there is also a systematic and significant association between higher rates of income inequality and lower life expectancy.

With regard to the relation between the municipalities' populations and life expectancy at birth, the years 1980, 1991, and 2000 indicated a statistically significant association between municipalities with larger populations and lower life expectancy. In 2010, the relationship changed direction and municipalities with larger populations showed higher life expectancy, although the value of this association was low and without statistical significance.

These models also yield information on the association between life expectancy at birth and sanitation variables. It was expected that the greater the supply of such public services, the longer the life expectancy at birth. That relationship was corroborated only in 2010 in relation to drinking water supply, and even so, at very low values.

Model 2A incorporates the variables relating to the public health-care system. However, no statistically significant associations were observed between increased supply of SUS services and greater life expectancy at birth.

These results point in the same direction as the results discussed in relation to infant mortality. They suggest a strong association between higher mean income in the municipalities and greater life expectancy at birth. They also suggest that posi-

Models 2 and 2A: Life expectancy at birth, Brazilian municipalities, 1980–2010

	Model 2	Model 2A (Model 2 + health variables)					
	1980	1991	2000	2010	1991	2000	2010
Public drinking water system	−0.000	−0.010**	−0.005	−0.005***	−0.010**	−0.005	−0.005***
	(0.003)	(0.005)	(0.004)	(0.002)	(0.005)	(0.004)	(0.002)
Sewage, drainage, and septic tank	0.003	0.003	−0.001	0.004**	0.002	−0.001	0.003**
	(0.006)	(0.005)	(0.003)	(0.002)	(0.005)	(0.003)	(0.001)
Log population	−0.641***	−0.458***	−0.404***	0.063	−0.454***	−0.387***	0.063
	(0.129)	(0.073)	(0.087)	(0.038)	(0.079)	(0.097)	(0.038)
Theil index	0.004	−0.024***	−0.050***	−0.007***	−0.024***	−0.050***	−0.007***
	(0.006)	(0.008)	(0.005)	(0.002)	(0.008)	(0.005)	(0.002)
% over-14 women with complete basic education	0.092***	0.111***	0.060***	0.035***	0.110***	0.060***	0.034***
	(0.026)	(0.021)	(0.012)	(0.009)	(0.020)	(0.012)	(0.009)
Log mean income	0.563	3.193***	4.468***	2.372***	3.190***	4.489***	2.377***
	(0.632)	(0.409)	(0.233)	(0.360)	(0.414)	(0.226)	(0.358)
Doctors/1000 population					0.035	−0.020	−0.004
					(0.094)	(0.030)	(0.016)
% population covered by Family Health Program						−0.000	−0.001
						(0.001)	(0.001)
Public outpatient health facilities/10,000 inhabitants						0.176	0.062
						(0.136)	(0.067)
Constant	56.990***	63.625***	67.748***	73.089***	63.625***	67.748***	73.089***
	(0.000)	(0.000)	(0.000)	(0.000)	(0.000)	(0.000)	(0.000)
N	3991	4491	5507	5565	4491	5507	5565
r2	0.046	0.208	0.328	0.337	0.208	0.329	0.337
Rmse	2.675	2.636	2.434	1.277	2.637	2.434	1.277

Standard errors in parentheses
$*p < 0.10$; $**p < 0.05$; $***p < 0.01$

tive variations in income were associated with positive variations in life expectancy at birth. In the same way, positive variations in the percentage of women who had completed fundamental education displayed statistically significant associations with greater life expectancy at birth.

A statistically significant association was also observed between greater life expectancy at birth and intra-municipal income inequality, although it weakened over the course of the period. Lastly, these models found no significant associations between expanded supply of public sanitation and health services and increased life expectancy at birth. In sum, our analysis points to a reduction in health inequalities among Brazil's municipalities.

Challenges in Analyzing Health Inequalities

With a view toward encouraging debate on the kind of data necessary for this kind of analysis, this section presents an exercise designed to advance the discussion of health inequalities among population groups.

In addition to the variables of the previous section, skin color was included in the exercise. The aim was to compare mean mortality rates in municipal populations with those reported in different population groups (here, whites and non-whites with different levels of education) in the various periods (1980, 1991, 2000, and 2010).

The first step was to use direct methods to calculate the rates for all the municipalities in each period.[13] The results proved not only lacking in consistency, but also the rates calculated were quite different from those produced by nationwide studies (Szwarcwald et al. 2002; Victora 2001; Macinko et al. 2006). Previous studies that focused on inequality in Brazil's states have already pointed to the fragility of the information available from states, which have less well-organized information systems and tend to under-record health events (Duarte et al. 2002). The situation is even more complicated when – as in the analyses proposed here – municipalities in Brazil provide the information.

Graph 3 shows the results obtained by using raw and corrected regional mortality rates from DATASUS and by our calculations using the direct method.

The considerable differences between the lines on the graphs above reflects high rates of underreporting, particularly in the Northeast and North, and also points to the need to improve the recording system for births and deaths and to the difficulty in conducting more refined analyses of the behavior of health inequalities. This thus reinforces what other authors have written about investing in improved vital statistics recording: without that progress, researchers will continue to rely on primary

[13] These rates were calculated using, as numerator, data from the Ministry of Health Mortality Information System (SIM/MS) for each group and, as denominator, the population reported by the census for each group. This procedure is necessary because in order to proceed with the analysis proposed, there needs to be information on individual deaths, which are available in the SIM, but are not provided by the databases used in the previous section, which provide corrected mortality rates.

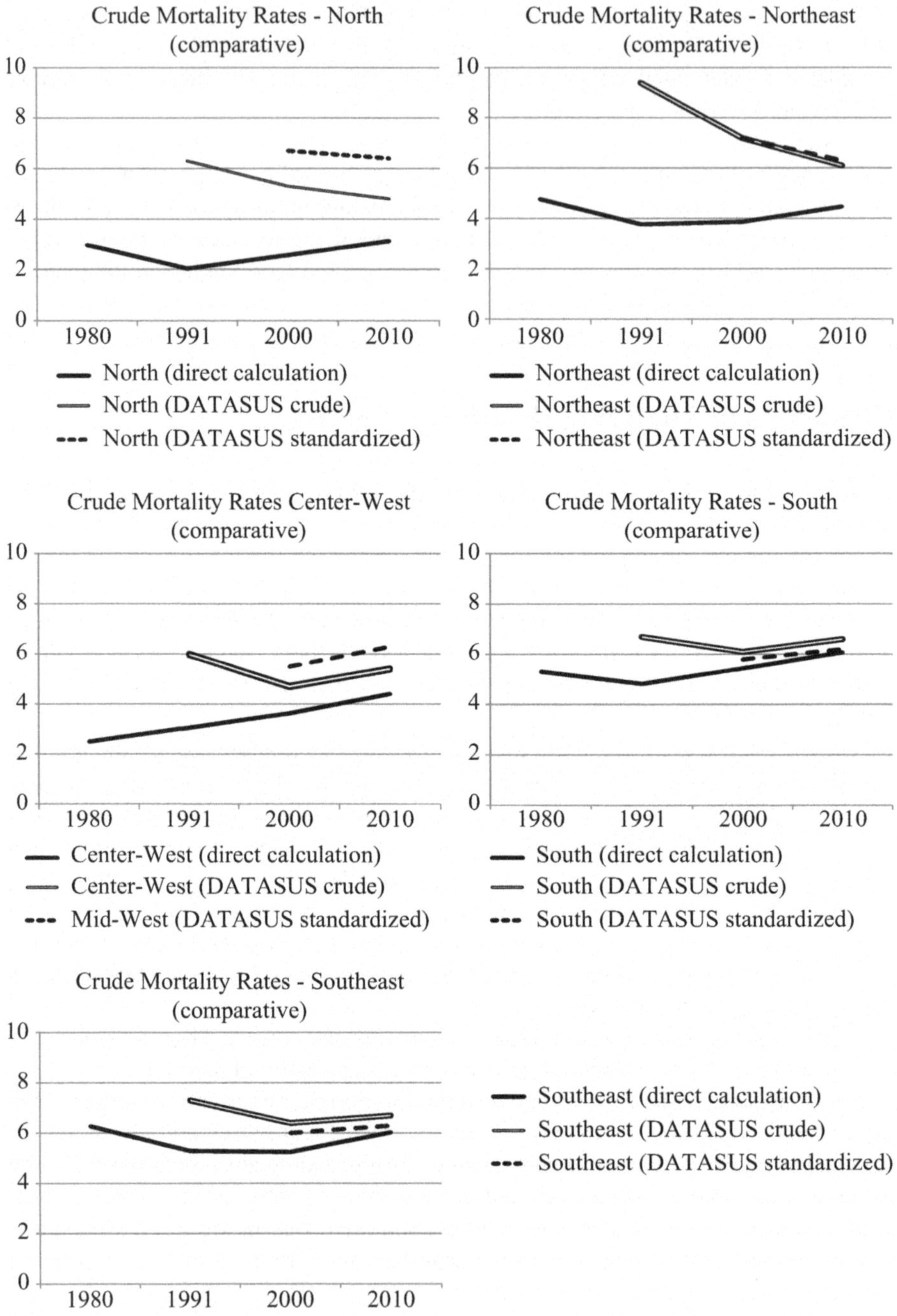

Graph 3 Comparison among mortality rates, major regions, Brazil, 1980–2010. (Sources: DATASUS, public health data system, (IDB 2011); mortality information system (SIM); live birth information system (SINASC))

data that are not robust, undermining efforts being made to achieve more detailed analyses of inequalities among population groups.

Conclusions

This study was designed to advance in describing the behavior of health inequalities between 1980 and 2010. Over the course of that period, considerable improvements were recorded in both infant mortality rates and life expectancy at birth as well as in reducing the inequalities in these indicators among Brazil's regions, states, and municipalities.

A robust and statistically significant association was also found between health indicators and mean income in the municipalities. Municipalities with higher mean income displayed lower infant mortality rates and greater life expectancy throughout the entire period. That association was also positive for women's level of education. Gains in income and educational level were accompanied by substantial health gains. These results suggest that the loss of income experienced by different groups of the Brazilian population after 2014 may, in the near future, negatively impact health indicators and contribute to worsening inequalities.

Municipalities with larger populations, which reported worse health indicators in 1980, showed better indicators than smaller municipalities in 2010. Income inequality, meanwhile, behaved in a manner compatible with descriptions provided in the literature: higher rates of inequality appeared in association with higher infant mortality rates and lower life expectancy. The strength of this association was modest and diminished over the course of the period.

However, these results reveal little about the dynamics of health inequalities between population groups. The exercise presented in section "Challenges in Analyzing Health Inequalities", which might have contributed to this analysis by calculating mortality rates directly, yielded unsubstantial results. Accordingly, the method should be used with caution, particularly in studies like the one described here, which seek to compare municipal results over long time periods.

Contrary to expectations, no association was found between expansion of public health-care service supply and improvement in health indicators. These results do confirm the findings of a good many studies that have addressed this relationship.[14] In this connection, Martin et al. (2008:827) remark "the failure to identify strong and consistent relationships between health care spending and health outcomes [...] has become a persistent theme in the literature, while – in contrast – socioeconomic factors are often found to be highly associated with health outcomes." The results obtained here, however, are seen, at least in part, to reflect methodological difficulties in measuring health interventions.

---

[14] McGuire (2005 mentions Przeworski et al. (2000), Rajkumar and Swaroop (2002), Gupta et al. (2003), and Wagstaff (2003) as exceptions that found positive associations between public health investment and lower infant mortality.

Improvement in Brazil's vital statistics recording systems will make it possible – beyond the reach of this study – to examine the contribution made by the SUS to improving health conditions and reducing health inequalities.

References

Adler, N. E., & Ostrove, J. M. (1999). Socioeconomic status and health: What we know and what we don't. In N. E. Adler, M. Marmot, B. S. McEwen, & J. Stewart (Eds.), *Socioeconomic status and health in industrial nations: Social, psychological, and biological pathways* (pp. 3–15). New York: New York Academy of Sciences.

AGÊNCIA NACIONAL EM SAÚDE SUPLEMENTAR. (2013). *Informações em Saúde Suplementar*. Available at: http://www.ans.gov.br/anstabnet/anstabnet/ materia_novo.htm.

Castro, M., & Simões, C. (2009). Spatio-temporal trends of infant mortality in Brazil. In *XXVI IUSSP International Population Conference*. Marrakech.

Chiavegatto Filho, A. D. P., Gotlieb, S. L. D., & Kawachi, I. (2012). Cause-specific mortality and income inequality in São Paulo, Brazil. *Revista Saúde Pública, 46*(4), 712–718.

Costa, M. C. N., Azi, P. A., Paim, J. S., & Silva, L. M. V. (2001). Mortalidade infantil e condições de vida: a reprodução das desigualdades sociais em saúde na década de 90. *Caderno de Saúde Pública, 17*(3), 555–567.

Crémieux, P. Y., Ouellette, P., & Pilon, C. (1999). Health care spending as determinants of health outcomes. *Health Economics, 8*, 627–639.

Cunha, E. M. G. P. (2008). O recorte racial no estudo das desigualdades em saúde. *São Paulo em Perspectiva, 22*(1), 79–91. (January/June).

DATASUS. *Sistema de Informações em saúde. Indicadores e Dados Básicos 2011*. Available at: http://tabnet.datasus.gov.br/cgi/idb2011/matriz.htm.

DATASUS. *Sistema de Informações de Mortalidade*. Available at: http://www2.datasus.gov.br/DATASUS/index.php?area=040701.

DATASUS. *Sistema de Informações de Nascidos Vivos*. Available at: http://www2.datasus.gov.br/DATASUS/index.php?area=040702.

Duarte, C. M. R. (2007). Reflexos das políticas de saúde sobre as tendências da mortalidade infantil no Brasil: revisão da literatura sobre a última década. *Caderno de Saúde Pública [online], 23*(7), 1511–1528. ISSN 0102-311X.

Duarte, E. C., Schneider, M. C., Paes-Sousa, R., da Silva, J. B., & Castillo-Salgado, C. (2002). Expectativa de vida ao nascer e mortalidade no Brasil em 1999: análise exploratória dos diferenciais regionais. *Revista Panamericana de Salud Pública, 12*(6).

Filmer, D., & Pritchett, L. (1999). The impact of public spending on health: Does money matter? *Social Science & Medicine, 49*, 1309–1323.

Garcia, L. P., & Santana, L. R. (2011). Evolução das desigualdades socioeconômicas na mortalidade infantil no Brasil, 1993–2008. *Ciência Saúde Coletiva [e-journal], 16*(9), 3717–3728.

Goldani, M. Z., Barbieri, M. A., Bettiol, H., Barbieri, M. R., & Tomkins, A. (2001). Infant mortality rates according to socioeconomic status in a Brazilian city. *Revista Saúde Pública, 35*(3), 256–261.

Gupta, S., Verhoeven, M., & Tiongson, E. R. (2003). Public spending on health care and the poor. *Health Economics, 12*, 685–696.

Hitris T and Posnett J (1992). The determinants and effects of health expenditure in developed countires. *Journal of Health Conomics, 11*(2), 173–81.

Holcman, M. M., Latorre, M. R. O., & Santos, J. L. (2004). Evolução da mortalidade infantil na região metropolitana de São Paulo, 1980-2000. *Revista Saúde Pública, 38*(2), 180–186.

IDB (2011). Indicadores e Dados Básicos. *DATASUS: Brasília*, Ministério da Saúde.

Kaplan, G. A., Pamuk, E. R., Lynch, J. W., Cohen, R. D., & Balfour, J. L. (1996). Inequality in income and mortality in the United States: Analysis of mortality and potential pathways. *BMJ, 312*, 999–1003.

Kennedy, B. P., Kawachi, I., & Prothrow-Stith, D. (1996). Income distribution and mortality: Cross-sectional ecological study of the Robin Hood index in the United States. *BMJ, 312*, 1004–1007.

Kondo, N., Sembajwe, G., Kawachi, I., Van Dam, R. M., Subramanian, S. V., & Yamagata, Z. (2009). Income inequality, mortality, and self-rated health: Meta-analysis of multilevel studies. *BMJ, 339*, b4471.

Macinko, J., & Lima-Costa, M. F. (2012). Horizontal equity in health care utilization in Brazil, 1998–2008. *International Journal for Equity in Health, 11*(1), 1–87.

Macinko, J., Guanais, F. C., & Souza, M. F. M. (2006). Evaluation of the impact of the Family Health Program on infant mortality in Brazil, 1990–2002. *Journal of Epidemiology & Community Health, 60*(1), 13–19.

Marmot, M. (2002). The influence of income on health. *Health Affairs, 21*(2), 31–46. Bethesda: Project HOPE.

Martin, S., Rice, N., & Smith, P. C. (2008). Does health care spending improve health outcomes? Evidence from English program budgeting data. *Journal of Health Economics, 27*(4), 826–842.

McGuire, J. W. (2005). Basic health care provision and under-5 mortality: A cross-national study of developing countries. *World Development, 34*(3), 405–425. Elsevier.

Menegolla, I. (2008). Perfil epidemiológico das populações indígenas do Brasil. In *Consórcio IDS-SSL-CEBRAP – Diagnóstico Situacional da Saúde Indígena no Brasil.* Consultancy report.

Moore, D., Castillo, E., Richardson, C., & Reid, R. J. (2003). Determinants of health status and the influence of primary health care services in Latin America, 1990-98. *International Journal of Health Planning and Management, 18*, 279–292.

Moreno-Serra, R., & Smith, P. C. (2012). Does progress towards universal health coverage improve population health? *The Lancet, 380*, 917–923.

Nolte, E., & McKee, M. (2004). *Does health care save lives? Avoidable mortality revisited.* London: The Nuffield Trust.

Pellegrini Filho, A., & Vettore, M. V. (2011). Estudos brasileiros sobre determinantes sociais das iniquidades em saúde. *Caderno de Saúde Pública, 27*(supl. 2), 132–133.

Przeworski, A., Alvarez, M. E., Cheiub, J. A., & Limongi, F. (2000). *Democracy and development: Political Institutions and well-being in the world, 1950–1990.* New York: Cambridge University Press.

Rajkumar, A. S., & Swaroop, V. (2002). Public spending and outcomes: Does governance matter? World Bank Policy Research Working Paper, No. 2840. Washington, DC: World Bank.

Rocha, R., & Soares, R. R. (2009). Evaluating the Impacts of Community-Based Health Interventions: Evidence from Brazil's Family Health Program. *IZA Discussion Paper*, No. 4119, April, Bonn: The Institute for the Study of Labor.

Singer, P., Campos, O., & Oliveira, E. M. (1988). *Prevenir e Curar: O controle social através dos serviços de saúde*. Forense Universitária: Rio de Janeiro.

Sousa, A., Hill, K., & Dal Poz, M. (2010). Sub-national assessment of inequality trends in neonatal and child mortality in Brazil. *International Journal for Equity in Health, 9*, 1–10.

Szwarcwald CL; Leal MC, Andrade CLT; Souza JR, PRB (2002). Estimação da mortalidade infantil no Brasil: o que dizem as informações, óbitos e nascimentos do Ministério da Saúde? *Cadernos de Saúde Pública, 18*, 1725–1736.

Victora CG (2001). Intervenções para reduzir a mortalidade infantil pré-escolar e materna no Brasil. *Revista Brasileira de Epidemiologia, 4*, 3–69.

Wagstaff, A. (2003). Child health on a dollar a day: Some tentative cross-country comparisons. *Social Science and Medicine, 57*(9), 1529–1538.

Wilkinson, R. G. (1996). *Unhealthy societies: The afflictions of inequality*. London: Routledge.

Wilkinson, R. G. (2000). *Mind the gap: Hierarchies, health and human evolution.* London: Weidenfeld and Nicolson.

World Bank. (2005). *The World Health Report.* Washington, DC: World Bank.

World Bank. (2012). *World development indicators 2013.* Washington, DC: World Bank. Available at: http://wdi.worldbank.org/tables.

Young F W (2001). An explanation of the persistent doctor-mortality association. *Journal of Epidemiology and Community Health*, 55, p80–84.

Part IV
Demographics

Internal Migration in Brazil over the Past 50 Years: (Dis)Continuities and Ruptures

José Marcos Pinto da Cunha

Somos muitos Severinos iguais em tudo e na sina:
a de abrandar estas pedras suando-se muito em cima,
a de tentar despertar terra sempre mais extinta,
a de querer arrancar algum roçado da cinza.
Mas, para que me conheçam melhor Vossas Senhorias
e melhor possam seguir a história de minha vida,
passo a ser o Severino que em vossa presença emigra.

(Morte e Vida Severina, de João Cabral de Melo Neto)

We are many Severinos and our destiny's the same:
to soften up these stones by sweating over them,
to try and bring to life a dead and deader land,
to try and wrest a farm out of burnt-over land.
But, so that Your Excellencies can recognize me better
and be able to follow better the story of my life,
I'll be the Severino you'll now see emigrate.

(The Death and Life of a Severino, by João Cabral de Melo Neto, translated by Elizabeth Bishop, Poetry Magazine, Chicago, October 1963)

Abstract Migration is among Brazil's most persistent phenomena that has had tremendous influence on the social dynamics of the country. Even more important is the fact that migration greatly expresses existing regional inequalities. Based on five demographic censuses (1970 to 2010), this chapter shows that this persistent divide impacts migration flows, especially those of longer distances. Such territorial inequalities were somehow attenuated in the 2000s, as a result not only of the recovery of the purchasing power of wages but also of advances in social policies. As a result, we witnessed the intensification of return migration, especially toward

J. M. P. da Cunha (✉)
Institute of Philosophy and Human Sciences (IFCH), Population Studies Center "Elza Berquó" (NEPO) – University of Campinas (UNICAMP) and Center for Metropolitan Studies (CEM), Campinas, Brazil
e-mail: zemarcos@nepo.unicamp.br

M. Arretche (ed.), *Paths of Inequality in Brazil*,
https://doi.org/10.1007/978-3-319-78184-6_10

the poorer Brazilian Northeast. On the other hand, the economic crisis of the 1990s also affected the national migration dynamics. Hence, longer distance movements (interstate) are influenced by regional differences, which are still far from being eradicated. This chapter attempts to show that a broader temporal view of the national migration process leads us to reflect on the nature of the actual ruptures and continuities of Brazilian social context, particularly the transition to an urban society. Describing and discussing these trends becomes an even more provocative experience when we are able to rely on several comparable demographic censuses, which allow us to examine the migratory phenomenon over the course of five decades.

Keywords Brazil · Migration flows · Interstate migration · Regional inequalities · Demographic census

There is no doubt that migration is among Brazil's most persistent phenomena because of the tremendous influence it has had on the social dynamics of the country. Perhaps, more important though is the fact that migration greatly expresses existing inequalities in the country, since migration flows reveal the depth of regional inequalities, not only in Brazil but also in Latin America.

Among the main causes of the most significant migration flows – the first involving the freed slaves and the most recent between the states – are regional inequalities that have been the driving force in migration trends in Brazil over the 50 years this study analyzed. As the chapter by Marta Arretche demonstrates, the military regime and the process of industrialization that came with it brought economic growth along with an immense divide between wealthy (South and Southeast) and poor (North and Northeast) regions.

This chapter shows that this persistent divide impacts migration flows, especially those between longer distances. Such territorial inequalities were somehow attenuated in the 2000s, as a result not only of the recovery of the purchasing power of wages but also from advances in social policies. As a result, we witnessed the intensification of return migration, especially toward the poorer Brazilian Northeast. On the other hand, the economic crisis of the 1990s also affected the national migration dynamics. Hence, longer distance movements (interstate) are influenced by regional differences, which are still far from being eradicated.

Analyses of census data, especially after the 1980s, a time preceded by a period demographers considered particularly "lethargic," have given rise to series of studies and consensus about the internal migration processes in Brazil.

Contributions from a large number of authors in the fields of demography and social science were crucial to achieving this knowledge threshold. Among the most important works, we find Lopes (1973), Balán (1973), Singer (1980), Graham and Holanda (1980), Moura (1980), Martine and Camargo (1984), Martine (1990, 1992 1994), Pacheco and Patarra (1997), Brito (2009), Matos (1995), Rigotti (2011), Cunha (2005, 2006), Cunha and Baeninger (2007), and Baeninger (2012, 1999). In effect, all literature on the subject up to the present day, particularly since the 1990s, has been vital for reaching conclusions that will certainly be shared by specialists.

In the 50 years covered by this chapter, the major significance of rural-urban migration set the "tone" for Brazil's internal migration. Graham and Holanda (1980), Martine (1994), and Martine and Camargo (1984) pointed out two processes associated with this type of migration: the first, "centripetal" in nature, was primarily related to population movements driven by industrialization and urbanization in the Southeast, especially in São Paulo; the second, "centrifugal" in nature, displaced large numbers of people in the South and Northeast toward agricultural border areas in the North and Central-West as an "escape valve" from areas suffering the impacts of economic stagnation as well as from locations subjected to changing factors (Singer 1980) such as agricultural modernization and land concentration.

The centrifugal movements were important both for a more extensive occupation of Brazilian territory and to curb, if only relatively, the population concentrated in the Southeast. It is worth remembering that movements toward agricultural border areas occurred together with trends that characterized occupation in areas such as the state of Pará, motivated by the so-called mineral borders defined by gold mining (the most ephemeral) and the exploration of other minerals.

As we will show below, the migratory effervescence of the 1970s occasioned the country's most intense demographic movement of these 50 years, giving rise to the metropolitan phenomenon, which undoubtedly reflects great changes in the country, and carries important implications with regard to its demographics.

There is also consensus regarding the fact that regional inequalities, especially the paltry retention power of some Brazilian regions not only in past decades but also today, were among the main drivers of an average volume of nearly 10 million people who engaged in interstate migration in the 1970s.

The 1990s were a time of significant change in internal migration. This reinforced a trend begun in the 1980s that saw declines in population losses in traditional sending areas such as the states of Minas Gerais, Paraná, and even in some in the Northeast, associated with the process of economic decentralization, particularly in the industrial sector, and with territorial growth and expansion of agribusiness and irrigated agriculture. Likewise, the emergence of "prosperity islands" (Pacheco 1998), the gradual recovery of the minimum wage (considered the country's foremost social policy), and income transfer policies, especially to the poorest areas (Cunha 2006), were all part of the debate about the constraints involved in regional and intraregional migration in the 1990s.

Influenced by the economic crisis, the 1990–2000 period also saw the reduced capacity to attract and retain internal migration in Brazil's major metropolitan areas, especially São Paulo and Rio de Janeiro. In an increasingly urbanized country, this period further witnessed the intensification of a phenomenon known as return migration.

A progressive "closure" of the agricultural border areas ran parallel to this process, which until the 1970s had a decisive impact on territorial occupation and population mobility. If the so-called mineral borders managed to survive, especially in Pará, they no longer exerted the same influence.

Other demographic trends may also have contributed to such changes in the national scenario. One of them concerns the widespread decline in fertility, which had an impact on growth and therefore on demographic pressure, especially in traditional expulsion areas, particularly in the Northeast (Brito 2009), a phenomenon little explored in migration studies.

The twenty-first century arrives with a very different economic, social, and demographic situation than the one that preceded it, one in which interstate migration apparently acquires new traits and even less relevance in the spatial redistribution process of the population (Baeninger 2012).

This chapter attempts to show that even in acknowledging such changes, a broader temporal view of the national migration process leads us to reflect on the nature of the actual ruptures and continuities, albeit enabled by changes in our society, particularly the transition to an eminently urban country with a very different economic, social, and political structure.

The 2010 census data do not provide much novelty regarding the migration trends outlined in the 1990s. Ruptures such as a reduction in rural-urban migration have certainly occurred, but these had already been happening since the mid-1980s. Likewise, the crisis that devastated the Southeast metropolitan areas helps us understand the intensification of return migration, which apparently decreases again during the period of economic recovery in the 2000s. There is also a clear reduction in demographic growth as well as qualitative and quantitative transformations in social policies.

Describing and discussing these trends becomes an even more provocative experience when we are able to rely on several comparable demographic censuses, which allow us to examine the migratory phenomenon over the course of five decades. This opportunity also represents a major challenge from an analytical standpoint, given that the large volume of information leads to many possibilities for interpretation. We therefore expect to take advantage of this abundance without falling into the trap of conducting an excessively dense and insufficiently objective analysis. The challenge is thus set.

Some Methodological Clarifications

This analysis is essentially based on direct migration data collected by the demographic censuses whose wealth of information for analyzing this issue is recognized by not only Brazilian researchers but also by many scholars abroad.

Rigotti (2011) skillfully presents all the possibilities censuses provided to a researcher studying Brazil's spatial mobility, particularly the variety of ways to identify migrants. Given the extended period involved in the analysis, we decided to use information regarding the "place of last residence" at the state level, available in all demographic censuses consulted.

We therefore consider a migrant as "an individual who has lived for less than 10 years in the federative unit (FU) where he or she was surveyed," also identifying the state of previous residence. The only exception to this definition refers to the 1970 census, which unfortunately introduces a problem for surveying migration using this criterion.[1] This study considered the data without this kind of correction, so 1970 census values will show slight "inflation"[2] compared to the reality of migration during the 1960–1970 period.

Cross-tabulations between the FU surveyed and the former residence provide a double entry matrix where we are able to see all interstate migration flows during the period between two censuses.[3] This study will prioritize the origins of the flows to distinguish them as follows:

- Interregional: between FUs belonging to major regions
- Intraregional: between FUs belonging to the same macroregion

With this in mind, we hope to better grasp the nature of demographic gains and losses for each FU and assess the interaction level among FUs within a same region.

Another category used refers to the status of being a return migrant, defined as an individual who, during an inter-census period, migrated from a given FU to his or her FU of birth. In addition, we should point out that for purposes of this study, we chose to disregard migrations from abroad, meaning that the migration matrix considers only those movements between FUs.

From this migratory matrix, we can therefore identify not only the volume of immigration, emigration, and net migration[4] but also the various flows among FUs. Similarly, we will use migration intensity measures (rates), the calculation of which has the average population for the period as its denominator (Hamilton 1975).

Another way of analyzing data derived from migration matrices refers to what we call "net migratory exchanges" between regions and FUs. If n people immigrate from region A to region B and the reverse flow (from B to A)[5] reaches value m, the

---

[1] In the 1970 census, the period of residence for individuals living in a given federative unit for more than 5 years was increased in a closed category called "6–10 years," which as can be easily seen, also included people with a period of up to 10 years of residence in federative units and, therefore, more migrants than those of the inter-census period (1960/1970).

[2] By tabulating migrants by period of residence and the approximate breakdown of the group "6–10 years," we found that migration during the inter-census period (i.e., migrants with period of residence between 0 and 9 years) corresponds, on average, to 95% of the FU total derived from the census, which caused us to discard this adjustment.

[3] With the exception of the 2000 census, this information is obtained by referring to the former municipality of residence for everyone living in the surveyed municipality for less than 10 years. Thus, the FU stated in the census as being the former residence would be the one that corresponds to the declared municipality of the former residence. Therefore, although living less than 10 years in a FU (and thus a migrant in the classification used), people who engaged in intrastate migration would be classified as nonmigrants, since their previous FU would be the same as the one surveyed. For this reason, it became necessary to distribute these people (present in the migration matrix diagonal) among the known sources. Therefore, migratory volumes and flows used in this chapter will indicate different totals from those presented by the IBGE.

[4] Net migration (the difference between immigration and emigration), obtained from the information about the "place of last residence," does not formally correspond to the real indicator value for the 10-year period, given that it is not possible to pinpoint the precise time period of moving from one FU to another. Nevertheless, they are reasonable approximations and usually deviate little from expected values.

[5] In demographic jargon, the terms used are "stream" or "dominant stream" and "counter-stream," where "stream" presents the higher volume.

resulting net migratory exchange would be the difference ($n - m$). Depending on the region, the value will be either positive or negative. This indicator is important since it allows us to break down the total migratory balance, making it possible to observe which flows have the greatest impact on a region's net earnings or losses.

We also use the migration effectiveness index (MEI)[6] adapted for the purposes of this study with a somewhat different intention from the one used in other studies on interstate migration (Baeninger 1999; Oliveira and Oliveira 2011). Proposed in the 1940s (Naciones Unidas 1972), this index, instead of characterizing the migratory pattern of a particular area as attraction or expulsion, attempts to grasp the result of migratory exchanges between the regions.

The index is calculated as follows:

$$\mathrm{IEM}(i) = \frac{\mathrm{SM}(i)}{\mathrm{MB}(i)}$$

where:

SM(i) refers to the net migration (the difference between immigration and emigration) of a certain FU.

MB(i) corresponds to the gross migration (sum of immigration and emigration) of the same FU.

The closer to 1, the more effective the FU, since its migratory movements (either inflow or outflow) occur predominantly toward its direction: on the other hand, the FU will be less effective if its registered migration is mostly composed of emigration, bringing index values closer to −1.

It is interesting to use the MEI when it reaches values close to zero as, for example, when measuring the circulation of migrants in the heart of São Paulo's Metropolitan Region, to understand age variations in migratory flows between São Paulo and Bahia (Cunha 1999) or, more recently, to suggest the concept of turnover as a proxy for the "coming and going" of migrants in the same flow (Baeninger 2012; Baeninger and Peres 2011). In this chapter, however, we resort to its original intention, namely, to classify predominance (values closer to 1) or otherwise (values closer to zero) from one direction to another for a given flow.[7]

The MEI will be used here to show that along with the reduction of population mobility in Brazil, no longer do we observe FUs where migration or emigration is predominant; therefore, within a framework of fewer internal displacements, flows and exchanges between FUs apparently become the dominant pattern in the national migration process.

---

[6]Calculated as the quotient between net migration (immigration minus emigration) and gross migration (immigration plus emigration).

[7]It is worth remembering that migration flows have a "direction" (connecting two specific areas) as well as a "course" (to/from). A MEI close to zero indicates no predominance of a specific course.

Internal Migration in Brazil: A Brief Contextual Analysis

In an evocative essay on the theoretical challenges faced by migration studies, Brito (2009) explores some of the main theoretical views used in Brazil for understanding this phenomenon. The author highlights the existence of two major paradigms guiding the literature on the subject – one that is economic and developmental in nature and the other that is associated with social modernization –and shows that there are important differences between the ways these two traditions explain migratory movements.

In a somewhat different way, but also acknowledging the existence of various paradigms for understanding migration, De Hass (2008) discusses the characteristics as well as the advantages and disadvantages of several forms of migration analyses, drawing particular contrast between what could be called the modernization and structural-historical approaches.

Similar to De Hass (2008), this research presents a contrast between at least two ways of understanding migration: first, as the inexorable result of capitalist development, particularly in late capitalist societies such as Brazil, which would engender social and regional inequalities, and second, as a product of society's modernization, which would lead to a certain rationality in the migration process. In the latter case, "migrants are considered individuals endowed with economic rationality in their decision to migrate and therefore, able to plan their own paths through the territory in a manner suitable to the needs of the labor market" (Brito 2009, p. 6).

While rational elements are always present in the decision to migrate, it is hard to imagine that they alone would be enough to reveal the actual causes for migration. As stated by Singer (1980), one must differentiate between causes (structural) and motivations (individual), since only the former allows us to understand the whole process that leads people to leave their place of residence in search of new life opportunities.

Therefore, to understand migration in Brazil over 50 years, we must take into account the process of economic, political, social, and territorial transformations Brazil has experienced. Internal migration is largely the result of urban/industrial changes that accompany development, especially since the 1960s. It was a modern Brazil that outweighed the traditional agricultural Brazil, generating a unique synthesis, far beyond any dualism: economic development and social modernization, with strong regional imbalances and acute social imbalances (Brito 2009, p. 12).

Graph 1 shows that the period analyzed here, and particularly the 1960s and 1970s, witnessed unprecedented growth in the urban population.

It is worth noting, however, that while the Brazilian population became urbanized, its demographic growth endured constant reduction, particularly since the 1980s and mostly due to a decline in fertility. The annual growth of almost 3% seen in the decade of 1960–1970 fell to less than 1.2% in the 2000s. The rate of decline also accelerated significantly during the 1980s when, as we will see, internal migration in Brazil witnessed its most dramatic period of change.

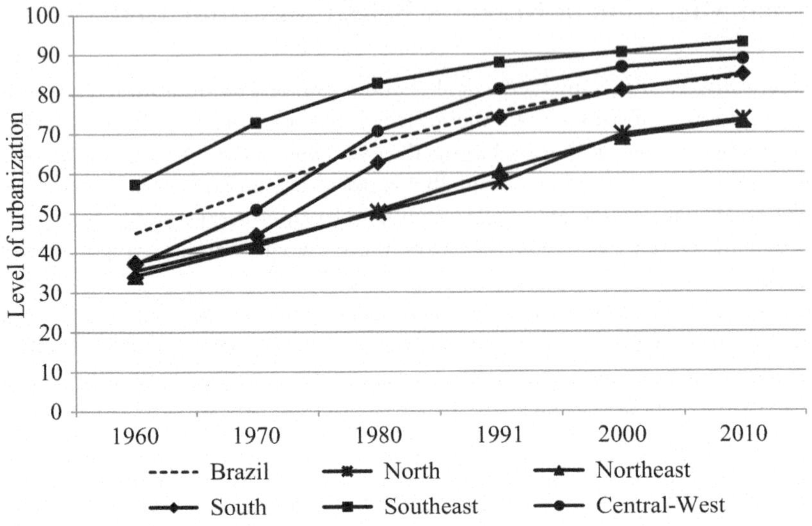

Graph 1 Level of urbanization: Regions of Brazil (1960–2010) (%). (Source: IBGE. Demographic Census (1960–2010). Special tabulations by NEPO)

Table 1 Average annual demographic growth rate: Regions of Brazil (1960–2010) (%)

	1960–1970	1970–1980	1980–1991	1991–2000	2000–2010
Brazil	2.90	2.51	1.77	1.61	1.18
North	3.64	4.91	3.85	2.57	2.10
Northeast	2.49	2.13	1.66	1.30	1.08
Southeast	2.65	2.69	1.61	1.60	1.06
South	3.44	1.51	1.21	1.41	0.88
Central-West	5.63	4.23	2.72	2.37	1.93

Source: IBGE. Demographic Census (1960–2010) (special tabulations by NEPO)

Population growth across the regions was unequal (Table 1), which ended up having only a slight impact on the territory's demographic redistribution because changes in the relative weight of the Brazilian regions proved to be of little consequence. While the Southeast reduced its share by nearly two percentage points, the Central-West and North registered an increase. The Northeast, in turn, lost relative weight, especially after the 1980s, as shown in Graph 2.

Lastly, the behavior of "Metropolitan Brazil" is noteworthy. While Brazil currently has a large number of metropolitan areas,[8] the data used refer only to federal metropolitan regions (MRs), which, with a few exceptions, accurately represent the country's actual metropolitan component.

[8]The 1988 Constitution gave states the authority to create metropolitan areas, which led to a large increase in official metropolitan regions in areas that did not actually undergo the process of metropolitization.

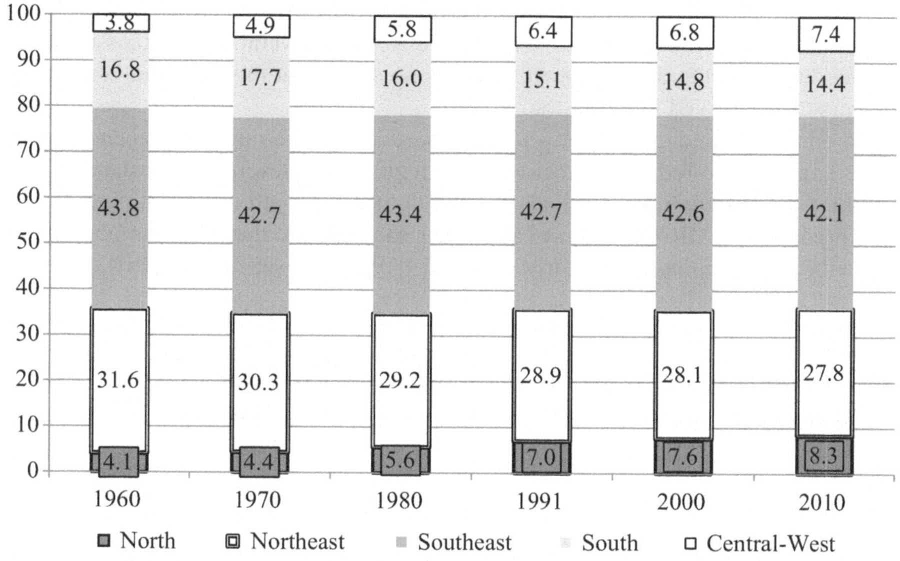

Graph 2 Population distribution: Regions of Brazil (1960–2010) (%). (Source: IBGE. Demographic Censuses from 1960 to 2010 (special tabulations by NEPO))

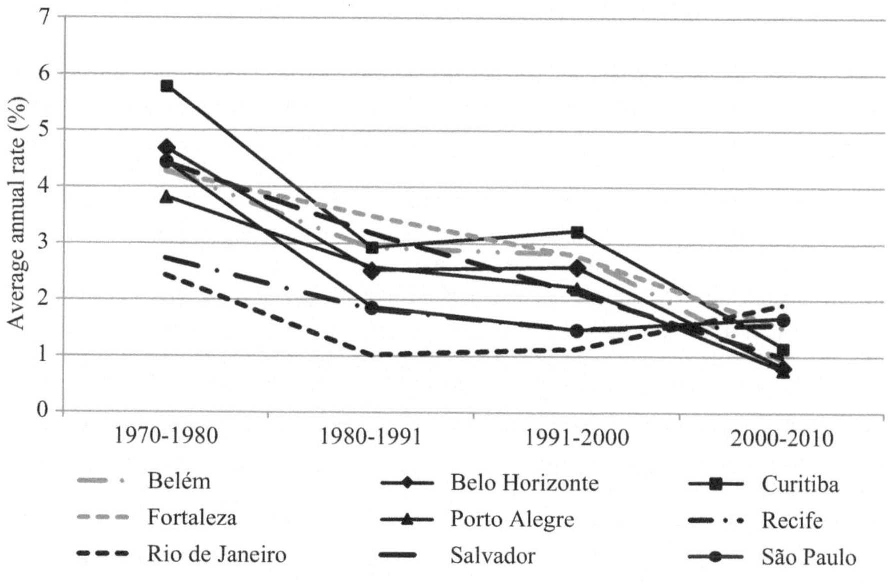

Graph 3 Average annual demographic growth rate (%): Federal metropolitan areas (1970–2010). (Source: IBGE. Censuses (1970–2010) (special tabulations by NEPO))

The data in Graph 3 clearly indicate that growth of these MRs was of great importance in the 1970s but less so in the 1980s, when several MRs witnessed sharp reductions in demographic growth. There is no doubt that this behavior essentially mirrors that observed in migration.

In other words, demographic changes, particularly the migratory phenomenon, were largely mirrored in the metropolitan regions. However, notwithstanding the central role these regions, particularly the Southeast, played in the national migration process, the MRs did little to alter their share within the Brazilian population since the 1970s, going from nearly 30% in 1980 to just over 31% in 2010.

The Evolution of Interstate Migration in Five Decades: Volume and Intensity

It is very exciting (and challenging) to observe the behavior of internal migration among Brazilian states[9] from such a broad temporal perspective. With a five-decade data record in hand, new questions invariably come up. As mentioned above, in addition to the contribution of national scholarly literature, larger temporal amplitude also enables us to better view the ruptures and continuities within Brazil's migration processes.

Evidently, this approach considers only the numbers in migratory trends since as already mentioned by Cano (2011), Baeninger (2012), and Brito (2009), the economic, social, and political processes affecting population movements have undergone major changes, particularly in the post-1980 period. Therefore, similarities or differences in volume, intensity, and flow should be interpreted in light of the major transformations Brazil has undergone throughout the period.

What can we observe from this data? From Graph 4 we can assume that while the volume of individuals who changed FU in the decade prior to each census has increased dramatically (from 6.9 to 11.4 million people), it is clear that there was a sharp reduction in this migratory movement over the period. Thus, the internal migration rate in the country decreased from 0.84% per annum (p.a.) in the 1960s to 0.63% p.a. in the 2000s.

In terms of intensity, Brazil's internal migration peak occurred between 1970 and 1980 when the rural exodus reached its highest levels. In fact, estimates drawn up by Carvalho and Garcia (2002) note that, during this period, rural Brazil's negative net migration (population losses) was 18 million compared with 13.6 million in the 1960s and 10 million in the 1980s.

Graph 4 also shows the behavior of return migration. While the phenomenon intensified since the 1980s, it had been present in the migration process for some time. Although return migration was insignificant in the 1960s and 1970s, the return to a person's area of birth was a regular practice, particularly among northeasterners.

[9] Readers are reminded that this chapter opted to prioritize migration between states, thus leaving aside an important dimension of internal migration within states and between Brazil's municipalities and subregions.

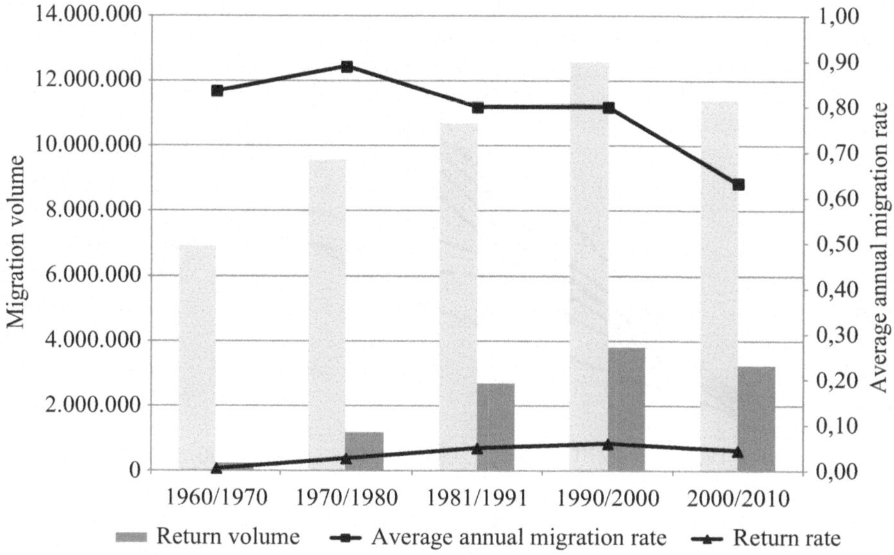

Graph 4 Annual volume and average rate (%) of total interstate migration and return migration: Brazil (1970–2010). (Source: IBGE. Demographic Censuses (1970–2010) (special tabulations by NEPO))

To understand the process, we need to consider the historic events that have affected the various regions, such as the droughts in the Northeast – particularly during the 1950s, which was one of the most punishing (Moura 1980, 1982; Ribemboim and Moreira 2008) – the occupation of the North (especially Rondônia) and western Paraná through the expansion of coffee operations, and the increasing industrialization of the Southeast.

Data in Graph 5 indicate that return migration occurred across all regions of Brazil, especially the Northeast and states such as São Paulo, Paraná, and Minas Gerais. Moreover, with regard to the Northeast and North, this phenomenon increased in intensity precisely during economic crises and the gradual closure of the agricultural border areas in the 1980s and 1990s. The higher return migration rates for the Central-West are also noteworthy, a behavior that largely reflects what took place in Goiás and the Federal District.

The need to take with caution the novelty introduced by return migration (Cunha 2005) is confirmed in the data in Graph 5. In the 1980s and especially during the 1990s, there is indeed a significant increase in this type of migration, since during the 1970s this phenomenon was contained by the dynamics of industrialization, urbanization, and economic growth (Cano 2011), resulting in nearly full employment, particularly in the country's most attractive areas. During the Brazilian Miracle – a term coined by the military regime – jobs and occupations multiplied, and the hope of migrants could often become reality (Brito 2009, p. 13).

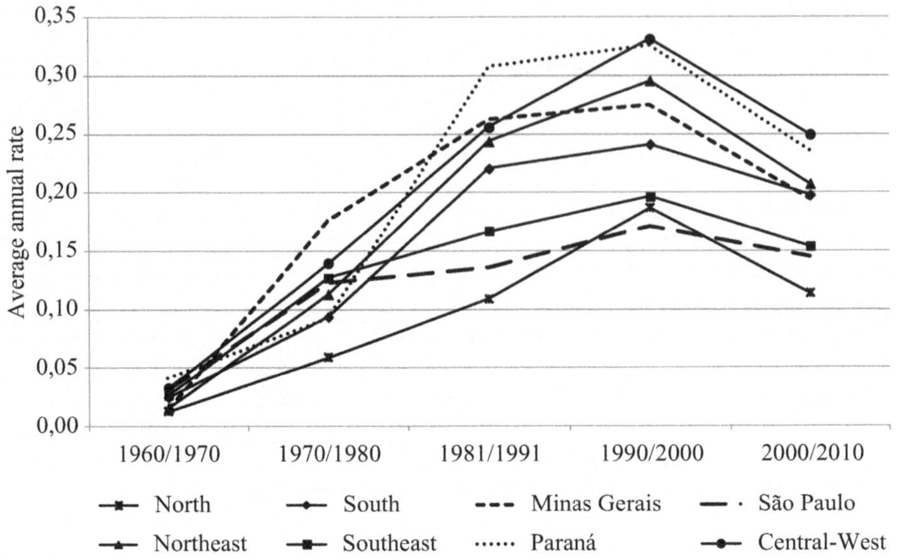

Graph 5 Average annual rate of return migration (%): Regions of Brazil and selected states (1960–2010). (Source: IBGE. Censuses (1970–2010) (special tabulations by NEPO))

After this period, return migration rates began to grow more quickly. The country faced a critical situation where social mobility through spatial mobility was questioned for the first time. Among other things, this period was marked by "truncated mobility," as conceived by Vilmar Faria (1992). This seems to have contributed to the impoverishment of the labor market (rising unemployment, underemployment, flexibilization of production, etc.). In the 2000s, economic recovery – now in a democratic context – could once again account for the downward trend in both the volume and intensity of return migration. Therefore, when seen in perspective, return migration appears to be an excellent barometer of the country's dynamic economic growth and, thus, the possibilities for upward mobility.

Graph 6 provides an overview of the behavior of immigration and emigration volumes in Brazilian states.

The number of people arriving in Northern states increased steadily until the 1980s before decreasing in subsequent periods. However, this trend is mostly due to the declining appeal of Rondônia – the embodiment of the process of gradual closure of the agricultural border areas – since other areas such as Roraima, Amapá, and Pará, the latter also a mineral border, maintained significant attractiveness. This evolution led to annual immigration rates of 0.5% p.a. in the 1960s, reaching a peak in the next decade (1.63% p.a.), until decreasing to a level close to 0.8% p.a. in 2000. In this region, emigration volumes increased significantly, up to the point where, in most states, especially the most attractive ones, the intensity of population gains suffered a sharp decline in the 2000s (Graph 6).

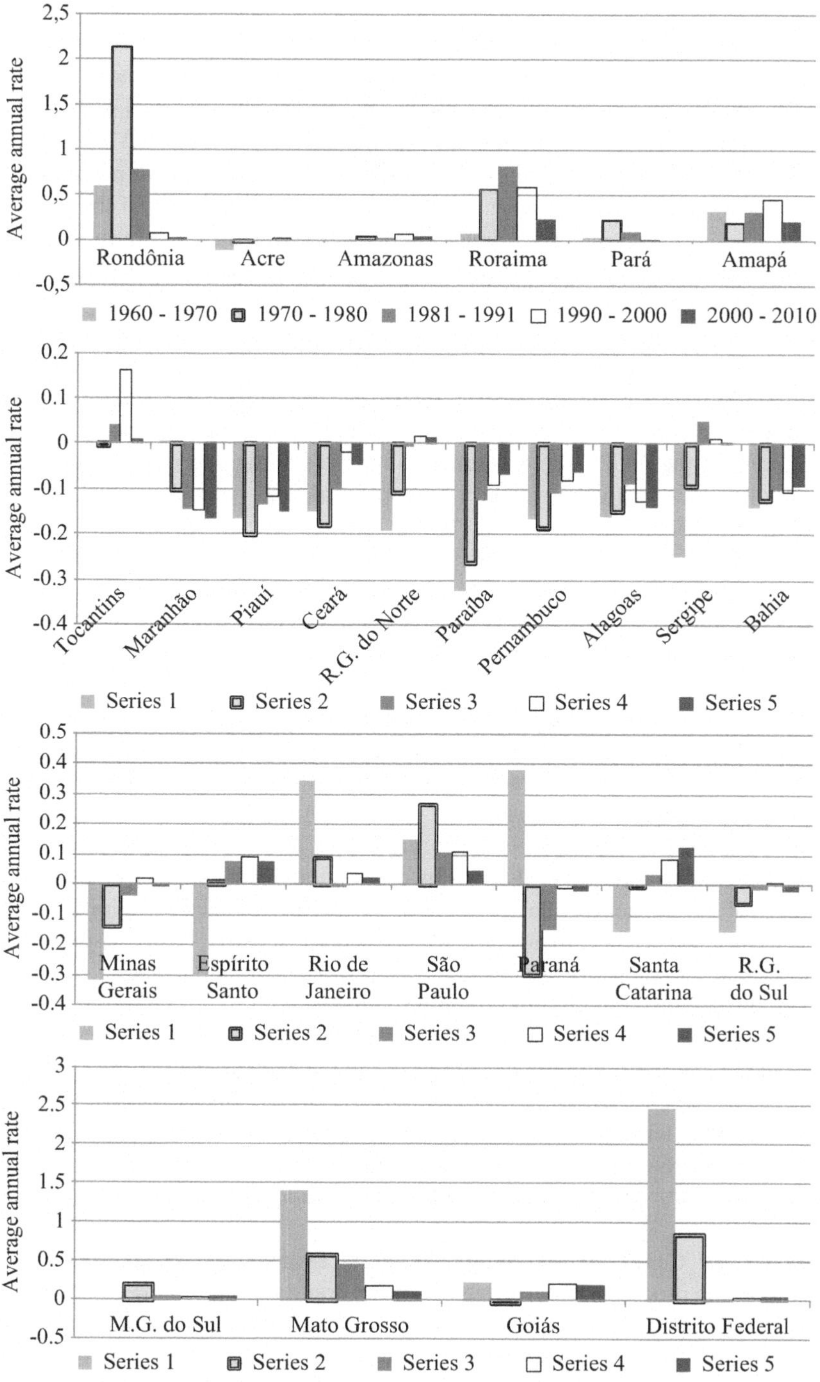

Graph 6 Average annual "net migration" rate (%): Brazilian states (1960–2010). (Source: IBGE. Censuses (1970–2010) (special tabulations by NEPO/UNICAMP) Note: The term in quotes means that the estimate used here, while approximate, does not formally correspond to the actual net migration (see section "Some Methodological Clarifications"))

The marked increase in Northeast immigration starting in the 1980s, as a result of an increase in return migration, was not enough to have a significant effect on the intensity of the migratory phenomenon, which fluctuated between 0.33% and 0.55% p.a. throughout the entire period. At the same time, its emigration witnessed growth, albeit once again this did not have a major impact on the intensity of the phenomenon: in the 1960s, the average annual rate was 0.95% p.a., a figure that remained practically unchanged in the following decades, suffering a slight decline in the 2000s (0.81% p.a.).

In practically every state – except for Sergipe and Rio Grande do Norte – net migration rates remained negative, and some states, such as Maranhão, Piauí, Alagoas, and Bahia, even experienced increases. Therefore, even when considering a slight demographic recovery in traditional emigration states such as Pernambuco and Paraíba in the 2000s, there seems to have been some sort of resumption of its population losses, with the states of Ceará, Piauí, and Alagoas serving as prime examples (Graph 6).

In contrast, the Southeast region, where immigration intensity reached a record rate of over 1.06% p.a. in the 1970s, followed by a progressive decline of at least 0.6% p.a. in the 2000s, shows very heterogeneous behavior among its states. If, on the one hand, São Paulo – despite reductions in the intensity of its net migration gains, especially after the 2000s (Graph 6) – has registered significant immigration volumes consistently above 2 million people, on the other hand, Minas Gerais virtually eliminated its net population losses without, however, indicating that it had become a new area of attraction. In this case, this can be said to be simply a situation of demographic recovery due mainly to such factors as return migration (Graph 5) and the reduced levels of emigration.

Rio de Janeiro's behavior is also worthy of attention. Even with an increase in immigration (with no impact on rate) in recent decades, Rio de Janeiro is a long way from reprising its 1960s role as major pole of attraction (Graph 6). Lastly, Espírito Santo, albeit with increasing gains, sees relatively little movement of population groups.

Data pertaining to the South region provides us with at least two very thought-provoking points. The first refers to demographic occupation, emptying, and recovery of Paraná. In both volume and intensity, the state established itself as a major demographic pole of attraction in the 1960s, but later witnessed hefty losses, and since the 1990s, has significantly reduced its negative rates (Graph 6). The second point relates to the emergence of Santa Catarina as an area of population gain in recent decades. As for Rio Grande do Sul, population loss was much more intense in the 1960s.

Finally, the Central-West region is home to some of the most important FUs involved in the process of interiorization of the population since the 1950s, whether through the construction of Brasília or through public and private colonization projects. In this case, high immigration rates (over 3% p.a.) registered during peak occupation in the 1960s weakened over time, to the point of reaching close to 1.5% p.a. in the 2000s, although this is in no way a negligible rate when compared to other regions of the country.

Thus, with the exception of Goiás – certainly due to the dynamism of two urban clusters represented by the metropolitan areas of Goiânia and the Integrated Development Region of the Federal District (RIDE)[10] – where growth and migration gains remain significant, the remaining states show a significant slowdown in their migration. In addition, emigration intensity in the Central-West has been dropping across all five decades analyzed, indicating that regional demographic dynamic was strongly characterized by the cycle involving occupation of border areas. Even with the current impact (more urban in nature) of agribusiness and significant growth of some cities, we no longer witness the demographic and migratory dynamics of the past.

It can therefore be said that the national migration process during the period analyzed underwent a series of ruptures, particularly in the progressive loss of attractiveness of the agricultural border areas and mineral borders (Central-West and North), and continuities, as in the Northeast, where almost all states continue to be the country's main areas of escape.

However, this has to be viewed in a context in which there is a decrease in the volume and particularly the intensity of interstate migration. Return migration, especially to the Northeast, witnesses growth into the 1990s after which it again declines in the 2000s. For the heterogeneous Southeast region, the migration framework witnessed significant changes since the 1990s, whether due to São Paulo's decreased power of attraction/retention, or the indisputable demographic recovery of Minas Gerais, which until the 1980s had belonged in the same category as the Northeast and Paraná, as one of the country's main areas of population escape. Finally, in the South, the already underscored recovery of Paraná and emergence of Santa Catarina may be the most important events in terms of ruptures in trends before the 1990s.

Interstate Migration Flows: The Comings and Goings of the Brazilian Population

How can we understand the overall trends thus far in light of the volume and intensity of Brazil's internal migration? Certainly, indicators of stock as previously analyzed allow us to view "who's who" within the national migration dynamic, but they are not enough to paint a more complete portrait of what took place in Brazil in 50 years.

Considering the broad time frame we have adopted and the number of FUs, it would be quite difficult to attempt to observe all migratory flows. Therefore, our analysis is conducted at the macroregional level in order to depict the most important aspects in migratory exchanges in Brazil during the period under research.

[10] RIDE is an abbreviation for "Integrated Development Region of the Federal District," a particular format of official metropolitan region.

Table 2 Migratory exchanges between regions: Brazil (1960, 2010)[a]

	Residence region at the time of the census and migration period				
	1960/1970	1970/1980	1981/1991	1990/2000	2000/2010
Former residence region	North				
Northeast	58.680	262.356	328.123	248.953	208.250
Southeast	−29.197	75.214	72.889	−4.405	627
South	3.825	131.340	97.772	1.454	988
Central-West	13.667	91.567	31.144	−49.597	−62.906
	Northeast				
North	−58.680	−262.356	−328.123	−248.953	−208.250
Southeast	−1.154.943	−1.767.947	−966.143	−1.405.378	−1.063.799
South	−99.284	−6.207	−9.310	−19.484	−46.155
	−279.171	−244936	−236543	−284788	−380108
	Southeast				
North	29.197	−75.214	−72.889	4.405	−627
Northeast	1.154.943	1.767.947	966.143	1.405.378	1.063.799
South	−289.299	694.038	201.790	71.465	−114.368
Central-West	−474.400	−171.709	−98.399	−26.096	−135.658
	South				
North	−3.825	−131.340	−97.772	−1.454	−988
Northeast	99.284	6.207	9.310	19.484	46.155
Southeast	289.299	−694.038	−201.790	−71.465	114.368
Central-West	−53.016	−259.681	−197.792	−48.119	−50.474
	Central-West				
North	−13.667	−91.567	−31.144	49.597	62.906
Northeast	279.171	244.936	236.543	284.788	380.108
Southeast	474.400	171.709	98.399	26.096	135.658
South	53.016	259.681	197.792	48.119	50.474

Source: IBGE. 1970–2010 censuses (special tabulations by NEPO/Unicamp)
Note: [a]Positive values correspond to a net gain for the area of residence at the time of the census. The table appears to be incomplete since it does not include all paired exchanges. However, this is unnecessary since the values repeat themselves with mixed signals (for further details, see section "Some Methodological Clarifications")

The first aspect of interstate migration flows refers to migrations between states within the same region (intraregional). The relative weight of this type of migration in the total movements registered decreased over the period, going from 45% of all interstate internal migration in the decade of 1960–1970 to less than 35% in the 2000s, a fact that reflects how spatial redistribution of population in Brazil has expanded over the period. Nonetheless, migration to or from FUs within the same region is not insignificant in the total registered migration. However, on average, over 60% of all migration captured by the demographic censuses came from distant regions and states.

Table 2 shows the flows that had greater influence on the migratory profile of Brazilian regions. With regard to the North, we can see that most of its population

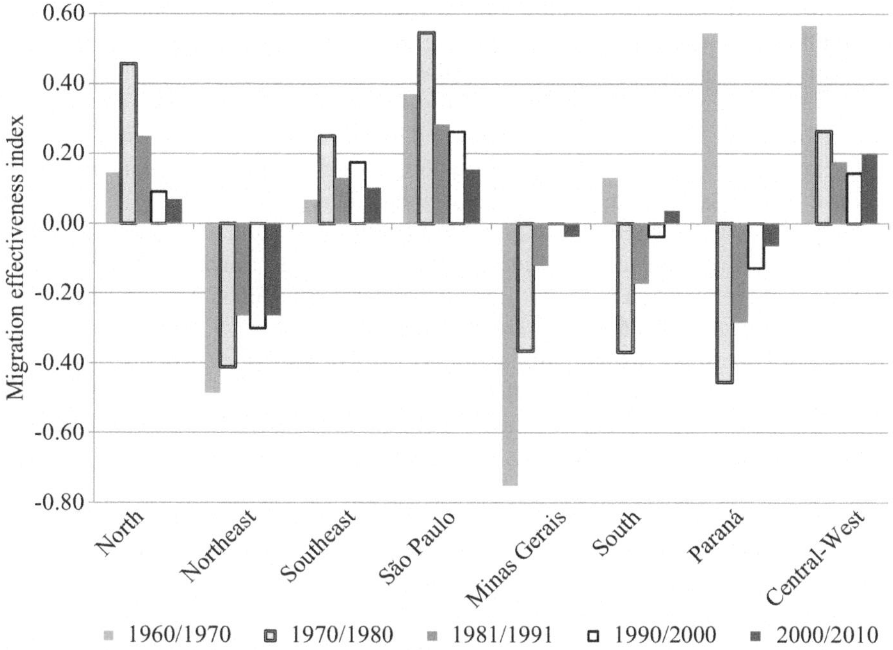

Graph 7 Migration effectiveness index: Regions of Brazil (1960–2010). (Source: IBGE. Censuses (1970–2010) (special tabulations by NEPO/UNICAMP))

came from the Northeast, especially since the 1970s. It is also interesting to note the role that the South played in this region during the 1970s and 1980s, particularly because it comprises the period with the greatest losses of old border areas, especially in the state of Paraná. In recent decades, the Central-West appears as the region that presents population gains in its exchanges with the North, reversing the trends seen in previous decades.

In the Northeast, in addition to the previously mentioned losses to the North, the Southeast is the major beneficiary of migratory exchanges registered in the region. Also noteworthy are the losses in exchanges with the Central-West, which finds the Northeast to be an important population provider.

In contrast, while the Southeast has gained large population volumes in its exchanges with the Northeast throughout the period analyzed, and with the South (mainly Paraná) in the 1970s and 1980s, it was also a major population "exporter" for the Central-West (especially when first occupied the 1960s). For the other regions, the results were not significant with regard to their impact on the population.

In the South, data in Table 2 merely confirm what several studies on migration in Brazil have indicated. The South has lost much of its population to interregional migratory exchanges, especially to the Southeast (mainly to São Paulo) and to border areas: first the Central-West and then the North. Either way, the trend in net losses has witnessed a significant slowdown since the 1990s, with Parana's economic and demographic recovery and the emergence of Santa Catarina as a regional hub. Moreover, these factors certainly explain the reversal of the historic trend in its exchanges with the Southeast, first affording a loss before registering demographic gains in the 2000s.

Lastly, the Central-West witnesses gains from all regions of Brazil in almost every period analyzed. This behavior is justified by the fact that it was an area of intense border occupation until the 1980s and, more recently, of agribusiness expansion. No less important was the growth and expansion of two major regional conurbations: Brasilia and its surrounding areas and Goiânia.

Graph 7 shows the MEI, which helps describe the evolution of internal migration across the period analyzed. Considering that the Southeast and South are regions that register greater heterogeneity in the behavior of their FUs, data on São Paulo, Minas Gerais, and Paraná are presented separately.

The MEI measures the predominant directions[11] of migratory flows. Positive values indicate the predominance of flows toward the Southeast (particularly toward São Paulo), the Central-West, and the North in the 1960s and 1970s, which certainly did not hold up after the 1980s. Not only do we see a reduction in the volume and intensity of interstate internal migration, but we also see a significant decline in the hegemony of certain areas in their migratory exchanges. Thus, while the Northeast could be considered an exception, since it maintains significant negative values throughout the period, there is no doubt that migratory movements in the post-1980 period have experienced significant changes.

Baeninger aptly defines the differentiated nature of migration after this period in the following excerpt:

> Internal migrations thus assumed greater complexity from the 1980s on, particularly due to the predominance of migration between urban areas... The understanding of the population's process of reorganization in space moves from the analytical axis via rural-urban migration, the driving force of centripetal analyses. (Baeninger 2012, p. 47)

In other words, the centripetal pattern (urban-industrial) and the centrifugal pattern (expansion and consolidation of agricultural borders) are well characterized until 1980; from then on, there is a significant reduction in the predominance of certain directions in migration flows.

In Graph 7, the behavior of São Paulo is noteworthy – its MEI value in 1970 has shown a gradual reduction. The opposite happened in Minas Gerais and Paraná, where data strongly suggest a recovery of losses rather than a change in profile to an area of migratory attraction.

In short, these data suggest that it is the circulation of people – or turnover according to Baeninger (2012) – and not, as in the past, the predominance of certain destinations and migratory origins that appears to be the new pattern in Brazil's migratory phenomenon.

[11] See footnote 7.

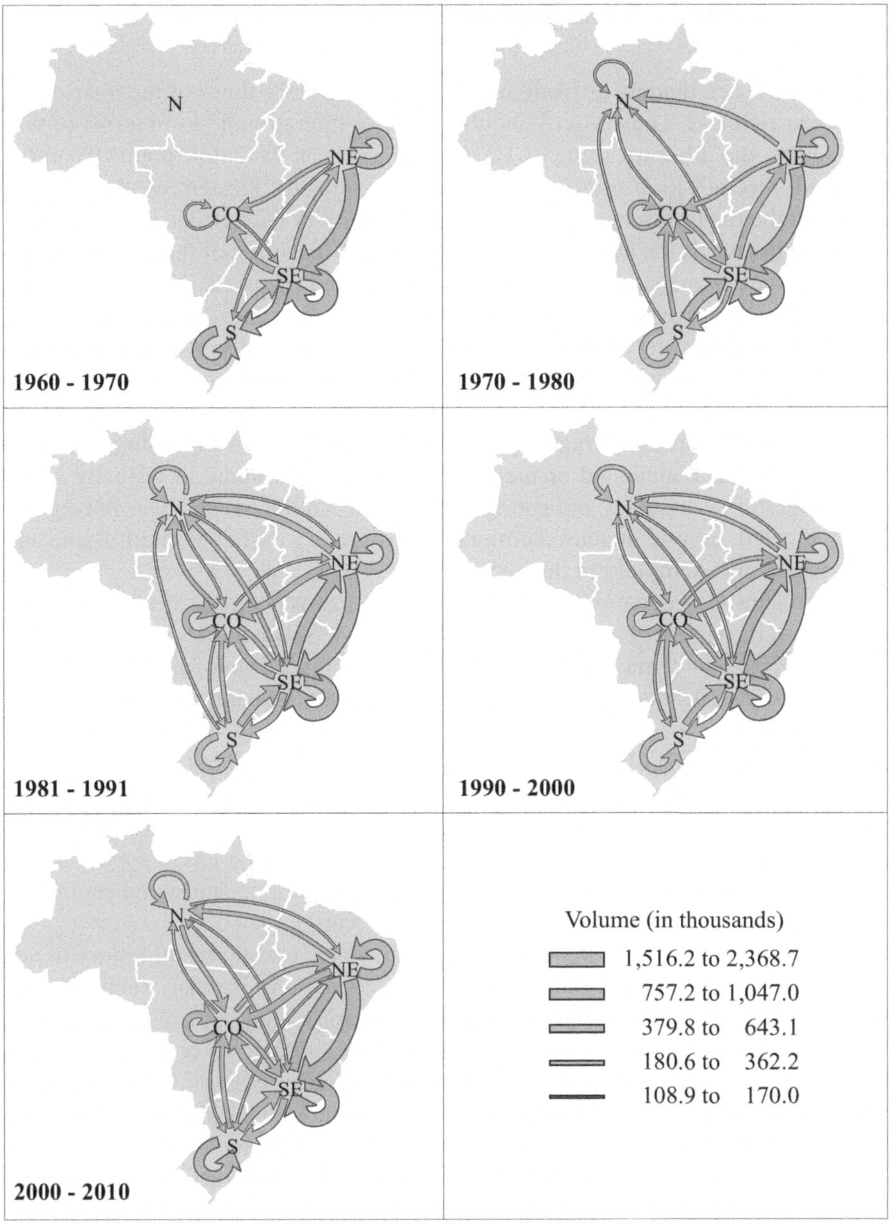

Map 1 Interregional and intraregional migration flows (*): Brazil (1970–2010). (Source: IBGE. Censuses (1970–2010) (special tabulations by NEPO/UNICAMP) and CEM cartographic database. Map elaboration by José Donizete Cazzolato) (*) only flows over 100 thousand people

Migratory Flows: Some Typical Cases

Our limited space hinders us from exploring the migratory flows of the matrices in all of their richness. Thus, Map 1 shows the major migration flows in terms of volume, setting the arbitrary value of 100,000 migrants as the cutoff point. If, on the one hand, this selection presents processes as regionally located, on the other, it points out the major directions in Brazilian migration in the five decades analyzed.

This map reveals the key points in the spatial redistribution of the Brazilian population in the 50 years analyzed: the centripetal trend (from the Northeast, Minas Gerais and Paraná, especially toward São Paulo); the centrifugal trend (at first toward Paraná, then to the Central-West, and, more recently, to the North); the demographic recovery of Minas Gerais and Paraná; the counterparts, largely due to return migration from São Paulo with its main migratory exchange areas, especially to the Northeast; and the increased growth of Brasília and its surrounding areas.

São Paulo has maintained or increased immigration volume in virtually all its major migratory exchanges, indicating that the state's attractiveness was not significantly affected, despite increased emigration. Migratory exchanges with Bahia and Pernambuco are exemplary in this regard.

With regard to occupation of border areas, the major boom occurred during the 1960s, with the state of Paraná acting as protagonist. Subsequently, especially during the 1970s, Rondônia and Mato Grosso do Sul played that role before finally turning it over to the state of Mato Grosso in the 1980s through the mid-1990s. As we can see, Pará is the only state in the North to appear among the main flows, a fact that reflects expansion of both the agricultural and the mineral borders.

First and foremost, the 1960s and especially the 1970s were times of increased internal migration in Brazil. This was driven by urban-industrial development in the Southeast, especially in São Paulo, by the opening of border areas in such states as Paraná, Rondônia, and Mato Grosso, as well as by economic and social stagnation of large areas of the country, as in the case of the Northeast.

In much the same way, a major rupture occurs in the traditional migratory trends observed beginning in the 1980s. This entails a decrease in intensity (and volume) of internal migration flows and an increase in return migration, especially toward the Northeast. Such trends, which intensify in the 1990s, by no coincidence occur simultaneously with crises in the economy and labor market, particularly in metropolitan areas inclined toward industry deconcentration and a clear decline in the border occupation process. On the other hand, the economic recovery of Paraná and Minas Gerais and the emergence of opportunities in traditional areas of demographic escape, such as social policies that granted pension benefits to many rural and urban workers and even specific income transfer policies, may have contributed toward enhancing the retention power over potential migrants.

However, 2010 census data indicate that although the reduction of internal movements in Brazil has remained steady, return migration (largely toward the Northeast) seems to present an uptick in growth, which can be explained by the economic recovery, especially the improved labor market in large urban cities.

Map 1 shows the changes in Brazil's interstate internal migration over the past 50 years. We can now say that the migratory effervescence seen in Brazil up to 1980 has ceased to exist, a fact that although does not diminish the social, economic, or even political importance of the phenomenon, at least makes us think about its new characteristics and implications. As shown in Graph 6, there are increasingly fewer origins or destinations that predominate. Unfortunately, the major constant over the course of these 50 years is the Northeast region, which continues to be a source of demographic escape, albeit one with less intensity.

By Way of Conclusion

The data analyzed in this study show that Brazil has witnessed significant changes in the behavior of its internal migration over 50 years. This has not resulted in major variations in the directions of migratory flows but has led to losses within certain regional hegemonies in terms of both the origin and the destination of migrants.

The gradual closing of borders; decentralization of economic activities; economic performance, permeated by periods of crisis and recovery; reduced demographic growth, especially in traditional areas of demographic escape; the vast emptying of rural areas; and subsequent urbanization have embodied major changes which, since the 1980s, have clearly altered the face of migration in the country.

Nonetheless, we cannot say for sure that such changes are here to stay: the decreased intensity in interstate mobility between 1990 and 2000 was much lower than that observed between 1980 and 1990. In the 2000s, return migration shows signs of decline in both volume and intensity.

Therefore, even if under a different guise, set of constraints, or implications, even if at different levels of intensity and volume, or even in a very different time in the country's migration history (Baeninger 2012; Brito 2009), the changes observed in recent decades do not appear to be permanent.

It is very hard to predict Brazil's interstate migratory behavior in the next few decades with any certainty. Two facts – the decreased intensity of return migration in the 2000s following a period of increased intensification and the small drop in internal migration rates since 1980 – suggest that during times of crisis or recovery (whether in the origin or destination), migration at some point responds, even if with time lags.

It is possible that as Baeninger (2012) suggests, the migration-employment relationship no longer carries the same explanatory value it once did to account for population movements. Yet how can we understand the fact that even today, thousands of people travel huge distances in search of social inclusion? If not for this reason, what are they looking for?

Even if we take into account the fact that our society has changed and that certain paradigms (such as those explaining the rural exodus) need to be revisited (BRITO 2009), spatial inequalities – regional and intraregional – and the resulting socioeconomic opportunities still seem to set a benchmark for migratory movements in the country. At the same time, it is important to keep in mind that Brazil has not only become urbanized, but it has also experienced a reduction in population growth that occurred at an accelerated pace, which, from a demographic standpoint, should have a considerable impact on the intensity of mobility, which, as we have seen, is much lower today than it was 50 years ago.

Part of the discussion presented here, however, refers to a way of thinking nurtured by the reading of a classic piece of literature, whose introduction features remarks by journalist Clóvis Rossi. In a new edition of the beautiful book *Morte e Vida Severina*, by João Cabral de Melo Neto,[12] Rossi writes:

> This book is eternal, both fortunately and unfortunately. Fortunately, because very rarely do we find texts that can be read 30 years later [...] and evoke the same pleasure as did its first reading [...] Unfortunately, because the story told by the poem continues to be lived by countless "*severinos*" half a century after the book was written. Furthermore, it is impossible to see ahead to the end of the saga of northeastern migrants seeking a new life in order to escape [...]

This study shows that despite major changes in the national migration process, at least one characteristic seems to persist: the Northeast region as a demographic escape area. Even as we tread into the twenty-first century, current news about the worst drought in the history of Northeast shows that, as Clovis Rossi wrote, we are still far from changing this situation. Nevertheless, Brazil's internal migration does have a different face, which needs to be better understood and explained.

Lastly, one cannot forget that even at the peak of Brazil's interstate migration (1970s), the percentage of migrants in one decade represented slightly less than 8% of the population, a number that was even smaller in 2010 (6%). Perhaps, starting to consider the factors and reasons that make people stay might be much more useful than trying to understand why some people migrate.

References

Baeninger, R. Região, (1999). Metrópole e Interior: espaços ganhadores e espaços perdedores nas migrações recentes – Brasil, 1980–1996. Campinas, 1999. 231f. Tese (Doutorado) – IFCH/UNICAMP.

Baeninger, R. (2012). *Fases e faces da migração em São Paulo*. Campinas: NEPO/Unicamp.

Baeninger, R., & Peres, R. (2011). Metrópoles brasileiras no século 21: evidências do Censo Demográfico de 2010. *Informe Gepec, Toledo, vol., 15*(Special Issue), 634–648.

Balán, J. (1973). Migrações e desenvolvimento capitalista no Brasil: ensaio de interpretação histórico comparativa. *Estudos Cebrap*, no. 5.

Brito, F. (2009). *As migrações internas no Brasil: um ensaio sobre os desafios teóricos recentes*. Belo Horizonte: CEDEPLAR/UFMG (Text for discussion, no. 366).

Cano, W. (2011). *Novas determinações sobre as questões regional e urbana após 1980*. Campinas: Instituto de Economia, Unicamp (Text for discussion, no. 193).

Carvalho, J. A. M., & Garcia, R. A. (2002). *Estimativas decenais e qüinqüenais de saldos migratórios e taxas líquidas de migração do Brasil, por situação do domicílio, sexo e idade, segundo unidade da federação e macrorregião, entre 1960 e 1990, e estimativas de emigrantes*

[12] *Coleção Folha Grandes Escritores Brasileiros*, vol. 2, 2008.

internacionais do período 1985/1990. Belo Horizonte: CEDEPLAR/UFMG. Available from: http://www.cedeplar.ufmg.br/pesquisas/saldos_migratorios/Estimativas_saldos_migratorios.pdf.

Cunha, J. M. (1999). (Des)continuidades no padrão demográfico do fluxo São Paulo/Bahia no período 1970/91: qual o efeito da crise? *Revista Brasileira de Estudos de População, 16*(1/2), 83–98. (Jan./Dec.).

Cunha, J. M. P. (2005). Migração e Urbanização no Brasil: alguns desafios metodológicos para a análise. Revista São Paulo em Perspectiva. São Paulo, v.19 n.4, p.03-20, out./dez.

Cunha, J. M. (2006). A migração no Brasil no começo do século 21: continuidades e novidades trazidas pela PNAD 2004. *Parcerias Estratégicas, 22*, 381–439. June.

Cunha, J. M. P., & Baeninger, R. A. (2007). Las migraciones internas en el Brasil contemporâneo. *Notas de Población*, Santiago de Chile, ano. XXXIII, no. 82.

De Haas, H. (2008). *Migration and development: A theoretical perspective*. United Kingdom: International Migration Institute, University of Oxford, (Working papers, no. 9).

Faria, V. (1992). A conjuntura social brasileira: dilemas e perspectivas. *Novos Estudos Cebrap*, no. 33.

Graham, D. H., & Holanda, S. B. (1980). As migrações interregionais e urbanas e o crescimento econômico do Brasil. In Moura H. (Org.) *Migração interna: textos selecionados*. Fortaleza: Banco do Nordeste do Brasil S.A.

Hamilton, H. (1975). Consideraciones prácticas y matemáticas en la formulación y selección de tasas de migración. In Elizaga, J. C. & Macisco Jr., J. J. (Orgs.). *Migraciones internas: teoria, método y factores sociológicos* (pp. 171–198). Santiago de Chile: CELADE.

Lopes, J. R. B. (1973). Desenvolvimento e migrações: uma abordagem histórico-estrutural. Cadernos CEBRAP, n.5, São Paulo, CEBRAP.

Martine, G. & Camargo, (1984). Crescimento e Distribuição da População Brasileira: tendências recentes. Revista Brasileira de Estudos de População, v.1,n.1 (1/2), jan/dez.

Martine, G. (1990). As migrações de origem rural no Brasil: uma perspectiva histórica. In *História e população: estudos sobre a América Latina*. São Paulo: Fundação Seade.

Martine, G. (1992). *Ciclos e destinos da migração para áreas de fronteira na era moderna: uma visão geral*. Brasília: ISPN. (Documento de trabalho, no. 12).

Martine, G. (1994). *A redistribuição espacial da população brasileira durante a década de 80*. Brasília: IPEA (Text for discussion, no. 329).

Matos, R. (1995). Questões teóricas acerca dos processos de concentração e desconcentração da população no espaço. *Revista Brasileira de Estudos de População, 12*(1–2.) (Jan./Dec.).

Moura, H. A. (1980). O balanço migratório do nordeste no período de 1950/70. In *Migração interna: textos selecionados* (pp. 1025–1071). Fortaleza: Banco do Nordeste do Brasil.

Moura, H. A. (1982). Nordeste: migrações internas e desequilíbrios regionais. *Revista Pernambucana de Desenvolvimento, 9*(2).

Naciones Unidas. (1972). Métodos de Medición de la Migración Interna, Manual VI, Nueva York.

Oliveira, L. A. P. and Oliveira, A. T. R. (Org). (2011). Reflexões sobre os deslocamentos populacionais no Brasil. IBGE, Estudos e Análises Informação Demográfica e Socioeconômica, n.1, Rio de Janeiro.

Pacheco, C. A. (1998). *Fragmentação da nação*. Campinas: Instituto de Economia/Unicamp.

Pacheco, C. A., & Patarra, N. (1997). Movimentos migratórios nos anos 80: novos padrões. In Patarra, N. L. et al. (Orgs.). *Migração, condições de vida e dinâmica urbana: São Paulo 1980–1993*. Campinas: IE/Unicamp.

Ribemboim, J., & Moreira, F. G. L. (2008). O fenômeno da chegada urbana em contraponto ao do êxodo rural durante a segunda metade do século XX. In *Encontro Nacional De Estudos Populacionais,. 16 Anais*. Belo Horizonte: ABEP.

Rigotti, J. I. (2011). Dados censitários e técnicas de análise das migrações no Brasil: avanços e lacunas. In Cunha, J. M. P. (Org.). *Mobilidade espacial da população: desafios teóricos e metodológicos para o seu estudo*. Campinas: NEPO/Unicamp.

Singer, P. (1980). Migrações internas: considerações teóricas sobre o seu estudo. In: MOURA, H. (Org.). *Migração interna: textos selecionados*. Fortaleza: Banco do Nordeste do Brasil S.A.

Fifty Years of Gender and Generational Relations in Brazil: Changes and Continuities

Maria Coleta Ferreira Albino de Oliveira, Joice Melo Vieira, and Glaucia dos Santos Marcondes

Abstract This chapter gathers evidence and interpretations regarding demographic changes within the broad and complex process of transformation in the life of Brazilian families since the second half of the twentieth century. Social transformations were both cause and consequence of profound changes in the demographic system, especially after the 1960s. The main demographic factors affecting private life – mortality, fertility, and marriage rates – reflect the increasingly multifaceted conformation of contemporary families, especially those housing children under the age of 15. There is evidence of a growing heterogeneity of family arrangements resulting from a convergence toward low fertility levels across all social groups. Increased plurality does not mean loss of relevance of the nuclear family model, especially when raising children. The information used is derived mostly from demographic censuses since 1970. The historical series of demographic censuses display significant achievements for the public and private lives of the Brazilian citizens and, at the same time, help us understand a country with a long path ahead in overcoming inequalities. Concerning families, the recognition of their plural and metamorphic condition in the 1988 Brazilian Constitution – and reiterated by subsequent laws – sets the tone of the force, intensity, and speed of changes addressed in this chapter.

Keywords Fertility · Nuptiality · Children · Family arrangements · Demographic dynamics

M. C. F. A. de Oliveira (✉) · J. M. Vieira
Population Studies Center (Nepo), Department of Demography,
State University of Campinas (Unicamp), Campinas, Brazil
e-mail: mcoleta@nepo.unicamp.br; jmvieira@nepo.unicamp.br

G. dos Santos Marcondes
Population Studies Center (Nepo), State University of Campinas (Unicamp),
Campinas, Brazil
e-mail: gal@nepo.unicamp.br

M. Arretche (ed.), *Paths of Inequality in Brazil*,
https://doi.org/10.1007/978-3-319-78184-6_11

The decades that followed the end of World War II were witness to intense changes in the private lives of the Brazilian population. New opportunities brought alternative choices for men and women and left a strong impression on postwar generations.

Structural factors both material and cultural established the scenario of driving forces that pushed new generations toward modernity. Two of them are particularly important: education and women in the labor market. Undoubtedly, the powerful engine behind both factors was an urban revolution, which relocated huge population contingents toward cities, categorically changing living arrangements as well as expectations for the future.

Various authors have drawn attention to a characteristic feature of social change in Brazil and Latin America, one filled with ambivalence, asynchrony, and contradiction that qualify modernity as incomplete, unfinished, peripheral, late, or anomalous, among many other expressions implying deformations or distortions in the transition process experienced by the most advanced capitalist societies (Bacha and Klein 1986; Oliveira 2001; Martins 2000; Pintor 2000; Souza 2003; Marín and Morales 2010). Oftentimes, change trends are not explicit or fully consummated, apparently ceasing at a halfway point, which produces heterogeneities when faced with an apparent homogenization of patterns and behavior, a type of modernity capable of engendering new inequalities, sometimes mistakenly taken as signs of the past (Martins 1994). This observation is important to keep in mind. Structural changes, modernization, increased living standards, and changes in ways of life do not mean social equality or homogenization.

Nevertheless, transformations run their course, destroying old Brazilian sociability and establishing a new one, overcoming known solutions and making room for social creativity.

With regard to the family and private life, transformations gradually introduced in gender relations were the main transformative dimension. Postwar generations, especially urbanites, echoed the emblems of European and North American feminism, enveloped in the libertarian wave that has captivated young cohorts in almost all of the West. New values and practices continue to defy concepts and create opportunities for social experimentation as we move forward in the twenty-first century.

Social transformations were both cause and consequence of profound changes in the demographic system. These changes became entrenched in the second half of the twentieth century, especially after the 1960s. An intense decline in fertility accompanied by simultaneous changes in the private lives of individuals resulted in an increase in the aging population. A reduction in the size of younger cohorts and extensions of the lifespans of both men and women paved the way for redefining generational transitions and their relationships.

These structural changes include an increase in the availability of modern methods of contraception and a growing demand for their use. This is the result of different social groups who incorporated the idea that having children was a matter of choice and not predestination.

In this chapter, we gather evidence and interpretations regarding demographic changes within the broad and complex process of transformation in the life of Brazilian families since the second half of the twentieth century. We believe that the main demographic factors affecting private life – mortality, fertility, and marriage rates – reflect the increasingly multifaceted conformation of contemporary families, especially those housing children under the age of 15.

The information used is derived mostly from demographic censuses since 1970. Data from previous periods are incorporated when needed to better understand processes.

Sociodemographic Regimes in the Second Half of the Twentieth Century

Prolonging Life

The prolongation of life is a key aspect of the demographic regime that gradually took shape in Brazil in the second half of the twentieth century. Following the general trend in most countries, Brazilians were living increasingly longer. Life expectancy at birth did not exceed 41.5 years in 1940, reaching 51.6 years in 1960, 61.7 years in 1980, 66 years in 1991, and 73.5 years in 2010. In seven decades, the average life expectancy of the Brazilian population increased by over 30 years, with the greatest advances occurring in the 1970s and 1980s, which coincided with an intense period of urbanization.

Primarily the result of the control and reduction of child mortality, increased life expectancy at birth reduced the differences between those with more and fewer chances of survival. What took place was not merely the extension of the lifespans of average Brazilians, but rather a decrease in inequality in the survival rates of contemporary individuals.

Graph 1 shows the reduction in differences in life expectancy over the past 30 years. The double line corresponds to the age that divides the population into two equal parts: the survivors and those who had died up to that point. We can observe that in 1980, 20% of the population would have died before reaching the age of 47, with this threshold being extended to age 60 in 2010. In contrast, the 20% of the population living longer in 1980 surpassed 80 years of age, a limit which swelled to nearly 90 years of age in 2010. This shows a remarkable change over the course of just 30 years; the gap between the 20% of Brazilians living longer and the 20% living less had decreased from 35 to 28.9 years.

In Brazil, as in Latin America, mortality reduction in the postwar period largely benefited from importation of the means for endemic disease control without, however, leading to considerable improvements in the population's well-being. This reduction especially favored more affluent social groups and residents of the country's most developed regions, thus heightening social and regional inequalities. Improvements in mortality conditions were therefore selective.

In the mid-1970s, under the centralizing policies of the military regime and demands driven by the increasing incorporation of the population into an urban-industrial economy, government action expanded basic sanitation as well as maternal and child health programs, such as those targeting pregnancy, childbirth and

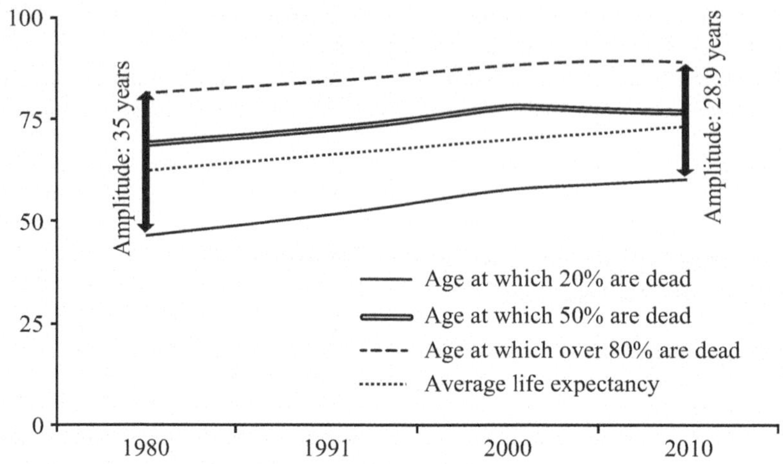

Graph 1 Life extension and reduction of life expectancy differences among people from the same cohort: Brazil (1980–2010). (Source: Albuquerque and Senna 2005; IBGE 2011)

postpartum, immunization campaigns, breastfeeding, and oral rehydration. Deprived areas where state action was lacking or precarious began to receive attention.

The continuity of these programs in the following decades was crucial for expanding access to public health services. The expansion of vaccination coverage, especially during childhood, provided significant gains in life opportunities, increasingly benefiting larger contingents, not just the more affluent groups (Prata 1992). Investments in health and sanitation, along with increased schooling rates and declining fertility rates, contributed to reductions and changes in Brazilian mortality and reduction of historical social and regional inequalities (IBGE 1999).

Declining Offspring

If significant advances in controlling death rates in Brazil date back to the early decades of the twentieth century, significant changes in the behavior of fertility would appear only 30 years later. While evidence indicates that urban elites within predominantly agricultural societies were the precursors of restricted fertility, only in the 1960s did the practice of reduced families undergo broader expansions (Guzmán and Rodríguez 1993; Souza 1995). The beginning of the decline in fact precedes the date considered as the start of the drop in fertility rates.

Estimates for the early twentieth century (Frias and Oliveira 1991; Horta et al. 2000; Rio-Neto 2000) indicate that the reduction in Brazilian fertility rates was in motion prior to the 1930s, especially in the country's more developed regions. The data in Graph 2 suggest a slow process of decline, possibly because the population at the forefront of change did not have sufficient weight to significantly alter the rates for the entire population. If the decline seems to have been

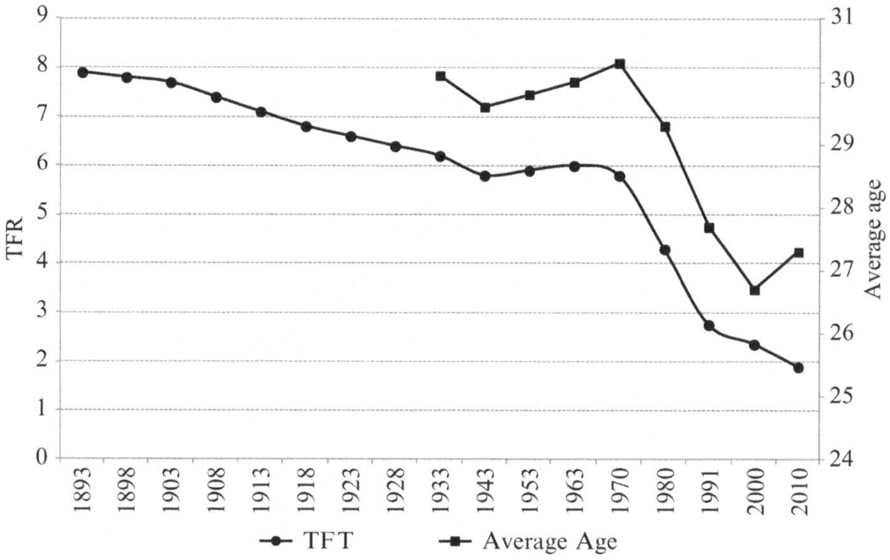

Graph 2 Total fertility rates (TFR) (The total fertility rate is the average number of live births by a woman at the end of the reproductive period, expressed by the formula $TFT_j = n \times \sum_{x=15}^{45} {}_{n}TFE_{x,j}$) and average fertility age: Brazil (1893–2010) (Sources: Horta et al. 2000; IBGE. Demographic Censuses 1970–2010

consistent up to 1940, there would have been a pre-transitional growth of total fertility rates (TFR) from this date until 1960, albeit mild. For this reason, Rios-Neto (2000) argues that the behavior of Brazilian fertility, from the early twentieth century until the mid-1960s, would be compatible with the slow decline type of transition observed in the European experience. Since 1968, however, the downward trend is dramatically accentuated, distancing the Brazilian transition from the classic European model.

The characteristics of the transition process in Brazil's fertility rates prior to the second half of the twentieth century are due to the combined effect of persistence and increased fertility rates in less developed regions, with significant reductions in more developed ones. Rio de Janeiro and São Paulo showed signs of a transition to lower fertility rates from the 1950s, with rates below the 1970 national TFR. In contrast, the Northeast maintained high fertility levels during the same period (Carvalho and Wood 1994). Nonetheless, there was a general 20% decline between 1930 and 1960, and, in the early 1970s, all regions registered a significant reduction in fertility rates compared to the early 1960s (Frias and Oliveira 1991; Carvalho and Wood 1994).

Since the 1970s, the decline in Brazilian fertility leaves no room for doubt. The turning point seems to coincide with the introduction of the pill in 1965 (Carvalho et al. 1981; Merrick and Berquó 1983). The data indicate, however, that reduction gained momentum in the 1980s when a restricted fertility pattern became well established and reached average rates below two children per woman

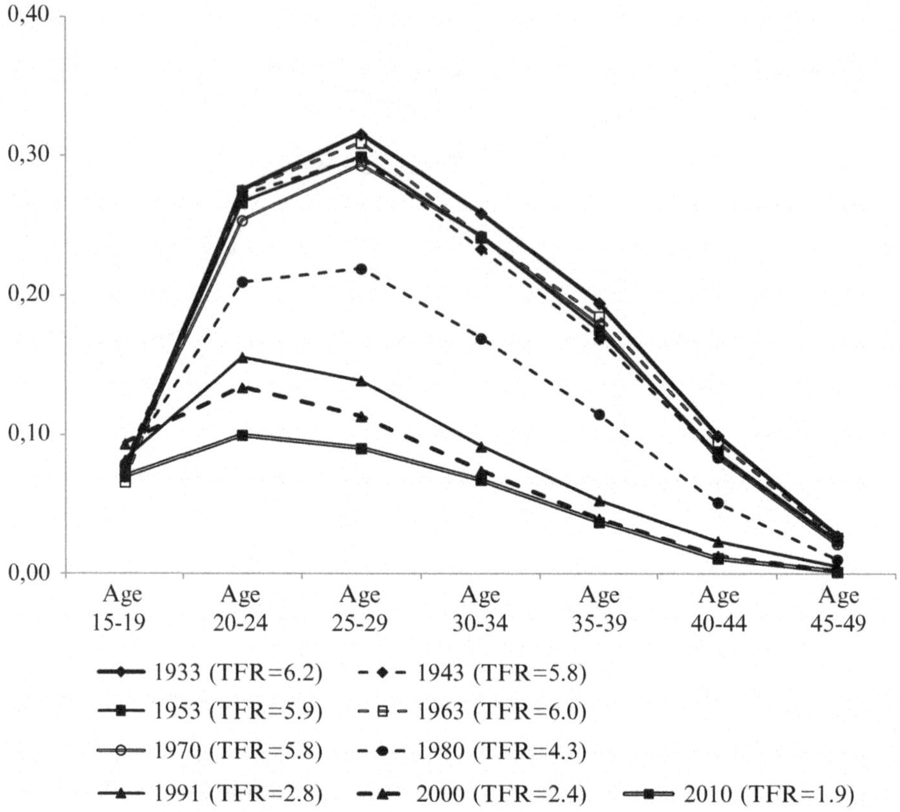

Graph 3 Specific fertility rates by age: Brazil (1930–2010). (Source: Horta et al. 2000; IBGE. Demographic Censuses (1970–2010)

in the first decade of the twenty-first century, lower than the population replacement level (Graph 2).

This intense decline was accompanied by a reduction in the average age of childbearing women, revealing fertility concentration behavior at younger ages (see Graph 3, below), which changes in 2010 with a rise in the average age, indicating possible postponement of fertility.

More recent analyses show some distinctive aspects of the transition process. In a study evaluating the *time effect* and *parturition effect*[1] of the TFR, Miranda-Ribeiro et al. (2010) show that Brazilian fertility rates between 1976 and 1998 witnessed a reduction in the average ages of fertility (fertility postponement) and an increase in the relative weight of lower-order births (first and

[1]The study applies the Kohler and Ortega model to obtain a more accurate fertility indicator than conventional measures, allowing us to measure the distortions caused by the *time effect* – changes occurring in the average fertility age – and the *parturition effect*, changes in composition of fertility due to parturition. By knowing these effects, it is possible to adjust the fertility calculation by obtaining a hypothetical value free of such distortions known as the *quantum*.

second children). The late 1990s witnessed an interruption of the downward movement in the average fertility age, which remained constant at 26.5 years, while similar reductions occurred in the proportions of lower- and higher-order births. These characteristics indicate the possible beginning of a process of fertility postponement that would mark the twenty-first century.

Some of the forces at work in the decline of fertility rates are obvious such as urbanization, which changed the living environment for millions of Brazilians. Even though major urban transformations were still a recent phenomenon in 1970, the TFR discrepancy between rural and urban women was quite marked (Table 1): the former had three more children on average than the latter. The historical series reveals, however, that changes were in motion throughout the country. In 40 years, there has been a *rapprochement* in the behavior of rural and urban women: the average fertility rate of the former decreased by more than five children, while for urban women, the decline was by almost three. While it still makes a difference whether one lives in cities or otherwise, changes in Brazil during the second half of the twentieth century confronted limits and undoubtedly brought opportunities, demands, and even access to services.

It is worth remembering that the very meaning of the word rural underwent substantial changes in Brazil, leading experts to refer to a "new rural" (Abramovay 1992; Campanhola and Graziano da Silva 2000), a phenomenon with similar references outside of the country (Barlett 1986; Arnalte 1989).

Urbanization expanded the labor market for women in a process of female worker individualization (Oliveira 1984). The service sector, particularly domestic but commerce as well, opened up possibilities for female labor outside the home, a process that continues to this day (Bruschini 1994; Hoffmann and Leone 2004). Educational expansion, along with market forces, benefited urban women by promoting lower average fertility rates. The data in Table 1 indicate that a portion of the female population – the working population with high educational levels – present a marked trend for having fewer children, reaching rates close to or below two children per woman at an earlier point in time.

The fertility rate of Brazilian women in 2010 (1.9 children on average) was equivalent to that observed in 1970 among women with a college degree. Differences waned after 40 years, although women with higher levels of education have almost one child less than their contemporaries with incomplete primary education (Table 1).

Evidence strongly indicates that the trajectory of change is not linear, but instead involves multiple transitions (Patarra and Oliveira 1988). The data suggest that women of the social elite were the vanguard of fertility change, as shown by the results from a pioneering research project in São Paulo (Berquó et al. 1977) as well as a research study by Souza (1995) on women with higher educational levels in Bahia. Recent studies confirm the belief that the educated elite commanded the fertility decline process in Brazil as well as in other contexts, as shown by Livi-Bacci (1986) regarding Venetian aristocracy and others in Europe.

Along with female educational levels, labor market integration meant that women had fewer children. Whether because life brings them fewer children or because they choose to limit their offspring due to an interest in and/or need for a

Table 1 TFRs[a] and average fertility age by selected characteristics: Brazil (1970–2010)

Years	Household situation				Occupation				Schooling				Household monthly per capita income			
	Rural		Urban		Does not work		Works		No instruction incomplete primary		Completed higher education		40% with less income		20% with the highest income	
	TFR	Average age	TFR	Average age	TFR	Average age	TFR	Average age	TFR	Average age	TFR	Average age	TFR	Average age	TFR	Average age
1970	7.7	30.7	4.6	29.9	6.7	30	3.2	31.6	6.3	30.2	1.9	30.7	9.1	31.1	2.2	28.5
1980	6.2	30.0	3.6	28.9	5.3	29	2.7	30.3	4.9	29.1	2.3	30.2	7.4	30.0	2.0	28.4
1991	4.3	28.8	2.4	27.4	3.6	27.7	1.9	28.4	3.5	27.5	2.5	29.9	4.7	28.5	1.5	27.9
2000	3.5	27.2	2.2	26.7	3.1	26.9	1.8	27.4	3.4	26.0	1.9	31.0	3.7	26.8	1.3	28.8
2010	2.6	26.7	1.8	27.4	2.6	27.4	1.6	27.9	3.0	25.8	1.9	32.1	3.0	26.7	1.2	30.4

Source: IBGE, Demographic Censuses (1970–2010)

[a]The TFRs were adjusted by the Brass' P/F method (United Nations 1983), and the fertility of women age 20–24 is used as reference for the adjustment, except for the cut using household monthly per capita income, in which average fertility of women aged 20–24 and 25–29 provides the best adjustment

job, working women tend to have a lower average number of children than those who do not work (Table 1).

Moreover, throughout the period analyzed, the composition of working women changed significantly: it went from young, single, female workers, to age 30 or older, mostly married or in a consensual union, with children. This trend brings into the discussion implications for fertility differentials regarding tensions between work and family for women from different social sectors (Bruschini and Ricoldi 2009; Dedecca et al. 2009; Marri and Wajnman 2006; Montali 2012).

Table 1 shows that educational level and income seem to have their own effects on how fertility behaves. The extreme ends of the income scale show sharper divergences in fertility levels over time than similar extremes of the educational scale. This is a tricky observation, since what may have happened is that educational progress would tend to approach similar fertility levels of a larger group of women who are already at lower thresholds across all educational degrees, except for those with a college degree whose leading position was demonstrated in 1970. Therefore, it is income perhaps more than education that exposes inequality in recent times in Brazil. The polarization of fertility at income extremes now seems more pronounced than at educational extremes.

Our hypothesis is that education has rapidly promoted a reduction in inequality, especially for women, in the past two decades. Extremes from the past currently tend toward less pronounced differences, especially among the younger generations and young adults. Income, on the other hand, does not depend solely on education. Educational thresholds that act as requirements for better jobs have increased and, despite recent growth in formal employment rates, wages have not necessarily increased. Wage mass as a whole is one issue; another issue is to individually assess inequality in labor income (Cunha and Vasconcelos 2012).

One cannot ignore the role of marriage in this equation. The increase in the average age of marriage for women since the 1990s is also related to an increase in education and women's participation in the labor market, processes that resulted in changes in the timing of the formation of marital partnerships and, consequently, of families. Equally noteworthy are the repercussions within the marriage market. Increased education and economic participation of women in the workforce would tend to reduce potential partner opportunities under conditions that combine male excess mortality rates and persistent cultural values that prescribe adherence to the older men/younger women model (Berquó 1986; Camargo and Oliveira 1977; Oliveira 1977). These constraints particularly affect women. If restricted to seeking older men, women would eventually include less educated men or men that are somehow below their social expectations in their roster of possible male partners. It bears emphasizing that such partners, prospective older men, tend to look for increasingly younger women, reinforcing the vicious circle of the marriage market.

Information regarding these 50 years in Brazil allows for other considerations. Given widespread lower fertility rates across various segments of the population, Berquó and Cavenaghi (2009) consider the importance of assessing which groups persist with higher fertility patterns (an average of more than four children). By comparing data from 1991 and 2000, the authors show that the reduced proportion of women with high fertility rates (an average of five or more children) corresponded to those with the lowest educational levels (up to 3 years of schooling) and per capita household income (up to one-half of the minimum wage). Stating similar findings, Rios-Neto (2005) argues that along with the positive role of fertility decline in families' adaptation to pressure for resources in Brazil, fertility differentials persist or even intensify. From the author's perspective, it seems that the accumulation of shortages would lead to preservation, most likely residual, of population segments that retain behaviors outside the more general trend curve.

Establishing Families

It is impossible to continue debating this issue without evaluating the characteristics and implications of the timing of household formation processes. After all, families have to be addressed when dealing with fertility, regardless of the characteristics of the relationship or the legal status of the unions.

The reduction in the average fertility age in Brazil (Graph 2) reveals that children tend to be born to young women, producing a rejuvenation of fertility, which is a characteristic that distinguishes the Brazilian fertility transition process (Berquó and Cavenaghi 2009). The data in Table 1, however, indicate at least one situation that departs from the rule: highly educated women tend to have a higher average age at childbirth than other women. Differences between educational groups in terms of average age at childbirth have increased since the 1980s, the period that witnessed Brazil's greatest decline in fertility. In 2010, high income also appears to differentiate the average age of women more clearly at childbirth (Berquó and Cavenaghi 2009; Rios-Neto 2005; Miranda-Ribeiro et al. 2008).

Graph 3 shows that changes occur in the fertility behavior of women over the course of their lives, conveying different timing for the formation of family units. Until 1980, childbirth was concentrated in the group, age 25–29; from this decade on, women began having children earlier, so childbirth after the age of 30 became increasingly more infrequent. However, there is an ongoing change: a reduction of fertility in the first decade of the twenty-first century can be credited to younger women (Table 1). A reduction occurs in the rates of children born to women under the age of 30, while their more mature contemporaries remain just as fertile as they were 10 years before.

Various authors (Berquó and Cavenaghi 2009; Miranda-Ribeiro et al. 2008; Alves and Cavenaghi 2009) suggest that Brazil is currently witnessing a postponement of the childbearing age. In fact, there are currently two patterns equally associated with reduced fertility: women who begin and end their reproductive life relatively early and those who start later, after age 30, thus, ultimately having fewer offspring than their contemporaries. However, the widening of the fertility curve by age also raises the hypothesis of a "third route": a portion of women – among the more educated and more integrated into the labor market – adhere to their generation's pattern of postponing reproduction, but eventually establish a higher fertility rate after the age of 30 (women with two to three children).

We must emphasize the importance of the widespread dissemination of modern contraceptive methods both in shaping the rejuvenated pattern as well as in the postponement of offspring formation. While the pill is an important factor, female sterilization ultimately assumed the lead role in controlling the fertility of women in Brazil (Berquó 1999; Goldani 2001; Perpétuo and Wong 2009).

Until Death Do Us Part

The exploration of the relationship between vital events (births and deaths) and family ties is nothing new. The expansion or contraction of families largely depends upon these events. Studies by Ariès (1978) are examples of the extent and depth of the implications of reducing child mortality and the voluntary limitation of the number of children in terms of the growing appreciation of children and the centrality they acquired within Western European families after the eighteenth century.

In addition, the increase in life expectancy has expanded the potential period for family life or, at least, the coexistence of two or three generations. It has also opened up possibilities for redefining the stages between crucial time markers already in existence, extending some while others emerge, such as between childhood and adulthood (adolescence) or between adulthood and old age (maturity), or even changing the order of events that define life stages, such as family formation, school completion, or entry into the labor market.

Graph 4 summarizes some of the major demographic changes observed in Brazil in the second half of the twentieth century, allowing us to visualize the intensity and timing of urbanization and to highlight the association between this process and the decline in fertility rates in the country.

In terms of trends, Graph 4 displays information about marital unions with data on marital breakdowns (*desquites,*[2] separations, and divorces), which are increasingly important events in redefining family ties due to expanded lifespans, enabling us to get a glimpse into what takes places in this area.[3]

The systematic decrease in the gross rate of legal marriage[4] seems evident since the early 1980s, with a slight recovery in the early 2000s. Also in 1980, the proportion of people consensually united exceeds the 10% threshold, reaching 36.4% in 2010. As for marital breakdowns, Berquó and Oliveira (1992) call attention to the increase in separation rates between 1960 and 1970. Until the late 1980s, separation rates were higher than divorce rates, probably because of the time lag required by law between legal separation and divorce, spawning an accumulated demand for marriage dissolutions upon approval of the 1977 Divorce Act (Marcondes 2011).

[2] *Desquite* refers to the legal form of marriage dissolution before the 1977 Divorce Act.

[3] Information on marriage rates is generated through the civil registry offices, while data on consensual unions come from the demographic census and are therefore not strictly comparable.

[4] Marriage rate is the ratio between the number of marriages in a year and the total population in that same year expressed per 1000 inhabitants. The gross rates for *desquites*, legal separations, and divorces are established analogously.

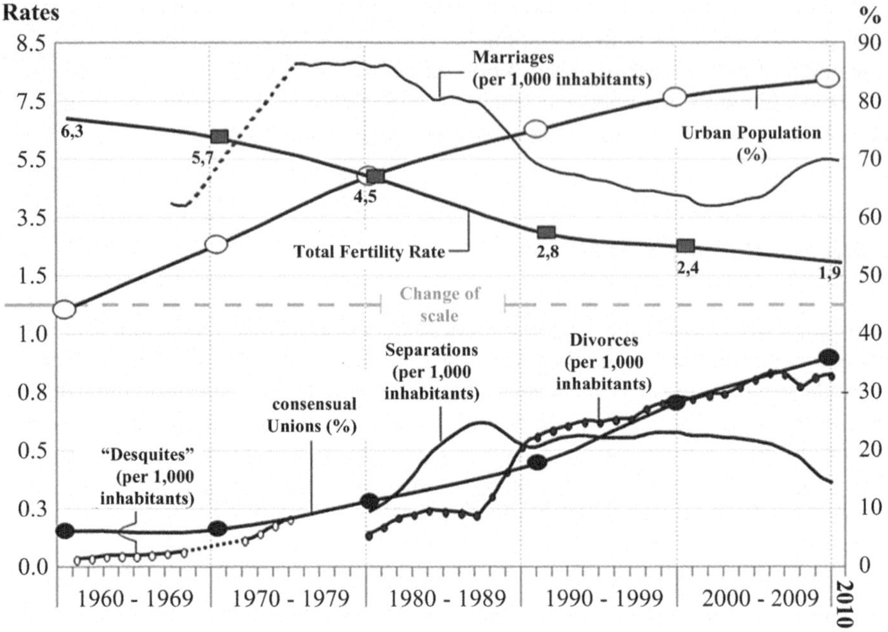

Graph 4 Crude rates for marriage, *desquite*, legal separation and divorce, degree of urbanization, total fertility, and evolution of consensual unions: Brazil (1960–2010). (Source: IBGE, Demographic Census, Civil Registry Statistics, Population Estimates and Projections (1960–2010))

In Graph 5, we can observe a significant increase in the separated/divorced population since 1980, highlighting the ever-higher proportion of women who are separated, divorced, and widowed, with implications on the conformation of families. Two factors contribute to the maintenance of these gender differences: high mortality of males and a higher incidence of male remarriages.

The decline in marriage rates and increased marital breakdowns seem at first glance to suggest a reduced propensity toward conjugal life. However, the data indicate that people continue to opt to have a life partner, progressively more so in conjugal unions other than marriage. In the past 40 years, there has been little change in the proportion of people living with a partner, with a particular reduction in the share of married couples compared to consensual unions in the population over the age of 15 (Graph 4).

Although more frequently present in the lives of individuals and Brazilian families, separations and divorces still affect the lives of men, women, children, and ultimately, families. The persistence of gender inequalities in income and childcare responsibilities and domestic space is a stronger burden for women and children. However, the increase in separations and divorces does not seem to indicate a weakening of marital partnerships to the point of endangering the family institution itself. The facts do not suggest a rejection of union, but rather the incorporation of marital breakdown as a legitimate possibility within the general conjugal model.

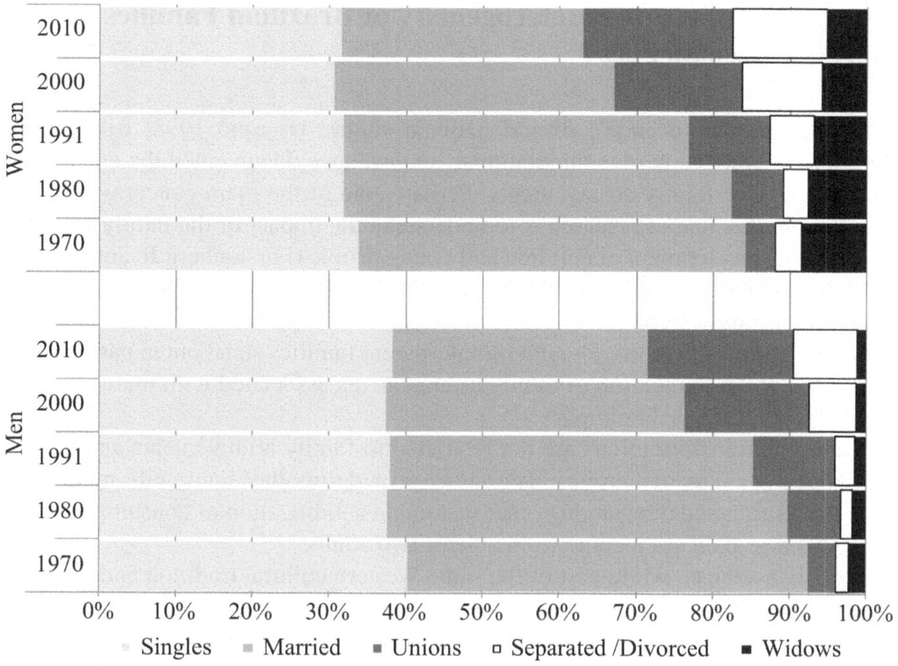

Graph 5 Distribution of persons, age 15 and over, by gender and marital status (1): Brazil (1970–2010) (Source: IBGE, Demographic Censuses (1970–2010), (1) Data standardized by the age structure of the population in 1970)

Formal marriages continue to be important alternatives to consensual unions and family formation, while at the same time the social legitimacy of consensual unions is expanding across all social environments.

The increase in cohabitation, low fertility levels, rising divorce rates, and other private life events established a different demographic development stage (a second demographic transition), in which practices, projects, and choices are steered by an individualistic *ethos* that values autonomy and personal fulfillment (Lesthaeghe 1995; Van De Kaa 2002). Far from being a new phenomenon in Brazil or Latin America (Oliveira 1979, 1982; Quilodrán 1992, 2011; Marcondes 2008), consensual unions have been historically associated with poverty, in social exclusion contexts, far removed from conditions that would suggest personal emancipation or lifestyle choice. However, the latest increase in these types of unions and their presence in different social segments indicate the existence of more than one conjugal pattern. Either way, cohabitation has been a constant within the dynamics of family formation and family structuring in Brazil (Oliveira 1996).

Family, Families: The Heterogeneity of Brazilian Families and Its Consequences

Over the past few decades, several national studies (Berquó 1998; Bilac 1991, 2000), as well as numerous international studies, have documented the emergence of a plurality of family arrangements. Perhaps one of the main concerns of those engaging in this line of research is to understand the impact of the family environment on the development of children and young people (Furstenberg Jr. and Cherlin 1991; Furstenberg Jr. 2007; Phelps et al. 2002; Mclanahan 2006). More and more children are raised in homes outside the conjugal two-parent model entrenched in Western culture, where the so-called single-parent families stand out in particular in a scenario of diversification of family arrangements associated with marital breakdowns and/or informal unions.

However, transformations are not restricted to family arrangements and impact the inner dynamics of families. The father-provider/mother-housewife model has long been surpassed due, among other factors, to solidification of consumption patterns that now demand income from at least two adults.

Brazilian society, while part of the same Western cultural tradition and subordinated to the laws of development of capitalist market economies, displays particularities not easily assimilated to the social formation of other countries in the Americas, with which it bears similarities. Cohabitation without marriage, in a society with a strong family tradition such as Brazil, is a prime example. The notion of *geoculture* (Therborn 2004) helps us discriminate features incorporated into the local *ethos*, whose origin and permanence stem from a "combination of Portuguese Iberian tradition with the native population and that brought from Africa under the slave system" (Oliveira 2009, p. 78).

However, research lines primarily interested in the effects of family arrangement on child development and well-being, or which adopt a cultural-historical perspective, coexist with one another, are inspired by Becker's contributions (1981) and are focused on family size. These refer to the relationship between fertility and human capital investment and the role of fertility reduction in the strengthening of family relationships. The latter is understood as the growing importance of emotional bonds and the pursuit of satisfaction as a motivation to have children and a relative mitigation of motivation grounded on utilitarianism and short-term economic benefits. According to Becker, the decision to have children is a rational choice, and the choice for a small number of descendants implies a shift from quantity to quality. Investing in the quality of children means instilling in them socially valued characteristics regarding education, health, and capacity for social mobility, resulting in rising educational gains and advances in child health indicators over time.

Such logic manifests itself in the daily lives of ordinary citizens within contemporary Brazilian society. People who have four or five children sometimes are considered "irresponsible" because according to one type of perception and particularly among the middle class, the capacity to provide adequate support, assistance, and care for so many children comes into question.

Is Family No Longer the Same?

The "couple with children" arrangement – the most common form of family life in Brazil during the twentieth century – no longer represents the absolute majority of the population in 2010. The reduced proportion of people living in this arrangement is without doubt one of the most striking transformations that has taken place in Brazilian families between 1970 and 2010. In 1970, 67% of Brazilians lived in this type of family structure, a figure that fell to 48.3% in 2010.

The category "single parent with relatives" expanded the most: in 1970, it encompassed 2.4% of Brazilians, reaching 8.1% in 2010. At that time, 9% of the population lived in arrangements which comprises the mother and her children, a slightly higher rate than in 1970 (7.2%). At the same time, there is a significant upward trend in the number of individuals living alone (1.6% in 1970 and 4.3% in 2010). It is worth noting, however, that from the point of view of children, the nuclear family[5] remains the dominant child-rearing environment. In 1970, 77.5% of children lived in homes of this type, decreasing to about 62% in 2010.

The hypothesis that the Brazilian family has become more heterogeneous or plural is the leading thread of the following studies. They established synthetic indicators to express the degree of heterogeneity of the events or phenomena – the so-called entropy indexes (Theil 1972; Billari 2001; Fussell 2005; Vieira 2008; Vieira and Miret 2010) – here used to measure the diversity of family arrangements across four decades. Ranging from 0 to 100, the interpretation of the indicator is straightforward: the closer to zero, the more homogeneous the familiar environment, consequently, the greater the entropy index, the greater the level of heterogeneity in family arrangements.[6]

---

[5] In this chapter, the terms "nuclear family" and "couple with children" are used interchangeably.

[6] The entropy index measures how individuals are scattered across different family arrangement categories. The more dispersed people are in different possible arrangements, the more heterogeneous the family environment. In this study we consider eight types of arrangements based on the "census family" concept: single-person household, childless couples, couples without children and with relatives, couples with children, single parents, two parents with relatives, single parents with relatives, and others. The index is calculated with the formula $E = \Sigma\ P_{s,x} * \ln\ (1/P_{s,x})$, where s indicates a certain family arrangement category, x is the social group analyzed (color, PCHI quintile, etc.), and $P_{s,x}$ is the proportion of individuals in social group x in family arrangement category s in a given year. Therefore, if all individuals are concentrated in one single family arrangement category, the entropy value will be equal to zero. Since this study considered eight possible family arrangement categories, the maximum amount the entropy index could reach is given by $E_{max} = \Sigma\ (1/C_s)* \ln\ [1/(1/\ C_s)]$, where C_s is the total number of family arrangement categories. In the present study, since there are eight familial arrangement categories, the maximum entropy is in the formula $E = \Sigma\ (1/8)*$ in $[1/(1/\ 8)] = 2079$. In a hypothetical situation with the exact same number of people in each of the eight living arrangement categories, the maximum entropy of 2079 would synthesize this reality. Since values ranging from 0 to 2079 are not very easy to grasp or interpret, we transformed each group's entropy indexes into a percentage of maximum entropy. Therefore, our indicators for heterogeneity level (the entropy indexes) ranges from 0 to 100.

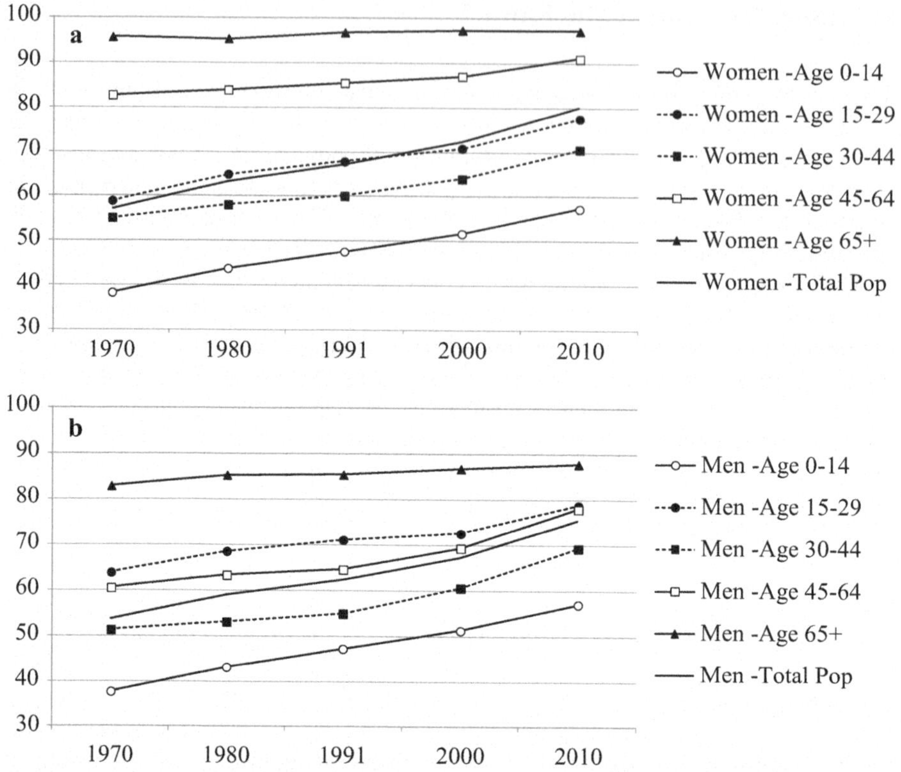

Graph 6 Evolution of the heterogeneity level of family arrangements by gender, according to age groups: Brazil (1970–2010) (**a**) Women, (**b**) Men (Source: IBGE, Demographic Censuses (1970–2010))

Measuring the diversity of family structures through entropy analysis allows us to compare the behavior of specific social groups, opening up the possibility for identifying which ones have indeed become more plural.

Graph 6 describes different movements in the ways men and women travel through family arrangements over the course of their lives. The plurality of family arrangements increases as the cycles of life progress, although not linearly. This trend is much stronger among women. Indeed, men and women show differences in this respect. Female family structures are more complex (Oliveira 1992). Adult men adhere more to the nuclear family model and have low participation in single-parent arrangements in a fatherly position, and, therefore, the family configurations in which they operate are less heterogeneous. It becomes clear how female family formations from the age of 45 are much more plural than their male counterparts.

The group, age 65 and over, has the highest plurality of family arrangements, with women reaching higher levels of heterogeneity than men. The elderly presented relatively stable behavior over time, displaying high heterogeneity indexes. This characteristic derives from the fact that the chance of changing the composition of the group in which one lives increases with age. This trend is a reflection of the distribution or scattering of this aging group across different family arrangements.

At age 0–14 and 30–44, both men and women tend to gather in nuclear families, either at the expansion or consolidation stages. At age 15–29, many have begun to establish their own households, while others continue to live with their parents. Multiple possible scripts increase heterogeneity. Though with similar plurality levels, this stage of life is the second most heterogeneous among men and third most heterogeneous among women. During youth, male family arrangements are more plural than at age 45–64, while the opposite occurs among women.

The group, age 0–14, follows the general trend observed in other groups with regard to increased plurality in household arrangements. However, the slope of the sharpest curve for this group reveals a more intense heterogeneity increase among children.

Regional differences remain very much present among children. Graph 7 shows that the North and Northeast regions appear to have more plural family configurations than the South. Although heterogeneity has increased across all regions, regional thresholds witness sharper distinctions when it comes to children rather than the population as a whole. This suggests that contrary to what one might think, family structure heterogeneity is not necessarily associated with more favorable social and economic conditions.

Children who live in homes where the head of the household is black (Graph 8) or has a low educational level tend to live in more diverse family structures compared to those living in arrangements where the head of the household has a university degree or belongs to a higher-income stratum.

Interestingly, when considering the wealthiest people among all age groups, we see that they seem to be more scattered across different family arrangements, with the exception that in the ages between childhood and early adolescence, the residential pattern is almost exclusively couples with children.

Greater heterogeneity can possibly indicate lower adherence to a normative-ideal model. Thus, the reduced heterogeneity identified among the most privileged children compared to underprivileged ones may be credited to the fact that, when people with higher incomes choose to have children, they are more likely to fit the nuclear family mold. Among the poorest children, arrangements tend to be more heterogeneous, either because of marital breakdowns, child circulation, or cohabitation with other relatives (Oliveira 1992).

Final Considerations

It is no easy task to analyze the changes and continuities of Brazilian families in the past 50 years. The phenomenon encompasses social, cultural, political, and economic processes at multiple levels, establishing a more complex approach between the micro and macro spheres of society. Many of the changes intensified after the 1990s, a period marked by economic stabilization due to the real plan and progress in universal access to health and basic education, the latter accompanied by an intensive campaign to eradicate child labor. Women are certainly the protagonists of a silent revolution at the micro level: increasingly involved in the labor market and more educated than their male counterparts, women seem to live in a new Brazil, especially when we contrast the 2010 generation with their 1970 counterparts.

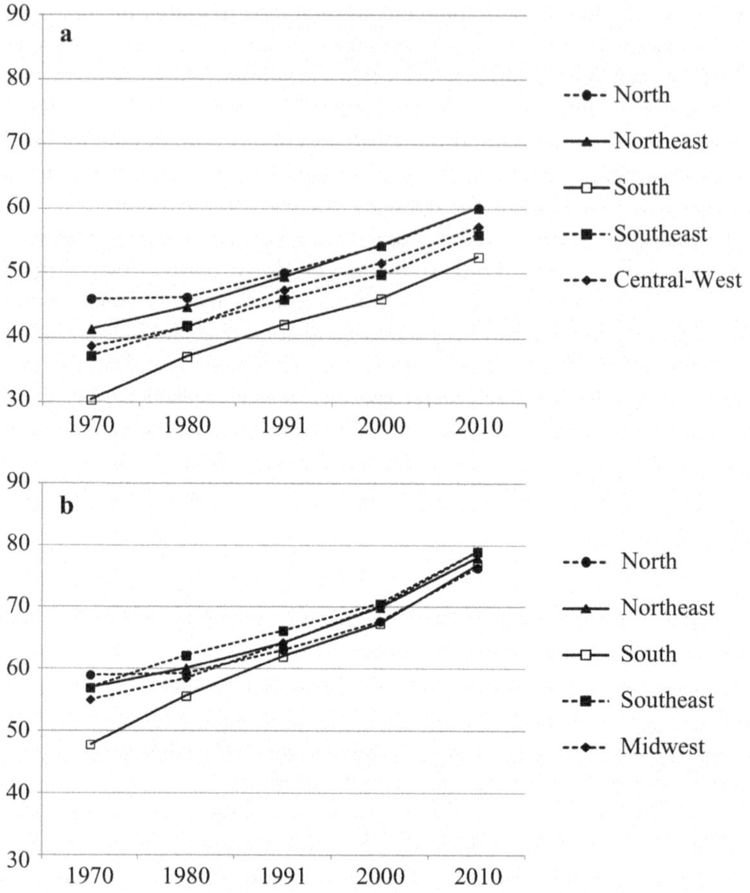

Graph 7 Family structure heterogeneity level according to major regions: Brazil (1970–2010). (Source: IBGE, Demographic Censuses (1970–2010))

The historical series of demographic censuses help us understand a country with a long path ahead in overcoming inequalities, albeit displaying significant achievements for the public and private lives of its citizens. Concerning families, the recognition of their plural and metamorphic condition in the 1988 Constitution – and reiterated by subsequent laws – sets the tone of the force, intensity, and speed of changes addressed in this chapter.

Maintaining very low fertility levels not only implies the need to review the social welfare model but also occasions reconfigurations in human relations and within the fundamental bonds of sociability and support networks (Oliveira 1997). Increased longevity also increases possibilities for longer periods of intergenerational coexistence (great-grandparents, grandparents, parents, grandchildren, great-grandchildren), but the drastic reduction of fertility decreases the presence of collaterals (siblings, cousins, uncles) and, consequently, chances of intragenerational family solidarity. It may be that friendship bonds replace family ties – and conventional wisdom often maintains that friends are the family we choose.

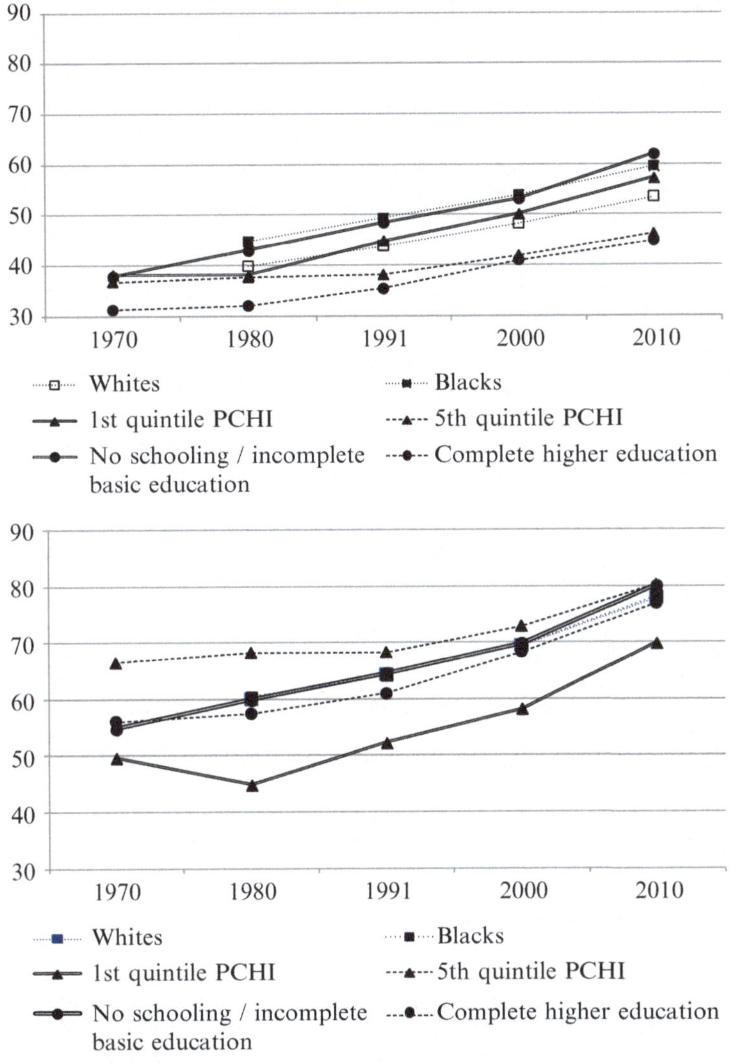

Graph 8 Degree of family structure heterogeneity according to color, per capita household income, and educational level of the head of the household: Brazil (1970–2010). (Source: IBGE, Demographic Censuses (1970–2010))

There is evidence of a growing heterogeneity of family arrangements resulting from a convergence toward low fertility levels across all social groups. Increased plurality does not mean loss of relevance of the nuclear family model, especially when raising children. There is still much to be discovered as to the place reproduction holds in the trajectory of life and its influence on decision-making regarding other aspects of life.

The inexorable theme underlying this chapter pertains to the content of the choices governing contemporary life, a long-standing questioning about the awareness, designs, and/or constraints imposed over the lives of individuals. To what extent are fertility restrictions or rejection, tensions between family and professional life, educational training and maintenance of affective-sexual partnerships, support, care, and sociability networks dictated by conditions external to people, or are they simply the product of preferences? Progress in data collection enabling us to comprehend trajectories and to explore the values that guide individual and familial decision-making is an essential public task.

References

Abramoway, R. (1992). *Paradigmas do capitalismo agrário em questão*. São Paulo: Anpocs/ Hucitec.

Albuquerque, F. R. P. C., & Senna, J. R. X. (2005). *Tábuas de mortalidade por sexo e grupos de idade – Grandes Regiões e Unidades da Federação – 1980, 1991 e 2000*. Rio de Janeiro: IBGE (Discussion papers, 20).

Alves, J. E. D., & Cavenaghi, S. (2009). Timing of childbearing in below replacement fertility regimes: How and why Brazil is different? In *IUSSP International population conference*, 26. *Proceedings*.... Paris: International Union for the Scientific Study of Population. Available at: http://iussp2009.princeton.edu/papers/92527.

Ariès, P. (1978). *História social da criança e da família*. Rio de Janeiro: Zahar Editores.

Arnalte, A. E. V. (1989). Estructura de las explotaciones agrarias y externalización del proceso productivo. *Revista de Economía, 66*, 101–117.

Bacha, E., & Klein, H. S. (Orgs.). (1986). A transição incompleta: Brasil desde 1945. Rio de Janeiro: Paz e Terra.

Barlett, P. (1986). Part-time farming: Saving the farm or saving the life-style? *Rural Sociology, 51*(3), 289–313.

Berquó, E. (1986). *Pirâmide da solidão*. Campinas: Núcleo de Estudos de População/Unicamp. Mimeografado.

Berquó, E. (1998). Arranjos familiares no Brasil: uma visão demográfica. In Schwarcz, L. M. (Org.). *História da vida privada no Brasil: contrastes da intimidade contemporânea*. (5ª ed., pp. 411–441). São Paulo: Companhia das Letras.

Berquó, E. (1999). Ainda a questão da esterilização feminina no Brasil. In K. Giffin & Costa, S. H. (Orgs.). *Questões da saúde reprodutiva* (pp. 113–126). Rio de Janeiro: Editora Fiocruz.

Berquó, E., & Cavenaghi, S. (2009). Brazilian fertility regimes:Profiles of women below and above replacement levels. In *IUSSP International population conference*, 25. *Proceedings*.... Paris: International Union for the Scientific Study of Population. Available at: http://iussp2005.princeton.edu/download.aspx?submissionId=51864.

Berquó, E., & Oliveira, M. C. F. A. (1992). Casamento em tempos de crise. *Revista Brasileira de Estudos de População, 9*(2), 155–167.

Berquó, E., Oliveira, M. C. F. A., & Camargo, C. P. F. (Orgs.). (1977). A fecundidade em São Paulo: características demográficas, biológicas e sócio-econômicas. São Paulo: CEBRAP/ Editora Brasileira de Ciências.

Bilac, E. D. (1991). Convergências e divergências nas estruturas familiares no Brasil. *Ciências Sociais Hoje* (pp. 70–94). São Paulo: Vértice/Editora Revista dos Tribunais.

Bilac, E. D. (2000). Família: algumas inquietações. In Carvalho, M do C. B. (Org.). *A família contemporânea em debate* (pp. 29–38). São Paulo: Educ/Cortez.

Billari, F. (2001). The analysis of early life courses: Complex descriptions of the transition to adulthood. *Journal of Population Research, 18*(2), 119–142.

Bruschini, C. (1994). O trabalho da mulher brasileira nas décadas recentes. *Estudos Feministas, 2*(3), 179–199.

Bruschini, C., & Ricoldi, A. M. (2009). Família e trabalho: difícil conciliação para mães trabalhadoras de baixa renda. *Cadernos de Pesquisa, 39*(136), 93–123.
Camargo, C. P. F., & Oliveira, M. C. F. A. (1977). Padrões de casamento. In E. S. Berquó, M. C. F. A. Oliveira, & C. P. F. Camargo (Eds.), *A fecundidade em São Paulo: características demográficas, biológicas e sócio-econômicas* (pp. 86–110). CEBRAP/Ed. Brasileira de Ciências: São Paulo.
Campanhola, C., & Graziano Da Silva, J. (2000). *O novo rural brasileiro: uma análise nacional e regional.* Campinas: Embrapa/Unicamp (4 volumes).
Carvalho, J. A. M., & Wood, C. H. (1994). *A demografia da desigualdade no Brasil.* Rio de Janeiro: IPEA.
Carvalho, J. A. M., Paiva, P. T. A., & Sawyer, D. R. (1981). *The recent sharp decline in fertility in Brazil: Economic boom, social inequality and baby bust.* México: Population Council, Latin America and Caribbean Regional Office (Working papers, 8).
Cunha, M. S., & Vasconcelos, M. R. (2012). Evolução da desigualdade na distribuição dos salários no Brasil. *Economia Aplicada, 16*(1), 105–136. Available at: http://www.scielo.br/scielo.php?script=sci_arttext&pid=S1413-80502012000100005&lng=en&nrm=iso.
de Souza, G. A. A. (1995). Difusión de prácticas para limitar la procreación: momentos, mecanismos y determinantes. *Notas de Población, 61*, 9–28.
Dedecca, C. S., Ribeiro, C. S. M. F., & ISHII, F. H. (2009). Gênero e jornada de trabalho: análise das relações entre mercado de trabalho e família. *Trabalho Educação e Saúde, 7*(1), 65–90.
Frias, L. A. D. M., & Oliveira, J. C. (1991). Níveis, tendências e diferenciais de fecundidade do Brasil a partir da década de 30. *Revista Brasileira de Estudos de População, 8*(1/2), 72–111.
Furstenberg, F. F., Jr. (2007). *Destinies of the disadvantaged: The politics of teenage childbearing.* New York: Russell Sage Foundation.
Furstenberg, F., Jr., & Cherlin, A. J., Jr. (1991). *Divided families: What happens to children when parents part.* Cambridge: Harvard University Press.
Fussell, E. (2005). Measuring the early adult life course in Mexico: An application of the entropy index. In R. MacMillan (Ed.), *The structure of life course: Standardized? Individualized? Differentiated?* (pp. 91–122). Minneapolis: University of Minnesota. (Advances in life course research, vol. 9).
Goldani, A. M. (2001). Rethinking Brazilian fertility decline. In *IUSSP International population conference, 24. Proceedings....* Paris: International Union for the Scientific Study of Population. Available at: http://www.abep.nepo.unicamp.br/iussp2001/cd/Sessao_Especial_Goldani_Text.pdf.
Guzmán, J. M., & Rodríguez, J. (1993). La fecundidad pre-transicional en América Latina: un capítulo olvidado. *Notas de Población, 21*(57), 217–246.
Hoffmann, R., & Leone, E. T. (2004). Participação da mulher no mercado de trabalho e desigualdade da renda domiciliar per capita no Brasil: 1981–2002. *Nova Economia, 14*(2), 35–58.
Horta, C. J. G., Carvalho, J. A. M., & Frias, L. A. (2000). Recomposição da fecundidade por geração para Brasil e Regiões: atualização e revisão. In *Encontro Nacional De Estudos Populacionais, 12 Anais....* Belo Horizonte: ABEP. Available at: http://www.abep.nepo.unicamp.br/docs/anais/pdf/2000/Todos/rept10_1.pdf.
IBGE. (1999). *Evolução e perspectivas da mortalidade infantil no Brasil.* Rio de Janeiro: O Departamento.
IBGE. (2011). *Tábuas Completas de Mortalidade 2010.* Rio de Janeiro: IBGE. Available at: http://www.ibge.gov.br/home/estatistica/populacao/tabuadevida/2010/defaulttab.shtm.
Lesthaeghe, R. (1995). The second demographic transition in western countries: An interpretation. In K. O. Masony & A. Jensen (Eds.), *Gender and family change in industrialized countries* (pp. 17–62). New York: Oxford University Press.
Livi-Bacci, M. (1986). Social-group forerunners of fertility control in Europe. In A. J. Coale & S. C. Watkins (Eds.), *The decline of fertility in Europe* (pp. 82–200). Princeton University Press: Princeton.
Marcondes, G. S. (2008). *Recasamento formal no Brasil: alguns achados do Registro Civil.* Campinas: Unicamp (NEPO Papers, 58).

Marcondes, G. S. (2011). La normalización jurídica de la familia, vida conyugal y reproducción en Brasil. In G. Binstock &, J. M. Vieira (Orgs.). *Nupcialidad y familia en la América Latina actual* (1ed. Alap. pp. 255–280). (Serie Investigaciones, 11).

Marín, Á., & Morales, J. J. (2010). Modernidad y modernización en América Latina: una aventura inacabada. *Nómadas: Revista Crítica de Ciencias Sociales y Jurídicas, 26*(2), 1–20.

Marri, I., & Wajnman, S. (2006). Esposas como principais provedoras de renda familiar. In *Encontro Nacional De Estudos Populacionais, 15. Anais....* Belo Horizonte: ABEP. Available at: http://www.abep.nepo.unicamp.br/encontro2006/docspdf/ABEP2006_731.pdf.

Martins, J de S. (1994). A reprodução do capital na frente pioneira e o renascimento da escravidão no Brasil. *Tempo Social: Revista de Sociologia da USP, 6*(1–2), 1–25.

Martins, J de S. (2000). *A sociabilidade do homem simples: cotidiano e história na modernidade anômala.* São Paulo: Hucitec.

McLanahan, S. S. (2006). Fragile families and the marriage agenda. In L. Kowaleski-Jones & N. H. Wolfinger (Eds.), *Fragile families and the marriage agenda* (pp. 1–21). New York: Springer.

Merrick, T., & Berquó, E. (1983). *The determinants of Brazil's rapid decline in fertility.* Washington, D.C.: National Academy of Science Press.

Miranda-Ribeiro, A., Rios-Neto, E. L. G., & Ortega, J. A. (2008). Declínio da fecundidade no Brasil e México e o nível de reposição: efeitos tempo, parturição e quantum. In Wong, L. R. R. (Org.). *Población y salud sexual y reproductiva en América Latina* (1ª ed. pp. 81–100). Rio de Janeiro: Alap. (Serie Investigaciones, 4).

Miranda-Ribeiro, A., Rios-Neto, E. L. G., & Carvalho, J. A. M. (2010). Tempo e quantum no Brasil: indicadores e evidências empíricas. In *Encontro Nacional De Estudos Populacionais, 16. Anais....* Belo Horizonte: ABEP. Available at: http://www.abep.nepo.unicamp.br/encontro2010/docs_pdf/tema_5/abep2010_2399.pdf.

Montali, L. (2012). Família e trabalho: os desafios da equidade para as famílias metropolitanas na recuperação da economia nos anos 2000. In Turra, C. M., & Cunha, J. M. P. (Orgs.). *População e desenvolvimento em debate: contribuições da Associação Brasileira de Estudos Populacionais* (pp. 177–186). Belo Horizonte: ABEP.

Oliveira, M. C. F. A. (1977). Os grupos ocupacionais em São Paulo: características sociais, demográficas e o comportamento reprodutivo. In E. S. Berquó, M. C. F. A. Oliveira, & C. P. F. Camargo (Eds.), *A fecundidade em São Paulo: características demográficas, biológicas e sócio-econômicas* (pp. 161–212). CEBRAP/Ed. Brasileira de Ciências: São Paulo.

Oliveira, M. C. F. A. (1979). *Classe social, família e reprodução: reflexões teóricas e referências empíricas.* São Paulo: FAU-USP.

Oliveira, M. C. F. A. (1982). Notas sobre união dos sexos e família: tipos e fundamentos de legitimidade. In CLASCO. *Reproducción de la población y desarrollo 2* (pp. 275–319). São Paulo: Clacso.

Oliveira, M. C. F. A. (1984). A individualização da força de trabalho e o trabalho feminino familiar: um estudo de caso de Pederneiras, SP. In Aguiar, N. (Coord.). *Mulheres na força de trabalho na América Latina: análises qualitativas* (pp. 99–122). Rio de Janeiro: Vozes.

Oliveira, M. C. F. A. (1992). Condição feminina e alternativas de organização doméstica: as mulheres sem companheiro em São Paulo. *Revista de Estudios Demográficos y Urbanos, 7*(2–3), 511–537.

Oliveira, M. C. F. A. (1996). A família brasileira no limiar do ano 2000. *Estudos Feministas, 4*(1), 55–63.

Oliveira, M. C. F. A. (1997). Some notes on the family as a mechanism of social protection in Brazil. In Cosio-Zavala, M. E. (Org.). *Women and families: The evolution of the status of woman as a factor in and a consequence of changes in family dynamics* (pp. 118–128). Paris: Cicred/UNFPA/Unesco.

Oliveira, M. C. F. A. (2001). Women's status and labor regimes: The demand for fertility regulation. In Hogan D. (Org.). *Population change in Brazil: contemporary perspectives* (pp. 53–60). Campinas: NEPO/Unicamp.

Oliveira, M. C. F. A. (2009). Constrangimentos e motivações: a propósito da queda da fecundidade em Göran Therborn. In Menezes, J. E. X.; Castro, M. G. (Orgs.). *Família, população, sexo e poder: entre saberes e polêmicas* (pp. 73–96). São Paulo: Paulinas. (Coleção Família na Sociedade Contemporânea).

Patarra, N. L., & Oliveira, M. C. F. A. (1988). Transição, transições. In *Encontro Nacional De Estudos Populacionais, 6* (pp. 17–36). *Anais....* Belo Horizonte: ABEP. Available at: http://www.abep.org.br/?q=publicacoes/anais/anais-do-vi-encontro-nacional-de-estudos-populacionais-1988-volume-1.

Perpétuo, I. H. O., & Wong, L. L. R. (2009). Desigualdade socioeconômica na utilização de métodos anticoncepcionais no Brasil: uma análise comparativa com base nas PNDS 1996 e 2006. In M. da Saúde (Ed.), *Pesquisa Nacional de Demografia e Saúde da Criança e da Mulher – PNDS 2006: dimensões do processo reprodutivo e da saúde da criança* (pp. 87–104). Ministério da Saúde: Brasília.

Phelps, E.; Furstenberg Jr., F. F.; Colby, A. (Eds.). 2002. Looking at lives: American longitudinal studies of the twentieth century. New York: Russell Sage Foundation.

Pintor, A. (2000). Modernización, escuela e identidad en América Latina. *Investigación y Desarrollo, no., 11*(July), 106–121.

Prata, P. R. (1992). A transição epidemiológica no Brasil. *Cadernos de Saúde Pública, 8*(2), 168–175.

Quilodrán, J. (1992). La vida conyugal en América Latina: contrastes y semejanzas. In *Conferencia de el Poblamiento de Las Américas. Actas....* Paris: International Union for the Scientific Study of Population.

Quilodrán, J. (2011). Un modelo de nupcialidade postransicional en América Latina? In Binstock, G., Vieira, J. M. (Orgs.). *Nupcialidad y familia en la America Latina actual* (1ª ed. pp. 11–34): Alap (Serie Investigaciones, 11).

Rios-Neto, E. L. G. (2000). Passado, presente e futuro da fecundidade: uma visão de idade, período e coorte. *Revista Brasileira de Estudos Populacionais, 17*(1–2), 5–15.

Rios-Neto, E. L. G. (2005). Questões emergentes na análise demográfica. *Revista Brasileira de Estudos de População, 22*(2), 371–408.

Souza, J. (2003). *A construção social da subcidadania: para uma sociologia política da modernidade periférica*. Belo Horizonte: Editora da UFMG.

Theil, H. (1972). *Statistical decomposition analysis: With applications in the social and administrative sciences*. Amsterdam/London: North-Holland Publishing Company.

Therborn, G. (2004). *Between sex and power: Family in the world, 1900–2000*. London: Routledge.

United Nations. (1983). *Manual X: Indirect techniques for demographic estimation*. New York: Department of International Economic and Social Affairs (Population Studies n° 81).

Van De Kaa, D. (2002). The idea of a second demographic transition in industrialized countries. In *Welfare policy seminar, 6. Proceedings....* Tokyo: National Institute of Population and Social Security. Available at: http://websv.ipss.go.jp/webj-ad/WebJournal.files/population/2003_4/Kaa.pdf.

Vieira, J. M. (2008). Transição para a vida adulta no Brasil: análise comparada entre 1970 e 2000. *Revista Brasileira de Estudos de População, 25*, 27–48.

Vieira, J. M., & Miret, P. (2010). Transición a la vida adulta en España: una comparación en el tiempo y en el territorio utilizando el análisis de entropía. *Revista Española de Investigaciones Sociológicas, 131*, 75–107.

Religious Transition in Brazil

Ronaldo Romulo Machado de Almeida and Rogério Jerônimo Barbosa

Abstract The chapter describes the long path of changes in the religious distribution of the Brazilian population over 50 years between 1960 and 2010, analyzing how such changes correlate to broader socioeconomic transformations. We call "religious transition" the sum of these three trends: (i) the major change in the country's religious landscape, from being predominantly Catholic to increasingly Evangelical, (ii) the Christianity's tendency to boost its internal segmentation (especially among the Evangelicals) and to foster different ways of being a participant/believer, and (iii) the substantive pluralization and growth of non-Christians (people of other religions and also without religion). The analysis is divided into four parts. First, a basic descriptive overview indicates tendencies of growth, decline, continuity, and points of inflection. Then, the socioeconomic characteristics of major religious groups are presented. Afterward, an age-period-cohort analysis proceeds in order to identify how the probabilities of being part of each religious group changes for each person across the life course and for the whole population through the decades and generations. Lastly, religion reproduction within families through the transmission from parents to child is analyzed along with how this changed in the last decades. The religious transition is not just the differential growth between denominations – it is deeply rooted in changes in the socioeconomic characteristics and in the probabilities of reproduction inside the households, and it is taking place for a long time.

Keywords Religion · Pluralism · Demographic changes · Brazil · Transition

The authors are grateful for the thoughtful comments received from Ricardo Mariano, Marcelo Camurça, Eduardo Rios-Neto, and Marta Arretche.

R. R. M. de Almeida (✉)
Department of Anthropology, University of Campinas (Unicamp), Campinas, Brazil

Brazilian Center of Analysis and Planning (Cebrap), São Paulo, Brazil

R. J. Barbosa
Center for Metropolitan Studies (CEM), São Paulo, Brazil
e-mail: antrologos@gmail.com

M. Arretche (ed.), *Paths of Inequality in Brazil*,
https://doi.org/10.1007/978-3-319-78184-6_12

After undergoing numerous transitions in its past (economic, demographic, epidemiologic), Brazil is now clearly in the midst of yet another: in the religious realm. It has been taking place for some time – a few decades – but has now gained macroscopic proportions in just the last 20 years or so. It is characterized by several major components: a huge drop on the part of traditional religions (especially Catholicism), a significant increase in Evangelicals (accompanied by growing number of denominations and transit among religions under this designation), and some gains in terms of diversity and pluralization. But these do not tell the entire story. There are endogenous vectors (forces determined inside the field of religion) as well as exogenous ones driving these changes. And if their causes are not restricted to the religious realm, neither are their consequences.

From the perspective of a sociologist, among other things, such a change in religious aspects is a symptom of a deep societal change. Acceleration of the urbanization process has profoundly altered the structures of sociability and interpersonal trust. For the sake of a preliminary example, consider the case of the rise of Pentecostalism and Evangelicals. Classic studies in this field in Brazil and Latin America (César 1974; de Souza 1969; D'Épinay 1975) have emphasized the importance of these new religions for integration of rural migrants into urban centers, especially during the 1960s and 1970s. Fostering social networks and creating institutional frameworks for the development of interpersonal relationships were certainly essential not only for adjusting to the subjectivities of the new environment (religion has always been a very important source of social ties) (Marques and Bichir 2012) but also for spreading information and opportunities (Granovetter 1973, 1974). Traditional Catholic rituals and organizations were too impersonal and distant from the everyday emotional and social needs of those newcomers.

From the perspective of a political scientist, religious transition is an event that shakes the very foundation of the formation of preferences – and as a consequence, has an effect on electoral behavior. Again we can use the example of Evangelicals. Since redemocratization in Brazil, the number of evangelical candidates (mostly members of Pentecostal churches) running for offices at all levels of the state has increased in each election. It is widely known that being an evangelical dramatically raises the probability of voting for these candidates (Freston 1993; Fernandes et al. 1998; Fonseca 2002; Bohn 2004; Peixoto and Rennó 2011). Moreover, religion has an independent effect, even after controlling for socioeconomic, educational, and locational characteristics. Since the first major study on the topic (Pierucci 1989), the number of seats occupied by purportedly religious people (who carry religiously oriented agendas) has increased significantly, reaching more than 70 in 2014. Pierucci (1989) argued that they – Pentecostal leaders and followers – lay the basis for a "new right" in the ideological spectrum, mixing traditional values and liberal-conservative orientations (see also Pierucci and Mariano 1992; Pierucci and Prandi 1995). Of course, this fact has important consequences on distributive politics and should not be underestimated. Evangelicals are a strong political force in contemporary Brazil – and studying religious transition may add to this field. One cannot simply deduce political affinities directly from beliefs and theodicies though – a point we cannot stress enough. There are considerable variations among the denominations, and the political position of one is not always defined as antagonistic to another – that is why the field of religious studies remains important in and of itself.

In this chapter, we describe the long path of changes in the religious distribution of the Brazilian population in 50 years between 1960 and 2010, analyzing how such changes correlate to broader socioeconomic transformations. We do not intend to establish a direct and functional link between religion and economic inequalities. For now, politics and the economy will take a backseat – in part because our main source of data (the censuses) do not allow for this kind of investigation. However, sometimes, when it seems appropriate and necessary, we rely on other studies and conclusions to interpret the empirical trends. It should be quite clear that religion is a way of living and experiencing inequality as well as confronting it (through mutual support, beliefs and subjective comfort, and political participation). It is simply not possible to understand Brazil without a discussion of this realm.

We divided the analysis into four parts. First, we present a basic descriptive overview, indicating growth, decline, continuity, and inflection. We then explore the socioeconomic characteristics of major religious groupings before turning to a more sophisticated empirical exercise, which aims to identify how the Brazilian religious scenario (un)tangles aspects that are part of the normal life cycles of individuals, the situational/contextual effects (of each period), and long-term trends (generational and intergenerational). Lastly, we analyze the characteristics of contemporary reproduction of religions through the topic of religious transmission.

Pluralism and Transition

Censuses are commonly used when analyzing religion in Brazil, although their information is limited to the question "what is your religion?" In addition, until very recently and because of several restrictions, researchers could only rely on preprocessed data from the Brazilian Institute of Geography and Statistics (IBGE), aggregated by category and geographic location. More recently, the direct use of microdata has become possible (information at the individual level), allowing us to retrace the steps of previous researchers and undertake new ventures without having to rely on documents that often explored the subject of religion without the desired level of detail.

Graph 1 shows the general outline of Brazil's religious field. Since the classifications of religions varied greatly between censuses, groupings were established to maximize comparability over time.

The general trend is clear: continuous (non-moderate) decline of Catholicism and (accelerated) growth of other groups, particularly Evangelicals. Non-Catholics (including those without religion) account for 35.5% of the population in 2010.[1] Since our intention is to observe possible ruptures and continuities within this period, Table 1 presents the detailed categories. In the 1980 census, there is differentiation among Evangelicals (between Traditional and Pentecostal Protestants) and

[1]There is no longer a Catholic majority in two Brazilian states: Rondônia and Rio de Janeiro, where Catholics represent 47.9% and 46.3%, respectively.

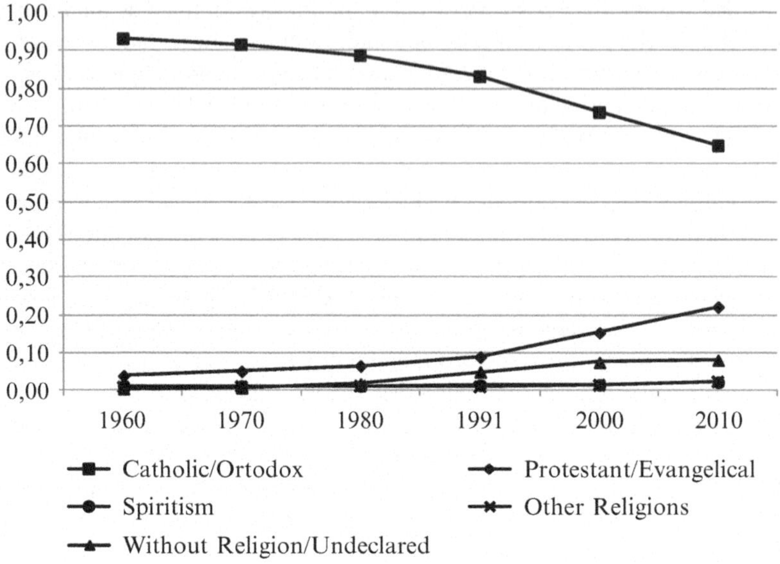

Graph 1 Population distribution according to stated religions. Brazil – 1960–2010. (Source: IBGE. Demographic Censuses 1960–2010. (Special tabulations by CEM))

Spiritists (between Kardecism and African-Brazilian religions). Further distinctions are created within these groups after the 1991 Census.

Until the year 2000, the decrease in Catholics had always been accompanied by an increase in the absolute number of individuals declaring themselves to be Catholics. However, the last decade witnessed decreases both in percentage (from 73.9% to 64.5%) and absolute terms (from 125.5 million to 123.9 million). Catholics have always presented positive growth rates, albeit lower than the total population. In the last decade, however, this rate was negative.

By separating Evangelicals into Traditional and Pentecostal, we see that recent growth is concentrated in the latter segment, confirming trends already observed in censuses since the 1980s. By the late 1990s, one could easily believe that the Pentecostal field tended toward polarization within a limited number of denominations. The last decade, however, has shown a different behavior. The Christian Congregation of Brazil, the oldest Pentecostal denomination in the country, halted its advance. The same occurred with the Universal Church of the Kingdom of God, which until that point had displayed uninterrupted and accelerated growth trends, having increased its followers almost sevenfold between 1991 and 2000.

The reasons behind the deceleration in the Universal Church require further study, but we have a few preliminary hypotheses. Firstly, its proselytizing strategy lends less emphasis to strengthening community ties, since it is anchored in a client relationship between pastors and a congregation that seek religious services for everyday life problems. This makes it quite vulnerable to the appeals of other churches with the religiosity pattern of the Universal Church of the Kingdom of

Table 1 Population, according to stated religions. Brazil – 1960–2010[a]

Religions	1960	1970	1980	1991	2000	2010
Catholic	65,377,921	85,475,431	105,861,113	122,366,762	125,527,349	123,986,727
Roman Catholic	65,329,520			121,812,831	124,977,528	123,256,665
Brazilian Roman Catholic				518,534	500,582	560,781
Orthodox Catholic and other	48,401			35,397	49,239	169,281
Evangelicals	2,824,775	4,813,676	7,885,846	13,189,272	26,184,941	42,275,440
Traditional protestant			4,022,343	4,388,311	6,943,510	7,688,555
Lutheran				1,029,680	1,062,145	999,498
Presbyterian				498,207	981,064	921,209
Methodist				138,885	340,963	340,938
Baptist				1,532,675	3,162,691	3,723,853
Adventist				706,407	1,209,842	1,561,071
Other protestant traditional				482,456	186,805	141,985
Pentecostals			3,863,503	8,211,502	18,515,165	26,305,121
Assemblies of god				2,439,770	8,418,140	12,314,410
Christian congregation of Brazil				1,635,952	2,489,113	2,289,634
Brazil for Christ				48,240	175,618	196,665
International Church of the Foursquare Gospel				303,267	1,318,805	1,808,389
Universal Church of the Kingdom of God				268,955	2,101,887	1,873,243
God is love				233,920	1,052,172	1,201,404
Other pentecostals				3,281,97	2,959,430	6,621,376
Evangelicals without institutional ties or belonging to multiple congregations or undetermined				589,459	726,267	8,281,764
Spiritist or "mediumistic" religions	977,561	1,178,685	1,538,230	2,292,819	2,767,898	4,437,674
Spiritist Kardecism			859,516	1,644,344	2,242,886	3,848,876
African-Brazilian religions			678,714	648,475	525,012	588,797

(continued)

Table 1 (continued)

Religions	1960	1970	1980	1991	2000	2010
Umbanda				541,519	397,431	407,331
Candomblé				106,956	118,097	167,363
Other African-Brazilian religions					9484	14,103
Other religions	622,987	954,911	1,473,091	1,512,648	2,496,796	4,478,510
Mormons				93,193	199,645	226,509
Jehovah's witnesses				752,575	1,104,886	1,393,208
Judaism	96,199		91,795	86,422	86,825	107,329
Islamism	7745			236,403	214,873	243,966
Buddhism	179,464			132,177	161,817	171,301
Oriental religions			257,006	22,449	27,239	35,167
Other	339,579		1,124,290	189,429	701,512	2,301,030
Without religion/undeclared	388,126	717,163	2,252,782	7,454,285	12,876,356	15,577,449
Total	70,191,370	93,139,866	119,011,062	146,815,786	169,853,340	190,755,799

Source: IBGE. Demographic Censuses 1960–2010. (Special Tabulations by CEM)

[a]As we accessed census microdata, we devised our own categories for religious nomenclatures. Thus, some of the data differ from those officially presented by the IBGE. For example, the number of nondenominational Evangelicals calculated in this study is 8,281,764 people, while the number published by the IBGE is 9,218,129. The difference is because we classify code "499 – other Evangelical" (which accounts for 936,365 individuals) as "other Pentecostals," while the IBGE grouped them together with undetermined Evangelicals or belonging to multiple denominations

God, such as the World Church of the Power of God, which has not only attracted followers but also ministers and workers. Secondly, despite the drop in the number of followers during the 2000s, Rede Record, a television station owned by the Universal Church, has established itself as Brazil's second major television channel, and its political structure was strengthened even further by serving as a base of support during the administration of President Luis Inácio Lula da Silva. Lastly, it has expanded significantly in recent years in Latin America, Africa, Europe (and on a smaller but no less significant scale), and Asia. The census numbers in this case reflect changes in evangelism priorities. In short, the Universal Church has lost followers internally in absolute numbers but has strengthened itself in terms of politics, business, and the media and become more global externally by directing a portion of its efforts and human resources (missionaries and ministers) out of the country.

In contrast, the Assemblies of God have maintained their growth rates, totaling more than 12 million Brazilians in 2010 (46.8% of Pentecostals). In recent decades, the Assembly of God has fragmented itself into various conventions and ministries (Belém, Madureira, etc.). One way to compete and demonstrate power among conventions is through the recruitment of dissenting or newly formed temple communities. Because of the broad autonomy enjoyed by temples, institutional fragmentation is a recurring phenomenon that does not yet compromise "assembly" doctrine and identity. As a result, this universe is comprised of large conventions scattered across small ministries differentiated by minor doctrinal issues, political disputes, and, most recently, the addition of words to the church's name: Assembly of God for the Victory of Christ, Assembly of God of the Latter Day, Assembly of God Berean, etc. In this regard, the assembly becomes increasingly diversified within its own Pentecostal environment (Alencar 2012).

In the last decade, the group "other Pentecostal religions" went from just over 2.9 to an impressive 6.6 million people, and the group "Evangelicals without institutional ties or belonging to multiple congregations or undetermined" grew from just over 700,000 people to more than 8 million, increasing its representation from 3.8% to 23.9% of Evangelicals.

Such a sudden increase raises the suspicion of data collection errors in the last census.[2] However, even if this hypothesis holds true, several qualitative studies conducted in the 1990s and 2000s point toward a small-scale upsurge of people generically identified as Evangelical as they circulate among institutions, making use of their religious services. Thus, it is no longer the norm for followers of the same religion to match their identity, connection, behavior, and doctrine to a specific Evangelical church. This identification with the broader Evangelical universe allows for an interdenominational flow and weakens the ties to a particular religious community.

As previously mentioned, the 1960 and 1970 censuses did not distinguish Kardecism from African-Brazilian religions. This is partially explained by the fact that official classifications did not recognize the existence of Umbanda, Candomblé, Xango, and other religions, which were registered as "Spiritist Centers" (Negrão 1996; Montero 2006). It also partially reflects the influence of sociological and

[2] Hypothesis raised by Ricardo Mariano when discussing an earlier version of this chapter during the first internal seminar of the project.

anthropological studies, which classified this set of religions as belonging to a "psychic continuum": Candomblé, Umbanda, and Kardecism (de Camargo 1961). However, despite the syncretic similarities in both segments, these are very different religions that embrace completely different social groups.

Classic studies expected that Umbanda would become a universal religion, open to converting anyone (Levy 1967), and therefore embedded with the task of adapting individuals to a modern, industrial urban context (de Camargo 1973; Fry and Howe 1975). Ortiz's work (1979) is one of the first references of how Umbanda had established itself amid urbanization. Candomblé, although considered an "ethnic religion" (Prandi 1991), would also have acquired universalist traits in the context of the metropolis (da Silva 1995). However, as early as the 1980s, African-Brazilian religions began to wane. Candomblé continued to grow in absolute numbers (at least since 1991), but at a slow pace, and lost ground in the overall picture (as shown by the 2000 census). Umbanda witnessed a more serious case of decline in terms of percentages and absolute numbers until 2000, and the slight recovery it saw in 2010 was not enough to boost its relative numbers. Since, unlike the Evangelicals, the African-Brazilian religions did not engage in proselytism, they were at a competitive disadvantage. Camargo's prognosis as well as the views of other scholars of the 1960s and 1970s is not valid for Umbanda followers. It was supposed to be for everyone, but it never had that many followers. The growth surge, however, was indeed accurate when it came to Kardecism, whose numbers have almost doubled in size in the past decade.

The "other religions"[3] category has shown sinuous upward movement, growing from 0.89% of the population in 1960 to 2.33% in 2010 (Table 1). No single religion exerts major dominance, although Jehovah's Witnesses have considerably enhanced their participation in the last two decades. Buddhism had its golden moment during periods of intense Japanese immigration; however, despite its growth in recent decades, it does not currently reach the same levels witnessed at the beginning of the analyzed period.

Those "without religion" or "undeclared" now make up a larger share in official records, especially since 1980 and 1991. Growth has tapered off in the past decade, however, albeit with increases in absolute terms (nearly 2.7 million people) and percentages (from 7.58% to 8.92%).

A preliminary interpretation would suggest that this group would be synonymous with the advance of atheism, resulting from urbanization and increased educational levels.[4] But, as we will see, this population does not stand out in terms of occupation, income, and education – in fact, they are below the national average for some of these indicators, making it therefore impossible to ascertain that they

[3] Ethnic religions (Judaism, Islam, Hinduism, etc.), Eastern religions (Buddhism, Seicho No-Ie, Hare Krishna, etc.), indigenous religions (Santo Daime, União do Vegetal, Barquinha, etc.), and others.

[4] The 2010 census introduced differentiation between atheists (those who do not believe in the supernatural/are not religious) and agnostics (those who have suspended their questioning on the matter). But the reliability of this information is suspect. We cannot reasonably presume that the entire population knows how to properly differentiate between "without religion," "atheist," and "agnostic."

belong to any "club of disenchanted intellectuals" (Negrão 2005). On the other hand, some qualitative studies (Almeida and Rumstain 2009; Almeida 2011) have shown that the majority of nonreligious corresponds to people who engage in a heavy transit between denominations and religiosities – or merely religious people without religion. Other studies have also signaled a clear association between youth and the statement "without religion" (Novaes 2004), providing evidence that this phenomenon is associated with a life stage that may have become more accentuated in recent generations. It refers to an extensive and heterogeneous contingent. These are not the "pilgrims of faith" of whom Hervieu-Léger spoke of (1999), nor do they signal the end of religion.

In summary, the data describe phenomena that occur at both large-scale and small-scale levels. The first encompasses the decline of Catholicism and the increase in Pentecostal religions and those without religion. While the phenomena at the second level are quantitatively less significant, they are no less important since they provide continuity and reaffirm their regularity throughout the period: slight replenishment of Traditional Protestants, some preservation of African-Brazilian religions in the last decade, and an almost doubling (decennial) of Kardecism and other religions.

These two thresholds of change brought pluralism, which has been growing within a field historically marked by traditionalism and syncretism (Sanchis 1995, 2001).[5] Pierucci (1997, p. 116) referred to pluralism as the "trick" to understanding religious transformations in Brazil in recent decades by reinforcing the notion of competition and, therefore, the religious market as a consequence of a secularization process.[6] On another occasion, however, Pierucci (2006b) asked "Where is our religious diversity?" warning that pluralism in Brazil (diversity and institutional competitiveness) has very specific contours: the majority of the population still declares itself to be Christian, Catholic, or Evangelical. That is to say, plurality in Brazil does not equal diversity.

However, the diversity branch (Kardecism, African-Brazilian religions, other religions, and nonreligious) already makes up 13.6% of the population and has witnessed steady growth, going from 2.8% in 1960 to 3.1% in 1970, 4.4% in 1980,

[5] We understand pluralism to mean the fragmentation of the religious field into several denominations within a larger scenario of competitiveness, which implies adherence by individual choice, where belonging to one religion implies not belonging to or practicing another. Traditionalism, in turn, refers to religious behavior as a result of social and particularly family heritage. Traditional religious behavior is commonly not internalized (Camargo 1971). Lastly, syncretism encompasses the fusions between cosmological systems and different ritual practices, which may lead to a double religious affiliation or the development of new systems rooted in previous ones (Almeida 2009).

[6] Strictly speaking, secularization refers to the process of separating church and state, in which religious parameters do not dictate laws or secular institutions. The state deregulates the religious field (or vice versa), paving the way for competition between religions in an environment previously marked by a denominational monopoly (Pierucci 1998; Stark and Iannaconne 1994). Thus, pluralism is a result of secularization. In a broad sense, secularization involves the loss of plausibility of the religious worldview and, consequently, the weakening of religions and religiosity (Berger 1985).

7.7% in 1991, and 10.7% in 2000. This progress shows no signs of slowing down. Thus, while the Christian matrix remains hegemonic, phenomena occurring on a smaller demographic scale (other religions) combined with the growth of those without religion ultimately produced a scenario of considerable dimensions. Pluralism gradually engendered diversity.

Generally speaking, religious transition in Brazil consists of three forces for change: Christianity's internal pluralization, with increasing fragmentation of Evangelical denominations and ways to be a believer (Cin 1992; Fernandes et al. 1998; Mariano 1999), accompanied by a proliferation of ways that one can be Catholic (Camurça 2006; Faustino and Menezes 2009; Fernandes 2009; Carranza et al. 2009); an internal transition within the Christian segment, from predominantly Catholic to increasingly Evangelical; and a general pluralization with the increase of non-Christians (other religions and without religion).

Socioeconomic Trends in Religion

Graph 2 indicates changes in the socioeconomic characteristics of religious followers. This data allows us to contrast the current scenario with the various expectations of authors who have analyzed religious trends in Brazil.

The literature in the 1960s and 1970s was unanimous in establishing a correlation (or causality) between ever-increasing urbanization and the growth of certain religions. According to Waldo César (1974), Pentecostalism was essentially an urban phenomenon, a suitable response to the existing behavioral turmoil in large cities. To de Souza (1969) and de Camargo (1973), Pentecostalism provided the migrant with a better way to adapt to urban thinking. Willems (1967) realized that the rapid change in value systems left the migrant without referents, facilitating the acceptance of teachings from Pentecostalism. According to D'Epinay (1970) when analyzing Pentecostalism in Chile, the traditional social order would be restored in a conservative manner (the pastor replacing the figure of the farmer). In the rural to urban transition, social values and patterns shifted. This set of interpretations suggests that the new social environment consequently posed material and emotional challenges to migrants, and certain religions were more effective than Catholicism in providing answers to those needs. From a Durkheimian perspective, the growing religions would have a social integration function in the face of the risk of anomie.

The urban environment also encouraged social diversity, and the possibility for opting between rupture and continuity within a particular religion was a sign of individual autonomy. This scenario would favor the internalization of religion not only among Traditional and Pentecostal Protestants but also within Catholic segments (de Camargo 1971).[7] As a result, religious followers as a matter of conviction

[7] Camargo (1971) contrasts traditional religions with internalized religions, the former characterized by their ritualistic and procedural aspects that are strongly linked to established powers (and often legitimizers of the social order). In internalized religions, individual adherence occurs through conviction (the *rapprochement* to the Weberian concept of ethics of conviction is not ran-

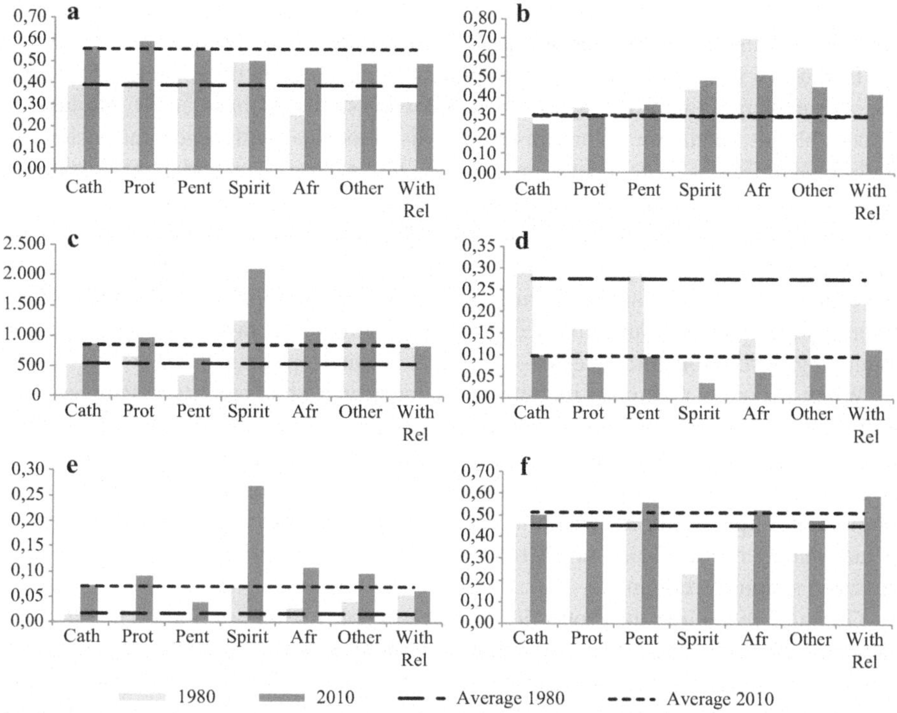

Graph 2 Population, by religion, according to socioeconomic characteristics. Brazil – 1980–2010. (**a**) Urban non-metropolitan population. (**b**) Urban metropolitan population (9 MRs and FD). (**c**) Average per capita household income. (**d**) Illiterates (%). (**e**) Higher education (%). (**f**) Black people (black + brown) (%). (Source: IBGE. Demographic Censuses 1980–2010. (Special tabulations by CEM). Note: We only considered metropolitan areas in existence before 1988: São Paulo, Rio de Janeiro, Salvador, Belo Horizonte, Porto Alegre, Curitiba, Recife, Fortaleza, Belem, and the Federal District)

were viewed as being more appropriately slanted toward economic modernity, which the country entered through industrialization. For religious scholars during the 1950s, 1960s, and 1970s, internalization would be an adaptive response to the psychosocial needs of urban, industrial, peripheral, and marginal environments.

Catholicism is less concentrated than average in metropolitan and non-metropolitan urban areas. Therefore, it is the only religion that has proportionally more followers in rural areas than among the total population. Catholics always numbered slightly below the national average in urban areas and, in the last decade, they also recorded a quantitative decline in metropolitan areas (Graph 2b). Rural areas continue to be the locus of resistance to Catholicism, where Catholicism would be organically linked to worldviews and familial and communal organization

dom), which to a large extent can be based on criticism of traditional behaviors, leading to possible shocks or clashes.

(de Camargo 1971). However, the current rural environment is not the same as it was in 1960 and can no longer be equated with the term "traditional."[8]

Traditional Protestants increased slightly above average in urban areas and below average in metropolitan areas, a movement relatively similar to that seen in Catholicism. A possible interpretation is that this process is associated with a general decline of traditional religions. The fastest-growing religions, Spiritism and Pentecostalism, were precisely those that increased their proportions in metropolitan areas.

Among African-Brazilian religions, other religions, and without religion, we still find a greater proportion of individuals in metropolitan areas, but their growth rates have slowed in such locations. In turn, in non-metropolitan urban areas, they registered a slight increase but remained below the national average. This indicates the spreading of religious practices once restricted to metropolitan areas.

When it comes to family income and educational characteristics, Pentecostals and Kardecists stood at opposite extremes. While the former is located at the bottom of both dimensions (education and income), Spiritists are a highly educated group with high per capita income.[9] It is important to remember that the entire Brazilian population improved its income and educational levels during the period analyzed, a fact that is reflected across all religions. However, to a large extent, distances between religions remained.

Graph 2f also shows the proportion of black people in every religion. The religion/race binomial is a classic factor in debates on religion in Brazil. Race is a key factor when analyzing African-Brazilian religions since ethnicity and nationality were central when analyzing immigration religions (Reformed Protestants) or, according to the jargon, religions which, in the countries of arrival, assumed the role of preserving ethno-cultural heritage, such as Buddhism and Judaism (de Camargo 1973).

Issues pertaining to race, ethnicity, and nationality were initially considered within the context of openness or reticence to mass conversions. By definition, an ethnic religion or a religion aimed toward national identity ties would not be universal. Candomblé seemed to have assumed this role within the African-Brazilian spectrum, since its belief system was strongly anchored in African traditions and its practitioners were mostly black. Umbanda, although African, was syncretic at its roots and would therefore be for everyone. These definitions, however, were strongly questioned at the time of the waning of Umbanda and Candomblé and the growth and whitening of Candomblé in the 1980s. Thus, Candomblé could also be universal.

The subsequent scenario brought further classificatory challenges when, in the year 2000, Pentecostals became a majority among blacks and blacks became a majority among Pentecostals (Pierucci 2006a). Data from the 2010 census shows the strength of the black Evangelical phenomenon. However, in the last 10 years, Brazil has become more black: there was an above-average increase in the number of people self-identified as black or brown – which had an impact on all religious groups; they all became darker. Spiritists are the whitest, followed by Protestants,

[8] There were intense transformations in labor relations and economic organization in rural areas, displacing the former centrality of subsistence agriculture (anchored in family organization) and instituting "more modern" work and social organization models.

[9] Income variables were deflated according to the suggestion by Corseuil and Foguel (2002).

and then other religions, and finally Catholics. Regarding the last two groups, we should note that they became less black than the average population.

Another important aspect in the racial distribution of religions is the fact that those without religion also became blacker. This segment already had more blacks than the average population, but this proportion became considerably larger. According to income and education, those without religion have also become poorer and less educated: in 1980 they stood out as a group with above-average attributes, which corroborated interpretations that saw them as a modern segment; now they are either below or exactly equal to the general population. Those without religion are no longer the same. One hypothesis is that the self-declaration of without religion has become less stigmatized, much like what happened with African-Brazilian religions, enabling other segments (poorer, less educated, more black, and less metropolitan) to declare themselves as such. Another suggestion is that these poorer, less educated, and metropolitan segments also underwent processes of modernization, despite material deprivation. This approach avoids the stigma that the religion, especially those that make use of the supernatural and magic, belongs to the most disadvantaged social strata.

In short, if religions have changed, so too have other aspects of Brazilian social reality. A more pivotal question of change refers to the rural-urban transition, which in recent decades has accentuated the metropolitanization of parts of the country through the formation of large areas of poor living in the periphery of cities, as such transformations occurred within the process of reproducing social inequalities. In turn, religions expressed, legitimized, accommodated, resisted, and reproduced the country's social stratification during the past 50 years.

Life Cycles and Long-Term Trends

Recent outcomes of the changes within the religious field are a blend of short-, medium-, and long-term processes associated with structural transformations across generations. This section analyzes these dynamics using an age-period-cohort approach (Yang et al. 2008), dividing the notion of time into three components.

The first component, age, pertains to the course of life. More or less stable regularities exist within age groups across several dimensions: school entry, market entry, marriage, etc. Our interest lies in representing regularities in religious behavior associated with life cycles, which does not imply that the exact age of experience will be the same for all individuals or that all people go through the same experiences. We will then trace an average profile that indicates the age at which religious adherence or leaving is more likely.

The period component expresses historical points that affect all individuals living within them, regardless of age, such as wars, epidemics, political events, etc. However, the effects of the period may indicate longer-lasting movements, such as political processes and industrialization, among others. Thus, the notion of period will be understood as contexts in which affiliation or adherence to a religion can be more or less favorable or likely.

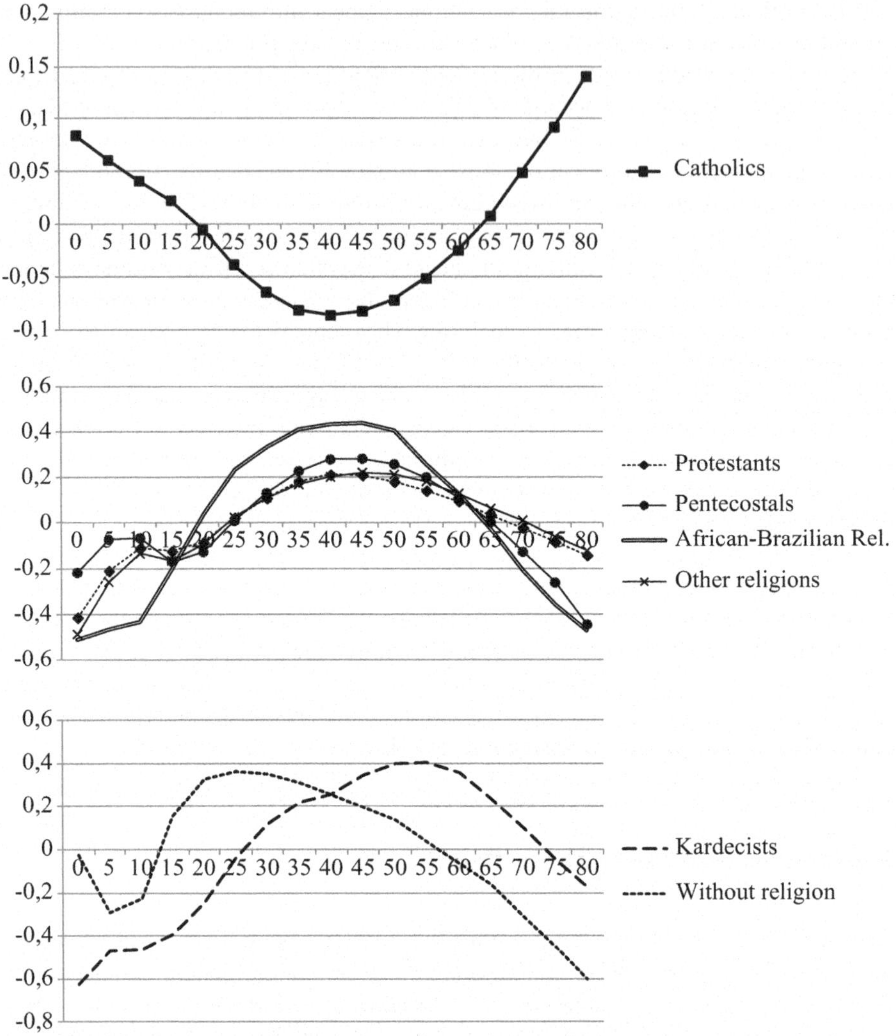

Graph 3 Effects of age on the probability of belonging to each religion. Brazil – 1980–2010. (Source: IBGE. Demographic Censuses 1980–2010. (Special Tabulations by CEM))

The third component is birth cohort, which we can associate with the notion of generation. Individuals born in the same era jointly experience the effects of age and period (together they experience regularities associated with their life cycles). Thus, this dimension relates to the consequences of a formative experience within the same context (Ryder 1965; Coutinho and Golgher 2012).

We considered individuals between the ages of 0 and 80 in the 1980–2010 censuses, thus encompassing generations born since 1900 – a fairly long period of time.[10] Graphs 3, 4 and 5 present the results of the statistical models.

[10]The model used was the intrinsic estimator (Yang et al. 2008). It is a Poisson regression with

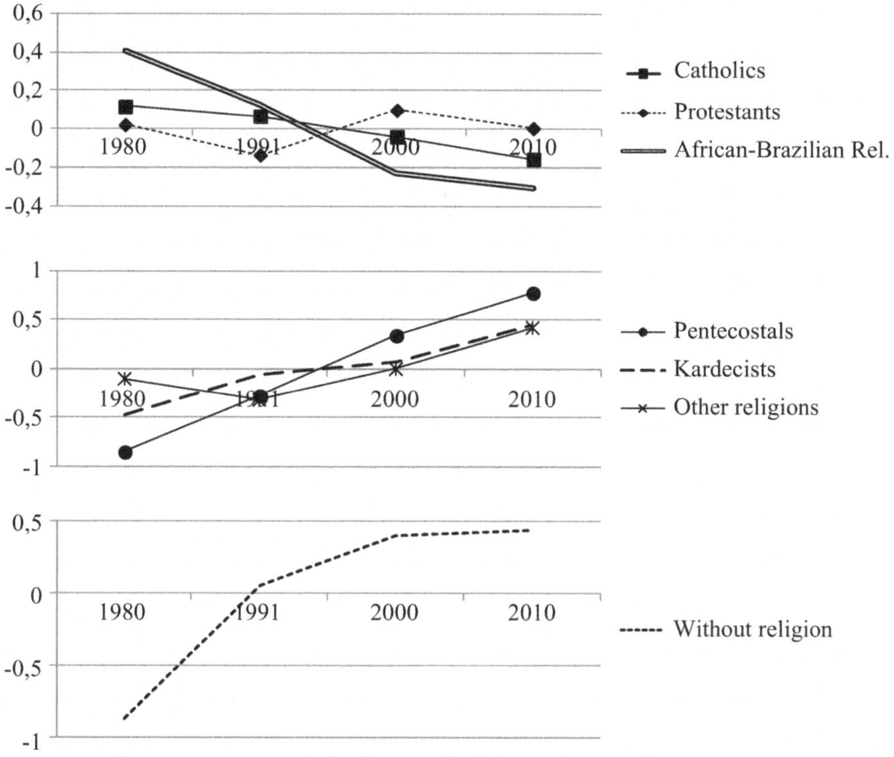

Graph 4 Period effects on the probability of belonging to each religion. Brazil – 1980–2010. (Source: IBGE. Demographic Censuses 1980–2010. (Special tabulations by CEM))

Graph 3 shows the effects of age on religious declaration. The horizontal axis provides the age groups, and each line on the graph represents a religious group. The zero figure on the vertical axis represents the average number of individuals in each religion for all ages. The vertical axis scale represents the measurement unit of the statistical model. Simply stated, positive values indicate above-average probabilities, and negative values indicate below-average probability. For this analysis, we are solely concerned with (+/−) signs and behavioral trends.

We observed that, on average, it has always been, and still remains, more likely that an individual will be born Catholic in Brazil. However, the probability of remaining Catholic drops in the early stages of one's life cycle, a movement contrary to other religions. Among people ages 20–65, we found lower percentages of Catholics when compared with the population average, and the negative peak occurs around age 40.

---

modifications that allow us to isolate the separate influence of each component. Its specificity allows for the use of these three perfectly related variables (period = age + cohort) without the mathematical limitations inherent in regression analysis. Details for the estimate may be requested to the authors.

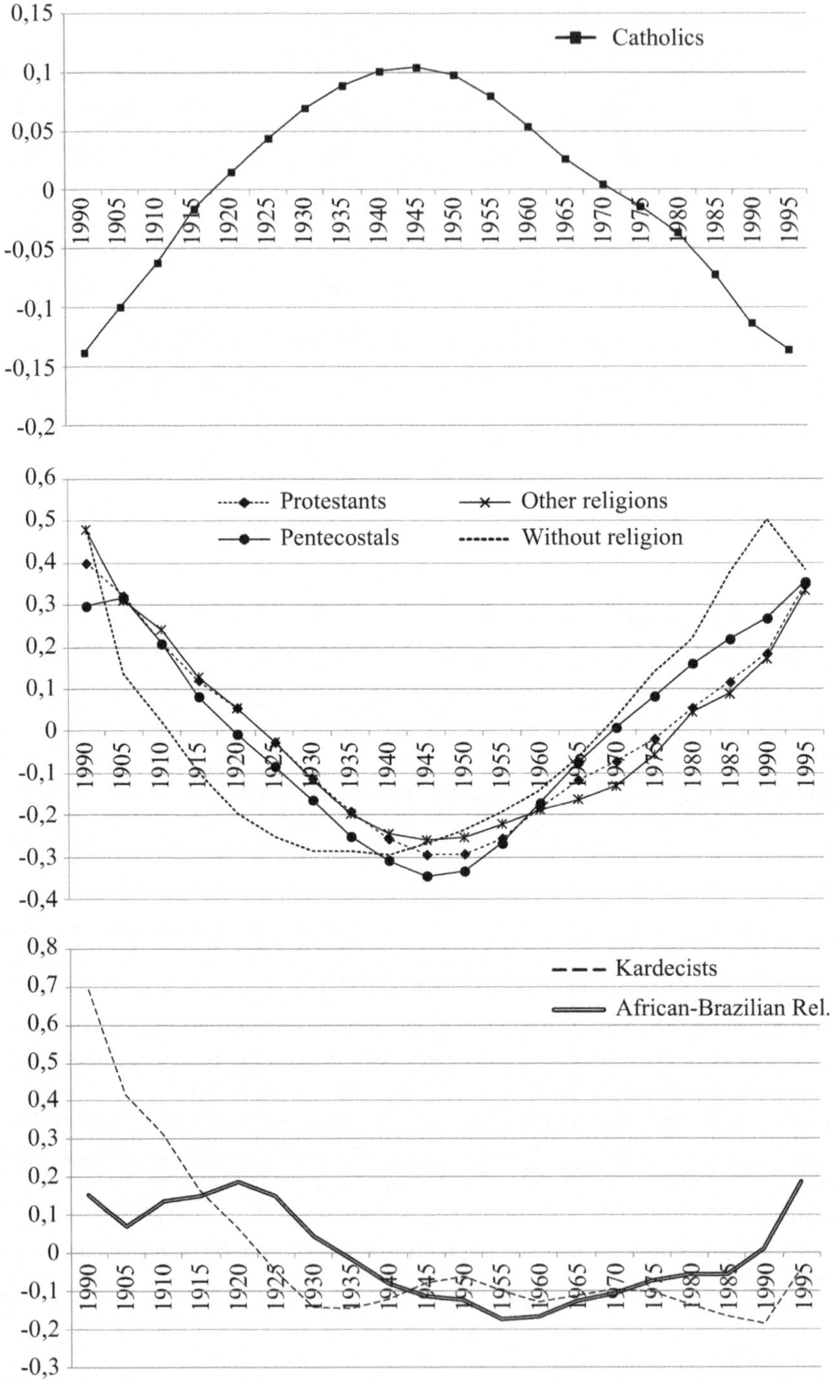

Graph 5 Cohort effects on the probability of belonging to each religion. Brazil – 1980–2010. (Source: IBGE. Demographic Censuses 1980–2010. (Special tabulations by CEM))

The remaining religious groups begin to increase precisely when the odds of being Catholic are already greatly reduced. The odds of belonging to an African-Brazilian religion greatly increase from the age of 20 – which leads us to describe it as a late phenomenon of youth. The odds of belonging to Traditional Protestants, Pentecostals, and the group other religions also follow a similar trend, but these phenomena occur even later in life, affecting the adult population between ages 30 and 45.

The group without religion seems to be a phenomenon strongly associated with youth: the likelihood of not having a religion rapidly increases from the age of 15, reaching its peak around the age of 25, but decreases over the course of life, becoming greatly reduced in older ages. It is as if the individual is born Catholic, over the course of building their own identity she feels a certain need to break free from the religion inherited from their parents during adolescence, which would lead her to declare herself without religion during a period. However, the probability of continuing in this group decreases rapidly, suggesting that this may be a common transitional phase for many people. This is when the likelihood of belonging to any other religions increases.

Kardecism, in turn, is a phenomenon of late adulthood. Although the odds of belonging to this group also increase after age 25 (as in other religions), there is some variation and acceleration after age 45, and its peak occurs between the ages of 50 and 60.

However, the positive odds of all groups are greatly reduced after age 65 – while Catholicism increases precisely during this life stage. This is a result of the fact that the expansion of all non-Catholic groups is still recent, and the population belonging to them has not yet aged. The average number of Catholics among the elderly is always higher than in the general population, reflecting the dominance of this religion throughout Brazil's history.

The behavior of the period effects is not different from the general movement of religions. The zero value in Graph 4 expresses the average frequency of each religion, considering all periods together. Positive values indicate periods where a certain religion was more frequent than all other periods, whereas negative values indicate the opposite. Thus, all religions were placed on a single scale, allowing the discernment of trends concealed in Graph 1.

Religions were divided into three groups according to behavioral similarities. The first one, in the words of Pierucci (2004), shows the "decline of traditional religions": Catholicism, Traditional Protestantism, and African-Brazilian religions (in fact, Umbanda). We see that the period's trends for Traditional Protestants were sinuous, beginning its recovery in the 1990s when the group went from 4.4 million to nearly 7 million individuals (thanks to Baptists, Presbyterians, Methodists, and Adventists, all of which became more heterogeneous, partly because a portion of them became Pentecostal) and witnessing quite an intense reduction in the 2000s. The drop in African religions (led by Umbanda) experienced a slowdown in the last decade but showed no signs of reversal.

In the group of religions exhibiting intense growth (Pentecostalism, Kardecism, and other religions), we witnessed acceleration of Kardecism in the last decade and

Table 2 Cross-tabulation between the religion of children and mothers. Brazil – 1980

Religion of son/daughter		Mother's religion							Total
		Catholic	Protestant	Pentecostal	Spiritism	African-Brazilian	Other	Without religion	
Catholic	Observed	52.630.378	346.147	493.012	100.785	123.326	147.712	130.230	53.971.590
	Expected	47.522.077	2.050.935	2.354.272	392.940	340.110	719.185	592.071	
Protestant	Observed	84.375	1.832.732	17.230	2.195	1.739	4.399	9.684	1.952.354
	Expected	1.719.051	74.190	85.163	14.214	12.303	26.016	21.417	
Pentecostal	Observed	51.805	11.829	1.988.243	685	1.523	2.856	7.710	2.064.651
	Expected	1.817.929	78.457	90.061	15.032	13.011	27.512	22.649	
Spiritism	Observed	22.334	1.312	793	311.394	1.553	1.027	1.699	340.112
	Expected	299.469	12.924	14.836	2.476	2.143	4.532	3.731	
African-Brazilian	Observed	22.206	1.283	1.777	1.846	225.911	1.065	1.686	255.774
	Expected	225.209	9.719	11.157	1.862	1.612	3.408	2.806	
Other	Observed	40.744	6.164	5.771	1.816	1.903	611.268	5.140	672.806
	Expected	592.407	25.567	29.348	4.898	4.240	8.965	7.381	
Without religion	Observed	205.128	90.340	121.648	19.985	23.768	34.621	504.880	1.000.370
	Expected	880.827	38.014	43.637	7.283	6.304	13.330	10.974	
Total		53.056.970	2.289.807	2.628.474	438.706	379.723	802.948	661.029	60.257.657

Source: IBGE. Demographic Census – 1980. (Special Tabulations by CEM)

some swings in other religions, which had been in decline until the early 1990s (pluralism establishes itself sinuously). The third group clearly shows deceleration of those without religion, which had been occurring for at least 20 years.

In terms of the effects of birth cohort on religious declaration, the results of this analysis are more counterintuitive and novel given the lack of studies that employ this approach in the field of religious studies.

The results were also divided into three groups according to similarities. Interestingly, the first and second graphs are perfect counterpoints. Generations born in the early twentieth century were more likely to belong to other religions than the average of the generations included in the analysis (which does not mean that in absolute terms there were more people in these groups than today). This is likely a result of the immigration climate, responsible for implementing nearly every branch of non-Catholic religions in the country. However, the interval between 1890 and 1930 is precise when an autonomous and Romanized Catholicism established itself, primarily through state and local agreements (Miceli 2009), and since then, it has been guided by a central leadership – initially the individual figure of Dom Leme and later the National Conference of Bishops of Brazil (CNBB).

Generations born during this period of Catholicism had an increased likelihood of participating and remaining in the religion, i.e., the Romanizing investment paid off. This is probably why the decline of Catholicism was not even more pronounced. The counterpart to Catholicism's internal organization was the reduced probability of belonging to other groups in subsequent generations. However, the power of this Catholic strategy seems to have affected those born in the 1930s, notably the period in which Brazilian urbanization truly began. Those born in urban areas became increasingly non-Catholic, confirming previous analyses regarding the limits of traditional Catholicism and the strong affinity of other religious groups with the modern environment.

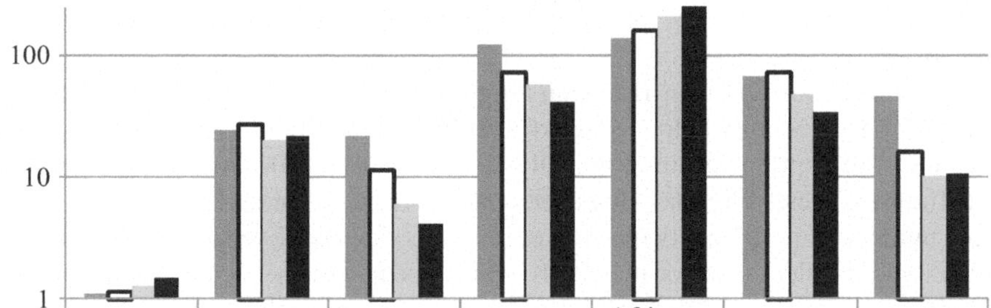

	Catholicism	Traditional Protest.	Pentecostal Protest.	Kardecist Spir.	African-Brazilian religions	Other Religions	Without Religion
1980	1	25	22	126	140	68	46
1991	1	27	12	73	161	74	17
2000	1	20	6	58	209	49	10
2010	1	22	4	41	256	34	11

Graph 6 Ratio between observed and expected frequencies in religious concordance between mothers and children. Brazil – 1980–2010. (Source: IBGE. Demographic Census – 1980 (Special tabulations by CEM))

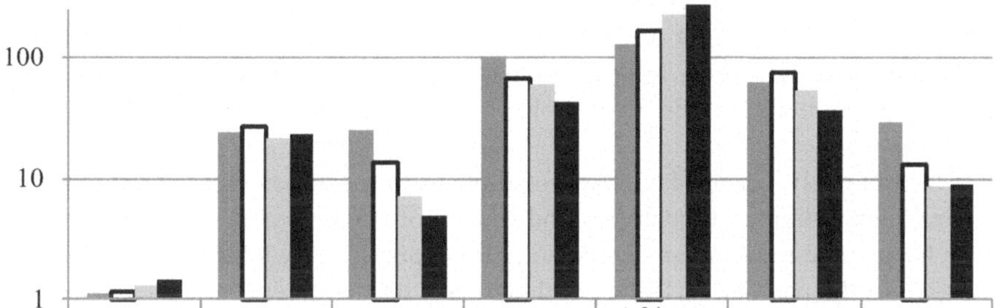

	Catholicism	Traditional Protest.	Pentecostal Protest.	Kardecist Spir.	African-Brazilian religions	Other Religions	Without Religion
1980	1	24	25	100	131	63	29
1991	1	28	13	68	167	77	13
2000	1	22	7	59	228	54	9
2010	1	23	5	42	277	37	9

Graph 7 Ratio between observed and expected frequencies in religious concordance between fathers and children. Brazil – 1980–2010. (Source: IBGE. Demographic Census – 1980 (Special tabulations by CEM))

The generations that experienced a higher proportion of Spiritists were those of the nineteenth century, although the likelihood of belonging to Kardecism suffers a sharp decline until the 1930s in contrast with Catholicism and presents no significant recovery since that time – just a slight increase among those born in the past 20 years. This indicates that the current growth of Kardecism is a phenomenon of period, that is, the growing likelihood of converting to Kardecism affects everyone, regardless of generation.

The behavior of African-Brazilian religions is very peculiar. Those born up until the 1920s increasingly belonged to African-Brazilian religions. This certainly justifies all of the optimism found in analyses during the 1960s and 1970s concerning the future of these religions. However, changes occurred in this trend and the absolute number of participants of African religions displayed vegetative growth, with only a slight inflection since the 1960s, which became further accentuated in the late 1990s. This indicates growth horizons for these groups in the future.

Transmission: Household Arrangements and Religious Concordance

The three dimensions observed (age, period, and cohort) were established as average profiles of the potential life trajectories of individuals over 50 years, indicating trends in how religion in Brazil is preserved. However, by focusing on the individual aspect, these dimensions fail to include another crucial aspect in the reproduction of religion: family ties.[11] If a fragmentation in the religious field does indeed exist, one would also expect family arrangements to engender new religious arrangements within households. Thus, religious adherence should also be viewed in terms of family interactions in the household, which becomes a unit of demographic analysis.

Unfortunately, census data does not allow us to accompany these individuals and follow their religious trajectories and modes of transmission. The religion under which someone is raised in a household, for example, may no longer be the current religion of the parents; or if the youth agrees with her parents at a later stage, both may have transitioned, and it is likely that one party may have influenced the other. Conscious of these limitations, we address the notion of transmission from the point of view of religious concordance within households. Religious diversity acts upon everyday household relations, even if partially, and can lead to conflicts or increased affection between people, among other possibilities.

In addition, two age dimensions stand out. First, after age 20, children increasingly begin to leave their parents' home. Second, differences in religious identities only begin to appear during preadolescence, when an individual becomes more capable of opting for something other than what their parents opted for. In the analysis we cross-tabulated the children's religion with their parents' religion when both live in the same household (a limitation posed by the census data) – i.e., from preadolescence to the age at which children still live with their parents, which tends not

[11] Qualitative research has found that family exerts influence on the acceptance or rejection of a religion. In this case, a differentiated religious adherence in a single household may signal conflicts among members of a family (Almeida and Rumstain 2011).

to exceed somewhere between ages 25 and 30. The data presented here refers to religious concordance between fathers/mothers and children.

In Table 2, derived from the 1980 census, the diagonal cells marked in gray indicate the absolute number of sons/daughters with the same religion as their mothers. We can see that the highest figures pertain to Catholics – and they have always been a majority in Brazil. But that does not mean that Catholics have greater transmission power in households. Therefore, these observations should be controlled by the size of each religion compared to the observed and expected frequency. The expected values are those that would be found if statistical independence existed between the religions of mothers and children – if concordance happened purely by chance. Since religious concordance is the result of social processes and mechanisms (rather than randomness), the observed concordance is always higher than expected for all religions, even for those without religion. The division between observed and expected is an excellent dimension for revealing the strength of such social mechanisms that engender concordance.[12]

Graphs 6 and 7 present the ratios between expected and observed frequencies for all religions, among mother and children and fathers and children.

There are major similarities in the concordance rates between fathers and children and mothers and children, but as one would expect, rates are higher among mothers and children since, according to census data, women are more religious than men. They are the majority across all six categories of religion analyzed here, losing out to men only among the nonreligious. However, data pertaining to the nonreligious also show that greater concordance of children occurs with their mothers rather than their fathers. Thus, we can deduce that mothers are not only dominant in defining their children's religion, but they are also responsible for non-transmission of religious *habitus*.

It is worth mentioning that the difference between the transmission capacity of fathers and mothers decreased significantly up to the 2000 census and remained the same in 2010. To a large extent, this change is related to changes in the behavior associated with contemporary fatherhood, which tend to decrease the emotional distance between fathers and children.

The smallest concordance rates were found among Catholics. Temporal trends show, however, that these scenarios are quite fluid and the framework of some religions has changed rapidly. Concordance rates began to strengthen among Catholics, quite possibly indicating intrafamily religious transmission. As Catholicism loses ground on the national stage, it is quite possible that the remaining followers are merely the most devout and therefore the ones with greater potential for religious transmission and heritage. But until when will Catholicism suffer this loss of followers and how strong is the potential reaction from Charismatics and other contemporary Catholic expressions? These are difficult issues to answer through the censuses, precisely because there are still many Catholics and they are an internally diverse group.

---

[12] This same methodology was used by Barbosa (2009).

Among followers of African-Brazilian religions, intrafamily concordance increased, and we can go so far as to hypothesize that this indeed occurred via religious transmission. Without having increased during the period, maintenance of the size and space taken up by these groups in the religious field is most likely due to their ability to reproduce themselves in households. In turn, concordance rates decreased among Traditional Protestantism, which probably indicates a reduction in its domestic transmission capacity, as percentage and absolute declines within this group have widened.

Concordance rates have also dropped among Kardecists and the nonreligious. Pentecostals, Kardecists, and nonreligious are precisely the three groups that witnessed the most growth during the period analyzed. On a smaller scale, the same phenomenon occurs in the other religions group, which also experienced some expansion.

Concordance rates are declining among Pentecostals, expressing the strong dynamic nature of a segment driven by large-scale conversion. In other words, this probably relates not to a potential for low religious transmission but to the fact that most Pentecostals are individuals who converted and not individuals who were raised under such religions. They are known for their emphasis on family ties and proselytism, resulting in the Christian duty toward the evangelization of family members, the religious education of their children, and the preference for marriages with other Evangelicals. In short, relatives become brothers in faith, and brothers in faith become relatives. If the transmission capacity of Evangelicals is more intense, this means that growth occurs both through proselytism and heritage. However, even if there is a growing trend toward transmission of the Evangelical religion through heritage, growth through proselytism is quite substantial. According to this trend, we can expect the maximum age of 45 for Evangelicals to decrease every census year as the number of people born Evangelical increases.

Still according to Graph 6, the ratio between Pentecostal children and Protestant mothers is very similar to the ratio between Protestant children and Pentecostal mothers (7:5 to be precise). This is a strong indication of internal movement within the Evangelical universe, with no predominance of either segment.

According to Pierucci (2006a), conversion religions, or so-called universal religions, appeal to people as individuals, causing them to detach themselves from religious family ties in pursuit of salvation, which at first is an individual movement (and, it seems, the hypothesis can also be applied to the without religion group). According to his diagnosis, the trajectory of the contemporary Brazilian religious field is marked by an individual logic that breaks primary kinship ties. The author summarized it as an individual salvation, universal in nature. Contemporary religion is a solvent of ethnic, racial, national, and family ties, further away from Durkheim's moral community and closer to the Weberian congregation.

However, family ties are effective in religious transmission across both directions: parents who transmit to their children via heritage and children who evangelize their parents via proselytism. If Evangelical conversion can lead to ruptures in family ties (Duarte and Gomes 2008), once they become Evangelicals, they may acquire further consistency in reproducing the religion (Almeida 2010, p. 379).

The censuses do not allow for a direct observation of these phenomena and behaviors, but there are several indicators that support this interpretation. Analysis of life cycles has shown that different religions are presented in a certain way at every stage of individuals' lives.

Those without religion are a youth phenomenon, and African-Brazilian religions have a stronger appeal among young adults. Pentecostalism and Protestantism advance especially among adults, ages 30 and older. Kardecism is in tune with older people, and Catholicism may have special appeal among the elderly (increasing the chances of return transmission). These specificities indicate that parents and children, at different periods in their lives, may be more likely to religiously approach or distance themselves – and that religious transmission is not a one-way street phenomenon. The phrase "my mother converted to Pentecostalism," often heard during field research, is supported by the quantitative analysis of life cycles, since Protestantism and Pentecostalism appeal mainly to people the age of the respondents' parents.

Closing Remarks

This dynamic within the Brazilian religious realm has led Catholicism to no longer behave and think as *the* religion of Brazilians but as one among many alternatives. This is one of the many effects of religious pluralism. The outcome may be that Catholicism will have an increasing number of followers by choice, since it continues to lose them mostly among those who merely inherited the religion: the so-called non-practicing Catholics, according to a very precise native category in defining a way of being Catholic.

If Catholicism mostly loses non-practicing members, there is a growing number of people among Evangelicals identified as Evangelical without belonging to any specific denomination, circulating among different religious services. Common among "non-practicing Catholics and circulating Evangelicals" is the non-institutionalization of religious practice (Almeida and Rumstain 2009; Almeida 2011). The direction is the same, but the meanings are different. Non-practitioners tend to rid themselves of their inherited religion, declaring themselves nonreligious or converting to Evangelism. Evangelicals, in turn, attract Catholics, followers from other institutions, and the nonreligious, but an increasingly significant number of them are not affiliated with a particular denomination. In other words, as alternatives become more numerous, many people are becoming less loyal to a single religion.

If the religious pluralism initially introduced by the Protestant presence presumes that religious adherence should be exclusive, this becomes increasingly less true in Brazil. The notion of religious pluralism, in its classical postulation (Troeltsch 1987; Neiburh 1992), acquires a different configuration. Diversity and mixture are processes that feed each other, and one may presume that some of the contemporary dynamics occur as a kind of syncretic pluralism, especially in the transition relating to the Christian matrix (Almeida 2010). Diversity and competition among alternative faiths, circulation of followers, and the non-institutionalization of practices and beliefs are some of the dimensions of the religious transitions in Brazil in recent decades.

All these movements have been accelerating over the decades – sometimes exponentially, as in the case of Evangelicals. In part, they are connected to life course dynamics, in part to secular trends related to cohort replacement. Mostly though they are driven by period effects: they can affect everyone living in a historical era (independent of age or generation). That is why it became more common to encounter converted parents and find decreasing rates of religious concordance inside a family in all groups that are growing: they are not just reproducing themselves, but expanding outwardly.

Now, with all these figures, we can go back to some of the points we made in the introduction and also open the door to some possibilities for further investigation. Religious persons, like anyone else, do not have just ideal interests but also quite material ones – as Max Weber noted. Very often religions move individuals toward rejection of the world in its current state, inspiring reactions, reforms, and changes in one's own behavior. And all of this may have profound implications on the political and economic organization of society – not surprisingly, Weber framed those aspects as part of the economic ethic of religions. However, we think it is not possible to deduce probable political preferences over distributive matters solely on the basis of beliefs in this kind of study. In specific places and in the short-term (decades), the historical noise may be a lot stronger than the theological signal. Weber's study of world religions relied on regularities abstracted over the course of centuries or millennia. What transpired in Brazil in the last 50–100 years is more properly explained by examining its history, institutions, and characteristics of society, and not its religious ideas alone.

For a long time, Catholicism was considered – formally or informally – the official religion of Brazil. Until 1890, priests were actually public servants and received payments from the government. After legal separation of church and state, Catholicism continued to assume responsibilities concerning the provision and management of services, especially in education and health. That increased the likelihood that some church members would assume a political stance of soft reformism, based mainly on traditional values concerning welfarism. Emphasis was never placed on criticism of the inequalities of this world. Of course this fit between religion and state is a characteristic feature of Catholicism throughout the history of Western civilization. But as the Brazilian state became stronger, it assumed responsibility for those types of public provision.

It is certainly not easy (nor even possible) to speak generically about Catholics. In the period from the early 1960s to the late 1980s, we can find at least three more important branches and/or guiding principles inside the church. First, there was a very conservative group composed of a considerable number of priests, bishops, and lay middle class members to whom redistributive policies always resembled or sounded like Communism (hence atheism and anticlericalism). Some of these people even supported the military and the dictatorship. Secondly, there was liberation theology, a set of ideas and practices that organically communicated with leftist and socialist ideals, defending equality and especially the poor. It was born and took hold in Latin America but was considered subversive by ecclesiastic authorities and often by states as well. Liberation theologians and leftist militants frequently associated, and this helped the establishment and survival of political parties – most importantly the Workers' Party (PT) in Brazil. Finally, after redemocratization, Charismatic Renewal – a spiritual movement inside the Catholic Church – gained considerable ground, reinforcing traditional values and conservative ideas. In order to oppose the characteristic political activism liberation theology entailed, Charismatic Renewal emphasized subjective spiritual and emotional experiences. There is surely a significant correlation between these three religious perspectives and political preferences. However, they have never reached the majority of church members, who were and continued to be largely non-practicing Catholics.

Classical analysis of Protestantism, drawn from the Weberian interpretation, continued to corroborate the affinity between its ethics and modern economic behavior. But as we have seen in Brazil, Traditional Protestants always enjoyed better material conditions than the average population. In addition to being restricted to a minority, they were also geographically concentrated in the South – where immigrants as well as their descendants who introduced these practices are still present in large numbers. That is, their influence over culture and politics as a whole was never very strong, even as a result of spillover effects.

Conversely, traditional Pentecostal denominations have always been more universalistic, while at the same time, their members have been more subject to poverty and instability. They embrace the idea of divine providence (that God will directly and intentionally help in times of material need) along with the magical notion of potential manipulation of the sacred (that God answers prayers) – but are not certain how these two can be reconciled to generate specific political views, especially concerning inequality. On the one hand, one can think it may help to legitimize the status quo and foster conformity; on the other hand, it can also imply that reality can be changed by fiat. In fact, both situations occur, although not necessarily at the same time. One of the main foundations of the so-called neo-Pentecostal denominations is the theology of prosperity: the idea that God can provide economic prosperity in this world – mainly in return for, or exchange of, tithes, donations, and material sacrifices. Moreover, that discourse encourages individual initiatives and provides legitimate justification for those who are willing to consume. Analysts found these ideas quite adapted to the logic of capitalism in an environment of flexible labor relations. Thus, the neo-Pentecostal churches offered a strong religious meaning to frame experiences that were widely disseminated during the decades of 1980, 1990, and 2000. In a sense, the theology of prosperity is quite the antagonist of the Catholic liberation theology. The former emphasizes individual action, and its ideas hold strong affinity with liberal ideologies concerning merit and achievement. The latter is founded on collectivist assumptions and sees inequalities as arising from a social structure that, instead of being conformed to, must be modified through mundane action (not by praying).

As usual though, things are hardly as straightforward as they appear. We must remember traditional Pentecostals and neo-Pentecostals are mostly in the lowest socioeconomic strata. These beliefs then interact with very concrete and urgent material needs. By being poor, they largely benefited from government social programs involving income transfers during the 2000s, among other policies. Their electoral preferences in recent elections were a mix of favoring religious candidates (often their first choice) and voting for leftist agendas (Peixoto and Rennó 2011) – usually preferring the latter if the election has a second round. Religious leaders in congress themselves were divided between alliances with the right (that favor conservative and traditional values) and PT governments.

Religion has increasingly become part of the public sphere. For a long time (at least since publication of the precursor work of Pierucci in 1989), almost no social scientists, save for experts on the topic, saw it coming. Now it looms large, and one can scarcely deny its importance to the way people face and react to inequalities. The end of religion did not come and it probably will not. In fact, recent chapters in our history give us the impression that a lot of new things are just beginning in this realm.

References

Alencar, G. (2012). *Assembleias Brasileiras de Deus: teorização, história e tipologia (1911–2011)*. Dissertation PhD. São Paulo: PUC/SP.

Almeida, R., & Rumstain, A. (2009). Católicos no trânsito religioso. In F. Texeira & R. Menezes (Eds.), *Catolicismo plural: dinâmicas contemporâneas*. Petrópolis: Vozes.

Almeida, R. (2010). Religião em transição. *Novos Horizontes Antropológicos* (Antropologia). São Paulo: Anpocs.

Almeida, R. (2011). Evangélicos no trânsito religioso. In R. Cabanes, I. Géorges, C. Rizek, & V. Telles (Eds.), *Saídas de emergência: ganhar/perder a vida na periferia de São Paulo*. São Paulo: Boitempo.

Barbosa, R. J. (2009). Transmissão e participação religiosa sob rupturas e continuidades: interpretações. In L. F. Perez, F. Tavares, & F. Camurça (Eds.), *Ser jovem em Minas Gerais: religião, cultura e política*. Belo Horizonte: Argumentum.

Berger, P. (1985). *O dossel sagrado*. São Paulo: Paulinas.

Bohn, S. R. (2004). Evangélicos no Brasil. Perfil socioeconômico, afinidades ideológicas e determinantes do comportamento eleitoral. *Opinião Pública, Campinas, X*(2), 288–338.

Camurça, M. (2006). A realidade das religiões no Brasil no Censo do IBGE. In F. Texeira & R. Menezes (Orgs.). *As religiões no Brasil: continuidades e rupturas*. Petrópolis: Vozes.

Carranza, B., Mariz, C., & Camurça, M. (Orgs.). (2009). *Novas comunidades católicas: em busca do espaço pós-moderno*. São Paulo: Ideias & Letras.

César, W. (1974). Urbanização e religiosidade popular: um estudo da função da doutrina pentecostal na sociedade urbana. *Revista Vozes*, (7). pp. 19–28.

Coutinho, R., & Golgher, A. (2012). The changing landscape of religious affiliation in Brazil 1980–2010: Age, period and cohort perspectives. In Xviii Encontro Nacional De Estudos Populacionais (Ed.), *Anais*.... Águas de Lindóia: ABEP.

D'Epinay, C. L. (1970). *O refúgio das massas* (pp. 1954–1994). Rio de Janeiro: Paz e Terra.

D'epinay, C. L. (1975). *O refúgio das massas: estudo sociológico do protestantismo chileno*. Rio de Janeiro: Paz e Terra.

da Silva, V. G. (1995). *Orixás da metrópole*. 1. ed. Petrópolis: Vozes.

de Camargo, C. P. F. (1961). *Kardecismo e Umbanda*. São Paulo: Ed. Pioneira.
de Camargo, C. P. F. (1971). *Igreja e desenvolvimento*. São Paulo: Cebrap.
de Camargo, C. P. F. (Org.). (1973). Católicos, protestantes, espíritas. Petrópolis: Vozes.
de Souza, B. M. (1969). *A experiência da salvação: pentecostais em São Paulo*. São Paulo: Duas Cidades.
Duarte, L. F. D., & Gomes, E. (Orgs.). (2008). *Três famílias: identidades e trajetórias transgeracionais nas classes populares*. Rio de Janeiro: FGV.
Fernandes, R. C. (1992). *Censo Institucional Evangélico CIN* (p. 1992). Rio de Janeiro: ISER.
Fernandes, S. R. A. (2009). *Novas formas de crer: católicos, evangélicos e sem-religião nas cidades*. São Paulo: Ceris.
Fernandes, R. C., et al. (1998). *Novo nascimento: os evangélicos em casa, na política e na igreja*. Rio de Janeiro: Mauad.
Fonseca, A. (2002). *Secularização, pluralismo religioso e democracia no Brasil: um estudo sobre a participação dos principais atores evangélicos na política*. Dissertation PhD, University of São Paulo.
Freston, P. (1993). *Protestantes e política no Brasil: da constituinte ao impeachment*. Dissertation PhD, University of Campinas.
Fry, P., & Howe, G. N. (1975). Duas respostas à aflição: Umbanda e Pentecostalismo. *Debate e Crítica, 6*, 25–39.
Granovetter, M. (1973). The strength of weak ties. *American Journal of Sociology, 78*(6), 1360–1380.
Granovetter, M. (1974). *Getting a job: A Study of networks and careers*. Cambridge: Harvard University Press.
Hérvieu-Léger, D. (2005). *O peregrino e o Convertido: a religião em movimento* (p. 187). Lisboa: Editora Gradita.
Levy, M. S. F. (1967). Umbanda is for all of us: an alternative dimension of socialization (Master dissertation) University of Wisconsin, Madison.
Mariano, R. (1999). *Neopentecostais: sociologia do novo pentecostalismo no Brasil*. São Paulo: Loyola.
Marques, E., & Bichir, R. (2012). As redes pessoais em São Paulo. In E. Marques (Org.). *Redes sociais no Brasil: sociabilidade, organizações civis e políticas públicas* (pp. 45–68). São Paulo: Ed. Fino Traço.
Miceli, S. (2009). *A elite eclesiástica brasileira*. São Paulo: Companhia das Letras.
Montero, P. (2006). Religião, modernidade e cultura:novas questões. In F. Teixeira & R. Menezes (Eds.), *As religiões no Brasil: continuidades e rupturas* (1st ed., pp. 249–263). Petrópolis: Vozes.
Niebuhr, H. R. (1992). As origens sociais das denominações cristãs, São Paulo, Aste.
Negrão, L. N. (1996). *Entre a cruz e a encruzilhada: formação do campo umbandista em São Paulo*. São Paulo: Edusp.
Negrão, L. N. (2005). Nem "jardim encantado", nem "clube dos intelectuais desencantados." *Revista Brasileria de Ciencias Sociais, 20*(59), pp. 23–36.
Novaes, R. (2004). Os jovens "sem religião": ventos secularizantes, "espírito de época" e novos sincretismos. Notas preliminares. *Estudos Avançados, 18*(52), pp. 321–330.
Ortiz, R. (1979). *A morte branca do feiticeiro negro*. Petrópolis: Vozes.
Peixoto, V., & Rennó, L. (2011). Mobilidade social ascendente e voto: as eleições presidenciais de 2010 no Brasil. *Opinião Pública, Campinas, 17*(2), 304–332.
Pierucci, A. F. (1989). Representantes de Deus em Brasília: a bancada evangélica na constituinte. *Ciências Sociais Hoje*. São Paulo, *11*, 104–132.
Pierucci, A. F. (1997). A propósito do autoengano em sociologia da religião. *Novos Estudos*, (49), 99–117.
Pierucci, A. F. (1998). Secularização em Max Weber: da contemporânea serventia de voltarmos a acessar aquele velho sentido. *Revista Brasileira de Ciências Sociais, 13*(37), pp. 43–73.
Pierucci, A. F. (2004). "Bye bye, Brasil": o declínio das religiões tradicionais no Censo 2000. *Estudos Avançados, 18*(52), pp. 17–28.

Pierucci, A. F. (2006a). Religião como solvente – uma aula. *Novos Estudos*, (75), 111–127. http://www.scielo.br/scielo.php?script=sci_arttext&pid=S0101-33002006000200008
Pierucci, A. F. (2006b). Cadê nossa diversidade religiosa? – comentários ao texto de Marcelo Camurça. In F. Texeira & R. Menezes (Orgs.). *As religiões no Brasil: continuidades e rupturas* (pp. 17–34). Petrópolis: Vozes.
Pierucci, A. F. O., & Mariano, R. (1992). O envolvimento dos pentecostais na eleição de Collor. *Novos Estudos Cebrao, 34*, 92–106.
Pierucci, A. F. O., & Prandi, J. R. (1995). Religiões e voto: a eleição presidencial de 1994. *Opinião Pública, 3*(1), 20–43.
Prandi, R. (1991). *Os candomblés de São Paulo: a velha magia na metrópole nova*. São Paulo: Hucitec e Edusp.
Ryder, N. (1965). The cohort as a concept in the study of social change. *American Sociological Review, 30*(6), 843–861.
Sanchis, P. (1995). As tramas sincréticas da história: sincretismo e modernidades no espaço luso-brasileiro. *Revista Brasileira de Ciências Sociais*, (28).
Sanchis, Pierre. (2001). Religião, religiões. Alguns problemas do sincretismo no campo religioso brasileiro. In Pierre Sanchis. *Fiéis e cidadãos. Percursos de sincretismo no Brasil*. Rio de Janeiro: Editora da Univ. Est. do Rio de J. (EDUERJ), (p. 9–58).
Stark, R., & Iannaccone, L. (1994). A supply-side reinterpretation of the "secularization" of Europe. *Journal for the Scientific Study of Religion*, pp. 230–252.
Teixeira, F., & Menezes, R. (2009). *Catolicismo no Plural*. Vozes: Petrópolis.
Troeltsch, Ernest. (1987). Igreja e Seitas. In Religião e Sociedade, ISER, Rio de Janeiro, 14/3.
Yang, Y., Schulhofer-Wohl, S., Fu, W. J., & Land, K. C. (2008). The intrinsic estimator for age-period-cohort analysis: What it is and how to use it. *American Journal of Sociology, 113*(6).

Part V
Labor Market

Economic Development and Inequalities in Brazil: 1960–2010

Alvaro A. Comin

Abstract The chapter examines social inequalities in Brazil from the perspective of changes in productive and occupational structures and their relationship to economic development. A brief theoretical discussion drawing upon the "Kuznets curve" debate is followed by an analysis of censuses data from 1960 to 2010, focusing on how rural-urban transition shaped the actual socio-occupational stratification. The role of two key factors is highlighted in the analysis: the high levels of concentration in land ownership and the import substitution industrialization model. The role of education in shaping inequalities is examined indirectly through the evolution of the educational profile of the workforce, with an emphasis on its effects on the rural population and nonwhite racial groups. One section specifically addresses the rise of occupation polarization among women as they massively joined the labor market. Lastly, the chapter analyzes inequalities through the lens of labor and welfare rights. Although the overall trends found along this study converge with the Kuznets thesis, the trend toward less income inequality in Brazil is much weaker than that observed among developed countries; as a matter of conclusion, it is argued that the main obstacles to the decline in inequality in Brazil are to be found in political rather than economic processes.

Keywords Urbanization · Social stratification · Inequality · Education · Economic development

Since the mid-1970s, when systematic data became available for measuring inequality in Brazil, the Gini coefficient for income experienced only slight variations, holding at around 0.6 between 1976 and 1999 before dipping to 0.53. This threshold is nonetheless extremely high when compared to countries whose economic development

I am grateful to Rogério Barbosa for his careful preparation of all data used in this article. I am also grateful to Marta Arretche, the editor of this volume, for her careful reading and helpful comments for improving the accuracy of the text.

A. A. Comin (✉)
Department of Sociology, University of São Paulo, São Paulo, Brazil
e-mail: alvcomin@usp.br

M. Arretche (ed.), *Paths of Inequality in Brazil*,
https://doi.org/10.1007/978-3-319-78184-6_13

is similar to Brazil's. The period between 1960 and 2010 witnessed significant changes in the economic structure, the institutional framework, demographic dynamics, and women's professional insertion patterns in contrast to the relative stability of income distribution. Most importantly for the purposes of this chapter, income inequality has endured the exponential increase in per capita income.

Most studies concerning the recent decline in Brazil's income inequality point to the labor market as the main explanatory factor, since it experienced a positive cycle of increase in formal jobs along with improvements in formal education. Conditional income transfer programs also played an important role, as did the continuous provision of benefits and retirement pensions indexed to the minimum wage (Soares 2010), in addition to demographic factors, particularly the cumulative decline in fertility and the resulting decrease in the number of younger cohorts, leading to a reduction in the volume of new participants in the labor market.

This chapter examines inequality in Brazil from the perspective of changes in productive and occupational structures and their relationship to economic development. A brief theoretical discussion will be followed by an analysis of the censuses from 1960 to 2010, focusing on rural-urban transition and the resulting socio-occupational stratification. The influence of an existing agrarian structure and the industrialization model play a central role in the analysis. The choices made by successive Brazilian governments will be analyzed indirectly through the evolution of the educational profile of the workforce, with an emphasis on its effects on the rural population and nonwhite racial groups. One section will address the entry of women into the labor market. Lastly, we will analyze socio-occupational stratification and labor and welfare rights.

Economic Development and Inequalities

In an influential article published in 1955, Simon Kuznets (Kuznets, 1955) presented a theoretical framework to explain the relationship between economic development and inequality in the distribution of personal income. His starting point is a simple yet contemporary inquiry: does economic development magnify or reduce income inequality between individuals?

Two considerations led him to the answer that economic growth would, in its early stages, engender further concentration of income. The first derives from the fact that only the highest-income strata are able to save money and thus make productive investments that return more income and savings and further widen their distance from the lower strata. Intergenerational wealth is mainly passed down through inheritance. The second consideration stems from urbanization, typical of capitalist development processes. Agrarian economies tend to be less unequal than urban economies, where sectoral diversification and productivity differentials between sectors are much greater. Thus, the growth of the urban sector would prompt further inequality. Moreover, technological progress, while also present in rural areas, tends to occur more quickly in industrial activities, increasing the distance between rural and urban average incomes.

Based on data for the USA, the UK, and Germany regarding the last two decades of the nineteenth century and the immediate postwar period, Kuznets finds evidence of increasing income inequality. However, after a given point, each scenario witnessed a clear trend toward a decline in inequality. To explain this inverted U-shaped curve, Kuznets established an additional hypothesis, one political in nature that underscored political decisions, such as government actions that included such things as capital gains taxes, inheritance taxes, and prolonged maintenance of low interest rates. The propensity to tax the rich or establish limits for wealth increases insofar as democratic societies become more economically developed and citizens increasingly begin to question the usefulness of income concentration as an engine for productive investments.

For Galbraith (2011), this economic development trajectory seems to suit the USA, much of Europe, and Japan but does not necessarily repeat itself in other contexts where the sectoral component of the product has different characteristics, such as intensive economic activity in export agriculture or mining. Thus, Galbraith concludes (2011, p. 14): "Kuznets' lasting message is not that the same curve always applies, but that the essence of inequality is found in inter-sectoral transitions or in structural changes that constitute the economic growth process."

Like the Kuznets model, the theory of underdevelopment put forth by the Economic Commission for Latin America and the Caribbean (CEPAL), as found in Celso Furtado (1967), operates within a dual model that places modern (capitalist) and traditional (precapitalist) sectors in opposition. Such dualism found in underdeveloped economies would result in only a partial penetration of capitalist activities, juxtaposed with precapitalist production forms where vast segments of the workforce remain. Existing income concentration (inherited from the primary export model) led local elites to demand consumer goods typically found in advanced economies, giving shape to the import substitution industrialization (ISI) model. This, in turn, placed great emphasis on attracting companies that produced modern goods and used labor-saving technologies, with the automobile industry being the most iconic example of this strategy (Furtado 1967).

The fact remains that changes in the sectoral arrangement of productive activities entail changes in the occupational structure. An agricultural economy that only expands by incorporating more land, inputs, and labor force (like Brazil until the mid-twentieth century) tends to preserve the occupational structure, while industrialization and urbanization generate occupational diversification. Industrial development also triggers growth and diversification of services and activities complementary to the urban way of life, shifting segments of the agricultural workforce toward the cities. The pace and volume of these shifts depend on income differentials in these two sectors (rural and urban).

However, this is not the only factor that explains the rural-urban shift. The prevailing conditions of rural life play a crucial role in this process. Well-known is the pioneer history of England where centuries of direct actions by the State to fence off land and thus displace farmers from their means of livelihood were vital to generating the workforce for industry. In countries such as the USA and Brazil, the use of imported foreign labor played an important role in establishing an urban-industrial labor market. In all cases, however, the nature of labor relations and government policies was decisive in preserving or altering the existing agrarian structure.

In Brazil, the agrarian structure was and continues to be one of the most concentrated in the world. Frankema (2006, 2009) shows that Latin America presents land concentration ratios (Gini and Theil indices) consistently higher than any other parts of the world throughout the entire nineteenth and early twentieth centuries. In the mid-twentieth century, the Gini coefficient for land ownership in South America reached the level of 0.804 compared with 0.395 in East Asia, 0.554 in South Asia, 0.638 in North Africa and the Middle East, and 0.452 in West and Central Africa (Frankema 2009, p. 27). Between 1920 and 1985, the Gini coefficient for land in Brazil changed hardly at all, from 0.780 to 0.802 (Frankema 2006, Appendix, Table A.1), even though Brazilian agriculture had undergone major changes during this period.

The huge inequality in land distribution combined with low productivity in a large portion of Brazilian agriculture meant that given the miserable living conditions endured by rural workers, wages paid in urban occupations (including the industrial sector) were enough to prompt rural-urban migration. There was no need to go much beyond subsistence wages, as noted by Celso Furtado. The massive and continuous displacement of workers with little or no schooling from the countryside toward major cities produced what sociologists at the time called the "marginal mass" (Nun, 1969; Kowarick, 1975), a very low-income social stratum excluded from social protection and the labor market (Pinto 1972; Rodríguez 1986; Filgueira 2001).

The enormous relative shortage of a skilled workforce assured the more educated strata the best positions in the labor market and extremely high wages, in addition to benefits typical of social welfare states, such as social security coverage, subsidized housing credit, and health systems funded by companies. As with land, major inequality in educational access was a trait of Brazilian history and had profound consequences on income inequality levels. Benavot and Riddle (1988) estimate that in 1870 Brazil, only 5.8% of school-age children were enrolled in primary school compared to 72% in the USA, 48.7% in England, 67.4% in Germany, 39.8% in Hungary, 20.9% in Argentina, and 16% in Mexico. In 1940, this rate in Brazil was only 29.8%, when it had already reached 91.1% in the USA, 73.3% in England, 71.8% in Germany, 58.8% in Hungary, 58.2% in Argentina, and 37.5% in Mexico. Chaudhary, Musacchio, Nafziger, and Yan (2011) show that in 1910, when school enrollment rates among children aged 5–14 were close to 15%, Brazil spent more per student, in estimated absolute values, than countries such as England, Germany, and France where school enrollment rates were close to 80%. This data reveals an educational model aimed at catering to middle and upper social strata at the expense of the majority of the population.

Integration of the workforce from traditional sectors into higher productivity sectors was very limited; as a result, the entire occupational structure took on radically unequal features. In particular, workers in family subsistence agriculture or on the fringes of export agricultural production (*boias-frias*, sharecroppers, peasants) remained deprived of land ownership, credit, and access to modern technological

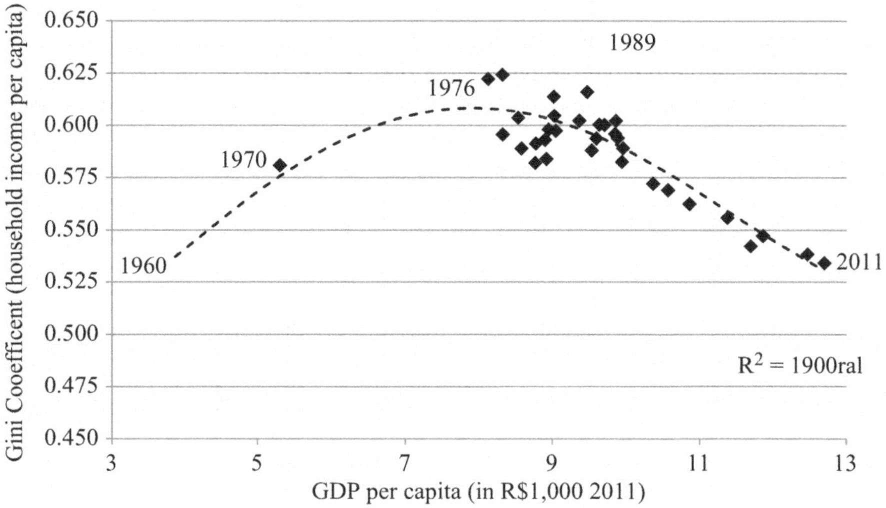

Graph 1 Relationship between GDP per capita and income inequality. Brazil (1960–2011). (Source: Institute for Applied Economic Research (IPEA-Data); Brazilian Institute of Geography and Statistics (IBGE). National Household Sample Surveys (PNADs), 1976–2011 (Special tabulations by CEM))

resources and were unable to save or invest any capital. Therefore, they did not become consumers of the products of emerging industry even when economic growth began to gather steam.

The relative depletion of the workforce in rural areas led to a slowdown in changes within the occupational structure. By the late 1980s, rural-urban transition and the demographic curve were already at a very advanced stage, which decisively contributed to the expansion of educational access. Low economic growth rates since 1981, and especially the loss of dynamism in the industrial sector beginning in the mid-1980s and worsening after 1990, resulted in deterioration of the labor market, with an increase in labor informality, unemployment, and income inequality. The most striking feature of the 1990s and 2000s was the transition toward a more job-intensive economy in the large and heterogeneous service sector. Between 2000 and 2010 alone, the effects of reduced migration flows, declining fertility rates, and an expanding education system combined with moderate acceleration of economic growth and a more consistent set of redistributive policies, both via the labor market and social policies, began to translate into reduced income inequality.

Graph 1 combines data from the 1960 and 1970 censuses with the National Household Sample Surveys (PNADs) for the 1976–2011 period, which seem to confirm Kuznets' hypothesis that economic development, and especially its acceleration period (referred to in Brazil as the "economic miracle"), led to escalating income inequality, a trend that lasted until the late 1990s when a more consistent drop begins. Taking into account the necessary methodological precautions, it should be noted that the Gini level in 2011 was still higher than in 1960.

If the trend observed over the past decade continues, Brazil could become a widely known case for confirming Kuznets' hypothesis. However, as Galbraith reminds us (2011), the lesson to be learned from Kuznets is not that development eventually reduces inequalities. Proof of this is the fact that countries that have developed through the famous curve resulting in greater equality, such as the USA and the UK, have experienced growing inequality in recent decades. The key lesson is that sectoral structure and employment opportunities matter greatly for income inequality. Whether economic development entails an increase or a decrease in inequality depends mainly on the strategies countries adopt and the results actually obtained.

The following sections examine how the rural exodus shaped the urban labor market; how this process affected the occupational integration of women, blacks, browns, and indigenous people, segments that make up for roughly half of the population; and finally, how the expansion of the service sector has reconfigured the occupational structure and, consequently, income inequality.

Evolution of the Brazilian Occupational Structure: 1960–2010

Economic Growth and Sectoral Shifts

While Brazilian economic growth rates throughout the period have witnessed wild swings, levels declined substantially after the so-called "economic miracle" (an expression used to describe the high levels of growth Brazil underwent from 1968 to 1973). In the 1960s and 1970s, Brazil's economy grew at the average rate of over 7% per year, reaching a peak of 14% in 1973. Between 1960 and 1980, Brazil's GDP per capita tripled. During the particularly turbulent 1980s, the Brazilian economy grew just over 3% on average, reaching 10% in 1980 and over 7% in 1985–1986. In 1981, it registered negative growth: −4.25%. GDP per capita ended the decade where it had begun. In the 1990s, economic growth declined further, averaging 1.4% in the first 4 years and just over 2% for the rest of the decade. Under the benefit of the demographic curve, GDP per capita varied by 5% between 1990 and 2000, never again attaining the peak reached in 1987. Finally, the 2000s witnessed a recovery in growth, averaging over 3% in the first half and more than 4% in the second. The result was a 20% expansion in GDP per capita (IPEA-Data).

The manufacturing industry's share in Brazil's GDP has grown steadily in the postwar years, reaching its peak in the mid-1980s when it then began to decline.[1]

[1] There are significant discrepancies in measuring the relative share of economic sectors in Brazil's GDP due to methodological changes made over time by the IBGE. The usual calculation, which uses current values, indicates that participation by industry would have reached a peak of 35% in 1985, as found in Pedersen (2008). By retroactively applying methodological changes introduced in the 1990s, which increased the share of the service sector, and using 2009 constant values, Bonelli, Pessoa, and Matos (2013) conclude that in 1985, the weight of the industry sector was close to 25%. Despite discrepancies, the trend is the same in both cases: accelerated growth of the

Table 1 Distribution of the workforce according to major economic sectors. Brazil: 1960–2010 (%)

Economic activity sectors	1960	1970	1980	1991	2000	2010
Agriculture, fishing, and livestock	55.2	45.4	30.0	22.8	18.7	11.3
Construction	3.3	6.0	7.6	6.7	7.1	8.1
Industry, mining, and public utilities	10.1	12.8	17.9	16.5	14.4	14.7
Trade, transportation, communication, and hospitality	14.4	14.9	17.7	20.5	24.3	26.2
Financial, real estate, and business	1.7	2.2	5.7	6.6	6.5	9.2
Public administration and defense	3.1	4.3	4.4	4.9	5.4	6.0
Education, health, and welfare	2.5	4.4	6.1	8.0	9.7	10.6
Domestic services	4.2	8.3	6.1	6.8	7.7	7.7
Other services	5.5	1.7	4.5	7.2	6.2	6.1

Source: IBGE. Demographic Censuses 1960–2010 (Special tabulations by CEM)

Between 1960 and 2010, the agricultural sector saw its share of GDP drop from about 18–5%. Until 1985, all ground lost by agriculture shifted toward manufacturing, constantly maintaining the large service sector at the level of 50% (Pedersen 2008). Since 1985, however, losses in both sectors (agriculture and industry) were transferred to the tertiary sector, which accounted for about two-thirds of GDP. These shifts are essential when analyzing changes in the occupational structure.[2]

Table 1 shows the cumulative effects of economic growth on the sectoral allocation of the workforce. The decline in employment in the primary sector between 1960 and 1991 was intense and even more proportional than the sector's decline in GDP. Until 1980, the industrial sector absorbed most of the workforce: its 8% expansion represented approximately half of what was lost by the primary sector. Virtually all other sectors experienced relative growth. Especially indicative of the movement in sector diversification is the remarkable expansion of modern services in the fields of finance and business, as well as the expansion of social services such as education and health.

Rural-Urban Transition

Table 2 shows the effects of sectoral changes on the occupational structure, now using the occupational classification system created by Erikson, Goldthorpe, and Portocarrero known as EGP. The last four lines of the table present two basic aggregates: rural and

industrial sector in the GDP until the mid-1970s and relative decline after 1985. After the 1995 methodological changes, the time series begin to coincide, and the point of arrival becomes consensual: in 2011 the weight of the industry sector stood at 15%.

[2]The reasons for these changes (the crisis of the 1980s and the liberal reforms of the 1990s) are well known and beyond the scope of this chapter. For an overview of the economic history of this period, see Fishlow (2011) and Love and Baer (2009).

Table 2 Evolution of the occupational structure, EGP classes. Brazil: 1960–2010 (including unpaid workers) (%)

	EGP classes	1960	1970	1980	1991	2000	2010	1960–1991	1991–2010
Non-manual	Professionals (high)	0.02	0.02	0.03	0.04	0.05	0.07	0.02	0.04
	Professionals (low)	0.04	0.05	0.06	0.08	0.09	0.07	0.04	0.00
	Routine non-manual (high)	0.05	0.07	0.09	0.10	0.10	0.10	0.05	0.00
	Routine non-manual (low)	0.04	0.06	0.08	0.07	0.11	0.15	0.03	0.07
	Owners and employers	0.01	0.01	0.02	0.03	0.03	0.02	0.02	−0.01
	Rural employers	0.01	0.01	0.01	0.01	0.00	0.00	0.00	−0.01
Manual	Subsistence agriculture and self-employed rural workers	0.40	0.33	0.18	0.11	0.12	0.10	−0.29	−0.01
	Manual labor technicians and supervisors	0.02	0.03	0.03	0.03	0.03	0.03	0.02	0.00
	Skilled workers	0.17	0.18	0.24	0.24	0.24	0.25	0.07	0.01
	Semi-skilled workers	0.12	0.13	0.15	0.18	0.17	0.16	0.06	−0.02
	Rural wage employees	0.14	0.11	0.11	0.11	0.06	0.04	−0.03	−0.07
	Non-manual	0.16	0.22	0.28	0.33	0.37	0.41	0.17	0.09
	Manual	0.84	0.78	0.72	0.67	0.63	0.59	−0.17	−0.09
	Rural	0.54	0.45	0.30	0.23	0.18	0.15	−0.32	−0.08
	Urban	0.46	0.55	0.70	0.77	0.82	0.85	0.32	0.08

Source: IBGE. Demographic Censuses 1960–2010 (Special tabulations by CEM)

urban, and manual and non-manual. Finally, the two columns on the far right present the variations between two major periods: 1960–1991 and 1991–2010.

The most significant share of rural-urban transition took place between 1960 and 1991 when, in the direction indicated by Kuznets' hypothesis, inequality measured by the Gini index increased until reaching its highest level. This transition was the result of the dissolution of vast parcels of small family subsistence farms. This group, which in 1960 accounted for almost 40% of all occupations in Brazil, was reduced to just over 10% in 1991. The same did not occur with rural workers or rural employers, however, whose negative growth in this period was quite modest. The share of both groups in the occupational structure shrank throughout the two most recent decades.

Paul Singer (1971) concluded that until 1960, the decline of occupations in the primary sector had been relatively slow, despite high growth rates in the industry sector. His explanation is that during the first industrialization period, concentrated growth in traditional industries, such as textiles, food, and furniture, led to the eradication of small artisanal businesses, greatly reducing their impact on new job creation. Only with further development of new industrial sectors (electronics, automobiles, etc.) did manufacturing begin to add new jobs on a massive scale, increasing its appeal to the rural workforce.

Singer's explanation (1971) is certainly part of this story. However, factors leading to the rural exodus were equally if not more responsible for the intense migratory flow. The modernization of Brazilian agriculture, which intensified after the 1960s, resulted in increased land concentration – through the violent expulsion of small family farmers from traditionally occupied areas and indigenous populations from agricultural border areas, especially in Brazil's Central-West and North regions – the deterioration of living conditions, and the increased concentration of agricultural income (Thiesenhusen and Melmed-Sanjak 1990). Bresser-Pereira estimates that the share of rural income appropriated by the poorest half of Brazil's families decreased from 17% in 1960 to 15% in 1970 and 13% in 1980.[3] The Gini coefficient for land, in turn, increased from 0.838 in 1960 to 0.853 in 1980 (Thiesenhusen and Melmed-Sanjak 1990). Nevertheless, Denslow and Tyler estimate that the average income gap in rural and urban areas decreased throughout the 1970s as a result of wage-squeeze policies pursued by the military governments.[4]

Internal migration data also corroborate this timeline.[5] During the interval from 1940 to 1950, 10% of the rural population at the beginning of period was part of the rural-urban movement; from 1950 to 1960, this figure represented 21% of those living in the countryside in 1950. In the 1960s and 1970s, no fewer than 31 million individuals left the countryside. Throughout the entire period analyzed, the 1990s was the only decade that saw an increase in both the absolute number as well as the relative share of individuals involved in subsistence agriculture.

The consequences of educational policies were much more dramatic for the rural population, condemning them to extremely unfavorable conditions for entering the urban labor market. Graph 2 shows the scale of the disadvantages experienced by this population segment. In 1960 and 1970, 60% of rural workers had never attended school, compared with 20% of workers in urban areas. Within the same period, only about 10% of urban workers had completed primary education, but this proportion increased steadily to 40% by 1991, while in rural areas, it remained close to 5%. In 2010, 70% of the urban employed had completed primary education, while in rural areas, this ratio barely exceeded 20%; in the same year, nearly 15% of the urban workforce held a college diploma compared to 0.8% of the rural population.

Even when compared only to urban manual labor groups, rural workers are at a considerable disadvantage. In 1960, in the group made up of semiskilled urban manual workers, there were nearly 50% fewer individuals who had not gone through the school system than in the group made up of rural workers; one-third of those in the group made up of skilled urban manual workers and only one-sixth of the group made up of technicians and industrial supervisors had no schooling compared to their rural counterparts. The hierarchy among these groups is sharply discernible and remains more or less unchanged over time. The data reinforces the

---

[3] Bresser-Pereira (1982) quoted in Thiesenhusen and Melmed-Sanjak (1990).

[4] Denslow and Tyler (1984) quoted in Thiesenhusen and Melmed-Sanjak (1990).

[5] In this volume, refer to the chapter "Internal migration in Brazil over the past 50 years: (dis) continuities and ruptures," by José Marcos Pinto da Cunha.

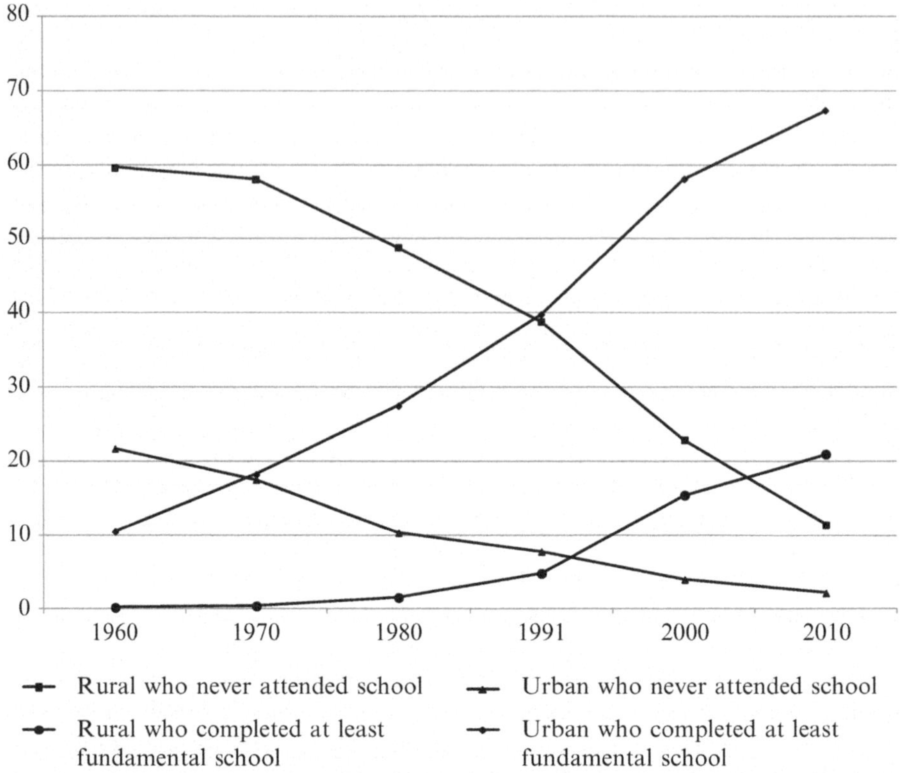

Graph 2 Workforce, according to skill level and occupational sector. Brazil: 1960–2010 (%). (Source: IBGE. Demographic Censuses 1960–2010 (Special tabulations by CEM))

thesis shared by the literature that the majority of rural migrants mostly comprised the lower strata of urban occupations and, so, is much less likely to benefit from the opportunities brought about by industrialization.[6] From the mid-1980s, when the industrialization cycle had dissipated, the best opportunities for upward mobility shifted to niche occupations in services, for which educational requirements tend to be higher.

The segment that consists of semiskilled workers (the lowest urban category, dominated by domestic workers and street vendors) increased by 60% between 1960 and 1991, going from 11.7% to 18.5% of the total employed population (Table 2). Skilled workers (mostly engaged in civil construction and more traditional industry jobs such as tailors and weavers) increased by almost 70% (from 17% to 25%), while technicians and supervisors (which brings together the highest skilled working class, associated with modern industries), although doubling their

[6] For a more comprehensive and comparative discussion regarding the effects of rural-urban migration on urban stratification, see Koo (1978).

relative share in the first period, accounted for less than 4% of the total employment in 1991, a level that persists until 2010.

Inequality and Racial Differences

Graph 3 allows us to observe the legacy of colonization and slavery and the subsequent marginalization of non-European ethnic groups across the hierarchy of Brazil's occupational structure. The black, brown, and indigenous population will be considered here as a single group: nonwhites. Its concentration in rural areas helps explain why it grew faster than the white population (fertility decline is slower in the countryside and among the poor than in cities and among the wealthiest); therefore, nonwhites are overrepresented in the lower manual occupations and underrepresented among the remaining occupational groups. Between 1960 and 2010, the share of nonwhites in the labor force expanded by about 10%, increasing from 40% to 50%. Among rural workers, nonwhites had a 7% higher share than their participation in the total workforce in 1960, rising to 12.5% in the 1980–2000 period. In 2010, nonwhites accounted for almost two-thirds of the workforce employed in the primary sector, whose labor income is the lowest among all groups, except for employers.

These figures indicate that the urbanization process has more than proportionally mobilized the white rural population. The reasons behind this are geographical,

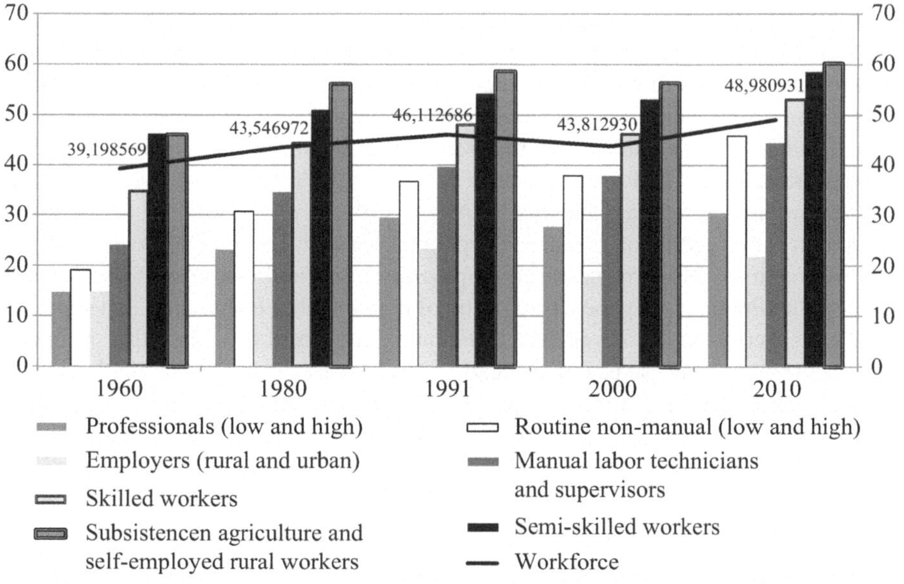

Graph 3 Participation of nonwhites in the workforce, according to EGP occupational groups. Brazil: 1960–2010. (Source: IBGE. Demographic Censuses 1960–2010. (Special tabulations by CEM))

industrialization was very concentrated in the South and Southeast regions where the participation of European immigrants is high, and historical, immigration waves in the late nineteenth and early twentieth centuries moved toward urban centers, whose strata consisted of skilled workers, non-manual workers, and entrepreneurs (Barbosa 2008).

Among urban occupations, the only group in which nonwhites were overrepresented in 1960 consisted of semiskilled manual workers, a fact that became more marked throughout the period. Among the remaining groups, participation was inferior to their weight in the workforce. Aside from the group made up of employers, where underrepresentation of nonwhites has increased over these 50 years, their participation in other groups has improved in relative terms, albeit following a clear hierarchy. Among skilled workers (the second lowest urban group), nonwhites exceeded their relative weight in the working population as early as 1970; among routine non-manual workers, underrepresentation was 20% in 1960, decreasing continuously to almost disappear in 2010. Improvement was very modest in high-skilled and prestigious occupations, however. In 2010, when nonwhites already made up half of the total workforce, they accounted for only about 30% of this group and were heavily concentrated in low-skilled occupations.

Inequality and Gender Differences

Graph 4 presents data on female participation in the workforce, a third major structural aspect. Statistically speaking, participation is significantly lower in rural activities than in urban activities.[7] Rural-urban transition constituted the key element of increased female participation in the labor market. Even so, female participation tended to be two to three times higher among those employed in family farming than among rural workers – the latter, at least conceptually speaking, already integrated into the labor market. On the other hand, women's participation in urban manual occupations had risen to nearly 30% in 1960, a level only reached by the total economically active population (EAP) in 1991.

Within the universe of manual occupations, women have mainly occupied the lowest positions. Modern industrial employment was and continues to be a male bastion. In 1960, virtually the entire group of manual labor technicians and supervisors consisted of men (over 95%). Female participation within this segment increased slowly over the past five decades, reaching less than 15% in 2010. Among skilled manual workers (civil construction, craftsmen, and workers in more traditional industries), women's participation is lower than their relative weight in the EAP and has decreased over time. The female haven among manual occupations was and continues to be domestic work, with participation nearly three times higher than its relative weight in the EAP.

[7] In all likelihood, female contribution to rural labor, especially in family farming, is obscured by the overlap between domestic work and productive work.

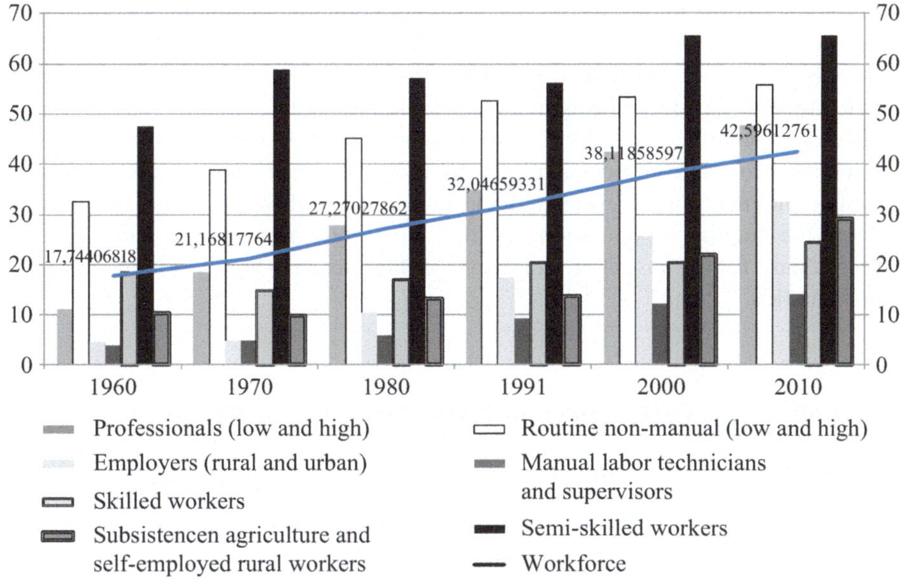

Graph 4 Female participation in the workforce, according to EGP occupational groups. Brazil: 1960–2010. (Source: IBGE. Demographic Censuses 1960–2010 (Special tabulations by CEM))

Unlike the nonwhite population, women are equally distributed among the social classes and have progressed faster than men in educational terms, which have ensured them a more significant presence in the universe of non-manual occupations. However, much like what occurred in the case of nonwhites, women tended to further concentrate in low-skilled low-wage occupations, especially routine non-manual occupations, encompassing a wide range of professions in the basic services (salesperson, clerk, cook, housekeeper, clothing presser, telephone operator, receptionists, and cashier), in high-skilled office occupations (secretary, typist, administrative and accounting assistant), and in social services (teaching assistant, preschool teacher, and teacher in the lower grades of elementary school). Among these occupations, women's participation in relation to their weight in the total employed population expanded from about 15% in 1960 to more than 20% in 1991, falling from then on until 2010, when it stopped slightly below the 1960 level.

Women have always had significant participation among highly skilled and prestigious occupations, and since 1980 they have come to represent a portion higher than their relative weight in total employed population, a fact mainly explained by the expansion of social services. The principal niches for female labor that carry higher educational requirements correspond to the field of education (teaching positions across various educational levels) and health (nursing assistants, midwives, and nurses). They also hold significant roles in occupations such as journalist, architect, artist, manager and administrator, psychologist, and physician, although they do not have a dominant presence in these fields. In terms of most science and technology professions (engineering, agronomy, mathematics, physics, and systems analysis), top-level legal careers, high-ranking corporate positions, and entrepreneurial endeavors, women's participation, although increasing over the period, has always been much lower than their relative weight in the workforce, especially in relation to their weight in the aggregate of professional occupations.

Broadly speaking, integration of women into the labor market follows a pattern concentrated in a narrower occupational arc than men. On the lower extreme, nearly 8% of employment in 2010 was in domestic services (where women make up over 80% of the employed population). At the upper extreme, technical and top-level professionals, the expansion of social services has created a highly skilled, typically female market.

Inequality and Differences in Labor and Social Rights

One key aspect that shapes inequality stems from the selectivity with which labor legislation and social rights have been applied by the Brazilian government to various occupational segments. It is a well-known fact that Brazil's labor regulation and social welfare apparatus followed a corporate model of selective coverage of legally recognized professions, i.e., those in modern and structured niches (workers in heavy industry, transportation systems operators, and employees of financial institutions) and, above all, civil servants (Draibe 2007). Wage employment rapidly expanded between 1960 and 1980, encompassing nearly 70% of the total employed population, a level that would only increase after 2000. In 2010, however, about a quarter of the employed population was either independent or self-employed, historically one of the main strongholds of informal work, i.e., not covered by labor or social protection laws. The mere status of wage employee has never been a guarantee of a formal labor contract. Informality rates have always been very high in activities such as civil construction, at small industrial firms and service companies, in rural employment, and, above all, in domestic employment.

It is very difficult to estimate how much additional income is earned by those with a formal employment contract compared to those without one. Contractual formality, however, does provide a broad universe of rights and benefits, which has been growing over time: different forms of indirect income (such as family allowances and food and transportation subsidies), layoff compensation (FGTS), unemployment insurance, private health insurance, protection against temporary or permanent inability to work caused by illness or accident, and the right to union representation.[8]

Unfortunately, information regarding formal employment is not adequately registered in the censuses, and, for this reason, we used data from the PNADs. Although formal labor contracts only apply to wage employment relationships, employers and

[8] One of the central premises of Esping-Andersen (1985) for expansion of the welfare state is that partial workforce decommodification mechanisms enabled workers to organize and pressure employers and the State for better income distribution.

Table 3 Proportion of formal employment according to EGP occupational classes. Brazil (selected years) (%)

EGP classes	1981	1992	2001	2006	2007	2008	2009	2011
Professionals (high)	0.79	0.85	0.76	0.75	0.76	0.76	0.79	0.81
Professionals (low)	0.70	0.78	0.68	0.48	0.50	0.50	0.53	0.55
Routine non-manual (high)	0.76	0.84	0.76	0.76	0.77	0.77	0.78	0.81
Routine non-manual (low)	0.60	0.54	0.50	0.58	0.60	0.59	0.62	0.71
Owners and employers	0.89	0.76	0.64	0.63	0.61	0.59	0.61	0.70
Rural employers	0.34	0.27	0.21	0.24	0.28	0.22	0.28	0.30
Subsistence agriculture and self-employed rural workers	0.05	0.02	0.02	0.04	0.04	0.03	0.04	0.05
Manual labor technicians and supervisors	0.85	0.73	0.58	0.63	0.64	0.75	0.73	0.77
Skilled workers	0.63	0.50	0.45	0.48	0.49	0.51	0.51	0.55
Semi-skilled workers	0.37	0.35	0.37	0.38	0.38	0.38	0.39	0.43
Rural waged employees	0.12	0.24	0.27	0.32	0.34	0.36	0.33	0.38
Total	0.46	0.43	0.43	0.46	0.47	0.48	0.50	0.55

Source: IBGE. PNADs 1981–2011 (Special tabulations by CEM)

individuals who are self-employed may also contribute to social security. Thus, in Table 3, the proportion of formal work contracts corresponds to the sum of individuals with formal wage employment contracts and those contributing to the national social security system.

Even by using this expanded definition of formality, only in the late 2000s did the share of formal employment reach half of the total employed population. The negative variation of the early 1980s and late 1990s gave rise to a formality rate that presents continuous growth from the mid-2000s; in 2011, it represented 55% of all occupational relationships, probably the highest rate in history, although still far from the universalization of labor and social rights, without which one can hardly speak of structural reduction of social inequalities in a broader sense.

There are many reasons for this change, and it is almost impossible to isolate them from each other. The decline in fertility rates associated with the increased length of time that children and young people are in school[9] is certainly among the most significant, as it reduces the absolute number of young people putting pressure on the labor market. Similarly, the decline in rural population and the resulting decrease in rural-urban migration limit the flow of the largest source of workers for the lowest occupational strata. A similar phenomenon is seen in terms of the participation of women, which tends to grow more slowly once it reaches a relatively high level.

Between 2000 and 2010, these macro trends along with accelerated economic growth affected the occupational structure and led to an increase in labor formalization. The occupational categories that shrank most in relative terms after 1991 are

[9] For more on demographic transformations, see Rodriguez Wong and Carvalho (2006). For an analysis regarding the evolution of Brazil's educational indicators in the past three decades, see Rios-Neto et al. (2010).

Table 4 Relationship between the income of EGP occupational groups and overall average income from main occupation. Brazil: 1960–2010

EGP classes	1960	1970	1980	1991	2000	2010
Professionals (high)	4.4	5.4	4.2	3.7	3.2	2.9
Professionals (low)	2.1	2.3	2.0	1.7	1.6	1.6
Routine non-manual (high)	1.7	1.5	1.0	1.0	1.0	1.0
Routine non-manual (low)	1.1	0.8	0.8	0.7	0.6	0.7
Owners and employers	4.5	5.8	4.3	3.9	5.0	3.9
Rural employers	3.0	3.2	3.8	2.6	4.9	4.8
Subsistence agriculture and self-employed rural workers	0.6	0.5	0.6	0.5	0.5	0.5
Manual labor technicians and supervisors	1.7	1.6	1.5	1.4	1.2	1.2
Skilled workers	1.1	0.9	0.8	0.8	0.7	0.7
Semi-skilled workers	0.7	0.6	0.5	0.5	0.4	0.5
Rural wage employees	0.4	0.4	0.3	0.3	0.3	0.4
Relative income (general average = 1)	1.0	1.0	1.0	1.0	1.0	1.0
Average income (in BRL R$ 06/2012)	617.04	749.46	1349.99	1147.19	1350.83	1424.58

Source: IBGE. Demographic Censuses 1960–2010 (Special tabulations by CEM)
The income variable in the 1960 census is categorical rather than continuous. Thus, when calculating this ratio, we take the midpoint of each income range as an estimate of the point value for the occupations. Another limitation concerns the fact that income variables in the 1960 and 1970 censuses refer to amounts earned by an individual from all sources (wages, pensions, rents, etc.) – i.e., not just from labor income. Nonetheless, this continues to be a good approximation, given that we only considered employed persons (for whom labor income represents more than 80% of monthly earnings).

rural workers, semiskilled workers in subsistence agriculture, rural employers, and less skilled workers (Table 2). With the exception of the latter, these categories also present the lowest levels of formal employment (Table 3). In addition, we find growing and continuous rates of formal employment among rural workers, whose share more than tripled between 1981 and 2011, although they still remain among the lowest. Similar behavior can be seen among semiskilled workers, although their starting point was much higher and progression less pronounced. In turn, top-level professionals and low-skilled routine non-manual workers are among the categories with the highest formalization rates in the last two census periods. In short, the progressive shrinkage of the base of the occupational pyramid, dense in low-skilled occupations, and the gradual relocation of the workforce mostly toward the two poles of non-manual occupations (highly skilled professionals and low-skilled routine non-manual workers) led to the expansion of formalized employment and contributed to the overall reduction of inequality, not only in direct income but also of rights involving indirect incomes.

Income Inequalities and the Effects of the Transition Toward Services

The hierarchy of income between major occupational groups can be seen in Table 4, where the average income of all those employed assumes the value of 1 and the income of different occupational groups is calculated as the relative share of this value. Thus, for example, in 1960, top-level professionals earned on average 4.4 times the average income of all wageworkers, while agricultural workers earned only 40% of that value. We should note that since we are dealing with large aggregates that internally are relatively heterogeneous, the averages are crude measures; but all the same, hierarchy between groups is pronounced and stable over time, serving as an approximation of the inequalities between them.

Average income increased substantially during the economic miracle, more than doubling in updated monetary values. However, it suffered a decline of about 15% in the 1980s, when inflation soared. It slowly recovered in the two decades that followed, and in 2010, average income stood at a level that was only around 5% higher than that seen in 1980.

Despite variations in income, low-skilled manual occupations maintain a stable relationship with average income levels: rural workers, a low-income category, saw nearly a 30–40% increase in average income over the entire period; subsistence farmers increased their average income nearly 50%, a level quite similar to that of semiskilled manual workers. The categories comprising the industrial working class, skilled manual workers, and technicians and supervisors, which had a major advantage compared to other manual occupations, have lost ground over time, especially since 1980 when industry lost momentum.

Contrary to what occurred with manual occupations from 1960 to 1970, occupations at the top of the occupational hierarchy, highly skilled and less skilled professionals, and rural and urban employers experienced gains in average income. Since then, the category of senior professionals has expanded substantially, absorbing the increased supply of mid- and upper-level labor, presumably becoming more heterogeneous. It presented a continuous trend of relative decline among the overall group in comparison with overall average income. In the 1990s, when labor market conditions deteriorated sharply, the only categories to experience relative gains in income were rural and urban employers. The latter witnessed the disappearance of these relative gains in the last decade. Rural employers, however, saw significant income growth, which indicates that Brazilian agriculture productivity gains contributed to the increase rather than the reduction of income inequality.

The sharp decline in the share of the two groups of rural workers (the poorest of all in the 1960–1991 occupational structure, as seen in Table 2) largely resulted from the growth of lower manual categories, which presented only slightly higher incomes. Since 1991, the reduction in the group of rural workers (from 11.2% to 4.6% of the total employed population) and the more modest decrease in the number of semiskilled manual workers were compensated by the growth in non-manual categories, particularly highly skilled professionals and low-skilled routine non-manual workers; together, they increased from 11.6% in 1991 to 23.1% of the total employed population in 2010. We therefore identify a clear upward shift in the occupational structure.

It is important to note that the expansion of Brazil's service sector (unlike what occurred in developed countries), at least thus far, is not occurring *primarily* at the expense of industrial employment but rather because of agricultural labor and, to a lesser extent, very low-skilled manual occupations. These shifts are collaborating toward a reduction of income inequalities. What prevented this trend from presenting itself as early as the 1990s was certainly economic stagnation, which generated few jobs, largely concentrated in the informal sector. In the past decade, intense job creation – formal jobs – has favored the convergence of structural trends identified with income distribution policies, especially minimum wage enhancement policies.

The expansion of non-manual occupations within the service sector is occurring at two extremes of the occupational structure: highly skilled professionals and low-skilled routine non-manual workers. As long as the relative growth of these sectors takes place at the expense of the participation of very low-skilled manual occupations (and there is still a lot of room for this), the result will most likely favor a decline in inequality. However, in a hypothetical scenario of continued low growth where the decline in manual labor is concentrated in higher productivity sectors, particularly the industrial sector – as has been the case in many developed countries – expansion of the service sector may result in a new type of polarization where the rewards for educational gains hard-won by the poorest fail to become established.

Conclusions

The process of urbanization represents the major turning point in the path of a nation's development. The diversification of economic activities and the increased productivity associated with this process, far from erasing existing social structures, are built upon them and in turn by them deeply and lastingly influenced. Therefore, claims to universality in many of the economic explanations concerning the capitalist modernization process are frustrated when faced with the diversity of actual experiences.

Brazil's colonial history and slavery produced an extremely polarized and unequal agrarian society, not just when compared to European peasant societies but also in comparison with colonized areas in Africa, the Middle East, and Asia. Brazil's trajectory of modernization broke away from neither the existing agrarian structure nor the regime of labor exploitation. The apparatus for labor market regulation and provision of social services (particularly education) strongly discriminated against the rural population. The expansion of labor and social rights for rural workers (recommended by the 1988 Constitution) is taking place at a very slow pace. The key innovation of recent decades has been the introduction of conditional cash transfer policies, particularly the *Bolsa Familia* program. Despite the significance of this kind of policy for poverty reduction, its impact on occupational insertion of the adult workforce remains very limited.

In the early decades of the period analyzed, this segment comprised the majority of the workforce; its massive displacement toward the cities exposed a largely illiterate population with very limited prospects for occupational insertion. Domestic work, street vending, menial occupations in civil construction, small traditional industries, commerce, and informal services increased with urbanization and still make up a significant proportion of existing occupations. Gradual educational development of this workforce could well result in advances in productivity and income among some niches, which could then lead to business improvement. However, in many other segments, such as domestic work, education rarely translates into productivity gains with an impact on income. In such cases, the increase in income depends on the relative scarcity of labor supply. However, the income elasticity of domestic workers or service providers in the home will always be subject to the availability of family income, and not directly to worker productivity as in industrial activity.

While the industrial sector still embodies a significant share of better income and formal labor opportunities (more so for men than for women), the higher-skilled occupational niches are very limited and become increasingly selective.

In recent decades, occupational niches that experienced greater increases in relative terms are primarily concentrated in low-skilled routine non-manual activities (commerce, food and hospitality services, and bureaucratic services). First of all, while there are no major income variances within these occupations when compared to skilled manual occupations, they do present much higher formalization levels. Secondly, there was an increase in the group that consists of highly skilled professionals associated with social services, activities related to science and technology, business administration, and the State apparatus. This growth is associated with the expansion of higher education, the pace of which increased significantly in the past 15 years, notwithstanding quality flaws and inequality in access to top-level institutions and careers. Thus, as a general trend, the increase of non-manual occupations benefited both lower and higher income and qualification occupational groups. Although the displacement of the workforce toward non-manual strata represents an important and in many ways positive qualitative change, it does not necessarily lead to a long-term reduction in inequalities, as attested by the recent trajectory of developed countries.[10]

The reduction in inequalities with regard to the dynamics of occupational structure will continue to depend on the shrinking low-skilled manual labor strata. While this has been the trend, it continues to be mostly due to the decline in rural labor, reduced to nearly 10% of all occupations in 2010. This segment does not represent much more than the nearly 8% of workers employed in domestic services, a group that shows no downward trend. Thus, the rural exodus, which at the beginning of the

[10] For a discussion regarding the trend toward polarization in advanced service economies, see Sassen (2001).

period analyzed resulted in widening inequalities (the upward part of the Kuznets curve), has collaborated in its own decline since the last decade (confirming the expected curve reversal). Some factors were instrumental in this result, such as demographic changes, the resumption of economic growth, distributive policies via the labor market (minimum wage, especially), and direct income distribution (*Bolsa Família*, noncontributory pensions and benefits). From this point on, however, even if employment in the primary sector continues to shrink, the effect of eliminating the worst jobs within the occupational structure will become increasingly marginal. Within the urban universe, the share of low-skilled manual occupations – and therefore low-income and low-formalization – is still vast and has only showed signs of shrinking in the last decade, and only then very tentatively. A mostly adult workforce with low levels of education has very limited chances for upward occupational mobility in the absence of bolder training policy initiatives and additional opportunities.

Economic growth – and the activity sectors that prevail – will continue to be an indispensable, albeit insufficient condition, for upholding the trend toward inequality decline as observed over the past decade. As Kuznets suspected, structural changes are vital for explaining the inequality curve, but political decisions that limited income accumulation at the top of the pyramid were crucial for producing the second leg of the curve, which marks the decline in inequality. Thus, in the field of redistributive and social policies, Brazil will have to do better and do more should it wish its Kuznets curve to be more than a mere successful theory but rather an actual victory over its own past.

References

Barbosa, A. F. (2008). *A formação do mercado de trabalho no Brasil*. São Paulo: Editora Alameda.

Benavot, A., & Riddle, P. (1988). The expansion of primary education, 1870-1940: Trends and issues. *Sociology of Education, 61*(3), 191–210.

Bonelli, R., Pessoa, S., & Matos, S. (2013). Desindustrialização no Brasil: fatos e interpretações. In E. Bacha & M. B. de Bolle (Eds.), *O futuro da indústria no Brasil: desindustrialização em debate*. Rio de Janeiro: Editora Civilização Brasileira. (Chapter 2, pp. 45–80).

Chaudhary, L., Musacchio, A., Nafziger, S., & Yan, S. (2011). *Big BRICs, weak foundations: The beginning of public elementary education in Brazil, Russia, India, and China* (NBER working paper no. 17852). Available at: http://www.nber.org/papers/w17852

Draibe, S. M. (2007). The Brazilian developmental welfare state: Rise, decline and perspectives. In M. Riesco (Ed.), *Latin America: A new developmental welfare state model in the making?* (pp. 239–281). New York: Palgrave Macmillan.

Esping-Andersen, G. (1985). Power and distributional regimes. *Politics and Society, 14*(2), 185–222.

Filgueira, C. 2001. *La actualidad de viejas temáticas: sobre los estudios de clase, estratificación y movilidad social en América Latina*. Santiago: CEPAL (Serie Políticas Sociales, no. 51).

Frankema, E. (2006). The colonial origins of inequality in Latin America: exploring the causes and consequences of land distribution. GGDC Research Memorandum, GD 88, Groeningen. *Growth and Development Center*.

Frankema, E. (2009). The colonial origins of inequality in Latin America: Exploring the causes and consequences of land distribution. In S. Klasen & F. Nowak-Lehmann (Eds.), *Poverty, inequality, and policy in Latin America* (pp. 19–46). Cambridge, MA: The MIT Press.

Fishlow, A. (2011). Starting Over: *Brazil since 1985 Chapter 3* (pp. 33–87). Washington: The Brookings Institution.

Furtado, C. (1967). *Teoria e política do desenvolvimento econômico*. São Paulo: Companhia Editora Nacional.

Galbraith, J. K. (2011). Inequality and economic and political change: a comparative perspective. *Cambridge Journal of Regions, Economy and Society, 4,* 13–27.

Koo, H. (1978). Rural-Urban migration and social mobility in third world metropolises: A cross-National study. *The Sociological Quarterly, 19*(2. (Spring, 1978)), 292–303.

Kowarick, L. (1975). *Capitalismo e marginalidade na América Latina*. Rio de Janeiro: Paz e Terra.

Kuznets, S. (1955). Economic growth and income inequality. *American Economic Review, 45*(1), 1–28.

Love, J. L., & Baer, W. (2009). *Brazil under Lula: Economy, Politics, and Society under the worker-President.* New York: Palgrave Macmillan.

Nun, J. (1969). Superpoblación relativa, ejército industrial de reserva y masa marginal. *Revista Latinoamericana de Ciencias Sociales, 2*(2), 1–43.

Pedersen, J. D. (2008). *Globalization, development and the state. The performance of India and Brazil since 1990.* New York: Palgrave MacMillan.

Pinto, A. (1972). Factores estructurales y modalidades del desarrollo; su incidencia sobre la distribución del ingreso. *Revista Latinoamericana de Ciencias Sociales, 4,* 162–184.

Rios-Neto, E. L. G., Guimarães, R. R. M., Pimenta, P. S. F., & Moraes, T. A. (2010). *Análise da evolução de indicadores educacionais no Brasil: 1981 a 2008.* Brasília: IPEA (Discussion papers, no. 386).

Rodriguez, O. (1986). O pensamento da Cepal: síntese e crítica. *Revista Novos Estudos Cebrap, 16*, 8–28.

Rodríguez Wong, L., & de Carvalho, J. A. M. (2006). Age-structural transition in Brazil. Demographic bonuses and emerging challenges. In I. Pool, L. R. Wong, & É. Vilquin (Eds.), *Age-structural transitions: Challenges for development* (pp. 159–200). Paris: Committee for International Cooperation in National Research in Demography.

Sassen, S. (2001). *The global city: New York, London and Tokyo* (2a ed.). Princeton, Princeton University Press.

Soares, S. (2010). *PNAD 2009 – Primeiras análises: distribuição de renda entre 1995 e 2009.* Brasília: IPEA (Comunicados IPEA, no. 63).

Thiesenhusen, W. C., & Melmed-Sanjak, J. (1990). Brazil's agrarian structure: Changes from 1970 through 1980. *World Development, 18*(3), 393–415.

Commodification of Labor in Brazil's Labor Market (1960–2010)

Nadya Araujo Guimarães, Murillo Marschner Alves de Brito, and Leonardo Sangali Barone

Abstract The past 50 years were decisive in reconfiguring Brazil's labor market. Individuals who once lived off agricultural work moved on to industrial activities and services in increasingly concentrated urban areas. The economically active population changed significantly. Such changes have not gone unnoticed and have stimulated multiple narratives from the literature, which also encouraged changes in the census metrics; the chapter's first section documents it. Section "Inflections" describes the labor commodification process as indicated by census data from 1960 to 2010, identifying the social segments that have increasingly resorted to the market and mapping the changes on the employment relations. The third section tests statistical models to identify differences in the propensity to resort to the labor market within the period analyzed. The comparison between census years demonstrated how the Brazilian labor market tends to be an increasingly relevant space for working-age individuals. However, individual characteristics also proved to be relevant. Particularly significant were the inflections in the number of women in the market. Despite race is an important determinant for wage inequalities in Brazil, there is no statistical evidence to believe it significantly differentiates individuals with regard to their propensity to engage in economic activity as gender does.

Keywords Labor market · Labor commodification · Gender · Race · Brazil

---

We appreciate the careful reading and thought-provoking insights provided by André Portela Souza, Claudio Amitrano, and Marta Arretche, the leading commentators for this chapter, as well as the methodological support team coordinated by Rogerio Barbosa himself, a constant discussion partner.

N. A. Guimarães (✉)
Department of Sociology, University of Sao Paulo, São Paulo, Brazil
e-mail: nadya@usp.br

M. M. A. de Brito
Department of Education, Pontifical Catholic University of Rio de Janeiro (PUC-Rio), Rio de Janeiro, Brazil
e-mail: murillo-marschner@puc-rio.br

L. S. Barone
Department of Political Science, University of São Paulo, São Paulo, Brazil

M. Arretche (ed.), *Paths of Inequality in Brazil*,
https://doi.org/10.1007/978-3-319-78184-6_14

The past 50 years were decisive in reconfiguring Brazil's labor market. Individuals who once lived off agricultural work moved on to industrial activities and services in increasingly concentrated urban areas. The economically active population (EAP) changed significantly as a result of a rapid inflection of female engagement in the labor market coupled with a notable decline in fertility rates as well as changes in the patterns of family and household organization. Workforce skill level also changed; educational gains on the part of those employed appeared in parallel with an abandonment of child labor. Lastly, mass unemployment that had gained a foothold in the 1980s as a socially significant phenomenon signaled that survival was a game to be played within the labor market.

Given this plethora of processes resulting from intense changes in Brazil's labor market structure, this chapter explores how the past 50 years heralded, among these important changes, entrenchment of Brazil's commodification of labor.

Our focus on the commodification of labor is an attempt to describe and explain the propensity of individuals to pursue their survival by means of engaging in the labor market. Our interest lies in understanding the movement by which the *potential labor supply*, composed of individuals deemed socially suitable according to their age, becomes the *effective labor supply*, composed of the labor force, whether employed or unemployed.

An investigation into labor commodification allows us to obtain a glimpse of the complexity involved in forming a market that matches buyers and sellers of labor in Brazil. While formal and universally free workers have been able to offer themselves in the labor market since the late nineteenth century, despite extensive rules regulating wage relationships through labor laws enacted since the first half of the twentieth century, and even though economic dynamics have relied upon increasingly globalized capitalist markets since the second half of the twentieth century, the propensity of workers to pursue their livelihood in the labor market cannot be reduced to an automatic response, be it legal or economic. On the contrary, it reflects how a normative construction – of labor and laws – becomes socially assimilated and gradually reconfigures the mechanisms of this very market.

Two preliminary observations are in order here. First, inequalities operating within the labor commodification process are of a specific nature, which neither extend nor can be reduced to the results that are subsequently obtained. Thus, if the likelihood of finding an occupation or earning higher wages is subject to the presence and profile of other individuals competing for positions and salaries within the market, the same does not occur with regard to movement into the market. Barriers, if any, arise from normative constructions, which establish, in every society and at different moments in time, those who can offer their labor in the market.

As a second observation, we recall that several variables can affect the pressure to seek survival through the market. In this chapter, we will discuss three dimensions:

- Individual characteristics: age and education (and the resulting experience associated with seniority, attributes with high market value), gender and racial status (attributes that have market value even though they should not), or position

within the family (and the socially expected responsibilities with regard to dependents), which compel individuals to return to the labor market
- Characteristics of the household group (size and weight of those economically and socially dependent) that determine the need for income obtained from the labor market
- Context in which one lives and competes (whether urban or rural, as well as region of the country) that signals a greater or lesser attractiveness of the market into which one enters

This set of variables will allow us to understand how labor supply grows over time as well as what determines this growth.

The chapter is divided into four sections. The first section, entitled "Clues", gathers evidence of the magnitude of these changes. On the one hand, we observe how the sociological literature has analyzed changes taking place at our starting point (1960) as well as at our ending point (2000s). On the other hand, we assess the impact of these new processes in the development of census statistics; it is assumed that in the wake of modifications to the way phenomena are measured using upgraded census classification structures and categories, we will be able to find indelible clues as to the changes occurring now.

The second section, "Inflections", describes the labor commodification process as indicated by census data from 1960 to 2010. At least two inflections are analyzed in this second section. First, we identify the social segments that have increasingly resorted to the market. Then we map the diversity of the social relationships of employment through which individuals became incorporated into economic activity. This diversity has provided the Brazilian labor market with a peculiar institutional configuration: although based on capitalist principles, the typical employment relationship (wage work) did not become widespread at the same time as labor supply expanded as it did in countries that served as archetypes to sacred interpretations regarding labor under capitalism.

The third section, "Engagement determinants and inequalities", tests statistical models to identify differences in the propensity to resort to the labor market within the period analyzed, exploring some key features in the range of propensity. This will conclusively allow us to integrate the diverse movements of our analysis in the final section.

Clues

Sociological literature has explored the idiosyncrasies of the Brazilian labor market extensively. Particular attention has been given, on the one hand, to its pronounced heterogeneity (given the way individuals engage themselves in the labor market) and, on the other hand, its initially reduced scope (in view of the proportion of the population included and, particularly, the agricultural workers excluded).

This is not the place for an exhaustive review of such literature. We have instead systematized some clues into two key instances: the starting point (1960s) and the ending point (2000s). If we assume that commodification of labor in Brazil takes root during this period, sociological interpretations regarding these two instances can be symptomatic of the transformations that may have occurred.[1]

The first of these instances takes place during the 1960s. Scholars at the time faced the challenge of explaining the singularity of a labor market that, while capitalist, did not make its typical employment relationship – a contractually established wage employment relationship – widespread across the entire workforce. This was a social relationship capable of subjecting workers to lasting employment contracts in such a way that the market would inescapably become the space in which these individuals would find the conditions for their survival.

In studies conducted in the 1950s and 1960s, Lopes (1964, 1967), Rodrigues (1970), and Durham (1973) pointed out how pendulous migration strategies toward major industrial centers revealed the importance of one's ties with places of origin and the backflow economic activity in the place of arrival. Accordingly, they indicated the coexistence of *loci* (and a fortiori of markets) where survival was in play. Furthermore, these authors underscored how the plans of these migrants, often precariously integrated into newly arrived urban centers, were guided by the search for a formal job (becoming a registered wageworker) that safeguarded the rights of those in industrial occupations and modern services,[2] which were nonexistent in rural areas. If the market and urban environment exerted undeniable attraction because of the assurance of rights, the continued recourse to return migration witnessed the fragile construction of this market order and the difficult access to such rights.[3]

[1] A vast sociological and historiographical literature explored the meaning and content of legislation regulating the labor market during Getulio Vargas' first administration (1930–1945), from which we highlight such authors as Gomes (1979, 1988), Santos (1979), Vianna (1976), and Erickson (1979). We should also mention analyses on the commodification of social and trade relations in Brazil during the late nineteenth century, carefully organized by Oliveira (1988).

[2] As acknowledged by Santos (1979) when coining the notion of regulated citizenship, significantly defined at first as occupational citizenship.

[3] Cardoso (2010, pp. 229–230) observed the movement of three variables for the period 1940–1976: the urban EAP, the number of individuals holding the labor contract booklet required to engage in formal jobs (*carteira do trabalho*), and the number of contributors to social security in Brazil. The last two are proxies for formal employment relationships, but in a rather different fashion compared to the United States. In Brazil, holding a *carteira do trabalho* just means having a license to search for formal jobs; once registered as a wageworker, the new employment relationship gets recorded in this document and provides access to all rights under labor legislation. This is not the case for informal employment relationships or self-employment. Cardoso showed that issuance of *carteiras do trabalho* grew 150% more than the increase in the EAP and 230% more than the expansion of welfare beneficiaries. Despite some caution when comparing those growth rates (since the number of *carteiras* was very low at the starting point), the growth in the issuance of labor contract booklets, i.e., in the number of holders of *carteiras*, signals a belief in the possibility of including oneself in the formal labor market. Although the use of *carteiras* had been established since 1932 and made compulsory 2 years later, it is significant that the first major inflection in their number issued only occurred from 1950 to 1960 (Cardoso 2010, p. 230), which

Machado da Silva (1971) enriched this narrative by emphasizing the role of the consumer market. Given the increasingly monetized nature of the Brazilian economy, apparent since the late nineteenth century and undeniable during the 1930s, individuals were pressed to find in the labor market the income needed for their own and family survival. However, according to Silva, there was a gap between this trend and the institutional construction of the labor market. Unlike what occurred in major capitalist countries, Brazil's fragile regulation fostered the convergence between population and economically active population, which stemmed from an unlimited labor supply (unlimited because it was unregulated). Brazilians were faced with a market that had no entry barriers, the so-called informal market, a theme with strong appeal in the debate at the time and central to understanding the disengagement caused by greater expansion of effective labor supply (our commodification indicator) without similar expansion of formal wage relationships.[4]

The 2000s offered a very different narrative, however, one indicative of the vast transformations that had taken place in the ties between market and labor commodification in Brazil. This changed the tone of the debates regarding both engagement and labor heterogeneity. When faced with the challenge of examining the effects of an extended scenario of ebbing economic growth (begun in the 1980s with the so-called lost decade), sociologists documented how formal wage retraction signaled the halting of a movement, which since the late 1940s had gradually included new contingents of workers into the labor market. It was then that unemployment was considered a problem that was here to stay (Cardoso 2000; Guimarães 2004).

Macroeconomic retraction in conjunction with increasing rationalization in the use of labor at the micro level, by companies, resulted in a marked increase in unemployment, which appeared as an urgent problem in need of a solution. In other words, when market engagement in search of survival offers no prospects for any return, unemployment evolves into a structural feature of the market, beginning with the major metropolitan labor markets. Do we need any better signal of this compulsory market engagement than therein remaining even without a regular occupation?[5]

---

signals a time of inflection in the individual propensity to engage within the market.

[4] It is not without reason that boundaries were also blurred when defining the category of EAP as operationally translated into the census metric of the time.

[5] Two other clues also signal the establishment of a compulsory pattern of labor market engagement at this time. On the one hand, there was the debate regarding unemployment measurement that galvanized sociologists and economists in the 1980s and 1990s and finally resulted in a new metric in the official statistics found in the IBGE's Monthly Research on Employment (PME) in 2002. On the other hand, there was trade union mobilization surrounding the measurement dispute, which proved so intense that an alternative measure for unemployment – the Employment and Unemployment Survey (PED) – was introduced by the Inter-Union Department of Statistics and Socioeconomic Studies (DIEESE); what's more, it was road-tested precisely in the largest metropolitan region, São Paulo, in 1984, just 2 years after a movement by unemployed people nearly overthrew the first opposition state government elected during the military dictatorship, amidst a deep economic crisis and a significant contraction of job opportunities.

Rising unemployment, a trademark of the 1980s and 1990s, was the result of intense micro-organizational restructuring. It occurred in a context of profound macroeconomic change associated with the crisis and the State's new regulatory policy on the economy, especially rapid trade liberalization. But this was not all. A majority and growing share of the workforce was now bound to the labor market, with no return (Hirata and Humphrey 1989). Engagement was no longer transient and/or pendulous, alternating between market and extra-market forms of subsistence.

While resources stemming from private social relationships could enable survival (through group solidarity) when threatened by unemployment – even though these resources aligned themselves to engagement and social relationships via the market[6] – the latter had become paramount. Individuals pressed on, tied to the market, even under different forms of unemployment; hence the reason why measuring and acting upon it came to be what society demanded of the State. In the 2000s, the market had ultimately become the necessary locus for survival. The process of labor commodification was thus firmly established.

Furthermore, the numerous forms of unemployment – especially the remarkable weight of hidden unemployment in precarious occupations or in desperation[7] – expressed another dimension of Brazil's labor commodification: the lack of a social policy for labor protection able to institutionalize minimal benefits (insurance, training, intermediation, and outplacement, etc.) and allow the unemployed to devote themselves to seeking work. Thus, it became impossible to express their labor market engagement status under the notion of *open unemployment*, as in countries with more inclusive (in terms of coverage) and generous (in terms of benefits) welfare regimes, which provided the means to what has become known as the decommodification of labor (Esping-Andersen 1990).[8]

The debate is equally revealing when we turn to the findings on employment. In the years 1960–1970, researchers turned their attention to the social heterogeneity that segmented workers between those in typically capitalist forms of employment and those unable to break into this circuit, or those who were transiently included in the market but outside the beating heart of modern industry and services. From 1990 to 2000, the debate assumed a different tone than that of 1960–1970, with the

[6] This has been registered by the wide and extensive literature produced by Brazilian sociology in the 1980s regarding the living conditions of the working class and the role of private, family, or community life. See Bilac (1978) and Fausto Neto (1982).

[7] Hidden unemployment was the fastest-growing modality in cities as soon as it began to be measured in the mid-1980s (Dedecca et al. 1993; Dedecca and Montagner 1993).

[8] Herein lies another peculiarity of the Brazilian case. While mainstream academics examined the international scale of the decommodification of labor, a correlate of social welfare regimes erected under Fordism, the "glorious years" (among Brazilians) of expanded Fordism (between 1950 and 1970), were free of these social considerations. In fact, in Brazil, this expansion occurred without universalization of wage work as a lasting employment relationship based on a system of limited protection in terms of benefit coverage, which left to private social relationships both the burden of providing the conditions for tackling unemployment as well as the responsibility for supporting and guiding the search of work.

emergence of new terms coined to name and rank individuals according to their various positions. Thus, the classification systems of companies placed permanent ahead of temporary, sometimes monthly ahead of hourly, and frequently regular ahead of subcontracted or cooperative members.

Thus, there emerges another novelty: no longer was the nature of the occupation (or the professional activity) or the job position itself paramount to differentiating workers. It was the type of employment relationship that became the socially significant label. Notions such as flexibility and precariousness came to the forefront, denoting how individuals were committed to their market engagement, through any form of employment relationship, be it more or less protected, more or less lasting. It also demonstrates the growing maturity of Brazil's labor commodification during the decade of 2000.[9]

This process is confirmed by the way the censuses updated their categories to account for the new reality that presented official statistics to production managers. To reflect this path, we consider the censuses to be sources with special meaning. We put aside the numbers (the results of the measurements) and focused on conceptual definitions found in the actual questions (their phrasing, sequence, the structure of possible answers) and even in the instructions provided to field researchers. Groundbreaking analysis by Paiva (1984), who investigated the censuses from 1940 to 1980, inspired us to observe the changes in the conceptual framework and enumeration of EAP. Like Paiva, we found a movement toward increasing complexity in the measurement of individuals' working conditions, which persists until 2010. That way, we find an increasing number of questions regarding work and income that seek to improve the mechanisms for understanding the phenomenon and providing more sophisticated measurements.

One could rightly argue that there is nothing exceptional about upgrading measurement tools, it being no more than the researcher's obligation. However, the actual process and its course over time may be illustrative of what changes in the reality one wishes to describe and evaluate. Some of these changes are eloquent in that they reveal the intent to better understand new phenomena. Three pieces of evidence are very suggestive in this regard.

The first and perhaps the most significant: the censuses change how they (re) define the EAP, i.e., how they account for the contingent of individuals who come into the labor market (the effective supply) and remain there as employed or unemployed (and as such, seeking work). Paiva (1984) showed that Brazilian censuses only adopted this methodology for accounting for the EAP after 1960. In 1940, the compulsion to offer work in the market was so low that the census did not even measure unemployment; in 1950, even though the unemployed were counted, they were excluded from the EAP and accounted for as inactive population (those who neither had, nor were seeking, work). This EAP until 1960, according to the census, pure and simply coincided with the employed population; it served more as an indicator of occupational structure than as an indicator of labor supply as is currently

[9] For further development of this argument, see Guimarães (2011).

the case. Rather than a counting error,[10] it reveals how unnecessary it was to measure unemployment. Given that there was little pressure for labor market engagement, unemployment was not yet a structural element of labor market organization.

The second piece of evidence: a significant change took place in the response categories regarding measurement of two other key variables dealing with market engagement: employment status, which tracks changes in the social relationship of employment, and the search for work, which documents unemployment as a key reality in a labor market in the midst of crisis and economic restructuring. Only after the 1990s, when unemployment surfaces as a social problem does the urgency to measure it appear in increasingly sophisticated forms. On the one hand, this took the form of further inquiries regarding job seeking, while on the other, it was by changing the reference period in order to account for activity (from 12 months to 1 week), as done in the censuses of 1991, 2000, and 2010.

The third piece of evidence: the 2000 census, particularly the 2010 census, begins to account for income from social protection policies, which also have an impact on pressure to engage in the labor market. Censuses begin to ask about income sources provided by the government that allow children and those outside the appropriate age to be excluded from the market (through policies to eradicate child labor, such as PETI and *Bolsa Escola*), [11] or policies for supporting the elderly through income supplements and, above all, income transfer mechanisms decoupled from the offer of labor *(Bolsa Família, Benefício de Longa Permanência)*. Enhancement of the censuses thus indicates the need to follow a movement that (in accordance with international literature) could potentially point to a decommodification of labor. This, however, occurs precisely when formal jobs expand, i.e., when the most visible element of commodification becomes entrenched, another peculiarity of the Brazilian case.

These examples also reveal how census inquiries had to upgrade their instruments in view of the significant changes at the time. Thus, the refinement of census statistics also reveals the widespread nature of labor commodification in Brazil.

Inflections

The clues identified thus far resonate when one looks at general trends in labor market engagement.

We begin with the behavior of activity rates. This quotient measures the connection between the EAP, our indicator for *effective* labor supply, and the working-age

[10] The difficulty in counting the EAP creates major problems when comparing censuses prior to 1960 with those after (Paiva 1984).

[11] PETI (Programa de Erradicação do Trabalho Infantil, Program to Eradicate Child Labor) and Bolsa Escola were conditional cash benefit programs adopted under President Fernando Henrique Cardoso.

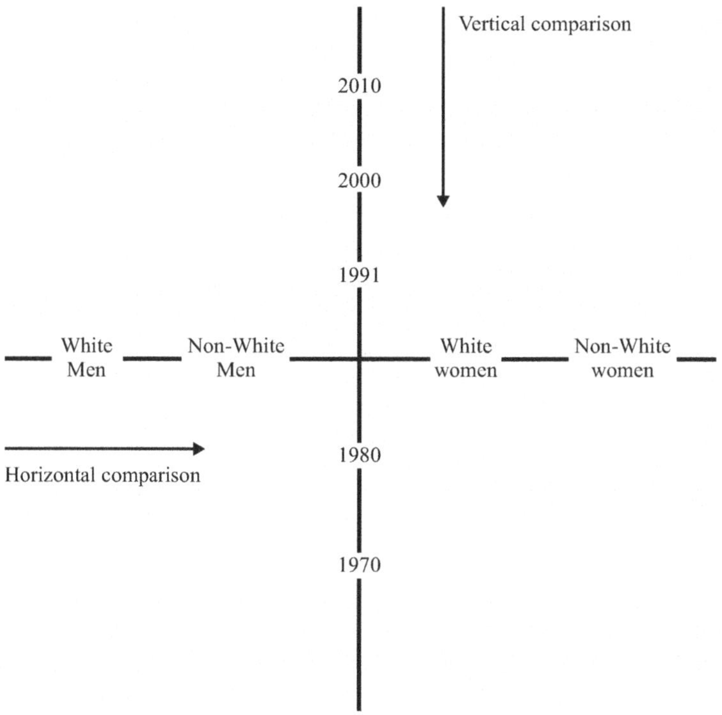

Graph 1 Effective labor supply by gender. Brazil: 1960–2010. (Source: IBGE. Demographic Census 1960–2010 (Special tabulations by CEM))

population (WAP), our indicator for *potential* labor supply: the higher the weight of the numerator, the greater the propensity of individuals to engage in the market, whether as employed or unemployed. We will now look at how labor supply has behaved in the past 50 years.

Graph 1 shows that until the late 1960s in Brazil, most working-age individuals survived without resorting to labor commodification. After 50 years, this situation reversed itself in 2010: 6 out of 10 Brazilians were pushed to engage in economic activity for a living. Systematic growth in the effective labor supply occurs during the period (the solid line goes from 0.47 to 0.61). However, it was not until 1980 that more than half of working-age individuals (potential supply) engaged in the labor market.

This average movement, while important, hides a significant dimension: commodification is mainly a female process. At the beginning of the period in 1960, men dominated the labor market, but by the end of the period, this situation had changed. Nearly 8 out of 10 men eligible to work in 1960 sought their living in the labor market, compared to fewer than 2 out of 10 women. Over the course of these 50 years, the integration of women into the EAP increased nearly fourfold, aligning with the male trend toward high commodification (the female activity rate reached 0.52). The period witnessed an expansion in the number of women entering the

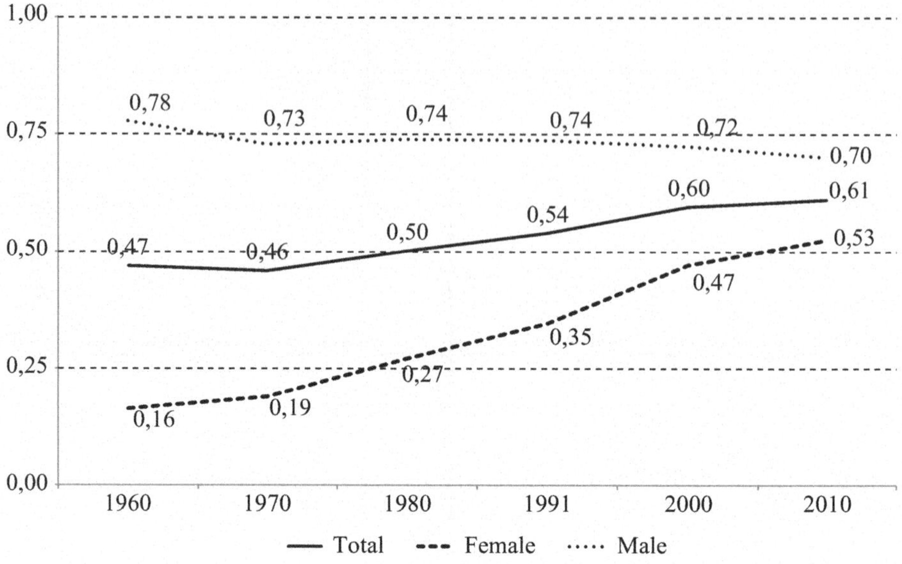

Graph 2 Engagement in the labor market by gender and color. Brazil: 1960–2010 (Note: (1) The absence of the option "color" in the 1970 census prevented its inclusion for this year). (Source: IBGE. Demographic Census 1960–2010 (Special tabulations by CEM))

labor market although a comparison with other countries reveals the particular speed with which this occurred in Brazil over the past 50 years.[12]

This differs from the male engagement pattern: high at the beginning of the period (activity rate of 0.77) with a slight decline in the last two decades (0.70 in 2010). As a result, we find significant convergence between male and female engagement curves (Graph 1), a movement driven by women's swift labor commodification.

Differentials by racial groups are also significant. Whites tend toward higher engagement rates than nonwhites, regardless of gender (Graph 2). Trends once again vary over the years, becoming particularly interesting when observed according to age group. Male engagement not only declines, but the manner in which the reduction occurs also differentiates engagement patterns between age groups: men, especially blacks, tend to accentuate the shape (in the inverted U-shape) of their activity curve due to changes in the age limits, i.e., later entry into, and early retirement from, economic activity.

[12]According to data from the International Labor Organization (ILO) (www.ilo.org) for the same period in France, women's incorporation increased from 0.42 to 0.66; in the United States, it went from 0.39 to 0.68, significantly higher in initial levels than the Brazilian case and much closer to Brazil in ending points. Even in Argentina, a country with late industrialization like Brazil, female engagement reached 0.24 as early as 1960, reaching 0.53 (almost equal to Brazil's level) over these same 50 years. That is, in every case, we find engagement levels higher than Brazilian rates, and growth occurs at a slower pace than ours. For further details on trends, see Costa (2000) and Cipollone et al. (2002).

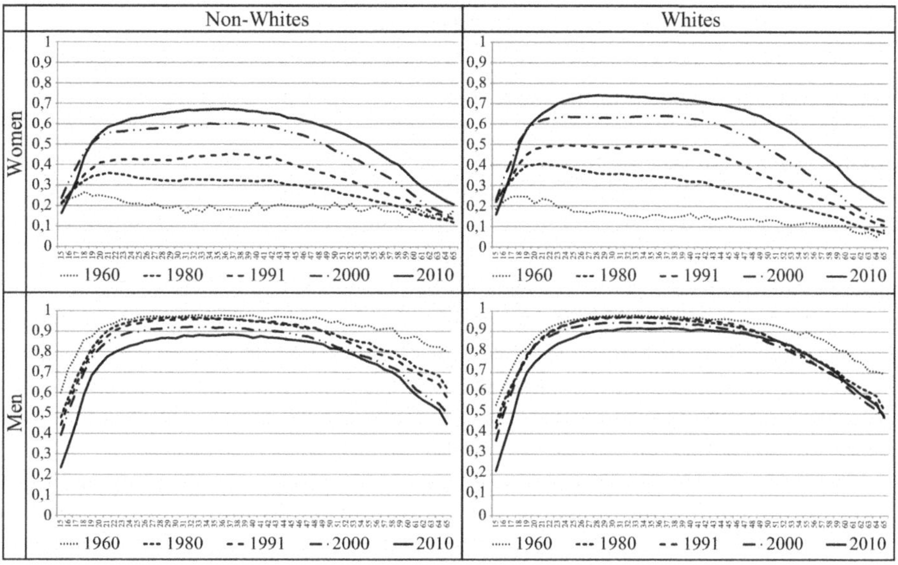

Note: (1) The absence of the option "color" in the 1970 census prevented itsinclusion for this year.

Graph 3 Changes in employment relationships and consolidation of the labor commodification process. Brazil: 1960–2010. (Source: IBGE. Demographic Censuses 1960–2010 (Special tabulations by CEM))

Among women, the expressive expansion in engagement results in an opposite motion. The increase in the labor supply of women – white and nonwhite – occurs precisely during the reproductive ages, making the inverted U-shaped curve increasingly similar to those of men since the 1990s. This growth, more pronounced among white women, is nonetheless also significant among nonwhite women, with swift acceleration in the last two decades.

Changes in the insertion pattern are also noticeable in the growth of effective labor supply within urban-metropolitan, urban nonmetropolitan, and rural contexts, with special emphasis on the dynamics of major cities, on the one hand, and intense transformations in rural areas, on the other.

Widespread labor commodification also reveals changes in employment relationships. Graph 3 shows the combination of two movements: on the one hand, the growing importance of wage employment (expressed in the advancement of the employee status), which since the 1980s encompasses the majority of those with an occupation, and, on the other hand, the systematic decline in the importance of self-employed workers, especially of unpaid family workers.[13]

[13] Commodification also varies according to the level of education. Those who achieved the highest educational transitions (entered into or completed higher education) indicate high rates of participation along with a higher presence of employees and employers, the typical dyad seen in capitalist labor markets. At the other extreme are illiterates, the self-employed, and those working without pay for family members who together are compared with wage employment until the late 1990s.

Engagement Determinants and Inequalities

The decision to compete in the labor market is always an individual prospect, not one limited by the decisions of others. Even in a scenario marked by unequal results among gender and race groups within the labor market, it is possible that there are no differences in the likelihood of competing for a job among such groups. This is because all individuals are able to offer their labor and join the EAP while not all individuals are able to secure the work or position they aspire to or be paid the amount they desire. Therefore, an analysis of engagement odds differs from an analysis of the results obtained in the labor market (e.g., employment rate, position, or income), which run into limitations in terms of the availability of jobs and resources distributed among the number of people offering their labor to the market. In this case, the opportunities and advantages of a group have a direct impact on other groups; this is not the case when we observe labor market engagement.

This particularity is significant for our goal in this section: evolution of the likelihood of engaging in the Brazilian labor market when looking at the population qualified to offer its labor.[14] A focus on the likelihood of an individual opting to turn to the market, prior to observing the results of their inclusion, may indicate the evolutionary direction of Brazil's labor market institutionalization. For this reason, we are interested in analyzing the entire population between the ages of 15 and 65.

Clearly, labor market's appeal to this population is not constant over time. First of all, this is due to the fact that the market structure varies within the system of occupational positions. An occupational structure with a higher proportion of high-skilled occupations tends to have a different appeal than a structure that focuses on low-skilled occupations. Thus, by observing variations in the propensity to engage in the market, one needs to initially consider that individuals make their decisions by considering the differences between occupational structures.

These differences correspond to differences in the performance of the labor market itself. Thus, for example, high unemployment, which indicates a high proportion of individuals unsuccessfully trying to sell their labor, affects the attractiveness of the market and influences the odds of individuals offering their labor, regardless of the occupational structure in which the scenario occurs.

Thus, the likelihood of engagement depends on the form assumed by the link between occupational structure and labor market performance. In our analysis, this comparative approach will be vertical, since it compares the attractiveness of the

[14] For this purpose, we use a version of the Oaxaca-Blinder decomposition (Oaxaca 1973; Blinder 1973) for nonlinear models, according to Fairlie (1999, 2005). Strictly speaking, this decomposition has been designed for linear regression models where the explained variable is continuous, such as income. Since our interest here lies in the individual propensity to engage in the labor market, we need to use nonlinear methods of estimation, hence the use of Fairlie's adaptation. The dependent variable in the model is binary, where 1 is for individuals who make up the EAP, regardless of their employment status, and 0 is for other individuals outside the EAP, albeit considered socially eligible according to their age (between 15 and 65 years).

Fig. 1 Comparison modalities: vertical and horizontal axes

labor market, which is the result of the specific scenario that links its performance and its occupational structure for each census year.

The likelihood of engagement varies between different social segments when the circumstances in which job seeking occurs are kept constant. Given the same scenario of market performance and structure, there are certain characteristics that distinguish the attractiveness of the market among social segments: it matters whether one is male or female, younger or older, black or white, or living in the Northeast or the Southeast. Thus, the characteristics of the population also determine the attractiveness of the market. To understand how labor commodification moves forward in Brazil, we have to investigate the evolution of differences in the likelihood of engagement among different social groups within the same scenario. We call this *horizontal* comparison since we compare the likelihood of engagement for different individual characteristics within a single year. Figure 1 schematically illustrates this argument with vertical and horizontal axes:

The first question refers to the vertical comparison: did the likelihood of resorting to the labor market remain constant between 1970[15] and 2010? Or did varying the link between occupational structure and labor market performance lead to an increase (or decrease) in the likelihood of individuals between the ages of 15 and 65 resorting to the market for their living?

[15] Due to the difficulties faced by the IBGE in processing census information in 1960 (the first planned census to take place with the support of modern computers) and our ignorance regarding the sampling procedure used, which defined the microdata sample, we chose to exclude the year 1960 from the results presented in this section. For more details on the particularities of the 1960 census microdata that formed a basis for this decision, see Barbosa et al. (2013) and Barbosa (2013).

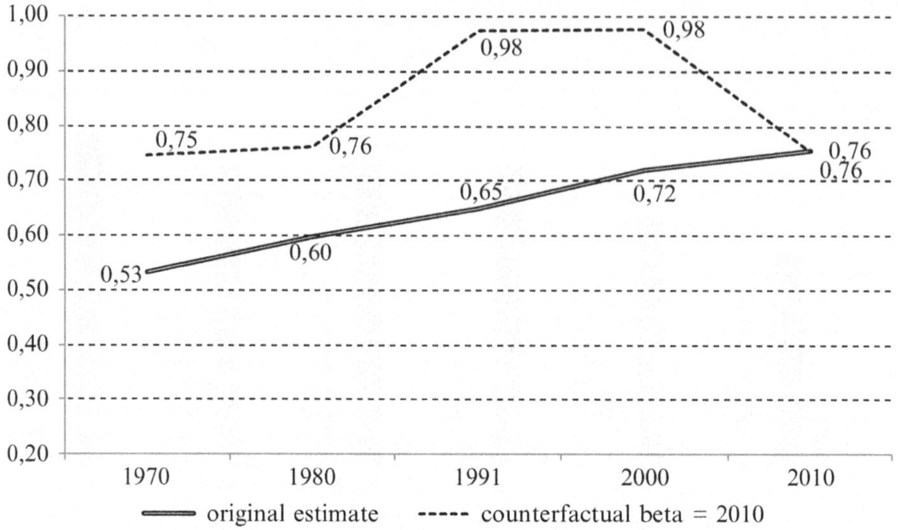

Graph 4 Likelihood of engaging in the labor market among individuals, ages 15–65 years, and the 2010 counterfactual population – vertical comparison. Brazil: 1970–2010. (Source: IBGE. Demographic Censuses 1970–2010 (Special Tabulations by CEM))

In this vertical analytical strategy, we compare the census years as if they were groups. The result allows us to capture market and individual movements within each group, separating them into two components: variations between the years in terms of the propensity to enter the labor market because individuals change over time, and we can observe more characteristics that drive the population toward the market or variations between years in terms of the propensity to enter the labor market due to institutional or structural factors, and thus individuals with the same characteristics most often resort to the market in 1 year rather than in another.

To estimate the propensity of individuals to resort to the labor market, we used the same logistic regression model for every year and for the groups and subgroups of race and gender.[16] The set of variables used to estimate the logit model refer to individual characteristics considered relevant for their market engagement: age, education, and marital status. Others refer to the household setting in which the individual dwells, its size (number of household members), and the relationship between individual habits regarding income (dependency ratio between employed and residents). Still other variables are associated with the context in which individuals and households operate (region and urbanization).

Graph 4 presents the overall probabilities of being part of the EAP among individuals ages 15–65 and a counterfactual exercise, using the parameters observed for the population in 2010.

---

[16] To this end, the basic model does not include gender and race variables since they were used as criteria for defining groups in the counterfactual exercise.

We estimated the likelihood of engagement in each year to draw the vertical comparison; subsequently, by considering the effects observed in the variables used in the 2010 estimate, we estimated the parameters for the likelihood of engagement of the population in other years (Graph 4). In other words, we maintained a constant relationship between structure and performance of the labor market and varied the population characteristics for a counterfactual exercise that evaluates the effects of variables on the likelihood of engagement in 2010. We then applied these same effects to the population in 2000, 1991, etc. From this we obtained a counterfactual distribution of the likelihood of engagement, which can then be compared with the distribution originally observed.

Although the solid line in Graph 4 shows that likelihood of engagement increases between 1970 (53.3%) and 2010 (75.5%), if the distribution of the likelihood of engagement according to individual characteristics were the same as those observed in 2010, we would have very different participation probabilities from the ones empirically found. This indicates changes in the composition effect, i.e., the association between the observed characteristics (used in the estimates, which establish a common model for all years) and the likelihood of engagement – changes in both the specific events observed for each of the variables between years and in the model's capacity to predict the likelihood of engagement.[17] The 1990s and 2000s witnessed a higher likelihood of Brazil's WAP engaging in the labor market; in these decades the characteristics used for the estimates presented the highest association levels with the likelihood of engagement. In 2010 we witness the highest likelihood of engagement empirically observed (in terms of the average level of population) as opposed to 1970 and 1980, but the counterfactual exercise shows that the composition effect overrides the population's characteristics effect. If the likelihood of engagement in 1970 and 1980 had the same association pattern with the variables included in the 2010 estimation, the chances of engaging in the labor market would be much higher.[18] That is, we find a labor market that not only tends to attract an increasing number of individuals but also one in which changes occur over time in the effect of the variables used to analyze the likelihood of engagement (age, region of the country, level of education, census tract, and household composition).

However, to better describe engagement differentials, we should move toward a horizontal comparison, inquiring as to how these differences behave within certain social groups over the years.

---

[17] The results of the logit model estimation, from which we prepared the counterfactual exercise, show significant changes in the effect of age (which tends to rise, increasingly indicating that the older the individual, the greater the likelihood of participating in the labor market), just like the effect of age squared, which tends to be increasingly negative (indicating that advanced age increasingly tends to reduce the likelihood of individual engagement). These results show increasing barriers toward engagement among younger and older population, most likely related to the historical evolution in regulating labor supply among young people still of school age and among the elderly, closer to retirement.

[18] We should note that this difference is maintained even without incorporating the gender variable in the estimate. Here the results correspond to all individuals included in the analysis, regardless of gender.

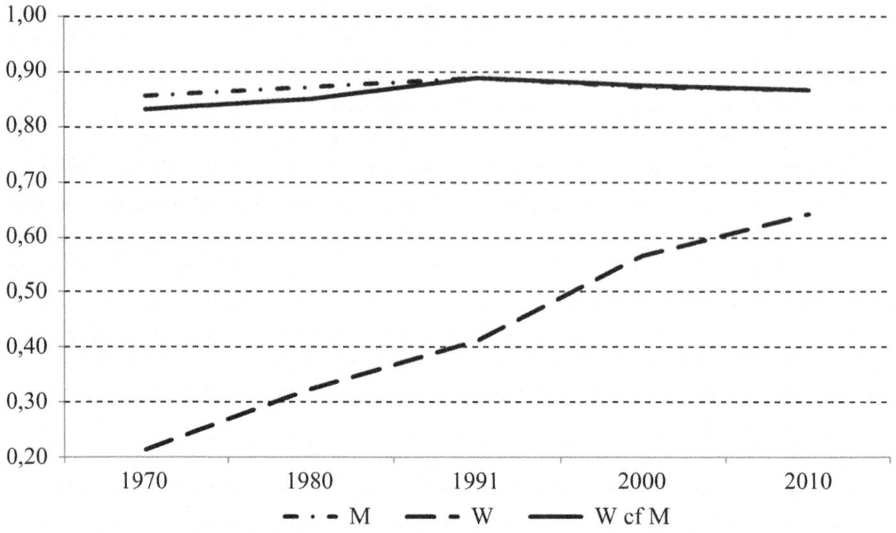

Graph 5 Likelihood of engaging in the labor market by gender and the male counterfactual – horizontal comparison. Brazil: 1970–2010. (Source: IBGE. Demographic Censuses 1970–2010 (Special tabulations by CEM))

The intuition behind the horizontal comparison is similar to the previous one. We estimate the likelihood of engagement per social group each year and apply the observed effects in the reference group to other groups, thus establishing the counterfactual exercise. The difference between the observed probabilities and the obtained counterfactuals may indicate segmentation between groups, since it eliminates the possibility that we are dealing with differences in the population characteristics within each group.

Graph 5 presents the results of likelihood of market engagement by gender. The clues concerning the weight of female engagement in consolidating labor commodification in Brazil led us to compare the observed and counterfactual probabilities by gender groups. Graph 5 shows the original likelihood for men and women (dotted lines) and the likelihood for women using male parameters (solid line).

The results show a clear increase in the likelihood of women engaging in the labor market, from just over 20% in 1970 to over 60% in 2010. However, if we assign them conditions similar to those of men, gender differences become almost nonexistent after 1991. This indicates that these differences are not based on the characteristics of the group; that is, the likelihood of engagement of men and women are different beginning in 1960, although these populations are not as different when we look at other characteristics.

These results point to significant changes in the determinants of the likelihood of engaging in the labor market. The likelihood of women's engagement constituted one of the main factors behind this change and significantly increased their likelihood to turn to the labor market, with gender segmentation becoming increasingly less important for participation in the market.

Could the same change be observed in the working-age population distinguished by gender and race?[19] Faced with the vast literature identifying different *results* in the labor market between men and women and between whites and nonwhites, always at the expense of women and nonwhites, could the same differences be found with regard to the change that preceded this one: the very decision to offer one's labor in exchange for monetary compensation?

Graph 6 presents, on the left, the likelihood of engaging in the labor market by gender and race.[20] Throughout the entire period, white and nonwhite men have a similar and stable likelihood of joining the workforce, ranging between 85.5% and 89.4%. In turn, white and nonwhite women in the early 1980s had a likelihood estimated at just over 30%, quite disparate from those of men. By 2010, after just 30 years, women's propensity for turning to the labor market, whatever their racial status, had doubled. Although effectively declining over the period, inequalities regarding men as well as the gap between white and nonwhite women increased.

Graph 6 also attempts to answer another question by means of the figure on the right: what would the result have been if factors determining one's propensity to resort to the labor market had the same effect on the likelihood of engagement of men and women, whites, and nonwhites? To this end, we present the likelihood of engagement for black men, white women, and black women as if there were no differences between these groups in the factors driving them to the labor market. Unlike the results obtained for the original probabilities (on the left), the distinction between gender and race groups now becomes much less clear.

This indicates that differences between these groups regarding their original and counterfactual likelihood of engagement cannot be explained by differences in individual characteristics but rather by differences in the return (likelihood of engagement) on these characteristics among the groups. Therefore, while race is an important determinant for the exchanges (between work and pay) that occur within the Brazilian labor market, there is no reason to believe it significantly differentiates individuals with regard to their propensity to engage in economic activity. Gender is considerably more significant than race.[21]

[19] Guimarães (2012) explores the sociological controversies over the use of the terms "race," "color," and "skin color" to define Brazil's racial classification system. His argument states that the Brazilian system is becoming increasingly based on physical traits and less on the "whitening ideology," which used to identify color more directly with social status. He argues that the Brazilian system was never based purely on skin color. On the other hand, Brazilian censuses (from 1960 to 2010) do not ask the question "what *race* are you" but instead "what *color* are you," up until 1980 and "what *color/race* are you," from 1991 on. That is why we will use the term "color" rather than "skin color," when dealing with racial self-identification as recorded in Brazilian censuses.

[20] We were unable to conduct the exercise involving gender and racial groups using 1970 census data because that year, the survey did not include questions about color or race. In order to conduct an Oaxaca-Blinder decomposition, models for all groups and years have to contain the same variables.

[21] Note, however, that even in the counterfactual exercise, some differences persist, especially since 1991, when nonwhites, male and female, displayed a slightly lower propensity than white groups. These differences can be attributed to inequalities in the average characteristics of people belonging to each of the racial groups.

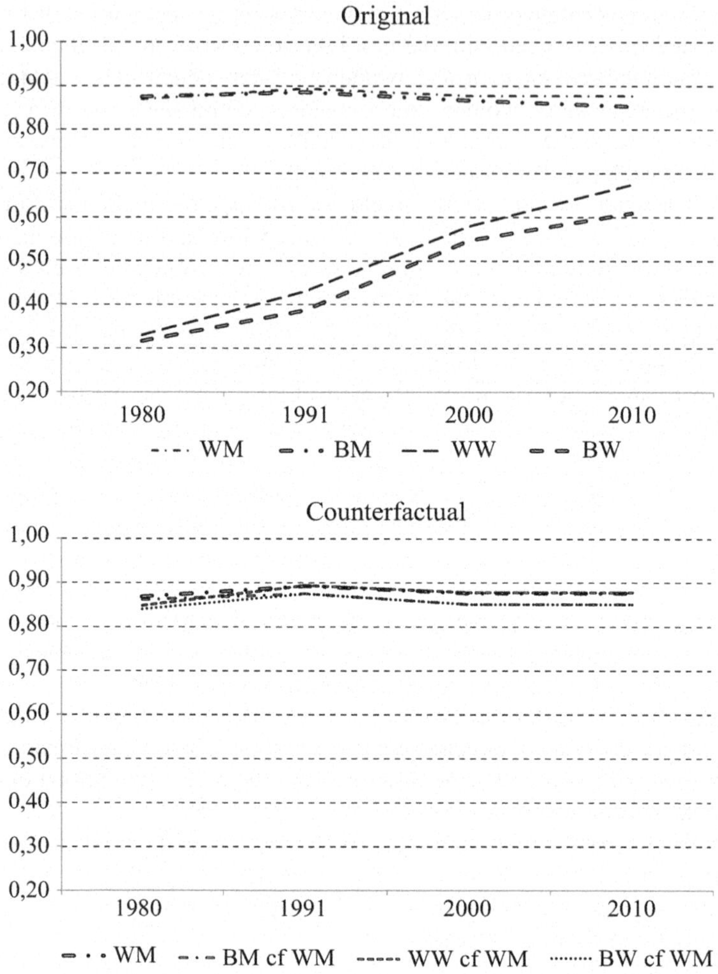

Graph 6 Likelihood of engaging in the labor market by gender and race and the likelihood of market engagement using the counterfactual analysis of white men for the same year (horizontal comparison). Brazil: 1980–2010. (Source: IBGE. Demographic Censuses 1980–2010 (Special tabulations by CEM))

Conclusion

In the past 50 years, the labor market in Brazil has established itself as a space in which individuals are pressed to seek a living. This process involves expanding the effective labor supply, which means increasing the weight of the EAP (employed and unemployed) among working-age individuals.

Specific circumstances resulting from the link between occupational structure and labor market performance define the parameters of market attractiveness since they derive from different returns. The vertical comparison – between census years –

demonstrated how the Brazilian labor market clearly tends to be an increasingly relevant space for working-age individuals. However, the return in terms of likelihood of market engagement due to individual characteristics (education, region, age, and household composition) has made participation levels in 2010 similar to those found in 1980, and well below those observed in 1991 and 2000, even with increased likelihood of participation. This points to a change in the parameters defining engagement rates, which occurs alongside an increase in the likelihood of participation and, above all, with advances in social policy measures, responsible, for the first time in the past 50 years, for reducing the compulsion to seek survival in the labor market.[22]

Individual characteristics also proved to be relevant. Particularly significant were the inflections in the number of women in the market. Data indicate that propensities were not only different but also varied in different ways over time. The evolution of the distinguishing features of gender groups shows that the likelihood of women resorting to the labor market varies greatly over the years. While women did not attain the same levels of participation as did men in 2010, there is a marked growth in their likelihood of participation. However, differences in the characteristics of men and women do not explain the distinguishing features of the engagement but rather the varied return on these characteristics between men and women across all census years. This helps us understand how, in the Brazilian labor market, the likelihood of participation greatly increases even if the variation explained by the characteristics is lower in 1970, 1980, and 2010 than in 1991 and 2000.

Once we learned about gender and race inequalities from the results obtained in the labor market, we tested whether there would be distinguishing features in play just prior to the market. That prelude often makes individuals unequal in terms of the likelihood of offering themselves as workers. Our question is, then, if such likelihood could be explained by factors specific to each gender and race group based on the variables used in the estimation (individual attributes, family group, and the context in which work is provided).

In short, the past 50 years were decisive for Brazil's achieving widespread commodification of its workforce. The labor market that in the 1960s retained only 4 out of 10 Brazilians by 2010 had become a compelling space for survival among nearly 7 out of 10 working-age Brazilians. Moreover, the market, once a male domain, substantially altered its gender composition through key interfaces with other processes analyzed in several chapters within this book, such as the reduction of fertility rates and the significant expansion of female education.

Such changes have not gone unnoticed and have stimulated multiple narratives from the academic literature, encouraging significant changes in the census metrics. But above all, they challenge current interpretations and inspire us to understand how labor commodification develops and becomes widespread.[23] While experiences

---

[22] Note that setbacks in social protection policies in a context of such intense commodification of labor may result in the expansion of poverty and inequality levels mainly by rising unemployment and/or poor-quality jobs.

[23] Sophisticated academic arguments indicate a reverse trend, i.e., the decommodification of labor in the wake of the construction of welfare regimes based on social policies allowing workers some autonomy with regard to the market circuit.

in protection seem to have exhausted themselves elsewhere, Brazil in the early 2000s provided a counterexample, increasing job opportunities and ensuring rights that no longer stem from labor market integration. As in any social process, reversals and setbacks can never be excluded from the horizon. Nevertheless, this recent combination between labor commodification and the enhancement of social protection challenges interpretations and underscores the complexity of national dynamics. Are we witnessing a Brazilian style of labor commodification?

References

Barbosa, R. J. (2013). *Nota Técnica: Instruções para o uso dos bancos de microdados das amostras dos Censos Demográficos Brasileiros (1960 a 2010)*. São Paulo. Disponível em. http://www.fflch.usp.br/centrodametropole/upload/aaa/517-nstru%C3%A7%C3% B5es_para_os_Censos_out_2013.pdf. Accessed Feb 2014.

Barbosa, R. J., Marschner, M., Ferrari, D., Silva, P., Prates, I., & Barone, L. S. (2013). Ciências sociais, censo e informação quantitativa no Brasil: entrevista com Elza Berquó e Nelson do Valle Silva. *Novos Estudos CEBRAP, 95*, 143–155.

Bilac, E. D. (1978). *Famílias de trabalhadores — estratégias de sobrevivência: a organização da vida familiar em uma cidade paulista*. São Paulo: Edições Símbolo.

Blinder, A. S. (1973). Wage discrimination: Reduced form and structural variables. *Journal of Human Resources, 8*, 436–455.

Cardoso, A. M. (2000). *Trabalhar, verbo transitivo. Destinos profissionais dos deserdados da indústria automobilística*. Rio de Janeiro: Editora FGV.

Cardoso, A. M. (2010). *A construção da sociedade do trabalho no Brasil. Sociabilidade capitalista, padrões de justiça e persistência das desigualdades*. Rio de Janeiro: Editora FGV.

Cipollone, A, Patacchini, E., & Vallanti, G. (2002). *Women labor market performance in Europe: Trends and shaping factors*. http://www.neujobs.eu/sites/default/files/event/2012/03/VALLANTI-REPORT_complete.pdf. Accessed July 2013.

Costa, D. (2000). From mill town to board room: The rise of women's paid labor. *Journal of Economic Perspectives, 14*(4), 101–122.

Dedecca, C., & Montagner, P. (1993). *Flexibilidade produtiva e das relações de trabalho: considerações sobre o caso brasileiro*. Campinas: Instituto de Economia da Unicamp (Discussion paper, no. 29).

Dedecca, C., Montagner, P., & Brandão, S. (1993). *Recessão e reestruturação econômica: as novas condições de funcionamento do mercado de trabalho na década de 90*. Campinas: Instituto de Economia da Unicamp.

Durham, E. (1973). *A caminho da cidade: a vida rural e a emigração para São Paulo*. São Paulo: Editora Perspectiva.

Erickson, K. (1979). *Sindicalismo no processo político do Brasil*. São Paulo: Brasiliense.

Esping-Andersen, G. (1990). *The three worlds of welfare capitalism*. Princeton: Princeton University Press.

Fairlie, R. W. (1999). The absence of the African-American owned business: An analysis of the dynamics of self-employment. *Journal of Labor Economics, 17*, 80–108.

Fairlie, R. W. (2005). An extension of the Blinder–Oaxaca decomposition technique to logit and probit models. *Journal of Economic and Social Measurement, 30*, 305–316.

Fausto Neto, A. M. Q. (1982). *Família operária e reprodução da força de trabalho*. Rio de Janeiro: Vozes.

Gomes, A. C. (1979). *Burguesia e trabalho: política e legislação social no Brasil, 1917–1937*. Rio de Janeiro: Editora Campus.

Gomes, A. C. (1988). *A invenção do trabalhismo*. Rio de Janeiro: Editora Vértice.
Guimarães, N. A. (2004). *Caminhos cruzados: estratégias de empresas e trajetórias de trabalhadores*. São Paulo: Ed. 34.
Guimarães, N. A. (2011). O que muda quando se expande o assalariamento (e em que o debate da sociologia pode nos ajudar a compreendê-lo)? *Dados, 54*, 97–130.
Guimarães, A. S. A. (2012). The Brazilian system of racial classification. *Ethnic and Racial Studies, 35*(7), 1157–1162.
Hirata, H., & Humphrey, J. (1989). Trabalhadores desempregados: trajetórias de operárias e operários industriais no Brasil. *Revista Brasileira de Ciências Sociais, 11*(4), 71–84.
Lopes, J. R. B. (1964). *Sociedade industrial no Brasil*. São Paulo: Difusão Européia do Livro.
Lopes, J. R. B. (1967). *A crise do Brasil arcaico*. Difusão Européia do Livro: São Paulo.
Machado Da Silva, L. A. (1971). *Mercados metropolitanos de trabalho manual e marginalidade*. Master's thesis. Universidade Federal do Rio de Janeiro, Programa de Pós-Graduação em Antropologia do Museu Nacional.
Oaxaca, R. (1973). Male-female wage differentials in urban labor markets. *International Economics Review, 14*(3), 693–709.
Oliveira, M. C. F. A. (1988). *Mercantilização e urbanização em São Paulo*. Campinas:Unicamp/NEPO (NEPO Papers, 14).
Paiva, P. T. A. (1984). A conceituação e a enumeração da população economicamente ativa nos censos demográficos brasileiros. In ABEP (Ed.), *Censos, consensos, contra-sensos* (pp. 9–66). Ouro Preto: ABEP.
Rodrigues, L. M. (1970). *Industrialização e atitudes operárias*. São Paulo: Brasiliense.
Santos, W. G. (1979). *Cidadania e justiça*. Rio de Janeiro: Campus.
Vianna, L. W. (1976). *Liberalismo e sindicato no Brasil*. Rio de Janeiro: Paz e Terra.

Conclusion: A Half-Century of Change

Marta Arretche

Abstract This concluding chapter summarizes some of the insights that have emerged from the study of a half-century of change presented along the chapters of the book *Paths of Inequality in Brazil – A Half-Century of Changes*. It shows that Brazil's democracy gave way to reductions in inequality in a number of significant dimensions. However, despite such dramatic changes, inequality has remained resilient in a number of relevant dimensions during the first decade of the twenty-first century. This chapter also addresses some theoretical controversies of the comparative literature on inequality. It discusses whether high inequality can lead to democracy and redistribution and whether wealth concentration is compatible with income redistribution. It demonstrates that well-being consists of more than just the income dimension, favoring then for the study of the multidimensionality of inequality in order to better understand the mechanisms through which accumulation of advantages/disadvantages remains. It finally argues that inequality reduction is the result of a combination of factors, which means that any monocausal theory of the phenomena cannot capture its encompassing dynamics.

Keywords Brazil · Inequality · Democracy · Redistribution · Social policy

Early twenty-first-century Brazil is tremendously different from the Brazil of the 1960s. This was evident in every dimension examined in our study. The lives of women have undergone a silent revolution in education, occupation, and income. The ways Brazilians organize themselves, as families or in their political lives outside the family, have taken on forms that could not have been foreseen in the 1960s. Religious affiliation has changed significantly as the century-old monopoly of Catholicism gave way to religious pluralism rather than agnosticism. Brazilians became much more educated, and as a result of better conditions in terms of health

M. Arretche (✉)
Department of Political Science, University of São Paulo, São Paulo, Brazil

Center for Metropolitan Studies, São Paulo, Brazil
e-mail: arretche@usp.br

M. Arretche (ed.), *Paths of Inequality in Brazil*,
https://doi.org/10.1007/978-3-319-78184-6_15

and sanitation, life expectancy at birth has increased about 20 years over the span of 50 years our study focused on.

Recognized throughout the world as a champion of inequality, Brazil, like many other Latin American countries, embarked upon a trajectory quite unlike that of many advanced democracies, which saw the rise of poverty and inequality from the 1970s on (Piketty and Saez 2014). From the early 1990s, Brazil's democracy gave way to reductions in inequality in a number of significant dimensions, such as income, access to schooling and health, as well as access to basic household services (electricity, garbage collection, water, and sanitation). Gender and race gaps also diminished. The transition to democracy was geared toward the *inclusion of outsiders*: nearly half of Brazilians who were once denied the right to health-care and pension benefits as a result of their precarious engagement in the job market are now entitled to such rights regardless of insurance contributions. Moreover, incremental access to basic household conditions has now reached those at the bottom strata of income distribution.

The *inclusion of outsiders* was brought about by paradigmatic changes to the conservative social policy regime (Esping-Andersen 1985) launched in the mid-1930s and preserved by the limited democratic regime (1946–1964) and the military regime (1964–1985) (Draibe 1994; Santos 1979). Such a model of social policy produced a great divide between *insiders* and *outsiders*, since it protected only those engaged in the formal labor market, within the context of a small urban industrial sector and high rates of unemployment (see the chapter by Alvaro Comin in this volume and Huber and Stephens 2012: 78; Roberts 2012). In addition, not only were *outsiders* excluded from benefits, but they also contributed to the funding of such benefits. Under the import substitution model, the costs of social protection of *insiders* were transferred to product prices and thus paid by all consumers. Family income then had a major effect on access to education (see chapter by Ribeiro, Ceneviva, and Brito, in this volume) and housing conditions (see chapter by Marques, in this volume), not to mention health care and pensions. Based on a mechanism of accumulation of advantages, *insiders* obtained channels of access to state policies from which *outsiders* were excluded. Social policies produced a sort of fusion of advantages/disadvantages upon the same individuals, meaning that income and state benefits could easily go hand in hand. From the early 1990s, economic inequality reduction, along with factors exogenous to policies themselves, was a by-product of the *inclusion of outsiders*, a mechanism through which access to different social benefits was incrementally, although at different speeds, de-linked from income and social background. Such a process entitled those at the middle and bottom strata of income distribution to social rights.

However, despite such dramatic changes, inequality has remained resilient in a number of relevant dimensions during the first decade of the twenty-first century. First of all, the gains described above appear as striking as they do because the point of departure was an outrageous level of exclusion, which cannot be justified on economic grounds (de Barros et al. 2000). Brazilian GDP tripled from 1960 to 1980, yet industrialization did not result in the rapid changes in the occupational structure Kuznets had predicted (1955). Accelerated de-ruralization translated into precarious engagement in the urban job market due to high rates of fertility among the poor (see the chapter by Oliveira et al., in this volume) and very low levels of schooling on the part of rural and urban workers (see chapter by Menezes-Filho and Kirschbaum as well as Alvaro Comin, in this volume), and both factors garnered a large supply of low-skilled workers. In 1980, nearly half (43%) of the Brazilian workforce was functionally illiterate, meaning that it had at most 3 years of education. One-third (33%) had not achieved complete primary education. Better jobs were of course held by the remaining one-fourth, among which only 3% of the total workforce had earned an academic degree (see Graph 3 in the chapter by Naercio Menezes-Filho and Charles Kirschbaum, in this volume). In 2010, functional illiteracy among the economically active population (EAP) fell nearly 30 points, to 17%, while the number of workers who had completed 8 years of education jumped from 4 to 17 million. Yet they still constituted just one-fifth of the workforce. The scarcity in the number of high school degree holders diminished, since their number had gone from 5.6 million in 1980 to 37.5 million in 2010. In spite of such an inclusion effort, they did not surpass one-fourth of the workforce in 2010 (see Graph 3 in Naercio Menezes-Filho and Charles Kirschbaum, in this volume).

In 1980, the average infant mortality rate was 85 per 1000 live births, but variation ranged from 133 per 1000 live births in Brazil's poorest Northeast to 54 per 1000 live births in its affluent South. In 2010, this indicator plummeted to 16 per 1000 live births and was accompanied by a reduction in the cross-region gap: the poorest Northeast showed a rate of 19, while the rate in the affluent South was 11.5 (see Graph 1 in the chapter by Coelho and Dias, in this volume). Despite an 81% decrease, Brazil was still some distance from OECD countries, whose rates are around 5 per 1000 live births (World Bank Data – IBRD-IDA).

Still, the mechanism of accumulation of disadvantages provided that in 1981, only 19% of households whose per capita income placed them at the 11th vintile had access to sewage collection. In 2015, those in the same condition, that is, at the 11th vintile with access to sanitation, numbered 55%. Despite a 65% rate of advancement in this indicator, nearly half of households still lacked access to basic sanitation services. In sum, although inclusion has been remarkable in several dimensions, conditions at the point of departure explain part of the remaining levels of inequality.

Second, some dimensions of inequality revealed themselves to be more resilient than others. Two social revolutions struck the world in the 1960s: the feminist movement and the civil rights movement. Both aimed at equality before the law as a way to eliminate discrimination and segregation according to either gender or race. Although both gaps diminished, in terms of either income or education, women fared much better than nonwhites. The Brazil of the 1960s, where the worlds of education and employment consisted mainly of white males, no longer exists. However, the distance between women and men in 2010 was much smaller than that between whites and nonwhites.

Graphs 1 and 2 depict the earning gap ratios by gender and race according to vintile from the early 1980s to 2015.[1] Low-skilled women, at the bottom strata of

[1] Annual data on earnings by race is available only from 1987 on.

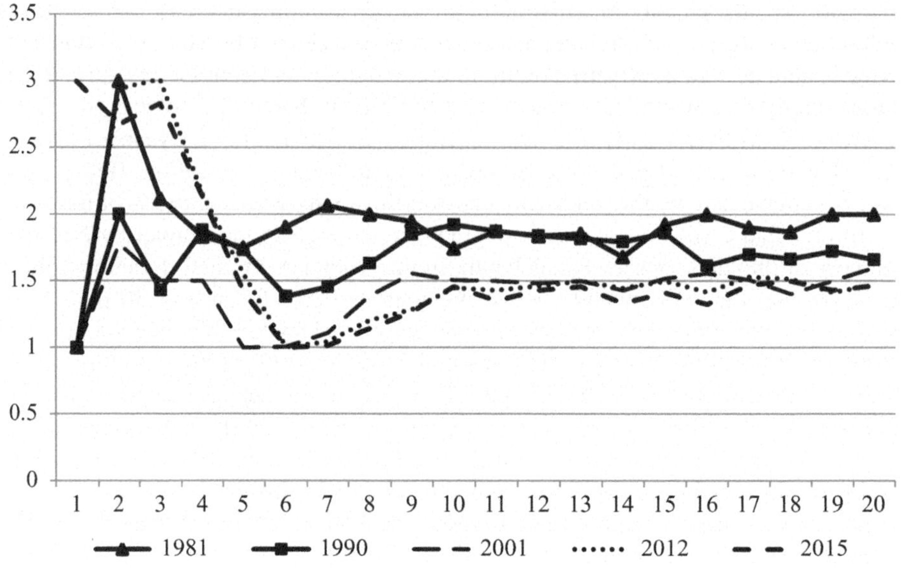

Graph 1 Gender earning gap ratios, Brazil, 1981–2015. (Source: National Household Sample Survey, 1981–2015 (IBGE). Note: Units of observation are individuals

income distribution, earn much less than men in the same strata. However, among those whose earnings are around the 6th vintile, which roughly corresponds to the statutory minimum wage, income inequality was eliminated if we compare 1981 and 1990 to the twenty-first century, when this ratio stood at 1. As for the rest of the scale, gender income gap ratios declined from 2 in 1981 to 1.5 beginning in 2001. In addition, values are more or less the same regardless of income distribution strata.

The earning gap in terms of color achieves higher values as income increases, meaning that the distance in incomes between whites and nonwhites becomes greater as nonwhites obtain higher earnings. Although values for the color earning gaps also decreased from the late twentieth to the early twenty-first centuries, they are higher than those found for gender: from 2 up to 3 in 1987 and 1991 while values for 2001 range from 1.5 to 2.5. A further step-down is obtained in 2012 and 2015, since at that point values range from 1.5 to 2. Although the path toward income inequality reduction is similar regarding either gender or race, baselines are quite different.

Nonwhites have usually been the last to be included in education, so much so that race inequality only disappears when access becomes universal. When school slots in primary education eventually become available to everyone, the gap between whites and nonwhites then shifts to high school. The white male university world of the 1960s was radically changed to incorporate women, but nonwhites did not share the same fate until 2010 (see the chapters by Ribeiro and Schlegel and Lima and Prates, in this volume).

Cross-region inequality also revealed itself as resilient. The industrialization Brazil underwent from the mid-1960s on produced a big divide between affluent

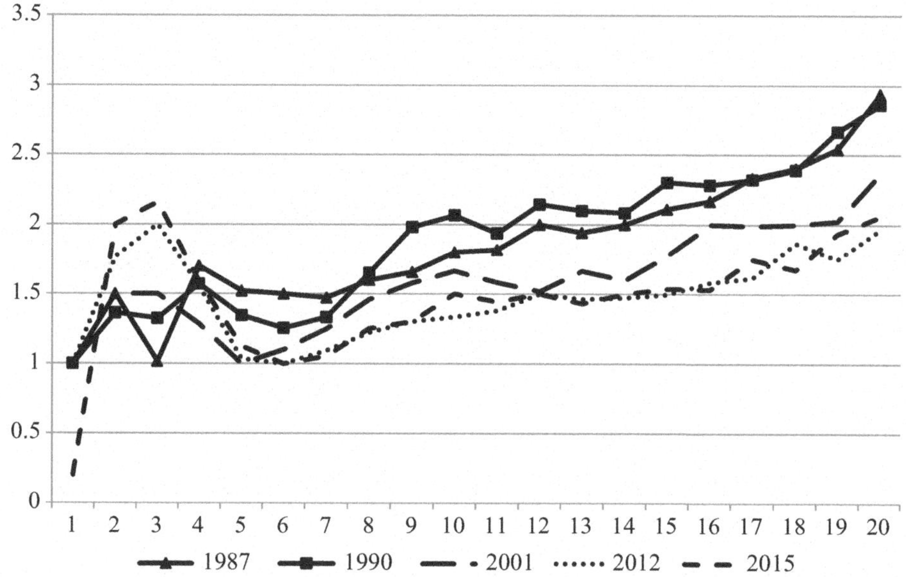

Graph 2 Color earning gap ratios, Brazil, 1987–2015. (Source: National Household Sample Survey, 1981–2015 (IBGE). Note: Units of observation are individuals

and poorer regions, meaning that job opportunities and access to basic household living conditions were concentrated in the former while the latter lacked both (see the chapter by Marta Arretche, in this volume). As a result, massive emigration flows from poorer regions to more affluent ones turned out to be a demographic characteristic of Brazil: an average of 10 million people by decade (see the chapter by Jose Marcos Pinto da Cunha, in this volume). Such a territorial divide only evened out in the equalizing period Brazil underwent starting in the mid-1990s. However, low income and inadequate service provision still prevail in the North and Northeast regions, while higher income and adequate service provision are seen in the South and Southern regions (see the chapters by Marta Arretche and by Eduardo Marques, in this volume).

Finally, the speed of inclusion has been all but even along different dimensions. Income (as shown above), health, and access to electricity fared better than other areas. Graph 3 presents the Gini coefficient for household per capita income, from 1981 to 2016, based on survey data collected by the Brazilian Institute of Geography and Statistics (IBGE). It shows that income inequality indeed climbed throughout the democratic transition, reaching a peak in 1989 at the end of President Sarney's term, before starting a steady decline. It accelerated from 2001 on, particularly throughout the two terms of left-wing President Lula and President Dilma Rousseff. Soares (2010), also using survey data, shows that such rates were comparable to those seen in Sweden as it began its long-term process of income inequality decline. However, the Brazilian path spanned just 15 years, being open what will happen in the future.

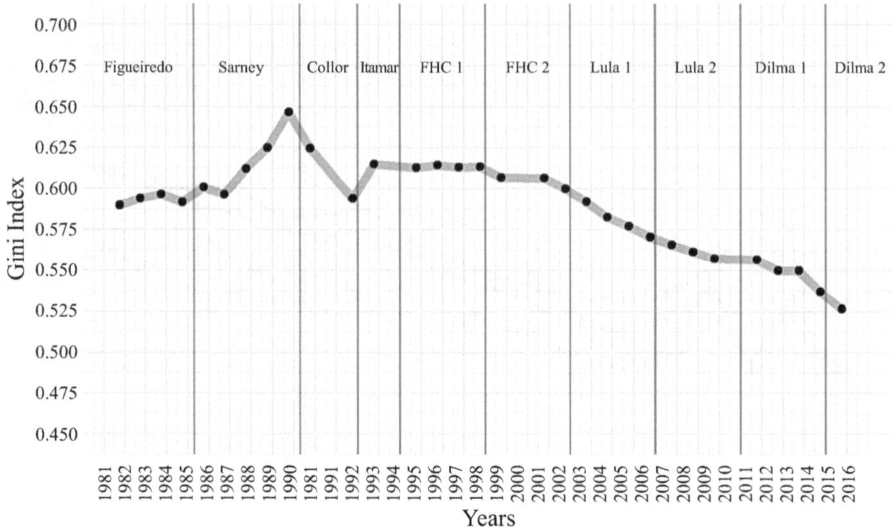

Graph 3 Gini coefficient – household per capita income, Brazil, 1981–2016. (Source: National Household Sample Survey, 1981–2016 (IBGE). Note: Units of observation are households, not individuals. Nonrelatives of household head were excluded. There was no data collection in 1991, 1994, 2000, and 2010.)

Graph 4 shows an example of the mechanism of accumulation of advantages/disadvantages, as it refers to the association between household income and access to electricity. Back in 1981, electricity was not a problem for better-off households, yet among those at the 2nd vintile of income distribution, more than 60% had no power connection. Among those at the 6th vintile, around 40% had no connection. The incremental inclusion of the worse off accompanied the transition to democracy, whereas those left behind went on to obtain access under the left-wing government of President Lula starting in 2003. This incorporation has a territorial expression due to the concentration of poor people in the North and Northeast regions (see the chapter by Marta Arretche, in this volume). In any case, with regard to this particular dimension, facts do not confirm the proposition that inclusion of the poor can be explained by power in the hands of a left-wing party in government. Instead, the inclusion process is one whose path is incremental and coincides with the transition to democracy and to democracy itself.

Other dimensions fared much worse, notably the inclusion of nonwhites, and sewage collection, whose pace, although improving, proved to be much slower. Graph 5 displays data on household access to sewage collection systems according to household income vintile from 1981 to 2015. While the path is like that of electricity, the pace is not. A similar association between household income and access to service and a similar incremental process of increasing incorporation are present, but baselines are much slower. The trajectory is one of resilient inequality, albeit

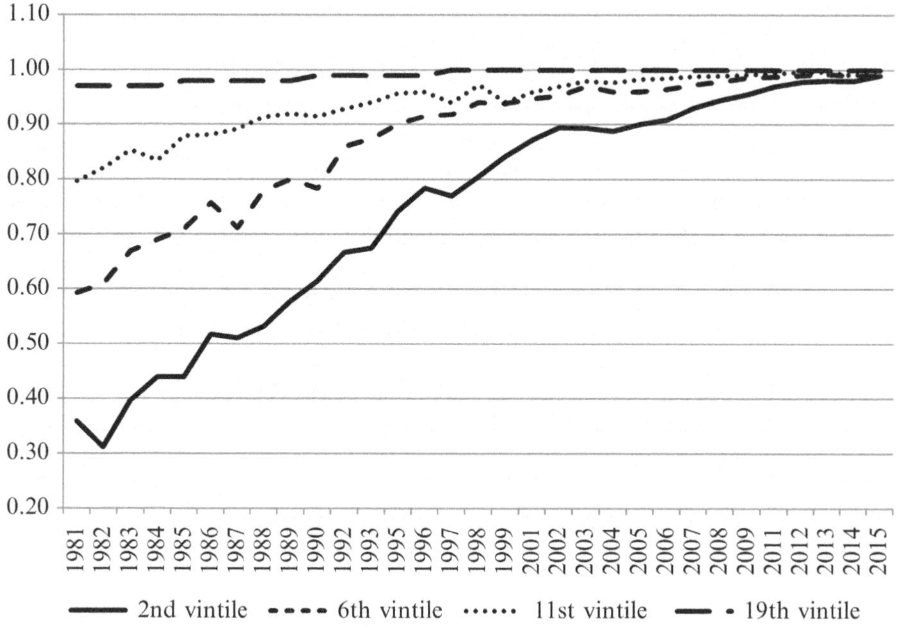

Graph 4 Access to electricity by household income vintile: 1981–2015. (Source: National Household Sample Survey, 1981–2015 (IBGE). Note: There was no data collection in 1991, 1994, 2000, or 2010)

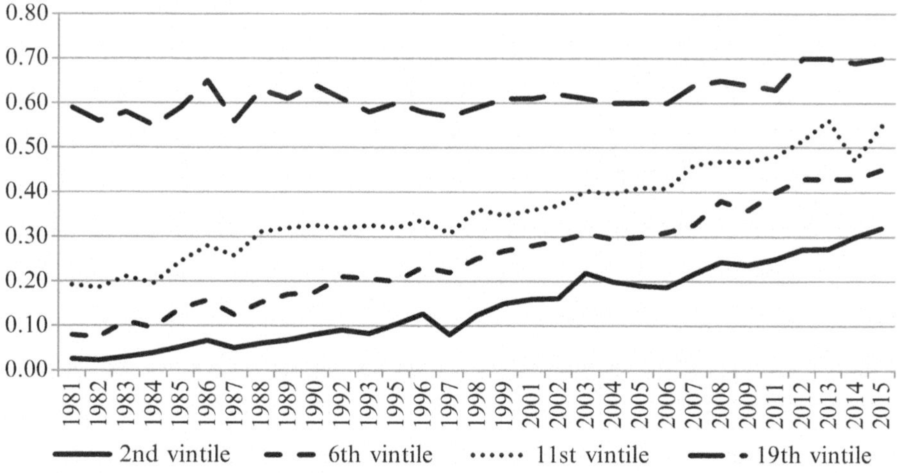

Graph 5 Access to sewage collection by household income vintile; 1981–2015. (Source: National Household Sample Survey, 1981–2015 (IBGE). Note: There was no data collection in 1991, 1994, 2000, or 2010)

with slow inclusion of those at the bottom strata of income distribution. In 2015, nearly 70% of households whose earnings were at the 2nd vintile lacked sanitation services. Even among median income households, nearly half had no access to such services. Many of them are spatially concentrated in the poorest regions.

The inevitable question a reader of this book might ask refers to what occurred after 2013, when Brazil experienced an economic downturn. Graph 6 shows data on annual growth in Brazilian GDP as well on unemployment from 1981 to 2016. Because the IBGE method for calculating unemployment has changed, two indexes are shown: one refers to 1981–2012 (based on the National Household Sample Survey – PNAD), and the other refers to 2012–2016 (based on the Continuous National Household Sample Survey). Data shows the dramatic drop in Brazilian GDP from 2013 on. It increased only 0.5% in 2014 and registered −3.8% in 2015, falling again in 2016 to −3.6%. Similar economic crises occurred between 1988 and 1992 as well as between 1981 and 1983, when annual GDP variation registered very small growth rates or was negative. Although the two unemployment indexes displayed are not directly comparable because of the different methodologies used, data indicates that from 2013 on, those seeking employment and not finding a job jumped from around 6% to nearly 12% of EAP. A similar jump occurred from 1995

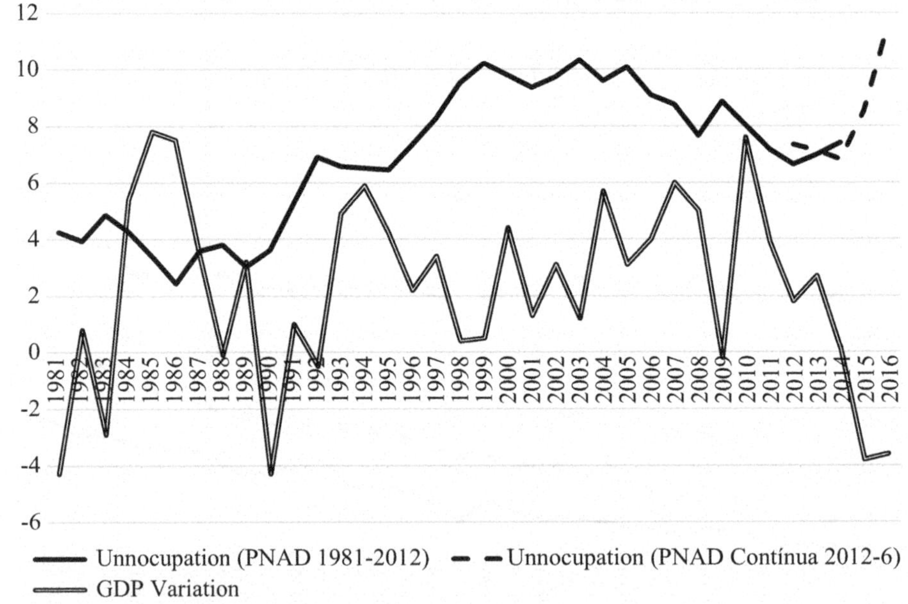

Graph 6 Annual growth rates in GDP and unemployment; 1981–2016. (Source: National Household Sample Survey, 1981–2012 (IBGE); Continuous National Household Sample Survey, 2012–2016 (IBGE); National Accounting System (IBGE). Note: (1) There was no data collection under the National Household Sample Survey in 1991, 1994, 2000, or 2010. For these years, unemployment was calculated by means of interpolation. (2) Underemployed refers to those individuals over the age of 15 who looked for a job and worked less than 1 hour, either in the formal or informal job market, during the week data was collected.)

to 1999, when unemployment behaved in a similar fashion. To make household earnings even more dramatic, annual inflation rates (as calculated by the IBGE's Extended National Consumer Price Index – IPCA) jumped from 6.4 in 2014 to 10.7 in 2015, before falling back to 6.4 in 2016. However, these inflation rates are quite low if compared to the 1987–1994 period, when the annual variation was around 2000 (IPCA/IBGE, available at IPEADATA).

It is possible to compare inequality of income losses in those adverse economic contexts. We can examine whether individuals' earnings declined or not and, more importantly, how these possible losses were distributed across different income strata. Graph 7 displays information about relative income gains by vintile (either from the job market or from government transfers) for these three different contexts. Earnings from the last year of recession/unemployment were compared to those for the year before the phenomenon of interest began. So, as GDP dropped from 1987 to 1988 and the economy started recovering in 1992, the earnings from each vintile in 1992 were compared to those obtained in 1987. The same calculation was used to compare 1999 to 1995 and 2015 to 2012.

Since this data was obtained through surveys, we know that the income of the wealthiest is underestimated, meaning that the extreme right of the lines would probably perform differently if we had more precise information on their earnings. In spite of that though, data primarily shows that unlike the 1995–1999 period, when unemployment increased at a similar rate, and the 1987–1992 period, when there was a similar economic downturn, there were no income losses when 2015 earnings are compared to those obtained in 2012, except for the extremely poor who indeed suffered loss income. For the remaining deciles, there were in fact some modest gains in earnings. Second, income losses/gains were not evenly distributed.

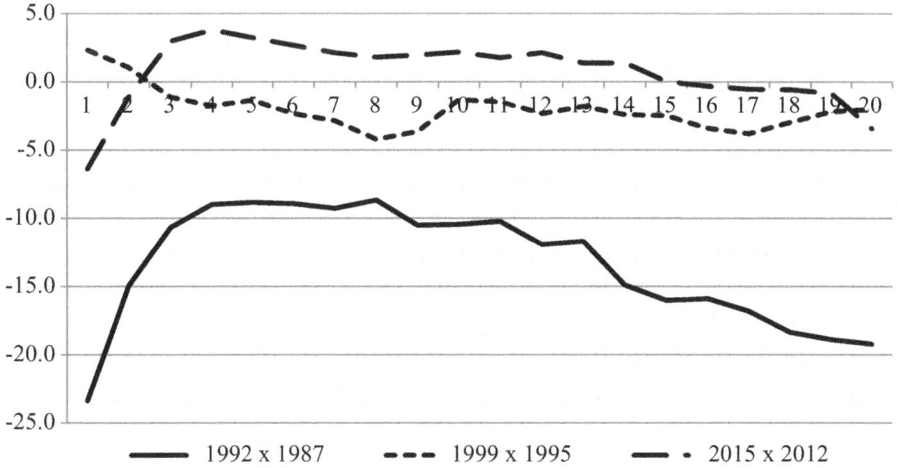

Graph 7 Relative earning gains by vintile for selected years. (Source: National Household Sample Survey, 1981–2015 (IBGE). Note: (1) Current values were deflated to 2016 values. (2) Units of observation are households, not individuals. Nonrelatives of head of household were excluded.)

The poorest, meaning either those whose education and skills imply obtaining very low earnings in the job market or those whose benefits are not indexed to the minimum wage, were the most penalized either by the combination of recession and hyperinflation in 1987–1992 or by the combination of recession and growing unemployment in 2012–2015. However, those whose earnings, either from the job market or from government benefits, are benchmarked to the statutory minimum wage, distributed from the third to 10th vintile, lost the least in every context, either in the case of decreases in GDP or increases in unemployment.

Unfortunately, data limitation recommends caution when extracting inferences. We have no data for 2016, when GDP fell 3.6 points and unemployment affected 11.5% of the EAP. We also have no data on earnings by vintile for the 1981–1983 period that would allow us to compare relative income gains in a context in which the policies of inclusion of outsiders were not yet in place. Despite such limitations, the fact is that the economic crisis that began in 2013 occurred *in the presence* and *after maturation* of (1) the *Bolsa Família* Program, a conditional cash program that targeted households whose per capita earnings are below the statutory minimum wage which reached 13.7 million households in 2015 (through the Brazilian Ministry of Social Development), and (2) the policy that sets a bottom limit to the value of government benefits benchmarked to the statutory minimum wage, which ended up reaching nearly 25% of Brazilian adults in 2015 (Flores 2017) along with a steady increase in its real amount from 1995 on (see Graph 9).

However, between 2012 and 2015, the value of *Bolsa Família* benefits was adjusted in 2014 by 10% – that is, below the inflation rate – while the value of the statutory minimum wage was adjusted on an annual basis according to a legal formula that fully replaces inflation and GDP variation. In other words, while the gains of the beneficiaries of the latter were protected against inflation, those entitled to the former were not.

In sum, the economic crisis affected the job market, while governmental income policies adopted different value adjustment rules from 2012 to 2015. Data displayed in Graph 7 suggests that these policies protected differently those at the bottom strata of the income distribution from becoming the big losers in the economic downturn that began in 2013.

Those interested in Brazil or in a specific dimension of inequality have found plenty of information throughout this book. This conclusion summarizes some of the insights that have emerged from our study of a half-century of change and presents some theoretical contributions that cut across specific chapter topics.

High Inequality Can Lead to Democracy and Redistribution

One of the controversies among political scientists regarding the origins of political institutions refers to whether inequality affects the transition to democracy. Acemoglu and Robinson (2000a) posit democratization as a response to the threat of revolution and social unrest. By extending the franchise, and thus changing the identity of the median voter, the rich commit to future redistribution. However, as the poor impose higher taxes on the rich, highly unequal societies are likely to fluctuate in and out of democracy, if coups are less costly than redistribution (Acemoglu and Robinson 2000a, b). Boix (2003: 235–6) in turn is skeptical about the probability of democratic transitions under a scenario of high inequality. For him, the rich restrict the franchise so as to avoid redistribution under excessive differences between the wealthy and the poor.

Brazil's successful democratization in the late 1980s confirms the proposition that democratic transitions are compatible with highly unequal distribution of income and assets. As the previous Fig. 3 shows, at the end of the military regime in Brazil during the first half of the Sarney administration, the Gini coefficient for income was around 0.600. Moreover, the mechanism of accumulation of advantages left behind voters in the bottom and the middle of income distribution. In 1980, more than 80% of the workforce had not completed 8 years of education (see Graph 3 in the chapter by Menezes-Filho and Kirschbaum). Comin's chapter (Table 3) estimates that less than half of the workforce had a job in the formal market in 1981, meaning, as we saw above, such individuals were not entitled to health care or social security. This is indisputable evidence of a highly unequal society.

However, such levels of exclusion did not translate into revolutionary threats. Instead, the Brazilian path toward democratization was a result of the ability of political elites, who, in learning from dramatic past conflicts in a context of acute economic crisis, opted for encompassing a broad pact (Almeida and Sorj 1983; Lamounier 1988; Martins and Cruz 1983; Stepan 1988). Indeed, evidence shown in the chapter by Fernando Limongi, José Cheibub, and Argelina Figueiredo (Graph 1) raises questions as to the argument that the transition to democracy radically changed the identity of the median voter. Voter registration was already close to 80% in 1980 before the transition to democracy was fully accomplished. The threat after that time was electoral defeat of the incumbent, since the selection of candidates was severely restricted by the rules of the military regime.

In any case, high levels of inequality did not prevent either the transition to democracy or pledges for future redistribution. The Brazilian transition to democracy ended up framing a Constitution that commits to paradigmatic changes in the entitlement to social rights as well as political participation. The *inclusion of outsiders* replaced a previously conservative model of social policies whose entitlement rules were restricted to workers in the formal job market. Noncontributory pensions benchmarked to the minimum wage, along with universal and free health and education, were introduced. Social rights were extended to what were then understood to be *outsiders*. The social wage, defined as the floor below which an individual's disposable income should not be allowed to fall (Boix 1998: 17), was raised considerably.

Moreover, as shown in the chapter by Adrian Lavalle and Leonardo Barone, in this volume, constitutional mandates established during the transition to democracy bind the regular operation of policy areas then considered strategic to extra-parliamentary forms of political participation, which took the form of policy councils. Far from remaining just a pledge, policy councils have now blossomed to include additional policy areas and increased in number.

Historical evidence shows that a combination of prevention of social unrest and institutional leverage was the driving mechanism behind this outcome. Poverty and limited political participation were highly politicized by the left-wing throughout the transition to democracy, on the grounds that both were causally connected. The pro-democratizing coalition blamed the economic policies of the military for the high level of exclusion that prevailed in Brazil (Almeida 1995; Draibe 1994). Indeed, even among right-wing sectors, the prevailing notion was that democracy would not survive if policies against poverty were not adopted (Lamounier 1987).

However, both politicization of poverty and concern over the stability of democracy by the political elite do not appear to be enough to explain the decision as to why the 1987–1989 Constituent Assembly favored the inclusion of *outsider*s. Indeed, redistribution policies turned out to be a very controversial issue in framing the Constitution, to the extent that the conservative majority, a right-wing group labeled "Centrão," rebelled in the midst of the deliberation process and successfully changed decision-making rules so as to prevent the final document from being too leftist in both the economic and social realms (Gomes 2006).

Left-wing parties were a tiny minority in the Assembly though. They held 48 of the total 559 seats.[2] How then do we explain the social-democratic leaning of the deliberations geared toward the *inclusion of outsiders*? They are explained by the strategic use of the Assembly's decision-making rules, for which a minority of parliamentarians held the positions of rapporteurs in the thematic committees related to the social issues (Gomes 2006).

The first version of the Constituent Assembly Bylaws, under which a good deal of what turned out to be final constitutional text was framed, allowed for a minority of parliamentarians to approve their preferences at the level of subcommittees and thematic committees. Mario Covas, leader of the Assembly's majority party, the Brazilian Democratic Movement Party (Partido do Movimento Democrático Brasileiro, PMDB), appointed progressive representatives to key positions as rapporteurs of committees charged with drafting proposals on social issues. Rapporteurs in these subcommittees and committees – subcommittees were composed of 21 members, while committees comprised 63 – not only wielded significant drafting power, but they benefited from the rule that required a simple majority for approval, meaning that either 11 or 32 votes were enough to approve a proposal.

Vetoing such decisions at subsequent points of the decision-making process was much harder, however, because the rules of the first version of Bylaws stated that plenary sessions required a simple majority to do so. In other words, 280 votes were needed to veto decisions made by subcommittees and committees. When the conservative majority realized the consequences of these rules, it successfully approved a second version of the Bylaws, but the status quo favored decisions made by sub-

[2] The Workers' Party (*Partido dos Trabalhadores*, PT) had 16 constituents; the Democratic Labor Party (*Partido Democrático Trabalhista*, PDT) had 26; the Brazilian Socialist Party (*Partido Socialista Brasileiro*, PSB) had 1; and the Communist Party of Brazil (*Partido Comunista do Brasil*, PCdoB) had 5.

committees and committees, since public opinion had acknowledged and approved them (Gomes 2006).

Thus, the redistribution pledged by the 1988 Constitution cannot be fully explained by concern on the part of the political elite over providing credible commitments to future redistribution so as to avoid social unrest. Although poverty and inequality were highly politicized throughout the democratic transition, it was up to the strategic use of the rules of the deliberation arena along with the high visibility of the resolutions favoring the *inclusion of outsiders* that explains why these measures were not vetoed by the conservative majority that eventually approved the final text of the Federal Constitution of 1988 (Gomes, 2006).

Wealth Concentration Is Compatible with Income Redistribution

To determine whether or not inequality was reduced, one inevitably needs metrics to compare different states of affairs. The choice of a particular metric in turn is invariably a matter of value judgment (Decancq et al. 2015: 70). Indeed, most prominent economists in the field of redistribution policy – from Adam Smith to Amartya Sen – have had a foot in both camps: the positive analysis of income distribution and the moral philosophy that refers to the principles one adopts to judge different income distributions (Sandmo 2015).

Analysis of income redistribution was largely influenced throughout the twentieth century by the Dalton-Pigou principle, which posited that income inequality is reduced if lower-income strata are benefited by transfers from higher-income ones (Atkinson 1970; Dalton 1920; Pigou 1920). Within this theoretical framework, the share of total income obtained by different quintiles, which can be observed through various indexes, came to be the metrics used to compare different income distributions. The book *Capital in the Twenty-First Century* (Piketty 2014) advanced an alternative metric, which turned out to be very influential as well: the share the richest quintiles obtain from total income.

The latter metric is indeed a practical solution to the statement that tax records are superior to surveys as data sources, since surveys underestimate the income of the richest, particularly earnings derived from ownership of capital, financial assets, and property (Piketty and Saez 2014). However, tax records hamper recovering the continuous scale of income distribution because they do not register the income of the lower strata (Medeiros et al. 2015c), which is a sort of underestimation whose extent must plausibly be larger in contexts where the poor make up the majority of the population.

The metric of the *top richest* implies a conceptual conflation between wealth concentration, on the one hand, which refers to the share of total income obtained by the richest and income redistribution, on the other hand, a concept that requires earnings of all strata to be taken into account. Although not explicitly stated, this conceptual conflation is based on a normative principle, according to which a reduction in income inequality is obtained only if the wealthiest are expropriated. In contrast, the Dalton-Pigou principle advances the notion that income redistribution is obtained when poorer strata obtain transfers from richer ones, no matter how small the transfer.

Empirical studies adopting the metrics of the *top richest* made an important contribution to our understanding of the path of income inequality in Brazil by showing that the level of inequality was much higher than that obtained by studies based on surveys. When earnings from financial assets and property are considered, the share of income earned by the richest 1% from 2006 to 2012 jumps to about 25% of total income as opposed to the nearly 15% obtained using the survey metric (Medeiros et al. 2015c: 24; 2015a; Souza and Medeiros 2015). Hence, what was up to then understood as the speed of the decline in income inequality was largely a result of the underestimation of the share of income obtained by the richest 1% (Medeiros et al. 2015b). According to this metric then, income inequality was not reduced in Brazil, even under the left-wing government of President Lula. Instead, it remained at its previously known high levels (Medeiros et al. 2015c).

What then do we get by focusing on the entire scale of earning distribution? Graph 8 displays information on the relative income gains by vintile from 1981 to 2015. Earnings include what comes from the job market as well as from government transfers. The transition to democracy, from 1981 to 1989,[3] penalized the bottom and middle strata of income distribution. Indeed, income distribution was regressive throughout the period. Not only were gains accumulated by households above the 10th vintile, but the higher the households' per capita earnings, the higher the relative gains were. In contrast, throughout the democratic period, from 1989 to 2015, the bottom and middle strata obtained larger relative gains, with those at the 3rd vintile benefitting the most. Relative gains were then progressively distributed: the lower the households' per capita earnings, the higher the relative gains were.

This outcome sums up the distribution of relative gains in different periods. Under the left-wing administration of President Lula, from 2003 to 2010,[4] relative income gains were not only progressive but the highest throughout the entire period. The commodity boom provided both for increased tax revenues, allowing expanded pro-poor spending without incurring fiscal deficits, and for very low unemployment rates, which positively impacted earnings from the job market. Relative gains during the left-wing administration of Dilma Rousseff, from 2011 to 2015,[5] were slightly redistributive, since values range from around 10–14% for the poorest to 4–7% for the richest. Finally, the administration of President Fernando Henrique

[3] I assume that the transition to democracy was completed in 1989, when, for the first time, illiterates were allowed to vote in free and competitive national elections and when the new Constitution was eventually approved.

[4] Although the comparison should preferably be made between the last year of the former president and the last year of the incumbent, in this case 2011 is considered, because 2010 was a census year and the National Household Sample Survey data was not collected.

[5] President Dilma Rousseff was reelected in 2013 and impeached in August 2016.

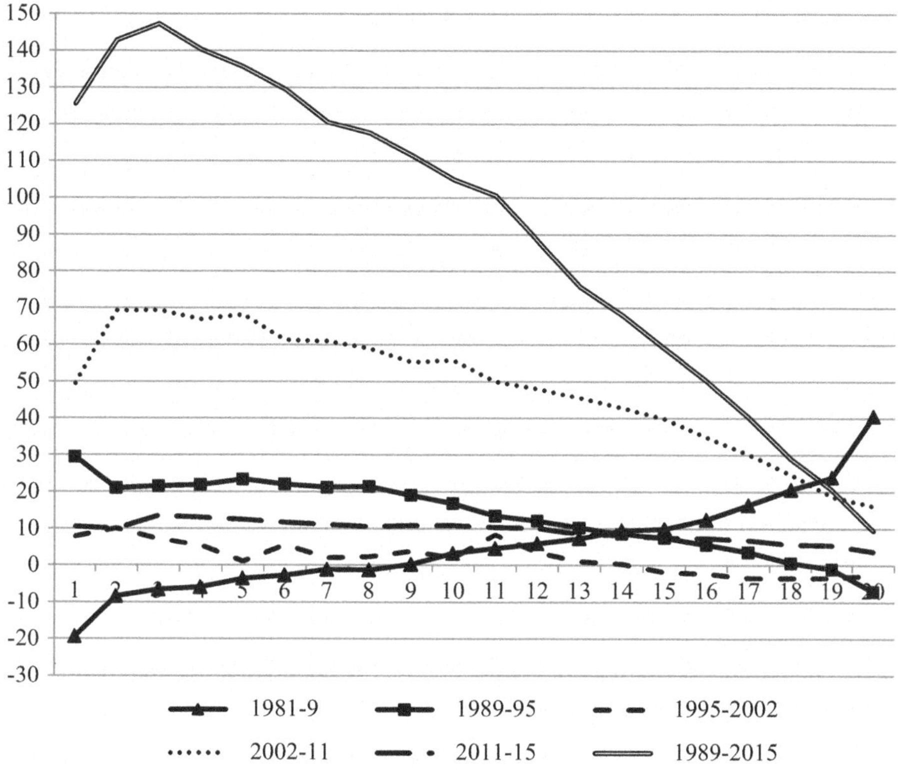

Graph 8 Relative earning gains by vintile: Brazil (1981–2015). (Source: National Household Sample Survey, 1981–2015 (IBGE), values adjusted for 2016. Note: Units of observation are households, not individuals. Nonrelatives of household head were excluded. There was no data collection in 1991, 1994, 2000, or 2010)

Cardoso, from 1995 to 2002, displayed a behavior similar to that of Rousseff, although with lower values: the poorest obtained 7–10% relative gains, while the richest lost around 3% of what they had obtained during the first year of his term.[6] Notice the impact of the monetary stabilization successfully achieved in 1994, highly favoring the election of Fernando Henrique Cardoso, who served as Minister of Finance under President Itamar Franco (1993–1994). It can be seen in the area comprising the line that refers to 1989–1993 and the line that refers to 1989–1995. The largest relative gains were obtained by the 1st decile, while those households whose earnings are around the statutory minimum wage, ranging from the 3rd to the 9th decile, were the least penalized by the combination of recession and inflation that occurred between 1989 and 1994.

[6] Although the comparison should preferably be made between the last year of the former president and the last year of the incumbent, in this case, 1995 is considered, because the National Household Sample Survey data was not collected in 1994, the final year of the Itamar Franco administration.

In sum, we have two different stories regarding the path of income distribution. One says that inequality remained stable and high, while the other says that the poorer benefited. The point is that each metric implies opposing conclusions. Indeed, they result from different normative conceptions about what requirements should be accomplished for redistribution to take place. From the positive perspective though, they reveal different aspects of the behavior of Brazil's income distribution. As each metric underestimates the earnings of different extremes of the income scale, all we can conclude is that both should be taken into account. Actually, methodologically sophisticated empirical efforts to reconcile data from tax records and surveys showed that the former underestimated the *level* of income inequality in Brazil but not its *trajectory* throughout the 2000s (Medeiros et al. 2015b).

Therefore, a comprehensive assessment of the path of income inequality in Brazil under democracy should state that the concentration of wealth and earnings by the richest 1% went along with income redistribution in favor of the bottom and middle strata. Focusing attention only on the richest would impede observing the relative gains received by the poorer, when they received it. Ignoring the gains of the 1% and their origins would also conceal an important portion of the inequality production dynamic.

The Statutory Minimum Wage Played a Key Role in Income Inequality Reduction

The statutory minimum wage has been the subject of theoretical and empirical controversy in the field of labor economics, the main question being whether its valorization by means of state regulation decreases inequality by raising wages at the bottom of the income distribution or, alternatively, ends up concentrating income since employers' adjustment strategy would be to eliminate low-wage jobs or simply not register their employees. Empirical studies point in both directions, meaning that the issue has not yet been resolved.

Far from solving the controversy, this concluding chapter presents empirical information about the role of the statutory minimum wage on income inequality reduction in the last two decades. To better understand the Brazilian case, two specific dimensions should be taken into account: multiplication of the number of beneficiaries from the early 1990s on and real valorization of the minimum wage beginning in the mid-1990s.

First, the minimum wage in Brazil does not just regulate the formal job market. As a result of the 1988 Federal Constitution, pensions as well as noncontributory cash benefits (to which are entitled only to handicapped and aged poor) are also benchmarked to its amount. The number of recipients of the Continuous Cash Benefit (BPC), which entitles the handicapped and aged poor to cash benefits, jumped from 346,200 in 1996, when it began to be implemented, to 4.2 million in 2015 (Araújo and Flores 2017). The number of workers in the formal job market earning 1 minimum wage surged from 2.5 to 15 million from 1995 to 2014, with women overrepresented among that number. In all, social security pensions and noncontributory cash benefits doubled in the same period: from 10 to 20 million (Flores 2017). In 2014, more than half of retirees and pensioners and one-fifth of formal workers received the minimum wage. Both are concentrated at the bottom and middle strata of income distribution (Brito et al. 2016).

As a result, a conservative estimation that takes into account only direct beneficiaries of the statutory minimum wage calculates for 2015 that around 25% of Brazilian voters had a direct interest in its amount (Flores 2017). No doubt the extent of such category of voters is associated with the valorization of the statutory minimum wage from the mid-1990s on, as we can see in Graph 9. From 1995 to 2015, the statutory minimum wage underwent a continuous increase in real value, so as to almost recover the real value it had at the end of the 1946–1964 democratic period. Indeed, the highest real values of statutory minimum wage in Brazil occurred between 1954 and 1964. From then on, it declined substantially, in a downward path that came at the beginning of the military regime as well as during the transition to democracy.

As a result, Brito et al. (2016: 17) estimate that 64.3% of the 14.6% reduction in household income inequality between 1995 and 2014, as measured by the Gini index, was due to the minimum wage policy.

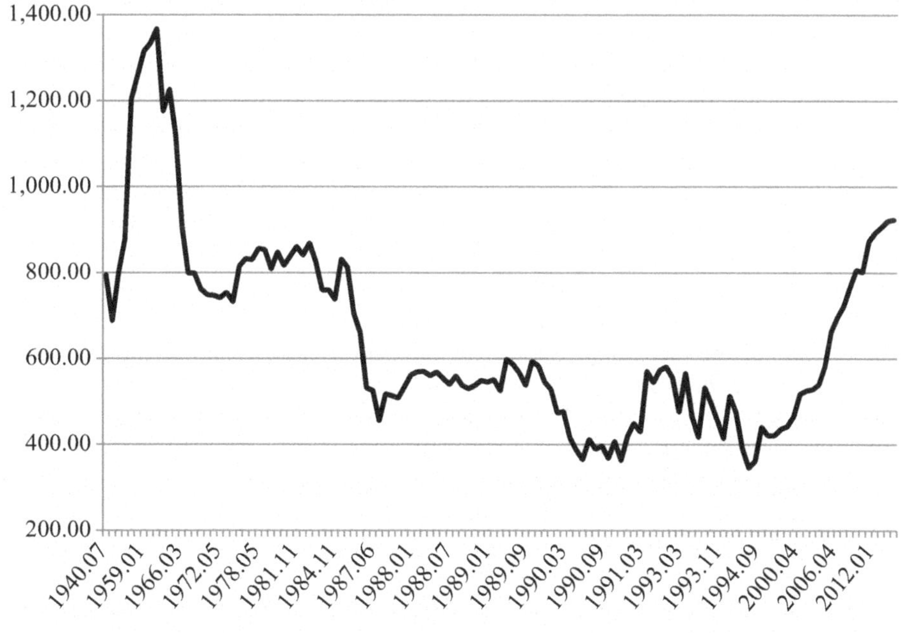

Graph 9 Statutory minimum wage, real values: 1960– 2012 (Source: IPEADATA and Ministry of Labor. Note: Real values were obtained by deflation of nominal values according to the IBGE's IPC, from March 1979 on. Deflators employed in previous years were IGPC-Mtb (January 1948–March 1979), IPC-RJ/FGV (January 1944–January 1948), and IPC-SP/FIPE (July 1940–January 1944).)

Well-Being Consists of More than Just the Income Dimension

The literature on inequality has usually focused on income, but the assumption that income is indeed an adequate proxy for an individual's well-being has been discussed by prominent economists such as Amartya Sen and Joseph Stiglitz. Diversity among individuals means that they have different needs, so can they have quite different lives in spite of similar incomes (Sen 1973, 1999). Other dimensions of life, such as health and living conditions, should be taken into account when evaluating an individual's well-being (Stiglitz et al. 2009).

Political scientists and sociologists have also called attention to how dimensions other than income affect the economy of households. First, income and access to services tend to reinforce each other. Income affects an individual's access to education, while schooling levels affect an individual's earnings (Autor 2014). Moreover, public policies affect household income, not only by means of government transfers but also because real income depends directly on how much families should spend on basic services, such as education and health, for instance (Marshall 1950). Social policies affect how a family's budget is distributed by means of the rules that entitle individuals to social services (Esping-Andersen 1990). Indeed, in 2009 the Brazilian Gini coefficient dropped from 0.565, if only nominal earnings, taxes, and government transfers were observed, to 0.479, when indirect earnings from public spending on health and education were included (Silveira et al. 2013). Thus, access to public services affects the present and future income of individuals, meaning that the nonmonetary dimension of inequality is as crucial as its monetary dimension.

Finally, many theoretical statements regarding the relationship between democracy and redistribution do not limit the scope of the former to income alone. Marshall's (1950) narrative of the impact of political rights on social rights in Britain is not limited to income but in fact refers to a package of benefits guaranteed by nation-states. Acemoglu's and Robinson's (2000a) account of the fall in inequality due to democratization includes access to education as an important dimension of redistribution. Milanovic (2000: 395–6) found weak empirical support for the median voter hypothesis (Meltzer and Richard 1981) as a mechanism of collective choice, connecting inequality to transfers in cash under universal suffrage. Hence, he suggests that analysis of the relationship between democratization and redistribution could benefit from the observation of the nonmonetary dimensions of States' action. In sum, the reasons to focus the analysis of well-being only on income are more practical than theoretical, due to the availability of data.

Our study on Brazil has indeed shown that the nonmonetary dimension of inequality is as fundamental as the monetary one. The former comprises access to services and living conditions, while the latter refers to income. By enlarging the dimensions through which inequality is examined, we could observe the mechanism of *fusion of advantages*, that is, the extent of benefits accumulated by some while others accumulate disadvantages. Because the fusion of advantages provides for an overlay of benefits upon the same categories of individuals, inequality, either in terms of well-being or economic opportunities, turns out to be greater than when it is observed only through the income dimension.

We could also observe that such an overlay of advantages upon roughly the same categories of individuals has largely been guided by particular types of social policies that prevailed from the early 1930s to the late 1980s, according to which entitlement to crucial rights, such as retirement and health care, was linked to formal engagement in the job market, in a context of limited size of the urban industrial sector and high levels of chronic unemployment. Being excluded from the formal job market, a fate whose possibility was by and large causally linked to educational opportunities (as shown in the chapters by Ribeiro, Ceneviva, and Brito et al., as well as by Alvaro Comin, in this volume) also resulted in being denied the right to health care as well as to retirement payments. Moreover (as shown by Marta Arretche's and Eduardo Marques's chapters, in this volume) households' access to urban infrastructure services, such as electricity, water, and sewage collection, was revealed as negatively associated with income.

That is why we should be very careful in making inferences about inequality based solely on the income dimension. The Gini coefficient for income in Brazil (based on survey data) was very similar for 1960 and 2009: 0.535 and 0.539, respectively (IPEA 2012). However, the evidence presented in this book shows that in the 1960s, more than three-quarters of Brazilian workers had 0–3 years of schooling (as shown in chapter by Menezes Filho and Kirschbaum, in this volume), and nearly 60% of workers engaged in rural and domestic jobs were not protected by labor laws (as shown by Comin's chapter, in this volume). The scarcity of skilled workers guaranteed them a premium in the labor market, in the form of higher wages and legislative protection. The right to health and pension insurance was attained by their engagement in the formal job market. As a result, the social protection system produced a great divide between *insiders* and *outsiders*, in which *outsiders* were not only excluded from the benefits but also contributed to funding such benefits, given that the costs of social protection of *insiders* were transferred to product prices and thus paid by all consumers.

By extending our scope of analysis from income to encompass other crucial dimensions of well-being, we can also observe how the mechanism of *inclusion of outsiders* unfolded under democracy. The constitutional entitlement to free and universal access to health and education as well as to noncontributory pensions at age 65[7] meant that such crucial dimensions of well-being eventually turned out to be de-linked from engagement in the job market and even from individuals' insurance payments. Individuals are entitled to the payments and services regardless of the monetary dimension. Besides that, endogenous layering changes (Thelen 2003) in the federal systems launched by the military regime to fund infrastructure also contributed to de-linking access to basic services from households' income. As a result, inequality reduction from the early 1990s to 2015 was not the result of income distribution alone. It also encompassed smoothing the mechanism of fusion of advantages.

---

[7] The 1988 version of the Constitution specified that those who reached the age of 70 were entitled to the benefit. Law 9720/1998 reduced the age to 67. Finally, in 2003, the Statute for the Elderly reduced the age of entitlement to noncontributory pensions to 65.

Expanding our understanding of well-being can also contribute to better assessing the electoral impact of redistribution policies. Studies on President Lula's performance in the 2006 national elections, for instance, have focused on the *Bolsa Família*, a conditional cash transfer program that at the time of the election was benefitting 11 million families. Many attributed the great change in the geography of Lula's voting in 2006, particularly the increase in number of supporters in the poor cities of the North and Northeast regions, to the electoral credits garnered by that program (Soares and Terron 2008; Zucco 2008, 2013). Yet, evidence shown by Marta Arretche's chapter (in this volume) reveals that the gains in well-being obtained by the North and Northeast regions under President Lula went well beyond income alone. Thus, by enlarging the dimensions through which redistribution can take place, political scientists can more precisely assess why and how voters reward incumbents.

In summary, our study suggests that analysis of the relationship between political regimes and redistribution can benefit by enlarging the dimensions through which the former is observed. There are good theoretical reasons to consider more than just income in a comparative analysis of what governments do when facing political pressure toward redistribution.

Inequality Reduction Is the Result of a Combination of Factors

Our study of Brazil revealed that inequality reduction is the result of a combination of factors. It has been guided by a variety of policies as well as by factors exogenous to policies.

Demographic changes, transformations in social behavior, and market factors were revealed to be as crucial as were the policies that serve as the driving forces behind the path of inequality reduction in Brazil, so much so that slight changes in the specification of econometric models aimed at disentangling the weight of each factor on outcomes tend to obtain contradictory results (as shown in Vera Schattan Coelho and Marcelo Dias's chapter, in this volume). The fact is that inequality reduction, either in its monetary or nonmonetary dimension, is the result of a combination of factors, some associated with policies but others exogenous to them. In addition, different factors can emerge on their own and can develop independently of one another. Moreover, there is a time lag between when some factors emerge and when their effects are felt, meaning effects are not necessarily contemporaneous with their emergence.

Some examples are useful in clarifying this proposition. From the 1970s on, poorer and less-schooled women adopted the patterns of reproductive behavior that prevailed at that time among highly schooled women. A steady decline in total fertility rates ensued (as shown in the chapter by Maria Coleta Oliveira, Joice Vieira, and Glaucia Marcondes, in this volume). As a result, the demographic pace of the supply of poor young people into the job market has diminished. Such impact only appeared from the mid-1980s on though, when the average geometric rate of EAP growth showed a downward trend (IBGE 2000). As demonstrated in Alvaro Comin's chapter (in this volume), the higher levels of fertility among the poor and their low schooling levels were key determinants of the historically high levels of income inequality in Brazil. Universalization of access to basic education in turn was only achieved in the late 1990s. Hence, the compression of wages in the job market from the early 2000s on (as shown by the Naercio Menezes Filho and Charles Kirschbaum chapter) was facilitated by the fact that the behavior of both factors – fertility rates and schooling levels – not only changed but was also combined at this time. Because each factor has an independent source and evolved at a different pace, it is the combination of the effect of both at one point in time that is relevant in understanding the speed of the decline of income inequality in the job market.

Second, women's incremental entry into the job market beginning in the 1970s (as shown in the chapter by Nadya Araújo Guimarães, Leonardo Sangali Barone, and Murillo Marschner Alves de Brito, in this volume) implied that large numbers of individuals without any income were able to obtain monetary earnings. Despite the gender income gap, total income inequality has fallen due to the fact that women went from receiving zero income to receiving some income (Souza 2016). Female engagement in the job market is part of the silent revolution in which women have been protagonists since the 1970s. As a sociological phenomenon, it can contribute to reducing gender inequality in different dimensions, including the domestic one (as shown in the chapter by Oliveira et al., in this volume). Yet evolution of the job market's gender composition can hardly be understood without taking into account its interfaces with other key independent dimensions, such as the expansion of female education and rewards that come from social policies. As shown in Guimarães et al., in this volume, these phenomena are not contemporaneous with one another, meaning that their combined effect on women's participation in the job market varied over time.

Third, Graph 8 above shows that it was under President Lula's two terms that the poorest benefited the most in terms of relative income gains. Aside from his ideological orientation, this achievement was largely helped by exogenous factors. The commodity boom greatly favored income inequality reduction through market forces. Wage gains resulted from the increasing demand for jobs, which favored the bargaining power of workers. Added to that, economic growth increased tax revenue collection, meaning that President Lula was able to augment spending on pro-poor policies without incurring fiscal deficits, despite avoiding pursuit of approval for unpopular policies that increased taxes. Moreover, reduction in wage differentials has also benefited from the increase in the supply of education, especially at the fundamental (as shown in Naercio Menezes-Filho and Charles Kirschbaum chapter, in this volume). Yet, this outcome was the result of the expansion of access whose origins date back to the mid-1990s. In the absence of these two driving forces – the commodity boom and the previous expansion of schooling levels – both beyond the reach of President Lula's own policies, his accomplishments would have been less generous than they in fact were.

In sum, the fact that inequality reduction results from a combination of factors whose evolution is independent of one another and whose effects have a time lag makes the causal explanation of the path of inequality a challenge for the social sciences. The examples above refer only to income. Yet if we extend our concept of well-being toward nonmonetary dimensions, as suggested, the factors to be included as potential causes include policy-specific elements. For example, a household's access to urban infrastructure seems to be better explained by the spatial concentration of poverty, not just by the individual's household income, meaning that living in a jurisdiction with concentration of the poor can be a better predictor of the lack of basic services than living in a poor household.

Our study also shows that different household infrastructure policies displayed different speeds in increasing supply, so that the poorer had access to them at quite different points in time. Such diverse pace requires an explanation. This seems to follow a cost hierarchy. Expansion of electricity distribution was favored by investments that were made during the military regime, thus reducing the volume of investments needed for power generation to reach universal access when President Lula opted for subsidy policies under the National Program for Universal Access and Use of Electric Power. Water and sewage disposal policies also followed a very different trend, even if implemented and financed under a single national system that was also launched during the military regime – PLANASA, established in 1971. Installation costs appear to be higher in the former than in the latter. If this is so, funding requirements are not commensurate among policies.

Thus, the fact that the path of inequality reduction in its various dimensions results from a combination of factors, associated with as well as exogenous to policies, whose evolution is independent of one another and whose effects have a time lag, does not seem to imply great methodological difficulties when one is committed to descriptive analysis. Instead, it poses nontrivial challenges to the study of its causal factors, particularly if one aims at long-term and comparative explanations.

Hence, social scientists have much work ahead in their efforts to better grasp the sources of inequality reduction. We hope to have put our imprimatur on this collective effort.

References

Acemoglu, D., & Robinson, J. A. (2000a). Why did the west extend the franchise? Democracy, inequality, and growth in historical perspective. *The Quarterly Journal of Economics*, 115(4), 1 November 2000, 1167–1199.

Acemoglu, D., & Robinson, J. A. (2000b). A Theory of Political Transitions. The American Economic Review, 91(4), 938–963.

Almeida, M. H. T. (1995). Federalismo e políticas sociais. *Revista Brasileira de Ciências Sociais, 10*(28), 88–108.

Almeida, M. H. T., & Sorj, B. (1983). *Sociedade e Política no Brasil pós* (p. 64). Brasiliense: São Paulo.

Araújo, V., & Flores, P. (2017). Redistribuição de Renda, Pobreza e Desigualdade Territorial no Brasil. *Revista de Sociologia e Política, 25*(63).

Atkinson, A. B. (1970). On the measurement of inequality. *Journal of Economic Theory, 2*(3), 244–263.

Autor, D. H. (2014). Skills, education, and the rise of earnings inequality among the 'other 99 percent'. *Science, 344*(6186), 843–850.
Boix, C. (1998). *Political parties, growth and equality. Conservative and social democratic economic strategies in the world economy*. Cambridge: Cambridge University Press.
Boix, C. (2003). *Democracy and redistribution*. Cambridge: Cambridge University Press.
Brito, A., Foguel, M., & Kerstenetzky, C. (2016, October). *Minimum wage valorization policy and the decline in income inequality in Brazil between 1995 and 2014: a decomposition approach*. Center for Studies on Inequality and Development (Discussion Paper no. 115).
Dalton, H. (1920). *Some aspects of the inequality of income in modern communities*. London: Routledge.
de Barros, R. P., Henriques, R., & Mendonça, R. (2000). Desigualdade e Pobreza no Brasil: retrato de uma estabilidade inaceitável. *Revista Brasileira de Ciências Sociais, 42*, 123–142.
Decancq, K., Fleurbaey, M., & Schokkaert, E. (2015). Inequality, income, and well-being. In A. B. Atkinson & F. Bourguignon (Eds.), *Handbook of income distribution*. Oxford/Amsterdam: Elsevier.
Draibe, S. (1994). As políticas sociais do regime militar brasileiro: 1964–84. In G. D. Soares & C. D'Araújo (Eds.), *21 Anos de Regime Militar*. Rio de Janeiro: FGV.
Esping-Andersen, G. (1985). *Politics against markets. The social democratic road to power*. Princeton: Princeton University.
Esping-Andersen, G. (1990). *The three worlds of welfare capitalism*. Princeton University: Princeton.
Flores, P. (2017). *A política da política do salário mínimo no Brasil*. Universidade de São Paulo. Dissertação. (Máster).
Gomes, S. C. (2006). O Impacto das Regras de Organização do Processo Legislativo no Comportamento dos Parlamentares: Um Estudo de Caso da Assembléia Constituinte (1987-88). *Dados, 49*(1), pp. 193–224.
Huber, E., & Stephens, J. D. (2012). *Democracy and the left. Social policy and inequality in Latin America*. Chicago: The University of Chicago Press.
IBGE. (2000). *Tendências demográficas no período de 1950/2000: Uma análise dos resultados da amostra do Censo Demográfico 2000*. Rio de Janeiro: IBGE.
IPEA. 2012. *A Década Inclusiva: 2001–2011: Desigualdade, Pobreza e Políticas de Renda*. No. 155, Brasília: IPEA.
Kuznets, S. (1955). Economic Growth and Income Inequality. *The American Economic Review, 45*(1), 1–28.
Lamounier, B. (1987). Perspectivas da Consolidação Democrática: o caso brasileiro. *Revista Brasileira de Ciência Sociais, 4*(2), 43–64.
Lamounier, B. (1988). O 'Brasil autoritário' revisitado: o impacto das eleições sobre a abertura. In S. Alfred (org.), *Democratizando o Brasil* (pp. 83–134). Rio de Janeiro: Paz e Terra.
Marshall, T. H. (1950). *Citizenship and social class and other essays*. London: Cambridge University Press.
Martins, C. E., & Cruz, S. V. (1983). De Castello a Figueiredo: uma incursão na pré-história da abertura. In M. H. T. Almeida & B. Sorj (Eds.), *Sociedade e Política no Brasil pós* (Vol. 64, pp. 13–61). Brasiliense: São Paulo.
Medeiros, M., de Souza, P. H. G. F., & de Castro, F. Á. (2015a). A estabilidade da desigualdade de renda no Brasil, 2006 a 2012: estimativa com dados do imposto de renda e pesquisas domiciliares. *Ciência & Saúde Coletiva, 20*(4), 971–986.
Medeiros, M., Galvão, J. C., & Nazareno, L. (2015b). *A Composição da Desigualdade no Brasil. Conciliando o Censo 2010 e os Dados do Imposto de Renda* (Texto para Discussão IPEA, no. 2147).
Medeiros, M., Souza, P. H. G. F., & Castro, F. A. (2015c). O Topo da Distribuição de Renda no Brasil: primeiras estimativas com dados tributários e comparação com pesquisas domiciliares, 2006–2012. *Dados.Revista de Ciências Sociais, 58*(1), 7–36.
Meltzer, A. H. and Richard, S. H. (1981), A rational theory of the size of government. *The Journal of Political Economy*, 89, 5: 914–27.

Milanovic, B. (2000). The median-voter hypothesis, income inequality, and income redistribution: An empirical test with the required data. *European Journal of Political Economy, 16*, 367–410.
Pigou, A. C. (1920). *The economics of welfare*. London: Macmillan.
Piketty, T. (2014). *Capital in the twenty-first century* (Kindle ed.). Cambridge, MA: Harvard University Press.
Piketty, T., & Saez, E. (2014). Inequality in the long run. *Science, 344*(6186), 838–842.
Roberts, K. (2012). *The politics of inequality and redistribution in Latin America's post-adjustment era* (WIDER working paper 2012/008). Helsinki: UNU-WIDER.
Sandmo, A. (2015). The principal problem in political economy: Income distribution in the history of economic thought. In A. B. Atkinson & F. Bourguignon (Eds.), *Handbook of income distribution*. Oxford/Amsterdam: Elsevier.
Santos, W. G. (1979). *Cidadania e Justiça*. Rio de Janeiro: Ed. Campus.
Sen, A. (1973). *On economic inequality*. Oxford: Oxford University Press.
Sen, A. (1999). *Development as freedom*. New York: Oxford University Press.
Soares, S. S. D. (2010). O ritmo na queda da desigualdade no Brasil é aceitável? *Revista de Economia Política, 30*(3 (119)), 364–380.
Soares, G. A. D., & Terron, S. L. (2008). Dois Lulas: a geografia eleitoral da reeleição (explorando conceitos, métodos e técnicas de análise geoespacial). *Opinião Pública, 14*(2), 269–301.
Souza, P. H.G. F. (2016). *Os ricos e a Desigualdade no Brasil ao longo de nove décadas*. PhD dissertation. Universidade de Brasília.
Souza, P. H. G. F., & Medeiros, M. (2015). Top income shares and inequality in Brazil, 1928–2012. *Sociologies in Dialogue, 1*(1), 119–132.
Stepan, A. (org.). (1988). *Democratizando o Brasil*. Rio de Janeiro: Paz e Terra.
Stiglitz, J. E., Sen, A., & Fitoussi, J.-P. (2009). *The measurement of economic performance and social progress revisited*. Paris: OFCE - Centre de Recherche en Economie de Sciences Po. Document de Travail No. 33.
Zucco, C. (2008). The president's 'new' constituency: Lula and the pragmatic vote in Brazil's 2006 presidential elections. *Journal of Latin American Studies, 40*(1), 29–49.
Zucco, C. (2013). When payouts pay off: Conditional cash transfers and voting behavior in Brazil, 2002–2010. *American Journal of Political Science*. https://doi.org/10.1111/ajps.12026.

Index

M. Arretche (ed.), *Paths of Inequality in Brazil*,
https://doi.org/10.1007/978-3-319-78184-6

The manufacturer's authorised representative in the EU is Springer Nature Customer Service Centre GmbH, Europaplatz 3, 69115 Heidelberg, Germany. If you have any concerns regarding our products, please contact ProductSafety@springernature.com

Printed and bound by CPI Group (UK) Ltd, Croydon, CR0 4YY
05/10/2026
02228144-0012